W9-BUZ-193

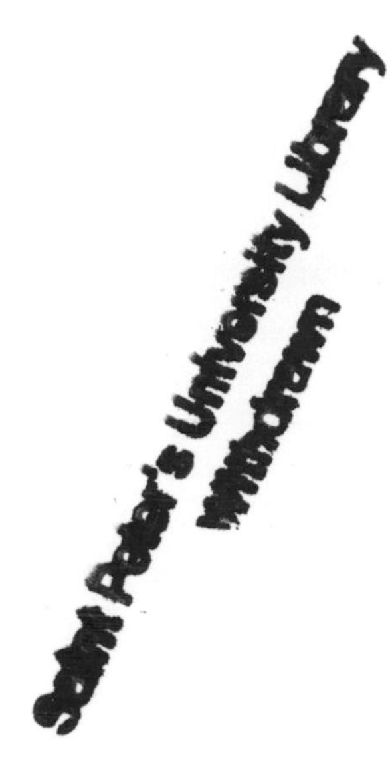
Saint Peter's University Library
Withdrawn

CAMBRIDGE CLASSICAL TEXTS AND COMMENTARIES

6

CICERO'S LETTERS TO ATTICUS

VOLUME IV

CICERO'S LETTERS TO ATTICUS

EDITED BY

D. R. SHACKLETON BAILEY

VOLUME IV

49 B.C.

133–210 (BOOKS VII. 10–X)

CAMBRIDGE
AT THE UNIVERSITY PRESS
1968

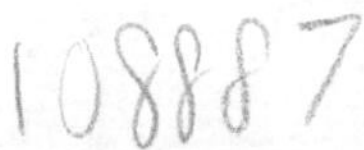

Published by the Syndics of the Cambridge University Press
Bentley House, 200 Euston Road, London, N.W.1
American Branch: 32 East 57th Street, New York, N.Y. 10022

Library of Congress Catalogue Card Number: 65-18929
Standard Book Number: 521 06928 9

Printed in Great Britain by
Alden & Mowbray Ltd
at the Alden Press, Oxford

CONTENTS

ABBREVIATIONS

The following may be noted:

Broughton = T. R. S. Broughton, *The Magistrates of the Roman Republic* (New York, 1951–60). References unless otherwise stated are to Vol. II.

Drumann–Groebe = K. W. Drumann and P. Groebe, *Geschichte Roms*. 2nd edition (Leipzig, 1899–1929).

K.–S. = R. Kühner and C. Stegmann, *Ausführliche Grammatik der lateinischen Sprache:* Satzlehre. 3rd edition (Leverkusen, 1955).

Lehmann, *de Cic. ad Att.* = C. A. Lehmann, *De Ciceronis ad Atticum epistulis recensendis et emendandis* (Berlin, 1892).

Lehmann, *Quaest.* = C. A. Lehmann, *Quaestiones Tullianae* (Prague and Leipzig, 1886).

L.–S.–J. = Liddell–Scott–Jones, Greek–English Lexicon, 9th edition.

Mommsen, *St.* = Th. Mommsen, *Römisches Staatsrecht*, 3rd edition (Leipzig, 1887–8).

Mommsen, *Str.* = Th. Mommsen, *Römisches Strafrecht* (Leipzig, 1899).

Otto, *Sprichwörter* = A. Otto, *Die Sprichwörter und sprichwörtlichen Redensarten der Römer* (Leipzig, 1890).

Propertiana = D. R. Shackleton Bailey, *Propertiana* (Cambridge, 1956).

RE. = Pauly–Wissowa, *Realencyklopädie.*

Schmidt, *Briefwechsel* = O. E. Schmidt, *Der Briefwechsel des M. Tullius Cicero von seinem Prokonsulat in Cilicien bis zu Caesars Ermordung (Leipzig,* 1893).

Sjögren, *Comm. Tull.* = H. Sjögren, *Commentationes Tullianae* (Uppsala, 1910).

Thes. = *Thesaurus Linguae Latinae.*

ABBREVIATIONS

Towards a Text = D. R. Shackleton Bailey, *Towards a Text of Cicero, ad Atticum* (Cambridge, 1960).

T.–P. = R. Y. Tyrrell and L. C. Purser, *The Correspondence of Cicero*, third and second editions (Dublin, 1904–1933).

The Letters to Quintus and to M. Brutus are cited from W. S. Watt's Oxford Text, Asconius by line and page from that of A. C. Clark.

TEXT AND TRANSLATION

133–210 (BOOKS VII. 10–X)

49 B.C.

INDEX SIGLORVM

E = Ambrosianus E 14 inf. (saec. XIV).
H = Landianus 8 (saec. XIV–XV).
N = Laurentianus (ex Conv. Suppr.) 49 (saec. XIV–XV).
V = Palatinus Lat. 1510 (saec. XV).
O = Taurinensis Lat. 495 (saec. XV).
R = Parisinus Lat. 8538 (anno 1419 scriptus).
P = Parisinus Lat. 8536 (saec. XV).
Ant. = Antonianus a Malaespina citatus.
F = Faërni codex a Malaespina vel Vrsino citatus.
codd. Mal. = Malaespinae codices ab ipso generatim citati.
Σ = consensus codicis E cum codicibus HNV (vel O deficiente V) R aut omnibus aut eis qui quoquo loco praesto sunt
M = Mediceus 49. 18 (anno 1393 scriptus).
b = Berolinensis (ex bibl. Hamiltoniana) 168 (saec. XV).
d = Laurentianus (ex bibl. aedilium) 217 (saec. XV).
m = Berolinensis (ex bibl. Hamiltoniana) 166 (anno 1408 scriptus).
s = Vrbinas 322 (saec. XV).
δ = consensus codicum *bdms*.
Δ = consensus codicis M cum codicibus *bdms*, aut omnibus aut tribus.
Ω = consensus codicum Σ (quotquot praesto sunt) et M = archetypum omnium quos supra nominavi codicum.
C = lectiones margini editionis Cratandrinae (an. 1528) adscriptae.
c = lectiones in textu eiusdem editionis primum prolatae.
Z = Tornesianus (de Z^l, $Z^{(l)}$, Z^b, $Z^{(b)}$, Z^β, $Z^{(\beta)}$, vide tom. I, p. 93).
λ = lectiones in margine alterius editionis Lambinianae (an. 1572–3) veteri codici (v.c.) adtributae.
Lamb. (*marg.*) = lectiones ibidem quibus littera 'L.' praefixa est.
ς = lectiones ex codicibus deterioribus, ut videntur, hic illic citatae vel in editionibus ante Cratandrinam primum inventae.
M^2, O^2, etc. = codicum M, O, etc. secundae manus.

133 (VII. 10)

Scr. ad urbem xiii Kal. Febr. an. 49

CICERO ATTICO SAL.

Subito consilium cepi ut ante quam luceret exirem, ne qui conspectus fieret aut sermo, lictoribus praesertim laureatis. de reliquo neque hercule quid agam neque quid acturus sim scio; ita sum perturbatus temeritate nostri amentissimi consili. tibi vero quid suadeam, cuius ipse consilium exspecto? Gnaeus noster quid consili ceperit capiatve nescio adhuc, in oppidis coartatus et stupens. omnes, si in Italia consistet, erimus una; sin cedet, consili res est. adhuc certe, nisi ego insanio, stulte omnia et incaute. tu, quaeso, crebro ad me scribe vel quod in buccam venerit.

134 (VII. 11)

Scr., ut vid., in Formiano x Kal. Febr. an. 49

CICERO ATTICO SAL.

1 Quaeso, quid est hoc? aut quid agitur? mihi enim tenebrae sunt. 'Cingulum' inquit 'nos tenemus, Anconem amisimus; Labienus discessit a Caesare.' utrum de imperatore populi Romani an de Hannibale loquimur? o hominem amentem et miserum, qui ne umbram quidem umquam τοῦ καλοῦ viderit! atque haec ait omnia facere se dignitatis causa. ubi est autem dignitas nisi ubi honestas? honestum igitur habere exercitum nullo publico consilio, occupare urbis civium quo facilior sit aditus ad patriam, χρεῶν ἀποκοπάς, φυγάδων

Ep. 133] 3 neque (*alt.*) *O*: ne *RMdm*: nec *Hbs* 4 amentissimi ς: aman- *HR*δ: *om. O* 7 et *M corr.*: sed Ω omnes] omnino *Watt* consistet *Pius*: -tat Ω 8 certe *Victorius*: -ta *M*: incerta *O*: -ti *R*δ

Ep. 134] **1,** 1 est hoc Σ: hoc est Δ 2 cingulum *OP*δ: si- *EHRM* inquis *PF* anconam *s* 7 honestum Σ: nisi h- *M*: num h- δ igitur *E*Δ: est i- *OR*

133 (VII. 10)

Near Rome, 18 January 49

CICERO TO ATTICUS

I have decided on the spur of the moment to leave before daybreak so as to avoid looks or talk, especially with these laurelled lictors. As for what is to follow, I really don't know what I am doing or going to do, I am so confounded by the rashness of this crazy proceeding of ours. As for yourself, what can I recommend—*I* am expecting advice from *you*. What our Gnaeus has decided or is deciding I don't yet know, cooped up there in the country towns in a daze. If he makes a stand in Italy we shall all be with him, but if he leaves, it's a matter for consideration. So far anyhow, unless I am out of my mind, there has been nothing but folly and recklessness. Pray write to me often, if only just what comes into your head.

134 (VII. 11)

Formiae (?), 21 January (?) 49

CICERO TO ATTICUS

1 Pray, what's all this? What is going on? I am in the dark. 'We hold Cingulum, we've lost Ancona, Labienus has deserted Caesar.' Is it a Roman general or Hannibal we are talking of? Deluded wretch, with never in his life a glimpse of even the shadow of Good! And he says he is doing all this for his honour's sake! Where is honour without moral good? And is it good to have an army without public authority, to seize Roman towns by way of opening the road to the mother city, to plan debt cancellations, recall of exiles, and

καθόδους, sescenta alia scelera moliri, 'τὴν θεῶν μεγίστην ὥστ'
ἔχειν τυραννίδα'? sibi habeat suam fortunam! unam mehercule
tecum apricationem in illo lucrativo tuo sole malim quam
omnia illius modi regna, vel potius mori miliens quam semel
2 illius modi quicquam cogitare. 'quid si tu velis?' inquis. age,
quis est cui velle non liceat? sed ego hoc ipsum velle miserius
esse duco quam in crucem tolli. una res est ea miserior, adipisci
quod ita volueris. sed haec hactenus; libenter enim in his
molestiis ἐνσχολάζω σοι.

3 Redeamus ad nostrum. per fortunas, quale tibi consilium
Pompei videtur? hoc quaero, quid urbem reliquerit; ego enim
ἀπορῶ. tum nihil absurdius. urbem tu relinquas? ergo
idem, si Galli venirent. 'non est' inquit 'in parietibus res
publica.' at in aris et focis. 'fecit Themistocles.' fluctum
enim totius barbariae ferre urbs una non poterat. at idem
Pericles non fecit anno fere post quinquagesimo, cum praeter
moenia nihil teneret; nostri olim urbe reliqua capta arcem
tamen retinuerunt. 'οὕτως που τῶν πρόσθεν ἐπευθόμεθα κλέα
4 ἀνδρῶν'. rursus autem ex dolore municipali sermonibusque
eorum quos convenio videtur hoc consilium exitum habiturum.
mira hominum querela est (nescio istic, sed facies ut sciam)
sine magistratibus urbem esse, sine senatu. fugiens denique
Pompeius mirabiliter homines movet. quid quaeris? alia causa
facta est. nihil iam concedendum putant Caesari. haec tu mihi
explica qualia sint.

---

14 illius *EORΔC*: istius *Hc* **2**, 5 σοι *Victorius*: COCON *RMm* **3**, 1 redeamus *s*: debe- Ω 2 quid *scripsi*: quod Ω reliquit *Watt* 3 tum] tamen ς 7 anno *EOR*: annum *HΔ* quinquagesimo *E*: -mum *HORΔ* 8 et nostri *Buecheler* **4**, 3 nescio ς: -is Ω isticine *Wesenberg* 6 facta est *Victorius*: -a si *H*: -as *EORM*: -a δ

a hundred other villainies 'all for that first of deities, Sole Power'? He is welcome to his greatness. I would rather a single hour with you, warming myself in that 'bonus' sunshine of yours, than all such autocracies, or rather I had sooner
2 die a thousand deaths than entertain one such thought. You may say 'But supposing you *did* wish for it?' Come! Anyone is allowed to *wish*. But I reckon the mere wish a sorrier thing than crucifixion. There is only one thing sorrier still, and that is for a man in such a case to get what he wishes for. But there's enough. In the midst of these disquietudes I like to make you my lecture class.

3 To come back to our friend. What *do* you think, for heaven's sake, of Pompey's line—I mean, why has he abandoned Rome? *I* don't know what to make of it. At the time it looked the most senseless thing. Abandon Rome? I suppose you would have done the same if the Gauls were coming? 'House walls' he might answer 'don't make the Republic.' But altars and hearthstones do. 'Themistocles did it.' Yes, because one city could not stand against the tide of the whole barbarian world. But Pericles did not half a century later, though he held nothing except the town walls. Our own forebears still held the citadel after the rest of Rome was in enemy hands. 'Such the brave tales we've heard of
4 men of old.' And yet again, to judge from the indignation in the towns and the talk of the people who come my way, it looks as though this proceeding may achieve something after all. The public outcry is astonishing (whether so in Rome I do not know, but you will inform me) at the thought of the capital without magistrates or Senate. Finally the picture of Pompey on the run affects people marvellously. In a word, the case is altered. They are now against any concessions to Caesar. You must explain to me what all this adds up to.

5 Ego negotio praesum non turbulento; vult enim me Pompeius esse quem tota haec Campania et maritima ora habeat ἐπίσκοπον, ad quem dilectus et negoti summa referatur; itaque vagus esse cogitabam. te puto iam videre quae sit ὁρμὴ Caesaris, qui populus, qui totius negoti status. ea velim scribas ad me, et quidem, quoniam mutabilia sunt, quam saepissime; acquiesco enim et scribens ad te et legens tua.

135 (VII. 12)

Scr. in Formiano ix Kal. Febr. an. 49

CICERO ATTICO SAL.

1 Vnam adhuc a te epistulam acceperam datam XII Kal. [Iun.], in qua significabatur aliam te ante dedisse, quam non acceperam. sed quaeso ut scribas quam saepissime, non modo si quid scies aut audieris sed etiam si quid suspicabere, maximeque quid nobis faciendum aut non faciendum putes.

Nam quod rogas curem ut scias quid Pompeius agat, ne
2 ipsum quidem scire puto; nostrum quidem nemo. vidi Lentulum consulem Formiis x Kal., vidi Libonem; plena timoris et erroris omnia. ille iter Larinum; ibi enim cohortes et Luceriae et Teani reliquaque in Apulia. inde utrum consistere uspiam velit an mare transire nescitur. si manet, vereor ne exercitum firmum habere non possit; sin discedit, quo aut qua, aut quid nobis agendum sit nescio. nam istum quidem cuius Φαλαρισμὸν times omnia taeterrime facturum puto; nec eum rerum prolatio nec senatus magistratuumque discessus

---

5, 2 campania et *H*δ: -na et *EORM*: et Campana *Sternkopf* habeat *ms*: -ent *HRMbd*: -eant *E* 4 quae] *anne* qua? 5 ὁρμὴ *Victorius*: hora me *EORM*: hora mei *H*: (h)ora vi(a)e δ

Ep. 135] 1, 1 kl'. (*sequ. spat.*) *E*: Kal. iun. *vel sim. HOR*Δ: Kal. Feb. *Corradus* 5 putes *Lambinus*: putas Ω **2,** 7 sit ς: est Ω 9 senatus *P*δ: senectus Ω

5 I have a fairly quiet job to look after. Pompey wants me to exercise supervision over all this part of Campania and the sea coast, with general authority over recruiting, etc. I therefore expect to be moving about from place to place. I imagine that by now you see the direction of Caesar's drive, the popular reaction, the state of the whole business. I hope you will write to me about these matters and as often as possible, since they won't stand still. Both when writing to you and when reading what you write I feel calmer.

135 (VII. 12)

Formiae, 22 January 49

CICERO TO ATTICUS

1 I have so far received one letter from you dispatched the 19th, in which you indicate that you had sent another earlier which I have not received. But I do beg you to write as often as you can, anything you know or hear or even just suspect; above all what you think I ought to do or not to do.

As for your request that I should let you know what Pompey
is about, I don't think he knows himself; certainly none of
2 us knows. I saw Consul Lentulus at Formiae on the 21st and
Libo also. No sign of anything but panic and bewilderment. Pompey is making for Larinum, where there are some cohorts, as also at Luceria and Teanum and in the rest of Apulia. Once there, whether he wants to make a stand at any point or to go overseas is unknown. If he stays, I am afraid it may be impossible for him to have a strong army. If he goes, I don't know his route or destination or what I am to do. As for the man whose Phalarism you dread, I expect nothing but atrocities from him. Neither the suspension of business nor the departure of Senate and magistrates nor the closure of the Treasury

3 nec aerarium clausum tardabit. sed haec, ut scribis, cito sciemus.

Interim velim mihi ignoscas quod ad te scribo tam multa totiens; acquiesco enim et tuas volo elicere litteras maximeque consilium quid agam aut quo me pacto geram. demittamne me penitus in causam? non deterreor periculo sed dirumpor dolore: tamne nullo consilio aut tam contra meum consilium gesta esse omnia! an cuncter et tergiverser et iis me dem qui tenent, qui potiuntur? 'αἰδέομαι Τρῶας', nec solum civis sed etiam amici officio revocor, etsi frangor saepe misericordia puerorum.

4 Vt igitur ita perturbato, etsi te eadem sollicitant, scribe aliquid, et maxime, si Pompeius Italia cedit, quid nobis agendum putes. M'. quidem Lepidus (nam fuimus una) eum finem statuit, L. Torquatus eundem. me cum multa tum etiam lictores impediunt. nihil vidi umquam quod minus explicari posset. itaque a te nihildum certi exquiro sed quid videatur, denique ipsam ἀπορίαν tuam cupio cognoscere.

5 Labienum ab illo discessisse prope modum constat. si ita factum esset ut ille Romam veniens magistratus et senatum Romae offenderet, magno usui causae nostrae fuisset. damnasse enim sceleris hominem amicum rei publicae causa videretur, quod nunc quoque videtur, sed minus prodest; non enim habet cui prosit, eumque arbitror paenitere, nisi forte id ipsum est falsum, discessisse illum. nos quidem pro certo habebamus.

6 Et velim, quamquam, ut scribis, domesticis te finibus tenes, formam mihi urbis exponas, ecquod Pompei desiderium,

---

3, 5 demittamne *Pius*: dim- Ω 7 tamne *HRMZ*[1]: tam *EOP codd. Mal.* δ 4, 3 M'. *Aldus nepos*: m. Ω 5, 2 magistratus *Wesenberg*: -um Ω 3 Romae *del. Manutius* 6, 1 ut *H*Δ: ut tu *EOR* 2 ecquod *et* ecquae (*v.* 3) *Victorius*: et q- *more suo* Ω

3 will put a brake on him. But as you say, we shall know shortly.

Meanwhile I hope you will forgive me for writing to you so much and so often. It calms me, and I want to elicit letters from you, above all advice on what to do or how to behave. Shall I fling myself whole-hearted into the cause? I am not deterred by the risk, but I *am* bursting with indignation at the utter lack of judgement, or shall I say the flouting of *my* judgement, in the whole proceedings. Or shall I temporize and sit on the fence and offer myself to those in actual possession of power? 'I fear the Trojans', and my obligations not only as a citizen but as a friend call me back. And yet pity for the boys often makes me waver.

4 You see my perplexity. You have similar anxieties, but write something, and above all tell me what you think I ought to do if Pompey leaves Italy. M'. Lepidus (we have been together) has fixed that as his limit, L. Torquatus likewise. I am hampered by my lictors among many other embarrassments. It is the most intractable problem I ever met. So I do not ask anything definite from you yet, merely your opinion. Failing that, I want to hear of your puzzlement.

5 It is pretty well established that Labienus has left Caesar. If it had worked out so that he came to Rome and found the magistrates and Senate there, he would have been of great use to our cause. He would have appeared as having pronounced the guilt of a friend for country's sake, as indeed he does even now, but he renders less service because he has nobody to render it to. I imagine he regrets his action, unless by any chance the report is untrue and he has not left at all. *We* have it for certain.

6 Although you say you are keeping inside your own gates, I should be grateful if you would make me a sketch of things

ecquae Caesaris invidia appareat, etiam quid censeas de Terentia et Tullia, Romae eas esse an mecum an aliquo tuto loco. haec et si quid aliud ad me scribas velim vel potius scriptites.

136 (VII. 13)

Scr. Minturnis viii Kal. Febr. an. 49

CICERO ATTICO SAL.

1 De Vennonianis rebus tibi adsentior. Labienum ἥρωα iudico. facinus iam diu nullum civile praeclarius, qui, ut aliud nihil, hoc tamen profecit, dedit illi dolorem; sed etiam ad summam profectum aliquid puto. amo etiam Pisonem, cuius iudicium de genero suspicor visum iri grave. quamquam genus belli quod sit vides: ita civile est ut non ex civium dissensione sed ex unius perditi civis audacia natum sit. is autem valet exercitu, tenet multos spe et promissis, omnia omnium concupivit. huic tradita urbs est nuda praesidio, referta copiis. quid est quod ab eo non metuas qui illa templa et tecta non patriam sed praedam putet? quid autem sit acturus aut quo modo nescio, sine senatu, sine magistratibus; ne simulare quidem poterit quicquam πολιτικῶς. nos autem ubi exsurgere poterimus aut quando? quorum dux quam ἀστρατήγητος tu quoque animadvertis, cui ne Picena quidem nota fuerint; quam autem sine consilio res testis. ut enim alia omittam decem annorum peccata, quae condicio non huic

---

3 invidia *Victorius*: invia *HRM*: iniuria *EPδ* 4 tuto *EH*: tuo *ORΔ* h(a)ec *EORM*: et h- *Hδ*

Ep. 136] 1, 1 ἥρωα *Hervagius*: ΠΡωΑ Ω 5 genus Ω: totius Z^1, *sed superscr.* genus: genus totius *Lambinus* 8 exercitu $Z^{(b)}$: -um Ω multos $Z^{(b)}$λ: -ta Ω 12 sine senatu *ERδ*: ne senatus (-tu *N*) *HNOM* magistratibus *Wesenberg*: -tu Ω 16 testis *Z*: stet Ω: est testis *Mueller*

in Rome. Is Pompey missed? Are there any signs of odium against Caesar? Also tell me what you think about Terentia and Tullia. Should they stay in Rome or with me or in some place of safety? Please let me have a letter about all this or anything else there may be, or rather a series of letters.

136 (VII. 13)

Minturnae, 23 January 49

CICERO TO ATTICUS

1 About Vennonius' affairs I agree with you. I call Labienus a hero. It is the finest political action we have seen for a long while. If he has achieved nothing else, he has made Caesar smart. But I think there is some general benefit as well. And bravo Piso! I suspect his verdict on his son-in-law will carry weight. But you see what kind of war we are fighting. A civil war if you will, but one that has arisen not from a conflict in the civic body but from the recklessness of one unscrupulous Roman, who, however, is strong in his army, has many folk tied to him by hopes and promises, and covets every man's all. The capital has been handed over to him undefended and full of wealth. Anything can be apprehended from a man who sees Rome's temples and homes not as his country but as so much plunder. But what he will do or how he will do it, without Senate or magistrates, I don't know. He will not be able to put up so much as a façade of constitutional procedure. As for us, where shall we hope to raise our heads or when? You too remark on our leader's bad generalship, who did not even know what was going on in Picenum. To his lack of judgement the facts themselves stand witness. To say nothing of his other errors over ten years, would not any terms have

2 fugae praestitit? nec vero nunc quid cogitet scio; ac non desino per litteras sciscitari. nihil esse timidius constat, nihil perturbatius. itaque nec praesidium, cuius parandi causa ad urbem retentus est, nec locum ac sedem praesidi ullam video. spes omnis in duabus invidiose retentis paene alienis leg⟨ion⟩ibus. nam dilectus adhuc quidem invitorum est et a pugnando abhorrentium; condicionum autem amissum tempus est. quid futurum sit non video; commissum quidem a nobis certe est sive a nostro duce ut e portu sine gubernaculis egressi tempestati nos traderemus.

3 Itaque de Ciceronibus nostris dubito quid agam; nam mihi interdum amandandi videntur in Graeciam. de Tullia autem et Terentia, cum mihi barbarorum adventus ad urbem proponitur, omnia timeo, cum autem Dolabellae venit in mentem, paulum respiro. sed velim consideres quid faciendum putes, primum πρὸς τὸ ἀσφαλές (aliter enim mihi de illis ac de me ipso consulendum est), deinde ad opiniones, ne reprehendamur quod eas Romae velimus esse in communi bonorum fuga. quin etiam tibi et Peducaeo (scripsit enim ad me) quid faciatis videndum est; is enim splendor est vestrum ut eadem postulentur a vobis quae ab amplissimis civibus. sed de hoc tu videbis, quippe cum de me ipso ac de meis te considerare velim.

4 Reliquum est ut et quid agatur quoad poteris explores scribasque ad me et quid ipse coniectura adsequare; quod etiam a te magis exspecto. nam acta omnibus nuntiantibus a te exspecto futura; 'μάντις δ' ἄριστος...'. loquacitati ignosces,

---

2, 5 insidiose ς 6 legionibus *P*δ: legibus Ω dilectus *Em*: del- *Pbds*: dilectis *HNOM* 3, 2 amandandi (amen-) *EHOR*: eman- (emen-) *P*Δ: commen- *N* 9 scripsit *Victorius*: -sti *Mm*: -sisti Σ*bds* 10 vester *Reid* 12 me *Z*: *om.* Ω meis te *Lambinus*, Z^b: me iste Z^l: me ista (isti *OR*) Ω **4**, 3 etiam a te Σ*bds*: a te e- *Mm*

2 been preferable to this flight? Nor can I say what his plans are now, though I am continually writing to enquire. It is generally agreed that he is in a state of utter panic and confusion. Accordingly I see no sign of the defensive force which he was kept at Rome to prepare nor of any place or rallying-point for such a force. The whole hope lies in two legions kept back not without discredit and scarcely his own. As for the levies, the men so far are reluctant and have no stomach for fighting. And the time for making terms has been let slip. What will come I cannot foresee, but it is certain that through our own fault or our leader's we have put to sea without a rudder and committed ourselves to the mercy of the storm.

3 And so I am in doubt what to do about our boys. Sometimes I feel it might be best to send them to Greece out of the way. As to Tullia and Terentia, when I picture the barbarians marching on Rome I fear all manner of things; but when I think of Dolabella I feel a little better. But I should be grateful to you if you would consider what you think should be done, making safety the first consideration (I have to apply a different standard to their case than to my own) and public opinion the second, lest I incur criticism for wanting them to stay in Rome in the general exodus of the honest folk. Indeed you too and Peducaeus, who has written to me, must see what you are going to do. Your distinction is such that as much is expected from you as from the highest in the land. But this I can leave to you—considering I want you to think about *my* position and my family's.

4 It remains for you to explore what is going on as far as you can and write it to me, and what you are able to guess yourself—I expect the latter from you even more than the former. Everyone tells me what *has* happened, from you I expect things to come. 'He prophesyeth best . . .'. You'll forgive

quae et me levat ad te quidem scribentem et elicit tuas litteras.

5 Aenigma succonum ex Velia plane non intellexi; est enim numero Platonis obscurius.

137 (VII. 13*a*)

Scr. Minturnis vii Kal. Febr. an. 49

⟨CICERO ATTICO SAL.⟩

1 Iam intellexi tuum aenigma; Oppios enim de Velia succones dices. in eo aestuavi diu. quo aperto reliqua patebant et cum Terentiae summa congruebant.

2 L. Caesarem vidi Minturnis a. d. VIII Kal. Febr. mane cum absurdissimis mandatis, non hominem sed scopas solutas, ut id ipsum mihi ille videatur irridendi causa fecisse, qui tantis de rebus huic mandata dederit; nisi forte non dedit et hic sermone aliquo adrepto pro mandatis abusus est.

3 Labienus, vir mea sententia magnus, Teanum venit a. d. VIIII Kal. ibi Pompeium consulesque convenit. qui sermo fuerit et quid actum sit scribam ad te cum certum sciam. Pompeius a Teano Larinum versus profectus est a. d. VIII Kal.; eo die mansit Venafri. aliquantum animi videtur nobis attulisse Labienus. sed ego nondum habeo quod ad te ex his locis scribam; ista magis exspecto, quid illinc adferatur, quo pacto de Labieno ferat, quid agat Domitius in Marsis, Iguvi Thermus, P. Attius Cinguli, quae sit populi urbani voluntas,

---

5, 1 *novam ep. Manutius* succonum *scripsi, duce Watt* (sacconum; *vide infra*): oppiorum Ω: tuum *Schütz* (ex Velia *del.*)

Ep. 137] *novam ep. Corradus*: *superiori coniungunt codd.* **1,** 1 succones *Bosius*: sac- ΩZ^b 2 dices ΩC: dicis Z^b aestuavi *Lambinus*: estu aut Ω **3,** 6 quod *Ernesti*: quid Ω 7 illim *M*(?)λ 8 Marsis ς: maresis ΩZ^l Iguvii *Malaespina*: i(n)gui ΩZ^l

my garrulity; it relieves me, writing to *you*, and draws your letters.

5 Your enigma of the juice-merchants from Velia has simply defeated me, it's darker than the Platonic Number.

137 (VII. 13 *a*)

Minturnae, 24 January 49

CICERO TO ATTICUS

1 *Now* I understand your enigma. By the 'juice-merchants of Velia' you must mean the Oppii. I cudgelled my brains over it a long while. Once that was solved the rest was plain and tallied with Terentia's figure.

2 Early on 23 January I saw L. Caesar at Minturnae bearing a ridiculous message—a loose broom if ever there was one. Indeed it looks to me as though Caesar were deliberately making mock of us in giving *him* a message on matters of such moment—unless perhaps he never gave one, and the fellow has caught up some piece of conversation which he has palmed off as a message.

3 Labienus, a great man *me iudice*, arrived at Teanum on the 22nd. There he met Pompey and the Consuls. Of what was said and done I shall write to you when I have definite information. Pompey left Teanum on his way to Larinum on the 23rd, staying over night at Venafrum. Labienus seems to have put a little fight into us. But I have nothing to write to you yet from this part of the world. I am rather expecting your news—what reports from Caesar, how he is taking it about Labienus, what Domitius is doing in the Marsian country and Thermus at Iguvium and P. Attius at Cingulum,

quae tua coniectura de rebus futuris. haec velim crebro et quid tibi de mulieribus nostris placeat et quid acturus ipse sis scribas.

Si scriberem ipse, longior epistula fuisset, sed dictavi propter lippitudinem.

138 (VII. 14)

Scr. Calibus vi Kal. Febr. an. 49 (§ 1)

CICERO ATTICO SAL.

1 A. d. VI Kal. Febr. Capuam Calibus proficiscens, cum leviter lippirem, has litteras dedi.

L. Caesar mandata Caesaris detulit ad Pompeium a. d. VIII Kal., cum is esset cum consulibus Teani. probata condicio est, sed ita ut ille de iis oppidis quae extra suam provinciam occupavisset praesidia deduceret; id si fecisset, responsum est ad urbem nos redituros esse et rem per senatum confecturos. spero posse in praesentia pacem nos habere; nam et illum furoris et hunc nostrum copiarum suppaenitet.

2 Me Pompeius Capuam venire voluit et adiuvare dilectum; in quo parum prolixe respondent Campani coloni. gladiatores Caesaris qui Capuae sunt, de quibus ante ad te falsum ex Torquati litteris scripseram, sane commode Pompeius distribuit binos singulis patribus familiarum. scutorum in ludo CIↃ fuerunt; eruptionem facturi fuisse dicebantur. sane multum in eo rei publicae provisum est.

3 De mulieribus nostris, in quibus est tua soror, quaeso videas ut satis honestum nobis sit eas Romae esse cum ceterae illa

---

Ep. 138 1, 2 dedi] *num* dictavi? 8 posse *Moser*: esse Ω (*om. O*) $Z^{(b)}$ **2,** 3 A. Torquati *c* 5 CIↃ Z^b: IↃↃ *OMm*: bis *bds*: IↃ *Schütz* 7 provisum *NORms*: prof(l)ixum *Mbd* **3,** 2 ceter(a)e *s*: -ri Ω illa *P*: illi Ω: ulla δ

what is the feeling among the city populace, what your forecast of things to come. Please write to me often about all this, also what you recommend anent my women-folk and what you yourself are going to do.

If I was writing myself this letter would have been longer, but I have dictated it because I am suffering from ophthalmia.

138 (VII. 14)

Cales, 25 January 49

CICERO TO ATTICUS

1 I am dispatching this letter, as I leave Cales for Capua (25 January), my eyes being slightly out of order.

L. Caesar brought Caesar's message to Pompey on 23 January, when he was with the Consuls at Teanum. The terms offered were approved, but on condition that Caesar withdrew his troops from the towns he had occupied outside his province. If he did that he was told that we should return to Rome and settle matters through the Senate. I hope there is a chance of peace for the time being. Caesar is not quite happy in his madness nor Pompey in the forces at his disposal.

2 Pompey has expressed a wish for me to go to Capua and help with the levy, in which the response among the Campanian settlers is far from enthusiastic. Caesar's gladiators at Capua, about whom I earlier sent you a false report based on Torquatus' letter, have been very sensibly distributed by Pompey among the population, two per household. There were 1,000 shields in the establishment and they were said to be going to break out. Certainly a valuable precaution in the public interest.

3 About our womenkind, among whom your sister is included, pray consider whether it is quite creditable to us that they

dignitate discesserint. hoc scripsi ad eas et ad te ipsum antea. velim eas cohortere ut exeant, praesertim cum ea praedia in ora maritima habeamus cui ego praesum ut in iis pro re nata non incommode possint esse. nam si quid offendimus in genero nostro, quod quidem ego praestare non debeo—sed id fit maius quod mulieres nostrae praeter ceteras Romae remanserunt. tu ipse cum Sexto scire velim quid cogites de exeundo de totaque re quid existimes. equidem ad pacem hortari non desino; quae vel iniusta utilior est quam iustissimum bellum cum civibus. sed haec ut fors tulerit.

139 (VII. 15)

Scr. Capuae v Kal. Febr. an. 49 (§ 2)

CICERO ATTICO SAL.

1 Vt ab urbe discessi, nullum adhuc intermisi diem quin aliquid ad te litterarum darem, non quo haberem magno opere quid scriberem sed ut loquerer tecum absens; quo mihi, cum coram id non licet, nihil est iucundius.

2 Capuam cum venissem a. d. VI Kal., pridie quam has litteras dedi, consules conveni multosque nostri ordinis. omnes cupiebant Caesarem abductis praesidiis stare condicionibus iis quas tulisset; uni Favonio leges ab illo nobis imponi non placebat, sed is ⟨non⟩ auditus in consilio. Cato enim ipse iam servire quam pugnare mavult; sed tamen ait in senatu se adesse velle cum de condicionibus agatur, si Caesar adductus sit ut praesidia deducat. ita, quod maxime

---

4 praedia λ: pr(a)esidia Ω   5 cui] quo λ   7 quod] quem *Watt*   10 equidem ad pacem *C*: quidem (eq- *O*) pacem Ω: p- q- δ   12 cum *c*: in Ω

Ep. 139] **1**, 3 quid] quod *Ernesti*   4 licet Σ: liceret Δ   **2**, 5 is] vix *Malaespina* non *add. F. Schmidt*: vix *Lambinus*: haud *Bosius*: non est (*post* auditus) ς

should stay in Rome when other ladies of their rank have left. I have written to them to that effect, as previously to yourself. I should like you to urge them to leave, especially as I have properties on the coast which is under my authority where they might stay without inconvenience (relatively speaking). If my son-in-law is a sore point with some, though really I should not have to answer for that, still the fact that my womenfolk of all others have remained in Rome makes it worse. I should be glad to know what you and Sextus mean to do about leaving and what you think about the whole business. I continue to urge peace. Even an unjust peace is better than the most just of wars against one's countrymen. But that's as fortune wills.

139 (VII. 15)

Capua, 26 January 49

CICERO TO ATTICUS

1 Since I left Rome I have not let a day pass so far without sending you some sort of letter, not that I have had a great deal to write about but just to talk to you in absence. Nothing gives me greater pleasure than that, when I can't do it face to face.

2 On arriving at Capua yesterday (the 25th) I met the Consuls and many members of the Senate. They were all hoping that Caesar would withdraw his garrisons and stand by the terms he has proposed, all except Favonius, who did not approve of letting Caesar dictate conditions to us. But he got no hearing in the conclave. Even Cato now prefers slavery to war. However he says he wants to be present in the Senate when the terms are debated, if Caesar is induced to withdraw

opus est, in Siciliam ire non curat; quod metuo ne obsit, in senatu esse vult. Postum⟨i⟩us autem, de quo nominatim senatus decrevit ut statim in Siciliam iret Fu⟨r⟩fan⟨i⟩oque succederet, negat se sine Catone iturum et suam in senatu operam auctoritatemque quam magni aestimat. ita res ad Fannium pervenit. is cum imperio in Siciliam praemittitur.

3 In disputationibus nostris summa varietas est. plerique negant Caesarem in condicione mansurum, postulataque haec ab eo interposita esse quo minus quod opus esset ad bellum a nobis pararetur. ego autem eum puto facturum ut praesidia deducat; vicerit enim si consul factus erit, et minore scelere vicerit quam quo ingressus est. sed accipienda plaga est; sumus enim flagitiose imparati cum a militibus tum a pecunia, quam quidem omnem non modo privatam quae in urbe est sed etiam publicam quae in aerario est illi reliquimus. Pompeius ad legiones Appianas est profectus; Labienum secum habet. ego tuas opiniones de his rebus exspecto. Formias me continuo recipere cogitabam.

140 (VII. 16)

Scr. Calibus iii Kal. Febr. an. 49 (§ 2)

CICERO ATTICO SAL.

1 Omnis arbitror mihi tuas litteras redditas esse, sed primas praepostere, reliquas ordine quo sunt missae per Terentiam. de mandatis Caesaris adventuque Labieni et responsis con-

---

9 metuo *C*: metu Ω 10 Postumius *Ascensius*: -mus Ω 11 Furfanio *Vrsinus*: fufano *vel sim.* Ω 13 quam *N*Δ: *om. EOR* **3**, 1 varietas *EOR*: veritas *HNR*Δ 2 condicionibus *N* 6 quod *Reid* 7 imparati *O*Δ: impati *ENR*: imperati *HP* 10 Appianas *Lipsius*: ac(c)i- *vel* at(t)i- *vel* acti- Ω 11 secum *R*: cum se *EHNO*Δ

his garrisons. So he does not trouble about going to Sicily, where his presence is urgently needed, but wants to be in the Senate, where I am afraid it will be in the way. Postumius, who was specifically directed by the Senate to proceed immediately to Sicily and take over from Furfanius, refuses to go without Cato, and sets no small store by his own activity and influence in the House. So it came to Fannius. He is being sent ahead to Sicily with military authority.

3 There is a wide variety of opinion in our debates. Most people say that Caesar will not keep to his terms and that he has only put forward these demands to stop us making the necessary preparations for war. My own opinion is that he will in fact withdraw his garrisons. After all, if he is elected Consul he will have won, and with a lesser measure of criminality than that on which he has embarked. But we must take our medicine. We are scandalously ill prepared both in men and money; indeed we have left Caesar all there is of the latter in Rome, public, in the Treasury, as well as private. Pompey has left to join Appius' legions, taking Labienus with him. I am waiting for your views about all this. I intend to return to Formiae at once.

140 (VII. 16)

Cales, 28 January 49

CICERO TO ATTICUS

1 I think all your letters have reached me, but the first in the wrong order, the rest in the order you sent them through Terentia. I wrote to you about Caesar's message, Labienus'

sulum ac Pompei scripsi ad te litteris iis quas a. d. v Kal.
Capua dedi, pluraque praeterea in eandem epistulam conieci.
2 Nunc has exspectationes habemus duas, unam quid Caesar
acturus sit cum acceperit ea quae referenda ad illum data
sunt L. Caesari, alteram quid Pompeius agat; qui quidem
ad me scribit paucis diebus se firmum exercitum habiturum
spemque adfert, si in Picenum agrum ipse venerit, nos Romam
redituros esse. Labienum secum habet non dubitantem de
imbecillitate Caesaris copiarum; cuius adventu Gnaeus noster
multo animi plus habet.

Nos a consulibus Capuam venire iussi sumus ad Non. Febr.
Capua profectus sum Formias a. d. III Kal.; eodem die cum
Calibus tuas litteras hora fere nona accepissem, has statim
3 dedi. de Terentia et Tullia tibi adsentior; ad quas scripseram
ad te ut referrent. si nondum profectae sunt, nihil est quod
se moveant quoad perspiciamus quo loci sit res.

141 (VII. 17)

Scr. in Formiano iv Non. Febr. an. 49 (§ 5)

⟨CICERO ATTICO SAL.⟩

1 Tuae litterae mihi gratae iucundaeque sunt. de pueris in Graeciam transportandis tum cogitabam cum fuga ex Italia quaeri videbatur; nos enim Hispaniam peteremus, illis hoc aeque commodum non erat. tu ipse cum Sexto etiam nunc mihi videris Romae recte esse posse. etenim minime amici Pompeio nostro esse debetis; nemo enim umquam tantum de urbanis praediis detraxit. videsne me etiam iocari?

Ep. 140] **1**, 4 ac Pompei *Manutius*: ad pompeium Ω 5 Capua *anon. ap. Pium*: -u(a)e Ω **2**, 10 eodem *C*: eo Ω (ea *H*)

Ep. 141] *novam ep. Pius*: *superiori coniungunt codd.* **1**, 4 etiam *deletum vellem* 7 praediis λ: praesid- Ω

arrival, and the answer given by the Consuls and Pompey in a letter I dispatched from Capua on the 26th, and I threw a number of other items into the same letter.

2 We now have two things to wait for: one, what is Caesar going to do when he gets the reply which L. Caesar has been given to transmit to him, two, what is Pompey doing. He writes to me that within a few days he will have a strong army and holds out the hope that once he himself gets to Picenum we shall go back to Rome. He has Labienus with him, confident in the weakness of Caesar's forces. His arrival has put much more heart into our Gnaeus.

We have been instructed by the Consuls to return to Capua by the Nones of February. I left Capua for Formiae on the 28th, and received your letter at Cales the same day, about
3 3 o'clock, so I am sending this straight away. I agree with you about Terentia and Tullia. I had written to tell them to consult you. If they have not yet set out there is no call for them to move until we see how things stand.

141 (VII. 17)

Formiae, 2 February 49

CICERO TO ATTICUS

1 I am grateful for your letters and enjoy them. I thought of shipping the boys over to Greece when it looked as though flight from Italy was in view. We should in that case have gone to Spain, which would not have been so suitable for them. It looks to me as though you yourself and Sextus can properly stay on in Rome. You certainly have little cause to love our friend Pompey. Nobody has ever knocked so much off property values in town. I still have my joke, you see.

2 Scire iam te oportet L. Caesar quae responsa referat a Pompeio, quas ab eodem ad Caesarem ferat litteras; scriptae enim et datae ita sunt ut proponerentur in publico. in quo accusavi mecum ipse Pompeium qui, cum scriptor luculentus esset, tantas res atque eas quae in omnium manus venturae essent Sestio nostro scribendas dederit; itaque nihil umquam legi scriptum Σηστιωδέστερον. perspici tamen ex litteris Pompei potest nihil Caesari negari omniaque et cumulate quae postulet dari. quae ille amentissimus fuerit nisi acceperit, praesertim cum impudentissime postulaverit. quis enim tu es qui dicas 'si in Hispaniam profectus erit', 'si praesidia dimiserit'? tamen conceditur, minus honeste nunc quidem violata iam ab illo re publica illatoque bello quam si olim de ratione habenda impetrasset. et tamen vereor ut his ipsis contentus sit. nam cum ista mandata dedisset L. Caesari, debuit esse paulo quietior dum responsa referrentur; dicitur autem nunc esse acerrimus.

3 Trebatius quidem scribit se ab illo VIIII Kal. Febr. rogatum esse ut scriberet ad me ut essem ad urbem; nihil ei me gratius facere posse. haec verbis plurimis. intellexi ex dierum ratione, ut primum de discessu nostro Caesar audisset, laborare eum coepisse ne omnes abessemus. itaque non dubito quin ad Pisonem, quin ad Servium scripserit. illud admiror, non ipsum ad me scripsisse, non per Dolabellam, non per Caelium egisse; quamquam non aspernor Trebati litteras, a quo me
4 unice diligi scio. rescripsi ad Trebatium (nam ad ipsum Caesarem, qui mihi nihil scripsisset, nolui) quam illud hoc tempore esset difficile; me tamen in praediis meis esse neque

---

2, 14 et *NO*Δ: *om. ER*: ei *Koch* **3,** 1 VIIII Σ: VIII Δ

2 You ought to know by now the reply which L. Caesar is taking back from Pompey and the letter which he is carrying from Pompey to Caesar, as it was written and dispatched for public display. In my own mind I blamed Pompey, who is an excellent writer, for giving our friend Sestius the job of composing documents of such importance, which will come into general circulation. And in fact I have never read anything more typically Sestian. But it is plain from Pompey's letter that Caesar is refused nothing, all his demands are met and more than met. It will be sheer lunacy for him not to accept, especially as his demands are the height of impudence. Who is he to say 'on condition that Pompey goes to Spain, that he dismisses his garrisons'? Nevertheless it's conceded, with less dignity it is true, now that he has committed treason and made war on the state, than if he had been allowed his point about his candidature earlier on. And yet I fear even this may not satisfy him. After giving that message to L. Caesar he might have been expected to keep a little quieter until the answer came back, but in fact he is said to be extremely active just now.

3 Trebatius writes that on 22 January Caesar asked him to write urging me to stay near Rome. He says I could do nothing that would please Caesar more, and develops the subject at great length. Counting up the days I perceived that as soon as Caesar heard of our departure he began to be anxious lest we should all be gone. Accordingly I don't doubt that he has written to Piso and to Servius. What surprises me is that he did not write to me himself, or through Dolabella or Caelius. Not that I despise Trebatius' letter. I know he has a peculiar
4 regard for me. I wrote back to Trebatius (I did not care to write to Caesar himself as he had written nothing to me) pointing out how difficult that would be for me at the present

dilectum ullum neque negotium suscepisse. in quo quidem manebo dum spes pacis erit; sin bellum geretur, non deero officio nec dignitati meae, pueros ὑπεκθέμενος in Graeciam. totam enim Italiam flagraturam bello intellego; tantum mali ⟨est⟩ excitatum partim ex improbis, partim ex invidis civibus. sed haec paucis diebus ex illius ad nostra responsa responsis intellegentur quorsum evasura sint. tum ad te scribam plura, si erit bellum; sin autem ⟨otium aut⟩ etiam indutiae, te ipsum, ut spero, videbo.

5 Ego IIII Non. Febr., quo die has litteras dedi, in Formiano, quo Capua redieram, mulieres exspectabam; quibus quidem scripseram tuis litteris admonitus ut Romae manerent. sed audio maiorem quendam in urbe timorem esse. Capuae Non. Febr. esse volebam, quia consules iusserant. quicquid huc erit a Pompeio adlatum, statim ad te scribam, tuasque de istis rebus litteras exspectabo.

142 (VII. 18)

Scr. in Formiano iii Non. Febr. an. 49 (§ 1)

CICERO ATTICO SAL.

1 IIII Non. Febr. mulieres nostrae Formias venerunt tuaque erga se officia plena tui suavissimi studi ad me pertulerunt. eas ego, quoad sciremus utrum turpi pace nobis an misero bello esset utendum, in Formiano esse volui et una Cicerones. ipse cum fratre Capuam ad consules (Nonis enim adesse iussi sumus) III Non. profectus sum, cum has litteras dedi.

4, 6 ὑπεκθέμενος ς: ΕΠ- Ω 7 mali ΣC: malum Δ 8 est *add. Lambinus post* excitatum, *hoc loco Klotz* improvidis *scribere nolui* 11 autem] aut O otium aut *addidi* (*pro* autem *Tyrrell*), *alii alia*

Ep. 142] *nova ep. in HNOR: cum superiore in Δ cohaeret* 1, 2 ad me pertulerunt C: attulerunt Ω

time, but adding that I was staying on my estates and had not undertaken any recruitment of troops or other activity. I shall hold to that as long as there is hope of peace. But if war is to be waged I shall not fall short of my duty and position, having put the boys out of harm's way in Greece. It is evident to me that the whole of Italy will be caught up in the fighting. Such is the holocaust kindled by our countrymen, some wicked, some jealous. But in a few days' time we shall see from Caesar's reply to our reply which way things are going to turn out. I shall write to you further if it's to be war; if peace, or even an armistice, I shall hope to see you in person.

5 I am expecting my wife and daughter today (2 February) at Formiae, where I have returned from Capua. I did write to tell them to stay in Rome, prompted by your letter, but I hear that nervousness there has increased for some reason. I want to be in Capua on the Nones of February because the Consuls have so instructed. I shall write to you at once of any news that comes in here from Pompey and shall expect your letters about affairs in town.

142 (VII. 18)

Formiae, 3 February 49

CICERO TO ATTICUS

1 On 2 February our ladies arrived at Formiae and brought me news of all your characteristically kind and zealous offices towards them. Until we know whether we are to have peace without honour or war with its calamities I have thought it best for them to stay in my house at Formiae and the boys too. My brother and I are leaving for Capua today (the 3rd) to join the Consuls, having been instructed to report there on the Nones.

Responsa Pompei grata populo et probata contioni esse dicuntur; ita putaram. quae quidem ille ⟨si⟩ repudiarit, iacebit; si acceperit, ⟨vicerit⟩. 'utrum igitur' inquies 'mavis?' responderem si quem ad modum parati essemus scirem.

2 Cassium erat hic auditum expulsum Ancona eamque urbem a nobis teneri. si bellum futurum est, negotium utile. Caesarem quidem L. Caesare cum mandatis de pace misso tamen aiunt acerrime dilectum habere, loca occupare, vincire praesidiis. o perditum latronem! ⟨o⟩ vix ullo otio compensandam hanc rei publicae turpitudinem! sed stomachari desinamus, tempori pareamus, cum Pompeio in Hispaniam eamus. haec optima in malis, quoniam illius alterum consulatum a re publica ne data quidem occasione reppulimus. sed haec hactenus.

3 De Dionysio fugit me ad te antea scribere; sed ita constitui, exspectare responsa Caesaris, ut, si ad urbem rediremus, ibi nos exspectaret, sin tardius id fieret, tum eum arcesseremus. omnino quid ille facere debuerit in nostra illa fuga, quid docto homine et amico dignum fuerit, cum praesertim rogatus esset, scio, sed haec non nimis exquiro a Graecis. tu tamen videbis, si erit, quod nolim, arcessendus, ne molesti simus invito.

4 Quintus frater laborat ut tibi quod debet ab Egnatio solvat; nec Egnatio voluntas deest nec parum locuples est, sed cum tale tempus sit ut Q. Titinius (multum enim est nobiscum) viaticum se neget habere idemque debitoribus suis denuntiarit ut eodem faenore uterentur, atque hoc idem etiam L. Ligus

---

8 si *PF*: *om.* Ω 9 iacebit *R*: ta- *NO*Δ vicerit *addidi* (*subaudierat Corradus*) igitur inquies Δ: in- ig- *N*: in- *OR* **2,** 1 ancone *Rm* 4 vincire *P*: -ri (-ceri *N*) Ωλ: devincire *Mueller*: munire *Gronovius* 5 o ς: *om.* Ω 8 optima *Lipsius*: opto Ω **3,** 4 quid δ: quod Ω 5 amico *Pbs*: -cum Ω 6 esset *P*: -em Ω*C* scio *NORCZ*^{l}: *om.* Δ nimis *OP*: minus *NR*Δ 7 si] *fort.* nisi 8 molesti simus *Victorius*: -issimus Ω **4,** 1 frater ς: -tre Ω

Pompey's reply is said to be popular and to have gained the approval of a public meeting. This is what I expected. If Caesar rejects it, he will be generally condemned; if he accepts, he will have won the game. You will ask which I prefer. I should answer that if I knew the state of our preparations.

2 There is a report here that Cassius has been thrown out of Ancona and that the town is in our hands. A useful bit of work, if it is to be war. As for Caesar, they say that notwithstanding L. Caesar's peace mission he is intensely active in raising troops, occupying positions, and securing them with garrisons. Unscrupulous brigand! Can any peace make up for this national disgrace? But I must curb my temper, accept the necessities of the hour, and go to Spain with Pompey. That is the best to be made of a bad job, seeing that we did not protect the commonwealth from Caesar's second Consulship even when we were given the chance. But enough of this.

3 I forgot to write to you before about Dionysius, but what I have decided to do is to wait for Caesar's reply. If we return to Rome he can wait for us there; if that is postponed, I shall send for him then. To be sure I know what he ought to have done when I fled the capital, what was becoming in a man of his attainments and a friend, especially when he was asked; but I don't expect too much in this way from Greeks. You will however take care not to trouble him against his will if I have to send for him, which I hope will be unnecessary.

4 My brother Quintus is much concerned to pay his debt to you through Egnatius, nor does Egnatius lack the will and he is sufficiently well off. But considering the times are such that Q. Titinius, of whom we see a good deal, says he has no money for travel expenses and has informed his debtors that their loans are to be extended at the same rate (a step which L. Ligus

fecisse dicatur, nec hoc tempore aut domi nummos Quintus habeat aut exi⟨ge⟩re ab Egnatio aut versuram usquam facere possit, miratur te non habuisse rationem huius publicae difficultatis. ego autem etsi illud ψευδησιόδειον (ita enim putatur) observo, 'μηδὲ δίκην . . .', praesertim in te, a quo nihil umquam vidi temere fieri, tamen illius querela movebar. hoc, quicquid est, te scire volui.

143 (VII. 19)

Scr. in Formiano iii Non. Febr. an. 49

CICERO ATTICO SAL.

Nihil habeo quod ad te scribam, qui etiam eam epistulam quam eram elucubratus ad te non dederim; erat enim plena spei bonae, quod et contionis voluntatem audieram et illum condicionibus usurum putabam, praesertim suis. ecce tibi III Non. Febr. mane accepi litteras tuas, Philotimi, Furni, Curionis ad Furnium, quibus irridet L. Caesaris legationem. plane oppressi videmur nec quid consili capiam scio. nec mehercule de me laboro; de pueris quid agam non habeo. Capuam tamen proficiscebar haec scribens, quo facilius de Pompei rebus cognoscerem.

144 (VII. 20)

Scr. Capuae Non. Febr. an. 49 (§ 1)

CICERO ATTICO SAL.

1 Breviloquentem iam me tempus ipsum facit. pacem enim desperavi, bellum nostri nullum administrant; cave enim

---

7 exigere ς: exire Ω   8 te ς: *om.* Ω   11 illius *Victorius*: nul- Ω
Ep. 143] 1, 1 quod *Nbms*: quid *HORMd*   qui *cod. Ball.*: quin Ω   2 dedi δ

is said to have taken too), considering too that at the present time Quintus does not have the ready cash and cannot get it out of Egnatius nor yet borrow it in any quarter, he is surprised that you have not made allowance for this general stringency. As for me, I like to follow the maxim, attributed (wrongly, as is thought) to Hesiod, 'judge not a cause . . .', especially in your case, for I have never known you do anything without good reason. But still I have some sympathy with his grievance. I thought I should mention this, be it as it may.

143 (VII. 19)

Formiae, 3 February 49

CICERO TO ATTICUS

I have nothing to write to you about, indeed I have not dispatched a letter which I had already written to you by lamp light. It was full of optimism because I had heard of the feeling in the public meeting and thought Caesar would take the terms, particularly as they were of his own making. Then, at daybreak on 3 February, comes your letter along with others from Philotimus and Furnius and one from Curio to Furnius, in which he ridicules L. Caesar's embassy. We seem to be quite crushed, and I don't know what course to take. It's really not myself I am worried about but the boys; I don't know what to do about them. However I am leaving for Capua as I write this, hoping there to come by information about Pompey's affairs more easily.

144 (VII. 20)

Capua, 5 February 49

CICERO TO ATTICUS

1 The facts of the situation now make me laconic. I have given up hope of peace, and our people are doing nothing to wage

putes quicquam esse minoris his consulibus, quorum ego * * * spe audiendi aliquid et cognoscendi nostri apparatus maximo imbri Capuam veni prid. Non., ut eram iussus. illi autem adhuc, id est Nonis, nondum venerant, sed erant venturi inanes, imparati. Gnaeus autem Luceriae dicebatur esse et adire cohortis legionum Appianarum non firmissimarum. at illum ruere nuntiant et iam iamque adesse, non ut manum conserat (quicum enim?) sed ut fugam intercludat.

2 Ego autem in Italia 'καὶ συναποθανεῖν', nec te id consulo; sin extra, quid ago? ad manendum hiems, lictores, improvidi et neglegentes duces, ad fugam hortatur amicitia Gnaei, causa bonorum, turpitudo coniungendi cum tyranno; qui quidem incertum est Phalarimne an Pisistratum sit imitaturus. haec velim explices et me iuves consilio, etsi te ipsum istic iam calere puto; sed tamen quantum poteris. ego si quid hic hodie novi cognoro, scies; iam enim aderunt consules ad suas Nonas. tuas cottidie litteras exspectabo; ad has autem cum poteris rescribes. mulieres et Cicerones in Formiano reliqui.

145 (VII. 21)

Scr. Calibus vi Id. Febr. an. 49 (§ 1)

CICERO ATTICO SAL.

1 De malis nostris tu prius audis quam ego; istinc enim emanant. boni autem hinc quod exspectes nihil est. veni Capuam ad Non. Febr., ita ut iusserant consules. eo die Lentulus venit sero. alter consul omnino non venerat VII Id.; eo enim die ego Capua discessi et mansi Calibus. inde has litteras postridie

---

Ep. 144] 1, 3 *post* ego *excidisse aliquid videtur velut* ad congressum 6 adhuc id est Nonis *C*: *om.* Ω 8 Appianarum *Lipsius*: atin- *E*: itin- *ORMm*: itinerum (-ris *b*) *Nbds*: actinarum λ: Attian- *Bosius*

Ep. 145] 1, 1 istinc *EOR*δ: -im *N*: -i *H*: istum *M*

war—don't imagine these Consuls are worth twopence. To meet them (?), in the hope of getting some news and acquainting myself with our preparations, I arrived at Capua in pouring rain on the 4th, as instructed. They have as yet (i.e. on the Nones) not arrived, but are on their way, empty-handed and unprepared. Gnaeus is said to be at Luceria, visiting cohorts of Appius' legions, which are none too reliable. As for Caesar, they say he is plunging, will be down on us any minute, not to join battle (who is there for him to fight with?) but to cut off escape.

2 For my part in Italy I am ready 'e'en to die with him', and on that I don't ask your advice. But out of Italy? What do I do? 'Stay' say winter, lictors, improvident and negligent leadership: 'go' say my friendship for Gnaeus, the cause of the honest men, the dishonour of alliance with a despot, as to whom it is doubtful whether he will take Phalaris or Pisistratus as his model. Please sort it all out and help me with your advice, though I suppose you yourself have now got plenty to think about in Rome. But do your best. If I hear any news here today you shall know of it—the Consuls will be here presently for their Nones. I shall expect a letter from you every day. Please reply to this when you can. I have left the ladies and the boys at Formiae.

145 (VII. 21)

Cales, 8 February 49

CICERO TO ATTICUS

1 You hear of our misfortunes sooner than I, for they flow from your quarter. Of good news you need expect none from here. I went to Capua for the Nones of February as the Consuls had directed. Lentulus arrived late that day. The other Consul had not arrived at all on the 7th, on which day I left Capua and stayed the night at Cales. From there I am dispatching

ante lucem dedi. haec Capuae dum fui cognovi: nihil in consulibus, nullum usquam dilectum; nec enim conquisitores φαινοπροσωπεῖν audent, cum ille adsit, contraque noster dux nusquam sit, nihil agat, nec nomina dant; deficit enim non voluntas sed spes. Gnaeus autem noster (o rem miseram et incredibilem!) ut totus iacet! non animus est, non consilium, non copiae, non diligentia. mittam illa, fugam ab urbe turpissimam, timidissimas in oppidis contiones, ignorationem non solum adversari sed etiam suarum copiarum: hoc cuius
2 modi est? VII Id. Febr. Capuam C. Cassius tribunus pl. venit, attulit mandata ad consules ut Romam venirent, pecuniam de sanctiore aerario auferrent, statim exirent. urbe relicta redeant; quo praesidio? deinde exeant; quis sinat? consul ei rescripsit ut prius ipse in Picenum. at illud totum erat amissum; sciebat nemo praeter me ex litteris Dolabellae. mihi dubium non erat quin ille iam iamque foret in Apulia, Gnaeus noster in navi.

3 Ego quid agam σκέμμα magnum, neque mehercule mihi quidem ullum, nisi omnia essent acta turpissime neque ego ullius consili particeps—sed tamen, quid me deceat. ipse me Caesar ad pacem hortatur, sed antiquiores litterae quam ruere coepit. Dolabella, Caelius me illi valde satis facere. mira me ἀπορία torquet. iuva me consilio si potes, et tamen ista quantum potes provide. nihil habeo tanta rerum perturbatione quod scribam; tuas litteras exspecto.

---

7 conquisitores] *hic desinit N* 8 adsit *s*: ad se Ω contraque *Boot*: -a quem Ω **2**, 3 auferrent *Pms*: aff- Ω 4 consul ei rescripsit *P*: -lere scripsit Ω **3**, 3 quid *scripsi*: quod Ω 6 tamen] *fort.* tantum

this letter before daybreak on the 8th. While in Capua I learnt this much, that the Consuls are worthless and that there is no troop-levying anywhere. The recruiting officers dare not show their noses with Caesar in the offing, while our leader by contrast is nowhere and does nothing; and there are no volunteers. It is not loyalty they lack but hope. As for our Gnaeus, it is a lamentable and incredible thing. How utterly down he is! No courage, no plan, no forces, no energy. I won't dwell on what is past—the disgraceful flight from Rome, the craven speeches in the towns, the ignorance of his own forces, let
2 alone the enemy's. What do you make of this latest? On 7 February C. Cassius the Tribune arrived in Capua with a message for the Consuls instructing them to go to Rome, remove the money from the Inner Treasury, and leave again at once. So having abandoned the capital they are expected to go back without any military force and then leave with every chance that they may be prevented! The Consul replied asking Pompey to go himself to Picenum first. But Picenum is completely lost—no one knows except me, from a letter of Dolabella's. I have no doubt that Caesar will be in Apulia any minute and our Gnaeus on board ship.

3 What I am to do is a great question, though I should not find it a question at all, believe me, but for the disgraceful mishandling of our affairs at every point and my own complete exclusion from their conduct—all the same it is a question what is the fitting course for me. Caesar himself urges me to peace, but the letter was written before he started plunging. Dolabella and Caelius say he is very well satisfied with my behaviour. I am at my wits' end. Help me with your advice if you can, and anyhow look after things in Rome as far as you can. With everything in the melting pot like this I have nothing to write. I expect a letter from you.

146 (VII. 22)

Scr. in Formiano v Id. Febr. an. 49

CICERO ATTICO SAL.

1 Pedem in Italia video esse nullum qui non in istius potestate sit. de Pompeio scio nihil, eumque, nisi in navim se contulerit, exceptum iri puto. o celeritatem incredibilem! huius autem nostri—sed non possum sine dolore accusare eum de quo angor et crucior. tu caedem non sine causa times, non quo minus quicquam Caesari expediat ad diuturnitatem victoriae et dominationis sed video quorum arbitrio sit acturus. recte †sit† censeo cedendum.

2 De Oppiis egeo consili. quod optimum factu videbitur facies. cum Philotimo loquere, atque adeo Terentiam habebis Idibus.

Ego quid agam? qua aut terra aut mari persequar eum qui ubi sit nescio? etsi terra quidem qui possum? mari quo? tradam igitur isti me? fac posse tuto (multi enim hortantur), num etiam honeste? nullo modo quidem. a te petam consilium, ut soleo? explicari res non potest. sed tamen si quid in mentem venit velim scribas, et ipse quid sis acturus.

147 (VII. 23)

Scr. in Formiano iv Id. Febr. an. 49

CICERO ATTICO SAL.

1 v Id. Febr. vesperi a Philotimo litteras accepi Domitium exercitum firmum habere, cohortis ex Piceno Lentulo et Thermo ducentibus cum Domiti exercitu coniunctas esse,

Ep. 146] **1**, 1 esse nullum *HOR*: n- e- Δ 2 navem λ 7 vides *Watt* recte sit. sed censeo *Tyrrell–Purser* **2**, 1 Oppiis *Boot*: oppidis *HOR*: -dis iis Δ consilii *HO*Δ: -io *R Ant.* 7 etiam Z^b*ms*: et tam Ω quidem] quid Z^b 9 acturus] *hic desinit H*

Ep. 147] **1**, 1 vesperi a *c*: -ri e Σδ (-ris e *m*): -ris *M*

146 (VII. 22)

Formiae, 9 February 49

CICERO TO ATTICUS

1 Clearly there is not a foot of Italian soil which is not in Caesar's grasp. Of Pompey I know nothing, and unless he takes refuge aboard ship I expect he will be caught. The rapidity of movement is beyond belief. As for our man—but it is painful for me to complain of him when I am so desperately anxious about his fate. You may well be afraid of a massacre, not that anything would be less in Caesar's interests if he wants his victory and personal power to last, but I can easily see the kind of people at whose beck he will be acting. Let us hope it will be all right (?); but (?) my advice is to leave.

2 As regards the Oppii I have nothing to suggest. You will do what seems best. Talk to Philotimus—or rather you will have Terentia on the Ides.

For myself, what am I to do? How am I to follow, be it by land or sea, a man whose whereabouts I don't know?—though as to following him by land, that's impossible. If by sea, to what destination? Shall I then hand myself over to Caesar? Supposing I could do so safely (many urge me that way), can I also do it honourably? Most decidedly not. Well, shall I seek advice from you as usual? The problem is insoluble. None the less if anything occurs to you, please write, and tell me what you yourself are going to do.

147 (VII. 23)

Formiae, 10 February 49

CICERO TO ATTICUS

1 On the evening of 9 February I had a letter from Philotimus to the effect that Domitius has a strong army, that the cohorts from Picenum under Lentulus and Thermus have joined

Caesarem intercludi posse eumque id timere, bonorum animos recreatos Romae, improbos quasi perculsos. haec metuo equidem ne sint somnia, sed tamen M'. Lepidum, L. Torquatum, C. Cassium tribunum pl. (hi enim sunt nobiscum, id est in Formiano) Philotimi litterae ad vitam revocaverunt. ego autem illa metuo ne veriora sint, nos omnis plane iam captos esse, Pompeium Italia cedere; quem quidem (o rem acerbam!) persequi Caesar dicitur. persequi Caesar Pompeium? quid? ut interficiat? o me miserum! et non omnes nostra corpora opponimus? in quo tu quoque ingemiscis. sed quid faciamus? victi, oppressi, capti plane sumus.

2 Ego tamen Philotimi litteris lectis mutavi consilium de mulieribus. quas, ut scripseram ad te, Romam remittebam; sed mihi venit in mentem multum fore sermonem: me iudicium iam de causa publica fecisse, qua desperata quasi hunc gradum mei reditus esse quod mulieres revertissent. de me autem ipso tibi adsentior, ne me dem incertae et periculosae fugae, cum rei publicae nihil prosim, nihil Pompeio; pro quo emori cum pie possum tum libenter. manebo igitur, etsi vivere ....

3 Quod quaeris hic quid agatur, tota Capua et omnis hic dilectus iacet; desperata res est, in fuga omnes sunt, nisi quid eius modi fuerit ut Pompeius istas Domiti copias cum suis coniungat. sed videbamur omnia biduo triduove scituri.

[L.] Caesaris litterarum exemplum tibi misi; rogaras enim.

6 M'. *Aldus nepos*: m. Ω 10 plane *Wesenberg*: p(a)ene Ω **2**, 4 hunc quasi *Boot* 6 ipso *Manutius*: ipse Ω **3**, 2 quid eius modi fuerit *ER*: q- eius f- *O*Δ: q- f- eius modi λ: quis (qui *Tyrrell*) deus iuverit (fecerit *Boot*) *anon. ap. Pium* 5 L. *del. Victorius*

Domitius' army, that Caesar may be, and is afraid of being, cut off, that the honest men in Rome have taken fresh heart and the villains are pretty well floored. For my part I fear this is all fancy, but M'. Lepidus, L. Torquatus, and C. Cassius the Tribune, who are with me (i.e. in my house near Formiae) have been brought back to life by Philotimus' letter. But I am afraid the other tale has more truth in it, that we are all prisoners outright and Pompey leaving Italy. Caesar (I hate to write it) is said to be in pursuit of him. Caesar pursuing Pompey? For what? To kill him? Oh, God! Why are we not all throwing our bodies in the way? You too must be groaning at the thought. But what can we do? We are beaten, overwhelmed, prisoners pure and simple.

2 However after reading Philotimus' letter I changed my mind about the ladies. I was going to send them back to Rome as I wrote to you, but it occurred to me that there would be a great deal of talk. It would be said that I had now passed judgement on the national cause, that I had despaired of it, and that the return of my wife and daughter was a prelude to my own. As for me personally, I agree with you that I ought not to abandon myself to a doubtful and dangerous flight overseas since I should do no good to the state and no good to Pompey—for whom I can die not only dutifully but gladly. So I shall stay, though the thought of living. . . .

3 You ask what is toward here. Capua and the whole recruiting effort here is absolutely at a standstill. Hope is dead, everyone is in flight, unless something happens such as Pompey joining up those forces of Domitius' with his own. But it looks as though we shall know everything in two or three days' time.

I am sending you a copy of Caesar's letter as you requested.

cui nos valde satis facere multi ad me scripserunt; quod patior facile, dum, ut adhuc, nihil faciam turpiter.

148 (VII. 24)

Scr. in Formiano iii Id. Febr. an. 49

CICERO ATTICO SAL.

Philotimi litterae me quidem non nimis sed eos qui in his locis erant admodum delectarunt. ecce postridie Cassio litterae Capua a Lucretio, familiari eius, Nigidium a Domitio Capuam venisse; eum dicere Vibullium cum paucis militibus e Piceno currere ad Gnaeum, confestim insequi Caesarem, Domitium non habere militum VI milia. idem scripsit Capua consules discessisse. non dubito quin Gnaeus in fuga sit; modo effugiat. ego a consilio fugiendi, ut tu censes, absum.

149 (VII. 25)

Scr. in Formiano iii aut prid. Id. Febr. an. 49

CICERO ATTICO SAL.

Cum dedissem ad te litteras tristis et metuo ne veras de Lucreti ad Cassium litteris Capua missis, Cephalio venit a vobis; attulit etiam a te litteras hilariores nec tamen firmas, ut soles. omnia facilius credere possum quam quod scribitis, Pompeium exercitum ⟨firmum⟩ habere. nemo huc ita adfert omniaque quae nolim. o rem miseram! malas causas semper obtinuit, in optima concidit. quid dicam nisi illud eum scisse (neque enim erat difficile), hoc nescisse? erat enim ars difficilis

---

Ep. 148] 2 Cassio $Z^{b}\lambda$: -si(i) Ω: ad Cassium *Victorius* 6 VI milia *Wesenberg*: vim Δ: III *ORλ* (*addito* 'id est tria millia'): *anne* V milia? 8 ego a *Klotz*: ego *C*: e *OM*: o *R*: a δ

Ep. 149] 2 capua *OPc*: -am *R*Δ 5 firmum *m*: *om.* Ω 6 o $ORZ^{(b)}$: *om.* Δ

Many people have written telling me that he is very well satisfied with me. I have no objection to his being so, provided that, as hitherto, there is nothing in my conduct to blush for.

148 (VII. 24)

Formiae, 11 February 49

CICERO TO ATTICUS

Philotimus' letter gave great pleasure not so much to me as to those hereabouts. Then next day comes a letter from Capua to Cassius from his friend Lucretius, stating that Nigidius has arrived at Capua from Domitius and that according to him Vibullius is scurrying to Gnaeus from Picenum with a handful of troops and with Caesar in close pursuit. Domitius is said not to have 6,000 men. Lucretius also wrote that the Consuls had left Capua. I have no doubt that Gnaeus is a fugitive. I only hope he gets away. Personally, as you advise, I am not thinking of flight.

149 (VII. 25)

Formiae, 11 or 12 February 49

CICERO TO ATTICUS

After I had dispatched a gloomy and I fear veracious letter about Lucretius' letter to Cassius sent from Capua, Cephalio arrived from you people in Rome. He brought a more cheerful letter from you too, though not so solidly based as yours generally are. I can believe anything sooner than what you and the others write, that Pompey has a strong army. Nobody who comes here so reports, rather all manner of bad news. It is a melancholy story. Invariably successful in bad causes, he has fallen down in the best of all. What can one say except that there he knew his way (it was not difficult) and

recte rem publicam regere. sed iam iamque omnia sciemus et scribemus ad te statim.

150 (VII. 26)

Scr. in Formiano Id. Febr., ut vid., an. 49

CICERO ATTICO SAL.

1 Non venit idem usu mihi quod tu tibi scribis, 'quotiens exorior'; ego enim nunc ⟨primum⟩ paulum exorior, et maxime quidem iis litteris quae Roma adferuntur de Domitio, de Picentium cohortibus. omnia erant facta hoc biduo laetiora. itaque fuga quae parabatur repressa est. Caesaris interdicta, 'si te secundo lumine hic offendero . . .', respuuntur; bona de Domitio, praeclara de Afranio fama est.

2 Quod me amicissime admones ut me integrum quoad possim servem, gratum est; quod addis, ne propensior ad turpem causam videar, certe videri possum. ego me ducem in civili bello quoad de pace ageretur n⟨eg⟩avi esse, non quin rectum esset sed quia, quod multo rectius fuit, id mihi fraudem tulit. plane eum cui noster alterum consulatum deferret et triumphum (at quibus verbis! 'pro tuis rebus gestis amplissimis') inimicum habere nolueram. ego scio et quem metuam et quam ob rem. sin erit bellum, ut video fore, partes meae non desiderabuntur.

3 De HS $\overline{\text{XX}}$ Terentia tibi rescripsit. Dionysio, dum existimabam vagos nos fore, nolui molestus esse; tibi autem crebro ad me scribenti de eius officio nihil rescripsi, quod diem ex

---

Ep. 150] *nova ep. in* Σ: *cum superiore in* Δ *cohaeret* **1**, 2 primum *add. Tyrrell–Purser* **2**, 3 videri ς: -re Ω non possum ς certen videri possum? *conieceram* 4 in OΔ: *om. ER* negavi *Victorius*: navi Δ: nam *R* 6 cui *C*: quin OΔ: cum *R* 7 deferret *Victorius*: de ea ref- Ω at ς: a Ω pro tuis rebus *Lambinus*: ut prorsus Ω: pro rebus *Corradus* **3**, 3 scribenti *Ps*: scienti Ω

here he did not? To guide the state aright was not an easy art. However I shall know everything any day now and shall write to you at once.

150 (VII. 26)

Formiae, 13 February (?) 49

CICERO TO ATTICUS

1 My experience differs from yours. You say 'whenever I pluck up spirit'. *I* am plucking up spirit a little now for the first time, chiefly because of the letters I am getting from Rome about Domitius and the Picene cohorts. In the last couple of days everything has taken on a brighter look. Accordingly the flight which was in preparation has been checked. Caesar's interdicts ('If on a second dawn I find thee here') are scornfully rejected. Domitius is in good, Afranius in splendid repute.

2 Thank you for your most friendly advice to keep my hands free as long as possible. You add a warning against seeming partial to the discreditable cause. Certainly it is possible that I may seem so. I refused to take a leading role in a civil war so long as peace negotiations were proceeding, not that it would not have been proper to do so but because an action much more proper had been my undoing. Frankly I did not care to make an enemy of a man to whom our friend was offering a second Consulship and a Triumph (and in what terms! 'In recognition of your splendid achievements'). I know whom to fear and why. But if it is to be war, as I see it will be, my part shall not be found wanting.

3 Terentia has written back to you about the HS 20,000. As for Dionysius, while I thought I should be on the move I did not choose to trouble him, and I did not reply to your frequent mention of his loyal disposition because I was

die exspectabam ut statuerem quid esset faciendum. nunc, ut video, pueri certe in Formiano videntur hiematuri. et ego? nescio. si enim erit bellum, cum Pompeio esse constitui. quod habebo certi, faciam ut scias. ego bellum foedissimum futurum puto, nisi qui, ut tu sc⟨rib⟩is, Parthicus casus exstiterit.

151 (viii. 1)

Scr. in Formiano xv vel xiv Kal. Mart. an. 49

CICERO ATTICO SAL.

1 Cum ad te litteras dedissem, redditae mihi litterae sunt a Pompeio: cetera de rebus in Piceno gestis quas ad se Vibullius scripsisset, de dilectu Domiti, quae sunt vobis nota, nec tam laeta erant in iis litteris quam ad me Philotimus ⟨scrips⟩erat. ipsam tibi epistulam misissem sed iam subito fratris puer proficiscebatur; cras igitur mittam. sed in ea Pompei epistula erat in extremo ipsius manu 'tu censeo Luceriam venias; nusquam eris tutius'. id ego in eam partem accepi, haec oppida atque oram maritimam illum pro relicto habere, nec sum miratus eum qui caput ipsum reliquisset reliquis membris
2 non parcere. ei statim rescripsi, hominemque certum misi de comitibus meis, ⟨me⟩ non quaerere ubi tutissimo essem; si me vellet sua aut rei publicae causa Luceriam venire, statim esse venturum; hortatusque sum ut oram maritimam retineret, si rem frumentariam sibi ex provinciis suppeditari vellet. hoc me frustra scribere videbam; sed uti in urbe retinenda

---

6 egone, nescio *Wesenberg*: *fort.* an (num ς) et ego nescio 7 quod ς: quid Ω: si quid ς faciam ut scias *s*: sciam ut sciebam Ω: sciam *bd* 8 scribis *Orelli*: scis Ω
Ep. 151] **1**, 2 quas *scripsi*: qu(a)e Ω 3 tam *M corr.*: tamen Ω: tamen tam *Bosius* 4 quam Ω: quas *Ps*: quam quae *Orelli* scripserat *s*: erat Ω: mise- *P* 5 sed *Ps*: miser Ω 9 relicto *OMZ*^{b}: der- *ER*δ **2**, 2 me *add.* ς tutissimo *C*, *Charisius* (*v. comm.*): turpis- *Z*^{l}: tu pes- *M*: tutissime Σδ essent *Charisius*

waiting from one day to the next to decide what should be done. Now, as I see it, the boys at any rate are likely to spend the winter at Formiae. And I? I don't know. If it is to be war I have decided to be with Pompey. I shall let you know anything definite. I think there will be an atrocious war unless, as you say, some Parthian stroke of luck intervenes.

151 (VIII. 1)

Formiae, 15 or 16 February 49

CICERO TO ATTICUS

1 After I had dispatched a letter to you I received one from Pompey. The bulk of it concerned operations in Picenum as reported by Vibullius and Domitius' levying of troops, things which you in Rome already know. They were not however so cheerful-sounding in this letter as Philotimus had represented them to me in his. I should have sent you the letter itself, but my brother's boy is leaving now suddenly, so I shall send it tomorrow. However in that letter of Pompey's, at the end and in his own hand, are the words 'As for yourself, I advise you to come to Luceria. You will be as safe there as anywhere'. I took this to mean that he has given up the towns here and the coast for lost, nor am I surprised that having
2 abandoned the head he does not spare the limbs. I am writing back at once and sending a trusty person, one of my staff, to tell him that I am not looking for the safest place I can find. If he wants me to go to Luceria either on his own or the public account, I say I shall go at once. I also urge him to hold on to the sea coast if he wants to be supplied with grain from the provinces. I realize I write this to no purpose, but as formerly

tunc, sic nunc in Italia non reliquenda testificabar sententiam
meam. sic enim parari video, ut Luceriam omnes copiae con-
trahantur et ne is quidem locus ⟨sit⟩ stabilis sed ex eo ipso, si
3 urgeamur, paretur fuga; quo minus mirere si invitus in eam
causam descendo in qua neque pacis neque victoriae ratio
quaesita sit umquam sed semper flagitiosae et calamitosae
fugae. eundum, ut quemcumque fors tulerit casum subeam
potius cum iis qui dicuntur esse boni quam videar a bonis
dissentire. etsi prope diem video bonorum, id est lautorum
et locupletum, urbem refertam fore, municipiis vero his
relictis refertissimam; quo ego in numero essem, si hos lictores
molestissimos non haberem, nec me M'. Lepidi, L. Vulcati,
Ser. Sulpici comitum paeniteret, quorum nemo nec stultior
est quam L. Domitius nec inconstantior quam Ap. Claudius.
4 unus Pompeius me movet, beneficio non auctoritate; quam
enim ille habeat auctoritatem in hac causa? qui, cum omnes
Caesarem metuebamus, ipse eum diligebat, postquam ipse
metuere coepit, putat omnis hostis illi esse oportere. ibimus
tamen Luceriam, nec eum fortasse delectabit noster adventus;
dissimulare enim non potero mihi quae adhuc acta sint
displicere.

Ego si somnum capere possem, tam longis te epistulis non obtunderem. tu, si tibi eadem causa est, me remunerere sane velim.

---

9 sit *add. Mueller* (*post* stabilis *Ernesti*) 10 mirere *E*δ: -eris *OR*: -e res *M* si Σ: et *M*: si et δ **3,** 4 *fort.* sed eundum *vel* eundum tamen 5 a bonis *EOP*: ab omnibus *R*Δ 7 locupletium *E* 9 me M'. *Aldus nepos*: me an *ER*: mea u *M*: me auli (A.) δ L. *b*: luce *M*: luc(c)ei(i) *ERdms* 11 domitius *Obms*: do. *ERMd* **4,** 2 habet *Kayser* 4 esse oportere Σ: o- e- Δ 5 luceriam *O*δ: nuc- *ERM* 6 sunt *Em*

on holding the capital so now on not abandoning Italy I am putting my view on record. Clearly the plan is to concentrate all our forces at Luceria and not to make even that a firm point, but to prepare for flight from Luceria itself if we are pressed—
3 so you may be the less surprised if I embark with reluctance in a cause in which there has at no time been any attempt to plan either peace or victory, but always infamous and disastrous flight. I must go, so that rather than appear to be at variance with the honest men I may meet whatever fate fortune brings in company with those who are so called. And yet I can see that Rome will soon be full of honest men, i.e. men of style and substance, full to bursting indeed when the townships here are given up. I should be one of them if I did not have these confounded nuisances of lictors, and I should not be ashamed to be in company with M'. Lepidus, L. Vulcatius, and Ser. Sulpicius. None of them is more stupid than L.
4 Domitius or more fickle than Ap. Claudius. Pompey alone counts with me, because of what he did for me, not because of the weight of his name. What weight after all could it carry in this cause? When all of us feared Caesar, Pompey was his friend; now that *he* has started to fear him he expects us all to be Caesar's enemies. However I shall go to Luceria, and it may be that my coming won't make him any happier, for I shall not be able to conceal my disapproval of what has been done so far.

If I could get any sleep I should not bore you with such long letters. If you are in the same case, I very much hope you will repay me in kind.

152 (VIII. 2)

Scr. in Formiano xiii Kal. Mart. an. 49 (§ 4)

CICERO ATTICO SAL.

1 Mihi vero omnia grata, et quod scripsisti ad me quae audieras
et quod non credi⟨di⟩sti quae digna diligentia mea non erant
et quod monuisti quod sentiebas. ego ad Caesarem unas
Capua litteras dedi, quibus ad ea rescripsi quae mecum ille
de gladiatoribus suis egerat, brevis sed benevolentiam signifi-
cantis, non modo sine contumelia sed etiam cum maxima
laude Pompei; id enim illa sententia postulabat qua illum ad
concordiam hortabar. eas si quo ille misit, in publico proponat
velim. alteras eodem die dedi quo has ad te; non potui non
2 dare, cum et ipse ad me scripsisset et Balbus. earum exemplum
ad te misi. nihil arbitror fore quod reprehendas; si qua erunt,
doce me quo modo μέμψιν effugere possim. 'nihil' inquies
'omnino scripseris.' qui magis effugiam eos qui volent fingere?
verum tamen ita faciam, quoad fieri poterit.

Nam quod me hortaris ad memoriam factorum, dictorum
scriptorum etiam meorum, facis amice tu quidem mihique
gratissimum, sed mihi videris aliud tu honestum meque
dignum in hac causa iudicare atque ego existimem. mihi enim
nihil ulla in gente umquam ab ullo auctore rei publicae ac
duce turpius factum esse videtur quam a nostro amico factum
est, cuius ego vicem doleo; qui urbem reliquit, id est patriam,
3 pro qua et in qua mori praeclarum fuit. ignorare mihi videris
haec quanta sit clades; es enim etiam nunc domi tuae, sed invitis
perditissimis hominibus esse diutius non potes. hoc miserius,

---

Ep. 152] **1,** 2 credidisti *s corr.*: credis te Ω: -is ea *P*   digna *Ps*: -na a Ω   3 unas δ: unus Ω   6 cum ς: huius Ω   7 id enim *Manutius*: idem in *RM*: idem enim δ   **2,** 3 μέμψιν *Gronovius*: esse *RMZ*[b]: enim *ms*: ego *bd*   possim *d Ant.*: -sum Ω   4 qui *C*: quo *R*Δ   effugiam *scripsi*: -as Ω   9 existimo *Wesenberg*

152 (VIII. 2)

Formiae, 17 February 49

CICERO TO ATTICUS

1 On the contrary I thank you for everything: for letting me know what you heard, for not believing reports which made me out less punctilious than I am, and for telling me your opinion. I sent Caesar one letter from Capua in reply to the representations he made to me about his gladiators. It was short but friendly, and so far from abusing Pompey praised him highly, as my argument, urging him to a settlement, required. If he has sent the letter to third parties, well, I should be happy to have him post it up in public. I am dispatching another today. I could not do otherwise since both he and
2 Balbus had written to me. I am sending you a copy of my letter. I don't think you will find anything to censure. If you do, then show me how I am to escape adverse criticism. 'Don't write at all', you may say. How would that help me to escape people who will be willing to *fabricate*? However, that is what I shall do as far as I can.

You urge me to remember what I have done and said and even written. That is friendly of you and I appreciate it very much, but you seem to have a different idea of what is honourable and fitting for me in the present struggle than that which I hold myself. In my view no statesman or general of any nation has ever behaved more disgracefully than our friend. I grieve for him. He has abandoned Rome, his country, for which and in which it would have been glorious to die.
3 You don't seem to realize what a disaster this is, for you are still in your own house, though you cannot stay there except by sufferance of utter reprobates. But *this* is the last word in

hoc turpius quicquam? vagamur egentes cum coniugibus et liberis; in unius hominis quotannis periculose aegrotantis anima positas omnis nostras spes habemus, ⟨non⟩ expulsi sed evocati ex patria; quam non servandam ad reditum nostrum sed diripiendam et inflammandam reliquimus. ita multi nobiscum sunt? non in suburbanis, non in hortis, non in ipsa ⟨urbe⟩? et, si non sunt, non erunt? nos interea ne Capuae quidem sed Luceriae, et oram quidem maritimam iam relinquemus, Afranium exspectabimus ⟨et⟩ Petreium; nam in Labieno parum est dignitatis. hic tu in me * * * illud desideras? nihil de me dico, alii viderint; hic quidem quae est * * * ? domi vestrae estis et eritis omnes boni. quis istic se mihi non ostendit? quis nunc adest hoc bello (sic enim
4 iam appellandum est)? Vibulli res gestae sunt adhuc maximae. id ex Pompei litteris cognosces, in quibus animadvertito illum locum ubi erit διπλῆ: videbis de Gnaeo nostro ipse Vibullius quid existimet. quo igitur haec spectat oratio? ego pro Pompeio libenter emori possum, facio pluris omnium hominum neminem; sed non ita uno in eo iudico spem de salute rei publicae. significas enim aliquanto secus quam solebas, ut etiam Italia, si ille cedat, putes cedendum; quod ego nec rei publicae puto esse utile nec liberis meis, praeterea neque rectum neque honestum. †sed cur† 'poterisne igitur videre tyrannum?' quasi intersit audiam an videam, aut locupletior mihi sit quaerendus auctor quam Socrates, qui, cum XXX tyranni essent, pedem porta non extulit. est mihi praeterea

---

3, 6 non *add. M corr.* 8 *ante* ita *fort.* at *vel* et *addendum* 10 urbe *add.* ς 11 sed *Rs*: sed in OΔ 12 et *add.* ς 13 *post* me *spat. rel. OMm codd. Mal., nullum RbdsZ*^{1} 15 *post* est *spat. rel. Mms, nullum ORbdZ*^{1} istic λ: tu Ω: tamen *P*: tum *cod. Bod.* **4,** 3 διπλῆ *Victorius*: diple Ω 6 ita OΔ: tamen ita *P*: t- etiam *R*: ut tu *Wesenberg* uno *Bosius*: non OΔ: *om. R* in eo iudico *Corradus*: meo iudicio Ω 10 sed cur] *fort.* sequitur

misery and shame. We wander about in penury with our wives and children, our entire hopes dependent on the life of a man who falls dangerously ill once a year, not expelled but summoned out of our mother city. And we leave her not in safe keeping against our return but a prey to loot and arson. Are there so many with us? Are they not on their estates near Rome or in the suburbs or in the city itself? And if not now, won't they be soon? We meanwhile are not in Capua even, but in Luceria. We shall presently be giving up the coast, we shall wait for Afranius and Petreius—Labienus is not grand enough for us. Are such the circumstances in which you would like to see 'my old * * * '? I say nothing of myself, let others do that. What * * * is there here? All you honest men are in your own homes and mean to stay there. Who but professed his readiness to me back in Rome, and who is reporting present
4 *now* in this war, as it already has to be called? Vibullius' operations have been highly successful so far. You will see that from Pompey's letter. Note the place where you will find an arrow. You'll see what Vibullius himself thinks of our Gnaeus. Well, where does all this tend? I can willingly lay down my life for Pompey, there is not a man living I value more highly. But I do not, as you do, judge him to be the Republic's only hope of salvation. For you suggest, somewhat out of keeping with your previous attitude, that you think I ought even to leave Italy if Pompey does so. Now *I* do not think this would be in the public interest or in that of my children, nor yet right and honourable. Follows the question(?): 'Can you then bear the sight of a tyrant?' As though it mattered whether I hear of him or see him, or as though I needed a better precedent than Socrates, who never put a foot outside the gates when there were thirty tyrants in Athens! Moreover I have a reason for

praecipua causa manendi; de qua utinam aliquando tecum loquar!

Ego XIII Kal., cum eadem lucerna hanc epistulam scripsissem qua inflammaram tuam, Formiis ad Pompeium, si de pace ageretur, profecturus; si de bello, quid ero?

153 (VIII. 3)

Scr. in Caleno noctu xii–xi Kal. Mart. an. 49

CICERO ATTICO SAL.

1 Maximis et miserrimis rebus perturbatus, cum coram tecum mihi potestas deliberandi non esset, uti tamen tuo consilio volui. deliberatio autem omnis haec est, si Pompeius Italia excedat, quod eum facturum esse suspicor, quid mihi agendum putes. et quo facilius consilium dare possis, quid in utramque partem mihi in mentem veniat explicabo brevi.

2 Cum merita Pompei summa erga salutem meam familiaritasque quae mihi cum eo est, tum ipsa rei publicae causa me adducit ut mihi vel consilium meum cum illius consilio vel fortuna ⟨cum fortuna⟩ coniungenda esse videatur. accedit illud: si maneo et illum comitatum optimorum et clarissimorum civium desero, cadendum est in unius potestatem; qui etsi multis rebus significat se nobis esse amicum (et ut esset a me est, tute scis, propter suspicionem huius impendentis tempestatis multo ante provisum), tamen utrumque considerandum est, et quanta fides ei sit habenda et, si maxime exploratum sit eum nobis amicum fore, sitne viri fortis et

---

17 qua inflammaram ς: qua in (quam *OR*) flammarum Ω *post* Pompeium *fort.* profectus sum *addendum* 18 agetur *Victorius* profecturus ς: -tus Ω: praefectus λ quid ero *O*Δλ: quid erit *R*: videro ς

Ep. 153] **1**, 1 cum *Victorius*: sum Ω 2 esset *M*: est sed *E*δ: esset sed *OR* 3 italia *EP*δ: -am *ORM* 4 excedat *ER*δ: acce- *OM*: ce- *Victorius* **2**, 4 cum fortuna *add. Malaespina*: mea cum illius f- *Klotz* 8 tute] ut *Lamb.* (*marg.*): ut tute *Wesenberg* 10 fides ei sit *E*Δ: sit ei f- *O*: ei f- sit *R*

staying peculiar to myself, which I only wish I may some day be able to discuss with you.

I am leaving Formiae today, 17 February, having written this letter by the light of the same lamp with which I burned yours, to join Pompey. If peace be our business I shall help, but if war, what is my position going to be?

153 (VIII. 3)

Cales, night of 18–19 February 49

CICERO TO ATTICUS

1 Troubled as I am by matters of the gravest and saddest consequence and lacking the opportunity of consulting with you in person, I still want the benefit of your advice. The whole question at issue is this: if Pompey leaves Italy, as I suspect he will, what do you think I ought to do? It may help you to advise me if I set out briefly the points which occur to my mind in favour of either course.

2 Besides the signal obligations to Pompey under which I lie in the matter of my restoration and my personal friendship with him, the public cause itself leads me to feel that my course and my fortunes should be linked with his. There is a further point. If I stay and desert that company of right-minded and illustrious Romans, I must needs fall into the hands of one man. That man it is true lets it appear in many ways that he is my friend, and, as you know, I set myself long ago to make him such because of my premonition of the storm that was brewing, but two things are to be considered: first, how far he is to be trusted, second, no matter how definitely his amity is assured, whether it is the part of a brave man and

boni civis esse in ea urbe in qua cum summis honoribus imperiisque usus sit, res maximas gesserit, sacerdotio sit amplissimo praeditus, non futurus ⟨sit qui fuerit⟩, subeundumque periculum sit cum aliquo †fore dedecore, si quando
3 Pompeius rem publicam recuperarit. in hac parte haec sunt.

Vide nunc quae sint in altera. nihil actum est a Pompeio nostro sapienter, nihil fortiter, addo etiam nihil ni⟨si⟩ contra consilium auctoritatemque meam. omitto illa vetera, quod istum in rem publicam ille aluit, auxit, armavit, ille legibus per vim et contra auspicia ferendis auctor, ille Galliae ulterioris adiunctor, ille gener, ille in ⟨ad⟩optando P. Clodio augur, ille restituendi mei quam retinendi studiosior, ille provinciae propagator, ille absentis in omnibus adiutor, idem etiam tertio consulatu, postquam esse defensor rei publicae coepit, contendit ut decem tribuni pl. ferrent ut absentis ratio haberetur, quod idem ipse sanxit lege quadam sua, Marcoque Marcello consuli finienti provincias Gallias Kal. Mart. die restitit—sed ut haec omittam, quid foedius, quid perturbatius hoc ab urbe discessu sive potius turpissima in qua sum⟨us⟩ fuga? quae condicio non accipienda fuit potius quam relinquenda patria? malae condiciones erant, fateor, sed num quid hoc peius?

4 At recuperabit rem publicam. quando? aut quid ad eam spem est parati? non ager Picenus amissus? non patefactum

---

14 sit qui fuerit *add. Lehmann* 15 forte *s*: *an* si forte? dedecore *s*: dec- *b*: docere *ERMdm*: dolore *P* **3**, 3 nisi *P*: ni *EOMdm*: in *R*: non *s* 6 per vim et *M corr.*: servi(i) mei *OΔC*: *om. ER* 7 adoptando *ς*: op- Ω 9 prorogator *b* omnibus rebus *Wesenberg* idem *P*: fi- Ω 13 Gallicas *c* 15 turpissima in qua sumus *scripsi*: -mam que sum *M*: -ma Σδ **4**,1 reciperabit *P*δ: -avit *ORM*: recubit *E*

a patriot to remain in a city in which he has held the highest offices and commands, has done great things, and been invested with an exalted priestly function, in a reduced status and in prospect of danger along perhaps with some discredit (?)
3 should Pompey ever restore the constitution. So much on one side.

Now look at what can be said on the other. Our friend Pompey's proceedings have throughout been destitute alike of wisdom and of courage; and, I may add, contrary throughout to my advice and influence. I say nothing of ancient history—his building up and aggrandizing and arming Caesar against the state, his backing the violent and unconstitutional passage of Caesar's laws, his addition of Transalpine Gaul to Caesar's command, his marriage to Caesar's daughter, his appearance as Augur at P. Clodius' adoption, his greater concern for my restoration than for the prevention of my banishment, his prolongation of Caesar's tenure, his consistent support during Caesar's absence, his pressure (even during his third Consulship, after he had taken up the role of champion of the constitution) on the ten Tribunes to propose their law enabling Caesar to stand *in absentia*, a privilege which he confirmed after a fashion by a law of his own, his opposition to Consul M. Marcellus when he tried to fix the Kalends of March as the term of Caesar's command in Gaul—to say nothing of all this, what could be more undignified or more disorderly than this withdrawal from the capital or rather this disgraceful flight in which we are now involved? Would not *any* peace terms have been preferable to the abandonment of the mother city? The terms were bad I grant, but was anything worse than this?

4 You may say that he will restore the constitution. When? What provision is there for implementing such hopes? Picenum

iter ad urbem? non pecunia omnis et publica et privata adversario tradita? denique nulla causa, nullae vires, nulla sedes quo concurrant qui rem publicam defensam velint. Apulia delecta est, inanissima pars Italiae et ab impetu huius belli remotissima; fuga et maritima opportunitas visa quaeri desperatione. †invite cepit† Capuam, non quo munus illud defugerem, sed sine * * * causa in qua nullus esset ordinum, nullus apertus privatorum dolor, bonorum autem esset aliquis sed hebes, ut solet, et, ut ipse sensissem, multitudo et infimus quisque propensus in alteram partem, multi mu-
5 tationis rerum cupidi. dixi ipsi me nihil suscepturum sine praesidio et sine pecunia. itaque habui nihil omnino negoti, quod ab initio vidi nihil quaeri praeter fugam. eam si nunc sequor, quanam? cum illo non; ad quem cum essem profectus, cognovi in iis locis esse Caesarem, ut tuto Luceriam venire non possem. infero mari nobis incerto cursu hieme maxima navigandum est. age iam, cum fratre an sine eo cum filio an quo modo? in utraque enim re summa difficultas erit, summus animi dolor. qui autem illius impetus erit in nos absentis fortunasque nostras! acrior quam in ceterorum, quod putabit fortasse in nobis violandis aliquid se habere populare. age iam, has compedes, fascis, inquam, hos laureatos efferre ex Italia quam molestum est! qui autem locus erit nobis tutus, ut iam placatis utamur fluctibus, ante quam ad illum venerimus? qua autem aut quo nihil scimus.

---

4 null(a)e vires *Pδ*: -la viris *ERM* 8 -one invite *EPδ*: -onem in te *ORM*: -one. non *Hofmann*: -one. hinc *Sternkopf* cepi δ: recepi *Hofmann*: reieci *Sternkopf* 9 sine] in ea *Lambinus* *lac. indicavi* (*vide comm.*) 11 sensi *Lambinus*: sensi, esset *Bentivolius* 5, 2 habui *C*: habuit Ω negotii *P*: -io Ω 3 eam *EF Ant.ms*: meam *ORλ*: mea *M* 4 quanam *Frederking*: quon(i)am Ω 7 eo *Scheller*: et Ω an] aut *R* 9 illius impetus Σ: im- il- Δ 10 putabit *P*: -avit Ω 12 efferre *Hervagius*: h(a)ec f- Ω: ecf- *Victorius* 15 scimus ς: sciemus Ω

has been lost, the road to the capital left open, its entire wealth, public and private, handed over to the enemy. To cap all, there is no organization, no power, no rallying-point for would-be defenders of the constitution. Apulia was selected, the most sparsely populated area in Italy and the most remote from the onset of this war, apparently in despair as a coastal region convenient for flight. I declined (?) Capua, not that I shirked the post, but I did not want to be a leader without a force (?) in a cause which aroused no passion either in any order or, overtly, among private individuals, and in which the feelings of the honest men, though not wholly inactive, were as usual far from keen, whereas the populace and the lower orders sympathized, as I myself observed, with the other
5 side and many were eager for revolution. I told Pompey to his face that I would undertake nothing without troops and money. Accordingly I have had nothing whatever to do, because I saw from the start that flight pure and simple was intended. If I now follow it, what is to be my route? I cannot go with Pompey. When I set out to join him I learned that Caesar's whereabouts made it unsafe for me to go to Luceria. I must take ship by the Western Sea to an uncertain destination in the depths of winter. Then again, am I to go with my brother or without him with my son, or how? Either way will involve the greatest embarrassment and distress of mind. And imagine Caesar's fury against me and my possessions when I am away. It will be more bitter than in other cases because he will perhaps reckon that an attack on me will bring him a measure of popularity. Then look at the awkwardness of taking these shackles of mine, I mean these laurelled *fasces*, overseas. And what place will be safe for us, even supposing we have calm seas, until we reach Pompey?—and we know neither route nor destination.

6 At si restitero et fuerit nobis in hac parte locus, idem fecero quod in Cinnae dominatione ⟨L.⟩ Philippus, quod L. Flaccus, quod Q. Mucius, quoquo modo ea res huic quidem cecidit; qui tamen ita dicere solebat, se id fore videre quod factum est sed malle quam armatum ad patriae moenia accedere. aliter Thrasybulus, et fortasse melius; sed est certa quaedam illa Muci ratio atque sententia, est illa etiam Philippi, et, cum sit necesse, servire tempori et non amittere tempus cum sit datum. sed in hoc ipso habent tamen idem fasces molestiam. sit enim nobis amicus, quod incertum est, sed sit; deferet triumphum. non accipere ne periculosum sit, ⟨accipere⟩ invidiosum ad bonos. 'o rem' inquis 'difficilem et inexplicabilem!' atqui explicanda est; quid enim fieri potest? ac ne me existimaris ad manendum esse propensiorem quod plura in eam partem verba fecerim, potest fieri, quod fit in multis quaestionibus, ut res verbosior haec fuerit, illa verior. quam ob rem, ut maxima de re aequo animo deliberanti, ita mihi des consilium velim. navis et in Caieta est parata nobis et Brundisi.

7 Sed ecce nuntii scribente me haec ipsa noctu in Caleno, ecce litterae Caesarem ad Corfinium, Domitium Corfini cum firmo exercitu et pugnare cupiente. non puto etiam hoc Gnaeum nostrum commissurum, ut Domitium relinquat; etsi Brundisium Scipionem cum cohortibus duabus praemiserat, legionem Fausto conscriptam in Siciliam sibi placere a consule duci scripserat ad consules. sed turpe Domitium deserere erit implorantem eius auxilium. est quaedam spes,

---

6, 2 L. *add. Lambinus* 5 sed hoc malle ς 6 certa ς: -te Ω*C* 11 vereor *post* accipere *add. Klotz*, vide *Mueller* accipere *add. Orelli* (an acc- *P*) 13 quid *P*: qui Ω 15 in eam partem Σ*s*: in ea (mea in *M*) parte Δ 7, 6 a Fausto *Manutius* 7 consule *Manutius*: -libus Ω 8 est *Manutius*: et Ω: et est *Lehmann*

6 Supposing on the other hand I stay behind and find a place in Caesar's party, I shall be doing what L. Philippus and L. Flaccus and Q. Mucius did during Cinna's régime—however it turned out for the last named. And yet Mucius used to say that he saw his fate would be what it actually was but preferred it to marching in arms against the walls of his native city. Thrasybulus chose otherwise and perhaps better. Still there is something to be said for Mucius' line and point of view, something too for Philippus'—trimming one's sails when necessary, but taking one's opportunity when it comes. But there too these same *fasces* get in my way. Supposing Caesar is friendly to me, which is not certain, but suppose it: he will offer me my Triumph. To refuse may be dangerous, to accept will damage me with the honest men. 'A difficult, an insoluble problem', you may say. Yet solved it has to be. What alternative is there? And in case you think I am more inclined towards staying because I have argued at greater length that way, it may be, as is often the case in controversies, that there are more words on one side but more truth on the other. Therefore, as a man calmly weighing in his mind a matter of the greatest importance, I ask your advice. I have a ship in readiness at Caieta and another at Brundisium.

7 But lo and behold! As I write this very letter at night in my lodge at Cales, here come messengers and a letter to announce that Caesar is before Corfinium and Domitius inside the town, with a powerful army eager for battle. I don't believe that Gnaeus will crown all by leaving Domitius in the lurch—though he *had* sent Scipio with two cohorts to Brundisium and written to the Consuls that he wished one of them to take the legion raised by Faustus to Sicily. But it will be a disgraceful thing to desert Domitius when he is begging for help. There is a hope of sorts, not much so far as I am concerned

mihi quidem non magna sed in his locis firma, Afranium in Pyrenaeo cum Trebonio pugnasse, pulsum Trebonium, etiam Fabium tuum transisse cum * cohortibus; summa autem Afranium cum magnis copiis adventare. id si est, in Italia fortasse manebitur. ego autem, cum esset incertum iter Caesaris quod vel ad Capuam vel ad Luceriam iturus putabatur, Leptam misi ad Pompeium ⟨et⟩ litteras; ipse, ne quo inciderem, reverti Formias.

Haec te scire volui scripsique sedatiore animo quam proxime scripseram, nullum meum iudicium interponens sed exquirens tuum.

154 (VIII. 6)

Scr. in Formiano x Kal. Mart. an. 49

CICERO ATTICO SAL.

1 Obsignata iam ista epistula quam de nocte daturus eram, sicut dedi (nam eam vesperi scripseram), C. Sosius praetor in Formianum venit ad M'. Lepidum, vicinum nostrum, cuius quaestor fuit. Pompei litterarum ad consules exemplum attulit:

2 Litterae mihi a L. Domitio a. d. XIII Kal. Mart. adlatae sunt; earum exemplum infra scripsi. nunc, ut ego non scribam, tua sponte te intellegere scio quanti rei publicae in⟨tersit⟩ omnis copias in unum locum primo quoque tempore convenire. tu, si tibi videbitur, dabis operam ut quam primum ad nos venias, praesidi Capuae quantum constitueris satis esse relinquas.

---

10 trebonium *cod. Bod.*: petro- Ω*C* 11 *ante vel post* cohortibus *numerum excidisse puto* summa Σ*m*: suum Δ 15 misi ad pompeium Σλ: ad p- m- Δ et litteras ς: l- Ω: cum litteris *s*

Ep. 154] **1**, 2 praetor *cod. Bod.*: pr. (p.r.) Ω: praet. *c* 3 M'. *Aldus nepos*: m. Ω **2**, 1 XIII *Corradus*: VIII Ω 2 scribam *Sturmius*: sciebam Ω tua *C*: sua Ω 3 te *C*: *om.* Ω intersit *Victorius*: in Ω: sit *m* 5 ut *ORc*: *om.* Δ 6 constitueris *bds*: -ritis Ωλ

but strongly held hereabouts, that Afranius has engaged and beaten Trebonius in the Pyrenees, further that your friend Fabius has changed sides with * cohorts; and the long and short of it is that Afranius is on his way here with a large force. If that is true perhaps there will be no evacuation of Italy after all. As for me, since Caesar's movements are uncertain—it is thought he may march either on Capua or on Luceria—I have sent Lepta to Pompey with a letter. I myself am returning to Formiae to avoid falling into a trap.

I desired you to know this. I have written in a more composed frame of mind than when I last wrote, not intruding any opinion of my own but seeking yours.

154 (VIII. 6)

Formiae, 20 February 49

CICERO TO ATTICUS

1 I had already sealed the letter I was going to dispatch to you before daybreak, as I actually did (I wrote it the previous evening), when C. Sosius the Praetor arrived at my house at Formiae to see my neighbour M'. Lepidus, under whom he served as Quaestor. He brought a copy of Pompey's letter to the Consuls:

2 I have received a letter from L. Domitius on 17 February, a copy of which I append. As matters now stand I know that you will realize for yourself without any prompting from me how important it is for the public interest that all forces should be concentrated at the earliest possible moment. You will take steps, if you see fit, to join us as soon as possible, leaving in Capua as large a garrison as you judge to be sufficient.

3 Deinde supposuit exemplum epistulae Domiti quod ego ad te pridie miseram. di immortales, qui me horror perfudit! quam sum sollicitus quidnam futurum sit! hoc tamen spero, magnum nomen imperatoris fore, magnum in adventu terrorem. spero etiam, quoniam adhuc nihil nobis obfuit nisi timiditas et neglegentia, hoc quod cum fortiter et diligenter tum etiam mehercule * * *.

4 * * * modo enim audivi quartanam a te discessisse; moriar si magis gauderem si id mihi accidisset. Piliae dic non esse aequum eam diutius habere nec id esse vestrae concordiae.

5 Tironem nostrum ab altera relictum audio. sed eum video in sumptum ab aliis mutuatum; ego autem Curium nostrum si quid opus esset rogaram. malo Tironis verecundiam in culpa esse quam illiberalitatem Curi.

155 (VIII. 7)

Scr. in Formiano ix Kal. Mart. an. 49

CICERO ATTICO SAL.

1 Vnum etiam restat amico nostro ad omne dedecus, ut Domitio non subveniat. 'at nemo dubitat quin subsidio venturus sit.' ego non puto. 'deseret igitur talem civem et eos ⟨quos⟩ una sci⟨t e⟩sse, cum habeat praesertim XX ipse cohortis, XXX Domitius?' nisi me omnia fallunt, deseret. incredibiliter pertimuit, nihil spectat nisi fugam; cui tu (video enim quid

---

3 *nova ep. in* Ω, *non in ms* 5 nisi *Boot*: nihil ΩZ^1 6 timiditas et *Madvig*: imitasset Z^1: immut- *P*: mut- Ω neglegentia *Pius*: nec teg- ΩZ^1 cum *om.* Z^1: nunc fit *Boot* diligenter gestum iri. etiam me hercule gaudeo *Boot* 7 hercule Z^1 mehercule bonis (*melius* firmis) copiis suscipiatur (*melius* suscipi vide(a)tur), bene eventurum. de te quoque mehercule; modo *Madvig* **4,** 1 a *OP*: nam *R*: in Δ decessisse *Baiter* **5,** 3 verecundiam *OPms*: -ia *RMbd* culpa *Pms*: -am Ω

Ep. 155] 1, 3 quos *add. Victorius* (*post* una ς) 4 scit esse cum *scripsi*: scisse secum Ω: scis secum *C*: scis esse cum *Victorius* habere *C* XX *Sjögren*: ex Ω 5 fallunt ς: -lant Ω deseret *M corr.*: deser *M*: de se *ER*δ

3 He then appended a copy of Domitius' letter which I sent you yesterday. Gods above, I am shivering all over with suspense. What is going to happen? Still I am hopeful that there will be great power in our general's name, great terror in his advent. I hope too that, since only cowardice and negligence have stood in our way hitherto, the present operation, which seems likely to be (?) conducted with resolution and energy and also let me add * * *

4 * * * for I have just heard that your quartan has left you. Hang me if I am not as delighted as if it had happened to me. Tell Pilia it is not fair that she should keep hers any longer,
5 nor proper in so united a couple. I hear that Tiro has lost one of his. But I see he has been borrowing money outside to meet his expenses. I had asked our friend Curius to advance anything required. I would rather think the fault lies with Tiro's bashfulness than with any stinginess on Curius' part.

155 (VIII. 7)

Formiae, 21 February 49

CICERO TO ATTICUS

1 Only one thing remains to fill up the cup of our friend's dishonour—not to go to Domitius' help. 'But nobody doubts that he will go.' *I* don't think so. 'Is he then going to leave such a Roman in the lurch, and those whom he knows are with him, and that too when he himself has twenty cohorts and Domitius thirty?' Unless I am altogether out, yes. He is shaking in his shoes and aims at nothing but flight, in which you think

2 sentias) me comitem putas debere esse. ego vero quem fugiam habeo, quem sequar non habeo. quod enim tu meum laudas et memorandum dicis, malle quod dixerim me cum Pompeio vinci quam cum istis vincere, ego vero malo, sed cum illo Pompeio qui tum erat aut qui mihi esse videbatur; cum hoc vero qui ante fugit quam scit aut quem fugiat aut quo, qui nostra tradidit, qui patriam reliquit, Italiam relinquit, si malui, contigit: victus sum. quod superest, nec ista videre possum, quae numquam timui ne viderem, nec mehercule istum, propter quem mihi non modo meis sed memet ipso carendum est.

3 Ad Philotimum scripsi de viatico sive a Moneta (nemo enim solvit) sive ab Oppiis, tuis contubernalibus. cetera apposita tibi mandabo.

156 (VIII. 4)

Scr. in Formiano viii Kal. Mart. an. 49

CICERO ATTICO SAL.

1 Dionysius quidem tuus potius quam noster, cuius ego cum satis cognossem mores tuo tamen potius stabam iudicio quam meo, ne tui quidem testimoni, quod ei saepe apud me dederas, veritus superbum se praebuit in fortuna quam putavit nostram fore; cuius fortunae nos, quantum humano consilio effici poterit, motum ratione quadam gubernabimus. cui qui noster honos, quod obsequium, quae etiam ad ceteros contempti cuiusdam hominis commendatio defuit? ut meum iudicium reprehendi a Quinto fratre vulgoque ab omnibus mallem quam illum non efferrem laudibus, Ciceronesque nostros

---

2, 10 memet δ: meomet Ω **3**, 3 apposita Δ: po- Σ

Ep. 156] **1**, 3 testimonii *EO*Δλ: -ium *R* 10 efferre ς: -re me *Wesenberg*

2 (for I see what you feel) I ought to keep him company. Well, I know whom to flee but I don't know whom to follow. You praise that 'memorable' saying of mine, that I prefer defeat with Pompey to victory with those others. Why, so I do, but with Pompey as he then was or as I thought him to be. But *this* Pompey, who takes to his heels before he knows where he is running or whom he is running from, who has surrendered all that is ours, has abandoned Rome, is abandoning Italy – well, if I preferred defeat with him I have my wish, defeated I am. For the rest, I can't bear the sight of things I never feared to see, nor, I will add, of the man who has robbed me not only of what I had but of what I was.

3 I have written to Philotimus about travel-money, telling him to get it either from the Mint, as no one is paying debts, or from your cronies the Oppii. I shall give you other commissions as may be requisite.

156 (VIII. 4)

Formiae, 22 February 49

CICERO TO ATTICUS

1 Your friend (better not say 'our') Dionysius, on whose character I preferred your judgement to my own even after I had come to know it pretty well, has not been deterred even by consideration for the testimonials which you have so often given me on his behalf from a display of bumptiousness in what he thought would be my changed fortunes—the vicissitudes of which I intend to govern with some measure of rational calculation so far as that is humanly possible. From me he has had every possible compliment and compliance; I have even recommended this rather dingy figure to others on every occasion, preferring to let my brother Quintus and the world in general find fault with my judgement rather than refrain from singing his praises, preferring that our boys

meo potius labore subdoceri quam me alium magistrum
quaerere; ad quem ego quas litteras, di immortales, miseram,
quantum honoris significantis, quantum amoris! Dicaearchum
mehercule aut Aristoxenum diceres arcessi, non unum
hominem omnium loquacissimum et minime aptum ad
2 docendum. sed sit memoria bona: me dicet esse meliore.
quibus litteris ita respondit ut ego nemini cuius causam non
reciperem. semper enim 'si potero', 'si ante suscepta causa
non impediar'; numquam reo cuiquam tam humili, tam
sordido, tam nocenti, tam alieno tam praecise negavi quam
hic mihi plane ⟨sine⟩ ulla exceptione praecidit. nihil cognovi
ingratius; in quo vitio nihil mali non inest. sed de hoc nimis
multa.

3 Ego navem paravi. tuas litteras tamen exspecto, ut sciam quid respondeant consultationi meae.

4 Sulmone C. Atium Paelignum aperuisse Antonio portas, cum essent cohortes quinque, Q. Lucretium inde fugisse scis, Gnaeum ire Brundisium, ⟨Domitium⟩ desertum. confecta res est.

157 (VIII. 5)

Scr. in Formiano viii Kal. Mart. an. 49

CICERO ATTICO SAL.

1 Cum ante lucem VIII Kal. litteras ad te de Dionysio dedissem, vesperi ad nos eodem die venit ipse Dionysius, auctoritate tua permotus, ut suspicor; quid enim putem aliud? etsi solet

11 alium Σδ: -m vis *M*: -m iis *M corr.* 14 non unum hominem *Purser*: novi u- h- *s*: non u- Σ: hominem *Md*: -num *bm* **2**, 1 sed sit *scripsi*: sed est Ω: scilicet (*vel* si) est *Mueller* 6 sine *s*: *om.* Ω nulla *Pm* **3**, 1 navem ς: autem Ω tuas ς: duas Ω **4**, 1 Atium *Malaespina*: att- (act-) Ω 2 fugisse *ORMC*: eff- *E*δ 3 scito *Schmidt* Domitium *Lipsius*: *om.* Ω*C* *post* desertum *interrog. notam posuit Wesenberg*

Ep. 157] 1, 1 litteras ad te *ORm*Z^{b}: lit- ad te lit- *M*: ad te l- *bds* de Dionysio Z^{b}: di- *OR*: *om.* Δ

should be taught on the side by my own labour rather than to look for another tutor for them. And the letter I sent him, heavens above, what a complimentary, affectionate letter it was! It might have been Dicaearchus or Aristoxenus I was asking to join me, instead of an arrant chatterbox and a
2 thoroughly incompetent teacher. But let it be admitted he has a good memory: he shall find that I have a better! He answered my letter as I should never answer a man whose case I was not going to take. One always says 'if I can manage it', 'if I am not hindered by another case already undertaken'. I have never given any defendant, no matter how humble, how abject, how guilty, how complete a stranger, such a blank refusal as this quite unqualified 'no' I have had from Dionysius. It is the most ungrateful piece of behaviour I ever knew, and ingratitude contains all the vices. But that's more than enough about him.

3 I have a ship ready, but I am waiting for a letter from you to know your answer to my consultation.

4 You know that C. Atius Paelignus at Sulmo has opened the gates to Antony, though he had five cohorts, that Q. Lucretius has fled the town, that Gnaeus is *en route* for Brundisium and Domitius left in the lurch. It's all over.

157 (VIII. 5)

Formiae, 22 February 49

CICERO TO ATTICUS

1 After I had dispatched a letter to you about Dionysius before daybreak on the 22nd, Dionysius himself arrived at my house that same evening, induced by your promptings as I suspect—

eum, cum aliquid furiose fecit, paenitere. numquam autem cerritior fuit quam in hoc negotio. nam quod ad te non scripseram, postea audivi a tertio miliario tum eum isse 'πολλὰ μάτην κεράεσσιν ἐς ἠέρα θυμήναντα', multa, inquam, mala cum dixisset: suo capiti, ut aiunt. sed ⟨vid⟩e meam mansuetudinem: conieceram in fasciculum una cum tua vehementem ad illum epistulam; hanc ad me referri volo, nec ullam ob aliam causam Pollicem servum a pedibus meis Romam misi. eo autem ad te scripsi ut, si tibi forte reddita esset, mihi curares referendam, ne in illius manus perveniret.

2 Novi si quid esset scripsissem. pendeo animi exspectatione Corfiniensi, [in] qua de salute rei publicae decernetur.

Tu fasciculum qui est 'M'. Curio' inscriptus velim cures ad eum perferendum Tironemque Curio commendes et ut det ei si quid opus erit in sumptum roges.

158 (VIII. 8)

Scr. in Formiano vii Kal. Mart. an. 49

CICERO ATTICO SAL.

1 O rem turpem et ea re miseram! sic enim sentio, id demum aut potius id solum esse miserum quod turpe sit. aluerat Caesarem, eundem repente timere coeperat, condicionem pacis nullam probarat, nihil ad bellum pararat, urbem reliquerat, Picenum ⟨a⟩miserat culpa, in Apuliam se compegerat, ibat in Graeciam, omnis nos ἀπροσφωνήτους, expertis sui

---

5 cerritior *Bosius*: cert- Ω 6 isse] ipse Z^b 8 capiti ς: -te Ω sed vide *Mueller*: sede *OR*: sed *P*Δ: sed o Z^b meam *Rs*Z^b: in eam *O*Δ 10 vehementem *Ernesti*: venien- Ω: vemen- *cod. Bos.* **2**, 2 in *seclusi* decernetur *P*δ: -nitur *R*: -neret *M* 3 tu ς: ut Ω est *C*: est de ΩZ^b M'. *Manutius*: m(arco) Ω*C*Z^b 4 Curio inscriptus *C*: -oni scriptus *R*Δ: -one scriptus *Ps* et *Victorius*: ut *M*: *om.* *OR*δ 5 det ei *Boot*: peti Ω

Ep. 158] **1**, 4 pararat *Rs*: parat *O*Δ 5 amiserat *P*δ: m- Ω 6 ἀπροσφωνήτους *C*: -τος Ω: -τως *P*

what else am I to think? Though to be sure he is apt to be sorry after one of his crazy outbursts; and he has never shown himself more crackbrained than in this affair. I did not tell you, but I heard afterwards that he went from the third milestone on that occasion after 'full many an idle, angry toss of horn', i.e. after much cursing and swearing, which I hope may come home to roost, as they say. But admire my gentle nature! I put a strongly worded letter to him in the bundle along with yours. I should like that restored to me, and for this and no other purpose I have sent Pollex, one of my personal attendants, to Rome. And I am writing to you so that if by chance it has been delivered to you you may see it is returned to me to make sure it does not get into his hands.

2 If there was any news I should tell you. I am in suspense waiting for the outcome at Corfinium, where the existence of the Republic is at stake.

Would you see that the package addressed 'to M'. Curius' is duly forwarded to him and commend Tiro to Curius and ask him to advance Tiro anything that may be required to meet expenses?

158 (VIII. 8)

Formiae, 23 February 49

CICERO TO ATTICUS

1 What a dishonourable and *therefore* miserable business! For I hold that misery lies chiefly or rather solely in dishonour. He built Caesar up, then suddenly began to fear him, rejected all terms of peace, made no preparations for war, abandoned Rome, culpably lost Picenum, squeezed himself into Apulia, was off to Greece leaving us all without a word, without any

2 tanti, tam inusitati consili relinquebat. ecce subito litterae Domiti ad illum, ipsius ad consules! fulsisse mihi videbatur τὸ καλὸν ad oculos eius, et exclamasse ille vir qui esse debuit

> ‘πρὸς ταῦθ’ ὅ τι χρὴ καὶ παλαμάσθων
> καὶ πάντ’ ἐπ’ ἐμοὶ τεκταινέσθων·
> τὸ γὰρ εὖ μετ’ ἐμοῦ.’

at ille tibi πολλὰ χαίρειν τῷ καλῷ dicens pergit Brundisium. Domitium autem aiunt re audita et eos qui una essent se tradidisse. o rem lugubrem! itaque intercludor dolore quo minus ad te plura scribam; tuas litteras exspecto.

159 (VIII. 10)

Scr. in Formiano vi Kal. Mart. an. 49

CICERO ATTICO SAL.

Dionysius cum ad me praeter opinionem meam venisset, locutus sum cum eo liberalissime; tempora exposui, rogavi ut diceret quid haberet in animo; me nihil ab eo ipso invito contendere. respondit se quod in nummis haberet nescire quo loci esset; alios non solvere, aliorum diem nondum esse. dixit etiam alia quaedam de servulis suis qua re nobiscum esse non posset. morem gessi. dimisi a me, ut magistrum Ciceronum non libenter, ut hominem ingratum non invitus. volui te scire, et quid ego de eius facto iudicarem.

2, 3 ad] ob ς 5 ἐπ’ ς: EH *M*: ἐν *OR*δ 10 minus *Z*(b)λ: *om.* Ω
Ep. 159] 3 ab eo *OR*: ab Δ 4 quod *OR*: quot Δ 5 solvere *P*: -ret Ω 9 volui te *s*: solvite Ω: volui id te *Purser* et *del.* ς

2 part in so momentous and extraordinary a plan. Then of a sudden comes Domitius' letter to him and his to the Consuls. It seemed to me as though the light of Honour had shone before his eyes and the man he should have been had cried aloud

> 'So let them scheme what they must,
> And contrive to my bane what they may:
> Right is with me.'

But Pompey, waving adieu to Honour, is making for Brundisium. As for Domitius, they say that on hearing the news he and those with him have given themselves up. A tragic business! Sorrow prevents me from writing more. I wait to hear from you.

159 (VIII. 10)

Formiae, 24 February 49

CICERO TO ATTICUS

Dionysius having come to me contrary to my expectation, I spoke to him in the most liberal way. I explained the circumstances and asked him to tell me what he had in mind, saying that I was not demanding anything of him against his own free will. He replied that he did not know what shape his investments were in. Some of his debtors were not paying, others were not yet due to pay. He added some stuff about his slaves as a reason why he could not keep us company. I let him have his way and dismissed him. As a teacher for the boys I was sorry to lose him, as an ungrateful fellow I let him go without reluctance. I wanted you to know, and to know my opinion of his behaviour.

160 (VIII. 9*a*)

Scr. in Formiano v Kal. Mart. an. 49 (§ 2)

⟨CICERO ATTICO SAL.⟩

1 Εὐγενῆ tua consilia et tamen pro temporibus non incauta mihi valde probantur. Lepido quidem (nam fere συνδιημερεύομεν, quod gratissimum illi est) numquam placuit ex Italia exire, Tullo multo minus; crebro enim illius litterae ab aliis ad nos commeant. sed me illorum sententiae minus movebant; minus multa dederant illi rei publicae pignora. tua mehercule auctoritas vehementer movet; adfert enim et reliqui temporis recuperandi rationem et praesentis tuendi. sed obsecro te, quid hoc miserius quam alterum plausus in foedissima causa quaerere, alterum offensiones in optima? alterum existimari conservatorem inimicorum, alterum desertorem amicorum? et mehercule quamvis amemus Gnaeum nostrum, ut et facimus et debemus, tamen hoc, quod talibus viris non subvenit, laudare non possum. nam sive timuit, quid ignavius? sive, ut quidam putant, meliorem suam causam illorum caede fore putavit, quid iniustius? sed haec omittamus; augemus enim dolorem retractando.

2 VI Kal. vesperi Balbus minor ad me venit occulta via currens ad Lentulum consulem missu Caesaris cum litteris, cum mandatis, cum promissione provinciae, Romam ut redeat; cui persuaderi posse non arbitror, [ni]si erit conventus. idem aiebat nihil malle Caesarem quam ut Pompeium adsequeretur (id credo) et rediret in gratiam (id non credo, et metuo ne omnis haec clementia ad unam illam crudelitatem

---

Ep. 160] *novam ep. Rubenius ap. Graevium*: *superiori coniungunt codd.* **1**, 4 minus Σ*C*: minus movebant minus Δ 5 me illorum ς: melio- Ω: illo-*P*. **2**, 1 occulta via *Manutius*: -tavit Ω 2 currens *Victorius*: occ- Ω: acc- *anon. ap. Iunium* 4 cui *ER*: quoi *s*: qui Δ si *Nipperdey* (*sed del.* non): nisi Ω 5 malle δ: male Σ: mali *M* 7 crudelitatem Σ: credul- Δ

160 (VIII. 9*a*)

Formiae, 25 February 49

CICERO TO ATTICUS

1 Your counsels, honourable and yet not imprudent or regardless of the times we live in, are very much to my mind. Lepidus (we spend pretty well all day in one another's company, which he is very glad to do) never meant to leave Italy, Tullus much less—his letters often come my way from others. But their views do not weigh with me so much; they have not given so many pledges to the state as I. *Your* advice does weigh with me heavily, I do assure you. It offers a plan for redeeming the future and keeping the present uncompromised. But I ask you, could anything be more lamentable than the way one of the two is earning applause in a foul cause while the other earns unpopularity in a fine one—one is looked upon as the preserver of his enemies, the other as the forsaker of his friends? And really, love our friend Gnaeus as I may and do and ought to do, I cannot commend his failure to come to the aid of such men as these. If he was afraid, what could be more craven? Or if, as some think, he thought their massacre would be good propaganda for his own side, what could be more cynical? But let us leave all this, we only make it worse for ourselves by harping upon it.

2 On the evening of the 24th Balbus junior visited me. He was travelling post-haste on a secret mission from Caesar to Consul Lentulus, bearing a letter, a verbal message, and the promise of a province to induce him to return to Rome. I don't think he can be persuaded, if the meeting takes place. Balbus also said that Caesar would like nothing better than to come up with Pompey (I believe him there) and be reconciled —there I don't believe him, and I am afraid that all this piling up of clemency may be simply a prelude to the cruelty we

colligatur). Balbus quidem maior ad me scribit nihil malle Caesarem quam principe Pompeio sine metu vivere. tu, puto, hoc credis. sed cum haec scribebam v Kal., Pompeius iam Brundisium venisse poterat; expeditus enim antecesserat legiones XI ⟨Kal.⟩ Luceria. sed hoc τέρας horribili vigilantia, celeritate, diligentia est. plane quid futurum sit nescio.

161 (VIII. 11)

Scr. in Formiano iii Kal. Mart. an. 49

CICERO ATTICO SAL.

1 Quod me magno animi motu perturbatum putas, sum equidem, sed non tam magno quam tibi fortasse videor; levatur enim omnis cura cum aut constitit consilium aut cogitando nihil explicatur. lamentari autem licet illud quidem totos dies; sed vereor ne, nihil cum proficiam, etiam dedecori sim studiis ac litteris nostris. consumo igitur omne tempus considerans quanta vis sit illius viri quem nostris ⟨libris⟩ satis diligenter, ut tibi quidem videmur, expressimus. tenesne igitur moderatorem illum rei publicae quo referre velimus omnia? nam sic quinto, ut opinor, in libro loquitur Scipio: 'ut enim gubernatori cursus secundus, medico salus, imperatori victoria, sic huic moderatori rei publicae beata civium vita proposita est, ut opibus firma, copiis locuples, gloria ampla, virtute honesta sit; huius enim operis maximi inter homines

---

8 malle δ: male Ω 10 hoc *Graevii cod.*: h(a)ec Σδ: et *M* 12 Kal. *add. Orelli* 13 plane *Victorius*: plena Ω: -num δ

Ep. 161] **1**, 3 constitit *EP*Δλ: -stent *ORC*: -stant *Corradus* consilium *EP*δ: -ia *ORMC* 4 tamen lari *M* quidem *Boot*: tamen Ω 5 dedecori sim *m*: -ris in *ORM*: -ri sim in *Ebds* 7 libris δ: .s. (*i.e.* scilicet) l- *R*: *om. EOPM* 9 velimus *M* (*sed -i- ex corr.*): volumus *ER codd. Mal. ms*: volemus *bd*

feared. Balbus senior for his part writes to me that Caesar would like nothing more than to live without fear under Pompey's primacy. You believe this of course! But as I write on the 25th Pompey can already have reached Brundisium. He set off ahead of his troops on the 19th from Luceria, travelling light. But this portent is horribly wide-awake and swift and thorough. What will happen I simply don't know.

161 (VIII. 11)

Formiae, 27 February 49

CICERO TO ATTICUS

1 You say you suppose I am in great perturbation and uneasiness of mind. So I am, but not so much so as perhaps you think. Anxiety is always relieved when one has reached a firm decision or alternatively when thinking proves futile. One can lament to be sure all day long. But I do no good by that, and I fear I may even be a discredit to my studies and writings. I therefore spend all my time reflecting on the essential greatness of the figure I have portrayed conscientiously enough, in your opinion at least, in my volumes. Do you remember the standard which I want my ideal statesman to apply to all his actions? This is what Scipio says in Book V, I think: 'Just as a fair voyage is the object of the pilot, health of the physician, victory of the general, so our statesman's object is the happiness of his countrymen—to promote power for their security, wealth for their abundance, fame for their dignity, virtue for their good name. This is the work I would have him accomplish, the greatest and noblest in human

2 atque optimi illum esse perfectorem volo'. hoc Gnaeus noster cum antea numquam tum in hac causa minime cogitavit. dominatio quaesita ab utroque est, non id actum, beata et honesta civitas ut esset. nec vero ille urbem reliquit quod eam tueri non posset nec Italiam quod ea pelleretur, sed hoc a primo cogitavit, omnis terras, omnia maria movere, reges barbaros incitare, gentis feras in Italiam armatas adducere, exercitus conficere maximos. genus illud Sullani regni iam pridem appetitur, multis qui una sunt cupientibus. an censes nihil inter eos convenire, nullam pactionem fieri potuisse? hodie potest. sed neutri σκοπὸς est ille, ut nos beati simus; uterque regnare vult.

3 Haec a te invitatus breviter exposui; voluisti enim me quid de his malis sentirem ostendere. προθεσπίζω igitur, noster Attice, non hariolans, ut illa cui nemo credidit, sed coniectura prospiciens: 'iamque mari magno ...'; non multo, inquam, secus possum vaticinari; tanta malorum impendet Ἰλιάς. atque hoc nostra gravior est causa qui domi sumus quam illorum qui una transierunt, quod illi [qui]
4 alterum metuunt, nos utrumque. cur igitur, inquis, remansimus? vel tibi paruimus vel non occurrimus vel hoc fuit rectius. conculcari, inquam, miseram Italiam videbis proxima aestate ⟨aut alterius⟩ aut utriusque [in] mancipiis ex omni genere collectis, nec tam ⟨singulorum proscr⟩iptio pertimescenda, quae Luceriae multis sermonibus denuntiata esse dicitur, quam universae interitus; tantas in confligendo

---

2, 7 in Italiam armatas *Σ*: a- in it- *Δ*   10 an *EΔ*: an tu *OR*   12 beati simus *ms*: -issimus *Ω*   **3**, 3 ariolans *OPδ*: -las *ERM*   ut illa *Pius*: utilia *Ω*   4 mari *Hervagius*: -ia *Ω*   7 qui *del. Buecheler*: quidem *ς*   8 metuunt *cod. Bod.*: manu- *Ω*   nos utrumque *ς*: nostr- *ORΔ*: vestr- *E*   **4**, 4 aut alterius *add. Madvig*   in *del. ς*   5 singulorum *add. Boot*: singulis est *Buecheler*   proscriptio *Victorius*: iptio *EOΔ*: ipse *R*: emptio Z^b: direptio *Muretus*   6 pertimescenda *ς*: -endam *EOΔ*: -ebam *R*   7 esse dicitur *Gronovius*: est igitur *Ω* universae *ς*: -am *Ω*: *alii aliter (vide comm.)*   confligendo *Victorius*: oblig- *Ω*

2 society.' To this our Gnaeus has never given a thought, least of all in the present context. Both of the pair have aimed at personal domination, not the happiness and fair fame of the community. Pompey did not abandon Rome because he could not have defended her, nor Italy because he was driven from her shores. His plan from the first has been to ransack every land and sea, to stir up foreign kings, to bring savage races in arms to Italy, to raise enormous armies. He has been hankering for a long while after despotism on the Sullan model, and many of his companions are eager for it. Or would you maintain that no agreement or settlement between them was possible? It is possible today. But neither sees our happiness as his mark. Both want to reign.

3 I have briefly set this out at your invitation—you wanted me to declare what I feel about these afflictions. So I prophesy, my dear Atticus, not inspired like the girl whom nobody believed but by rational forecast:— 'And now on the great sea . . .'. Yes, I can vaticinate in pretty much the same strain on this vast impending Iliad of evils. And we who have stayed at home are worse off than those who have crossed overseas in that they fear one of the pair while we fear both.

4 Why then have I stayed? Perhaps it was that I followed your advice, perhaps that I did not fall in with Pompey, perhaps that it was the better thing to do. Yes, you will see our poor Italy trampled over this summer by the bondslaves of one or both the protagonists, scraped together from every species of humanity. It is not so much the proscription of individuals that we have to fear, the threat of which is said to be common talk at Luceria, as the destruction of the whole country—so enormous will be the power on either side when the clash

utriusque viris video futuras. habes coniecturam meam. tu autem consolationis fortasse aliquid exspectasti. nihil invenio; nihil fieri potest miserius, nihil perditius, nihil foedius.

5 Quod quaeris quid Caesar ad me scrips⟨er⟩it, quod saepe, gratissimum sibi esse quod quierim, oratque in eo ut perseverem. Balbus minor haec eadem mandata. iter autem erat eius ad Lentulum consulem cum litteris Caesaris praemiorumque promissis si Romam revertisset. verum cum habeo rationem dierum, ante puto tramissurum quam potuerit conveniri.

6 Epistularum Pompei duarum quas ad me misit neglegentiam meamque in rescribendo diligentiam volui tibi notam esse. earum exempla ad te misi.

7 Caesaris hic per Apuliam ad Brundisium cursus quid efficiat exspecto. utinam aliquid simile Parthicis rebus! simul aliquid audiero, scribam ad te. tu ad me velim bonorum sermones; Romae frequentes esse dicuntur. scio equidem te in publicum non prodire, sed tamen audire te multa necesse est.

Memini librum tibi adferri a Demetrio Magnete ad te missum περὶ ὁμονοίας. eum mihi velim mittas. vides quam causam mediter.

161A (VIII. 11A)

Scr. Luceriae iv Id. Febr. an. 49

CN. MAGNVS PROCOS. S. D. M. CICERONI IMP.

Q. Fabius ad me venit a. d. IIII Id. Febr. is nuntiat L. Domitium cum suis cohortibus XI⟨I⟩ et cum cohortibus XIIII quas Vibullius adduxit ad me iter habere; habuisse in animo

8 habes Σ*m*: habe Δ 5, 1 scripserit ς: -psit Ω: scripserit, scripsit *Allen* idem (id *Baiter*) quod *Wesenberg* 3 erat eius Σ: eius erat Δ 6 habeo *E*δ: ab eo *ORM* 7, 6 magnete *s*: -nite (-ni te) Ω 7 mis(s)um Σ: -um scio Δ eum *ERm*: enim Δ velim *Pms*: vellem Ω

Ep. 161A] MAGNVS $Z^{(b)}$λ *codd. Mal.*: POM(PEIVS) Ω 2 XII *Boot*: XI Ω

comes. Such is my forecast. Perhaps you expected some comfort. I can find none. A more miserable, hopeless, horrible situation there could not be.

5 You ask me what Caesar said in his letter. The usual thing, that he is greatly obliged for my quiescence and begs me to continue therein. Balbus junior brought a message from him to the same effect. He was travelling to Consul Lentulus with a letter from Caesar and promises of rewards if he returned to Rome. But reckoning up the days I think he will cross before a meeting can take place.

6 I wanted you to know the off-hand style of two letters sent me by Pompey and the care with which I answered them. I am sending you copies.

7 I am waiting to hear the result of this rapid march of Caesar's through Apulia on Brundisium. If only there could be something like the Parthian business! As soon as I hear anything I shall write to you. Please let me know how the honest men are talking. They are said to be in Rome in good muster. I know you don't go out in public, but still you must hear a lot.

I remember a book 'On Concord' being brought to you by Demetrius of Magnesia, dedicated to yourself. Would you kindly send it to me? You see the sort of brief I am getting up.

161 A (VIII. 11 A)

Luceria, 10 February 49

CN. MAGNUS PROCONSUL TO M. CICERO IMPERATOR

Q. Fabius came to me on 10 February. He reports that L. Domitius is on his way to join me with twelve cohorts of his own and fourteen brought in by Vibullius, that he intended

proficisci Corfinio a. d. v Id. Febr.; C. Hirrum cum v cohortibus subsequi. censeo ad nos Luceriam venias; nam te hic tutissime puto fore.

161B (VIII. 11B)

Scr. in Formiano xv vel xiv Kal. Mart. an. 49

M. CICERO IMP. S. D. CN. MAGNO PROCOS.

1 A. d. xv Kal. Mart. Formiis accepi tuas litteras; ex quibus ea quae in agro Piceno gesta erant cognovi commodiora esse multo quam ut erat nobis nuntiatum, Vibullique virtutem industriamque libenter agnovi.

Nos adhuc in ea ora ubi praepositi sumus ita fuimus ut navem paratam haberemus. ea enim audiebamus et ea verebamur ut, quodcumque tu consilium cepisses, id nobis persequendum putaremus. nunc quoniam auctoritate et consilio tuo in spe firmiore sumus, si teneri posse putas Tarracinam ⟨et⟩ oram maritimam, in ea manebo, etsi praesidia in oppidis nulla sunt. nemo enim nostri ordinis in his locis est praeter M. Eppium, quem ego Minturnis esse volui, vigilantem hominem et industrium. nam L. Torquatum, virum fortem et cum auctoritate, Formiis non habemus; ad te profectum arbitramur.

2 Ego omnino, ut tibi proxime placuerat, Capuam veni eo ipso die quo tu Teano Sidicino es profectus; volueras enim me cum M. Considio pro praetore illa negotia tueri. cum eo venissem, vidi T. Ampium dilectum habere diligentissime, ab eo accipere ⟨L.⟩ Libonem, summa item diligentia et in illa

---

Ep. 161B] **1**, 7 cepisses *Baiter*: perc- Ω 9 posse putas *Eδ*: pu- po- *ORM* 10 et ς: *om.* Ω 12 eppium *M(?)*: opp- Σδ **2**, 1 tibi proxime Σ: p- t- Δ 4 vidi T. Ampium *Victorius*: vidi (-it *M*) amplum Ω 5 L. *addidi*

to leave Corfinium on 9 February, and that C. Hirrus is following with five cohorts. I advise you to join us at Luceria, as I think you will be safest here.

161B (VIII. 11B)

Formiae, 15 or 16 February 49

M. CICERO IMPERATOR TO CN. MAGNUS PROCONSUL

1 I received your letter on 15 February at Formiae, from which I learned that the operations in Picenum have gone much more favourably than had been reported to us, and was glad to note the spirit and energy shown by Vibullius.

I have hitherto remained at my post of responsibility on the coast, but have kept a ship in readiness. From what I heard and from what I feared I felt that I must follow whatever plan you might adopt. Now that thanks to your initiative and planning our prospects are brighter, if you think Tarracina and the coastal area can be held, I shall stay there, though the towns are without garrisons, none of our order being in this area except M. Eppius, whom I desired to stay at Minturnae—he is an alert, energetic fellow. L. Torquatus, a brave gentleman whose name carries weight, is not with me at Formiae. I think he has set out to join you.

2 For myself, pursuant to your wish expressed shortly beforehand, I went to Capua the very day you left Teanum Sidicinum—you had asked me to look after affairs there with Propraetor M. Considius. On my arrival I found T. Ampius zealously engaged in raising troops and handing them over to L. Libo, whose zeal was no less conspicuous and who is

colonia auctoritate. fui Capuae quoad consules. iterum, ut erat ⟨e⟩dictum a consulibus, veni Capuam ad Non. Febr.; cum fuissem triduum, recepi me Formias.

3 Nunc quod tuum consilium aut quae ratio belli sit ignoro. si tenendam hanc oram putas, quae et opportunitatem et dignitatem habet et civis egregios et, ut arbitror, teneri potest, opus est esse qui praesit; sin omnia unum in locum contrahenda sunt, non dubito quin ad te statim veniam, quo mihi nihil optatius est, idque tecum quo die ab urbe discessimus locutus sum. ego si cui adhuc videor segnior fuisse, dum ne tibi videar non laboro, et tamen si, ut video, bellum gerendum est, confido me omnibus facile satis facturum.

4 M. Tullium, meum necessarium, ad te misi cui tu, si tibi videretur, ad me litteras dares.

161C (VIII. 11C)

Scr. Canusi x Kal. Mart. an. 49

CN. MAGNVS PROCOS. S. D. M. CICERONI IMP.

S.v.b. Tuas litteras libenter legi; recognovi enim tuam pristinam virtutem etiam in salute communi. consules ad eum exercitum quem in Apulia habui venerunt. magno opere te hortor pro tuo singulari perpetuoque studio in rem publicam ut te ad nos conferas, ut communi consilio rei publicae adflictae opem atque auxilium feramus. censeo via Appia iter facias et celeriter Brundisium venias.

---

7 edictum *Lambinus*: d- Ω **3**, 3 cives egregios Σ: e- c- Δ 4 praesit δ: praeest Ω sin *P*: in *M*: *om.* *ER*δ unum in *ER*: in unum *O*δ: unum *M* 6 quo die δ: quod te Ω 8 videar *ER*: -eor *O*Δ

Ep. 161C] 1 s.v.b. *nescioquis*: S.V.B.E. $Z^{(b)}$: sub *OM*: *om.* *R*δ

very highly respected in the colony. I remained at Capua as long as the Consuls. I visited the town a second time, in accordance with the Consuls' edict, for the Nones of February, and after a stay of three days returned to Formiae.

3 At the present time I am ignorant of your intentions and plan of campaign. If you think this coast line should be held (it has value both practical and sentimental, also an outstandingly loyal population, and in my opinion, it *can* be held), someone must be in command. If on the other hand everything is to be concentrated at one point, I am in no doubt about joining you immediately. Nothing would please me better, and I told you so the day we left Rome. If some think me insufficiently active hitherto, I do not care, so long as you do not share their opinion. At the same time, if war must be waged, as evidently it must, I am confident that I shall have no difficulty in meeting all expectations.

4 I am sending you M. Tullius, a familiar of mine, so that you may give him a letter for me if you are so disposed.

161C (VIII. 11C)

Canusium, 20 February 49

CN. MAGNUS PROCONSUL TO M. CICERO IMPERATOR

Greetings. I was glad to read your letter, recognizing your old spirit still forward in the public welfare. The Consuls have joined the army under my command in Apulia. I strongly urge you, in view of your outstanding and unwavering patriotism, to make your way over to us, so that in concert we may bring aid and comfort to our afflicted country. I advise you to travel by the Appian Way and come quickly to Brundisium.

161D (VIII. 11D)

Scr. in Formiano iii Kal. Mart. an. 49 (§ 4)

M. CICERO IMP. S. D. CN. MAGNO PROCOS.

1 Cum ad te litteras misissem quae tibi Canusi redditae sunt,
suspicionem nullam habebam te rei publicae causa mare
transiturum, eramque in spe magna fore ut in Italia possemus
aut concordiam constituere, qua mihi nihil utilius videbatur,
aut rem publicam summa cum dignitate defendere. inter-
im nondum meis litteris ad te perlatis ex iis mandatis quae
D. Laelio ad consules dederas certior tui consili factus non
exspectavi dum mihi a te litterae redderentur, confestimque
cum Quinto fratre et cum liberis nostris iter ad te in Apuliam
2 facere coepi. cum Teanum Sidicinum venissem, C. Messius,
familiaris tuus, mihi dixit aliique complures Caesarem iter
habere Capuam et eo ipso die mansurum esse Aeserniae.
sane sum commotus quod, si ita esset, non modo iter meum
interclusum sed me ipsum plane exceptum putabam. itaque
tum Cales processi, ut ibi potissimum consisterem, dum certum nobis ab Aesernia de eo quod audieram referretur.

3 At mihi, cum Calibus essem, adfertur litterarum tuarum exemplum quas tu ad Lentulum consulem misisses. hae scriptae sic erant, litteras tibi a L. Domitio a. d. XIII Kal. Mart. adlatas esse, earumque exemplum subscripseras; magnique interesse rei publicae scripseras omnis copias primo quoque tempore in unum locum convenire, et ut praesidio quod satis esset Capuae relinqueret. his ego litteris lectis in eadem opinione fui qua reliqui omnes, te cum omnibus copiis ad Corfinium

---

Ep. 161D] **1**, 3 italia *E*δ: -am *ORM* 7 D. Laelio *Corradus*: dialio *vel sim.* Ω 8 confestimque *ERms*: -im *OMbd* 9 q (que) fratre Δ: fratre Σ **2**, 1 Messius *Manutius*: mis- Ω 2 dixit *C*: *om.* Ω 4 si est non *Nonius* (*Lindsay, p.* 455) 5 putabat *Nonius* **3**, 1 at δ: ac Ω 6 praesidio Ω*C*: -dium *b*: -dii *P* quod *P*δ: quo Ω

161D (VIII. 11D)

Formiae, 27 February 49

M. CICERO IMPERATOR TO CN. MAGNUS PROCONSUL

1 When I sent you the letter which you received at Canusium it did not enter my mind that in the state's interests you would be going overseas. I was in high hopes that we should succeed either in establishing peace, which appeared to me the most expedient course, or in honourably defending the state in Italy. In the meanwhile, before my letter reached you, I learned of your intentions from the message you sent to the Consuls by D. Laelius. I did not wait to receive a reply from you, but started out immediately to join you in Apulia together
2 with my brother Quintus and our children. When I got to Teanum Sidicinum, your friend C. Messius and several others told me that Caesar was marching on Capua and would be stopping that very night at Aesernia. I was considerably alarmed, for if this was true I thought that not only was my route cut but I myself nothing but a prisoner. I therefore proceeded to Cales, which seemed the best place to stay until reliable news came in from Aesernia about what I had heard.

3 However, while at Cales, I was brought a copy of a letter which you had sent to Consul Lentulus. It was to the effect that a letter from L. Domitius had been brought to you on 17 February, and of this you appended a copy and wrote that it was of great public importance that all forces should be concentrated in one place at the earliest possible moment. You further asked him to leave an adequate garrison in Capua. On reading this I conceived, as did everyone else, that you intended to march on Corfinium with your entire force, and

esse venturum; quo mihi, cum Caesar ad oppidum castra haberet, tutum iter esse non arbitrabar.

Cum res in summa exspectatione esset, utrumque simul audivimus, et quae Corfini acta essent et te iter Brundisium facere coepisse; cumque nec mihi nec fratri meo dubium esset quin Brundisium contenderemus, a multis qui e Samnio Apuliaque veniebant admoniti sumus ut caveremus ne exciperemur a Caesare, quod is in eadem loca quae nos petebamus profectus celerius etiam quam nos possemus eo quo intenderet venturus esset. quod cum ita esset, nec mihi nec fratri meo nec cuiquam amicorum placuit committere ut temeritas nostra non solum nobis sed etiam rei publicae noceret, cum praesertim non dubitaremus quin, si etiam tutum nobis iter fuisset, te tamen iam consequi non possemus.

4 Interim accepimus tuas litteras Canusio a. d. x Kal. Mart. datas, quibus nos hortaris ut celerius Brundisium veniamus. quas cum accepissemus a. d. III Kal. Mart., non dubitabamus quin tu iam Brundisium pervenisses, nobisque iter illud omnino interclusum videbamus neque minus nos esse captos quam qui Corfini fuissent; neque enim eos solos arbitrabamur capi qui in armatorum manus incidissent sed eos nihilo minus qui regionibus exclusi intra praesidia atque intra arma aliena venissent.

5 Quod cum ita sit, maxime vellem primum semper tecum fuissem, quod quidem tibi ostenderam cum a me Capuam reiciebam; quod feci non vitandi oneris causa sed quod videbam teneri illam urbem sine exercitu non posse, accidere autem mihi nolebam quod doleo viris fortissimis accidisse.

---

12 audivimus Σ: audimus Δ   18 intenderet ς: -rat Ω   **4**, 1 interim *C*: inde prim *E*: inde (inte *R*) primas (*sed* c(o)epimus) *ORP*: inde primo Δ   5 videbamus *E*δ: -atur *OR*: -atur in iis *M*   6 fuissent *C*: venis- Ω   **5**, 2 fuissem *OM*λ: -sse *ER*δ

I did not think it would be safe for me to travel there with Caesar encamped before the town.

At the height of our suspense news arrived simultaneously of the outcome at Corfinium on the one hand and on the other that you had set out for Brundisium. Neither I nor my brother thought twice about pressing on to Brundisium, until we were advised by many persons coming from Samnium and Apulia to beware of falling into Caesar's hands, since he had started for the same area that we were making for and might be expected to reach his destination even more rapidly than we could do. In these circumstances neither I nor my brother nor any of our friends thought it right to run the risk of injuring the state as well as ourselves by our own imprudence, particularly as we felt sure that even if the journey had been safe for us it was now too late for us to catch up with you.

4 Meanwhile I have received your letter of 20 February from Canusium in which you urge me to come quickly to Brundisium. By the date of its receipt, 27 February, I feel sure that you have already arrived at Brundisium. It is clear to me that our route there is now completely cut and that we are taken prisoner no less than the men in Corfinium. For I put in that category not only those who have fallen into the hands of enemy troops but also and equally those who are cut off territorially and find themselves on the wrong side of enemy garrisons and armies.

5 In these circumstances my chief wish is that I had stayed with you all along, as indeed I made clear to you when I was declining the Capuan command. This I did, not to avoid responsibility, but because I saw that the town could not be held without an army and did not wish to happen to me what to my regret has happened to some very gallant gentlemen.

quoniam autem tecum ut essem non contigit, utinam tui consili certior factus essem! nam suspicione adsequi non potui, quod omnia prius arbitratus sum fore quam ut haec rei publicae causa in Italia non posset duce te consistere. neque vero nunc consilium tuum reprehendo, sed fortunam rei publicae lugeo; nec, si ego quid tu secutus sis non perspicio, idcirco minus existimo te nihil nisi summa ratione fecisse.

6 Mea quae semper fuerit sententia primum de pace vel iniqua condicione retinenda, deinde de urbe (nam de Italia quidem nihil mihi umquam ostenderas), meminisse te arbitror. sed mihi non sumo ut meum consilium valere debuerit; secutus sum tuum, neque id rei publicae causa, de qua desperavi, quae et nunc adflicta est nec excitari sine civili perniciosissimo bello potest, sed te quaerebam, tecum esse cupiebam, neque eius rei facultatem, si qua erit, praetermittam.

7 Ego me in hac omni causa facile intellegebam pugnandi cupidis hominibus non satis facere. primum enim prae me tuli me nihil malle quam pacem, non quin eadem timerem quae illi sed ea bello civili leviora ducebam. deinde suscepto bello, cum pacis condiciones ad te adferri a teque ad ea⟨s⟩ honorifice et large responderi viderem, duxi meam rationem; quam tibi facile me probaturum pro tuo in me beneficio arbitrabar. memineram me esse unum qui pro meis maximis in rem publicam meritis supplicia miserrima et crudelissima pertulissem, me esse unum qui, si offendissem eius animum

---

11 secutus sis Σ: sis se- Δ 12 ratione *E*Δ: cum r- *OR* **6**, 1 qu(a)e *OP*: -que *ER*Δ fuerit *O*Δ: -rat *ER* 7 civili *om. b* bello perniciosissimo *Purser* 8 qu(a)e *M*λ **7**, 4 deinde *C*: inde Ω 5 eas *Corradus*: ea Ω 6 large *M corr.*: ta- *EM*(?): tarde *OR*δ

Since however it was not my good fortune to be with you, I do wish I had been informed of your plans. It was impossible for me to fathom them by guesswork, since the last thing I thought could happen was that our national cause should prove unable to maintain itself in Italy under your leadership. Nor am I now criticizing your decision; I only mourn the plight of the Republic. And if I am unable to perceive what is behind your action, I am not on that account any the less confident that you have had excellent reasons for all you have done.

6 I think you remember what my opinion has always been, first as to preserving peace even on bad terms and second as to the capital (I do not say Italy, for you never told me anything about that). But I do not presume to suggest that my view ought to have prevailed. I have followed yours, not for the sake of the Republic, of which I have despaired and which now lies in the dust only to be revived by a calamitous civil war, but seeking you and desiring to be with you. And if I find opportunity to effect that, I shall not let it slip.

7 Throughout the present struggle it has been easy for me to see that the bellicose among us are dissatisfied with my conduct. To begin with I made no secret of my preference for peace above any other outcome, not that their fears for the consequences were not also mine but holding these consequences a lesser evil than civil war. Then after the commencement of hostilities, observing that terms of peace were presented to you and that you replied to them in complimentary and handsome fashion, I took stock of my own position; and in view of your past kindness to me I did not think I should have any difficulty in justifying my conclusions in your eyes. I bore in mind that my situation was exceptional. My important services to the state had earned me a cruel and savage punishment. If I gave offence to a personage who, even when

cui tum cum iam in armis essemus consulatus tamen alter et triumphus amplissimus deferebatur, subicerer isdem proeliis, ut mea persona semper ad improborum civium impetus aliquid videretur habere populare. atque haec non ego prius sum suspicatus quam mihi palam denuntiata sunt, neque ea tam pertimui, si subeunda essent, quam declinanda putavi, si honeste vitare possem.

8 Quam ob rem illius temporis, dum in spe pax fuit, rationem nostram vides, reliqui facultatem res ademit. iis autem quibus non satis facio facile respondeo; neque enim ego amicior C. Caesari umquam fui quam illi neque illi amiciores rei publicae quam ego. hoc inter me et illos interest, quod, cum et illi cives optimi sint et ego ab ista laude non absim, ego condicionibus, quod idem te intellexeram velle, illi armis disceptari maluerunt; quae quoniam ratio vicit, perficiam profecto ut neque res publica civis a me animum neque tu amici desideres.

162 (VIII. 12)

Scr. in Formiano prid. Kal. Mart. an. 49

CICERO ATTICO SAL.

1 Mihi molestior ⟨lippitudo⟩ erat etiam quam ante fuerat; dictare tamen hanc epistulam malui quam Gallo Fabio amantissimo utriusque nostrum nihil ad te litterarum dare. nam pridie quidem, quoquo modo potueram, scripseram ipse eas litteras quarum vaticinationem falsam esse cupio. huius autem epistulae non solum ea causa est, ut ne quis a me

---

11 tum *ERms*: tu *OΔ* 12 *num* amplissime ? 12 subicerer λ: -re Ω: -rem *Ps* procellis *anon. ap. Corradum*: periculis ς 13 ut] cum *Reid* 14 atque] neque *Mueller* **8,** 1 quam ob rem *scripsi*: quam brevem ΩZ^b: brevem *Madvig* 8 vicit *Brunus* (M^4): misit Ωλ
Ep. 162] 1, 1 lippitudo *add.* ς: λήμη *Orelli*

we were already in arms, was being offered a second Consulship and a most glorious Triumph, I should have to fight my battles over again, for further demonstration that bad citizens somehow find me a popular figure to attack. I did not have to guess these consequences, I was openly threatened with them. Nor was I so much afraid of incurring them if duty required as desirous of avoiding them if I honourably could.

8 There then you have my account of the period when peace might still be hoped for; over what followed circumstances deprived me of any power. To my critics I have a simple answer. I have never loved C. Caesar better than they, nor have they loved the Republic better than I. The difference between us is this: while they are very good patriots and I have some claim to that honourable title, I preferred that differences should be settled by negotiations, which I understood to be your desire also, they by force. Since their policy has triumphed, I need hardly say that I shall give the state no cause to complain of my patriotism nor you of my friendship.

162 (VIII. 12)

Formiae, 28 February 49

CICERO TO ATTICUS

1 My eyes are even more troublesome than formerly, but I prefer to dictate this letter rather than not to give a line to our common and very good friend Fabius Gallus to take to you. Yesterday to be sure I wrote in my own hand as best I could a letter of prophecy which I hope may prove false. My reason for writing now is not merely my reluctance to let a day pass

dies intermittatur quin dem ad te litteras, sed etiam haec iustior,
ut a te impetrarem ut sumeres aliquid temporis †quo tibi
quia perexiguo tempore† opus est. explicari mihi tuum
consilium plane volo, ut penitus intellegam.

2 Omnia sunt integra nobis; nihil praetermissum est quod
non habeat sapientem excusationem, non modo probabilem.
nam certe neque tum peccavi cum imperatam iam Capuam
non solum ignaviae dedecus sed etiam perfidiae suspicionem
fugiens accipere nolui, neque cum post condiciones pacis per
L. Caesarem et Fabatum adlatas cavi ne animum eius
offenderem cui Pompeius iam armatus armato consulatum
3 triumphumque deferret. nec vero haec extrema quisquam
potest iure reprehendere, quod mare non transierim. id enim,
etsi erat deliberationis, tamen obire non potui; neque enim
suspicari debui, cum praesertim ex ipsius Pompei litteris, idem
quod te video existimasse, non dubitarim quin is Domitio
subventurus esset, et plane quid rectum et quid faciendum
mihi esset diutius cogitare malui.

4 Primum igitur haec qualia tibi esse videantur, etsi significata sunt a te, tamen accuratius mihi perscribas velim, deinde aliquid etiam in posterum prospicias fingasque quem me esse deceat et ubi me plurimum prodesse rei publicae sentias, ecquae pacifica persona desideretur an in bellatore sint omnia.

5 Atque ego, qui omnia officio metior, recordor tamen tua consilia, quibus si paruissem, tristitiam illorum temporum

---

8 quo *ER*δ: quod *M* tibi quia *R*: tibi et q- *M*: q- t- *E*δ 9 tempore *om. s* (*vide comm.*) **2**, 3 imperatam (impa- *ER*) Ω*CZ*: impar- δ iam *del. Manutius* 4 dedecus *Orelli*: deiectus Ω: dele- *ms*: delictum *M corr.* 6 fabatum *MZ*^{l}λ: fabium Σδ: L. Fabatum *Wesenberg* **3**, 4 cum praesertim Σ*c*: p- c- Δ id quod *nescioquis*: quod idem *Faërnus* 5 te video Σ: v- te Δ **4**, 4 prodesse posse *Wesenberg*

without sending you a letter but a more valid one, namely to induce you to do me the favour of devoting some of your time * * * . I certainly do want to have your advice set out for me so that I thoroughly understand it.

2 My position is quite uncompromised. For any past omissions on my part I have a rationally just, and not merely plausible, excuse. I was not wrong when, avoiding not only the discredit of cowardice but the suspicion of treachery, I refused to take the Capuan command when actually ordered to do so. Neither was I wrong when after L. Caesar and Fabatus had brought Caesar's peace terms I was chary of offending a man to whom Pompey was offering a Consulship and a Triumph while both
3 had arms in their hands. Nor can anyone fairly blame me in this last phase for not going overseas. That would have needed thinking about in any case, but in fact I could not manage it. Indeed I could not be expected to guess the plan, particularly as from Pompey's own letter I was firmly under the impression (and I see you thought the same) that he would go to Domitius' rescue; and frankly I wanted more time to consider what was the right and proper thing to do.

4 First therefore I should like your opinion on these points. You have already indicated it, but I should be glad if you would write it out for me in greater detail. Secondly I hope you will also take a look into the future and sketch the figure I ought to present and the capacity in which you think I could best serve the country—is a peacemaking role required or does all rest with the warrior?

5 Duty is my yardstick in all things, but still I remember advice of yours which, if I had heeded it, would have spared me the sorrow of those old days. I remember what you urged upon

non subissem. memini quid mihi tum suaseris per Theophanem, per Culleonem, idque saepe ingemiscens sum recordatus. qua re nunc saltem ad illos calculos revertamur quos tum abiecimus, ut non solum gloriosis consiliis utamur sed etiam paulo salubri⟨ori⟩bus. sed nihil praescribo; accurate

6 velim perscribas tuam ad me sententiam. volo etiam exquiras quam diligentissime poteris (habebis autem per quos possis) quid Lentulus noster, quid Domitius agat, quid acturus sit, quem ad modum nunc se gerant, num quem accusent, num cui suscenseant—quid dico num cui? num Pompeio. omnino culpam omnem Pompeius in Domitium confert, quod ipsius litteris cognosci potest quarum exemplum ad te misi. haec igitur videbis et, quod ante ad te scripsi, Demetri Magnetis librum quem ad te misit de concordia velim mihi mittas.

162A (VIII. 12A)

Scr. Luceriae xii Kal. Mart., ut vid., an. 49

CN. MAGNVS PROCOS. S. D. C. MARCELLO L. LENTVLO COSS.

1 Ego quod existimabam dispersos nos neque rei publicae utilis neque nobis praesidio esse posse, idcirco ad L. Domitium litteras misi, primum ut ipse cum omni copia ad nos veniret; si de se dubitaret, ut cohortis XVIIII quae ex Piceno ad me iter habebant ad nos mitteret. quod veritus sum factum est, ut Domitius implicaretur, ut neque ipse satis firmus esset ad castra facienda, quod meas XVIIII et suas XII

5, 7 salubrioribus *cod. Ball.*: -bribus ΩZ^1 pr(a)escribo *Ps*: pers- Ω
6, 5 quid *P*: quod Ω 8 ante ad te Σ: ad te ante Δ
Ep. 162A] C. *Manutius*: m. Ω **1**, 6 ut neque *OM*: neque *R*δ: et n- *Madvig*

me at that time through Theophanes and through Culleo, and I have often recalled it with bitter remorse. So let me now at all events return to the standards I then rejected and take counsels of safety (in some slight degree) as well as of glory. But I am not telling you what to say. I want you to write out

6 your opinion in detail for me to read. I also want you to make every effort (you have those through whom you can make enquiries) to find out what our friend Lentulus and Domitius are doing and what their plans are, how they are behaving now, whether they blame anyone or have a grievance against anybody—I do not know why I say 'anybody' when I mean Pompey. To be sure Pompey puts all the blame on Domitius, as can be seen from his own letter of which I am sending you a copy. All right then, you will look into this, and as I wrote to you earlier, please send me the book Demetrius of Magnesia dedicated to you on Concord.

162A (VIII. 12A)

Luceria, 18 February (?) 49

CN. MAGNUS PROCONSUL TO C. MARCELLUS AND L. LENTULUS CONSULS

1 Holding as I do that while we are scattered we can neither be of use to the state nor any protection to one another, I wrote to L. Domitius asking him first to join me himself with his entire force; and if he hesitated for himself I asked him to send me the nineteen cohorts which were on their way to me from Picenum. What I feared has happened. Domitius is in the toils, and has neither the strength to take the field himself,

cohortis in tribus oppidis distributas haberet (nam partim Albae, partim Sulmone collocavit), neque ⟨se⟩, si vellet, expedire posset.

2 Nunc scitote me esse in summa sollicitudine. nam et tot et talis viros periculo obsidionis liberare cupio neque subsidio ire possum, quod his duabus legionibus non puto esse committendum ut illuc ducantur; ex quibus tamen non amplius XIIII cohortis contrahere potui, quod Brundisium praesidium misi neque Canusium sine praesidio, dum abessem, putavi esse dimittendum.

3 D. Laelio mandaram, quod maiores copias sperabam nos habituros, ut, si vobis videretur, alter uter vestrum ad me veniret, alter in Siciliam cum ea copia quam Capuae et circum Capuam comparastis et cum iis militibus quos Faustus legit proficisceretur, Domitius cum XII suis cohortibus eodem adiungeretur, reliquae copiae omnes Brundisium cogerentur et inde navibus Dyrrachium transportarentur. nunc cum hoc tempore nihilo magis ego quam vos subsidio Domitio ire possim * * * se per montis explicare, non est nobis committendum ut ad has XIIII cohortis quas dubio animo habeo hostis accedere aut in itinere me consequi possit.

4 Quam ob rem placitum est mihi (†altia† video censeri M. Marcello et ceteris nostri ordinis qui hic sunt) ut Brundisium ducerem hanc copiam quam mecum habeo. vos hortor ut quodcumque militum contrahere poteritis contrahatis et eodem Brundisium veniatis quam primum. arma quae ad me missuri eratis, iis censeo armetis milites quos vobis-

8 in tribus Σ: t- in Δ 9 se *add. Lambinus* **2,** 5 quod *ERΔ*: quod his duabus *O*: quas $Z^{(b)}$λ (*sed vide comm.*): quod duas *Mueller, duce Buecheler* praesidium $Z^{(b)}$λ: *om.* Ω **3,** 1 D. Laelio *Corradus*: de (a)elio Σ: del(l)io Δ 9 ipse autem fortasse possit *add. Wesenberg*: possit ipse *Castiglioni*: *minus apta alii* se per EZ^{1} (*ut vid.*) $Z^{(b)}$: semper *RΔ* **4,** 1 altia ΩZ^{b}: alcia Z^{l}: aliter O^{2}: nec al- ς: atque (*sed is* ac) ita *Manutius*: talia *Tyrrell* censeri Z^{b} *codd. Mal.*: -sori $\Sigma\delta Z^{l}$: -sorî (= -sori M.?) *M* 2 M. *M(?)ms Z*: *om.* Σ*bd*: a *Lambinus*

having distributed my nineteen and his own twelve cohorts between three towns (he stationed some at Alba and some at Sulmo), nor the means of extricating himself if he wished.

2 I must tell you that I am now in the utmost anxiety. On the one hand I am eager to free so many brave men of such quality from the danger of a siege. On the other, I cannot go to their assistance because I do not think I can trust the two legions at my disposal so far as to take them there. Actually I have not been able to assemble more than fourteen cohorts out of their complement because I have sent a garrison to Brundisium and did not think that Canusium should be left empty of a garrison during my absence.

3 Hoping to have a larger force I sent you word by D. Laelius that, if you saw fit, one or other of you should join me, while his colleague should proceed to Sicily with the force which you raised in Capua and the surrounding area and with the troops recruited by Faustus, that Domitius with his own twelve cohorts should be attached to this force, and that all remaining forces should be concentrated at Brundisium and transported from there by sea to Dyrrachium. As matters now stand, since I cannot go to Domitius' assistance any more than yourselves at the present time * * * get away through the mountains, I must not risk letting the enemy approach these fourteen cohorts of whose loyalty I am doubtful or overtake me on the march.

4 I have therefore decided (and I find that M. Marcellus and those others of our order who are here approve this course) to take the force I have with me to Brundisium. I urge you on your part to muster all the troops you can and come likewise to Brundisium as soon as possible. I advise that you use the arms which you were going to send me to equip the men

cum habetis. quae arma superabunt, ea si Brundisium iumentis deportaritis vehementer rei publicae profueritis. de hac re velim nostros certiores faciatis. ego ad P. Lupum et C. Coponium praetores misi ut se vobis coniungerent et militum quod haberent ad vos deducerent.

162B (VIII. 12B)

Scr. Luceriae iii Id. Febr. an. 49

CN. MAGNVS PROCOS. S. D. L. DOMITIO PROCOS.

1 Valde miror te ad me nihil scribere et potius ab aliis quam a te de re publica me certiorem fieri. nos disiecta manu pares adversariis esse non possumus; contractis nostris copiis spero nos et rei publicae et communi saluti prodesse posse. quam ob rem cum constituisses, ut Vibullius mihi scripserat, a. d. V Id. Febr. Corfinio proficisci cum exercitu et ad me venire, miror quid causae fuerit qua re consilium mutaris. nam illa causa quam mihi Vibullius scribit levis est, te propterea moratum esse quod audieris Caesarem Firmo progressum in Castrum Truentinum venisse; quanto enim magis appropinquare adversarius coepit, eo tibi celerius agendum erat ut te mecum coniungeres prius quam Caesar aut tuum iter impedire aut me abs te excludere posset.

2 Quam ob rem etiam te rogo et hortor, id quod non destiti superioribus litteris a te petere, ut primo quoque die Luceriam ad ⟨me⟩ venires, ante quam copiae quas instituit Caesar contrahere in unum locum coactae vos a nobis distrahant.

---

8 deportaritis ϛ: -aretis Ω 9 velim *EP*: vellim *R*: vellem *O*Δ 11 *post* deducerent *habent* valde Ω, valete *bds*

Ep. 162B] **1**, 1 valde *huc transp. Klotz* 9 progressum *EOZ*[1]: -su *R*Δ **2**, 1 etiam atque etiam *Lamb.* (*marg.*) 3 ad me venires *Otto*: adven- Ω: ven- *R* copiae s^2: -as Ω 4 vos *Hervagius*: nos Ω

you have with you. It will be an important service to the state if you will bring any arms left over by mule to Brundisium. Please inform our friends of this. I have sent instructions to Praetors P. Lupus and C. Coponius to join you with such troops as they have.

162B (VIII. 12B)

Luceria, 11 February 49

CN. MAGNUS PROCONSUL TO L. DOMITIUS PROCONSUL

1 I am very much surprised that you do not write to me and that I am informed of the public concerns by others rather than by you. With our power split we cannot be a match for the enemy; concentrating our forces I hope we may be able to serve the state and the general welfare. Accordingly I am at a loss to understand why, having decided as Vibullius wrote to me to leave Corfinium with your army on 9 February and join me, you subsequently changed your plans. The reason which Vibullius gives me, that you delayed because you heard Caesar had advanced from Firmum and reached Castrum Truentinum, is of no validity, for the nearer the enemy's approach the faster you should have acted in order to join me before Caesar was in a position either to interfere with your march or to cut me off from you.

2 Accordingly I once again beg and urge you, as I have continually asked you in my previous letters, to come to me at Luceria on the earliest possible day before those forces which Caesar has begun to muster are collected at one point so as to cut you off from us. If however you are held back by certain

sed si erunt qui te impediant ut villas suas servent, aequum est me a te impetrare ut cohortis quae ex Piceno et Camerino venerunt, quae fortunas suas reliquerunt, ad me missum facias.

162C (VIII. 12C)

Scr. Luceriae xiv Kal. Mart. an. 49

CN. MAGNVS PROCOS. S. D. L. DOMITIO PROCOS.

1 Litteras abs te M. Calenius ad me attulit a. d. XIIII Kal. Mart.; in quibus litteris scribis tibi in animo esse observare Caesarem et, si secundum mare ad me ire coepisset, confestim in Samnium ad me venturum, sin autem ille circum istaec loca commoraretur, te ei, si propius accessisset, resistere velle.

Te animo magno et forti istam rem agere existimo, sed diligentius nobis est videndum ne distracti pares esse adversario non possimus, cum ille magnas copias habeat et maiores brevi habiturus sit. non enim pro tua providentia debes illud solum animadvertere, quot in praesentia cohortis contra te habeat Caesar, sed quantas brevi tempore equitum et peditum copias contracturus sit. cui rei testimonio sunt litterae quas Bussenius ad me misit; in quibus scribit, id quod ab aliis quoque mihi scribitur, praesidia Curionem quae in Vmbria et Tuscis erant contrahere et ad Caesarem iter facere. quae si copiae in unum locum fuerint coactae, ut pars exercitus ad Album mittatur, pars ad te accedat, ut non pugnet sed locis suis repugnet, haerebis, neque solus cum ista copia tantam multitudinem sustinere poteris ut frumentatum eas.

5 villas *Graevius*: il- Ω 7 missas *O*
Ep. 162C] 1, 1 calenius Σ: call- Δ 4 ist(a)ec *bms*: istic *EOMd*: ista *R* 9 providentia *C*: prudentia Ω 13 bussenius *OMm*: buse- *ER*: bisse- *bds* 14 aliis ς: illis Ω 19 ut *s*: et Ω

persons anxious to save their farms, I am surely entitled to expect you to release the cohorts which have come in from Picenum and Camerinum, leaving their own possessions behind them, and let them join me.

162C (VIII. 12C)

Luceria, 16 February 49

CN. MAGNUS PROCONSUL TO L. DOMITIUS PROCONSUL

1 M. Calenius has brought me a letter from you on 16 February. In that letter you write that you propose to watch Caesar, and that if he starts to move in my direction along the coast you will at once march into Samnium to join me, whereas if he stays in your neighbourhood you wish to stand against him should he approach nearer.

I appreciate your generous and courageous spirit in this matter, but we must be careful to avoid a situation in which we are divided and therefore no match for the enemy, since he has large forces and will soon have larger. It would ill befit your foresight to consider only how many cohorts Caesar has against you at the present moment without regard to the size of the forces, both horse and foot, which he will shortly muster. That is attested by a letter sent to me by Bussenius, in which he says, as do others of my correspondents also, that Curio is mustering the garrisons which were in Umbria and Etruria and marching to join Caesar. If these forces are concentrated at one point, with part of his army sent against Alba and part advancing upon you, Caesar not offering battle but repelling attack from favourable positions, you will find yourself in a trap, unable single-handed with your present force to stand against such numbers for foraging purposes.

2 Quam ob rem te magno opere hortor ut quam primum cum omnibus copiis hoc venias; consules constituerunt idem facere. ego M. Tuscilio ad te mandata dedi providendum esse ne duae legiones sine Picentinis cohortibus in conspectum Caesaris committerentur. quam ob rem nolito commoveri si audieris me regredi, si forte Caesar ad me veniet; cavendum enim puto esse ne implicatus haeream. nam neque castra propter anni tempus et militum animos facere possum neque ex omnibus oppidis contrahere copias expedit, ne receptum amittam; itaque non amplius XIIII cohortis Luceriam coegi.

3 Consules praesidia omnia deducturi sunt aut in Siciliam ituri; nam aut exercitum firmum habere oportet quo confidamus perrumpere nos posse aut regiones eius modi obtinere e quibus repugnemus, id quod neutrum nobis hoc tempore contigit, quod et magnam partem Italiae Caesar occupavit et nos non habemus exercitum tam amplum neque tam magnum quam ille. itaque nobis providendum est ut summae rei publicae rationem habeamus. etiam atque etiam te hortor ut cum omni copia quam primum ad me venias. possumus etiam nunc rem publicam erigere, si communi consilio negotium administrabimus; si distrahemur, infirmi erimus. mihi hoc constitutum est.

4 His litteris scriptis †sic adpoete† mihi litteras et mandata attulit. quod me hortare ut istuc veniam, id me facere non arbitror posse, quod non magno opere his legionibus confido.

2, 2 hoc *Mm*: huc Σ*bds* 3 M. Tuscilio *Corradus*: metu- Σ*C*: metu stileo Δ 4 ne hae duae *Lehmann* 6 veniat *R*: venit *O* **3,** 8 summae *Lambinus*: -am Ω **4,** 1 sic adpoete (ad p-) *R*Δ: ad poete *E*: Sicca (*Hofmann*) abs te *Boot* (a te ς) et mandata attulit Σ: a- et m- Δ

2 Therefore I earnestly urge you to come here as soon as possible with your entire force. The Consuls have decided to do likewise. I sent you word by M. Tuscilius that I must be careful not to let the two legions into sight of Caesar without the cohorts from Picenum. Do not therefore be disturbed if you hear of my retiring should Caesar march against me. I feel I must be on my guard against falling into a trap. I cannot take the field because of the time of year and the disposition of my men, nor would it be wise to collect the garrisons out of all the towns in case I lose my line of retreat. For that reason I have gathered no more than fourteen cohorts at Luceria.

3 The Consuls will bring off all the garrisons or go to Sicily. We must either have an army strong enough to allow us to feel confident of breaking through or we must hold areas from which we can fight back. Neither advantage is ours at present because on the one hand Caesar has occupied a great part of Italy and on the other we do not have an army as ample and as numerous as his. We must therefore see that we take account of the main interests of the state. Yet again I urge you to join me as soon as possible with your whole force. Even now we can put the country on her feet if we apply ourselves to the task in concert. If we are divided we shall be weak. That is my fixed opinion.

4 After I had written this letter * brought me your letter and message. I do not think I can comply with your request that I should join you because I have no great confidence in these legions.

162D (VIII. 12D)

Scr. Luceriae xiii Kal. Mart. an. 49

CN. MAGNVS PROCOS. S. D. L. DOMITIO PROCOS.

1 Litterae mihi a te redditae sunt a. d. XIII Kal. Mart., in quibus scribis Caesarem apud Corfinium castra posuisse. quod putavi et praemonui fit, ut nec in praesentia committere tecum proelium velit et omnibus copiis conductis [per] te implicet, ne ad me iter tibi expeditum sit atque istas copias coniungere optimorum civium possis cum his legionibus de quarum voluntate dubitamus. quo etiam magis tuis litteris sum commotus; neque enim eorum militum quos mecum habeo voluntate satis confido ut de omnibus fortunis rei publicae dimicem neque etiam qui ex dilectibus conscripti sunt consulibus convenerunt.

2 Qua re da operam, si ulla ratione etiam nunc efficere potes, ut te explices, hoc quam primum venias, ante quam omnes copiae adversarium conveniant. neque enim celeriter ex dilectibus hoc homines convenire possunt et, si convenirent, quantum iis committendum sit qui inter se ne noti ⟨quidem⟩ sunt contra veteranas legiones non te praeterit.

163 (VIII. 13)

Scr. in Formiano Kal. Mart. an. 49

CICERO ATTICO SAL.

1 Lippitudinis meae signum tibi sit librari manus et eadem causa brevitatis; etsi nunc quidem quod scriberem nihil erat. omnis exspectatio nostra erat in nuntiis Brundisinis; si nactus

---

Ep. 162D] **1,** 4 per *E*Δ: pr(a)eter *OR*: *del.* ς 11 a consulibus ς **2,** 2 hoc *nescioquis*: huc Ω: et huc ς 4 hoc *ORM*: huc *E*δ 5 qui *Manutius*: quod Ω ne noti quidem ς: nec q- n- *P* (q- n- *Ant. F*): ne noti *E*δ: noti *ORM*
Ep. 163] **1,** 3 si *P*: i *E*: nisi *ORM*: *om.* δ

162D (VIII. 12D)

Luceria, 17 February 49

CN. MAGNUS PROCONSUL TO L. DOMITIUS PROCONSUL

1 A letter of yours has been delivered to me on 17 February in which you say that Caesar has encamped at Corfinium. What I thought and predicted is happening. He is unwilling to join battle with you at present and having collected all his forces hems you in, obstructing your road to me and preventing you from joining your own thoroughly loyal forces with the legions here whose disposition is doubtful. I am therefore all the more disturbed by your letter. I do not have enough confidence in the disposition of the men I have with me to fight a battle on which the whole future of the commonwealth would be staked, and the levies raised for the Consuls have not yet mustered.

2 Therefore do your best, if even at this stage you can by any means manage it, to extricate yourself and to come here as soon as possible before the entire enemy forces have joined up. The men from the levies cannot muster here rapidly, and if they did, you will appreciate how little confidence could be placed in troops who do not even know one another against veteran legions.

163 (VIII. 13)

Formiae, 1 March 49

CICERO TO ATTICUS

1 My clerk's hand will serve as an indication of my ophthalmia and likewise as an excuse for brevity, not that there is anything to say *now*. My whole mind is fixed in expectation of news from Brundisium. If Caesar has found our Gnaeus there, there

hic esset Gnaeum nostrum, spes dubia pacis, sin ille ante tramisisset, exitiosi belli metus.

Sed videsne in quem hominem inciderit res publica, quam acutum, quam vigilantem, quam paratum? si mehercule neminem occiderit neque cuiquam quicquam ademerit, ab
2 iis qui eum maxime timuerant maxime diligetur. multum mecum municipales homines loquuntur, multum rusticani; nihil prorsus aliud curant nisi agros, nisi villulas, nisi nummulos suos. et vide quam conversa res sit: illum quo antea confidebant metuunt, hunc amant quem timebant. id quantis nostris peccatis vitiisque ⟨e⟩venerit non possum sine molestia cogitare. quae autem impendere putarem scripseram ad te, et iam tuas litteras exspectabam.

164 (VIII. 14)

Scr. in Formiano vi Non. Mart. an. 49

CICERO ATTICO SAL.

1 Non dubito quin tibi odiosae sint epistulae cottidianae, cum praesertim neque nova de re aliqua certiorem te faciam neque novam denique iam reperiam scribendi ullam sententiam. sed si dedita opera, cum causa nulla esset, tabellarios ad te cum inanibus epistulis mitterem, facerem inepte; euntibus vero, domesticis praesertim, ut nihil ad te dem litterarum facere non possum, et simul, crede mihi, requiesco paulum in his miseriis cum quasi tecum loquor, cum vero tuas epistulas lego, multo etiam magis. omnino intellego nullum fuisse tempus post has fugas et formidines quod magis debuerit mutum esse a litteris, propterea quod neque Romae quicquam auditur novi nec in his locis, quae a Brundisio

8 neque Σ*c*: ne *M*: nec δ **2**, 4 sit *Lambinus*: est Ω 6 evenerit *cod. Bod.*: ven- Ω
Ep. 164] **1**, 8 paulum *EOMdm*: -lulum *Rbs* 10 formidines nostras *c* 11 debuerit mutum *Brunus* (M^4): defu- (desu-) multum Ω

is a faint hope of peace, but if he has crossed over beforehand, there is the fear of a deadly war.

But do you see what sort of man this is into whose hands the state has fallen, how clever, alert, well prepared? I verily believe that if he takes no lives and touches no man's property those who dreaded him most will become his warmest
2 admirers. Both town and country people talk to me a great deal. They really think of nothing except their fields and their bits of farms and investments. And look how the tables are turned! They fear the man they used to trust and love the man they used to dread. I cannot think without distress of the blunders and faults on our side which have led to this result. My forecast of what impends I have already given you and I am now waiting to hear from you.

164 (VIII. 14)

Formiae, 2 March 49

CICERO TO ATTICUS

1 I am sure you find daily letters a bore, especially as I give you no news and indeed can no longer think of any new theme to write about. But while it would certainly be silly of me to send you special couriers with empty letters and for no reason, I can't bring myself not to give a line for you to those who are going anyway, especially if they are of the family, and at the same time I do, believe me, find a modicum of relaxation in these miseries when I am as it were talking to you, much more still when I am reading your letters. I do of course realize that since these flights and alarms of ours began there has never been a time when epistolary silence would have been more appropriate in that there is no news either in Rome or in this part of the world, which is two or three days' journey closer than you to Brundisium. And Brundisium is the focus

absunt propius quam tu bidui aut tridui. Brundisi autem
omne certamen vertitur huius pr⟨ox⟩imi temporis; qua
quidem exspectatione torqueor. sed omnia ante Nonas
sciemus. eodem enim die video Caesarem a Corfinio post
meridiem profectum esse, id est Feralibus, quo Canusio mane
Pompeium; eo modo autem ambulat Caesar et iis diariis
militum celeritatem incitat ut timeam ne citius ad Brundisium
2 quam opus sit accesserit. dices 'quid igitur proficis, qui
anticipes eius rei molestiam quam triduo sciturus sis?' nihil
equidem; sed, ut supra dixi, tecum perlibenter loquor, et
simul scito labare meum consilium illud quod satis iam fixum
videbatur. non mihi satis idonei sunt auctores ii qui a te
probantur. quod enim umquam eorum in re publica forte
factum exstitit? aut quis ab iis ullam rem laude dignam
desiderat? nec mehercule laudandos existimo qui trans mare
belli parandi causa profecti sunt, quamquam haec ferenda
non erant; video enim quantum id bellum et quam pesti-
ferum futurum sit. sed me movet unus vir, cuius fugientis
comes, rem publicam recuperantis socius videor esse debere.
'totiensne igitur sententiam mutas?' ego tecum tamquam
mecum loquor. quis autem est tanta quidem de re quin varie
secum ipse disputet? simul et elicere cupio sententiam tuam,
3 si manet, ut firmior sim, si mutata est, ut tibi adsentiar. omnino
ad id de quo dubito pertinet me scire quid Domitius acturus
sit, quid noster Lentulus. de Domitio varia audimus: * * *
modo esse in Tiburti aut† lepidi quo cum lepidus accessisse†

---

13 bidui aut tridui *Lambinus*: biduum aut triduum Ω 14 proximi *scripsi*: primi Ω 15 Nonas *Boot*: nos Ω 18 diari(i)s Ω: dictis δ: congiariis *Victorius* **2**, 7 extitit *s*: existit *Ebdm*: ex istis *M*: ex illis *R* 15 elicere *Ps*: eligere Ω **3**, 3 audimus *E*δ: -iemus *ORM*: -ivimus ς *de lacuna vide comm.* 4 modo . . . accessisse(t) ad urbem *sic etiam* Z^1, quo cum *etiam C* Tiburti aut] Tiburtino *Corradus* accessisset *Ps*Z^1

of the whole struggle so far as the immediate future is concerned. I am racked with suspense on that account. But we shall know all before the Nones, for I see that Caesar left Corfinium on the afternoon of the same day, All Souls' Feast, on which Pompey left Canusium at dawn. In view of Caesar's marching habits and the rations with which he stimulates his men to speed I am afraid he may reach Brundisium sooner
2 than desirable. You will ask me what good I do by anticipating the unpleasantness of something that I shall know in three days' time. None at all to be sure. But as I said above, I love talking to you. Besides I must tell you that my decision, which seemed by now pretty well settled, is wavering. The examples which you approve are not quite good enough for me. What act of political courage have these people ever performed and who expects anything laudable from them? Not to be sure that I regard as laudable those who have left to prepare war overseas, intolerable as things here were; I see too well what a terrible, baneful war it will be. But the thought of one man weighs with me. On the face of it I ought to be his companion in flight and his fellow-worker in restoring the Republic. If you complain of my chopping and changing, I answer that I talk to you as to myself. In so great a matter must not any man argue with himself this way and that? Besides I want to draw *your* opinion—if it is still the same I shall be the steadier, if it has
3 changed I shall agree with you. Of course it is relevant to my problem to know what Domitius and our friend Lentulus are going to do. Of Domitius there are different reports ***. According to another he is at Tibur or in the neighbourhood

ad urbem, quod item falsum video esse; ait enim Lepidus eum nescio quo penetrasse itineribus ⟨occultis⟩, occultandi sui causa an maris a⟨di⟩ipiscendi—ne id quidem scit; ignorat etiam de filio. addit illud sane molestum, pecuniam Domitio satis grandem quam is Corfini habuerit non esse redditam. de Lentulo autem nihil audimus. haec velim exquiras ad meque perscribas.

165 (VIII. 15)

Scr. in Formiano v Non. Mart. an. 49

CICERO ATTICO SAL.

1 A. d. v Non. Mart. epistulas mihi tuas Aegypta reddidit, unam veterem, IIII Kal. quam te scribis dedisse Pinario, quem non vidimus; in qua ⟨ex⟩spectas quidnam praemissus agat Vibullius, qui omnino non est visus a Caesare (id altera epistula video te scire ita esse), et quem ad modum redeuntem excipiam Caesarem, quem omnino vitare cogito, et †aut hemonis† fugam intendis commutationemque vitae tuae, quod tibi puto esse faciendum, et ignoras Domitius cum fascibusne sit; quod cum scies, facies ut sciamus. habes ad primam epistulam.

2 Secutae sunt duae prid. Kal. ambae datae, quae me convellerunt de pristino statu, iam tamen, ut ante ad te scripsi, labantem. nec me movet quod scribis 'Iovi ipsi iniquum'; nam periculum in utriusque iracundia positum est, victoria

---

5 ait *s*: in te *R*Δ: sed *Em* 6 occultis *add. Lambinus* 7 adipiscendi *P*δ: ap- Ω id] is *Madvig* 8 etiam *Madvig*: enim Ω 9 corfini *Brunus* (M^4): coreni Ω 10 audivimus *O*

Ep. 165] **1**, 3 vidimus *P*δ: videmus Ω qua *s*: que *RMm*: quem *Pbd* exspectas ϛ: sp- Ω 7 aut hemonis Δ: haud ahem- *P*: haud hac hem- *R*: αὐθήμερον *Winstedt*: ad Thyamin *Lehmann*: αὐθαίρετον *Watt* fugam intendis *Malaespina*: fuga int- *OR*: fugam t- Δ -que ϛ: qui Ω **2**, 3 scribis Ω: scripsi *C*: -psti *Klotz*

of the capital (?). That too is evidently untrue, since Lepidus says he has made his way secretly somewhere to stay in hiding or it may be to gain the coast—that too he does not know. Neither has he any news of the son. He adds that a fairly large sum of money which Domitius had in Corfinium has not been restored to him. Very tiresome! Of Lentulus we hear nothing. I should be grateful if you would go into this and write to me in detail.

165 (VIII. 15)

Formiae, 3 March 49

CICERO TO ATTICUS

1 On 3 March Aegypta delivered your letters. One was an old letter of 26 February which you say you gave to Pinarius, whom I have not seen. In it you wonder how Vibullius is getting on with his mission (Caesar never even saw him, and I see from your second letter that you know this), and how I am going to receive Caesar on his way back (I mean to avoid him altogether). You also purpose flight 'that very day' (?) and a change in your way of life (I think you are right), and you don't know whether Domitius has the *fasces* with him (when you do you will tell me). So there's your first letter answered.

2 Two letters followed, both dated 28 February, which tore me from my earlier stance—though as I wrote to you I was already wavering. It is not what you say about 'bearing hard on Jove himself' that influences me—there is danger in the anger of either and victory is uncertain, except that the worse

autem ita incerta ut deterior causa paratior mihi esse videatur. nec me consules movent, qui ipsi pluma aut folio facilius moventur. offici me deliberatio cruciat cruciavitque adhuc. cautior certe est mansio, honestior existimatur traiectio; malo interdum multi me non caute quam pauci non honeste fecisse existiment. de Lepido et Tullo quod quaeris, illi vero non dubitant quin Caesari praesto futuri in senatumque venturi sint.

3 Recentissima tua est epistula Kalendis data, in qua optas congressum pacemque non desperas; sed ego cum haec scribebam nec illos congressuros nec, si congressi essent, Pompeium ad ullam condicionem accessurum putabam. quod videris non dubitare, si consules transeant, quid nos facere oporteat, certe transeunt vel, quo modo nunc est, transierunt. sed memento praeter Appium neminem esse fere qui non ius habeat transeundi; nam aut cum imperio sunt, ut Pompeius, ut Scipio, Sufenas, Fannius, Voconius, Sestius, ipsi consules, quibus more maiorum concessum est vel omnis adire provincias, aut legati sunt eorum. sed nihil differo; quid placeat tibi et quid prope modum rectum sit intellego.

Plura scriberem, si ipse possem; sed, ut mihi videor, potero biduo. Balbi Corneli litterarum exemplum quas eodem die accepi quo tuas misi ad te, ut meam vicem doleres, cum me deri⟨deri⟩ videres.

---

10 tullo *d*: tulio *E*: tullio *OR*Δ   3, 9 Sufenas *Vrsinus*: setenas Ω   Voconius] Copo- *Manutius*   11 differo *scripsi*: desero Ωλ: distero '*antiquus liber*' *teste Manutio*: decerno *Pius*   13 possem Σ: -sim Δ   15 me derideri *Brunus* (*M*⁴): me deri (med-) Ω

cause seems to me to be the better equipped. Nor am I influenced by the Consuls, who are themselves as unstable as a feather or a leaf. What tortures me, and has all along, is the question of duty. To stay is certainly the more prudent course, to go overseas is thought the more honourable. Sometimes I feel as though I had rather be thought to have acted imprudently by many than dishonourably by a few. As for your question about Lepidus and Tullus, they have quite made up their minds to meet Caesar and take their seats in the Senate.

3 The most recent of the batch was dispatched on the Kalends, in which you pray for a meeting and do not despair of peace. But at the time I write I don't think they will meet, or that if they do Pompey will agree to any terms. You seem to be in no doubt what I ought to do if the Consuls cross the water. Well, they are certainly crossing, or as things now stand have crossed already. But remember that except for Appius there is practically no one among them not legally entitled to go overseas, being either in military command, like Pompey, Scipio, Fannius, Voconius, Sestius, and the Consuls themselves, who by ancient custom have the right to visit any province they please, or else Legates of these. But I am not postponing the issue. I see what you favour and what, broadly speaking, is right.

I should write more if I could write myself. However I think I shall be able to do so in a couple of days. I am sending you a copy of a letter from Cornelius Balbus which I received the same day as yours, so you can be sorry for me when you see how I am mocked.

165 A (VIII. 15 A)

Scr. Romae c. Kal. Mart. an. 49

BALBVS CICERONI IMP. SAL.

1 Obsecro te, Cicero, suscipe curam et cogitationem dignissimam tuae virtutis, ut Caesarem et Pompeium perfidia hominum distractos rursus in pristinam concordiam reducas. crede mihi Caesarem non solum fore in tua potestate sed etiam maximum beneficium te sibi dedisse iudicaturum, si huc te reicis. velim idem Pompeius faciat; qui ut adduci tali tempore ad ullam condicionem possit magis opto quam spero. sed cum constiterit et timere desierit, tum incipiam non desperare et tuam auctoritatem plurimum apud eum valituram.

2 Quod Lentulum consulem meum voluisti hic remanere, Caesari gratum, mihi vero gratissimum me dius fidius fecisti; nam illum tanti facio qui non Caesarem magis diligam. qui si passus esset nos secum, ut consueveramus, loqui et non se totum etiam et etiam ab sermone nostro avertisset, minus miser quam sum essem. nam cave putes hoc tempore plus me quemquam cruciari, quod eum, quem ante me diligo, video in consulatu quidvis potius esse quam consulem. quod si voluerit tibi obtemperare et nobis de Caesare credere et consulatum reliquum Romae peragere, incipiam sperare etiam consilio senatus auctore te, illo relatore Pompeium et Caesarem coniungi posse; quod si factum erit, satis me vixisse putabo.

Ep. 165A] **1**, 6 hoc *M, fort. recte* 8 et *om. M* **2**, 1 *nova ep. in* Ω, *uno tenore codd. Bod. et Ball.* consulem *del. Weiske* mecum *s* 3 qui] ut *Lambinus* 4 cons(u)everamus *O*Δ: consuer- *ER* 5 etiam et *ERbdm*: et tam *OM*: etiam atque *s* 8 consulem *s*: -ul Ω 12 satis me Σ: me s- Δ

165A (VIII. 15A)

Rome, c.1 March 49

BALBUS TO CICERO IMPERATOR

1 I beg you, dear Cicero, put your thoughts and concern upon a design eminently worthy of your character, I mean the restitution of the old happy relations between Caesar and Pompey, now that intriguers have set them at variance. Believe me when I say that Caesar will not only put himself in your hands but will consider himself under the deepest obligation to you if you will bend your mind that way. I only wish that Pompey may do the like; but I rather pray than hope that he may be brought to any sort of accommodation at such a time. But when he settles down and regains a sense of security, *then* I shall begin not to despair of your influence counting heavily with him.

2 Caesar is grateful to you for desiring my friend Consul Lentulus to stay here, and I am indeed more than grateful. I have so high a regard for him that Caesar himself is no dearer to me. If he had let me talk to him as I used to do and had not repeatedly and absolutely declined conversation with me, I should be less unhappy than I am. For you must not think that anyone at the present time suffers more keenly than I do when I see a man who is dearer to me than myself become in his Consulship the sorry travesty of a Consul. But if he will listen to you and believe me about Caesar and serve out the rest of his term of office in Rome, I shall begin to hope that by the Senate's advice, with you to inspire and him to propose, Pompey and Caesar may yet come to be reconciled. If and when that happens I shall feel I have lived long enough.

3 Factum Caesaris de Corfinio totum te probaturum scio; et, quo modo in eius modi re, commodius cadere non potuit quam ut res sine sanguine confieret.

Balbi mei tuique adventu ⟨te⟩ delectatum valde gaudeo. is quaecumque tibi de Caesare dixit quaeque Caesar scripsit, scio, re tibi probabit, quaecumque fortuna eius fuerit, verissime scripsisse.

166 (VIII. 16)

Scr. in Formiano iv Non. Mart. an. 49 (§ 2)

CICERO ATTICO SAL.

1 Omnia mihi provisa sunt praeter occultum et tutum iter ad mare superum; hoc enim mari uti non possumus hoc tempore anni. illuc autem quo spectat animus et quo res vocat qua veniam? cedendum enim est celeriter, ne forte qua re impediar atque adliger. nec vero ille me ducit qui videtur; quem ego hominem ἀπολιτικώτατον omnium iam ante cognoram, nunc vero etiam ἀστρατηγητότατον. non me igitur is ducit sed sermo hominum qui ad me ⟨a⟩ Philotimo scribitur; is enim me ab optimatibus ait conscindi. quibus optimatibus, di boni? qui nunc quo modo occurrunt, quo modo etiam se venditant Caesari! municipia vero deum,
2 nec simulant, ut cum de illo aegroto vota faciebant. sed plane

---

3, 1 te ς: me Ω scio et *Corradus*: sciet *E*Δ: sciet et *R* 4 *nova ep. in ORδ, uno tenore EM* mei tuique *Brunus* (*M*[4]): me illud que *vel sim.* Ω te *hic add. Watt, ante* valde *Brunus* (*M*[4]) 6 scio re *Victorius*: scire *OR*Δ: si ire *E*: si re *C* verissime *Manutius*: velis- *E*: bel(l)is- *OR*: velis summe Δ*C*: *fort.* verissime se

Ep. 166] 1, 1 et tutum *Manutius*: et tum *MZ*[l]: metum Σδ 8 a *P*: *om.* Ω 11 etiam *scripsi*: autem Ω venditant *Budaeus*(?): -icant Ω deum *M*: ad eum Σ*bms*: ad deum *d*: *fort.* ad caelum

3 I know that Caesar's action over Corfinium will have your entire approval; and in such circumstances a bloodless finish to the business was the best possible outcome.

I was very glad to hear that you were pleased to see my (and your) dear boy. Whatever he told you about Caesar and whatever Caesar wrote to you, Caesar will, I am sure, prove to you by his actions, however fortune may go with him, that he wrote it in all sincerity.

166 (VIII. 16)

Formiae, 4 March 49

CICERO TO ATTICUS

1 I have provided for everything except a safe and secret journey to the Adriatic. I cannot go by this sea at this time of year. But how to go where my heart would be and where duty calls? I must leave and quickly, or I may somehow be obstructed and tied down. Nor, appearances notwithstanding, is it Pompey who draws me. I already knew him to be a hopeless failure as a statesman, and I now find him an equally bad general. It is not he therefore who draws me but the things people are saying, which I learn from Philotimus. He says the optimates are tearing me to shreds. What sort of optimates, in heaven's name? Look at the way they are now going out to meet Caesar and positively currying his favour. As for the towns, they make a god of him, and no pretence about it either, as there was when they were offering their prayers for Pompey's

quicquid mali hic Pisistratus non fecit tam gratum est quam si alium facere prohibuerit. ⟨hunc⟩ propitium sperant, illum iratum putant. quas fieri censes ἀπαντήσεις ex oppidis, quos honores? 'metuunt' inquies. credo, sed mehercule illum magis; huius insidiosa clementia delectantur, illius iracundiam formidant. iudices de CCCL⟨X⟩, qui praecipue Gnaeo nostro delectabantur, ex quibus cottidie aliquem video, nescio quas eius minas horrent. itaque quaero qui sint isti optimates qui me exturbent cum ipsi domi maneant. sed tamen, quicumque sunt, 'αἰδέομαι Τρῶας'. etsi qua spe proficiscar video coniungoque me cum homine magis ad vastandam Italiam quam ad vincendum parato dominumque exspecto. et quidem cum haec scribebam IIII Non. iam exspectabam aliquid a Brundisio. quid autem 'aliquid'? quam inde turpiter fugisset, et victor hic qua se referret et quo; quod ubi audissem, si ille Appia veniret, ego Arpinum cogitabam.

167 (IX. 1)

Scr. in Formiano prid. Non. Mart. an. 49 (§ 1)

CICERO ATTICO SAL.

1 Etsi cum tu has litteras legeres putabam fore ut scirem iam quid Brundisi actum esset (nam Canusio VIII⟨I⟩ Kal. profectus erat Gnaeus; haec autem scribebam prid. Non., XIIII die postquam ille Canusio moverat), tamen angebar singularum horarum exspectatione mirabarque nihil adlatum esse ne

2, 2 mali hic Δ: hic m- Σ fecit *Sedgwick*: fecerit Ω est] erit *Wesenberg* 3 hunc *s*: *om.* Ω: *ante* sperant *Wesenberg* 4 quas ς: cum Ω 6 illius ς: huius Ω 7 de *del. Wesenberg* CCCLX *Iunius*: CCCL Ω 9 minas *C*: lucerias Ω 10 cum ipsi *s*: cum (h)is (cumis) si Ω 13 dominumque *P*: domum (donum) quem Ω*C* et quidem *O*Δ: eq- *ER* 14 IIII *s*: illi Ω 15 inde] ille *Sedgwick* 16 quod ubi Σ*s*: qua (d)ubi *bd*: modo dubii *Mm*
Ep. 167] **1,** 2 VIIII *Pontedera*: VIII Ω

2 recovery. But the truth is that any evil this Pisistratus has not done is earning him as much popularity as if he were to have stopped someone else doing it. In him they hope to find a gracious power, while Pompey they think is an angry one. You can imagine the town deputations and official compliments. You will say they are frightened. I dare say they are, but I'll be bound they're more frightened of Pompey than of Caesar. They are delighted with *his* artful clemency and fear the other's wrath. Jurors of the panel of 360, who were our Gnaeus' especial admirers (I see one or other of them every day), are shuddering at certain threats of his. So I ask you, what sort of optimates are these that thrust me out while they themselves stay at home? And yet, be they what they may, 'I fear the Trojans', although I am only too well aware with what prospects I shall set out, and although I am allying myself with a man who is better prepared for the devastation of Italy than for victory, and although I expect to find myself a slave. And indeed as I write this on the 4th I am already expecting some news from Brundisium. Why do I say 'some'? I mean news of his disgraceful flight and the victor's return—his route and destination. When I hear that, if he is travelling by the Appian Way, I am for Arpinum.

167 (IX. 1)

Formiae, 6 March 49

CICERO TO ATTICUS

1 Although by the time you read this letter I expect I shall already know the outcome at Brundisium (for Gnaeus set out from Canusium on 21 February and I am writing this on the 6th, thirteen days after he marched from Canusium), I am tortured none the less by suspense from hour to hour. It is

rumoris quidem; nam erat mirum silentium. sed haec fortasse κενόσπουδα sunt, quae tamen iam sciantur necesse est;
2 illud molestum, me adhuc investigare non posse ubi P. Lentulus noster sit, ubi Domitius. quaero autem, quo facilius scire possim quid acturi sint, iturine ad Pompeium et, si sunt, qua quandove ituri sint.

Vrbem quidem iam refertam esse optimatium audio, Sosium et Lupum, quos Gnaeus noster ante putabat Brundisium venturos esse quam se, ius dicere. hinc vero vulgo vadunt; etiam M'. Lepidus, quocum diem conterere solebam,
3 cras cogitabat. nos autem in Formiano morabamur, quo citius audiremus, deinde Arpinum volebamus; inde iter qua maxime ἀναπάντητον esset ad mare superum, remotis sive omnino missis lictoribus. audio enim bonis viris, qui et nunc et saepe antea magno praesidio rei publicae fuerunt, hanc cunctationem nostram non probari multaque mihi et severe in conviviis, tempestivis quidem, disputari.

Cedamus igitur et, ut boni cives simus, bellum Italiae terra marique inferamus et odia improborum rursus in nos, quae iam exstincta erant, incendamus et Luccei consilia ac
4 Theophani persequamur. nam Scipio vel in Syriam proficiscitur sorte vel cum genero honeste vel Caesarem fugit iratum. Marcelli quidem, nisi gladium Caesaris timuissent, manerent. Appius et eodem timore et inimicitiarum recentium. et tamen praeter hunc et C. Cassium reliqui legati, Faustus pro quaestore; ego unus cui utrumvis liceret. frater accedit, quem socium huius fortunae esse non erat aequum;

2, 8 M'. *Manutius*: M. Ω **3**, 2 qua *Victorius*: quam Ω 6 mihi Ω: in me ς et severe ς: esse vere Ω 7 conviviis ς: conviciis (-tiis) Ω 8 simus *ERs*: sumus *O*Δ **4**, 4 et (*prius*) Ω: est ς, *Madvig* eodem] eodem modo *M* (*sed* modo *del.*): eodem in *Boot* recentium etiam; praeter *Madvig* 6 licet *Kayser* 7 accedit *C*: accesserit Σ*ms*: accederet *Mbd*

extraordinary that nothing has come through, not even a rumour. The silence is uncanny. But perhaps all this is worry
2 to no purpose, and after all the truth must soon be out. What *does* trouble me is that I still cannot discover the whereabouts of our friend P. Lentulus or of Domitius. I am looking for them in order to learn their plans, whether they are going to join Pompey, and if so, when and by what route.

Rome I hear is now full of optimates, and Sosius and Lupus, who our Gnaeus thought would arrive at Brundisium before him, are sitting on the bench. Here there is a general exodus; even my daily companion M'. Lepidus is off tomorrow. I
3 am staying on at Formiae to get the news quicker. Then I want to go to Arpinum and from there by the least frequented route to the Adriatic, putting my lictors out of the way or discharging them outright. For I hear that the honest men, who now and so often in the past have been such a tower of strength to the constitution, disapprove of this dallying of mine and that there is a deal of severe comment at dinner-parties, lengthy ones too!

So I had best leave and show myself a good citizen by carrying war into Italy by land and sea, and once again stir up against myself the hatred of the rascals, which had by now died out,
4 and execute the counsels of Lucceius and Theophanes. Scipio goes to Syria as his allotted province, or if you like he is accompanying his son-in-law, which is a respectable reason, or he is escaping Caesar's anger. As for the Marcelli, they would have stayed behind if they had not been afraid of Caesar's sword. Appius has the same reason for fear, and recent enmities besides. And anyhow, apart from him and C. Cassius, the others are all Legates, Faustus is Proquaestor. I am the only one who might take either way. Then there is my brother, who should not in fairness have been associated

cui magis etiam Caesar irascetur, sed impetrare non possum ut maneat. dabimus hoc Pompeio, cui debemus. nam me quidem alius nemo movet, non sermo bonorum, qui nulli sunt, non causa, quae acta timide est, agetur improbe. uni, uni hoc damus, ne id quidem roganti nec suam causam, ut ait, agenti sed publicam.

Tu quid cogites de transeundo in Epirum scire sane velim.

168 (IX. 2)

Scr. in Formiano Non. Mart. an. 49

CICERO ATTICO SAL.

Etsi Non. Mart., die tuo, ut opinor, exspectabam epistulam a te longiorem, tamen ad eam ipsam brevem quam III⟨I⟩ Non. ὑπὸ τὴν διάλειψιν dedisti rescribendum putavi. gaudere ais te mansisse me et scribis in sententia te manere. mihi autem superioribus litteris videbare non dubitare quin cederem, ita si et Gnaeus bene comitatus conscendisset et consules transissent. utrum hoc tu parum commeministi, an ego non satis intellexi, an mutasti sententiam? sed aut ex epistula quam exspecto perspiciam quid sentias aut alias abs te litteras eliciam. Brundisio nihildum erat adlatum.

169 (IX. 2*a*)

Scr. in Formiano viii Id. Mart. an. 49

CICERO ATTICO SAL.

1 O rem difficilem planeque perditam! quam nihil praetermittis in consilio dando! quam nihil tamen quod tibi ipsi

---

8 irascetur Σ*d*: -ceretur Δ 9 cui (quoi) *Schmidt*: quod Σδ: quo *M*

Ep. 168] *accedit V* 3 IIII *Corradus*: III Ω διάλειψιν *Orelli*: ΔΙΑΛΗΨΙΝ *vel sim.* Ω 5 in sup- *V*

Ep. 169] *novam ep. constituit Schütz: cum superiore in codd. cohaeret* **1**, 2 in *om. C*

with me in this plight. Caesar will be even angrier with him than with me; but I cannot induce him to stay. I shall do this for Pompey; it is what I owe him. No one else influences *me*, neither the honest men's talk (there *are* no honest men) nor the cause, which has been conducted without courage and will be conducted without scruple. I do it simply and solely for Pompey, who does not even ask it of me and is, so he says, fighting not for himself but for the country.

I should be very glad to know what you have in mind about crossing to Epirus.

168 (IX. 2)

Formiae, 7 March 49

CICERO TO ATTICUS

Though I am expecting a longer letter from you today (Nones of March), your bad day I believe, I thought I ought first to reply to that short letter which you sent on the 4th, just after the intermission. You say you are glad I have stayed and write that you hold to your opinion. But in your previous letter I thought you were clear that I should leave, provided that Gnaeus had embarked with a large following and that the Consuls had crossed. Don't you remember this? Or did I not fully understand? Or have you changed your mind? But I shall see from the letter I am waiting for what you think, or I shall make you write another. No news yet from Brundisium.

169 (IX. 2*a*)

Formiae, 8 March 49

CICERO TO ATTICUS

1 What a difficult, what an absolutely desperate business! How completely you cover the ground in giving your advice! But how completely you fail to find a solution with which

placeat explicas! non esse me una cum Pompeio gaudes: ac proponis quam sit turpe me adesse cum quid de illo detrahatur; nefas esse approbare. certe. contra igitur? 'di' inquis 'averruncent!' quid ergo fiet si in altero scelus est, in altero supplicium? 'impetrabis' inquis 'a Caesare ut tibi abesse liceat et esse otioso.' supplicandum igitur? miserum. quid si non impetraro? 'et de triumpho erit' inquis 'integrum.' quid si hoc ipso premar? accipiam? quid foedius? negem? repudiari se totum, magis etiam quam olim in xxviratu, putabit. ac solet, cum se purgat, in me conferre omnem illorum temporum culpam: ita me sibi fuisse inimicum ut ne honorem quidem a se accipere vellem. quanto nunc hoc idem accipiet asperius! tanto scilicet quanto et honos hic illo est amplior et ipse

2 robustior. nam quod negas te dubitare quin magna in offensa sim apud Pompeium hoc tempore, non video causam cur ita sit hoc quidem tempore. qui enim amisso Corfinio denique certiorem me sui consili fecit, is queretur Brundisium me non venisse cum inter me et Brundisium Caesar esset? deinde etiam scit ἀπαρρησίαστον esse in ea causa querelam suam. me putat de municipiorum imbecillitate, de dilectibus, de pace, de urbe, de pecunia, de Piceno occupando plus vidisse quam se. sin cum potuero non venero, tum erit inimicus; quod ego non eo vereor ne mihi noceat (quid enim faciet?

---

6 averruncent ς: *varia, velut* annerun(t)cent Ω 11 xxviratu *Ms*: -tum Σ*bdm* (iratum *V*) 15 honos *Wesenberg*: -or Ω **2**, 6 ea *ORΔ*: mea *EVm*

you yourself can be satisfied! You are glad that I am not with Pompey; and you point out how discreditable it would be for me to be present at any proceedings derogatory to him. 'It would be criminal to approve.' No doubt. Should I oppose then? 'Heaven forfend!' say you. Well, what *am* I to do then, with crime on the one side and punishment on the other? Caesar, you say, will give me permission to stay away, out of public life. Am I to beg then? Miserable! Supposing the permission is refused? And you point out that the Triumph will remain open. Suppose he presses me with that very thing? Am I to accept? Could anything be uglier? Refuse? He will feel utterly spurned, even more than over the place on the agrarian board in the old days. In his own excuse he always lays the whole blame for what happened then on my shoulders, says that I was so bitterly hostile to him that I would not even accept an honour at his hands. How much harder he will take a similar rebuff now! Obviously in proportion to the greater importance of the honour and the greater strength
2 of his own position. You say you don't doubt that I am in very bad odour with Pompey at present. I do not see any reason why this should be so *at present*. Having informed me of his plans only after the loss of Corfinium, he is surely not going to complain of my not having gone to Brundisium when there was Caesar between me and there. Furthermore he knows that a complaint from him on that subject would be out of court. He thinks I judged better than himself on the weakness of the municipalities, on the levies, on peace, on the capital, on the money, on occupying Picenum. But if I don't go when I can, *then* he will be angry. I am not afraid of that because of any harm that may come to me—after all, what

'τίς δ' ἐστὶ δοῦλος τοῦ θανεῖν ἄφροντις ὤν;'), sed quia ingrati animi crimen horreo. confido igitur adventum nostrum illi, quoquo tempore fuerit, ut scribis, ἀσμενιστὸν fore. nam quod ais, si hic temperatius egerit, consideratius te consilium daturum, qui hic potest se gerere non perdite? ⟨vetat⟩ vita, mores, ante facta, ratio suscepti negoti, socii, vires bonorum aut etiam constantia.

3 Vixdum epistulam tuam legeram cum ad me currens ad illum Postumus Curtius venit, nihil nisi classis loquens et exercitus. eripiebat Hispanias, tenebat Asiam, Siciliam, Africam, Sardiniam, confestim in Graeciam persequebatur. eundum igitur est, nec tam ut belli quam ut fugae socii simus. nec enim ferre potero sermones istorum, quicumque sunt; non sunt enim certe, ut appellantur, boni. sed tamen id ipsum scire cupio, quid loquantur, idque ut exquiras meque certiorem facias te vehementer rogo. nos adhuc quid Brundisi actum esset plane nesciebamus. cum sciemus, tum ex re et ex tempore consilium capiemus, sed utemur tuo.

170 (IX. 3)

Scr. in Formiano vii Id. Mart. an. 49 (§ 2)

CICERO ATTICO SAL.

1 Domiti filius transiit Formias viii Id. currens ad matrem Neapolim mihique nuntiari iussit patrem ad urbem esse, cum ex eo curiose quaesisset servus noster Dionysius. nos autem

---

14 temperatius *V*: -antius *EORΔ* te consilium Σ: consilium te Δ 15 vetat vita *scripsi* (vetant vita *Purser*): vita *EORΔ*: quoi vita *V*: vetant *Boot* 17 *post* constantia *add.* nihil impenditur *V*, cogent *Lehmann*

Ep. 170] *novam ep. faciunt RP*: *in cett. cum superiore cohaeret* **1**, 1 transiit *Vms*: -sit *ERMbd* 3 ex Σδ(*om. s*)λ: de *M*

can he do? 'What man's a slave that nothing recks of death?' —, but because I dread the charge of ingratitude. So I am confident that my coming will, as you say, be acceptable to him, happen when it may. You add that if Caesar shows moderation you will consider your advice more carefully; but how can he behave otherwise than as a desperado? That is precluded by his life, his character, his past, the nature of his present enterprise, his associates, the strength of the honest men or just their persistence.

3 I had hardly read your letter when Curtius Postumus arrived at my door hurrying to join Caesar and with nothing but fleets and armies on his tongue. His talk was of snatching Spain, holding Asia, Sicily, Africa, Sardinia, pursuing Pompey hot-foot into Greece. So I must be off to take my part, not so much in fighting as in running away. For I shall not be able to bear the talk of your friends in Rome—I don't know what name to give them, for they certainly are not what they are usually called, honest men. Be that as it may, I am anxious for information on this very point, what they are saying, and I particularly request you to find out and let me know. So far I am completely in the dark about what has happened at Brundisium. As soon as I know I shall take counsel according to the event and the hour, but I shall follow yours.

170 (IX. 3)

Formiae, 9 March 49

CICERO TO ATTICUS

1 Domitius' son passed through Formiae on the 8th, hastening to join his mother in Naples, and sent me word that his father was in the neighbourhood of Rome, in answer to a particular enquiry by my slave Dionysius. I had heard that he had left

audieramus eum profectum sive ad Pompeium sive in Hispaniam. id cuius modi sit scire sane velim. nam ad id quod delibero pertinet, si ille certe nusquam discessit, intellegere Gnaeum non esse facilis nobis ex Italia exitus, cum ea tota armis praesidiisque teneatur, hieme praesertim. nam si commodius anni tempus esset, vel infero mari liceret uti. nunc nihil potest nisi supero tramitti, quo iter interclusum est. quaeres igitur et de Domitio et de Lentulo.

2 A Brundisio nulla adhuc fama venerat, et erat hic dies VII Id., quo die suspicabamur aut pridie ad Brundisium venisse Caesarem. nam Kalendis Arpis manserat. sed si Postumum audire velles, persecuturus erat Gnaeum; transisse enim iam putabat coniectura tempestatum ac dierum. ego nautas eum non putabam habiturum; ille confidebat, et eo magis quod audita naviculariis hominis liberalitas esset. sed tota res Brundisina quo modo habeat se diutius nescire non possum.

171 (IX. 5)

Scr. in Formiano vi Id. Mart. an. 49

CICERO ATTICO SAL.

1 [Natali] die tuo scripsisti epistulam ad me plenam consili summaeque cum benevolentiae tum etiam prudentiae. eam mihi Philotimus postridie quam a te acceperat reddidit. sunt ista quidem quae disputas difficillima, iter ad superum, navigatio infero, discessus Arpinum ne hunc fugisse, mansio

---

11 et de . . . et de *E*Δ: et de . . . et *OR*: de . . . et *V* **2**, 2 ad Σ: *om.* Δ
Ep. 171] *haec ep. et quae sequitur usque ad* transiit (§ 3, 9) *desunt in V*
1, 1 natali *secl. Sternkopf*

Italy, either to join Pompey or for Spain. I should much like to know the truth of the matter; for it is relevant to my own problem, if he definitely has not gone away, that Gnaeus should understand that it is not so easy for us to get out of Italy, held down as the entire country is by garrisons and armies, in winter especially. If the season were more favourable, one could go by the Western Sea at a pinch. As it is, nothing can be got across except by the Adriatic, and the road to that is blocked. So please enquire both about Domitius and about Lentulus.

2 No report has come in yet from Brundisium, and today is the 9th, that or yesterday being the day on which according to my idea Caesar should have reached Brundisium, since he spent the night of the Kalends at Arpi. But if one cared to believe Postumus, Caesar was intending to pursue Gnaeus, who he thought had already crossed, judging by the weather and the number of days. I did not think Caesar would have the sailors; but Postumus was confident that he would, all the more so because, as he said, the shipowners had heard of the man's liberality. But I can't have long to wait before I know how the whole business at Brundisium stands.

171 (IX. 5)

Formiae, 10 March 49

CICERO TO ATTICUS

1 On your bad day you wrote to me a most kind and also most wise letter, full of advice. Philotimus delivered it to me the day after he had received it from you. The problems you discuss are indeed very difficult, journey by road to the Eastern Sea, by ship on the Western, departure to Arpinum,

Formiis ne obtulisse nos gratulationi videamur, sed miserius nihil quam ea videre quae tamen iam, inquam, videnda erunt.

Fuit apud me Postumus, scripsi ad te quam gravis, venit ad me etiam Q. Fufius quo vultu, quo spiritu! properans Brundisium, scelus accusans Pompei, levitatem et stultitiam senatus. haec qui in mea villa non feram †cur tum† in curia
2 potero ferre? age, finge me quamvis εὐστομάχως haec ferentem; quid illa 'dic, M. Tulli'? quem habebunt exitum? et omitto causam rei publicae, quam ego amissam puto cum vulneribus suis tum medicamentis iis quae parantur; de Pompeio quid agam? cui plane (quid enim hoc negem?) suscensui. semper enim ⟨me⟩ causae eventorum magis movent quam ipsa eventa. haec igitur mala (quibus maiora esse quae possunt?) considerans vel potius iudicans eius opera accidisse et culpa inimicior huic eram quam ipsi Caesari. ut maiores nostri funestiorem diem esse voluerunt Alliensis pugnae quam urbis captae, quod hoc malum ex illo (itaque alter religiosus etiam nunc dies, alter in vulgus ignotus), sic ego decem annorum peccata recordans, in quibus inerat ille etiam annus qui nos hoc ⟨non⟩ defendente, ne dicam gravius, adflixerat, praesentisque temporis cognoscens temeritatem, ignaviam,
3 neglegentiam suscensebam. sed ea iam mihi exciderunt; beneficia eiusdem cogito, cogito etiam dignitatem; intellego, serius equidem quam vellem propter epistulas sermonesque Balbi, sed video plane nihil aliud agi, nihil actum ab initio, ⟨nisi⟩

---

7 iam iam ς 12 cur tum Ω: cur eum *Pbd*: Curtium *anon. ap. Corradum*: *del.* Boot **2**, 6 me *add.* Casaubon 9 huic eram Σ*bs*: eram huic *Mdm* 14 non *Victorius*: *om.* Ω $Z^{(1)}$ **3**, 4 nihil (*prius*) *bs*: mi(c)hi Ω nisi *add. Wesenberg*: quam ς

which might look like flight from Caesar, remaining at Formiae, which might look like putting myself in the way of congratulating him; but the most wretched thing of all is the sight of what all the same (I repeat it) we must presently see.

Postumus has paid me a visit, how disagreeable you know from my letter. Another caller was Q. Fufius (imagine the look of him, the arrogance!), hastening through to Brundisium, loud against Pompey's wickedness and the Senate's fickleness and folly. If I can't stand this sort of thing under my own
2 roof shall I be able to stand it (?) in the Senate-House? Well, suppose I do stand it as phlegmatically as you please. What then? 'Speak M. Tullius!' Where is my way out? And I leave aside the cause of the Republic, which I take for lost, what with its own hurts and the remedies now in preparation; what am I to do about Pompey? I was frankly incensed against him—why should I deny it? I always attach more importance to the causes of events than to the events themselves. So considering these unparalleled disasters, or rather determining that they happened by his agency and fault, I felt a greater resentment against him than against Caesar himself. Our ancestors made the day of the battle of the Allia of blacker memory than that of the capture of the city, because the second calamity arose from the first, so that the former is even now a day of ill omen while the other is generally unknown. On the same principle I was angry when I remembered the mistakes of the past ten years, including the year of my own disaster in which *he* did not defend me (to use no harsher phrase), and when I perceived his recklessness, inertia, and
3 negligence at the present time. But now all that has gone out of my mind. I think of Pompey's services to me, and his greatness too. I understand, later indeed than I could have wished because of Balbus' letters and talk, but I do see clearly that

ut hunc occideret. ego igitur, sicut apud Homerum cui et mater et dea dixisset 'αὐτίκα γάρ τοι ἔπειτα μεθ' Ἕκτορα πότμος ἕτοιμος' matri ipse respondit

> 'αὐτίκα τεθναίην, ἐπεὶ οὐκ ἄρ' ἔμελλον ἑταίρῳ
> κτεινομένῳ ἐπαμῦναι,'—

quid si non ἑταίρῳ solum sed etiam εὐεργέτῃ, adde tali viro talem causam agenti?—ego vero haec officia mercanda vita puto. optimatibus vero tuis nihil confido, nihil iam ne inservio quidem. video ut se huic dent, ut daturi sint. quicquam tu illa putas fuisse de valetudine decreta municipiorum prae his de victoria gratulationibus? 'timent' inquies. at ipsi tum se timuisse dicunt. sed videamus quid actum sit Brundisi. ex eo fortasse alia consilia nascentur aliaeque litterae.

172 (IX. 6)

Scr. in Formiano v Id. Mart. an. 49

⟨CICERO ATTICO SAL.⟩

1 Nos adhuc Brundisio nihil. Roma scripsit Balbus putare iam Lentulum consulem tramisisse [me] nec eum a minore Balbo conventum, quod is hoc iam Canusi audisset; inde ad se eum scripsisse; cohortisque sex quae Albae fuissent ad Curium via Minucia transisse; id Caesarem ad se scripsisse et brevi

---

5 ego *ms*: eo Ω sicut *Faërnus*: si quid Ω: si quidem *Vrsinus*: sicut is *Iunius*: sicut ille *Schmidt* 7 ipse *OR*: ipsi *Ms* (matri ipse resp- *om. bdm*) 11 agenti ς: -ndi Ω ego *C*: et ego Ω officia . . . puto *ita Victorius*: officia mercanda puto *C*: officiam (eff- *Rbms*) ei candida (et canda *R*) vita puto Ω 13 vide *m* 17 alia *Lambinus* (nova *idem*): ea *ORMZ*^{1}: mea *E*δ

Ep. 172] *novam ep. agnovit Corradus: cum superiore in codd. cohaeret* 1, 1 putari *Orelli* 2 me *om. c* 4 curium *m*: curtum *EOMd* (*silent RPbs*) 5 via *Z*^{1}: in via *EOdm*: *om. M*

Caesar's whole purpose is and has been from the first to destroy him. I think of how in Homer a mother and a goddess says to her son

> 'Thy doom awaits thee after Hector's end.'

And her son replies

> 'Let me die quickly, since my friend is slain
> And I not there to aid.'

It is not only a friend in my case but a benefactor too; add the greatness of the man and of the cause he champions. Truly I think life worth losing for these duties' sake. As for your optimate friends, I don't put any faith in them, I don't even seek their good opinion any more. I see how they are kow-towing to Caesar, and will so continue. Those municipal decrees during Pompey's illness—are they to be compared, do you think, with these victory congratulations? You will say they are afraid; but by their own account they were afraid last year. But let us see what has happened at Brundisium. Perhaps that will give rise to other plans and other letters.

172 (IX. 6)

Formiae, 11 March 49

CICERO TO ATTICUS

1 Still nothing from Brundisium. Balbus wrote from Rome that he thought Consul Lentulus had already crossed, without having had an interview with Balbus junior, because the latter had heard this when he got to Canusium and had written to himself from there; also that six cohorts stationed at Alba had come over to Curius by the Minucian Way. Caesar, he

tempore eum ad urbem futurum. ergo utar tuo consilio neque me Arpinum hoc tempore abdam, etsi, Ciceroni meo togam puram cum dare Arpini vellem, hanc eram ipsam excusationem relicturus ad Caesarem. sed fortasse in eo ipso offendetur, cur non Romae potius. sed tamen, si est conveniendus, hic potissimum. tum reliqua videbimus, id est et quo et qua et quando.

2 Domitius, ut audio, in Cosano est ⟨et⟩ quidem, ut aiunt, paratus ad navigandum, si in Hispaniam, non ⟨im⟩probo, si ad Gnaeum, laudo; quovis potius certe quam ut Curtium videat quem ego patronus aspicere non possum. quid alios? sed, opinor, quiescamus, ne nostram culpam coarguamus qui, dum urbem, id est patriam, amamus dumque rem conventuram putamus, ita nos gessimus ut plane interclusi captique simus.

3 Scripta iam epistula Capua litterae sunt adlatae hoc exemplo:

'Pompeius mare transiit cum omnibus militibus quos secum habuit. hic numerus est hominum milia triginta et consules duo et tribuni pl. et senatores qui fuerunt cum eo omnes cum uxoribus et liberis. conscendisse dicitur a. d. IIII Non. Mart. ex ea die fuere septemtriones venti. navis quibus usus non est omnis aut praecidisse aut incendisse dicunt. de hac re litterae L. Metello tribuno pl. Capuam adlatae sunt a Clodia socru, quae ipsa transiit.'

4 Ante sollicitus eram et angebar, sicut res scilicet ipsa cogebat, cum consilio explicare nihil possem; nunc autem, postquam

---

2, 1 est et quidem *Lambinus*: est q- *RM*: est quidam *EO*δ: et quidem *Manutius* 2 improbo *scripsi*: probo Ω 3 Curtium *Victorius*: Curium *C*: certum Ω **3,** 1 capua *P*: -u(a)e Ω 4 duo et] et duo *Manutius*: *anne* duo et praetores et ? 8 de . . . transiit *Ciceroni dabant vulg.* 9 Capuam ς: -ua Ω: -u(a)e *bds* **4,** 1 ante] *hinc novam ep. incipit* Σ (*accedente V*) 5 cum (quum) . . . possem *ita C*: quo uti consilio possem Σδ: cum consilio possem *M* (*sed* cum *linea inductum*)

says, had so informed him by letter, and would be at Rome shortly. Accordingly I shall follow your advice and not hide myself away in Arpinum at present, though I wanted to give Marcus his white gown in Arpinum and that was the excuse I intended to leave with Caesar. But perhaps he will take offence at that too, because I am not doing it in Rome. But anyhow, if I must meet him, let it be here. Then we shall consider the next step, I mean where I am to go and how and when.

2 Domitius, I hear, is at his house near Cosa, and, so they say, ready to sail—if to Spain I do not blame him, if to join Gnaeus I commend him. Better go anywhere than have Curtius before his eyes, a sight too much for me his former counsel—not to speak of the others. But I had best lie low or I shall be convicting myself, in that for love of Rome, my country, and in the belief that there would be a compromise I got myself into the position of a prisoner, completely cut off.

3 After I had written this letter one came in from Capua. It reads as follows:—

'Pompey has crossed the sea with all the troops he had with him. They numbered 30,000 men, together with the two Consuls, and the Tribunes and Senators, all who were with him, along with their wives and children. He is said to have embarked on 4 March. The winds have been northerly from that day on. They say he disabled or burned all the ships he did not use. A letter on this subject was received in Capua by the Tribune L. Metellus from his mother-in-law Clodia, who was one of those to cross.'

4 I was anxious before and distressed, as one clearly could not but be in such a case, by my inability to think of any solution.

Pompeius et consules ex Italia exierunt, non angor sed ardeo dolore,

'οὐδέ μοι ἦτορ
ἔμπεδον, ἀλλ' ἀλαλύκτημαι.'

non sum, inquam, mihi crede, mentis compos; tantum mihi dedecoris admisisse videor. mene non primum cum Pompeio, qualicumque consilio usus ⟨est⟩, deinde cum bonis esse, quamvis causa temere instituta? praesertim cum ii ipsi quorum ego causa timidius me fortunae committebam, uxor, filia, Cicerones pueri, me illud sequi mallent, hoc turpe et me indignum putarent. nam Quintus quidem frater quicquid mihi placeret id rectum se putare aiebat, id animo aequissimo sequebatur.

5 Tuas nunc epistulas a primo lego. hae me paulum recreant. primae monent et rogant ne me proiciam, proximae gaudere te ostendunt me remansisse. eas cum lego, minus mihi turpis videor, sed tam diu dum lego. deinde emergit rursum dolor et αἰσχροῦ φαντασία. quam ob rem obsecro te, mi Tite, eripe hunc mihi dolorem aut minue saltem, aut consolatione aut consilio aut quacumque re potes. quid tu autem possis, aut quid homo quisquam? vix iam deus.

6 Equidem illud molior quod tu mones sperasque fieri posse, ut mihi Caesar concedat ut absim cum aliquid in senatu contra Gnaeum agatur. sed timeo ne non impetrem. venit ab eo Furnius. ut quidem scias quos sequamur, Q. Titini filium cum Caesare esse nuntiat—sed illum maiores mihi gratias agere quam vellem. quid autem me roget, paucis ille quidem

---

9 usus est *Wesenberg*: usus Ω: uso *Manutius* **5**, 3 gaudere te Σ*m*: te g- Δ 6 hunc mihi *ERc*: mihi *V*: mihi hunc Δ 8 vix deus. iam equidem Z^1
6, 4 ut *V*: et Ω 5 *sic distinxi*

But now that Pompey and the Consuls have left Italy, I am not merely distressed, I am consumed with grief:

'My heart
stands not, I am distraught.'

Yes, I give you my word I am beside myself at the thought of the dishonour I feel I have brought upon my head. To think that in the first place I am not with Pompey, whatever his mistakes, and in the second that I am not with the honest men, never mind how ill-advisedly they have managed our cause!—especially as the very ones for whose sake I hesitated to take the plunge, I mean my wife and daughter and the two boys, would have preferred me to follow the other course and thought this one discreditable and unworthy of me. As for my brother Quintus, he told me that whatever I thought best had his approval and followed it without qualm.

5 I now read over your letters from the beginning; they rouse my spirits a little. The earliest warn and beg me not to burn my boats; the most recent profess your satisfaction at my having stayed behind. When I read them I feel less ashamed, but only while I am actually reading; then pain and the spectre of dishonour rise afresh. So, my dear Titus, I implore you, rid me of this pain or at any rate relieve it, by consolation or advice or any way you can. And yet what could you do, what could any man do? A god could hardly help now.

6 For my part I am trying, as you advise and hope will be practicable, to obtain Caesar's consent to my absence from any proceedings in the Senate against Gnaeus. But I am afraid I may not succeed. Furnius has come from him—to show you models for our imitation, he reports that Q. Titinius' son is with Caesar. Anyway, according to Furnius Caesar expresses his gratitude to me, more than I could have wished. As for what he

verbis sed ἐν δυνάμει, cognosce ex ipsius epistula. me miserum quod tu non valuisti! una fuissemus; consilium certe non defuisset. 'σύν τε δύ' ἐρχομένω . . .'.

7 Sed acta ne agamus, reliqua paremus. me adhuc haec duo fefellerunt, initio spes compositionis, qua facta volebam ut⟨i⟩ populari via, sollicitudine senectutem nostram liberare; deinde bellum crudele et exitiosum suscipi a Pompeio intellegebam. melioris me dius fidius civis et viri putabam quovis supplicio adfici quam illi crudelitati non solum praeesse verum etiam interesse. ⟨sed⟩ videtur vel mori satius fuisse quam esse cum his. ad haec igitur cogita, mi Attice, vel potius excogita. quemvis eventum fortius feram quam hunc dolorem.

172A (IX. 6A)

Scr. in itinere Arpis Brundisium c. iii Non. Mart. an. 49

CAESAR IMP. S. D. CICERONI IMP.

Cum Furnium nostrum tantum vidissem neque loqui neque audire meo commodo potuissem, ⟨cum⟩ properarem atque essem in itinere praemissis iam legionibus, praeterire tamen non potui quin et scriberem ad te et illum mitterem gratiasque agerem, etsi hoc et feci saepe et saepius mihi facturus videor; ita de me mereris. in primis a te peto, quoniam confido me celeriter ad urbem venturum, ut te ibi videam, ut tuo consilio, gratia, dignitate, ope omnium rerum uti possim. ad propositum revertar; festinationi meae brevitatique litterarum ignosces. reliqua ex Furnio cognosces.

7, 3 uti *Bosius*: ut Ω via *Purser*: ut (et *V*) ea Ω: vita *Bosius* liberare *Wesenberg*: -ari *EOPΔ* (*vide Sjögren*): -arem *VR* 7 sed *addidi*

Ep. 172A] 2 meo *Z*: me Ω commodo Δ: -de Σ cum *add. Victorius, post* properarem *distinguens*: et *Koch* 5 et feci ς: effeci *O(?)RC*: feci *V*: effecit *M*: officium δ saepius] saepe *c*

asks of me, briefly but as one having authority, you will learn it from his own letter. If only you had not been ill! We should have been together. Assuredly we should have hit upon a plan. 'Two heads . . .'.

7 However let bygones be bygones and let us plan the future. Two things have misled me hitherto. At first there was the hope of a settlement, in which event I wanted to take a popular line and free my old age from anxiety. Then I saw that Pompey was embarking on a cruel and destructive war. Upon my word I thought that as a man and a citizen it was better to suffer any punishment rather than take a part, let alone a leading part, in such atrocity. But I feel even death would have been preferable to being with these people here. So think of all this, my dear Atticus, or rather think it out. I shall bear any outcome better than this pain.

172A (IX. 6A)

Between Arpi and Brundisium, c. 5 March 49

CAESAR IMPERATOR TO CICERO IMPERATOR

Though I have only just seen our friend Furnius and could neither speak nor listen to him at leisure since I am in haste and on the march with my army already sent ahead, yet I could not neglect to write to you and to send him and to express my thanks; though *that* I have often done and expect to do even oftener—you give me so much cause. Especially I ask of you, since I have every hope of getting to Rome in the near future, to let me see you there, so that I may be able to avail myself of your advice, influence, standing, and help in all matters. To return to my point: you must forgive my haste and the brevity of this letter. You will learn all else from Furnius.

173 (IX. 4)

Scr. in Formiano iv Id. Mart. an. 49

⟨CICERO ATTICO SAL.⟩

1 Ego etsi tam diu requiesco quam diu aut ad te scribo aut tuas litteras lego, tamen et ipse egeo argumento epistularum et tibi idem accidere certo scio; quae enim soluto animo familiariter scribi solent ea temporibus his excluduntur, quae autem sunt horum temporum ea iam contrivimus. sed tamen, ne me totum aegritudini dedam, sumpsi mihi quasdam tamquam θέσεις, quae et πολιτικαὶ sunt et temporum horum, ut et abducam animum a querelis et in eo ipso de quo agitur exercear. eae sunt huius modi:

2 Εἰ μενετέον ἐν τῇ πατρίδι τυραννουμένης αὐτῆς. εἰ παντὶ τρόπῳ τυραννίδος κατάλυσιν πραγματευτέον, κἂν μέλλῃ διὰ τοῦτο περὶ τῶν ὅλων ἡ πόλις κινδυνεύσειν. εἰ εὐλαβητέον τὸν καταλύοντα μὴ αὐτὸς αἴρηται. εἰ πειρατέον ἀρήγειν τῇ πατρίδι τυραννουμένῃ καιρῷ καὶ λόγῳ μᾶλλον ἢ πολέμῳ. εἰ πολιτικὸν τὸ ἡσυχάζειν ἀναχωρήσαντά ποι τῆς πατρίδος τυραννουμένης ἢ διὰ παντὸς ἰτέον κινδύνου τῆς ἐλευθερίας πέρι. εἰ πόλεμον ἐπακτέον τῇ χώρᾳ καὶ πολιορκητέον αὐτὴν τυραννουμένην. εἰ καὶ μὴ δοκιμάζοντα τὴν διὰ πολέμου κατάλυσιν τῆς τυραννίδος συναπογραπτέον ὅμως τοῖς ἀρίστοις. εἰ τοῖς εὐεργέταις καὶ φίλοις συγκινδυνευτέον ἐν τοῖς πολιτικοῖς κἂν μὴ δοκῶσιν εὖ βεβουλεῦσθαι περὶ τῶν ὅλων. εἰ ὁ μεγάλα τὴν πατρίδα εὐεργετήσας δι' αὐτό τε τοῦτο ἀνήκεστα παθὼν καὶ φθονηθεὶς κινδυνεύσειεν ἂν ἐθελοντὴς ὑπὲρ τῆς πατρίδος

Ep. 173] *hanc novam ep. 'in aliis exemplis' fuisse monet Lambinus in marg.: in nostris cum ep. 170 cohaeret* **1**, 2 egeo *OP*: ego *ERV*Δ 3 certo Δ*c*: -te Σ 4 ea ς: e *OR*Δ: et *EV* excluduntur ς: -dentur Ω 7 πολιτικαὶ *Orelli*: politic(a)e *vel sim.* Ω 8 a *ERbm*: ab *OMds* **2**, 3 εἰ] ἢ *Lambinus* τὸν . . . πατρίδος (*v.* 13) *om. RP* 4 αἵρηται *Bosius*: ΕΡΡΘΗΤΑΙ *M*: ἐγέρθηται *O*: ἄρθηται *C*: ΕΡΕΗΤΑΙ Z^b: *om.* δ: ἀρθῇ *Malaespina* 5 καιρῷ (-νῶ *O*) καὶ λόγῳ *OZc*: *om.* Δ 6 ἢ ς: εἰ *O*Δ 7 ἰτέον ς: ΕΙΤΕΟΗ *M*: θετέον *O*δ 8 αὐτὴν *c*: ταύτην *vel sim. O*Δ 12 τε τοῦτο *dm*: ΤΕΤΟΥ *M*: δὲ τοῦτο *bs*

173 (IX. 4)

Formiae, 12 March 49

CICERO TO ATTICUS

1 Though the time I spend writing to you or reading your letters brings me my only respite, I am at a loss for matter and I am sure it is the same with you. The kind of things friends usually write to one another when their minds are easy is ruled out by the times we live in, while we have already worn threadbare the topics appropriate to *them*. However, not to surrender myself wholly to bitterness of spirit, I have chosen some themes as it were, which are both political and topical, with the object of distracting my mind from its griefs and to keep it busy on the question at issue. This sort of thing:—

2 Ought a man to remain in his country under a despotism? Ought he to strive for the overthrow of a despotism by every means, even if the existence of the state is going to be endangered thereby? Ought he to beware of the overthrower lest *he* be set up as a despot? Ought he to try to help his country under a despotism by taking opportunity as it comes and by words rather than by war? Ought a statesman to live quietly in retirement while his country is under a depotism or ought he to take every risk for freedom's sake? Is it right to make war against one's country and blockade it when it is under despotic rule? Ought a man to enrol himself on the side of the best citizens even if he does not approve of overthrowing the despotism by war? Ought he in politics to join in the dangers of his friends and benefactors even though he does not approve of their actions in capital matters? Ought a man who has rendered his country great service and has on that account brought himself irreparable suffering and hostility voluntarily to incur danger on his country's behalf,

ἢ ἐφετέον αὐτῷ ἑαυτοῦ ποτε καὶ τῶν οἰκειοτάτων ποιεῖσθαι πρόνοιαν ἀφεμένῳ τὰς πρὸς τοὺς ἰσχύοντας διαπολιτείας.

3 In his ego me consultationibus exercens et disserens in utramque partem tum Graece tum Latine et abduco parumper animum a molestiis et τῶν προὔργου τι delibero. sed vereor ne tibi ἄκαιρος sim; si enim recte ambulavit is qui hanc epistulam tulit, in ipsum tuum diem incidit.

174 (IX. 7)

Scr. in Formiano iii Id. Mart. an. 49

CICERO ATTICO SAL.

1 Scripseram ad te epistulam quam darem IIII Id., sed eo die is cui dare volueram non est profectus. venit autem eo ipso die ille celeripes quem Salvius dixerat. attulit uberrimas tuas litteras, quae mihi quiddam quasi animulae restillarunt; recreatum enim me non queo dicere. sed plane τὸ συνέχον effecisti. ego enim non iam id ago, mihi crede, ut prosperos exitus consequar. sic enim video, nec duobus his vivis nec [hoc] uno nos umquam rem publicam habituros. ita neque de otio nostro spero iam nec ullam acerbitatem recuso. unum illud extimescebam, ne quid turpiter facerem vel dicam iam ne fecissem.

2 Sic ergo habeto, salutaris te mihi litteras misisse neque solum has longiores, quibus nihil potest esse explicatius, nihil

---

14 ἢ ς: εἰ Ω 15 τὰς] τῆς *Sjögren, auct. Daniellson* 3, 4 ambulavit is *Σbd*: -verit is *M* (-ritis) *ms*, *Mueller* 5 incidet *Mueller*

Ep. 174] *in inscriptione deficit V* 1, 1 darem *s*: parem Ω eo Σ: eos Δ die is *Ps*: dies *R*Δ: die *O* 3 celeriter pes Z^{1}: Callippides *Reid* 4 quasi animulae restillarunt *Lambinus* (*sed* instil-: stil- *Baiter*), *Bosius*: quastant mutaet estiliarunt $Z^{(1)}$: qua stant mutae test- Z^{b}: qua stant enim muta est illi aiunt (arunt *Mdm*) Ω (enim *om.* Δ) 8 hoc *seclusi* 11 ne fecissem *Schmidt* (*qui* iam, ne f-): effec- *OR*Δ: fec- *E*

or may he be allowed to begin to think of himself and his family, giving up political opposition to those in power?

3 Practising myself upon these questions and setting out the arguments on either side, now in Greek now in Latin, I take my mind for a while off my troubles and at the same time ponder matters of relevance. But I am afraid I come upon you at the wrong moment, for if the bearer of this letter has made decent time it will have reached you just on the day of your attack.

174 (IX. 7)

Formiae, 13 March 49

CICERO TO ATTICUS

1 I wrote a letter to you meaning to dispatch it on the 12th, but the man to whom I had meant to give it did not go. That same day Fleet-foot, as Salvius called him, arrived with a most substantial letter from you, which put back a *soupçon* of life into me—it would be too much to say that it set me up again. But you have certainly achieved the essential. Believe me, I no longer aim at finding a happy outcome. I realize that we shall never have a free state in the life-time of those two or of one singly. So I have no longer any hope of a quiet life for myself and I am ready to swallow every bitter pill. My one fear was of doing, or shall I say of having already done, something dishonourable.

2 So rest assured that your letters have done me good, not only this longer one, which could not have been better set out

perfectius, sed etiam illas breviores, in quibus hoc mihi
iucundissimum fuit, consilium factumque nostrum a Sexto
probari, pergratumque mihi tu fecisti; a quo et diligi me et
quid rectum sit intellegi scio. longior vero tua epistula non
me solum sed meos omnis aegritudine levavit. itaque utar tuo
consilio et ero in Formiano, ne aut ad urbem ἀπάντησις mea
animadvertatur aut, si nec hic nec illic eum videro, devita-
3 tum se a me putet. quod autem suades ut ab eo petam ut
mihi concedat ut idem tribuam Pompeio quod ipsi tribuerim,
id me iam pridem agere intelleges ex litteris Balbi et Oppi
quarum exempla tibi misi; misi etiam Caesaris ad eos sana
mente scriptas litteras quo modo in tanta insania. sin mihi Caesar
hoc non concedat, video tibi placere illud, me πολίτευμα
de pace suscipere; in quo non extimesco periculum (cum
enim tot impendeant, cur non honestissimo depecisci velim?)
sed vereor ne Pompeio quid oneris imponam, 'μή μοι
γοργείην κεφαλὴν δεινοῖο πελώρου' intorqueat. mirandum enim
in modum Gnaeus noster Sullani regni similitudinem con-
cupivit. εἰδώς σοι λέγω; nihil ille umquam minus obscure tulit.
'cum hocne igitur' inquies 'esse vis?' beneficium sequor, mihi
crede, non causam, ut in Milone, ut in—sed hactenus.
4 'causa igitur non bona est?' immo optima, sed agetur,
memento, foedissime. primum consilium est suffocare urbem
et Italiam fame, deinde agros vastare, urere, pecuniis locu-
pletum ⟨non⟩ abstinere. sed cum eadem metuam ab hac parte,
si illinc beneficium non sit, rectius putem quidvis domi perpeti.

2, 5 et diligi Σ: d- Δ **3**, 5 litteras *om.* *M* **4**, 3: locupletum *ORΔ*: -tium *Eλ* 4 non *add.* ς 5 illinc Σδ: illi *M*: illim *nescio quis*

or more complete, but the shorter one too, in which I was particularly pleased to read that my course and conduct have Sextus' approval. Thank you very much. I know his regard for me and his sound moral judgement. Your longer letter raised not only myself but all of us from our distress of mind. Accordingly I shall follow your advice and stay at Formiae, so that on the one hand I shall not attract notice by welcoming him at Rome and on the other he will not think I have deliberately avoided him, if I see him neither here nor there.
3 As for your suggestion that I ask him to allow me to pay as much regard to Pompey as I have paid to himself, you will see from Balbus' and Oppius' letters, copies of which I enclose, that this is what I have been doing for some time past—I also enclose a letter of Caesar's to them, a sane letter so far as there can be any sanity in such madness. If however Caesar should refuse me this, I see that you are in favour of my coming forward as an advocate of peace. I do not fear the danger involved (so many hang over me that I might as well settle for the most honourable), but I am afraid of causing Pompey embarrassment and of his turning on me 'the Gorgon's head, monster most terrible'. For our Gnaeus is marvellously covetous of despotism on Sullan lines. *experto crede*; he has been as open about it as he ever was about anything. 'And is that the man you want to be with?' you will ask. It is the obligation that moves me not the cause, as in Milo's case or—but enough.
4 'Is the cause not a good one then?' An excellent one, but remember that it will be abominably conducted. The plan is first to strangle Rome and Italy with hunger, then to carry fire and sword through the countryside and dip into the pockets of the rich. But since I fear the same from *this* quarter, if I did not have an obligation to repay in the other, I should think it better to take whatever may come at home. But I feel so

sed ita meruisse illum de me puto ut ἀχαριστίας crimen subire non audeam, quamquam a te eius quoque rei iusta defensio est explicata.

5 De triumpho tibi adsentior, quem quidem totum facile et libenter abiecero. egregie probo fore ut, dum agamus, 'ὁ πλόος ὡραῖος' obrepat. 'si modo' inquis 'satis ille erit firmus.' est firmior etiam quam putabamus. de isto licet bene speres. promitto tibi, si valebit, tegulam illum in Italia nullam relicturum. 'tene igitur socio?' contra mehercule meum iudicium et contra omnium antiquorum auctoritatem; nec tam ut illa adiuvem quam[quam] ut haec ne videam cupio discedere. noli enim putare tolerabilis horum insanias nec unius modi fore. etsi quid te horum fugit, legibus, iudiciis, senatu sublato libidines, audacias, sumptus, egestates tot egentissimorum hominum nec privatas posse res nec rem publicam sustinere? abeamus igitur inde qualibet navigatione; etsi id quidem ut tibi videbitur, sed certe abeamus. sciemus enim ⟨iam⟩, id quod exspectas, quid Brundisi actum sit.

6 Bonis viris quod ais probari quae adhuc fecerimus scirique ab iis ⟨non sine causa nos⟩ non profectos valde gaudeo, si est nunc ullus gaudendi locus. de Lentulo investigabo diligentius. id mandavi Philotimo, homini forti ac nimium optimati.

7 Extremum est ut tibi argumentum ad scribendum fortasse iam desit; nec enim alia de re nunc ulla scribi potest et de hac quid iam amplius inveniri potest? sed quoniam et

---

5, 2 *post* dum *excidisse aliquid* (*anne* id?) *coni. Goodyear* 4 putaramus *Wesenberg* 8 ut illa *s*: utilia Ω quam ς: quamquam Ω 9 noli *P*: nolui Ω 15 iam *add. Wesenberg* 6, 2 non sine causa nos *addidi* (nos *Lambinus*) profectos *PFZ*^{b}λ: -tis Ω

much beholden to Pompey that I dare not lay myself open to a charge of ingratitude, though there too you have made out a fair defence.

5 About the Triumph I agree with you. I shall throw the whole thing aside, lightly and willingly. I particularly like your remark that during the negotiations 'the seasonable sailing' may steal upon us. 'Provided only that Pompey is strong enough', you say. He is even stronger than we thought. On that point you can make your mind easy. I give you my word that if his health holds he won't leave one stone standing on another in Italy. And shall I be with him, you may ask. Yes, but against my own judgement and all ancient authority, nor is it so much to help there as to spare myself the sight of things here that I am anxious to leave. For take my word for it that the excesses of the men on the spot will be various and intolerable. But you must be well aware of all this—that after the subversion of laws, law-courts, and Senate neither private wealth nor common can satisfy the lusts, impudence, extravagance, and necessities of such a multitude of starvelings. So let's away from it all, by any sea that offers—though that shall be as you think best; but at all events let's away. We shall soon know what has happened at Brundisium, which is what you are waiting for.

6 You say that the honest men approve of my conduct thus far and know that I had good reason for not leaving. I am very glad to hear that, if one can be glad at anything nowadays. I shall make more thorough enquiries about Lentulus. I have entrusted that commission to Philotimus, a man of mettle and an ultra-optimate.

7 To end, it may be that you no longer have a theme for a letter, for one can't write about anything else at the present time and what more can one find to say about this? But since

ingenium suppeditat (dico mehercule ut sentio) et amor, quo et meum ingenium incitatur, perge, ut facis, et scribe quantum potest.

In Epirum quod me non invitas, comitem non molestum, subirascor. sed vale. nam ut tibi ambulandum, ungendum, sic mihi dormiendum. etenim litterae tuae mihi somnum attulerunt.

174A (IX. 7A)

Scr. Romae vi vel v Id. Mart. an. 49

BALBVS ET OPPIVS S. D. M. CICERONI

1 Nedum hominum humilium, ut nos sumus, sed etiam amplissimorum virorum consilia ex eventu, non ex voluntate a plerisque probari solent. tamen freti tua humanitate quod verissimum nobis videbitur de eo quod ad nos scripsisti tibi consilium dabimus. quod si non fuerit prudens, at certe ab optima fide et optimo animo proficiscetur.

Nos si id quod nostro iudicio Caesarem facere oportere existimamus, ut, simul Romam venerit, agat de reconciliatione gratiae suae et Pompei, id eum facturum ex ipso cognovissemus, ⟨non desineremus⟩ te hortari ut velles iis rebus interesse, quo facilius et maiore cum dignitate per te, qui utrique es coniunctus, res tota confieret; aut si ex contrario putaremus Caesarem id non facturum et etiam velle cum Pompeio bellum gerere sciremus, numquam tibi suaderemus contra hominem optime de te meritum arma ferres, sicuti te semper

---

7, 6 potest Z^1: -es Ω

post ep. 174 *sequitur in codd. ep.* 175 (*uno tenore in* Δ, *nova ep. in* Σ), *deinde* 174C, 174B, 174A: *transp. Schütz*

Ep. 174A] **1,** 7 nos si *Tunstall*: nos id *O*: nisi *E*δ: nos *PM*: vos *R* 10 non desineremus *hic addidi, post* hortari *add. Madvig* (desineremus *iam* ς): non desissemus *Tyrrell–Purser* 13 etiam *E*: etiam alias eum *O*(?)*R*: etiam eum *P*: eum δ: te *M*

you have both wit (I say as I think, you can be sure) and affection, which stimulates even *my* wits, carry on and write as much as you can.

I feel a little aggrieved that you don't invite me to Epirus, not being the most difficult of company. But good-bye. You to your exercise and massage, I to bed. And indeed your letter has brought sleep to my eyes.

174A (IX. 7A)

Rome, 10 or 11 March 49

BALBUS AND OPPIUS TO M. CICERO

1 Advice, even the advice of great men, let alone of humble folk like us, is generally judged by the event, not by the intention. None the less we shall rely on your charitable heart and give you the advice which seems to us the soundest on the matter about which you have written to us. It may or may not be wise, but at any rate it is offered in all sincerity and good will.

If we had learned from Caesar himself that he would do what in our judgement we think he ought to do, namely start negotiations for a reconciliation between himself and Pompey as soon as he gets to Rome, we should not cease to urge you to consent to take part in them, so that through you, who have ties with both, the whole matter might be settled with greater facility and dignity. Alternatively, if we thought on the contrary that Caesar would *not* do this and even knew that he wanted war with Pompey, we should never persuade you to bear arms against your benefactor, just as we have always

2 oravimus ne contra Caesarem pugnares. sed cum etiam nunc quid facturus Caesar sit magis ⟨sit⟩ opinari quam scire, non possumus nisi hoc, non videri eam tuam esse dignitatem neque fidem omnibus cognitam ut contra alterutrum, cum utrique sis maxime necessarius, arma feras, et hoc non dubitamus quin Caesar pro sua humanitate maxime sit probaturus. nos tamen, si tibi videbitur, ad Caesarem scribemus ut nos certiores faciat quid ⟨in⟩ hac re acturus sit. a quo si erit nobis rescriptum, statim quid sentiamus ad te scribemus et tibi fidem faciemus nos ea suadere quae nobis videntur tuae dignitati, non Caesaris actioni esse utilissima; et hoc Caesarem pro sua indulgentia in suos probaturum putamus.

174B (IX. 7B)

Scr. Romae vi vel v Id. Mart. an. 49

BALBVS CICERONI IMP. SAL.

1 S. v. b. Postea quam litteras communis cum Oppio ad te dedi, ab Caesare epistulam accepi cuius exemplum tibi misi; ex quibus perspicere poteris quam cupiat concordiam ⟨suam⟩ et Pompei reconciliare et quam remotus sit ab omni crudelitate; quod eum sentire, ut debeo, valde gaudeo. de te et tua fide et pietate idem mehercule, mi Cicero, sentio quod tu, non posse tuam famam et officium sustinere ut contra eum arma feras a quo tantum beneficium te accepisse

---

2, 2 sit caesar magis *R*: C- m- sit *Hellmuth* sit *post* magis *addidi* scire possimus ς: scire possimus, scribere *Wesenberg* 8 in hac re *P*: hac re Ω: hac de re *s* (*post* nos): de hac re *Baiter* 9 quid *Wesenberg*: quod *P*λ: quo *R*: quae δ: cum *M* sentiemus δ 11 actioni Ω*C*: rat- *P*

Ep. 174B] **1**, 1 S.V.B. *Mueller*: S.V.B.E. *Rivius* 3 quibus Ω: qua *nescio quis* suam *add. Wesenberg* 4 pompei *RM*: -ium *EOP*δ

2 besought you not to fight against Caesar. Since however Caesar's intentions are still a matter of conjecture rather than knowledge, all we can say is that it does not seem to us to suit your dignity and good faith, which all recognize, that you should bear arms against either, since you are a close friend of both; and we do not doubt that Caesar, with his sense of what is due to others, will thoroughly approve this view. However, if you think fit, we will write to Caesar asking him to let us know what he intends to do in this matter. When he replies, we shall immediately write to tell you our sentiments and we shall satisfy you that the course we recommend is what seems to us most serviceable to your dignity and not to Caesar's policy; and we think that Caesar, with the indulgence he always shows his friends, will approve.

174B (IX. 7B)

Rome, 10 or 11 March 49

BALBUS TO CICERO IMPERATOR

1 Greetings. After dispatching Oppius' and my joint letter I received a letter from Caesar of which I send you a copy. From it you will see how anxious he is to restore good relations with Pompey, and how far removed from any sort of cruelty. I am of course very pleased that these are his views. As regards yourself and your sentiments of loyalty and gratitude, I feel exactly as you do, my dear Cicero, that your reputation and duty do not allow of your bearing arms against one from whom you give out that you have received so

2 praedices. Caesarem hoc idem probaturum exploratum pro singulari eius humanitate habeo, eique cumulatissime satis facturum te certo scio cum nullam partem belli contra eum suscipias neque socius eius adversariis fueris. atque hoc non solum in te, tali et tanto viro, satis habebit, sed etiam mihi ipse sua concessit voluntate ne in iis castris essem quae contra Lentulum aut Pompeium futura essent, quorum beneficia maxima haberem, sibique satis esse dixit si togatus urbana officia sibi praestitissem quae etiam illis, si vellem, praestare possem. itaque nunc Romae omnia negotia Lentuli procuro, sustineo, meumque officium, fidem, pietatem ⟨in⟩ iis praesto. sed mehercule rursus iam abiectam compositionis spem non desperatissimam esse puto, quoniam Caesar est ea mente qua optare debemus.

Hac re mihi placet, si tibi videtur, te ad eum scribere et ab eo praesidium petere, ut petisti a Pompeio me quidem adprobante temporibus Milonianis. praestabo, si Caesarem bene novi, eum prius tuae dignitatis quam suae utilitatis rationem habiturum.

3 Haec quam prudenter tibi scribam nescio, sed illud certe scio, me ab singulari amore ac benevolentia quaecumque scribo tibi scribere, quod te (ita incolumi Caesare moriar!) tanti facio ut paucos aeque ac te caros habeam. de hac re cum aliquid constitueris, velim mihi scribas. nam non mediocriter laboro ⟨ut⟩ utrique, ut vis, tuam benevolentiam praestare possis quam mehercule te praestaturum confido. fac valeas.

2, 3 certo *s*: -te Ωλ   11 in *addidi*   12 iam *Corradus*: tam Ω   14 qua *O*(?)*RM*: quam *EP*δ   **3**, 2 ac *om.* Δ   6 ut *add. Manutius*   7 fac *EMm*: fac ut *O*(?)*Rbds*

2 great a service. That Caesar, the most considerate of men, will take the same view I am well assured, and I know for certain that he will be more than satisfied if you take no part in war against him and refrain from joining his adversaries. And not only will this satisfy him in the case of so distinguished a personage as yourself, but to me also he signified entirely of his own good will that I need not serve in any army which would be used against Lentulus or Pompey, to whom I am under the greatest obligations, and he told me that he would be content if I rendered him as a civilian in Rome the same good offices as I might, if I chose, render them. Accordingly I am now looking after all Lentulus' affairs in Rome and taking them upon myself, rendering therein my duty, loyalty, and gratitude. But really I begin once more to think that the hope of a composition, which I had given up, is not altogether forlorn, seeing that Caesar's sentiments are such as we must wish.

Therefore I am in favour, if you agree, of your writing to him and requesting him to provide you with a bodyguard, as you requested Pompey to do, very rightly as I thought, in the Milo period. I will guarantee, if I know Caesar, that he will think more of your position than of his own interests.

3 How wisely I have written I do not know, but this at least I do know, that whatever I write to you is written out of particular affection and good will, for, as I hope to die before Caesar, my regard for you is such that I hold few so dear. When you have come to any decision on this matter, perhaps you will write to me. I am in no little anxiety that you should be able to lend your good will to both parties as you wish to do and as indeed I do not doubt that you will do. Best wishes.

174C (IX. 7C)

Scr. in itinere c. iii Non. Mart. an. 49

CAESAR OPPIO CORNELIO SAL.

1 Gaudeo mehercule vos significare litteris quam valde probetis ea quae apud Corfinium sunt gesta. consilio vestro utar libenter et hoc libentius quod mea sponte facere constitueram ut quam lenissimum me praeberem et Pompeium darem operam ut reconciliarem. temptemus hoc modo si possimus omnium voluntates recuperare et diuturna victoria uti, quoniam reliqui crudelitate odium effugere non potuerunt neque victoriam diutius tenere praeter unum L. Sullam, quem imitaturus non sum. haec nova sit ratio vincendi ut misericordia et liberalitate nos muniamus. id quem ad modum fieri possit non nulla mihi in mentem veniunt et multa reperiri possunt. de his rebus rogo vos ut cogitationem suscipiatis.

2 N. Magium, Pompei praefectum, deprehendi. scilicet meo instituto usus sum et eum statim missum feci. iam duo praefecti fabrum Pompei in meam potestatem venerunt et a me missi sunt. si volent grati esse, debebunt Pompeium hortari ut malit mihi esse amicus quam iis qui et illi et mihi semper fuerunt inimicissimi, quorum artificiis effectum est ut res publica in hunc statum perveniret.

175 (IX. 8)

Scr. in Formiano prid. Id. Mart. an. 49

CICERO ATTICO SAL.

1 Cenantibus II⟨I⟩ Id. nobis ac noctu quidem Statius a te epistulam brevem attulit. de L. Torquato quod quaeris,

Ep. 174C] **1,** 5 possimus *Petrarcha*: -sumus Ω **2,** 1 N. *ERM*: CN. (Cn., GN., Gneum) *OP*δ scilicet et Δ 3 fabrum Δ: partium *OR*

Ep. 175] **1,** 1 III *scripsi*: II Σ*msZ*¹: .H. (*vel* .II.) d *M*: H II *bd* 2 quod Σ*C*: quod modo Δ

174C (IX. 7C)

On the march, c. 5 March 49

CAESAR TO OPPIUS AND CORNELIUS

1 I am indeed glad that you express in your letter such hearty approval of the proceedings at Corfinium. I shall willingly follow your advice, all the more willingly because I had of my own accord decided to show all possible clemency and to do my best to reconcile Pompey. Let us try whether by this means we can win back the good will of all and enjoy a lasting victory, seeing that others have not managed by cruelty to escape hatred or to make their victories endure, except only L. Sulla, whom I do not propose to imitate. Let this be the new style of conquest, to make mercy and generosity our shield. As to how that is to be done, certain possibilities occur to me and many more can be found. I request you to apply your thoughts to these matters.

2 I captured N. Magius, Pompey's Prefect. Naturally I followed my set practice and immediately discharged him. Two Prefects of Engineers of Pompey's have now fallen into my hands and been released by me. If they wish to show themselves grateful they should urge Pompey to prefer my friendship to that of those who have always been his and my bitter enemies, by whose machinations the country has been brought to its present pass.

175 (IX. 8)

Formiae, 14 March 49

CICERO TO ATTICUS

1 We were at dinner on the 13th and night had fallen, when Statius brought a short letter from you. You ask about L. Torquatus. Not only Lucius but Aulus too has left, the former

non modo Lucius sed etiam Aulus profectus est, alter multos ⟨ante dies, alter paucos⟩. de Reatinorum corona quod scribis, moleste fero in agro Sabino sementem fieri proscriptionis. senatores multos esse Romae nos quoque audieramus. ecquid potes dicere cur exierint?

2 In his locis opinio est coniectura magis quam nuntio aut litteris Caesarem Formiis a. d. XI Kal. Apr. fore. hic ego vellem habere Homeri illam Minervam simulatam Mentori cui dicerem 'Μέντορ, πῶς τ' ἄρ' ἴω, πῶς τ' ἂρ προσπτύξομαι αὐτόν;' nullam rem umquam difficiliorem cogitavi; sed cogito tamen, nec ero, ut in malis, imparatus. sed cura ut valeas. puto enim diem tuum heri fuisse.

176 (IX. 9)

Scr. in Formiano xvi Kal. Apr. an. 49 (§ *4*)

CICERO ATTICO SAL.

1 Tris epistulas tuas accepi postridie Id. erant autem IIII, III, prid. Id. datae. igitur antiquissimae cuique primum respondebo. adsentior tibi ut in Formiano potissimum commorer, etiam de supero mari, ⟨tem⟩ptaboque, ut antea ad te scripsi, ecquonam modo possim voluntate eius nullam rei publicae partem attingere. quod laudas quia oblivisci me scripsi ante facta et delicta nostri amici, ego vero ita facio; quin ea ipsa quae a te commemorantur secus ab eo in me ipsum facta esse non memini. tanto plus apud me valet benefici gratia

---

3 sed *om. C* 4 ante . . . paucos *addidi duce Castiglioni*

Ep. 176] I, 1 IIII ς: illi (ille, illic) Ω 3 adsentior *R*: -tio *EO*Δ commorer *P*: -rem Ω: -remur *bds* 4 temptaboque *Nipperdey*: plaboque OΔ: płabo que *R*: postulaboque *P*: laboque λ 5 possim *Corradus*: -sem Ω voluntate ς: -ati Ω 8 a te *Hervagius*: ante Ω 9 valet (-ent *R*) Σλ: -ete *M*: -ere δ gratia . . . dolor Σλ: -tiam . . . -rem Δ (-rem volo δ)

a long while ago, the latter within the last few days. As for what you write about the military auction at Reate, I am sorry that the seeds of proscription should be sown on Sabine land. We too have heard that there are many Senators in Rome. Can you tell me why they ever left?

2 It is thought hereabouts, rather by conjecture than from any report or letter, that Caesar will arrive at Formiae on 22 March. I wish I had Homer's Minerva here disguised as Mentor so that I could say to her 'Mentor, how shall I go, how greet him? Say.' I have never pondered a more difficult matter, but ponder it I do, and as far as a bad case allows I shall not be unprepared. But take care of yourself—I think yesterday was your bad day.

176 (IX. 9)

Formiae, 17 March 49

CICERO TO ATTICUS

1 I received three letters from you on the 16th, dispatched on the 12th, 13th, and 14th. So I shall answer them in chronological order. I agree with you that I should stay at Formiae for preference, also about the Adriatic, and as I wrote to you earlier I shall see whether by any means I can avoid taking part in public affairs with Caesar's good will. You praise me for writing that I forget the past actions and errors of our friend. Yes, I do forget them. Even those grievances of my own against him of which you remind me I do not remember. So far does gratitude for a service outweigh with me resentment of an injury. Let me then do as you recommend and

quam iniuriae dolor. faciamus igitur ut censes, colligamusque nos. σοφιστεύω enim simul ut rus decurro atque in decursu θέσεις meas commentari non desino; sed sunt quaedam earum perdifficiles ad iudicandum. de optimatibus, sit sane ita ut vis; sed nosti illud 'Διονύσιος ἐν Κορίνθῳ.' Titini filius apud Caesarem est. quod autem quasi vereri videris ne mihi tua consilia displiceant, me vero nihil delectat aliud nisi consilium et litterae tuae. qua re fac ut ostendis; ne destiteris ad me quicquid tibi in mentem venerit scribere. nihil mihi potest esse gratius.

2 Venio ad alteram nunc epistulam. recte non credis de numero militum; ipso dimidio plus scripsit Clodia. falsum etiam de corruptis navibus. quod consules laudas, ego quoque animum laudo, sed consilium reprehendo; discessu enim illorum actio de pace sublata est, quam quidem ego meditabar. itaque postea Demetri librum de concordia tibi remisi et Philotimo dedi. nec vero dubito quin exitiosum bellum impendeat, cuius initium ducetur a fame. et me tamen doleo non interesse huic bello! in quo tanta vis sceleris futura est ut, cum parentis non alere nefarium sit, nostri principes antiquissimam et sanctissimam parentem, patriam, fame necandam putent. atque hoc non opinione timeo sed interfui sermonibus. omnis haec classis Alexandria, Colchis, Tyro, Sidone, Arado, Cypro, Pamphylia, Lycia, Rhodo, Chio, Byzantio, Lesbo, Smyrna, Mileto, Coo ad intercludendos commeatus Italiae et ad occupandas frumentarias provincias comparatur. at quam veniet iratus! et iis quidem maxime qui eum maxime salvum volebant, quasi relictus ab iis quos

---

11 σοφιστεύω . . . rus *ita Bosius*: festivo enim simili urus Ω*Z* in decursu Z^1: cursu Ω 18 ni(c)hil mihi Σ: m- n- Δ **2**, 3 consulem *M*(?)*C* 4 discessu *s*: dispersu Ωλ 8 ducetur *EP*: -eretur *OR*Δ 17 at *Victorius*: ad Ω veniet *ER*: venit et *O*: venit Δ

collect my thoughts. For as soon as I run out into the country I play the sophist, and on the road I meditate my 'themes' all the time. But some of them are very hard to judge. About the optimates, let it be as you wish; but you know the saying 'Dionysius in Corinth'. Titinius' son is with Caesar. You almost seem afraid that your advice is disagreeable to me; why, your advice and letters are my only pleasure. So do as you promise; don't cease to write to me whatever comes into your mind. You can do me no greater kindness.

2 To come now to the second letter. You are right to be incredulous about the number of soldiers. Clodia multiplied by two. The report of the spoiled ships was also untrue. You praise the Consuls. I too praise their spirit, but I blame their action. Their departure has ruled out a peace initiative, of which I was thinking; so after the news I returned you Demetrius' book on Concord and gave it to Philotimus. Nor have I any doubt that a destructive war is ahead, to be introduced by famine. And yet I grieve that I am not participating in such a war! The criminality of it! To refuse to maintain one's parents is wicked, but our leaders think it right and proper to starve that older, more venerable parent, their country, to death. And this is no conjectural fear of mine; I was present when it was discussed. All this fleet from Alexandria, Colchis, Tyre, Sidon, Aradus, Cyprus, Pamphylia, Lycia, Rhodes, Chios, Byzantium, Lesbos, Smyrna, Miletus, Cos, is being collected with the object of cutting Italy's lifelines and occupying the grain-exporting provinces. How angry he will be when he comes!—most of all with those who wished him best, as though he had been deserted by

reliquit. itaque mihi dubitanti quid me facere par sit, permagnum pondus adfert benevolentia erga illum; qua dempta perire melius esset in patria quam patriam servando evertere. de septemtrione plane ita est; metuo ne vexetur Epirus. sed quem tu locum Graeciae non direptum iri putas? praedicat enim palam et militibus ostendit se largitione ipsa superiorem quam hunc fore. illud me praeclare admones, cum illum videro, ne nimis indulgenter et ut cum gravitate potius loquar. plane sic faciendum. Arpinum, cum eum convenero, cogito, ne forte aut absim cum veniet aut cursem huc illuc via deterrima. Bibulum, ut scribis, audio venisse et redisse prid. Id.

3 Philotimum, ut ais epistula tertia, exspectabas. at ille Idibus a me profectus est; eo serius ad tuam illam epistulam, cui ego statim rescripseram, redditae sunt meae litterae. de Domitio, ut scribis, ita opinor esse, ut et in Cosano sit et consilium eius ignoretur. iste omnium turpissimus ac sordidissimus qui consularia comitia a praetore ait haberi posse est idem qui semper in re publica fuit. itaque nimirum hoc illud est quod Caesar scribit in ea epistula cuius exemplum ad te misi, [et] se velle uti 'consilio' meo (age, esto; hoc commune est), 'gratia' (ineptum id quidem sed, puto, hoc simulat ad quasdam senatorum sententias), 'dignitate' (fortasse sententia consulari); illud extremum est, 'ope omnium rerum'. id ego suspicari coepi tum ex tuis litteris aut hoc ipsum esse aut non multo secus. nam permagni eius interest rem ad interregnum non venire; id adsequitur si per praetorem consules creantur. nos autem in libris habemus non modo consules a praetore sed ne

---

29 teterrima λ 3, 1 ut ais δ: ut aliis *M*: ut *OR*: in *P*: ut ais in *c* 2 ad Δ: tibi ad *OR* cui (quoi) δ: qui *M*: quoniam *OR* 5 ac Σ: et Δ 6 idem *OR*δ: ille *M*: ille idem *Orelli* 9 se ς: et se Ω 10 hoc Δ: id Σ 11 consulari *Corradus*: -is Ω 12 illud *Pms*: -um Ω 13 cepi tum *ms*: c(a)eptum Ω

those he abandoned. So as I consider where my duty lies, it is my good will towards him personally that weighs so heavily; that apart, it would be better to die in my country rather than by saving to destroy her. Yes, you are quite right about the North Wind; I am afraid Epirus may be in for a bad time. But what part of Greece do you think will *not* be plundered? He gives out openly and promises his men that even in largesse he will go one better than Caesar. Your admonition not to be too easy-going in what I say to the latter when I see him, to maintain my dignity rather, is excellent. Yes, that is the line to take. I mean to go to Arpinum after I have met him, so that I shall not happen to be away when he arrives or be rushing to and fro on a vile road. I hear that, as you say, Bibulus came and left again on the 14th.

3 In your third letter you say you are expecting Philotimus. But he left me on the Ides. That is why my reply to that other letter of yours, which I answered straight away, will have reached you a little late. As regards Domitius I think it is as you say—he is at Cosa and his plans are unknown. That squalid wretch who says that consular elections can be held by a Praetor is what he has always been throughout his political career. So *that* will be what Caesar means when he writes in the letter of which I have sent you a copy that he wants to avail himself of my 'advice' (well, let that pass as a commonplace), 'influence' (silly enough, but I suppose he affects here to be thinking of certain senatorial votes), 'standing' (my right to speak as an ex-Consul perhaps), and then at the end comes 'help in all matters'. I began to suspect from your letter at the time that it was either that or something not very different, for it's very important to him not to have an interregnum. This he achieves if Consuls are elected under a Praetor. But we have it in our books that it is illegal not only for Consuls

praetores quidem creari ius esse idque factum esse numquam; consules eo non esse ius quod maius imperium a minore rogari non sit ius, praetores autem cum ita rogentur ut collegae consulibus sint, quorum est maius imperium. aberit non longe quin hoc a me decerni velit neque sit contentus Galba,
4 Scaevola, Cassio, Antonio. 'τότε μοι χάνοι εὐρεῖα χθών'; sed quanta tempestas impendeat vides.

Qui transierint senatores scribam ad te cum certum habebo. de re frumentaria recte intellegis, quae nullo modo administrari sine vectigalibus potest; nec sine causa et eos qui circum illum sunt omnia postulantis et bellum nefarium times. Trebatium nostrum, etsi, ut scribis, nihil bene sperat, tamen videre sane velim. quem fac horteris ut properet; opportune enim ad me ante adventum Caesaris venerit.

De Lanuvino, statim ut audivi Phameam mortuum, optavi, si modo esset futura res publica, ut id aliquis emeret meorum, neque tamen de te, qui maxime meus, cogitavi. sciebam enim te quoto anno et quantum in solo solere quaerere, neque solum Romae sed etiam Deli tuum digamma videram. verum tamen ego illud, quamquam est bellum, minoris aestimo quam aestimabatur Marcellino consule, cum ego istos hortulos propter domum Anti quam tum habebam iucundiores mihi fore putabam et minore impensa quam si Tusculanum refecissem. volui HS Q. egi per †predum†, ille daret tanti, cum haberet venale. noluit. sed nunc omnia ista iacere puto propter

17 numquam *Manutius*: nusq- Ω **4**, 1 sed ... vides *ad sequentia pertinere putant vulg.* 11 aliquis emeret *OR*: aliquid Δ 12 meus es *Lambinus* sciebam enim te Z^l: scribam enim (eum Δ) de Ω 14 Deli tuum *C*: del(l)ituum *OR*: delitium (dil- *bd*) *Mbd*: delitum (-i tum) *ms* digamma Ω*C*: διάγραμμα *Corradus* 17 Anti(i) quam *Victorius*: antiquam Ω 19 egi ... venale *ita distinxit Mueller* pr(a)edem ς: *fort.* Precium daret tanti cum *Lehmann, duce Marshall*: daret antiquum Ω 20 venale *s*: -are Ω

but even Praetors to be elected under a Praetor, and that such a thing is without precedent—illegal for Consuls because it is illegal for a higher authority to be proposed by a lower, and for Praetors because they are proposed as colleagues of the Consuls, who possess higher authority. It won't be long before he wants me to sanction this, he won't be content with Galba, Scaevola, Cassius, Antony. 'Then may the earth gape wide
4 for me.' But you see what a storm is brewing.

I shall send you the names of the Senators who have crossed the water when I get them for certain. You are right about the grain supply, it cannot possibly be managed without the revenues. And you have good cause to fear both the uninhibited demands of his entourage and a wicked war. I should be very glad to see our friend Trebatius, though, so you say, he is most pessimistic. Please ask him to make haste. It will be convenient if his visit takes place before Caesar's arrival.

About the property at Lanuvium, as soon as I heard of Phamea's death I hoped—assuming that an ordered society was to continue—that one of my friends would buy it; but of you, my greatest friend, I did not think, being aware that you generally want to know about price-yield ratio and immovables and having seen your mark (?) in Delos as well as in Rome. Anyhow, nice as it is, I don't think it's worth as much as it was reckoned to be in Marcellinus' Consulship, when I thought that this little estate near Rome would be pleasanter for me on account of the house I had at Antium in those days, and less expensive than rebuilding my place at Tusculum. I offered HS 500,000, proposing through Precius (?) that he should let me have it for that price when he was ready to sell. He refused. But I imagine all these things have

nummorum caritatem. mihi quidem erit aptissimum vel nobis potius si tu emeris. sed eiusdem Antias cave contemnas; valde est venustum. quamquam mihi ista omnia iam addicta vastitati videntur.

Respondi epistulis tribus, sed exspecto alias; nam me adhuc tuae litterae sustentarunt. d. Liberalibus.

177 (IX. 10)

Scr. in Formiano xv Kal. Apr. an. 49 (§ 1)

⟨CICERO ATTICO SAL.⟩

1 Nihil habebam quod scriberem; neque enim novi quicquam audieram et ad tuas omnis rescripseram pridie. sed cum me aegritudo non solum somno privaret verum ne vigilare quidem sine summo dolore pateretur, tecum ut quasi loquerer, in quo uno acquiesco, hoc nescio quid nullo argumento proposito scribere institui.

2 Amens mihi fuisse a principio videor et me una haec res torquet quod non omnibus in rebus labentem vel potius ruentem Pompeium tamquam unus manipularis secutus sim. vidi hominem XIIII Kal. Febr. plenum formidinis. illo ipso die sensi quid ageret. numquam mihi postea placuit nec umquam aliud in alio peccare destitit. nihil interim ad me scribere, nihil nisi fugam cogitare. quid quaeris? sicut ἐν τοῖς ἐρωτικοῖς alienat ⟨quod⟩ immunde, insulse, indecore fit, sic me illius fugae neglegentiaeque deformitas avertit ab amore.

---

22 eiusdem antias (-ci-) *OR*: eius dementias Δ 25 alias Σ*m*: tuas *M*: tuas alias *bds* 26 *haec ep. in voce* sustentarunt *desinit in Ems, cum sequenti in cett. cohaeret* D *Mm* (d *M*): O *E*: De *Rbds* (*de O non liquet*)

Ep. 177] **1**, 1 nihil] *novam ep. hic indicavit Brunus* (M^4) enim *om.* λ **2**, 1 a principio videor Σ: v- a p- Δ 6 in] ex *Ernesti* 7 scribere *Corradus* (scrire *ed. Saliceti et Regii* (1499)): scire Ω 8 alienat quod *scripsi*: alienantur (-atur *R*) Ω: -amur si quid *Madvig* insulse *Madvig* (-sae *Victorius*): insulis Ω indecore *Madvig* (-rae *Victorius*): unde decore Ω

dropped in value because of the money shortage. It will suit me best, or rather us, if *you* buy it. But don't despise the same person's place at Antium. It is really charming; though I look on everything of this sort as already scheduled for destruction.

I have answered three letters, but I expect more. It is your letters that have kept me going till now. Dispatched on Bacchus' Day.

177 (IX. 10)

Formiae, 18 March 49

CICERO TO ATTICUS

1 I have nothing to write about, having heard no news and having replied to all your letters yesterday. But since my distress of mind is such that it is not only impossible to sleep but torment to be awake, I have started this scrawl without any subject in view, just in order as it were to talk to you, which is my only relief.

2 I think I have been out of my senses from the start, and the one thing that tortures me is that I have not followed Pompey like any private soldier in his drift or rather plunge to disaster. I saw him on 17 January, thoroughly cowed. That very day I realized what he was at. Nothing he did after that was to my liking. He went on blundering now here now there. Meanwhile not a line to me, not a thought except for flight. In short, just as *en choses d'amour*, anything uncleanly, uncouthly, unsuitably done alienates, so the ugliness of his flight and discourtesy turned me from my affection. Nothing in his conduct seemed

nihil enim dignum faciebat quare eius fugae comitem me adiungerem. nunc emergit amor, nunc desiderium ferre non possum, nunc mihi nihil libri, nihil litterae, nihil doctrina prodest. ita dies et noctes tamquam avis illa mare prospecto, evolare cupio. do, do poenas temeritatis meae. etsi quae fuit illa temeritas? quid feci non consideratissime? si enim nihil praeter fugam quaereretur, fugissem libentissime, sed genus belli crudelissimi et maximi, quod nondum vident homines quale futurum sit, perhorrui. quae minae municipiis, quae nominatim viris bonis, quae denique omnibus qui remansissent! quam crebro illud 'Sulla potuit, ego non potero?'

3 Mihi autem haeserunt illa: male Tarquinius qui Porsennam, qui Octavium Mamilium contra patriam, impie Coriolanus ⟨qui⟩ auxilium petiit a Volscis, recte Themistocles qui mori maluit, nefarius Hippias, Pisistrati filius, qui in Marathonia pugna cecidit arma contra patriam ferens. at Sulla, at Marius, at Cinna recte. immo iure fortasse; sed quid eorum victoria crudelius, quid funestius? huius belli genus fugi, et eo magis quod crudeliora etiam cogitari et parari videbam. me, quem non nulli conservatorem istius urbis parentemque esse dixerunt, Getarum et Armeniorum et Colchorum copias ad eam adducere? me meis civibus famem, vastitatem inferre Italiae? hunc primum mortalem esse, deinde etiam multis modis posse exstingui cogitabam, urbem autem et populum nostrum servandum ad immortalitatem, quantum in nobis esset, putabam; et tamen spes quaedam me oblectabat fore

---

11 nunc *EPbds*: ni(c)hil *ORMm* 13 dies et noctes *E*δ: die noctes *OR*: dies n- *P*: die nocte est *M* 19 nominatim *Victorius*: nomina etiam Ω **3**, 2 concitavit contra *Lehmann* 3 qui *add.* ς: *om.* Ωλ 9 parentemque Σ: quem parentem Δ 12 hunc *P*: nunc Ω 13 cogitabam *M corr.*: -aram Ω 15 oblectabat *Moser*: obtent- *OR*Δλ: obtempt- *EP* (-bant *E*): sustent- *anon. ap. Corradum*

to deserve that I should join him as his companion in flight. But now my affection comes to the surface, the sense of loss is unbearable, books, writing, philosophy are all to no purpose. Like Plato's bird I gaze out over the sea day and night, longing to take wing. Indeed and indeed I am punished for my thoughtlessness. And yet, what thoughtlessness? Was not everything I did most carefully considered? If flight had been the only object, I should have been perfectly ready to fly; but I shuddered at the kind of war intended, savage and vast beyond what men yet see. What threats to the municipalities, to honest men individually named, to everyone who stayed behind! 'What Sulla could do, I can do'—that was the refrain.

3 For myself I could not forget certain precedents. Tarquinius did wrong to stir up Porsenna and Octavius Mamilius against his country, Coriolanus committed an impiety in seeking help from the Volsci, Themistocles was right in preferring to die, Hippias, son of Pisistratus, who fell at Marathon in arms against his country, was a villain. It may be said that Sulla or Marius or Cinna acted rightly. Legally, perhaps; but their victorious régimes were the cruellest and most sinister episodes in our history. That was the kind of war from which I shrank, especially as I saw that even worse cruelties were contemplated and prepared. Was I, whom some have called Rome's saviour and father, to lead troops of Getae and Armenians and Colchians against her? Was I to bring famine upon my fellow-countrymen, devastation upon Italy? I reflected that Caesar was mortal to begin with and further that he might be eliminated in various ways, whereas our city and people should, as I thought, be preserved to eternity, so far as in us lay. And

ut aliquid conveniret potius quam aut hic tantum sceleris aut ille tantum flagiti admitteret. alia res nunc tota est, alia mens mea. sol, ut est in tua quadam epistula, excidisse mihi e mundo videtur. ut aegroto, dum anima est, spes esse dicitur, sic ego, quoad Pompeius in Italia fuit, sperare non destiti. haec, haec me fefellerunt et, ut verum loquar, aetas iam a diuturnis laboribus devexa ad otium domesticarum me rerum delectatione mollivit. nunc si vel periculose experiundum erit, experiar certe ut hinc avolem. ante oportuit fortasse; sed ea quae scrips[ist]i me tardarunt et auctoritas maxime tua.

4 Nam cum ad hunc locum venissem, evolvi volumen epistularum tuarum quod ego ⟨sub⟩ signo habeo servoque diligentissime. erat igitur in ea quam x Kal. Febr. dederas hoc modo: 'sed videamus et Gnaeus quid agat et illius rationes quorsum fluant. quod si iste Italiam relinquet, faciet omnino male et, ut ego existimo, ἀλογίστως, sed tum demum consilia nostra commutanda erunt.' hoc scribis post diem quartum quam ab urbe discessimus. deinde VIII Kal. Febr.: 'tantum modo Gnaeus noster ne, ut urbem ἀλογίστως reliquit, sic Italiam relinquat.' eodem die das alteras litteras quibus mihi consulenti planissime respondes; est enim sic: 'sed venio ad consultationem tuam. si Gnaeus Italia cedit, in urbem redeundum puto; quae enim finis peregrinationis?' hoc mihi plane haesit, et nunc ita video, infinitum bellum iunctum
5 miserrima fuga, quam tu peregrinationem ὑποκορίζῃ. sequitur χρησμὸς VI ⟨Kal.⟩ Febr.: 'ego, si Pompeius manet in Italia nec res ad pactionem venit, longius bellum puto fore; sin

---

21 haec haec $EOZ^b\lambda$: haec $R\Delta$ 23 si vel *Corradus*: sive ΩZ^1 periculose ΣZ^1: -lo Δ 25 scripsi ς: -sisti Ω 4, 2 sub *add.* ς 5, 2 Kal. *add.* ς

yet after all I was beguiled by a kind of hope that some agreement would be reached to save the one from such crime and the other from such infamy. Now the whole picture is changed and my mind with it. I feel as though the sun, as you put it in one of your letters, has fallen out of the universe. There is said to be hope for a sick man while there is life, and so long as Pompey was in Italy I kept on hoping. These things, I say, misled me. And also let me admit that in my declining years I am inclined to rest after my long labours and softened by the comforts of domestic life. But now, even if the attempt is dangerous, I shall at any rate try to fly away. Perhaps I ought to have done so earlier; but the considerations aforesaid and above all your advice held me back.

4 Having arrived at this point I unrolled the roll of your letters, which I keep under seal and preserve most carefully. Well, the one you dispatched on 21 January contains this passage: 'But let us see what Gnaeus is doing and where Caesar's plans tend. If your man abandons Italy, he will act wrongly and in my judgement irrationally; but then will be the time to change our plans.' You write this three days after our departure from Rome. Then on 23 January: 'Just so long as our friend Gnaeus does not abandon Italy in the same irrational way as he abandoned Rome.' On the same day you send another letter in which you make a categorical reply to my request for advice. It reads thus: 'But to come to your problem: if Gnaeus withdraws from Italy I think you should return to Rome. Otherwise where will your travels end?' That sank deep into my mind; and now I see it is so, war without limit combined with a
5 miserable exile which you euphemistically term 'travel'. Then follows an oracle, on 25 January: 'If Pompey remains in Italy and there is no composition, I think the war will last a

Italiam relinquit, ad posterum bellum ἄσπονδον strui existimo.' huius igitur belli ego particeps et socius et adiutor esse cogor quod et ἄσπονδον est ⟨et⟩ cum civibus! deinde VII Id. Febr., cum iam plura audires de Pompei consilio, concludis epistulam quandam hoc modo: 'ego quidem tibi non sim auctor, si Pompeius Italiam relinquit, te quoque profugere. summo enim periculo facies nec rei publicae proderis; cui quidem posterius poteris prodesse, si manseris.' quem φιλόπατριν ac πολιτικὸν hominis prudentis et amici tali admonitu

6 non moveret auctoritas? deinde III Id. Febr. iterum mihi respondes consulenti sic: 'quod quaeris a me fugamne foedam an moram nefandam utiliorem putem, ego vero in praesentia subitum discessum et praecipitem profectionem cum tibi tum ipsi Gnaeo inutilem et periculosam puto et satius esse existimo vos dispertitos et in speculis esse; sed me dius fidius turpe nobis puto esse de fuga cogitare.' hoc turpe Gnaeus noster biennio ante cogitavit; ita sullaturit animus eius et proscripturit iam diu. inde, ut opinor, cum tu ad me quaedam γενικώτερον scripsisses et ego mihi a te quaedam significari putassem ut Italia cederem, detestaris hoc diligenter XI Kal. Mart.: 'ego vero nulla epistula significavi, si Gnaeus Italia cederet, ut tu una cederes, aut si significavi, non dico fui inconstans sed demens.' in eadem epistula alio loco: 'nihil relinquitur nisi fuga, cui te socium neutiquam puto esse

7 oportere nec umquam putavi.' totam autem hanc deliberationem evolvis accuratius in litteris VIII Kal. Mart. datis: 'si

---

6 est et *Lambinus*: est Ω: et *Victorius* 10 facies ς: facis Ω cui (quoi) λ: quod Ω **6,** 1 deinde *EP*δ: deindceps *M*: deinceps *OR* 2 foedam *Lambinus*: fedam *M, ut vid.*: fidam (-em *b*) Σδλ 3 nefandam *Lambinus*: defendam Ωλ 6 dispertitos et ς: -tim eos et Ωλ (-ti meos) 8 sullaturit *Quintilianus* (*vide comm.*): -uri Ω 10 γενικώτερον *Victorius*: PEN- *ERM*: ἄρρεν- *O*δ quaedam *del. Schütz*: quodammodo *Orelli* 13 si *ERms*: *om. OMbd* 15 neutiquam ς: -que Ω **7,** 2 si M'. *Graevius*: si M. Δ: sin Σ

pretty long time; but if he leaves Italy, then I judge a war *à outrance* later on is in the making.' So I must needs be joint partaker and abettor in this war *à outrance* with my fellow-countrymen! Then on 7 February, when you were hearing more of Pompey's intention, you conclude a letter thus: 'I for my part would not advise you, in the event of Pompey leaving Italy, to flee too. You will be taking a very grave risk and doing no service to the state, whereas you may be able to serve it later on if you stay.' What patriotic public man would not be moved by the weight of such an admonition
6 from a wise friend? Then on 11 February you once more reply to my consultation as follows: 'You ask me which I think the more expedient, the ignominy of flight or the guilt of remaining. I think that for the present a sudden and precipitate departure would be inexpedient both for you and for Gnaeus himself and dangerous, and I consider it better that you people should stay apart on your watch-towers. But upon my soul I think it dishonourable for us to contemplate flight.' This dishonour our Gnaeus contemplated two years ago. He has been hankering after Sulla and proscriptions all that while. Then, I think it was after you had written to me in rather general terms and I had thought you were suggesting something to the effect that I should leave Italy, you were at pains to repudiate this on 19 February: 'No, I never in any letter suggested that if Gnaeus left Italy you should leave with him, or if I did I was—I won't say inconsistent, but out of my mind.' Elsewhere in the same letter: 'Nothing remains except flight, in which I by no means think and never have thought that
7 you should take part.' You develop this whole question in greater detail in a letter dispatched on 22 February: 'If M'.

M'. Lepidus et L. Vulcatius remanent, ⟨manen⟩dum puto, ita
ut, si salvus sit Pompeius et constiterit alicubi, hanc νέκυιαν
relinquas et te in certamine vinci cum illo facilius patiaris
quam cum hoc in ea quae perspicitur futura colluvie regnare.'
multa disputas huic sententiae convenientia. inde ad ex-
tremum: '"quid si" inquis "Lepidus et Vulcatius disce-
dunt?" plane ἀπορῶ. quod evenerit igitur et quod egeris id
στερκτέον putabo.' si tum dubitares, nunc certe non dubitas
8 istis manentibus. deinde in ipsa fuga v Kal. Mart.: 'interea
non dubito quin in Formiano mansurus sis. commodissime
enim τὸ μέλλον ibi καραδοκήσεις.' at Kal. Mart., cum ille
quintum iam diem Brundisi esset: 'tum poterimus delibe-
rare, non scilicet integra re sed certe minus infracta quam si
una proieceris te.' deinde IIII Non. Mart., ὑπὸ τὴ⟨ν διά⟩λειψιν
cum breviter scriberes, tamen ponis hoc: 'cras scribam plura
et ad omnia; hoc tamen dicam, non paenitere me consili de
tua mansione, et, quamquam magna sollicitudine, tamen quia
minus mali puto esse quam in illa profectione, maneo in
9 sententia et gaudeo te mansisse.' cum vero iam angerer et
timerem ne quid a me dedecoris esset admissum, III Non.
Mart.: 'te tamen non esse una cum Pompeio non fero
moleste. postea, si opus fuerit, non erit difficile, et illi, quo-
quo tempore fiet, erit ἀσμενιστόν. sed hoc ita dico, si hic qua
ratione initium fecit eadem cetera aget, sincere, temperate,
prudenter, valde videro et consideratius utilitati nostrae

---

3 remanent manendum *P*: -ent dum Ω 4 νεκυίαν (*sic*) *C* HEKYEIHA *et sim.* Ω (*talia ad epp.* 178.2, 187.2 *praeterii*) 8 quid si *MC*: si Σδ inquis *Ciceroni tribuunt vulg.* 10 dubitaras *Bosius*: -abas *Ernesti* 8, 3 at *Sjögren*: ad Ω: atque *Wesenberg* 5 integra *R*δ: in int- *EOM* 6 ὑπὸ τὴν διάλειψιν *Gurlitt* (ὑπὸ τὴν λῆψιν *Victorius*): ΥΠΟΤΠΑΠΨΙΝ Ω: ὑπογραφὴν *C* 9, 3 te tamen Σ*M*(?): tamen te δ una *om.* λ

Lepidus and L. Vulcatius stay behind, I think you should stay, with the proviso that, if nothing happens to Pompey and he establishes himself somewhere, you should leave this underworld and think defeat at his side a lesser evil than rule with Caesar in the sink of iniquity we can see ahead of us here.' You argue at length in accordance with this view. Then at the end: 'You may ask "What if Lepidus and Vulcatius leave?" I really don't know what to say. So whatever the event and you decide, I shall not quarrel.' If you would have been in doubt then, assuredly you are not now, since they are still in Italy.

8 Next, when the flight had already started, on 25 February: 'Meanwhile you will no doubt remain at Formiae. That is the most convenient place for you to wait upon events.' And on the Kalends of March, when Pompey had been at Brundisium for four days: 'Then we shall be able to take stock, not indeed with free hands but at any rate less hopelessly compromised than if you take the plunge with Pompey.' Then on 4 March, though the letter was a short one written just after your intermission, you write as follows: 'Tomorrow I shall write more at length and deal with all your points; but I will say this much, that I do not regret my advice about your remaining, and although very far from easy, still, thinking this as I do a lesser evil than departure with Pompey, I stand by my

9 opinion and am glad that you have stayed.' But when I was in agony of mind from anxiety lest I might have blemished my reputation, on 5 March: 'After all I am not sorry that you are not with Pompey. Later, if desirable, it won't be difficult, and come when it may it will be acceptable to him. But I say this with the reservation that if Caesar continues as he has begun, with sincerity, moderation, and prudence, I shall think

10 consuluero.' VII Id. Mart. scribis Peducaeo quoque nostro probari quod quierim, cuius auctoritas multum apud me valet.

His ego tuis scriptis me consolor ut nihil a me adhuc delictum putem. tu modo auctoritatem tuam defendito; adversus me nihil opus est, sed consciis egeo aliis. ego, si nihil peccavi, reliqua tuebor. ad ea tute hortare et me omnino tua cogitatione adiuva. hic nihildum de reditu Caesaris audiebatur. ego his litteris hoc tamen profeci; perlegi omnis tuas et in eo acquievi.

178 (IX. 11)

Scr. in Formiano xiii Kal. Apr. an. 49

⟨CICERO ATTICO SAL.⟩

1 Lentulum nostrum scis Puteolis esse? quod cum e viatore quodam esset auditum, qui se diceret eum in Appia via, cum is paulum lecticam aperuisset, cognosse, etsi vix veri simile ⟨visum est⟩, misi tamen Puteolos pueros qui pervestigarent et ad eum litteras. inventus est vix in hortis suis ⟨se⟩ occultans litterasque mihi remisit mirifice gratias agens Caesari; de suo autem consilio C. Caecio mandata ad me dedisse. eum ego hodie exspectabam, id est XIII[I] Kal. Apr.

2 Venit etiam ad me Matius Quinquatribus, homo mehercule, ut mihi visus est, temperatus et prudens; existimatus quidem est semper auctor oti. quam ille haec non probare mihi quidem visus est, quam illam νέκυιαν, ut tu appellas,

---

10, 6 est, sed *Bosius*: esse Ω egeo *Bosius*: ego Ω: *om. C*
Ep. 178] *novam ep. faciunt Ems*: *cum superiore in cett. cohaeret* **1**, 2 via *om. M* 4 visum est *addidi*: videbatur ς: est *Reid* 5 se *add. Victorius* 7 Caecio *Manutius*: cecio *vel* cetio Ω: Caesio *Schmidt* 8 XIII *Bosius*: XIIII Ω

10 hard and look more attentively to our interests.' On 9 March you write that my quiescence is also approved by our friend Peducaeus, whose judgement carries great weight with me.

I console myself with these passages in your letters, which make me think that I have done nothing amiss so far. But you must defend your own advice; there is no occasion to do so to me, but I want others in the picture. For my part, if I have done nothing wrong, I shall not fail in what remains. Encourage me in that, and in general help me with your deliberations. Nothing is heard here yet as to Caesar's return. By this letter I have done myself this much good at least: I have read all yours through, and found comfort in the reading.

178 (IX. 11)

Formiae, 20 March 49

CICERO TO ATTICUS

1 Do you know that our friend Lentulus is at Puteoli? I heard it from a traveller who said that he had recognized him on the Appian Way when he drew the curtain of his litter a little aside. Though it seemed scarcely probable, I sent some boys to Puteoli to make enquiries, along with a letter to him. After some trouble they found him hiding on his estate near the town, and he sent me a letter back containing glowing expressions of gratitude to Caesar. About his own plans he says that he has given C. Caecius a message for me. I am expecting him today, i.e. 20 March.

2 I also had a visit from Matius on Minerva's Day. I must say he impressed me as a man of moderation and good sense. Certainly he has always been looked upon as an advocate of peace. To me at any rate he seemed very far from approving what is going on, and very apprehensive of the Underworld, as you call them. In the course of a long talk I showed him

timere! huic ego in multo sermone epistulam ad me Caesaris ostendi, eam cuius exemplum ad te antea misi, rogavique ut interpretaretur quid esset quod ille scriberet 'consilio meo se uti velle, gratia, dignitate, ope rerum omnium'. respondit se ⟨non dubitare⟩ quin et opem et gratiam meam ille ad pacificationem quaereret. utinam aliquod in hac miseria rei publicae πολιτικὸν opus efficere et navare mihi liceat! Matius quidem et illum in ea sententia esse confidebat et se auctorem fore pollicebatur.

3 Pridie autem apud me Crassipes fuerat, qui se prid. Non. Mart. Brundisio profectum atque ibi Pompeium reliquisse dicebat, quod etiam qui VIII Id. illinc profecti erant nuntiabant; illa vero omnes, in quibus etiam Crassipes †qui prudentia potius† attendere, sermones minacis, inimicos optimatium, municipiorum hostis, meras proscriptiones, meros Sullas; quae Lucceium loqui, quae totam Graeciam, quae vero
4 Theophanem! et tamen omnis spes salutis in illis est, et ego excubo animo nec partem ullam capio quietis et, ut has pestis effugiam, cum dissimillimis nostri esse cupio! quid enim tu illic Scipionem, quid Faustum, quid Libonem prae⟨ter⟩missurum sceleris putas quorum creditores convenire dicuntur? quid eos autem, cum vicerint, in civis effecturos? quam vero μακροψυχίαν Gnaei nostri esse? nuntiant Aegyptum et Arabiam Εὐδαίμονα et Μεσοποταμίαν cogitare, iam Hispaniam

---

2, 9 non dubitare *P* (*sed post* quaereret), *Brunus* (M^4): *om.* Ω 10 aliquod in hac *s*: in hac (hoc *R*) aliquod Ω **3**, 4 qui Ω: qui pro sua *Lehmann* (qui pro *Madvig*): *fort.* quo(a)d 5 potius Ω$Z^{(l)}$: potuit *Hervagius* **4**, 2 has pestis ς: has petis *O*Δ: aspectis *R* 3 nostri *Manutius*: -is Ωλ 4 quid Faustum *C*: quidem austum *M*: quid emastium (-trum) δ: quid enustum *R* praetermissurum *s*: pr(a)em- Ω 5 sceleris *s*: cel- Ω 7 Gnaei *Victorius*: nec Δ: nam *O*: nec enim *R* 8 et μεσοποταμίαν *P* (-HAV) $Z^{(b)}$λ: et Mesopotamiam *c*: et (*spat.*) *O*: *om.* *R*Δ iam *Wesenberg*: in Ω: iter in *Sjögren*

Caesar's letter to me, the one of which I sent you a copy the other day, and asked him to interpret what Caesar meant by 'wanting to avail himself of my advice, influence, standing, and help in all matters'. He answered that he had no doubt Caesar was seeking both my help and my influence with a view to peace-making. If only I *could* do some political yeoman service to the state in this sorry pass! Matius at any rate was confident that Caesar was so minded and promised his personal support.

3 The previous day Crassipes had been with me. He said that he had set out from Brundisium on 6 March and left Pompey there—as was also reported by persons who started from Brundisium on the 8th. All, including Crassipes so far as his sagacity enabled him to pay attention (?), report threatening talk—enemies of the optimates, foes of the municipalities, proscriptions and Sulla in every sentence. The language attributed to Lucceius and to the whole Greek set, Theophanes
4 in particular—well! And yet all our hopes of salvation rest on these people, and I keep constantly on the alert without a moment's respite, longing to be with people utterly unlike myself in my desire to escape the horrors here. Do you suppose there are any criminal lengths over there to which Scipio and Faustus and Libo will not go?—their creditors are said to be meeting. What do you suppose they will do to their countrymen when they have won? And our Gnaeus' length of view, what of that? They report him as thinking of Egypt and Arabia Felix and Mesopotamia, as having already given up Spain.

abiecisse. monstra narrant; quae falsa esse possunt, sed certe et haec perdita sunt et illa non salutaria.

Tuas litteras iam desidero. post fugam nostram numquam tantum earum intervallum fuit. misi ad te exemplum litterarum mearum ad Caesarem, quibus me aliquid profecturum puto.

178A (IX. 11A)

Scr. in Formiano xiv aut xiii Kal. Apr. an. 49

CICERO IMP. S. D. CAESARI IMP.

1 Vt legi tuas litteras quas a Furnio nostro acceperam, quibus mecum agebas ut ad urbem essem, te velle uti 'consilio et dignitate mea' minus sum admiratus; de 'gratia' et de 'ope' quid significares mecum ipse quaerebam, spe tamen deducebar ad eam cogitationem ut te pro tua admirabili ac singulari sapientia de otio, de pace, de concordia civium agi velle arbitrarer, et ad eam rationem existimabam satis aptam esse
2 et naturam et personam meam. quod si ita est et si qua de Pompeio nostro tuendo et tibi ac rei publicae reconciliando cura te attingit, magis idoneum quam ego sum ad eam causam profecto reperies neminem, qui et illi semper et senatui cum primum potui pacis auctor fui nec sumptis armis belli ullam partem attigi iudicavique eo bello te violari, contra cuius honorem populi Romani beneficio concessum inimici atque invidi niterentur. sed ut eo tempore non modo ipse fautor dignitatis tuae fui verum etiam ceteris auctor ad te adiuvandum, sic me nunc Pompei dignitas vehementer movet. aliquot

---

12 tantum *scripsi*: iam nostrum Ω: iam tantum *Muretus*: tam longum *Corradus* earum *om. E*

Ep. 178A] **1**, 7 esse et (ei *bdm*) *O*Δ: esse *ER* **2**, 5 belli ullam *E*δ: bella in ul- *OR*: bellis nul- *M* 8 fautor $Z^{(b)}$: au(c)tor Ω: adiutor ς

They tell of monstrous things. These may not be true, but it is certain that there is no hope from this side and no salvation from the other.

I am now craving for a letter from you. Since we fled Rome there has never been so long a gap in the series. I send you a copy of my letter to Caesar, which I think will do some good.

178A (IX. 11A)

Formiae, 19 or 20 March 49

CICERO IMPERATOR TO CAESAR IMPERATOR

1 When I read your letter received from our friend Furnius in which you urge me to come to Rome, I was not so much surprised by your wish to 'avail yourself of my advice and standing', but I did ask myself what you meant by 'influence' and 'help'. However, hope led me towards the notion that, as suits the wisdom which you possess in so admirable and exceptional a degree, you might be desirous of instituting negotiations for peace, tranquillity, and civic harmony; and I conceived myself to be by nature and public image not ill fitted
2 to help in such an undertaking. If I am correct, and if you are at all concerned to maintain our friend Pompey and win him back to yourself and the Republic, you will surely find no more suitable person than myself for that purpose. I advocated peace to him always, and to the Senate as soon as I had opportunity. When arms were taken up, I had nothing to do with the war, and I judged you therein to be an injured party in that your enemies and those jealous of your success were striving to deprive you of a mark of favour accorded by the Roman people. But as then I not only gave my own support to your position but also urged others to come to your assistance, so now I am deeply concerned for Pompey's. It is some

enim sunt anni cum vos duo delegi quos praecipue colerem et quibus essem, sicut sum, amicissimus.

3 Quam ob rem a te peto vel potius omnibus te precibus oro et obtestor ut in tuis maximis curis aliquid impertias temporis huic quoque cogitationi ut tuo beneficio bonus vir, gratus, pius denique esse in maximi benefici memoria possim. quae si tantum ad me ipsum pertinerent, sperarem me a te tamen impetraturum, sed, ut arbitror, et ad tuam fidem et ad rem publicam pertinet me, et pacis et utriusque vestrum ⟨amicum, et ad vestram⟩ et ad civium concordiam per te quam accommodatissimum conservari.

Ego, cum antea tibi de Lentulo gratias egissem, cum ei saluti qui mihi fuerat fuisses, tum lectis eius litteris quas ad me gratissimo animo de tua liberalitate beneficioque misit, * * * eandem me salutem a te accepisse quam ille. in quem si me intellegis esse gratum, cura, obsecro, ut etiam in Pompeium esse possim.

179 (IX. 12)

Scr. in Formiano xiii vel xii Kal. Apr. an. 49

⟨CICERO ATTICO SAL.⟩

1 Legebam tuas litteras XIII Kal., cum mihi epistula adfertur a Lepta circumvallatum esse Pompeium, ratibus etiam exitus portus teneri. non me dius fidius prae lacrimis possum reliqua nec cogitare nec scribere. misi ad te exemplum. miseros nos! cur non omnes fatum illius una exsecuti sumus? ecce autem a Matio et Trebatio eadem, quibus Minturnis obvii

---

3, 1 te precibus Σ: et p- Δ 8 am- et ad v- *suppl. Lehmann* 12 *lacunam hic indicavi, versum ex archetypo excidisse suspicatus* (*vide comm.*): putavi *vel sim. infra addunt alii*

Ep. 179] *novam ep. faciunt Pms*: *superiori coniungit* Ω 1, 1 legerem *M*: -eram *Orelli* 3 possum *Manutius*: -sem Ω

years since I chose you and him as two men to cultivate above all others and as, what you are, my very dear friends.

3 Accordingly I ask you, or rather I beg and implore you with all my heart, to spare amid your grave preoccupations some time to consider how by your kindness I may meet the claims of honour, gratitude, and loyalty in the remembrance of a signal obligation. Even if my request concerned only myself I should hope that from you I should obtain it; but I believe it affects both your honour and the public welfare that I, as a friend of peace and of you both, should through you be preserved as the most appropriate agent for restoring harmony between yourself and Pompey and between Romans in general.

I have already thanked you concerning Lentulus, for saving as a citizen one who once saved me. But now that I have read the letter which he has sent me full of gratitude for your kindness and generosity * * * that in saving him you have saved me too. If my gratitude to Lentulus is apparent to you, then I beg you to let me show the like to Pompey.

179 (IX. 12)

Formiae, 20 or 21 March 49

CICERO TO ATTICUS

1 I was just reading your letter on 20 March when another came in from Lepta with the news that Pompey is besieged and that even the harbour outlets are blocked by ships. Upon my soul, tears prevent me thinking about the rest or writing it down. I send you a copy. Miserable that we are, why have we not all followed him to his doom? And now comes the same news from Matius and Trebatius, who met Caesar's messengers

Caesaris tabellarii. torqueor infelix, ut iam illum Mucianum exitum exoptem. at quam honesta, at quam expedita tua consilia, quam evigilata tuis cogitationibus, qua itineris, qua navigationis, qua congressus sermonisque cum Caesare! omnia cum honesta tum cauta. in Epirum vero invitatio quam suavis, quam liberalis, quam fraterna!

2 De Dionysio sum admiratus, qui apud me honoratior fuit quam apud Scipionem Panaetius; a quo impurissime haec nostra fortuna despecta est. odi hominem et odero; utinam ulcisci possem! sed illum ulciscentur mores sui.

3 Tu, quaeso, nunc vel maxime quid agendum nobis sit cogita. populi Romani exercitus Cn. Pompeium circumsedet, fossa et vallo saeptum tenet, fuga prohibet: nos vivimus, et stat urbs ista, praetores ius dicunt, aediles ludos parant, viri boni usuras perscribunt, ego ipse sedeo! coner illuc ire ut insanus, implorare fidem municipiorum? boni non sequentur, leves irridebunt, rerum novarum cupidi, victores praesertim
4 et armati, vim et manus adferent. quid censes igitur? ecquidnam est tui consili ad finem huius miserrimae vitae? nunc doleo, nunc torqueor, cum quidem aut sapiens videor quod una non ierim aut felix fuisse. mihi contra; numquam enim illius victoriae socius esse volui, calamitatis mallem fuisse. quid ego nunc tuas litteras, quid tuam prudentiam aut benevolentiam implorem? actum est. nulla re iam possum iuvari, qui ne quid optem quidem iam habeo nisi ut aliqua inimici misericordia liberemur.

---

7 illum *P*: ille Ω **2**, 2 haec *R*: h(a)ec h(a)ec *O*Δ **3**, 3 nos *Ps*: non Ω 6 consequentur *C* **4**, 2 ad finem *PF*: ad finis (-es *M*) Ω: ecquis finis ς: qui (*vel* quae) finis *Schmidt* 3 quidem *P*δ: quidam Ω: cuidam *Klotz* 9 liberemur ς: -rentur *R*: -retur *OP*Δ

at Minturnae. I am in such an agony of distress that I actually long for an end like Mucius'. And yet how well your advice sounds, how straightforward, how anxiously you have thought it out, whether as to my route or my time of sailing or my meeting and talk with Caesar! Everything honourable, everything prudent. And your invitation to Epirus, how agreeably put, how generous and brotherly!

2 As for Dionysius, I was surprised. He was treated with more consideration in my house than Panaetius in Scipio's; now he scorns me in my present plight. It is disgusting. I hate the fellow and always shall. I wish I could punish him. But his own character will do that.

3 Pray consider now of all times what I ought to do. A Roman army is besieging Cn. Pompeius, investing him with moat and rampart, stopping his escape; and we go on living, Rome stands, the Praetors sit on the bench, the Aediles prepare their games, the honest men book their receipts, I myself sit idle! Shall I make madly for Brundisium, appeal to the loyalty of the municipalities? The honest men will not follow, the triflers will laugh, the revolutionaries, victorious now with weapons
4 in their hands, will use violence. So what do you think? Have you any sort of advice to offer on how to end this miserable existence? *Now* the pain comes home and I am in torment, just when people think me either wise or lucky in not having gone with Pompey. I think the opposite. I never wanted a share in his victory but I would rather I had shared his disaster. What use is it now for me to beg you to write, appeal to your wisdom and good will? All is over. No one can help me now. I have nothing even to pray for except that one of my enemies may take pity on me and put me out of my misery.

180 (IX. 13)

Scr. in Formiano x Kal. Apr. an. 49 (§ 2)

⟨CICERO ATTICO SAL.⟩

1 ‘Οὐκ ἔστ’ ἔτυμος λόγος’, ut opinor, ille de ratibus. quid enim esset quod Dolabella iis litteris quas III Id. Mart. a Brundisio dedit hanc εὐημερίαν quasi Caesaris scriberet, Pompeium in fuga esse eumque primo vento navigaturum? quod valde discrepat ab iis epistulis quarum exempla antea ad te misi. hic quidem mera scelera loquuntur; sed non erat nec recentior auctor nec huius rei quidem melior Dolabella.

2 Tuas XI Kal. accepi litteras quibus omnia consilia differs in id tempus cum scierimus quid actum sit. et certe ita est, nec interim potest quicquam non modo statui sed ne cogitari quidem. quamquam hae me litterae Dolabellae iubent ad pristinas cogitationes reverti. fuit enim prid. Quinquatrus egregia tempestas; qua ego illum usum puto.

3 Συναγωγὴ consiliorum tuorum non est a me collecta ad querelam sed magis ad consolationem meam. nec enim me tam haec mala angebant quam suspicio culpae ac temeritatis meae. eam nullam puto esse, quoniam cum consiliis tuis mea facta et consilia consentiunt. quod mea praedicatione factum esse scribis magis quam illius merito ut tantum ei debere viderer, est ita. ego illa extuli semper, et eo quidem magis ne quid ille superiorum meminisse me putaret. quae si maxime meminissem, tamen illius temporis similitudinem iam sequi deberem. nihil me adiuvit cum posset; at postea fuit amicus, etiam valde, nec quam ob causam plane scio. ergo ego quoque

---

Ep. 180] *novam ep. constituit Schütz*: *cum superiore in codd. cohaeret* **1**, 2 esset *Wesenberg*: est Ω iis . . . iis (*v.* 5) *O*: is . . . is *R*: his . . . his (iis *m*) *P*Δ 3 εὐημερίαν quasi Caesaris Ω*c*: q- C- εὐ- *et* εὐ- C- q- ς: q- εὐ- C- *Lambinus* 7 quidem rei *Wesenberg* **2**, 4 me *Corradus*: mihi Ω **3**, 7 illa *bds*λ: illam Ω: illum *P* 10 me . . . posset δ: mea . . . possem Ω at *Corradus*: et Ω: sed *Wesenberg*: *secl. Boot* 11 etiam *Bosius*: et tam Ω nec *Madvig*: et Ω

180 (IX. 13)

Formiae, 23 March 49

CICERO TO ATTICUS

1 'It is not true, the tale', I think, about the ships. Why else should Dolabella in a letter dispatched from Brundisium on 13 March write that Pompey is in flight and will sail by the first wind, as though this were a coup for Caesar? That sounds very different from the letters of which I sent you copies the other day. Here the talk is all of horrors; but there is no more recent authority than Dolabella and none better, in this matter anyway.

2 I received a letter from you on the 22nd, in which you put off all plans until the time when we know what has happened. And certainly you are right, nothing can be decided or even considered in the meanwhile—though this letter of Dolabella's sends me back to my earlier ideas. For the weather was excellent on the 18th, and I expect he has taken advantage of it.

3 My *recueil* of your advice was not made in any spirit of recrimination but rather for my own comfort. The evils of the time distressed me less than the suspicion of fault and thoughtlessness on my own part. Of this I acquit myself, since my actions and plans accord with your counsels. You write that if I appear so greatly indebted to Pompey it is more because of my own public acknowledgements than through his deserts. That is true. I have always made much of them, all the more because he might otherwise have supposed that I had some memory of what went before. However well I remembered that I ought now to follow the pattern then set. He did not help me when he might; but afterwards he stood my friend, very much so even, I do not quite know why.

illi. quin etiam illud par in utroque nostrum, quod ab eisdem illecti sumus. sed utinam ⟨tan⟩tum ego ei prodesse potuissem quantum mihi ille potuit! mihi tamen quod fecit gratissimum. nec ego nunc eum iuvare qua re possim scio nec, si possem, cum tam pestiferum bellum pararet, adiuvandum

4 putarem; tantum offendere animum eius hic manens nolo, nec mehercule ista videre quae tu potes iam animo providere nec interesse istis malis possim. sed eo tardior ad discedendum fui quod difficile est de discessu voluntario sine ulla spe reditus cogitare. nam ego hunc ita paratum video peditatu, equitatu, classibus, auxiliis Gallorum, quos Matius ἐλάπιζεν, ut puto, sed certe dicebat peditum * * *, equitum sex polliceri sumptu suo annos decem—sed sit hoc λάπισμα; magnas habet certe copias, et habebit non Asiae vectigal sed civium bona. adde confidentiam hominis, adde imbecillitatem bonorum virorum, qui quidem, quod illum sibi merito iratum putant, oderunt, ut tu scribis, ludum. ac vellem †scribis quisnam hic significasset.† sed et iste, quia plus ostenderat quam fecit, et vulgo illum qui amarunt non amant; municipia vero et rustici Romani illum metuunt, hunc adhuc diligunt. qua re ita paratus est ut, etiam si vincere non possit, quo modo tamen vinci ipse possit non videam. ego autem non tam γοητείαν huius timeo quam πειθανάγκην. 'αἱ γὰρ τῶν τυράννων δεήσεις' inquit Πλάτων 'οἶσθ' ὅτι μεμιγμέναι ἀνάγκαις.'

---

13 illecti sumus *Lambinus*: -tissimus *M*: lecti sumus *PZ*[1]: dilecti s- *ORδ* tantum ς: tum Ω ei δ: et Ω 15 possim *P*: -sum Ω **4**, 1 offendere *Pδ*: -rem *RM*: *om.* *O* 3 possim *scripsi*: -sem Ω: -sum *Orelli* 7 ΕΛΑΠΙΖΕΝ *Z*: CAAΠ- *vel* CAΛΠ- Ω peditum CCIↃↃ *Bosius* 8 sex *Bosius*: se Ω*Z*[b] 9 Asiae *scripsi*: alie Ω: ille *Pδ*: ut ille *Bosius*: Italiae *Madvig*: Galliae *T. Frank*: alienum *Reid* 12 ludere *R* 13 *obelis inclusa melius quam ceteri refinxit Boot* scripsisses q- hoc s- 20 ἀνάγκαις ς (*sic Plat. Ep. vii. 329 D*): -κῃ *C*: *vel omittunt vel vestigia tantum praebent codd.*

Very well, I shall stand his. And there is another resemblance between us; we have both been taken in by the same set of people. But I only wish it had been in my power to help him as much as he could have helped me. Still for what he did I am truly thankful. And yet I don't know how I can help him now, nor even if I could should I feel that he *ought*
4 to be helped in preparing so baleful a war. It is simply that I do not want to hurt his feelings by remaining here, nor, be it added, could I bear to witness all that you can already see coming or be present at the mischief here. But I have been the slower to get away because it is difficult to put one's mind to a voluntary departure with no hope of return. For I see Caesar so well provided with infantry, cavalry, ships, and Gaulish auxiliaries, as to which last Matius said (*blague* I dare say, but he did say it) that they are promising * * * infantry and 6,000 cavalry at their own expense for ten years—but grant that was *blague;* he certainly has large forces and he will dispose, not indeed of the revenue of Asia, but of the property of his countrymen. Then consider the confidence of him and the feebleness of the honest men, who thinking that Pompey is justly angry with them, are bored with the game, as you say—I wish you had mentioned the name of the person who told you this (?). Anyhow *he* loves Pompey no longer, because he promised more than he performed, and it is the same with the generality of Pompey's erstwhile admirers; as for the municipalities and the country Romans, they fear Pompey and so far they like Caesar. So his resources are such that even if he cannot win I do not see how he can be beaten. I personally do not fear his beguilements so much as his *force majeure.* 'For the requests of despots' says Plato 'have, you know, an element of compulsion.'

5 Illa ἀλίμενα video tibi non probari; quae ne mihi quidem placebant, sed habebam in illis et occultationem et ὑπηρεσίαν fidelem. quae si mihi Brundisi suppetant, mallem; sed ibi occultatio nulla est. verum, ut scribis, cum sciemus.

6 Viris bonis me non nimis excuso. quas enim eos cenas et facere et obire scripsit ad me Sextus, quam lautas, quam tempestivas! sed sint quamvis boni, non sunt meliores quam nos; moverent me, si essent fortiores.

De Lanuvino Phameae erravi; Troianum somniabam. id ego volui Q., sed pluris est. istuc tamen [me] cuperem emeres, si ullam spem fruendi viderem.

7 Nos quae monstra cottidie legamus intelleges ex illo libello qui in epistulam coniectus est. Lentulus noster Puteolis est, ἀδημονῶν [is], ut Caecius narrat, quid agat. διατροπὴν Corfiniensem reformidat. Pompeio nunc putat satis factum, beneficio Caesaris movetur, sed tamen movetur magis prospecta re.

181 (IX. 13*a*)

Scr. in Formiano ix Kal. Apr. an. 49

⟨CICERO ATTICO SAL.⟩

Mene haec posse ferre? omnia misera, sed hoc nihil miserius: Pompeius N. Magium de pace misit et tamen oppugnatur.

5, 2 occultationem *Victorius*: occulte fio onem *vel sim.* Ω 3 suppeterent *Ernesti* 4 sciemus *Corradus*: scimus Δ: simus *OR* **6,** 4 me *Ps*: ne Ω: *fort. delendum* 5 Phameae *Victorius*: -mea Ω somniabam λ: -averam Ω 6 volui Q. *Bosius*: voluique (nol- *OP*) Ω cuperem emeres, si *Manutius*: me cupere memor est *O*(?)*R*: me cuperem me mei est Δ: mi cuperem emeres, si *Orelli*: cuperem emere, si *Ernesti*: *anne* te cuperem emere, si? 7 viderem *Manutius*: ut de re m (*vel* in) Δ: veterem *O*(?)*R* **7,** 1 legamus intelliges *Wesenberg*: intelligamus *R*Δ: -gebamus *O* ex illo libello *Beroaldus*: exilio libelli Ω 2 qui in *ms*: quin Ω 3 ut *Obds*: is ut *RMm* Caesius *Schmidt* 5 prospecta re (-tare *s*) *bs*: -taret *RMdm*: praespectaret *O*: perspecta re *Lambinus* **Ep. 181**] *novam ep. constituit Sternkopf*: *cum superiore in codd. cohaeret* 1 mene *Pius*: nec Ω: tene *Bosius* (*vide finem superioris ep.*) 2 numerium *R*: -rum (nūm *M*) *O*(?)*PM*: Numatium *C*: CN. (Cn., gneum) δ

5 I see that you don't like those harbourless places. Neither do I, but in them I have the means of hiding and a reliable crew. If the same were available at Brundisium I should prefer it; but there is no hiding there. However, as you say, wait till we know.

6 I don't make overmuch apology to the honest men. Sextus has written to me about the dinners they are giving and attending—such elegant, lengthy affairs! Anyway, let them be as honest as you please, they are no more so than I. I should be impressed if they were braver.

I was wrong about Phamea's place at Lanuvium. It was his property at Troy that I had dreamily in mind. I wanted it for 500,000, but it's worth more. Still I should be very glad for you to buy the other if I saw any prospect of enjoying it.

7 You will see from the enclosed paper what sort of horrors we are reading every day. Our friend Lentulus is at Puteoli, sorely perplexed, so Caecius says, what to do. The memory of the Corfinium *bouleversement* appals him. He thinks he has now done enough for Pompey and is affected by Caesar's generosity; but he is still more affected by foresight of the issue.

181 (IX. 13*a*)

Formiae, 24 March 49

CICERO TO ATTICUS

I should never have believed that I could bear this! Misery everywhere, but *this* is saddest of all: Pompey has sent N. Magius to treat for peace and is besieged just the same. I did

quod ego non credebam, sed habeo a Balbo litteras quarum ad te exemplum misi. lege, quaeso, et illud infimum caput ipsius Balbi optimi, cui Gnaeus noster locum ubi hortos aedificaret dedit, quem cui nostrum non saepe praetulit? itaque miser torquetur. sed ne bis eadem legas, ad ipsam te epistulam reicio. spem autem pacis habeo nullam. Dolabella suis litteris III Id. Mart. datis merum bellum loquitur. maneamus ergo in illa eadem sententia misera et desperata, quando hoc miserius esse nihil potest.

181 A (IX. 13 A)

Scr. Romae xi Kal. Apr. an. 49

BALBVS CICERONI IMP. SAL. DIC.

1 Caesar nobis litteras perbrevis misit, quarum exemplum subscripsi. brevitate epistulae scire poteris eum valde esse distentum qui tanta de re tam breviter scripserit. si quid praeterea novi fuerit, statim tibi scribam.

CAESAR OPPIO CORNELIO SAL.

A. d. VII Id. Mart. Brundisium veni; ad murum castra posui. Pompeius est Brundisi. misit ad me N. Magium de pace. quae visa sunt respondi. hoc vos statim scire volui. cum in spem venero de compositione aliquid me conficere, statim vos certiores faciam.'

2 Quo modo me nunc putas, mi Cicero, torqueri, postquam rursus in spem pacis veni, ne qua res eorum compositionem

---

5 balbi *Pb*: albi Ω 9 III *ORc*: *om.* Δ merum *P*: mecum Ω
Ep. 181A] CORNELIO *OM*: -LIOQVE *R*δ **1**, 6 N. *vulg.* : CN. (Cn., GN.) Ω
8 conficere posse *Lambinus*

not believe it, but I have a letter from Balbus of which I send you a copy. And pray read that final paragraph by the worthy Balbus himself, the man to whom Gnaeus gave a site for his suburban house, whom he often put before any one of us. So the poor fellow is on tenterhooks! But not to make you read the same text twice over, I refer you to the letter itself. Hope of peace I have none. Dolabella in his letter dispatched 13 March talks nothing but war. So let us stick to the old purpose, miserable and desperate as it is, since nothing can be more lamentable than this.

181A (IX. 13A)

Rome, 22 March 49

BALBUS TO CICERO IMPERATOR

1 Caesar has sent us a very short letter of which I append a copy. You will be able to see by its brevity that he is very busy indeed, to write so briefly about a matter of such importance. If there is any further news I shall write to you at once.

CAESAR TO OPPIUS AND CORNELIUS

On 9 March I reached Brundisium and encamped before the walls. Pompey is in Brundisium. He sent N. Magius to me to treat of peace. I replied as I thought proper. This I wanted you to know at once. As soon as I see any hope of achieving anything in the way of a composition I shall at once inform you.

You can imagine, my dear Cicero, how I am on tenter-hooks for fear anything should obstruct a composition between

impediat? namque quod absens facere possum, opto. quod si una essem, aliquid fortasse proficere posse mihi viderer. nunc exspectatione crucior.

182 (IX. 14)

Scr. in Formiano ix vel viii Kal. Apr. an. 49

CICERO ATTICO SAL.

1 Miseram ad te VIIII Kal. exemplum epistulae Balbi ad me et Caesaris ad eum. ecce tibi eodem die Capua litteras accepi a Q. Pedio Caesarem ad se prid. Id. Mart. misisse hoc exemplo:

Pompeius se oppido tenet. nos ad portas castra habemus. conamur opus magnum et multorum dierum propter altitudinem maris; sed tamen nihil est quod potius faciamus. ab utroque portus cornu moles iacimus, ut aut illum quam primum traicere quod habet Brundisi copiarum cogamus aut exitum prohibeamus.

2 Vbi est illa pax de qua Balbus scripserat torqueri se? ecquid acerbius, ecquid crudelius? atque eum loqui quidam αὐθεντικῶς narrabat Cn. Carbonis, M. Bruti se poenas persequi omniumque eorum in quos Sulla crudelis hoc socio fuisset; nihil Curionem se duce facere quod non hic Sulla duce fecisset; a ⟨se⟩ dam⟨natos am⟩bitus nomine, quibus exsili poena superioribus legibus non fuisset, ab illo patriae proditores de exsilio reductos esse; queri de Milone per vim expulso; neminem tamen se violaturum nisi qui arma contra. haec Baebius quidam a Curione III Id. profectus, homo non infans

---

2, 3 namque] *anne* nempe? 4 proficere *ORm*: -ciscere *M*: *om. bds* posse mihi viderer *Madvig*: -sem videri *ORd*: -sum videre *M*: -sem *bds*

Ep. 182] **1**, 8 exitu ς **2**, 6 a . . . nomine (*i.e.* a ⟨se⟩ dam⟨natos am⟩bit' noīe) *scripsi* (damnatos ambitus *iam Gronovius*, a se *iam Graevius*): ad ambitionem Ω 9 contra. haec *Lambinus*: h(a)ec c- *ORΔ*: habeat c- *EP* 10 b(a)ebius *ms*: barb- Ω

them, now that I see a hope of peace once more. I do indeed what I can, not being on the spot—pray. If I was with him I might perhaps flatter myself that I could be of some use. As it is I am tortured by suspense.

182 (IX. 14)

Formiae, 24 or 25 March 49

CICERO TO ATTICUS

1 I sent you on the 24th a copy of Balbus' letter to me and of Caesar's to him. Then on the same day what should come but a letter from Q. Pedius, from Capua, to say that Caesar had written to him on 14 March? Caesar wrote as follows:—

Pompey shuts himself up in the town. We have our camp at the gates. We are attempting a formidable task and one which will take us many days because of the depth of the sea; but there is nothing better we can do. We are sinking moles from both ends of the harbour so as either to oblige him to take his force at Brundisium overseas as soon as may be or to stop his way out.

2 Where is the peace about which Balbus wrote he was on tenterhooks? Could anything be harsher or more ruthless? And according to one first-hand authority he talks of avenging the deaths of Cn. Carbo and M. Brutus and of all the other victims of Sulla's cruelty, in which Pompey, as he says, participated. Curio, he says, is doing nothing as his lieutenant which Pompey did not do as Sulla's. He himself is restoring from exile men convicted on the charge of bribery who under previous laws would not have been liable to that penalty, whereas Sulla restored traitors to their country. He complains of Milo's extrusion by violence; but promises himself to injure no one who does not bear arms against him. All this comes from one Baebius, who left Curio on the 13th, something of

sed †quis ulli† non dicat. plane nescio quid agam. illim equidem Gnaeum profectum puto. quicquid est biduo sciemus. a te nihil ne Anteros quidem Quinti litterarum, nec mirum; quid enim est quod scribamus? ego tamen nullum diem praetermitto.

3 Scripta epistula litterae mihi ante lucem a Lepta Capua redditae sunt Id. Mart. Pompeium a Brundisio conscendisse, Caesarem a. d. VII Kal. Apr. Capuae fore.

183 (IX. 15)

Scr. in Formiano viii Kal. Apr. an. 49

CICERO ATTICO SAL.

1 Cum dedissem ad te litteras ut scires Caesarem Capuae VII Kal. fore, adlatae mihi Capua sunt eum hic VI et in Albano apud Curionem V Kal. fore. eum cum videro, Arpinum pergam. si mihi veniam quam peto dederit, utar illius condicione; si minus, impetrabo aliquid a me ipso. ille, ut ⟨Lepta⟩ ad me scripsit, legiones singulas posuit Brundisi, Tarenti, Siponti. claudere mihi videtur maritimos exitus et tamen ipse Graeciam spectare potius quam Hispanias. sed haec longius absunt.
2 me nunc et congressus huius stimulat (is vero adest) et prima eius actionis horreo. volet enim, credo, senatus consultum facere, volet augurum decretum (rapiemur aut absentes vexabimur) vel ut consules roget praetor vel dictatorem

---

11 quis ulli *Mds*: quis illi *mZ*[1]: quid si illi *O*(?)*R*: quis illa *Lambinus*: qui de suo illa *Tyrrell* illim equidem *Victorius*: illi me q- Ω 13 Anteros *Bosius*: ante pros. *Ant.*: a- pios Δ: a- prorsus *OR* Quinti *scripsi*: quin te Ω: *del. anon. ap. Corradum* **3**, 1 Capua *Manutius*: -u(a)e Ω 3 c(a)esarem Σ*bds*: ad c- *M*: at c- *m* capu(a)e *Rbs*: -ua *EOMdm*

Ep. 183] **1**, 2 capua Σ*s*: -u(a)e Δ eum hic *Schmidt*: et hoc Ω: et hic *Sjögren* VI *Sjögren* (VI Kal. *Schmidt*): mihi Ω 5 Lepta *hic addidi*, *post* scripsit *Ziehen* **2**, 1 is Σδ: id *Mc* primas eius actiones ς 4 vel ut dict- *Lambinus*

a chatterbox it is true, but * * * . I simply don't know what to do. For my part I think Gnaeus will have left Brundisium. Whatever the truth we shall know it in a couple of days. Not a word from you, not even by Quintus' boy Anteros. And no wonder. What is there for us to write? However I don't let a day pass.

3 P.S. A letter from Lepta in Capua has been delivered to me before daybreak saying that Pompey embarked from Brundisium on the Ides of March and that Caesar will be at Capua on the 26th.

183 (IX. 15)

Formiae, 25 March 49

CICERO TO ATTICUS

1 After I had sent off a letter to inform you that Caesar will be at Capua on the 26th, a letter from Capua was brought to me to the effect that he will stay here on the 27th and with Curio at Alba on the 28th. When I have seen him I shall go on to Arpinum. If he gives me the indulgence I ask, I shall accept his terms. If not, I shall get permission from myself. As Lepta has written to me, he has stationed separate legions at Brundisium, Tarentum, and Sipontum. It looks as if he wants to close the ways out by sea—though he himself seems to be more interested in Greece than in Spain. But this is all some
2 way ahead. What bothers me at the moment is the immediate prospect of meeting him, and also I dread his opening moves. I imagine he will want a decree of the Senate and another from the Augurs (I shall be hauled up or harried if I am not there) allowing a Praetor either to hold consular elections or to

dicat; quorum neutrum ius est. sed si Sulla potuit efficere ab interrege ut dictator diceretur et magister equitum, cur hic non possit? nihil expedio nisi ut aut ab hoc tamquam Q. Mucius aut ab illo tamquam L. Scipio.

3 Cum tu haec leges, ego illum fortasse convenero. 'τέτλα⟨θι⟩'. 'κύντερον' ne illud quidem nostrum proprium. erat enim spes propinqui reditus, erat hominum querela. nunc exire cupimus, qua spe reditus mihi quidem numquam in mentem venit. non modo autem nulla querela est municipalium hominum ac rusticorum sed contra metuunt ut crudelem, iratum. nec tamen mihi quicquam est miserius quam remansisse nec optatius quam evolare non tam ad belli quam ad fugae societatem. sed tu ⟨quid⟩, omnia qui consilia differebas in id tempus cum sciremus quae Brundisi acta essent? scimus nempe; haeremus nihilo minus. vix enim spero mihi hunc veniam daturum, etsi multa adfero iusta ad impetrandum. sed tibi omnem illius meumque sermonem omnibus verbis expressum statim mittam.

4 Tu nunc omni amore enitere ut nos cura et prudentia iuves. ita subito accurrit ut ne Trebatium quidem, ut constitueram, possim videre; omnia nobis imparatis agenda. sed tamen 'ἄλλα μὲν αὐτός,' ut ait ille, 'ἄλλα δὲ καὶ δαίμων ὑποθήσεται.' quicquid egero continuo scies. mandata Caesaris ad consules et ad Pompeium quae rogas, nulla habeo †et de-

---

5 sed si Z^bλ: et si (etsi) Ω 6 et magister equitum *om. m* **3,** 1 τέτλαθι *praeeunte Victorio Lambinus, qui recte distinxit*: ΤΕΤΑΛ *vel sim.* Ω*c* 2 at κύντ- *Schütz* 3 erat ς: erit Ω 9 sed . . . qui *ita scripsi*: sed tu omnia qui Ω: sed quid tu? omnia *Purser*: sed heus tu, omnia qui *Schmidt* **4,** 2 Trebatium ς: trabilius (cr- *R*) Ω: trebillum Z^b: T. Rebillum (C. Rebilum *debuit*) *Bosius* 6 habeo *OR*δ: ab eo *M* habeo: set rescripta attulit Matius (*vel aliud nom. propr.*); ea misi *Madvig*

nominate a Dictator, neither of which is legal. But if Sulla could arrange for a Dictator to be nominated by an Interrex, and a Master of the Horse, why not Caesar? All I can make out of it is a choice between Q. Mucius' fate at Caesar's hands or L. Scipio's at Pompey's.

3 When you read this I shall perhaps have met him. 'Bear it'—not even that disaster of my own was 'worse'. There was the hope of an early return, there was public murmuring. Now I am anxious to go, but with what hope of return I for one have not the least idea. And far from any murmuring in the municipalities and the country, they are afraid on the contrary of Pompey's cruelty and anger. And yet nothing makes me more wretched than having stayed behind and there is nothing I desire more than escape, to share not so much in fighting as in running away. But what do *you* say? You used to put off all planning until we knew the outcome at Brundisium. Well, we know; and we are as badly stuck as before. For I scarcely expect that Caesar will give me my request, though I have many good reasons to put forward in its favour. But I shall send you a complete verbatim report of all we say to one another straight away.

4 Now help me with your care and wisdom, and put all your affection into the effort. He is coming up in such a hurry that I cannot even see Trebatius as I had arranged. All must be without preparation. Never mind, 'some things myself', as the poet says, 'others a god shall rede'. However I get on, you shall know immediately. As for Caesar's messages to the Consuls and Pompey which you ask for, I have none * * * sent you

scripta attulit illa est via† misi ad te ante; e quibus mandata puto intellegi posse. Philippus Neapoli est, Lentulus Puteolis. de Domitio, ut facis, sciscitare ubi sit, quid cogitet.

5 Quod scribis asperius me quam mei patiantur mores de Dionysio scripsisse, vide quam sim antiquorum hominum: te me dius ⟨fidius⟩ hanc rem gravius putavi laturum esse quam me. nam praeter quam quod te moveri arbitror oportere iniuria quae mihi a quoquam facta sit, praeterea te ipsum quodam modo hic violavit cum in me tam improbus fuit. sed tu id quanti aestimes tuum iudicium est; nec tamen in hoc tibi quicquam oneris impono. ego autem illum male sanum semper putavi, nunc etiam impurum et sceleratum puto, nec tamen mihi inimiciorem quam sibi. Philargyro bene curasti; causam certe habuisti et veram et bonam, relictum me esse potius quam reliquisse.

184 (IX. 15*a*)

Scr. in Formiano viii Kal. Apr. an. 49

⟨CICERO ATTICO SAL.⟩

Cum dedissem iam litteras a. d. VIII Kal., pueri quos cum Matio et Trebatio miseram epistulam mihi attulerunt hoc exemplo:

MATIVS ET TREBATIVS CICERONI IMP. SAL.

Cum Capua exissemus, in itinere audivimus Pompeium Brundisio a. d. XVI Kal. Apr. cum omnibus copiis quas habuerit profectum

---

7 est via Ω: levia Z^b ante *ORZ*^{b}λ: *om.* Δ 5, 2 sim *Victorius*: sit Ω 3 te medius fidius δ: te medius *M*: timidius *OR* 5 quoquam *bds*: quoque Ω 6 quodam *c*: quonam Ω 10 puto ς: toto *OP*Δ: toti *R* mi(c)hi *Ps*: milit. *O*: militi *R*Δ 11 curasti *Z*^{b}λ*c*: *om.* Ω 12 me esse *OR*: esse me Δ

Ep. 184] *novam ep. agnovit Ziehen*: *cum superiore in codd. cohaeret* 1 VIII Δ: VII *OR* pueri *hic Malaespina* (*om.* cum): *post* Matio Ωλ 5 habuit λ

previously; from this I think the messages can be gathered. Philippus is at Naples, Lentulus at Puteoli. As for Domitius, please continue your enquiries about his whereabouts and plans.

5 You say that the harshness of my language about Dionysius is out of character. See now how old-fashioned I am! Upon my word I thought you would be more upset by this affair than I. For to leave aside that I think you ought to take a wrong against me to heart, no matter who commits it, there is the further point that his deplorable behaviour towards me is in a way an offence against yourself. But it is for you to judge how seriously you should take that, and do not think that I wish in any way to embarrass you in the matter. For my part I always thought him half crazy, and now think him a blackguardly scoundrel, but no more my enemy than his own. You were right to pay Philargyrus. You certainly had a fair and reasonable plea, that I had been left in the lurch rather than the other way about.

184 (IX. 15*a*)

Formiae, 25 March 49

CICERO TO ATTICUS

After I had dispatched my letter on 25 March, the boys whom I had sent with Matius and Trebatius brought me the following:—

MATIUS AND TREBATIUS TO CICERO IMPERATOR

After leaving Capua we heard on the road that Pompey left Brundisium on 17 March with his entire force, and that Caesar

esse; Caesarem postero die in oppidum introisse, contionatum esse, inde Romam contendisse, velle ante Kalendas esse ad urbem et pauculos dies ibi commorari, deinde in Hispanias proficisci. nobis non alienum visum est, quoniam de adventu Caesaris pro certo habebamus, pueros tuos ad te remittere, ut id tu quam primum scires. mandata tua nobis curae sunt eaque ut tempus postularit agemus. Trebatius sedulo facit ut antecedat.

Epistula conscripta nuntiatum est nobis Caesarem a. d. VIII Kal. Apr. Beneventi mansurum, a. d. VII Kal. Capuae, a. d. VI Sinuessae. haec pro certo putamus.

185 (IX. 16)

Scr. in Formiano vii Kal. Apr. an. 49 (§ 1)

⟨CICERO ATTICO SAL.⟩

1 Cum quod scriberem ad te nihil haberem, tamen ne quem diem intermitterem has dedi litteras. a. d. VI Kal. Caesarem Sinuessae mansurum nuntiabant. ab eo mihi litterae redditae sunt a. d. VII Kal., quibus iam 'opes' meas, non ut superioribus litteris 'opem', exspectat. cum eius clementiam Corfiniensem illam per litteras collaudavissem rescripsit hoc exemplo:

CAESAR IMP. CICERONI IMP. SAL. DIC.

2 Recte auguraris de me (bene enim tibi cognitus sum) nihil a me abesse longius crudelitate. atque ego cum ex ipsa re magnam capio voluptatem tum meum factum probari abs te triumpho

8 pauculos δ: paulos *MC*: paucos *OR* hispanias *OR*: -am δ (*de M non liquet*) 10 habebamus *ms*: -eamus Ω tuos *R*δ: *om. OM* 12 sedulo *c*: sc(a)evola *R*Δ: sevola *P* 14 Apr. ... Kal. *c* (*sed* Capuae ad VII. ad III. Sinuessae), *Lamb.* (*marg.*) (*sed* ad *pro* a.d.), *Bosius*: *om.* Ω

Ep. 185] *novam ep. faciunt ms* (*inscr. om. m*): *cum superiore cohaeret in* Ω **1,** 1 quod ς: quid Ω 5 expectat *E*δ: -to *ORMC* **2,** 1 auguraris *E*δ: -raturis *OR*: -raturi *M*: -raris tu ς, *fort. recte*

entered the town on the following day, made a public speech, and then left for Rome; further that he desires to reach the capital before the Kalends and to stay there only a few days, then to set out for Spain. Since we take the news of Caesar's coming as definite, we thought it as well to send your boys back to you, so that you should know of it at the first possible moment. Your commission is not forgotten and we shall attend to it as occasion requires. Trebatius is doing his best to reach you beforehand.

P.S. We have had word that Caesar is to stay at Beneventum on the 25th, at Capua on the 26th, at Sinuessa on the 27th. We regard this as definite.

185 (IX. 16)

Formiae, 26 March 49

CICERO TO ATTICUS

1 Though I have nothing to say to you I am sending this letter in order not to miss a day. They tell me that Caesar will stay the night of the 27th at Sinuessa. A letter from him was delivered to me on the 26th in which he now counts on my 'resources', not, as in his former letter, on my 'help'. I had written applauding his clemency at Corfinium and he has replied as follows:—

CAESAR IMPERATOR TO CICERO IMPERATOR

2 You rightly surmise of me (you know me well) that of all things I abhor cruelty. The incident gives me great pleasure in itself, and your approval of my action elates me beyond words. I am not

gaudio. neque illud me movet quod ii qui a me dimissi sunt discessisse dicuntur ut mihi rursus bellum inferrent; nihil enim malo quam et me mei similem esse et illos sui.

3 Tu velim mihi ad urbem praesto sis ut tuis consiliis atque opibus, ut consuevi, in omnibus rebus utar. Dolabella tuo nihil scito mihi esse iucundius. hanc adeo habebo gratiam illi; neque enim aliter facere poterit. tanta eius humanitas, is sensus, ea in me est benevolentia.

186 (IX. 17)

Scr. in Formiano vi Kal. Apr. an. 49 (§ 1)

CICERO ATTICO SAL.

1 Trebatium VI Kal., quo die has litteras dedi, exspectabam. ex eius nuntio Matique litteris meditabor quo modo cum illo loquar. o tempus miserum! nec dubito quin a me contendat ad urbem veniam; senatum enim Kalendis velle se frequentem adesse etiam Formiis proscribi iussit. ergo ei negandum est. sed quid praeripio? statim ad te perscribam omnia. ex illius sermone statuam Arpinumne mihi eundum sit an quo alio. volo Ciceroni meo togam puram dare, istic
2 puto. tu, quaeso, cogita quid deinde; nam me hebetem molestiae reddiderunt.

A Curio velim scire ecquid ad te scriptum sit de Tirone. ad me enim ipse Tiro ita scripsit ut verear quid agat; qui

---

4 gaudio *Lambinus*: -deo *MZ*: et gaudeo Σδ 5 dicuntur *ER*: se d- *M*: se dicunt *O*δ **3**, 3 hanc adeo] nec ideo *Madvig*

Ep. 186] **1**, 2 matiique *P*: malique *OM*: malimque *R*: manli(i)que δ 3 loquamur *M* 6 *post* negandum est *signum interrog. ponunt vulgo* praeripio ς: -ripi *OM*: -rupi *R*: percipiam *P*: pr(a)ecipit δ: praeripui *Schmidt* 8 istic ς: istum Ω **2**, 3 Curio *Hervagius*: curione Ω 4 ita *s* : ista Ω

disturbed by the fact that those whom I have released are said to have left the country in order to make war against me once more. Nothing pleases me better than that I should be true to my nature and they to theirs.

3 As for yourself, I hope I shall find you at Rome so that I can avail myself as usual of your advice and resources in all things. Let me add that I find your son-in-law Dolabella the most delightful of company. I shall owe him the more on this account—he will not be able to do otherwise; his kindness of heart, his good feeling, and his good will towards me guarantee it.

186 (IX. 17)

Formiae, 27 March 49

CICERO TO ATTICUS

1 I am expecting Trebatius on the 27th, the date of this letter. In the light of his report and Matius' letter I shall go over in my mind how I am to conduct the interview. It is a wretched time. I don't doubt that he will press me to come to Rome, seeing that he has given orders for notices to be put up at Formiae and elsewhere that he wants a full meeting of the Senate on the Kalends. So I must say no. But why anticipate? I shall send you a full account straight away. In the light of what he says I shall decide whether it is best for me to go to Arpinum or somewhere else. I want to give my boy his white
2 gown; there, I think. Pray consider what next, for my troubles have dulled my wits.

I should like to know whether you have had any word from Curius about Tiro. Tiro has written to me himself in a way

autem veniunt in⟨de, κινδυνώδη⟩ admodum nuntiant. sane in magnis curis etiam haec me sollicitat; in hac enim fortuna perutilis eius et opera et fidelitas esset.

187 (IX. 18)

Scr. in Formiano v Kal. Apr. an. 49

⟨CICERO ATTICO SAL.⟩

1 Vtrumque ex tuo consilio; nam et oratio fuit ea nostra ut bene potius ille de nobis existimaret quam gratias ageret, et in eo mansimus, ne ad urbem. illa fefellerunt, facilem quod putaramus; nihil vidi minus. damnari se nostro iudicio, tardiores fore reliquos, si nos non veniremus, dicere. ego dissimilem illorum esse causam. cum multa, 'veni igitur et age de pace.' 'meone' inquam 'arbitratu?' 'an tibi' inquit 'ego praescribam?' 'sic' inquam 'agam, senatui non placere in Hispanias iri nec exercitus in Graeciam transportari, multaque' inquam 'de Gnaeo deplorabo'. tum ille, 'ego vero ista dici nolo.' 'ita putabam' inquam, 'sed ego eo nolo adesse quod aut sic mihi dicendum est aut non veniendum, multaque quae nullo modo possem silere si adessem.' summa fuit ut ille, quasi exitum quaerens, ut deliberarem. non fuit negandum. ita discessimus. credo igitur hunc me non amare. at ego me amavi, quod mihi iam pridem usu non venit.

---

5 inde, κινδυνώδη admodum *scripsi, ducibus Ernesti* (*qui* inde, κινδυνώδη; inde κινδυνωδῶς *iam Bosius*) *et Lambino* (*qui* inania adm-: inania *iam Malaespina*): inni admodo Z^l: in id modo bZ^b: ni ad(?)modo *O*: ni (mihi *s*) id modo Δ: inanio *RF Ant.* 6 in ς: eo Ω sollicitat *Lambinus*: -ant Ω

Ep. 187] *novam ep.* (*inscr. om.*) *faciunt ms*: *uno tenore* Ω 1, 4 vidi minus Δ: vidimus *O*(?)*R* 5 reliquos *Victorius*: belli quos Ω si nos *F*: sinus *OR*: si in his Δ veniremus *Faërnus*: venerimus Ω 10 de Gnaeo (Cn.) *Victorius*: digne eo Ω 12 aut non veniendum *post* adessem δ 13 possem ς: -sim Ω 15 me amavi *Victorius*: meam aut *M*: mea aut *R*: me amabo δ

that makes me nervous about his condition, and people who come from over there say it is quite dangerous. Even among all my weighty anxieties this one really disturbs me. In my present plight his services and loyalty would be most useful.

187 (IX. 18)

Formiae, 28 March 49

CICERO TO ATTICUS

1 In both particulars I followed your advice. My language was such as to earn his respect rather than his thanks and I stood firm against going to Rome. But we were wrong in thinking him accommodating; I have never found anybody less so. He said I was passing judgement against him, that the rest would be slower to come if I did not. I replied that their position was different. After a long discussion: 'Come along then and work for peace.' 'At my own discretion?' I asked. 'Naturally' he answered. 'Who am I to lay down rules for you?' 'Well' I said, 'I shall take the line that the Senate does not approve of an expedition to Spain or of the transport of armies into Greece, and' I added 'I shall have much to say in commiseration of Pompey.' At that he protested that this was not the sort of thing he wanted said. 'So I supposed' I rejoined, 'but that is just why I don't want to be present. Either I must speak in that strain or stay away—and much besides which I could not possibly suppress if I were there.' The upshot was that he asked me to think the matter over, as though seeking a way to end the talk. I could not refuse. On that note we parted. So I imagine Caesar is not pleased with me. But I was pleased with myself, an experience I have not had for quite a long time.

2 Reliqua, o di! qui comitatus, quae, ut tu soles dicere, νέκυια! in qua erat ἥρως Celer. o rem perditam! o copias desperatas! quid quod Servi filius, quod Titini in iis castris fuerunt quibus Pompeius circumsederetur? sex legiones; multum vigilat, audet. nullum video finem mali. nunc certe promenda tibi sunt consilia. hoc fuerat extremum.

3 Illa tamen κατακλεὶς illius est odiosa, quam paene praeterii, si sibi consiliis nostris uti non liceret, usurum quorum posset ad omniaque esse descensurum. vidisti igitur virum, ut scripseras? ingemuisti certe. 'cedo reliqua.' quid? continuo ipse in †Pelanum†, ego Arpinum; inde exspecto equidem λαλαγεῦσαν illam tuam. 'tu malim' inquies 'actum ne agas; etiam illum ipsum quem sequimur multa fefellerunt.'

4 Sed ego tuas litteras exspecto. nihil est enim ut antea 'videamus hoc quorsum evadat'. extremum fuit de congressu nostro; quo quidem non dubito quin istum offenderim. eo maturius agendum est. amabo te, epistulam, et πολιτικήν. valde tuas litteras nunc exspecto.

188 (VIII. 9)

Scr. Formiis Arpinum iter faciens iv aut iii Kal. Apr. an. 49

CICERO ATTICO SAL.

1 Epistulam meam quod pervulgatam scribis esse non fero moleste, quin etiam ipse multis dedi describendam; ea enim

2, 2 ἥρως Celer *Lehmann*: eros celer Z^1: ero sceler *OR* (-rum): (a)ero sceleri Δ 3 quid . . . in iis *ita* Z^1: quid ser. servi(i) filius quot ut in his (*sed* ser. *non habet M*; quotti in iis *R*) *R*Δ: servius servii *et* in iis (*reliqua incerta*) *O* 4 sex legiones ς: sed legionis Ω **3,** 1 κατακλεὶς *Z*: KATAKIC *RMm* 3 *ita distinxi*: *at vulgo* 'vidisti . . . scripseras? ingemuisti?' certe. ut δ: aut *M*: aut ut *OP*: aut ūt *R* 5 pelanum (pell- *R*) Ω: pedanum ς: Pedi Norbanum *Schmidt* ego *R*δ: *om. OM* arpinum *Rm*: -no *OM*: in arpinum *bds* *post* inde *aposiopesin voluit Lehmann* equidem *Lambinus*: q- Ω 6 λαλαγεῦσαν *Bosius*: *varia, velut* ΛΛΛΤΕΛCAN Ω malim *Boot*: malem *R*: mallem *O*δ: malum *M*

2 For the rest, gods! What an *entourage*, what an Underworld, to use your favourite expression! Celer was there, as one of the Heroes. What an unprincipled adventure! What a gang of desperadoes! And then to think that Servius' son and Titinius' were in the army beleaguering Pompey! Six legions! He is alert and audacious. I see no end to the mischief. Now is the time for you to produce your advice. This was to have been the end.

3 But I nearly forgot to mention Caesar's disagreeable Parthian shot. If, he said, he could not avail himself of my counsels, he would take those he could get and stop at nothing. Well, have you 'seen the great man'? At any rate you must have groaned as you read. You ask for the rest of the story. Why, he left straight away for *, and I am leaving for Arpinum. From there I await that 'harbinger' of yours. You will say 'Can't you let bygones be bygones? Even our leader's forecasts were not always correct'.

4 But I am waiting to hear from you. It is no longer possible to say now, as formerly, 'see how this turns out'. Our meeting was to be the end. I don't doubt that it has put him out of humour with me. All the more reason for rapid action. Do let me have a letter, a political letter. I am eagerly waiting to hear from you now.

188 (VIII. 9)

Between Formiae and Arpinum, 29 or 30 March 49

CICERO TO ATTICUS

1 You write that my letter has been broadcast. I am not sorry to hear it, indeed I have myself let a number of people take

et acciderunt iam et impendent ut testatum esse velim de pace quid senserim. cum autem ad eam hortarer eum praesertim hominem, non videbar ullo modo facilius moturus quam si id quod eum hortarer convenire eius sapientiae dicerem. eam si admirabilem dixi cum eum ad salutem patriae hortabar, non sum veritus ne viderer adsentari, cui tali in re libenter me ad pedes abiecissem. qua autem est 'aliquid impertias temporis', non est de pace sed de me ipso et de meo officio ut aliquid cogitet. nam quod testificor me expertem belli fuisse, etsi id re perspectum est, tamen eo scripsi quo in suadendo plus auctoritatis haberem; eodemque pertinet quod causam eius probo.

2 Sed quid haec nunc? utinam aliquid profectum esset! ne ego istas litteras in contione recitari velim, si quidem ille ipse ad eundem scribens in publico proposuit epistulam illam in qua est 'pro tuis rebus gestis amplissimis' (amplioribusne quam suis, quam Africani? ita tempus ferebat), si quidem etiam vos duo tales ad quintum miliarium, quo nunc ipsum unde se recipienti, quid agenti, quid acturo? quanto autem ferocius ille causae suae confidet, cum vos, cum vestri similis non modo frequentis sed laeto vultu gratulantis viderit! 'num igitur peccamus?' minime vos quidem; sed tamen signa conturbantur quibus voluntas a simulatione distingui posset. quae vero senatus consulta video? sed apertius quam proposueram.

3 Ego Arpini volo esse prid. Kal., deinde circum villulas nostras errare, quas visurum me postea desperavi.

Ep. 188] **1**, 4 cum *Manutius*: quo Σδ: quem (*om.* eum) *M*: quoniam *Baiter* 8 cui] qui *M* 12 etsi (et si) Σ: si Δ **2**, 1 ne Σλ: nec Δ 4 -ne *EM*: -ve *R*δ 6 quo *Lambinus*: quod *C*λ: quod ad Ω: quid *Victorius*, *Boot* 7 unde] de *Boot* 12 posset Ω: potest *bs*: possit *Mueller* **3**, 1 kal. (k.) *ER*: *om.* *O*Δ

copies. In view of what has already happened and of what is coming I want to have my sentiments about peace upon record. In urging this particular person in its favour I saw no readier means of influencing his mind than by representing that the course I was urging upon him befitted his wisdom. If I called the latter 'admirable', in urging him to the salvation of our country, I had no fear of appearing to flatter; in such a cause I would gladly have thrown myself at his feet. In the passage where I ask him to 'spare some time' I was not referring to peace but requesting him to give some thought to myself and my obligations. As for my statement that I had taken no part in the war, the truth of it is sufficiently evident; but my object in so writing was to lend weight to my persuasions, and similarly with my approval of his cause.

2 But what does all this matter now? I wish enough that something had been achieved. I should be only too glad to have that letter read out at a public meeting, considering that Pompey himself, writing to the same personage, posted up in public a letter in which he used the phrase 'in recognition of your most brilliant achievements' (more brilliant than his own or Africanus'? The occasion required such language); considering also that men like you two are going to meet him five miles out of town, when he is at this very moment on his way from and to we all know where, doing and about to do we all know what. Don't you think he will be twice as bold and confident in his cause when he sees you and people like you in force, and what is more, smiling congratulations? Well, are you wrong? Not at all. Still all this blurs the signs that might distinguish sincerity from pretence. And the Senate's decrees in prospect! But I am writing more frankly than I intended.

3 I want to be at Arpinum on the 31st, and then to make a round of my little properties, which I never expect to see again.

189 (IX. 19)

Scr. Arpini Kal. vel iv Non. Apr. an. 49

CICERO ATTICO SAL.

1 Ego meo Ciceroni, quoniam Roma caremus, Arpini potissimum togam puram dedi, idque municipibus nostris fuit gratum. etsi omnis et illos et qua iter feci maestos adflictosque vidi; tam tristis et tam atrox est ἀναθεώρησις huius ingentis mali. dilectus habentur, in hiberna deducuntur. ea quae etiam cum a bonis viris, cum iusto in bello, cum modeste fiunt, tamen ipsa per se molesta sunt, quam censes acerba nunc esse, cum a perditis in civili nefario bello petulantissime fiant? cave autem putes quemquam hominem in Italia turpem esse qui hinc absit. vidi ipse Formiis universos neque mehercule [numquam] homines putavi; et noram omnis, sed numquam uno loco videram.

2 Pergamus igitur quo placet et nostra omnia relinquamus. proficiscamur ad eum cui gratior noster adventus erit quam si una fu⟨g⟩issemus. tum enim eramus in maxima spe, nunc ego quidem in nulla; nec praeter me quisquam Italia cessit nisi qui hunc inimicum sibi putaret. nec mehercule hoc facio rei publicae causa, quam funditus deletam puto, sed ne quis me putet ingratum in eum qui me levavit iis incommodis quibus idem adfecerat, et simul quod ea quae fiunt aut quae certe futura sunt videre non possum. etiam equidem senatus consulta facta quaedam iam puto, utinam in Vulcati sententiam! sed quid refert? est enim una sententia omnium. sed erit immitissimus Servius, qui filium misit ad effligendum Cn.

Ep. 189] *novam ep. faciunt Oms*: *cum superiore cohaeret im RMbd* **1**, 11 numquam *seclusi*: unq- *P* putavi *P*: -ari Ω **2**, 3 fugissemus *Gronovius*: fui- Ω 4 Italia cessit *Hervagius*: -am gessit Ω 5 facio δ: facto Ω 7 in *M corr.*: quin *OMms* (*de bd silet Sjögren*): erga *P*: *om. R* qui *om. M* 8 ea que fiunt aut *P*: (a)eque (aque *R*) fiunt. itaque Ω 9 possum *s*: -unt Ωλ: potero *P* 11 quid refert? est enim *Hervagius*: quid refert etenim *P*: qui referret enim Ω

189 (IX. 19)

Arpinum, 1 or 2 April 49

CICERO TO ATTICUS

1 Rome being impossible, I have given my son the white gown at Arpinum as the next best place, to the gratification of my fellow-townsmen. Not but what I find everyone both at Arpinum and on the road gloomy and downcast; so sad and terrible are the thoughts inspired by this vast mischief. Levies are in progress and men are led off into winter quarters. You can imagine how sorely such proceedings are felt. They are unpleasant enough in themselves, even when carried out with moderation by honest men in legitimate warfare; now they are carried out by ruffians in a wicked civil war with the utmost brutality. You may be sure that every disreputable character in Italy is with Caesar. I saw the whole crew at Formiae and upon my word I thought them more like beasts than men; and I knew them all, but I had never seen them all in one place.

2 So let me go the chosen way and leave all that is mine, let me set out to join one who will welcome my arrival more than if I had fled along with him. For then our hopes ran high, whereas now I for one have no hope at all; and nobody but I has left Italy who did not look upon Caesar as his personal enemy. Believe me I am not doing this for the sake of the Republic, which in my view has foundered utterly, but so that nobody shall think me ungrateful towards a man who brought me out of the troubles into which he himself had plunged me, and also because I can't bear to witness what is happening or what is certainly going to happen. I suppose that some senatorial decrees have actually been passed by now, I only hope on Vulcatius' motion. But what matter? They are all of one mind. But Servius will be implacable, after sending his son to crush

Pompeium aut certe capiendum cum Pontio Titiniano. etsi hic quidem timoris causa, ille vero—sed stomachari desinamus et aliquando sentiamus nihil nobis nisi, id quod minime vellem, spiritum reliquum esse.

3 Nos, quoniam superum mare obsidetur, infero navigabimus et, si Puteolis erit difficile, Crotonem petemus aut Thurios et boni cives amantes patriae mare infestum habebimus. aliam rationem huius belli gerendi nullam video. in Aegyptum nos abdemus. exercitu pares esse non possumus. pacis fides nulla est. sed haec satis deplorata sunt.

4 Tu velim litteras Cephalioni des de omnibus rebus actis, denique etiam de sermonibus hominum, nisi plane obmutuerunt. ego tuis consiliis usus sum maximeque quod et gravitatem in congressu nostro tenui quam debui et ut ad urbem non accederem perseveravi. quod superest, scribe, quaeso, quam accuratissime (iam enim extrema sunt) quid placeat, quid censeas; etsi iam nulla dubitatio est. tamen si quid vel potius quicquid veniet in mentem scribas velim.

190 (X. 1)

Scr. in Laterio Quinti fratris iii Non. Apr. an. 49 (§ 1)

CICERO ATTICO SAL.

1 III Non., cum in Laterium fratis venissem, accepi litteras et paulum lectis respiravi, quod post has ruinas mihi non acciderat; per enim magni aestimo tibi firmitudinem animi nostri et factum nostrum probari. Sexto etiam nostro quod

---

15 sentiamus nihil nobis *Gronovius*: sententiam ut ni(c)hil novi (non *R*) Ωλ minime *Gronovius*: -mum Ω **3**, 2 petemus *s*: petimus Ω 4 huius . . . nullam *R*δ: non huius . . . ullam *M*: huius . . . ullam *O* 5 abdemus ς: abdimus Ω exercitu *Rm*: -tum *OM*: in exercitu *bds* **4**, 3 et *om. M* 4 ut ad urbem non *RF Ant. m*: ad urbem ut non *bds*: ad urbem non *M*: ad urbem *O* 5 scribe *ms*: -bi Ω

Ep. 190] **1**, 1 litteras tuas *Wesenberg* 2 lectis $Z^b c$: *om.* Ω 4 etiam *scripsi*: enim Ω: autem *Watt, per litteras*

or at any rate capture Cn. Pompeius along with Pontius Titinianus! *He* acted out of fear to be sure, but Servius—however, no more spleen. It is time to face the truth, that nothing is left us except the breath in our bodies, and I only wish I had not been left that much.

3 Since the Adriatic is blocked we shall sail by the Western Sea, and if Puteoli proves difficult we shall make for Croton or Thurii and as loyal, patriotic citizens take to buccaneering. I see no other way of conducting this war. We shall bury ourselves in Egypt. On land we cannot hold our own. There is no genuine prospect of peace. But I have lamented over it all long enough.

4 Please give Cephalio a letter about all proceedings, even down to what people are saying, unless they have lost their tongues. I have followed your advice, especially in maintaining a fitting dignity during our interview and in holding out against going Romewards. For the rest, pray write with all care (we have now reached the final stage) what course you favour, what you advise—not that there is now any doubt. Still I should like you to write anything, or rather everything, that occurs to you.

190 (X. 1)

Laterium, 3 April 49

CICERO TO ATTICUS

1 I received your letter on the 3rd after I had arrived at my brother's place at Laterium and breathed a little more easily after reading it, for the first time since this collapse set in. I attach very great importance to your approval of my resolution and conduct. And when you tell me that our friend Sextus

scribis probari, ita laetor ut me quasi patris eius, cui semper uni plurimum tribui, iudicio comprobari putem; qui mihi, quod saepe soleo recordari, dixit olim Nonis illis ille Decembribus, cum ego 'Sexte, quidnam ergo?',

'μὴ μάν' inquit ille 'ἀσπουδί γε καὶ ἀκλειῶς,
ἀλλὰ μέγα ῥέξας τι καὶ ἐσσομένοισι πυθέσθαι.'

eius igitur mihi vivit auctoritas, et simillimus eius filius eodem est apud me pondere quo fuit ille; quem salvere velim iubeas plurimum.

2 Tu tuum consilium etsi non in longinquum tempus differs (iam enim illum emptum pacificatorem perorasse puto, iam actum aliquid esse in consessu senatorum; ⟨senatum⟩ enim non puto), tamen suspensum meum detines, sed eo minus quod non dubito quid nobis agendum putes; qui enim Flavio legionem et Siciliam dari scribas et id iam fieri, quae tu scelera partim parari iam et cogitari, partim ex tempore futura censes? ego vero Solonis, popularis tui (ut puto, ⟨iam⟩ etiam mei), legem neglegam, qui capite sanxit si qui in seditione non alterius utrius partis fuisset, ⟨et⟩ nisi si tu aliter censes, et hinc abero et illim. sed alterum mihi est certius, nec praeripiam tamen; exspectabo tuum consilium et eas litteras, nisi alias iam dedisti, quas scripsi ut Cephalioni dares.

3 Quod scribis, non quo alicunde audieris, sed te ipsum putare me attractum iri si de pace agatur, mihi omnino non

---

6 iudicio *Ms*: -io me *ORbdmc* 7 ille *om. P* 9 inquit *Victorius*: quid Ω ἀκλειῶς ἀπολοίμην ς 11 simil(l)imus δ: -ibus Ω **2,** 3 senatum *add. Malaespina* (*sed post* puto), *Graevius* enim non *Graevius*: non enim *OPFAnt.* ΔZ^b (non . . . putes *om. R*) 4 meum ΔZ^b: *om. OP*: me ς: meum animum *Wesenberg*: me animo *Sedgwick* de tenes Z^b, *unde* me inde tenes *Bosius* 5 qui *Wesenberg*: quid Ω Flavio] Asinio *Corradus* 8 ut puto, iam etiam *scripsi*: et (ς), ut puto, iam (iam iam *Gronovius*) *Orelli* 9 negligam *s*: nec legam Ω 10 et *add. Boot* si *om. P*δ 11 illim (-inc) *Orelli*: filii Ω

approves too, I am delighted—I feel as though I stood approved in the judgement of his father, for whom I always had the very highest respect. I often remember how long ago on that famous Nones of December I asked him 'Well, Sextus, what now?', and he replied

> 'No sluggard's fate, ingloriously to die,
> But daring that which men to be shall learn.'

So his influence lives on for me, and his son, who resembles him so much, carries the same weight with me as he did. Please give him my best regards.

2 Although you defer your advice only for a short time (for I suppose that purchased peacemaker has finished his speech by now and something has already been done in the convention of Senators—I don't call it a Senate), still you keep my plans in suspense—the less so, however, because I have no doubt as to what you think I ought to do. When you write that Sicily and a legion are being given to Flavius and that this is actually happening, what crimes do you suppose are either already in preparation and intention or only needing an occasion to be forthcoming? For my part I propose to ignore the law of your compatriot Solon (mine too soon, I imagine), who made it a capital offence to remain neutral in a strife of parties, and unless you think otherwise I shall stay away from either camp. But my resolution is more definite as regards *this* camp—however, I won't anticipate. I shall await your advice and the letter which I asked you to give Cephalio, unless you have already sent another.

3 You say, not as something that has come to your ears but as your own opinion, that if there are peace negotiations I shall

venit in mentem quae possit actio esse de pace, cum illi certissimum sit, si possit, exspoliare exercitu et provincia Pompeium; nisi forte iste nummarius ei potest persuadere ut, dum oratores eant et redeant, quiescat. nihil video quod sperem aut quod iam putem fieri posse. sed tamen hominis hoc ipsum probi est? est magnum et τῶν πολιτικωτάτων σκεμμάτων, veniendumne sit in consilium tyranni si is aliqua de re bona deliberaturus sit. qua re si quid eius modi evenerit ut arcessamur (quod equidem non puto; quid enim essem de pace dicturus dixi, ipse valde repudiavit), sed tamen si quid acciderit, quid censeas mihi faciendum utique scribito. nihil enim mihi adhuc accidit quod maioris consili esset.

Trebati, boni viri et civis, verbis te gaudeo delectatum, tuaque ista crebra ἐκφώνησις 'ὑπέρευ' me sola adhuc delectavit. litteras tuas vehementer exspecto; quas quidem credo iam datas esse.

191 (x. 1*a*)

Scr. in Laterio Quinti fratris prid. Non. Apr. an. 49

⟨CICERO ATTICO SAL.⟩

Tu cum Sexto servasti gravitatem eandem quam mihi praecipis. Celer tuus disertus magis est quam sapiens. de iuvenibus quae ex Tullia audisti vera sunt. †macum† istuc quod scribis non mihi videtur tam re esse triste quam verbo.

3, 4 exercitu et provincia *s*: -um et -iam Ω 5 nummarius *Manutius*: summ- Ω$Z^{(l)}$ ei *s*: et Ω 6 eant et redeant *Vrsinus*: cantent red- (rid- Δ) Ω: eant red- *Beroaldus* 7 sed . . . probi est *pro interrog. habui* 8 est magnum et τῶν *scripsi*: et (*om.* Δ) m- sit ωH (*vel* ωN) Ω: m- est et τῶν *Orelli* 9 σκεμμάτων *C*: σκέμματα *vel sim.* *R*Δ: σκέμμα *Tyrrell* 11 puto *Koch*: curo Ω: credo *Boot* 16 tuaque *s*: tuque (tu quae) Ω ὑπέρευ *Corradus*: ὑπέρει $Z^{(l)}$: IΠEPEI *M*: ΠEPEI *R*: τέρπει *O*δ delectavit *s*: -abit Ω

Ep. 191] *novam ep. constituendam esse viderunt Tyrrell–Purser, constituit Moricca: cum superiore in codd. cohaeret* 3 macum *R*Z^b (*de O non liquet*): maconi *Mbd*: M. antoni *ms*: Mucianum *Reid* istuc *OR*: -ud Δ 4 re Δ: in re *OR*

be drawn in. I cannot myself at all imagine how there *can* be any such negotiations, since Caesar is fully determined to deprive Pompey of his army and province if he is able—or can that hireling persuade him to keep quiet while envoys pass to and fro? I can see no ray of hope, no further conceivable chance. But in any case is the job itself one for a man of honour? It is a great question and an eminently political one whether it be right to enter a despot's council if he is going to deliberate something in the public interest. Therefore in case I receive some sort of summons (which *I* don't believe—I told him what I would have to say about peace, and he himself flatly rejected it)—however, in case anything of the sort happens, do be sure and tell me what you think I ought to do. Nothing has happened to me so far which needed more careful consideration.

I am glad Trebatius' language pleased you. He is a good man and a good citizen. Your oft repeated exclamation 'bravissimo' has pleased me like nothing else so far. I am eagerly awaiting a letter from you. I expect it is already dispatched.

191 (x. 1*a*)

Laterium, 4 April 49

CICERO TO ATTICUS

1 You and Sextus have preserved your dignity as you recommend me to do. Your relation Celer is more eloquent than wise. What Tullia has told you about the young men is true. I think the * you write of sounds sadder than it really is. This 'wander-

haec est ἄλη in qua nunc sumus mortis instar. aut enim mihi libere inter malos πολιτευτέον fuit aut vel periculose cum bonis. aut nos temeritatem bonorum sequamur aut audaciam improborum insectemur. utrumque periculosum est, at hoc quod agimus [nec] turpe nec tamen tutum.

Istum qui filium Brundisium [de pace] misit de pace (idem sentio quod tu, simulationem esse apertam, parari autem acerrime bellum), me legatum iri non arbitror, cuius adhuc, ut optavi, mentio facta nulla sit. eo minus habeo necesse scribere aut etiam cogitare quid sim facturus, si acciderit ut leger.

192 (x. 2)

Scr. in Laterio vel Arcano Quinti fratris Non. aut postridie Non. Apr. an. 49

CICERO ATTICO SAL.

1 Ego cum accepissem tuas litteras Non. Apr. quas Cephalio
attulerat essemque Minturnis postridie mansurus et inde
protinus, sustinui me in Arcano fratris, ut, dum aliquid cer-
tius adferretur, occultiore in loco essemus agerenturque nihilo
minus quae sine nobis agi possent. λαλαγεῦσα iam adest
2 et animus ardet, neque stat quicquam, quo et qua. sed haec
nostra erit cura et peritorum. tu tamen quod poteris, ut adhuc

---

7 sequamur *P*δ: sequimur Ωλ*c* 9 nec *del. Baiter*: et *Manutius* 10 de pace *secl. Boot, altero illo* de pace *in parenthesi posito*: misit de pace (de pace *e.q.s.*) *Corradus*: de pace misit (de pace *e.q.s.*) *vulgo* 12 acerrime bellum *ORC*: b- a- Δ me legatum iri *s*: eleg- iri Ω: legatum iri, non me *Wesenberg* 15 leger *Corradus*: legerer Ωλ

Ep. 192] 1, 2 et inde *ORM*: *om. E*δ: ut inde *Wesenberg* 5 possent *scripsi*: -sint Σ*Mbd*: -sunt *ms* λαλαγεῦσα *Bosius*: ΜΑΛΤΕΥϹΑ *vel sim.* Ω: μάντευμα, *dein* ἀλλὰ τελοῦσα *in cod. vet. legere sibi visus est Cratander* 6 stat *Purser*: est Ω

ing' in which I now find myself is as bad as death. I ought to have played a public part, either speaking my mind among the rascals or taking my risks if need were with the honest men. Let me either follow the honest men in their imprudence or denounce the insolence of the villains. There is danger either way, but my present line makes for dishonour without security.

I think the gentleman who sent his son to Brundisium will be the peace envoy (I see eye to eye with you, that it's a transparent sham and that preparations for war are in full swing), not I, seeing that, as I hoped, my name has not so far been mentioned in this connexion. So I feel the less bound to write or even think about what I shall do if by any chance I am commissioned.

192 (x. 2)

Laterium or Arcanum, 5 or 6 April 49

CICERO TO ATTICUS

1 After receiving your letter by Cephalio on 5 April, though I had intended to stay the next night at Minturnae and proceed thence directly, I stopped at Arcanum, my brother's place, so as to be in a more secluded spot pending more definite news, while such preparations as can proceed in my absence go forward none the less. Your 'harbinger' is nearly here now, and I am all impatience, though destination and
2 route have yet to be decided. But that will be my concern and that of the experts. All the same you must help me with

fecisti, nos consiliis iuvabis. res sunt inexplicabiles. fortunae sunt committenda omnia. sine spe conamur ulla. melius si quid acciderit, mirabimur. Dionysium nollem ad me profectum; de quo ad me Tullia mea scripsit. sed et tempus alienum est, et homini non amico nostra incommoda, tanta praesertim, spectaculo esse nolim; cui te meo nomine inimicum esse nolo.

193 (x. 3)

Scr. in Arcano vii Id. Apr. an. 49

CICERO ATTICO SAL.

Cum quod scriberem plane nihil haberem, haec autem reliqua essent quae scire cuperem, profectusne esset, quo in statu urbem reliquisset, in ipsa Italia quem cuique regioni aut negotio praefecisset, ecqui essent ad Pompeium et ad consules ex senatus consulto de pace legati, cum igitur haec scire ⟨cupere⟩m dedita opera has ad te litteras misi. feceris igitur commode mihique gratum si me de his rebus et si quid erit aliud quod scire opus sit feceris certiorem. ego in Arcano opperior dum ista cognosco. a. d. vii Id.

194 (x. 3 *a*)

Scr. in Arcano vii Id. Apr. an. 49 (§ 1)

⟨CICERO ATTICO SAL.⟩

1 Alteram tibi eodem die hanc epistulam dictavi et pridie dederam mea manu longiorem. visum te aiunt in Regia, nec

---

2, 4 melius si *ER*δ: melius *OM*: si m- λ 5 nollem *Wesenberg*: nolim Ω 8 nolim *Ernesti*: nolem *EP*: nollem *OR*Δ nolo *O*Δ: volo *ER*

Ep. 193] 1 quod *Malaespina*: quid Ω 5 cum *O*(?)*RM*: ut *E*δ scire cuperem *Lambinus*: scirem *ER*δ: -re *O*(?)*M*

Ep. 194] *novam ep. hic fecit Brunus* (*M*^{4}), *post* certiorem (*ep.* 193, *v.* 8) *Corradus*, *post* cognosco (*ibid. v.* 9) *Schütz*: *cum superiore in codd. cohaeret, spatio tamen ante* alteram *relicto in Mm*

your advice as you have done hitherto, so far as you can. There is no working it all out. Everything has to be committed to fortune. I make the venture quite without hope. Any better turn will surprise me. I am sorry Dionysius has set out to visit me. Tullia wrote to me about it, but the time is inconvenient and I would rather not parade our embarrassments, serious as they are, before other than friendly eyes. I have no wish for you to be his enemy on my account.

193 (x. 3)

Arcanum, 7 April 49

CICERO TO ATTICUS

I have really nothing to write, but there are a few things I should still like to know, namely whether he has set out, in what state he has left Rome, in Italy too whom he has put in charge of the various districts and jobs, whether any peace envoys to Pompey and the Consuls have been appointed under the Senate's decree. Anxious to learn these points I am sending this letter to you by special messenger. So I shall be grateful if you will kindly inform me about them and anything else I ought to know. I am waiting at Arcanum until I get your news. 7 April.

194 (x. 3*a*)

Arcanum, 7 April 49

CICERO TO ATTICUS

1 I am dictating a second letter to you this same day, having yesterday dispatched a longer one in my own hand. They say you have been seen in the Palace. I don't criticize, not having

reprehendo, quippe cum ipse istam reprehensionem non fugerim. sed exspecto tuas litteras, neque iam sane video quid exspectem, sed tamen, etiam si nihil erit, id ipsum ad me velim scribas.

2 Caesar mihi ignoscit per litteras quod non venerim, seseque in optimam partem id accipere dicit; facile patior. quod scribit secum Titinium et Servium questos esse quia non idem sibi quod mihi remisisset, homines ridiculos! qui cum filios misissent ad Cn. Pompeium circumsedendum, ipsi in senatum venire dubitarent. sed tamen exemplum misi ad te Caesaris litterarum.

195 (x. 4)

Scr. in Cumano xvii Kal. Mai. an. 49 (§ 7)

CICERO ATTICO SAL.

1 Multas a te accepi epistulas eodem die, omnis diligenter scriptas, eam vero quae voluminis instar erat saepe legendam, sicuti facio. in qua non frustra laborem suscepisti, mihi quidem pergratum fecisti. qua re ut id, quoad licebit, id est quoad scies ubi simus, quam saepissime facias te vehementer rogo.

Ac deplorandi quidem, quod cottidie facimus, sit iam nobis aut finis omnino, si potest, aut moderatio quaedam, quod profecto potest. non enim iam quam dignitatem, quos honores, quem vitae statum amiserim cogito, sed quid consecutus sim, quid praestiterim, qua in laude vixerim, his denique in malis quid intersit inter me et istos quos propter omnia amisimus. hi sunt qui, nisi me civitate expulissent,

---

1, 3 fugerim ς: -rem Ω 5 si *P*δ: et *OM*: *om. R* **2,** 3 Titinium *Koch*: tullium (tuli- *M*) Ω: Tullum *Corradus* 6 dubitarint *Wesenberg*

Ep. 195] **1,** 7 ac *Ernesti*: at *E*OΔ: id *R*: et *P* 9 iam $Z^{(b)}$: tam ΩZ^{β}: *om.* δ

escaped similar criticism myself. But I am waiting to hear from you, though I don't quite see now *what* I am waiting to hear; but all the same, even if you have nothing to tell me, please write and say so.

2 Caesar writes in forgiveness of my non-attendance and says he is not in the least offended on that account. No harm in that. He writes that Titinius and Servius have grumbled to him for not making them the same concession he has made me. Absurd creatures! After sending their sons to lay siege to Cn. Pompeius they boggle at attending the Senate themselves! Anyway I am sending you a copy of Caesar's letter.

195 (x. 4)

Cumae, 14 April 49

CICERO TO ATTICUS

1 I received a number of letters from you on the same day, all elaborate and one of volume size, to be read and re-read, as I do. You have not taken such pains over it for nothing. I am really grateful. And so I do entreat you to do this as often as you can for as long as you can, i.e. as long as you know my whereabouts.

Of my daily lamentations let there be an end for good and all if that is possible, or at least some measure of restraint, which is certainly possible. I no longer think of the rank, honours, and position in life that I have lost, but of what I have attained and what I have contributed, the high repute in which I have lived, and the distance which in these evil days separates me from those on whose account we have lost everything; I mean the men who thought that only by driving me

obtinere se non putaverunt posse licentiam cupiditatum
suarum; quorum societatis et sceleratae consensionis fides
2 quo eruperit vides. alter ardet furore et scelere nec remittit
aliquid sed in dies ingravescit; modo Italia expulit, nunc alia
ex parte persequi, ex alia provincia exspoliare conatur nec
iam recusat sed quodam modo postulat ut, quem ad modum
3 est, sic etiam appelletur tyrannus. alter, is qui nos sibi quon-
dam ad pedes stratos ne sublevabat quidem, qui se nihil
contra huius voluntatem facere posse, elapsus e soceri mani-
bus ac ferro bellum terra et mari comparat, non iniustum ille
quidem sed cum pium tum etiam necessarium, suis tamen
civibus exitiabile nisi vicerit, calamitosum etiam si vicerit.

4 Horum ego summorum imperatorum non modo res gestas non antepono meis sed ne fortunam quidem ipsam; qua illi florentissima, nos duriore conflictati videmur. quis enim potest aut deserta per se patria aut oppressa beatus esse? et si, ut nos a te admonemur, recte in illis libris diximus nihil esse bonum nisi quod honestum, nihil malum nisi quod turpe sit, certe uterque istorum est miserrimus, quorum utrique semper patriae salus et dignitas posterior sua dominatione et domesticis commodis fuit.

5 Praeclara igitur ⟨con⟩scientia sustentor, cum cogito me de re publica aut meruisse optime cum potuerim aut certe numquam nisi pie cogitasse, eaque ipsa tempestate eversam esse rem publicam quam ego XIIII annis ante prospexerim. hac igitur conscientia comite proficiscar, magno equidem cum dolore,

---

14 putaverunt (potue- *R*) posse Σ*m*: po- put- Δ **2**, 2 expulit generum *Kayser* **3**, 2 quidem qui se ς: qui (que *M*) se quidem Ω 4 ille] illud *Wesenberg* **5**, 1 conscientia *P*: sc- Σδ: sententia *M* 3 nisi pie *Bosius*: n- die Σ (diem *R*) Z^b: insidi(a)e Δ

out of the community could they gain free scope for their cupidities and whose plighted alliance and confederacy in
2 crime has ended in the results you see. One of the two is aflame with frenzy and wickedness. Far from any abatement the fit grows more violent every day. No sooner has he expelled his rival from Italy than he sets about pursuing him from one direction and stripping him of his province from another. He no longer objects, in a sense he demands, to be called what he
3 really is, a despot. The second, who once when I lay at his feet would not so much as ask me to rise, whose plea it was that he could do nothing against the other's wishes, has escaped from his father-in-law's hands and sword to prepare for war by land and sea; not it is true an unjust war, on the contrary a righteous and even necessary war, but one which will bring destruction on his fellow-countrymen if he loses and calamity even if he wins.

4 I do not rate the achievements of these great war-lords above my own, nor even their fortune, splendid though it appear, while mine looks hard and stormy. For what happiness is there for a deserter of his country on the one hand or an oppressor on the other? And if, as you remind me, I was right when I said in that book of mine that nothing is good but what is honourable and nothing bad but what is disgraceful, then assuredly they are both most unhappy, for both have always put personal power and private advantages before the safety and honour of their country.

5 So I have the comfort of an excellent conscience, reflecting that I gave the state good service while I was able, or at any rate that my thoughts were never other than loyal, and that this very storm which has overturned the state was foreseen by me fourteen years ago. So I shall go with this conscience to keep me company, though not without deep sorrow—

nec tam id propter me aut propter fratrem meum, quorum est iam acta aetas, quam propter pueros, quibus interdum videmur praestare etiam rem publicam debuisse. quorum quidem alter non tam ⟨quia filius quam⟩ quia maiore pietate est me mirabiliter excruciat, alter (o rem miseram! nihil enim mihi accidit in omni vita acerbius) indulgentia videlicet nostra depravatus eo progressus est quo non audeo dicere. et exspecto tuas litteras; scripsisti enim te scripturum esse plura cum ipsum vidisses.

6 Omne meum obsequium in illum fuit cum multa severitate, neque unum eius nec parvum sed multa ⟨et⟩ magna delicta compressi. patris autem lenitas amanda potius ab illo quam tam crudeliter neglegenda. nam litteras eius ad Caesarem missas ita graviter tulimus ut te quidem celaremus sed ipsius vide⟨re⟩mur vitam insuavem reddidisse. hoc vero eius iter simulatioque pietatis qualis fuerit non audeo dicere; tantum scio post Hirtium conventum arcessitum a Caesare, cum eo de meo animo a suis rationibus alienissimo et consilio relinquendi Italiam; et haec ipsa timide. sed nulla nostra culpa est, natura metuenda est. haec Curionem, haec Hortensi filium, non patrum culpa corrupit.

Iacet in maerore meus frater neque tam de sua vita quam de mea metuit. huic tu, huic tu malo adfer consolationes, si ullas potes; maxime quidem illam velim, ea quae ad nos delata sint aut falsa esse aut minora. quae si vera sint, quid futurum sit in hac vita et fuga nescio; nam si haberemus rem publicam,

---

6 tam *E*δ: tamen *ORM* 7 est *Lambinus*: ut *OMZ*^{l}: ut ut *Z*^{b}: *om. ER*δ: ut *ante* quorum *transp. Schmidt* 9 quia filius quam *add. Lambinus duce Malaespina* 10 excruciat δ: -ari Ω 13 et] sed *Malaespina* 14 plura *Orelli*: -rima Ω **6**, 2 et *P*: *om.* Ω 6 videremur *Madvig*: videmus Ω: -emur *Schütz* 8 eo de meo *Lambinus*: eodem eo Ω 14 huic tu huic tu *EOPMdm*: huic tu *Rbs* 17 vita et *ORF Ant.*: *om. E*Δ

not so much for myself or my brother, for we have had our time, but for our boys, who I sometimes feel had a right to expect from us a free constitution as part of their inheritance. For one of them I feel the most poignant distress, not so much because he is my son as because he is a better son. The other—it is a deplorable affair, the bitterest blow I have had to bear in all my life. Spoiled no doubt by our indulgence he has gone to I dare not say what lengths. And I await your letter; for you wrote that you would write more when you had seen the boy yourself.

6 My compliance towards him has always been seasoned with plenty of strictness and I have nipped many serious offences of his in the bud—not just the odd peccadillo. As for his father's mildness, it should have earned his affection rather than such callous disregard. We took so grave a view of his letter to Caesar that, while saying nothing to you, I think we made the boy's life pretty uncomfortable. But this journey of his and his pretence of filial duty is something I don't dare to characterize. So much I know, that after an interview with Hirtius he was summoned by Caesar, and spoke to him about my thorough hostility to his interests and my design of leaving Italy. Even this I write with hesitation. But it is no fault of ours, nature is the enemy. This, and not any fault on their father's part, was what ruined Curio and Hortensius' son.

My brother is plunged in misery, fearing more for my life than his own. In this calamity bring us, I beseech you, some comfort if you can find any. The best would be that what we have been told is either untrue or less serious than it has been represented. If it be true, then what is to happen in this life

consilium mihi non deesset nec ad severitatem nec ad diligentiam. nunc sive iracundia sive dolore sive metu permotus gravius scripsi quam aut tuus in illum amor aut meus postulabat, si vera sunt, ignosces, sin falsa, me libente eripies mihi hunc errorem. quoquo modo vero se res habebit, nihil adsignabis nec patruo nec patri.

7 Cum haec scripsissem, a Curione mihi nuntiatum est eum ad me venire. venerat enim is in Cumanum vesperi pridie, id est Idibus. si quid igitur eius modi sermo eius attulerit quod ad te scribendum sit, id his litteris adiungam.

8 Praeteriit villam meam Curio iussitque mihi nuntiari mox se venturum cucurritque Puteolos ut ibi contionaretur. contionatus est, rediit, fuit ad me sane diu. o rem foedam! nosti hominem; nihil occultabat, in primis nihil esse certius quam ut omnes qui lege Pompeia condemnati essent restituerentur; itaque se in Sicilia eorum opera usurum. de Hispaniis non dubitabat quin Caesaris essent. inde ipsum cum exercitu, ubicumque Pompeius esset. eius interitu⟨m⟩ finem illi fore. propius factum esse nihil. et plane iracundia elatum voluisse Caesarem occidi Metellum tribunum pl., quod si esset factum, caedem magnam futuram fuisse. permultos hortatores esse caedis, ipsum autem non voluntate aut natura non esse crudelem, sed quod ⟨putaret⟩ popularem esse clementiam. quod si populi studium amisisset, crudelem fore; eumque perturbatum quod intellegeret se apud ipsam plebem offen-

18 indulgentiam *Manutius* 19 nunc Σδ: M. nec *M*: nunc haec *c*: haec *Victorius* **7**, 3 igitur eius *Es*: e- (enim *R*) i- *OR*Δ sermo eius *ER*δ: e- s- *OPM*λ: sermo ϛ 4 his *Schütz*: in Ω **8**, 4 occultabat Σ: -abit *Md*: -avit *bms* 8 interitum *Lambinus*: -tu Ω belli *Manutius* 9 propius *s*: prope ius Σ*bdm*: pompeius *M* propius . . . nihil *post* tribunum pl. *transp. multi duce Malaespina*, *del.* ei et *scripsi*: ei Ω*Z* 11 fuisse *C*: esse Ω 13 putaret *add.* ϛ 15 plebem *Victorius*: legem Ω

of exiles we are leading I don't know. If we had a free country I should know how to act, failing neither in strictness nor in pains. As things are, if anger or sorrow or apprehension have made me write more sternly than suits your affection for him or my own, you must forgive me if the report is true and correct my error to my own rejoicing if it is false. However it turns out to be, I am sure you will not hold either his uncle or his father to blame.

7 I had written this much when a message arrived from Curio that he is coming to see me. He arrived at his place at Cumae yesterday evening, i.e. on the Ides. If he says anything worth writing to you I shall add it to this letter.

8 Curio passed my house and left word for me that he would be here shortly. He then rushed off to Puteoli to address a meeting there. He made his speech, returned, and paid me quite a lengthy visit. Horrible! You know what he is like. He kept nothing back. To begin with he says that nothing is more certain than that all persons condemned under the lex Pompeia are to be rehabilitated; so he himself would be using their services in Sicily. As for the Spanish provinces, he had no doubt they were Caesar's. From there Caesar and his army would go wherever Pompey was. Pompey's death would constitute his goal. It had been touch and go. He added that Caesar had been quite carried away with rage against the Tribune Metellus and had wanted to have him killed; in which case there would have been a great massacre. There were any number of people urging him that way, and as for Caesar himself, it was not by inclination or nature that he was not cruel but because he reckoned that clemency was the popular line. If he lost favour with the public he would be cruel. He was upset because he realized that even the populace had not liked his behaviour over the Treasury. So although

disse de aerario. itaque ei cum certissimum fuisset ante quam proficisceretur contionem habere, ausum non esse vehementerque animo perturbato profectum.

9 Cum autem ex eo quaererem quid videret, quem exitum, quam rem publicam, plane fatebatur nullam spem reliquam. Pompei classem timebat; quae si †esset†, se de Sicilia abiturum. 'quid isti' inquam 'sex tui fasces? si a senatu, cur laureati? si ab ipso, cur sex?' 'cupivi' inquit 'ex senatus consulto surrupto; nam aliter ⟨non⟩ poterat. at ille impendio nunc magis odit senatum. "a me" inquit "omnia proficiscentur." ' 'cur autem
10 sex?' 'quia duodecim nolui; nam licebat.' tum ego 'quam vellem' inquam 'petisse ab eo quod audio Philippum impetrasse! sed veritus sum, quia ille a me nihil impetrabat.' 'libenter' inquit 'tibi concessisset. verum puta te impetrasse; ego enim ad eum scribam, ut tu ipse voles, de ea re nos inter nos locutos. quid autem illius interest, quoniam in senatum non venis, ubi sis? quin nunc ipsum minime offendisses eius causam si in Italia non fuisses.' ad quae ego me recessum et solitudinem quaerere, maxime quod lictores haberem. laudabat consilium. 'quid ergo?' inquam, 'nam mihi cursus in Graeciam per tuam provinciam est, quoniam ad mare superum milites sunt.' quid mihi' inquit 'optatius?' hoc loco multa perliberaliter. ergo hoc quidem est [verum] profectum, ut non modo tuto verum etiam palam navigaremus.

9, 1 quem *M*: quod Σδ exitum *Malaespina*: exemplum Ω$Z^{(l)}$ 3 esset] exisset *Weiske*: adesset *Reid*: *fort.* accessisset 6 nam] non *R* non *add.* ς 7 senatum a me ς: senatum ad senatum a me ΩZ^{b} (*sed* a *om.* *OM*: a senatu a *Ebd*) quur autem sex? *C*: autem sex *EOMdm*: sex autem *s*: sex *Rb* (autem *ante* prof- *R*) **10**, 8 causam si *Lambinus*: causa si Σδ: causas *M* italia *E*δ: -am *ORM* ad quae *Lambinus*: atque Ω recessum *Victorius*: -surum Ω 9 laudabat Σ*ms*: -abit *Mbd*: -avit *Victorius* 13 profectum ς: verum profecto Ω

he had had every intention of holding a public meeting before he left, he had not dared to do so and had set off in a very agitated state of mind.

9 When I asked for his assessment—what way out, what constitution he foresaw—he frankly admitted that the situation is quite hopeless. He is afraid of Pompey's fleet. If it put to sea (?) he said he would leave Sicily. 'What about those six *fasces* of yours?' I asked. 'If they are from the Senate why the laurels? If from the great man, why six?' Answer: 'I wanted to get them by a snap decree of the Senate—it was impossible otherwise. But Caesar hates the Senate now far more than ever. "Everything shall come from me" is his motto.' 'But why six?' 'Because I didn't want twelve. I could have had them.'

10 Then I remarked: 'How I wish I had asked for the permission which I hear he has given to Philippus! But I did not like to because I was giving nothing to him.' 'He would have let you have it gladly' said Curio. 'But take it as granted. I shall write to him in terms approved by yourself that you and I have discussed the matter between us. After all, since you don't come to the Senate, what does it matter to him where you are? Indeed you would have done his cause least harm just now if you had not been in Italy.' To this I rejoined that I wanted retirement and solitude, especially because I had my lictors. He applauded my plan. 'What about it then?' I said. 'My way to Greece lies through your province, since there are troops stationed on the Adriatic.' 'Nothing I should like better' said he. So there is this much gained, that I shall sail not only without risk but without concealment.

11 Reliqua in posterum diem distulit; ex quibus scribam ad te si quid erit epistula dignum. sunt autem quae praeterii, interregnumne esset exspectaturus an quo modo dixerit ille quidem, ad se deferri consulatum sed se nolle in proximum annum. et alia sunt quae exquiram. iurabat ad summam, quod nullo negotio faceret, amicissimum mihi Caesarem esse debere. 'quid enim?' inquam. 'scripsit ad me Dolabella.' 'dic, quid?' adfirmabat eum scripsisse, quod me cuperet ad urbem venire, illum quidem gratias agere maximas et non modo probare sed etiam gaudere. quid quaeris? acquievi. levata est enim suspicio illa domestici mali et sermonis Hirtiani. quam cupio illum dignum esse nobis et quam ipse me invito †quae pro illo sit suspicandum†! sed opus fuit Hirtio convento? est profecto nescio quid, sed velim quam minimo. et tamen eum nondum redisse miramur. sed haec videbimus.

12 Tu †optimus† Terentiae dabis. iam enim urbis nullum periculum est. me tamen consilio iuva, pedibusne Regium an hinc statim in navem, et cetera, quoniam commoror. ego ad te [statim] habebo quod scribam simul et videro Curionem. de Tirone, cura, quaeso, quod facis, ut sciam quid is agat.

11, 3 dixerit . . . ad se *Ernesti* (ad se *et priores, ordine mutato*): -rim . . . sed ΩC 6 facere solet *Orelli* 7 debere *s*: debet Ω inquam *bds*: unq- Ω 8 dic *Hand*: dico Ω eum(?) scripsisse *E*: cum (quom *O*, eo *M*) scripsisset Ω 10 acquievi. levata *Bosius*: atque vi lebata *Z*: atque vilebat (iube- *Rbds*) Ω 12 esse *ms*: -et Ω 13 sit suspicandum Ω: si s- Z^l 14 sed *msC*: se Ω minimum *Lambinus* **12**, 1 optimus *OR*: -mos Δ: Oppios *Victorius*: hospitium *Muretus*: *anne* ab Oppiis? delegabis *Wesenberg* enim *OR*: cum Δ nullum *Pius*: unum Ω: vanum *Boot* (v- vel nullum *iam Gronovius*): minimum *Purser* 4 statim *del. Schütz* et $MdZ^{(b)}$: ut Σ*bms*: *del. Gronovius*

11 He put off further talk till next day. I shall write if any of it proves worth a letter. I omitted to raise certain points, as whether Caesar is going to wait for an interregnum or do as he hinted himself when he said that he was being offered the Consulship but did not want it for next year. And there are other questions I want to ask. To conclude, he took his oath, as he easily might, that Caesar must be very friendly to me. 'What do you mean?' I said. 'I have heard from Dolabella.' 'Tell me, what?' He stated that according to Dolabella's letter Caesar was profusely grateful to him for wishing me to come to Rome, and expressed not only approval but delight. So! It was a relief. My suspicions about our family trouble and that talk with Hirtius were allayed. How anxious I am to find him worthy of us and how much against my will * * * ! But why that interview with Hirtius? Yes, there must be something, but I hope it will come to as little as may be. And yet I am surprised that he has not yet returned. But we shall see.

12 You will please give * to Terentia, for there is now no danger in the capital. But help me with your advice, whether to go by land to Regium or to take ship direct from here, and write about other matters seeing that I am staying where I am. I shall have something to write to you about as soon as I have seen Curio. About Tiro, pray continue to make sure that I know how he is getting on.

196 (x. 5)

Scr. in Cumano xv Kal. Mai. an. 49 (§ 3)

⟨CICERO ATTICO SAL.⟩

1 De tota mea cogitatione scripsi ad te antea satis, ut mihi
visus sum, diligenter. de die nihil sane potest scribi certi
2 praeter hoc, non ante lunam novam. Curionis sermo postridie
eandem habuit fere summam, nisi quod apertius significavit
se harum rerum exitum non videre.

Quod mihi mandas de quodam regendo, ''Αρκαδίαν ...'.
tamen nihil praetermittam. atque utinam tu—sed molestior
non ero. epistulam ad Vestorium statim detuli, ac valde re-
3 quirere solebat. commodius tecum Vettienus est locutus quam
ad me scripserat. sed mirari satis hominis neglegentiam non queo. cum enim mihi Philotimus dixisset se HS $\overline{\text{L}}$ emere de Canuleio deversorium illud posse, minoris etiam empturum si Vettienum rogassem, rogavi ut, si quid posset, ex ea summa detraheret; promisit. ad me nuper se HS $\overline{\overline{\text{XXX}}}$ emisse; ut scriberem cui vellem addici; diem pecuniae Id. Nov. esse. rescripsi ei stomachosius, cum ioco tamen familiari. nunc, quoniam agit liberaliter, nihil accuso hominem scripsique ad eum me a te certiorem esse factum.

Tu de tuo itinere quid et quando cogites velim me certiorem facias. a. d. xv Kal. Mai.

Ep. 196] *novam ep. agnovit Corradus*: *cum superiore in codd. cohaeret* **1**, 2 potest scribi Σ*m*: s- p- Δ certi ς: -te Ω **2**, 4 quodam] Quinto *Victorius* 5 molestior *Victorius*: mode- Ω$Z^{(b)}$ 6 ero *nescio quis*: pro Δ: propter *O*: per *R* detuli *Graevius*: deculia Δ (-cidia *b*): de tullia *ORs* **3**, 1 Vettienus *Vrsinus*: vectinus Ω (*codicum in hoc nomine variationes amplius non curabo: vide comm.*) 2 satis δ: -is est Ω 6 se HS *Orelli*: esse Ω: sese HS ς 8 ei stomachosius *Manutius*: et in stomacho si vis *ORC* (et ist-): et isto madio si vis Δ ioco ς: loco Ω

196 (X. 5)

Cumae, 16 April 49

CICERO TO ATTICUS

1 About my plans in general I have already written to you, I think in sufficient detail. About the day nothing really can be said for certain except that it must not be before the new moon.
2 Curio's talk the next day was to much the same general effect, except that he intimated still more plainly that he sees no way out of the present situation.

As for what you enjoin upon me about governing a certain person—'Arcady . . .'! However, I shall leave no stone unturned. If only *you*—but I must not impose. I conveyed your letter to Vestorius at once. He had been wondering a
3 good deal why he had not heard. Vettienus' language to you was more suitable than his letter to me. But I really can't say how astonished I am at his off-handedness. When Philotimus told me that he could buy that lodge from Canuleius for HS 50,000 and that the price would be even less if I approached Vettienus, I did so, asking him to get it reduced if he could. He promised, then wrote to me the other day that he had bought the place for HS 30,000; I must write to say to whom I wanted it assigned; settlement day, Ides of November. I replied with some irritation, but in the way of friendly joking. Now, since he is behaving handsomely, I have nothing against him and have written to tell him that you have given me the facts.

Please let me know about your journey, what you plan and when. 16 April.

197 (x. 6)

Scr. in Cumano c. xi Kal. Mai. an. 49

CICERO ATTICO SAL.

1 Me adhuc nihil praeter tempestatem moratur. astute nihil sum acturus. fiat in Hispania quidlibet—et tamen recte sit. meas cogitationes omnis explicavi tibi superioribus litteris. quocirca hae sunt breves, et quia festinabam eramque occupatior.

2 De Quinto filio, fit a me quidem sedulo, sed—nosti reliqua. quod †dem† me mones, et amice et prudenter me mones, sed erunt omnia facilia si ab uno illo cavero. magnum opus est; mirabilia multa, nihil simplex, nihil sincerum. vellem suscepisses iuvenem regendum; pater enim nimis indulgens quicquid ego adstrinxi relaxat. si sine illo possem, regerem; quod tu potes. sed ignosco; magnum, inquam, opus est.

3 Pompeium pro certo habemus per Illyricum proficisci in Galliam. ego nunc qua et quo videbo.

198 (x. 7)

Scr. in Cumano fort. ix Kal. Mai. an. 49

⟨CICERO ATTICO SAL.⟩

1 Ego vero Apuliam et Sipontum et tergiversationem istam probo nec tuam rationem eandem esse duco quam meam,

---

Ep. 197] *hinc novam ep. incipit m, post* facias (*ep.* 196. 3, 12) *ePs*: *uno tenore ORMbd* **1**, 2 hispania *ms*: -am Ω recte sit *scripsi*: recitet et ΩZ^b: recite te Z^β (*sed del.*): reticeret Z^l: res stat; ἰτέον *Tyrrell* 4 et *OR*: et tamen Δ: *om. E* **2**, 1 filio *Corradus*: fratre Ω fit a *Bosius*: ita Ω: *fort.* fiet a 2 dem *C*: dein (?) *M*: de *E*δ: enim *O*(?)*R* me mones (*iterum*) *C*: memores *O*(?)*M*: -ras *ER*δ

Ep. 198] *novam ep. agnovit Corradus*: *cum superiore in codd. cohaeret*

197 (x. 6)

Cumae, c. 20 April 49

CICERO TO ATTICUS

1 Up to now nothing holds me up except the weather. I shall not try to be clever. Let the outcome in Spain be what it may—though I wish it may be all right. I have explained all my plans to you in an earlier letter. For that reason this one is brief, and because I am in a hurry and rather busy.

2 As regards young Quintus, *I* am sparing no pains but—you know what follows. Your admonition * * * is friendly and wise, but all will be easy if I only safeguard myself on *his* side. It is a great task. There is much in him that is extraordinary, but an utter lack of straightforwardness and sincerity. I wish you had taken the young man in hand. His too indulgent father undoes all my disciplinary measures. Without him, if that were possible, I could govern the lad. For *you* it is possible. But I don't insist. As I say, it is a great task.

3 We have it for certain that Pompey is on his way through Illyricum to Gaul. I shall now think about my own route and destination.

198 (x. 7)

CICERO TO ATTICUS

Cumae, 22 April (?) 49

1 Why certainly I approve of Apulia and Sipontum and this fence-sitting of yours, and I look upon your position as different

non quin in re publica rectum idem sit utrique nostrum, sed ea non agitur. regnandi contentio est, in qua pulsus est modestior rex et probior et integrior et is, qui nisi vincit, nomen populi Romani deleatur necesse est, sin autem vincit, Sullano more exemploque vincet. ergo hac in contentione neutrum tibi palam sentiendum et tempori serviendum est. mea causa autem alia est, quod beneficio vinctus ingratus esse non possum, nec tamen in acie ⟨me⟩ sed Melitae aut alio in loco simili ⟨vel⟩ oppidulo futurum puto. 'nihil' inquies 'iuvas eum in quem ingratus esse non vis?' immo minus fortasse voluisset. sed de hoc videbimus; exeamus modo. quod ut meliore tempore possimus facit Adriano mari Dolabella, Fretensi Curio.

2 Iniecta autem mihi spes quaedam est: 'velle mecum Ser. Sulpicium colloqui'. ad eum misi Philotimum libertum cum litteris. si vir esse volet, praeclara συνοδία, sin autem—.

3 erimus nos qui solemus. Curio mecum vixit, iacere Caesarem putans offensione populari Siciliaeque diffidens si Pompeius navigare coepisset.

Quintum puerum accepi vehementer. avaritiam video fuisse et spem magni congiari. magnum hoc malum est, sed scelus illud quod timueramus spero nullum fuisse. hoc autem vitium puto te existimare non ⟨a⟩ nostra indulgentia sed a natura profectum. quem tamen nos disciplina regimus.

1, 5 modestior Σδ: at(?) m- *M*: adm- *Z*[b]: et m- *Gronovius* 10 me *add. Wesenberg* (*post* tamen *Lambinus*) Melitae *Victorius*: militi(a)e Σ*m*: militia Δ aliquo *m* 11 simili Ω: sive *ms* vel oppidulo *scripsi* (vel oppido *Tyrrell–Purser*): oppidulo Ω sive in opp- *Lambinus* *aut* loco *aut* oppidulo *glossema fuisse suspicatus est Graevius* 12 ingratus *E*δ: gr- *ORM* 14 fretensi *ERMbdZ*[(b)] (*hoc in libris vett. constanter se legisse adfirmat Bosius; idem Tornesianum habuisse testatur Lambinus in ed. prima, at in altera* fretensi tensi, *fort. errore typographico*): cret- *Oms*: freto Siciliensi *Victorius* **2,** 1 *post* est *distinxit iam ed. Saliceti-Regii* (*1499*) 3 praeclara *Victorius*: decl- (de cl-) Ω συνοδία *Manutius*: synodia (sin-) Ω **3,** 7 a *add. Lambinus* 8 quam . . . regemus *Ernesti*

from mine. Not that right is not right for both of us as citizens of the Republic, but the Republic is not at issue. This is a fight for a throne. The expelled monarch is the more moderate, upright, and clean-handed, and unless he wins the name of the Roman people must inevitably be blotted out; but if he does win, his victory will be after the Sullan fashion and example. Therefore in such a conflict you should support neither side openly and trim your sails to the wind. My case however is different because I am bound by an obligation and cannot be ungrateful. Yet I don't think I shall stand in the line of battle, but rather stay in Malta or some similar place or little town. You may ask me whether I am doing nothing to help the person to whom I don't want to be ungrateful. On the contrary he would perhaps have preferred me to do less. But we shall see about this later on; only let me get away. I can do that at a better time of year, thanks to Dolabella on the Adriatic and Curio on the Straits.

2 I have been given a hope of sorts. Ser. Sulpicius is said to want to talk to me. I have sent my freedman Philotimus to him with a letter. If he chooses to be a man, it will be a notable
3 *rencontre;* if not, not. I shall take my usual line. Curio has been spending his time with me. He thinks Caesar is in bad odour because of the offence given to popular sentiment, and has no confidence in Sicily if Pompey should begin operations at sea.

I gave young Quintus a warm reception. I see it was greed and the hope of a handsome largesse. That is bad enough in all conscience, but I hope there was no such villainy as we feared. I think you will agree that this vice does not proceed from indulgence on our part but from nature. However I govern him with discipline.

De Oppiis Veliensibus quid placeat cum Philotimo videbis. Epirum nostram putabimus, sed alios cursus videbamur habituri.

199 (x. 8)

Scr. in Cumano vi Non. Mai. an. 49 (§ 10)

CICERO ATTICO SAL.

1 Et res ipsa monebat et tu ostenderas et ego videbam de iis rebus quas intercipi periculosum esset finem inter nos scribendi fieri tempus esse. sed cum ad me saepe mea Tullia scribat orans ut quid in Hispania geratur exspectem et semper adscribat idem videri tibi idque ipse etiam ex tuis litteris intellexerim, non puto esse alienum me ad te quid de ea re sentiam scribere.

2 Consilium istuc tunc esset prudens, ut mihi videtur, si nostras rationes ad Hispaniensem casum accommodaturi essemus; quod fieri * * *. necesse est enim aut, id quod maxime velim, pelli istum ab Hispania aut trahi id bellum aut istum, ut confidere videtur, apprehendere Hispanias. si pelletur, quam gratus aut quam honestus tum erit ad Pompeium noster adventus, cum ipsum Curionem ad eum transiturum putem? si trahitur bellum, quid exspectem aut quam diu? relinquitur ut, si vincimur in Hispania, quiescamus. id ego contra puto. istum enim victorem magis relinquendum puto quam victum, et dubitantem magis quam fidentem suis rebus. nam

---

9 oppiis *OR*: oppio Δ cum *OR*: quem Δ 10 nostram ς: -rum Ω videbamur ς: -eamur Ω (*sed ex* -ebimur *R*): -emur *s*

Ep. 199] **1,** 1 de iis *Om*: de hiis *R*: de his *bds*: denis *M* 5 adscribat (ass-) δ: -am Ω 6 ad *bds*: a Ω **2,** 1 istuc *OR*: -ud Δ 3 fieri Ωλ: f- non debet *P*: *alia add. alii* 4 ab hispania *R*δ: ad hispaniam *OM* 8 si *R*δ: si cum *OM*: sin *Lambinus*: sin autem *nescio quis*: si contra *Schmidt* 11 et] nec *Schütz*

Concerning the Oppii of Velia please consult with Philotimus as to the best arrangement. I shall regard Epirus as my own property, but it does not look as if I shall be going that way.

199 (x. 8)

Cumae, 2 May 49

CICERO TO ATTICUS

1 As the nature of the case warns us, as you have pointed out, and as I see for myself, it is time for us to give up writing on topics which would be dangerous if intercepted. But since my Tullia often writes begging me to wait and see what happens in Spain and always adds that you agree with her, and since I have gathered the same from your own letters, I think it may be as well for me to give you my views on the matter.

2 This advice would be sound, as I see it, if I were going to adapt my course to the fortune of war in Spain. But that * * *. For one of three things is bound to happen. Either, as I should most desire, Caesar will be driven from Spain, or the war there will drag on, or he will seize the Spanish provinces as he seems confident of doing. If he is driven out, what sort of welcome shall I get or what sort of figure shall I cut joining Pompey at a time when I imagine Curio himself will go over to him? But if the war drags on, what am I to wait for or how long? There remains the possibility that if we lose in Spain I do nothing. I take just the opposite view. I think there is more reason to leave Caesar in victory than in defeat, and more to leave while he is doubtful of success than when he is sure of it.

caedem video si vicerit et impetum in privatorum pecunias et exsulum reditum et tabulas novas et turpissimorum honores et regnum non modo Romano homini sed ne Persae quidem cuiquam tolerabile.

3 Tacita esse poterit indignitas nostra? pati poterunt oculi me cum Gabinio sententiam dicere, et quidem illum rogari prius? praesto esse clientem tuum Cloelium, †Cateli† Plaguleium, ceteros? sed cur inimicos colligo, qui meos necessarios a me defensos nec videre in curia sine dolore nec versari inter eos sine dedecore potero? quid si ne id quidem est exploratum, fore ut mihi liceat? scribunt enim ad me amici eius me illi nullo modo satis fecisse quod in senatum non venerim. tamenne dubitemus an ei nos etiam cum periculo venditemus quicum coniuncti ne cum praemio quidem volu⟨i⟩mus esse?

4 Deinde hoc vide, non esse iudicium de tota contentione in Hispaniis, nisi forte iis amissis arma Pompeium abiecturum putas; cuius omne consilium Themistocleum est. existimat enim qui mare teneat eum necesse ⟨esse⟩ rerum potiri. itaque [qui] numquam id egit ut Hispaniae per se tenerentur; navalis apparatus ei semper antiquissima cura fuit. navigabit igitur, cum erit tempus, maximis classibus et ad Italiam accedet, in qua nos sedentes quid erimus? nam medios esse iam non licebit. [classibus] adversabimur igitur? quod maius scelus

---

3, 1 tacita Ω: tanta PZ^1 indignitas *Victorius*: id indig- MZ^1: in id dig- *OR*δ poterunt *ms*: -rint *P*: potuerint Ω 3 cloelium *Mdm*: clocl- *R*: clodium *bs* (*de O non liquet*) cateli *OP*Δ: -elli *R*: catuli *s*: C. Ateii *Bosius* 8 senatum *bds*: -tu Ω venerim δ: venirem Ω 9 ei *Manutius*: et Ω: ut *bds* venditemus *C*: -icemus Ω 10 coniuncti ne *Hervagius*: -ctione Ω voluimus *Manutius*: -umus Ω **4,** 4 esse *add. Lambinus* 5 qui *del. Schütz* 6 cura *R*δ: *om. OM* navigabit *P*δ: -avit *OM*: -abat *R* 9 classibus *del. Manutius* maius δZ^{β}: malus Ω$Z^{1(b)}$ scelus aut *Malaespina*: scilicet Ω*Z*

For I foresee a massacre if he wins and an onslaught on private property and return of exiles and cancellation of debts and elevation of rapscallions to office and despotism worse than any Persian, let alone Roman, could endure.

3 Shall I be able to keep silence under such humiliation? Shall I be able to bear the sight of Gabinius speaking beside me in the Senate, and even called upon to speak before me? Can I stand the presence of your client Cloelius and * 's client Plaguleius and the rest? But I need not enumerate my enemies. What of my friends whom I have defended in the courts? I shall not be able to see them in the Senate House without distress nor to be in their company without discredit. And after all I cannot be certain that this will be open to me. Caesar's friends write to me that he is by no means satisfied with my conduct in not attending the Senate. Am I really to think of courting when it is dangerous to do so a man whose alliance I refused when it would have brought me profit?

4 Consider in the second place that the issue of the whole conflict will not be decided in Spain. Or do you think that if Spain goes Pompey will drop his weapons? No, his entire plan is Themistoclean. He reckons that whoever holds the sea is sure to be master. For that reason he was never interested in holding the Spanish provinces for their own sake; his main care was always to fit out a navy. So when the time comes he will put to sea with huge fleets and land in Italy, where I shall be quietly sitting. What will be my position then? Neutrality will no longer be possible. Shall I then take part against him? Could any crime be greater, or as great? What in fine could be more dishonourable? Am I, who have stood up all alone to Caesar's criminality, hard as he pressed me, not to stand up to it when I have Pompey and our other leaders

aut tantum? denique quid turpius? an qui valde incumbentis solus tuli scelus, eiusdem cum Pompeio et cum reliquis
5 principibus non feram? quod si iam misso officio periculi ratio habenda est, ab illis est periculum si peccaro, ab hoc si recte fecero, nec ullum in his malis consilium periculo vacuum inveniri potest, ut non sit dubium quin turpiter facere cum periculo fugiamus, quod fugeremus etiam cum salute. non simul cum Pompeio mare transi[er]imus. omnino ⟨non⟩ potuimus; exstat ratio dierum. sed tamen (fateamur enim quod est) ne con⟨ten⟩dimus quidem ut possemus. fefellit ea me res quae fortasse non debuit, sed fefellit: pacem putavi fore. quae si esset, iratum mihi Caesarem esse, cum idem amicus esset Pompeio, nolui. senseram enim quam idem essent. hoc verens in hanc tarditatem incidi. sed adsequar omnia si propero: si cunctor, amitto.

6 Et tamen, mi Attice, auguria quoque me incitant quaedam spe non dubia nec haec collegi nostri ab Atto sed illa Platonis de tyrannis. nullo enim modo posse video stare istum diutius quin ipse per se etiam languentibus nobis concidat, quippe qui florentis⟨simus⟩ ac novus sex, septem diebus ipsi illi egenti ac perditae multitudini in odium acerbissimum venerit, qui duarum rerum simulationem tam cito amiserit, mansuetudinis in Metello, divitiarum in aerario. iam quibus utatur vel sociis

---

10 quid] an quid Z^l an qui valde ς: an in (anin *M*: an tu *b*: an cum *s*) v- ΔZ^β: an invalide *O*: animal de *R* incumbentis *scripsi*: hic (hinc Z^β) in absentis Ω **5,** 5 salute *P*: -em Ω 6 transiimus *Nipperdey*: -ierimus Ω omnino non *Manutius*: non o- *P*: omnino Ω 8 contendimus *Nipperdey*: cond- Ω*C* possemus *Nipperdey*: -simus Ω ea me *Bosius*: eam OMZ^b: ea *R*δ 9 debuit *R*δ: -isset *M*: -i sed *O* 10 iratum ς: rata Ω 12 assequor *Lambinus* **6,** 1 qu(a)edam *OR*: quadam Δ 2 Atto *Orelli*: attico Ω 5 florentissimus *Manutius*: -ntis Ω vi, vii *Manutius*: ut uti *O*Δ: uti ut *R* 6 venerit *Corradus*: veniret Ω 7 tam *P*δ: tamen Ω 8 aerario *Victorius*: af(f)ranio Ωλ utetur *Kayser*

5 by my side? But now suppose I am to leave duty out of the question and take account of danger, there will be danger from Pompey's party if I do wrong and from Caesar if I do right, nor in these sorry times can any plan be devised that is free of risk. Therefore it is obviously better to avoid a dishonourable course fraught with danger when I would avoid it even if it carried security. I did not go abroad with Pompey; true, I did not have the opportunity—the dates are there to prove it. Still—I may as well acknowledge what is the fact—I did not try very hard to give myself the opportunity. One thing misled me, perhaps it ought not to have done but it did: I thought there would be peace. If that came about I did not want to have Caesar angry with me while on friendly terms with Pompey. I had learned by experience how hand in glove they were. This fear led me into such procrastination. But I shall gain all if I make haste; if I delay, I lose all.

6 And yet, my dear Atticus, I am also urged in this direction by a sure hope I have in certain auguries, not those of our College inherited from Attus, but Plato's on the subject of tyrants. As I see it, Caesar cannot last very long without falling by his own impulse, even though we are ineffective. Look how with all the advantage of novelty and brilliant success he has in a week become an object of bitter hatred even to the needy and reckless mob which supported him—how in so short a space of time he has lost two masks, the mask of clemency in dealing with Metellus and the mask of riches in the matter of the Treasury. Again, whom is he to take as his partners and

vel ministris? ii provincias, ii rem publicam regent quorum
nemo duo mensis potuit patrimonium suum gubernare?
7 non sunt omnia colligenda quae tu acutissime perspicis,
sed tamen ea pone ante oculos; iam intelleges id regnum vix
semenstre esse posse. quod si me fefellerit, feram, sicut multi
clarissimi homines in re publica excellentes tulerunt, nisi forte
me Sardanapali vicem in suo lectulo mori malle censueris
quam ⟨in⟩ exsilio Themistocleo. qui cum fuisset, ut ait
Thucydides, τῶν μὲν παρόντων δι' ἐλαχίστης βουλῆς κράτιστος
γνώμων, τῶν δὲ μελλόντων ἐς πλεῖστον τοῦ γενησομένου ἄριστος
εἰκαστής, tamen incidit in eos casus quos vitasset si eum nihil
fefellisset. etsi is erat, ut ait idem, qui τὸ ἄμεινον καὶ τὸ χεῖρον
ἐν τῷ ἀφανεῖ ἔτι ἑώρα μάλιστα, tamen non vidit nec quo modo
Lacedaemoniorum nec quo modo suorum civium invidiam
effugeret nec quid Artaxerxi pollice⟨re⟩tur. non fuisset illa nox
tam acerba Africano, sapientissimo viro, non tam dirus ille
dies Sullanus callidissimo viro, C. Mario, si nihil utrumque
eorum fefellisset. nos tamen hoc confirmamus illo augurio
8 quo diximus, nec nos fallit nec aliter accidet. corruat iste
necesse est aut per adversarios aut ipse per se, qui quidem
sibi est adversarius unus acerrimus. id spero vivis nobis fore;
quamquam tempus est nos de illa perpetua iam, non de hac
exigua vita cogitare. sin quid acciderit maturius, haud sane
mea multum interfuerit utrum factum [fiat] videam an futurum
esse multo ante viderim. quae cum ita sint, non est committendum ut iis paream quos contra me senatus, ne quid res
publica detrimenti acciperet, armavit.

---

9 ii . . . ii *Madvig*: si . . . si *OPM*: si ii . . . ii *R*: si ii (hi) . . . si ii (hi) δ **7**, 2 intelliges id δ: -gent *O(?)M*: -ges *R* 5 sardanapali *PMZ*[1]: -lli *OR*δ vicem *etiam Z*[1] suo *fort. delendum* (in suo lectulo *del. Nipperdey*): meo *Graevius* censueris *P*: -rint *Z*[b]: -runt Ω 6 in *add. Wesenberg* 7 *in Graecis codicum errores non perscripsi* 11 προεώρα *O* (*cf. Thuc. 1. 138. 3*) 13 polliceretur *bds*: -cetur Ω fuisset *s*: -e et *OM*: -et et *Rbdm* 17 quod *ms* fallet *Otto* accidet *Manutius*: -dit Ω **8**, 1 iste *R*δ: ista *OM* 6 factum δ: -tum fiat *OM*: -tum fuerit *R*

assistants? Are the provinces and the state to be governed by people not one of whom had the capacity to look after his own
7 family property for two months? I need not make a catalogue of points which are already apparent to your perspicacity, but do just call them to mind; you will soon see that this reign can hardly last six months. If I am wrong, I shall take the consequences, as many great men and eminent statesmen have done before me. Or do you think I would rather die in my bed like Sardanapalus than in exile like Themistocles? He was, Thucydides says, 'at once the best judge in those sudden crises which admit of little or no deliberation and the best prophet of the future, even to its most distant possibilities'. Yet he fell into misfortunes which he would have avoided if he had never forecast wrong. Although, to quote Thucydides again, 'he could excellently divine the good and evil which lay hidden in the unseen future',[1] yet he failed to see how to escape the jealousy of the Spartans or that of his own countrymen, or what promises he ought to make Artaxerxes. Africanus was a very wise man, C. Marius a very cunning one; yet if neither had ever forecast awry, there would never have come that cruel night for the one or that terrible day of Sulla's return for the other. But in the present case I confirm my forecast by the augury aforesaid. I am not wrong and it will not turn out
8 otherwise. He is bound to collapse either through his enemies' agency or his own; indeed he is his own worst enemy. I hope I may live to see it, though it is time for me to be thinking of eternity rather than this brief span. But if anything happens to me earlier, well, it will make little enough difference to me whether I see it come to pass or only saw long beforehand that it would come to pass one day. Therefore I must not stoop to yield obedience to men against whom the Senate placed arms in my hands 'lest harm come to the state'.

[1] Crawley's translation

9 Tibi sunt omnia commendata, quae commendationis meae pro tuo in nos amore non indigent. ne hercule ego quidem reperio quid scribam; sedeo enim πλουδοκῶν. etsi nihil umquam tam fuit scribendum quam nihil mihi umquam ex plurimis tuis iucunditatibus gratius accidisse quam quod meam Tulliam suavissime diligentissimeque coluisti. valde eo ipsa delectata est, ego autem non minus. cuius quidem virtus mirifica. quo modo illa fert publicam cladem, quo modo domesticas tricas! quantus autem animus in discessu nostro! est στοργή, est summa σύντηξις. tamen nos recte facere et
10 bene audire vult. sed hac super re mi⟨nu⟩s, ne meam ipse συμπάθειαν iam evocem.

Tu, si quid de Hispaniis certius et si quid aliud, dum adsumus, scribes, et ego fortasse discedens dabo ad te aliquid, eo etiam magis quod Tullia te non putabat hoc tempore ex Italia. cum An⟨ton⟩io item est agendum ut cum Curione, Melitae me velle esse, civili bello nolle interesse. eo velim tam facili uti possim et tam bono in me quam Curione. is ad Misenum VI Non. venturus dicebatur, id est hodie. sed praemisit mihi odiosas litteras hoc exemplo:

199 A (x. 8 A)

Scr. fort. Kal. Mai. an. 49

ANTONIVS TR. PL. PRO PR. CICERONI IMP. SAL.

1 Nisi te valde amarem et multo quidem plus quam tu putas, non extimuissem rumorem qui de te prolatus est, cum

---

9, 2 ne] nec *Hofmann* (nec mercule *Lamb.* (*marg.*)) 4 tam Δ: iam *OR* 5 accidisse δ: -et Ω 10 est στοργή, est λ : sit στοργῆς (*vel sim.*) sit Ω **10**, 1 re minus *scripsi*: remis Ω: re nimis ς: re ne nimis *Lehmann* 6 antonio *s*: an(n)io Ω 7 velle *OR*: -et Δ civili bello *scripsi duce Wesenberg*, *qui* huic c- b-: huic libello OΔ: huic b- *Rs* 8 uti ς: ut Ω possim *Pb*: -sem Ω: -se ς Curione. is *Beroaldus*: -onis *OM*: -onis is *R*δ

9 I have commended to you all my concerns, and your affection for me makes commendation on my part unnecessary. I too find nothing to write about—I am just sitting waiting to sail. And yet nothing ever needed writing more than this, that of all your many kindnesses there is none I have valued more than your tender and punctilious attention to my Tullia. It has given her the greatest pleasure, and me no less. Her courage and patience in face of public disaster and domestic worries is really wonderful. How brave she was when we parted! She combines natural affection with the most delicate sympathy. Yet she wishes me to do the right thing and to stand well in

10 men's eyes. But I say less than I might on this subject for fear I end by becoming my own sympathizer.

If you hear anything definite about Spain or anything else, please write as long as I am here, and perhaps I'll send you a line as I leave, especially as Tullia thinks you won't be going out of Italy for the time being. I must take the same line with Antony as with Curio, that I want to settle in Malta and keep out of civil war. I only hope I find him as amenable and well disposed towards me as Curio. He is said to be coming to Misenum on the 2nd, i.e. today. But he has sent me the following disagreeable epistle in advance:

199A (X. 8A)

Place uncertain, 1 May (?) 49

ANTONIUS TRIBUNE, PROPRAETOR

TO CICERO IMPERATOR

1 If I did not have a great affection for you, much more indeed than you suppose, I should not have been so alarmed at a

praesertim falsum esse existimarem. sed quia te nimio plus diligo, non possum dissimulare mihi famam quoque, quamvis sit falsa, falsam agnoscere magni esse. trans mare ⟨te iturum esse⟩ credere non possum, cum tanti facias Dolabellam ⟨et⟩ Tulliam tuam, feminam lectissimam, tantique ab omnibus nobis fias; quibus mehercule dignitas amplitudoque tua paene carior est quam tibi ipsi. sed tamen non sum arbitratus esse amici non commoveri etiam improborum sermone, atque eo feci studiosius quod iudicabam duriores partis mihi impositas esse ab offensione nostra, quae magis a ζηλοτυπίᾳ mea quam ab iniuria tua nata est. sic enim volo te tibi persuadere, mihi neminem esse cariorem te excepto Caesare meo, meque illud una iudicare, Caesarem maxime in suis M. Ciceronem reponere.

2 qua re, mi Cicero, te rogo ut tibi omnia integra serves, eius fidem improbes qui tibi ut beneficium daret prius iniuriam fecit, contra ne profugias qui te, etsi non amabit, quod accidere non potest, tamen salvum amplissimumque esse cupiet.

Dedita opera ad te Calpurnium, familiarissimum meum, misi, ut mihi magnae curae tuam vitam ac dignitatem esse scires.

Eodem die a Caesare Philotimus attulit hoc exemplo:

199B (X. 8B)

Scr. Massiliam iter faciens xv Kal. Mai. an. 49 (§ 2)

CAESAR IMP. SAL. D. CICERONI IMP.

1 Etsi te nihil temere, nihil imprudenter facturum iudicaram, tamen permotus hominum fama scribendum ad te

---

Ep. 199A] 1, 3 esse *om. c* 5 falsa falsam agnoscere Z^b: falsam agnosce *M*: falsa *OR*δ magni δZ^b: -no Ω te iturum esse *add. Baiter* (te iturum *P*), *sed post* esse 6 et *add.* ς 14 meo . . . iudicare *C*: *om.* Ω 15 c(a)esarem *R*δ: *om. OM* 2, 3 ne OΔ: eum ne *R*, *fort. recte*: ne ab eo *Lambinus* 5 -mum meum *P*δ: -mumque eum *O*(?)*M*: -mum *R* 8 attulit Ω$Z^{(b)}$: litteras at- *bds*
Ep. 199B] *hanc ep. habet etiam H*

report which has been put about concerning you, especially as I did not believe it. But because I have a quite peculiar regard for you, I cannot conceal my anxiety to be assured of the falsity of the rumour, rumour and false though it be. I cannot believe that you mean to go abroad, considering how fond you are of Dolabella and that most admirable young lady your daughter, and how fond we all are of you. I assure you that we care about your prestige and position more almost than you do yourself. However, I did not think it right as a friend to disregard even malicious talk, and I have been the more exercised because I considered that the coolness which has arisen between us, more from jealousy on my part than from any injury on yours, made my part harder. For I wish you to persuade yourself that no one means more to me than you except my friend Caesar, and that at the same time I believe Caesar gives the name of M. Cicero a place among his most particular
2 friends. Therefore, my dear Cicero, I beg you not to compromise yourself in any way, not to trust a man who to do you a service first did you an injury, and on the other hand not to shun one who, even if he ceases to love you (which cannot happen), will still desire your well-being and dignity.

I have specially sent Calpurnius, my intimate friend, to you so that you may know how deeply I care for your personal safety and position.

The same day Philotimus brought the following letter from Caesar:

199B (X. 8B)

En route to Massilia, 16 April 49

CAESAR IMPERATOR TO CICERO IMPERATOR

1 Persuaded as I am that you will do nothing hasty or imprudent, I am none the less troubled by current reports, and I therefore

existimavi et pro nostra benevolentia petendum ne quo progredereris proclinata iam re quo integra etiam progrediendum tibi non existimasses. namque et amicitae graviorem iniuriam feceris et tibi minus commode consulueris, si non fortunae obsecutus videberis (omnia enim secundissima nobis, adversissima illis accidisse videntur), nec causam secutus (eadem enim tum fuit cum ab eorum consiliis abesse iudicasti), sed meum aliquod factum condemnavisse; quo mihi gravius abs
2 te nihil accidere potest. quod ne facias pro iure nostrae amicitiae a te peto. postremo quid viro bono et quieto et bono civi magis convenit quam abesse a civilibus controversiis? quod non nulli cum probarent, periculi causa sequi non potuerunt; tu explorato et vitae meae testimonio et amicitiae iudicio neque tutius neque honestius reperies quicquam quam ab omni contentione abesse. XV Kal. Mai. ex itinere.

200 (X. 9)

Scr. in Cumano v Non. Mai. an. 49

⟨CICERO ATTICO SAL.⟩

1 Adventus Philotimi (at cuius hominis, quam insulsi et quam saepe pro Pompeio mentientis!) exanimavit omnis qui mecum erant; nam ipse obdurui. dubitabat nostrum nemo quin Caesar itinera repressisset—volare dicitur; Petreius cum Afranio coniunxisse⟨t se⟩—nihil adfert eius modi. quid quaeris? etiam illud erat persuasum, Pompeium cum magnis

---

1, 4 proclinata *RMbdCλ*: incl- *HOms* quo *ORM*: qua *HPδ* etiam *HΔ*: *om. OR* 7 videberis *Hbds*: ut deberes *OMm*: fueris ut deberes *R* (debes *P*): videbere *Victorius* 2, 5 tu explorato *Hδ*: quo expl- *O*: quo et pl- *M*: quo et expl- *R*

Ep. 200] *novam ep.* (*sed a verbis* XV Kal. *supra*) *facit P*: *uno tenore* Ω 1, 3 dubitabat *P*: -abit Ω: -avit δ 4 repressisset *Om*: oppr- *Rbds*: repressisset tuo *M*: -et. immo *Schmidt* 5 -isset se *Bosius*: -isse Ω 6 pompeium *Rδ*: -io *OM*

feel I ought to write and appeal to you in the name of our mutual good will not to take a step now that the scales have turned which you did not think fit to take even when they were level. You will be committing a graver offence against friendship and acting less advisedly from your own point of view if it appears that you have not bowed to fortune (since everything seems to have gone excellently for us and disastrously for our adversaries) nor yet followed a cause (since it was the same cause when you decided to keep aloof from their counsels), but that you have disapproved some action of mine, which is
2 the worst blow you could deal me. I appeal to you in the name of our friendship not to do this. Finally, to hold aloof from civil quarrels is surely the most fitting course for a good, peace-loving man and a good citizen. Some who favoured that course were prevented from following it by fear for their safety. But you have the witness of my career and the judgement implied in our friendship. Weigh them well, and you will find no safer and no more honourable way than to keep aloof from all conflict. 16 April, *en route*.

200 (X. 9)

Cumae, 3 May 49

CICERO TO ATTICUS

1 Philotimus' arrival (what an ass he is, and how many lies he tells on Pompey's behalf!) has thrown all my companions into consternation—I myself am hardened. None of us doubted that Caesar had checked speed—now he is said to be on wings; or that Petreius had joined Afranius—Philotimus brings nothing of the kind. Why, it was even believed that Pompey had

copiis iter in Germaniam per Illyricum fecisse; id enim αὐθεντικῶς nuntiabatur. Melitam igitur, opinor, capessamus, dum quid in Hispania. quod quidem prope modum videor ex Caesaris litteris ipsius voluntate facere posse, qui negat neque honestius neque tutius mihi quicquam esse quam ab omni contentione abesse.

2 Dices 'ubi ergo tuus ille animus quem proximis litteris?' adest et idem est; sed utinam meo solum capite decernerem! lacrimae meorum me interdum molliunt precantium ut de Hispaniis exspectemus. M. Caeli quidem epistulam scriptam miserabiliter, cum hoc idem obsecraret ut exspectarem, ne fortunas meas, ne unicum filium, ne meos omnis tam temere proderem, non sine magno fletu legerunt pueri nostri; etsi meus quidem est fortior eoque ipso vehementius commovet, nec quicquam nisi de dignatione laborat.

3 Melitam igitur, deinde quo videbitur. tu tamen etiam nunc mihi aliquid litterarum, et maxime si quid ab Afranio. ego si cum Antonio locutus ero, scribam ad te quid actum sit. ero tamen in credendo, ut mones, cautus; nam occultandi ratio cum difficilis tum etiam periculosa est. Servium exspecto ad Nonas et †adicit a† Postumia et Servius filius. quartanam leviorem esse gaudeo. misi ad te Caeli etiam litterarum exemplum.

---

9 quid *F*: quod Ω Hispania ς: -am Ω **2**, 1 ergo tuus ille bZ^b: i- e- t- Ω 6 unicum filium *Corradus*: -cam -iam Ω **3**, 1 quo *PF*: quod *O*Δ: cum *R* 6 adi(i)cit a Ω: adigit ita *Bosius*: *anne* agit ita*?* Servius filius *Bosius*: -vi (-vii, -bi) -li(i) Ω

marched through Illyricum into Germany with a large army; we had it on unimpeachable authority. Well then, best go to Malta till we know what happens in Spain. From Caesar's letter it almost looks as though I can do that with his blessing, since he says there is no more honourable or safer way for me than to hold aloof from all conflict.

2 You will ask what has become of the spirit I showed in my last letter. It is still here, the same as ever. But if only it was just my own life I was staking! The tears of those I love, who entreat me to wait for the outcome in Spain, sometimes sap my resolution. Our boys wept bitterly when they read a pathetic letter from M. Caelius in which he made the same plea, that I should wait and not so recklessly sacrifice my fortune, my only son, and all who are dear to me. My own son, it is true, is braver and for that very reason moves me more strongly. He thinks of nothing but my good name.

3 To Malta therefore, and then wherever seems best. Please send me a line or two even now, especially if you have any news from Afranius' quarter. If I talk to Antony, I shall let you know the result. But I shall follow your advice and be cautious in trusting him. As for a secret departure, it would be dangerous as well as difficult. I expect Servius for the Nones, as requested by (?) Postumia and Servius junior. I am glad your fever is easier. I am sending you a copy of Caelius' letter too.

200A (X. 9A)

Scr. in Liguria c. xv Kal. Mai. an. 49

CAELIVS CICERONI SAL.

1 Exanimatus tuis litteris, quibus te nihil nisi triste cogitare ostendisti neque id quid esset perscripsisti neque non tamen quale esset quod cogitares aperuisti, has ad te ilico litteras scripsi.

Per fortunas tuas, Cicero, per liberos te oro et obsecro ne quid gravius de salute et incolumitate tua consulas. nam deos hominesque amicitiamque nostram testificor me tibi praedixisse neque temere monuisse sed, postquam Caesarem convenerim sententiamque eius qualis futura esset parta victoria cognorim, te certiorem fecisse. si existimas eandem rationem fore Caesaris in dimittendis adversariis et condicionibus ferendis, erras. nihil nisi atrox et saevum cogitat atque etiam loquitur. iratus senatui exiit, his intercessionibus plane incitatus est; non mehercules erit deprecationi locus.

2 Qua re si tibi tu, si filius unicus, si domus, si spes tuae reliquae tibi carae sunt, si aliquid apud te nos, si vir optimus, gener tuus, valemus, quorum fortunam non debes velle conturbare, ut eam causam in cuius victoria salus nostra est odisse aut relinquere cogamur aut impiam cupiditatem contra salutem tuam habeamus * * * denique illud cogita, quod offensae fuerit in ista cunctatione te subisse. nunc te contra victorem

---

Ep. 200A] *reperitur haec ep. in epp. ad Fam.* (VIII. *16*). ψ = *cod. Mediceus 49. 9*
1, 1 tuis Ω: sum tuis ψ   nihil nisi *P* ψ: nihil Ω: non nihil δ   2 quid ψ: quod Ω: per quod *C*   5 te oro et Ω: oro ψ   11 fore *ms* ψ: forte Ω   13 exiit *O*²: exit Ω: exilit ψ   14 me hercules (meh-) Ω (-cule *Obds*): *om.* ψ   **2**, 2 curae *C*   3 valemus Ω: valet ψ   noli committere *ante* ut *olim add. Lehmann, post* habeamus *interpungens; melius, opinor,* haec omnia etiam atque etiam cogitabis *vel sim. post* habeamus *addideris*   6 offensae *P*δ ψ: def- Ω   7 fuerit ψ: -rint Ω: -runt *bs*   subisse *s* ψ: subesse Ω

200 A (X. 9 A)

Liguria (?), c. 16 April 49

CAELIUS TO CICERO

1 Much agitated as I am by your letter, in which you make it plain that you have none but gloomy ideas in mind but do not say in detail what they are, and yet do not conceal the general nature of your intentions, I am writing this letter to you straight away.

I beg and implore you, Cicero, in the name of your fortunes and your children, to take no step which will jeopardize your well-being and safety. I call gods and men and our friendship to witness that I have told you how it will be, and that it is no casual warning I give; having met Caesar and found what his disposition is likely to be once victory is won, I am telling you what I know. If you suppose that Caesar will continue his policy of letting opponents go free and offering terms, you are making a mistake. He thinks and even talks of nothing but ruthless severity. He left Rome angry with the Senate, he is thoroughly incensed by these vetoes. Believe me the time for intercession will be past.

2 Accordingly, if you care for yourself, for your only son, for your household, for your remaining hopes, if I and your excellent son-in-law have any influence with you, whose careers you surely do not wish to ruin by forcing us to hate or abandon the cause with which our welfare is bound up or else to harbour an undutiful wish contrary to *your* welfare * * * . Finally consider that any odium which may attach to

Caesarem facere quem dubiis rebus laedere noluisti et ad eos
fugatos accedere quos resistentis sequi nolueris summae stul-
titiae est. vide ne, dum pudet te parum optimatem esse,
3 parum diligenter quid optimum sit eligas. quod si totum tibi
persuadere non possum, saltem dum quid de Hispaniis agamus
scitur exspecta; quas tibi nuntio adventu Caesaris fore no-
stras. quam isti spem habeant amissis Hispaniis nescio; quod
porro tuum consilium sit ad desperatos accedere non me dius
fidius reperio.

4 Hoc quod tu non dicendo mihi significasti Caesar audierat ac, simul atque 'have' mihi dixit, statim quid de te audisset exposuit. negavi me scire, sed tamen ab eo petii ut ad te litteras mitteret, quibus maxime ad remanendum commoveri posses. me secum in Hispaniam ducit; nam nisi ita faceret, ego, prius quam ad urbem accederem, ubicumque esses, ad te percurrissem et hoc a te praesens contendissem atque omni vi te retinuissem.

5 Etiam atque etiam, Cicero, cogita ne te tuosque omnis funditus evertas, ne te sciens prudensque eo demittas unde exitum vides nullum esse. quod si te aut voces optimatium commovent aut non nullorum hominum insolentiam et iactationem ferre non potes, eligas censeo aliquod oppidum vacuum a bello dum haec decernuntur; quae iam erunt confecta. id si feceris, et ego te sapienter fecisse iudicabo et Caesarem non offendes.

---

8 Caesarem *om.* ψ 11 quid ψ: quod Ω **4**, 2 have ψ: habe Ω 3 exposuit *P* ψ: ea p- Ω sed ψ: *om.* Ω 6 esses Δ: esse ψ: tu esses *OR* 7 percurrissem *OR* ψ: percucurri- (-uri- *d*) δ*C*λ: pervicuri- *M* **5**, 2 ne] nec δ demittas *OPm* ψ: dim- *R*Δ

your hesitancy has already been incurred. When Caesar's prospects were doubtful you were unwilling to harm him; to go against him now, in the hour of victory, and to join a routed party which you did not choose to follow when they were fighting back, is the acme of folly. Don't be so much ashamed of failing the 'right' side as to think too little about
3 making the right choice. But if I cannot persuade you altogether, do at least wait until it is known how things go with us in Spain. You may take my word for it that these provinces will be ours as soon as Caesar arrives. What hope your friends have with Spain lost I do not know, and what sense it makes for you to join a hopeless party on my honour I cannot imagine.

4 What you conveyed to me without putting it into words Caesar had heard already. He scarcely said good day to me before he told me what he had heard about you. I professed ignorance, but asked him all the same to write to you in terms best adapted to induce you not to leave. He is taking me with him to Spain. Otherwise before returning to Rome I should have hurried to you wherever you were and urged my plea in person and held you back with all my might.

5 Think, Cicero, again and yet again before you bring utter ruin on yourself and your family, before you plunge with your eyes wide open into a situation from which you see there is no escape. If however you are worried by what the optimates may be saying or if you find the arrogance and bounce of certain people too much for you, my advice is to choose some town well away from the war while these issues are deciding. It will not be long before they are settled. If you do that I shall judge you to have acted wisely and you will not offend Caesar.

201 (x. 10)

Scr. in Cumano v Non. Mai. an. 49 (§ 3)

CICERO ATTICO SAL.

1 Me caecum qui haec ante non viderim! misi ad te epistulam Antoni. ei cum ego †saepissime† scripsissem nihil me contra Caesaris rationes cogitare, meminisse me generi mei, meminisse amicitiae, potuisse, si aliter sentirem, esse cum Pompeio, me autem, quia cum lictoribus invitus cursarem, abesse velle nec id ipsum certum etiam nunc habere, vide quam ad haec παραιν⟨ετ⟩ικῶς:

2 Tuum consilium †quia† verum est. nam qui se medium esse vult in patria manet, qui proficiscitur aliquid de altera utra parte iudicare videtur. sed ego is non sum qui statuere debeam iure quis proficiscatur necne; partis mihi Caesar has imposuit ne quem omnino discedere ex Italia paterer. qua re parvi refert me probare cogitationem tuam, si nihil tamen tibi remittere possum. ad Caesarem mittas censeo et ab eo hoc petas. non dubito quin impetraturus sis, cum praesertim te amicitiae nostrae rationem habiturum esse pollicearis.

3 Habes σκυτάλην Λακωνικήν. omnino excipiam hominem. erat autem v Non. venturus vesperi, id est hodie; cras igitur ad me fortasse veniet. temptabo, audiam: nihil properare, missurum ad Caesarem. clam agam, cum paucissimis alicubi occultabor; certe hinc istis invitissimis evolabo, atque uti-

---

Ep. 201] **1**, 2 ei *Faërnus*: et Ω saepissime *fort. delendum* 5 autem *R*δ: *om. OM* 6 vide δ: fide *OM*: -em *R* 7 παραινετικῶς *Lambinus*: παρηνικῶς Z^l, *et sim.* Ω: τυραννικῶς *c* **2**, 1 quia Ω: quam δ, *quo recepto vel* tuorum *pro* tuo *vel* ⟨nescio⟩ q- v- sit *legendum conieci* 5 paterer δ: preterea (-ter ea) Ω 8 *num* vestrae? **3**, 3 audiam *Moser*: audeam Ω 4 clam agam *Schmidt*: clamabam Ω 5 certe *ms*: carti ΩZ^β: cati Z^b (*errore typ., ut putavit Clark*)

201 (x. 10)

Cumae, 3 May 49

CICERO TO ATTICUS

1 Blind that I was not to have foreseen this! I sent you Antony's letter. I wrote to him to the effect that I had no thought of acting against Caesar's interests, that I bore my son-in-law in mind and also the claims of friendship, that if I had felt otherwise I might have been with Pompey now, but that finding it irksome to wander to and fro with my lictors I wished to stay at a distance, though even that I had still not definitely decided. This is his wise-acre reply:—

2 Your plan * * * sound. For a man who wishes to take neither side stays in his country; to leave it suggests that he is passing judgement on one side or the other. However it is not my responsibility to decide whether any person is entitled to leave or not. My instructions from Caesar are to allow nobody whosoever to go out of Italy. Therefore it matters little that I should approve your intention since even so I cannot grant you any concession. I advise you to send to Caesar and make your request of him. I do not doubt that he will accede to it, especially as you promise to take our friendship into consideration.

3 There's a Laconian dispatch for you! To be sure I shall lie in wait for him—he is coming on the evening of the 3rd, i.e. today, so perhaps he will call on me tomorrow. I shall sound him, listen to him. I shall say that I am in no hurry, that I shall send to Caesar. I shall act by stealth and conceal myself somewhere with a few companions. At all events I shall make my

nam ad Curionem! σύνες ὅ τοι λέγω. magnus dolor accessit.
efficietur aliquid dignum nobis.

Δυσουρία tua mihi valde molesta; medere, amabo, dum est
4 ἀρχή. de Massiliensibus gratae mihi tuae litterae; quaeso ut
sciam quicquid audieris. Ocellam cuperem, si possem palam,
quod a Curione effeceram. hic ego Servium exspecto; rogor
5 enim ab eius uxore et filio, et puto opus esse. hic tamen
Cytherida secum lectica aperta portat, alteram uxorem. se-
ptem praeterea coniunctae lecticae amicarum; et sunt ami-
corum. ⟨vi⟩de quam turpi leto pereamus, et dubita, si potes,
quin ille, seu victus seu victor redierit, caedem facturus sit.
ego vero vel luntriculo, si navis non erit, eripiam me ex
istorum parricidio. sed plura scribam cum illum convenero.
6 Iuvenem nostrum non possum non amare, sed ab eo nos
non amari plane intellego. nihil ego vidi tam ἀνηθοποίητον,
tam aversum a suis, tam nescio quid cogitans. vim incredi-
bilem molestiarum! sed erit curae et est ut regatur. mirum
est enim ingenium, ἤθους ἐπιμελητέον.

---

6 σύνες ὅ τοι λέγω *Cobet*: σύνες ὅτι λ- *c*: CINECωTΘIΛETω (-AETω) *RMm*: ουνετῷ σοι λέγω *anon. ap. Corradum* **4,** 2 ocellam *C*: soc- Ω 3 quod *Victorius*: quid Ω a curione *R*: acuone Δ **5,** 2 Cytherida *nescio quis*: -dam Ω (*nonnulla in prioribus litteris vacillatione*) *c*: -dem *Lambinus* portat *ms*: -tam Ω: -ta *bd* altera *ms* 3 et sunt *scripsi*: e(a)e s- *ORm*λ (sunt amicorum *etiam* Z^{β}): h(a)e s- *bds*: s- *M*: s- an *Bosius* 4 vide *s*: de Ω 6 vel luntriculo *Victorius*: vel lutridiculo $Z^{l\beta}$ (lintr- Z^{β}): velut rid- *vel sim.* Ω non erit *R*δ: non erat *O*: noverat *M* **6,** 3 aversum *ms*: adv- Ω tam nesc- *Manutius*: tamen sc- Ω o vim *Mueller*

escape from here, however much they want to stop me, and I only hope it will be to Curio. Mark my words. Intense vexation has been added to my other motives. I shall bring off something worthy of myself.

I am much concerned about your strangury. Do, I beg of
4 you, treat it while it is in the early stages. I am glad to hear from you about Massilia. Pray let me know whatever news comes your way. I should much like to take Ocella if I could travel openly, as I had arranged with Curio. I am waiting for Servius here; his wife and son ask me, and I think I ought.
5 But this worthy here is carrying Cytheris around with him in an open litter, a second wife. Seven other litters are attached, containing mistresses; and there are some containing *friends*. Look at the shame of the death we are dying and doubt if you can that Caesar will institute a massacre when he returns, victor or vanquished. I shall snatch myself from the clutches of these criminals in a rowing boat if I cannot get a ship. But I'll write more when I have met him.

6 As for our young man, I cannot help feeling affection for him, but I plainly see that he has none for us. I have never met with such a lack of moral constitution, such estrangement towards his family, such secretiveness. What an incredible spate of annoyances! But I shall take care that he gets some direction, and am already doing so. His abilities are extraordinary, it is his character that needs attention.

202 (X. 11)

Scr. in Cumano iv Non. Mai. an. 49

⟨CICERO ATTICO SAL.⟩

1 Obsignata iam epistula superiore non placuit ei dari cui constitueram quod erat alienus; itaque eo die data non est. interim venit Philotimus et mihi a te litteras reddidit. quibus quae de fratre meo scribis, sunt ea quidem parum firma sed habent nihil ὕπουλον, nihil fallax, nihil non flexibile ad bonitatem, nihil quod non quo velis uno sermone possis perducere; ne multa, omnis suos, etiam quibus irascitur crebrius, tamen caros habet, me quidem se ipso cariorem. quod de puero aliter ad te scripsit et ad matrem de filio, non reprehendo. de itinere et de sorore quae scribis molesta sunt eoque magis quod ea tempora nostra sunt ut ego iis mederi non possim. nam certe mederer; sed quibus in malis et qua in desperatione rerum simus vides.

2 Illa de ratione nummaria non sunt eius modi (saepe enim audio ex ipso) ut non cupiat tibi praestare et in eo laboret. sed si mihi Q. Axius in hac mea fuga HS $\overline{\text{xii}}$ non reddit quae dedi eius filio mutua et utitur excusatione temporis, si Lepta, si ceteri, soleo mirari de nescio quis HS $\overline{\text{xx}}$ cum audio ex illo se urgeri. vides enim profecto angustias. curari tamen ea tibi utique iubet. an existimas illum in isto genere lentu-
3 lum aut restrictum? nemo est minus. de fratre satis.

Ep. 202] *novam ep. faciunt E* (*inc. v.* 4, quae) *Pms*: *cum superiore cohaeret in ORMbd* **1**, 4 ea quidem Σ: eq- *Mm*: q- *bds* 5 non fl- *Manutius*: fl- non Ω 9 aliter ς: alter Ω 10 itinere *OR*δ: itine *MZ* scribis] *accedit W* 11 ea Σ*W*: ad *Mdm*: *om. bs* 12 qua in Δ: quam *W*: qua Σ **2**, 3 $\overline{\text{xii}}$ *Purser*: |$\overline{\text{xiii}}$| *M*: xiii *RbdsW*: $\overline{\text{xxiii}}$ *O*: $\overline{\text{xviii}}$ *m* 5 ceteri *bds*: -is Ω*W* 6 ex illo *Victorius*: exilio Ω*W* 7 utique *Manutius*: ubique Ω*W* lentum *W*

202 (X. 11)

Cumae, 4 May 49

CICERO TO ATTICUS

1 After I had sealed my last letter I decided not to give it to the man I had intended because he was not one of our own people, so it was not dispatched that day. Meanwhile Philotimus arrived and handed me a letter from you. What you say about my brother no doubt argues a certain infirmity, but nothing treacherous or *fourbe*, nothing that may not be bent over to good, nothing you could not lead where you liked in a single talk. In short, he is fond of all his own people, even those with whom he most often falls out of humour, and fonder of me than of himself. I do not think he is to be blamed for writing to you in terms different from those he used to the lad's mother about her son. What you say about the journey and your sister is tiresome, all the more so as our present circumstances do not allow me to put things right, as otherwise I certainly should. But you see what troubles we are in and how hopeless our fortunes.

2 As regards the money business, it is not (I often hear him talk about it) that he does not *want* to pay you and is unconcerned about it. But when Q. Axius does not repay me in this exile of mine the HS 12,000 I lent his son and pleads hard times, when Lepta and the rest do the like, I cannot help feeling surprised when I hear him say that he is being pressed about a matter of HS 20,000. You must see how tight things are. None the less he is giving categorical instructions to have you paid. Do you think him sticky or close about this sort of
3 thing? No one could be less so. Well, that's enough about my brother.

De eius filio, indulsit illi quidem suus pater semper, sed non facit indulgentia mendacem aut avarum aut non amantem suorum, ferocem fortasse atque adrogantem et infestum facit. itaque habet haec quoque quae nascuntur ex indulgentia, sed ea sunt tolerabilia (quid enim dicam?) hac iuventute; ea vero, quae mihi quidem qui illum amo sunt his ipsis malis in quis sumus miseriora, non sunt ab obsequio nostro; nam suas radices habent, quas tamen evellerem profecto, si liceret. sed ea tempora sunt ut omnia mihi sint patienda. ego meum facile teneo; nihil est enim eo tractabilius. cuius quidem misericordia languidiora adhuc consilia cepi et quo ille me certiorem vult esse eo magis timeo ne in eum exsistam crudelior.

4 Sed Antonius venit heri vesperi. iam fortasse ad me veniet aut ne id quidem, quoniam scripsit quid fieri vellet. sed scies continuo quid actum sit. nos iam nihil nisi occulte. de pueris quid agam? parvone navigio committam? quid mihi animi in navigando censes fore? recordor enim aestate cum ⟨illis⟩ illo Rhodiorum ἀφράκτῳ navigans quam fuerim sollicitus; quid duro tempore anni actuariola fore censes? o rem undique miseram!

Trebatius erat mecum, vir plane et civis bonus. quae ille monstra, di immortales! etiamne Balbus in senatum venire cogitet? sed ei ipsi cras ad te litteras dabo.

5 Vettienum mihi amicum, ut scribis, ita puto esse. cum eo, quod ἀποτόμως ad me scripserat de nummis curandis,

---

3, 2 de eius filio *ERs*: de eius inf- *O(?)W*: levis (lenis) in f- Δ 4 atque *Lambinus*: ac Δ: h(a)ec Σ*W* 9 nam *WZ*[b]: non Ω evellerem *ERms*: -re me *OMbdW* 10 ea Ω: ea omnia *W* tempora sunt ut *WZ*[b]: *om.* Ω sint *ORWZ*[b]: sunt *E*Δ 13 certiorem Σ*MbdW*: fort- *Pms* **4,** 3 occulte *ER*δ: -ti *OM(?)W* 4 agam Ω: -m de *W* 5 illis illo *Lehmann*: illo Ω*W* (illorum odi- *W*): illis *Boot* 7 actuariola *Victorius*: -uriora *MW*: -uaria Σδ 10 senatum *s*: -tu Ω*W* **5,** 1 scripsi *W* 2 ἀποτόμως *Victorius*: ΑΠΟΥΟΜΩ *RMmW*: ἀποθυμῶς *c*

As for his son, he has always been indulged by his father, but indulgence does not make a boy untruthful or grasping or wanting in natural affection, though it may make him headstrong, overbearing, and aggressive. Accordingly he has these faults too, the products of over-indulgence, but they are tolerable, at least I suppose I may call them so, young people being what they are nowadays. But the qualities that cause me, fond of him as I am, more pain even than the miseries of our present condition, do not arise from any compliance on our part. They have their own roots. No doubt I should tear them up if I had the opportunity. But the times are such that I must put up with all. I have no difficulty with my own boy, who is the most tractable of beings. It is out of pity for him that I have hitherto taken a weaker line, and the more positive he wants me to be the more I am afraid of proving an unkind father.

4 However Antony arrived yesterday evening. Presently perhaps he will call on me, or perhaps not even that as he has notified his wishes in writing. But you shall know the upshot at once. I shall now do nothing except by stealth. What am I to do about the boys? If I trust their lives to a small boat, how do you think I shall feel during the voyage? I remember how anxious I was last summer, sailing with them in that Rhodian open craft. What do you think it will be like at a bad season in a small dispatch boat? It's a wretched business, whichever way you look at it.

Trebatius is with me, a thoroughly good man and citizen. Ye gods, what monstrosities he has to tell! Can it really be that even Balbus is thinking of getting into the Senate? But I shall be giving Trebatius himself a letter for you tomorrow.

5 Yes, I think Vettienus is my good friend, as you say. As he had written to me brusquely about paying the cash, I put a

θυμικώτερον eram iocatus. id tu, si ille aliter acceperit ac debuit, lenies. 'monetali' autem adscripsi, quod ille ad me 'pro cos.' sed quoniam est homo et nos diligit, ipse quoque a nobis diligatur. vale.

203 (x. 12)

Scr. in Cumano iii Non. Mai. an. 49

⟨CICERO ATTICO SAL.⟩

1 Quidnam mihi futurum est aut quis me non solum infelicior sed iam etiam turpior? nominatim de me sibi imperatum dicit Antonius, nec me tamen ipse adhuc viderat sed hoc Trebatio narravit. quid agam nunc, cui nihil procedit caduntque ea quae diligentissime sunt cogitata taeterrime? ego enim Curionem nactus omnia me consecutum putavi. is de me ad Hortensium scripserat. Reginus erat totus noster. huic nihil suspicabamur cum hoc mari negoti fore. quo me nunc vertam? undique custodior.

2 Sed satis lacrimis. παραποπλευτέον igitur et occulte in aliquam onerariam corrependum, non committendum ut etiam compacto prohibiti videamur. Sicilia petenda; quam si erimus nacti, maiora quaedam consequemur. sit modo recte in Hispaniis! quamquam de ipsa Sicilia utinam sit verum!

3 eram *Corradus*: erat Ω*W* iocatus *c*: loc- *W*: *om.* Ω accepit *Wesenberg* 5 pro cos. *Manutius*: proconsulem Ω*W*

Ep. 203] *novam ep. faciunt* δ: *in* Ω*W cum superiore cohaeret* **1**, 2 imperatum δ: -turum Ω(impetr- *OR*)WZ^{1} 4 narravit *R*δ: -abit *OMW* cui *R*δ: qui *OMW* 6 nactus *ms*: -tu Ω*W* putavi. is *Victorius*: -abis Ω*W*: -abo. is *ms* 8 suspicabatur *W* cum *PC*: eum Ω*W* mari δ: mare Ω*W*λ **2**, 1 παραποπλευτέον *Emil Thomas*: ΠΑΡΑΟΤΑΕΥΤ- *RMmW*(-ΕΙΤ-): ΠΑΡΑ ΟΤΛΕΙΤ- Z^{b}: παραθ(τ)λειτ- $Z^{\beta}c$: παραβλεπτ- *O*: παρακλεπτ- *Woelfflin* 3 compacto *OW*: cum p- *R*Δ

touch of acerbity into my jests with him. If he has taken it amiss, please smooth him down. I put 'Moneyer' after his name because he put 'Proconsul' after mine. But since he is a good fellow and has a regard for me I am quite willing to reciprocate. Good-bye.

203 (X. 12)

Cumae, 5 May 49

CICERO TO ATTICUS

1 What is to become of me? Who is in a more unhappy, and not only that but by now in a more discreditable position than I? Antony says he has received specific orders about me—he has not yet seen me himself however, but so informed Trebatius. What am I to do now? Nothing goes right for me, and the most carefully laid plans turn out abominably. I thought that having gained Curio I had won the whole battle. He had written about me to Hortensius, and I can depend upon Reginus absolutely. I had no idea that this fellow would have anything to do with this sea. Where shall I turn now? I am watched on all sides.

2 But that's enough moaning. I must sail off on the sly then, and creep secretly on board some freighter. I must not let it appear that the prohibition is collusive. I must make for Sicily. Once I make Sicily bigger things will be in my grasp. If only things go right in Spain! Though as regards Sicily too I only

sed adhuc nihil secundi. concursus Siculorum ad Catonem dicitur factus, orasse ut resisteret, omnia pollicitos; commotum illum dilectum habere coepisse. non credo; at est luculentus auctor. potuisse certe teneri illam provinciam scio. ab Hispaniis autem iam audietur.

3 Hic nos C. Marcellum habemus eadem fere cogitantem aut bene simulantem; quamquam ipsum non videram sed ex familiarissimo eius audiebam. tu, quaeso, si quid habebis novi; ego, si quid moliti erimus, ad te statim scribam. Quintum filium severius adhibebo. utinam proficere possem! tu tamen eas epistulas quibus asperius de eo scripsi aliquando concerpito, ne quando quid emanet; ego item tuas.

4 Servium exspecto nec ab eo quicquam ὑγιές. scies quicquid erit.

204 (x. 12*a*)

Scr. in Cumano prid. Non. Mai. an. 49

⟨CICERO ATTICO SAL.⟩

1 Sine dubio errasse nos confitendum est. 'at semel, at una in re'. immo omnia quo diligentius cogitata eo facta sunt imprudentius. 'ἀλλὰ τὰ μὲν προτετύχθαι ἐάσομεν ἀχνύμενοί περ,' in reliquis modo ne ruamus. iubes enim de profectione me providere. quid provideam? ita patent omnia quae accidere possunt ut, ea si vitem, sedendum sit cum dedecore et dolore,

---

7 pollicitos λ: -tus Ω*W* 8 at *Purser*: ut Ω*W*: nec *Wesenberg* 9 teneri λ: -re Ω*W*
3, 1 fere *b*: e re Ω*W*: vere *Madvig* 4 Q. F. *OMW*λ: Q. fr. *R*: Q. fratrem δ
5 habebo *Corradus*: cohib- *Graevius* possem Ω: -se *W*(?): -sim *Pius*
4, 1 quicquid *W*: quid Ω

Ep. 204] *novam ep. constituit Wieland*: *cum superiore in codd. cohaeret* **1,** 4 iubes enim de Z^b: iubes de *W*: iubes enim Ω profectione me *Gronovius*: -ne mea Ω*W*Z^b (mea pr-): -nem meam δ 6 dedecore *R*δ: dec- *OMW*

hope it may be true, but so far we have had no luck—there's a report that the people have rallied to Cato, begged him to put up a fight, promised everything, and that he was sufficiently impressed to start raising troops. I don't believe it. Still the source is respectable. I know the province *could* have been held. From Spain we shall soon have news.

3 We have C. Marcellus here, who intends, or makes a good show of intending, pretty much the same as myself. Not that I have seen him in person, but I hear this from a close friend of his. Write, pray, if you have any news, and I shall write to you immediately if I put anything in hand. I shall handle young Quintus pretty strictly. I wish I was in a position to do good. But please tear up sometime the letters in which I have written sharply about him for fear something may some day leak out. I'll do the same with yours.

4 I am awaiting Servius, but don't expect anything good from him. You shall know whatever there may be to know.

204 (X. 12*a*)

Cumae, 6 May 49

CICERO TO ATTICUS

1 It must be admitted that I have been wrong, no doubt about it; and not on one occasion nor in one matter only. No, in everything alike, the more carefully I have planned the less wisely I have acted. 'But bygones, though in sadness, we'll let lie', and try only not to come to grief in what remains. You advise me to have a care about my departure. A care for what? Everything that can happen is obvious. If I avoid these risks I must accept an ignominious and painful inactivity, if I

si neglegam, periculum sit ne in manus incidam perditorum. sed vide quantis in miseriis simus: optandum interdum videtur ut aliquam accipiamus ab istis quamvis acerbam

2 iniuriam, ut tyranno in odio fuisse videamur. quod si nobis is cursus quem speraram pateret, effecissem aliquid profecto, ut tu optas et hortaris, dignum nostra mora. sed mirificae sunt custodiae et quidem ille ipse Curio suspectus. qua re vi aut clam agendum est, et si vi †forte ne cum tempestate clam autem istis†. in quo si quod σφάλμα, vides quam turpe sit. trahimur, nec fugiendum si quid violentius.

3 De Caelio saepe mecum agito nec, si quid habuero tale, dimittam. Hispanias spero firmas esse. Massiliensium factum cum ipsum per se luculentum est tum mihi argumento est recte esse in Hispaniis. minus enim auderent si aliter esset, et scirent; nam et vicini et diligentes sunt. odium autem recte animadvertis significatum ⟨in⟩ theatro. legiones etiam has quas in Italia assumpsit alienissimas esse video. sed tamen nihil inimicius quam sibi ipse. illud recte times ne ruat. si desperarit, certe ruet; quo magis efficiendum aliquid est, fortuna velim meliore, animo Caeliano. sed primum quidque; quod, qualecumque erit, continuo scies.

4 Nos iuveni, ut rogas, suppeditabimus et Peloponnesum ipsam sustinebimus. est enim indoles, modo aliquod †hoc sit ἦθος ἀκίμολον†. quod si adhuc nullum est, esse tamen potest, aut ἀρετὴ non est διδακτόν, quod mihi persuaderi non potest.

---

7 sit *Lambinus*: est Ω*W* **2**, 3 et *Manutius*: ut Ω 5 ne *O*Δ*W*: et *RFAnt.* pestate *M* clam autem istis *W*: -mant emistis (-tem i-) Δ: clam aut (autem *P*) cum isto (istis *P*) *R* 6 sit *Malaespina*: est Ω*W*: sed *Graevius* **3**, 1 tale *Pm*: -em Ω*W* 5 vicini *Victorius*: victi Ω*WZ* 6 in theatro *Boot*: theatrum Ω*W*: -ro *Victorius* 10 meliore *Lambinus*: -ri Ω*W* **4**, 1 ut *W*: *om.* Ω 2 indoles ϛ: -ens Ω*W*λ 3 AKIMOΛON (-AON *Mm*) *OMmZ*[β]*W*(?): AKI AΛΛOΛON *Z*[b]: AKIKTONMOAON *R*: ἀκίμωλον *c* (*fort.* huic adsit ἦθος ἄκακον καὶ ἄδολον (κακίᾳ ἄδολον *Gronovius*)) 4 quod *Hervagius*: quo Ω

disregard them, I am in danger of falling into the hands of desperadoes. But you can see what a miserable predicament I am in when I say that I sometimes feel inclined to *wish* for some injury, however grievous, at the hands of these people, so that I may appear to have been in bad odour with the tyrant.

2 If the route on which I had counted had been open to me, I should doubtless have achieved something to make my delay seem worth while, as you hope and urge. But the watch is marvellously close, and even Curio himself is suspect. So I must use force or stealth and if force * * * stealth. You will appreciate how ignominious any miscarriage in such an attempt would be. I am swept on by the stream, and I must not shrink from some violence if need be.

3 I often think about Caelius, and if I have any opportunity of that sort I shall not let it slip. I hope Spain is solid. The action of the Massilians is both valuable in itself and evidence to my mind that things are all right in Spain. Otherwise they would not be so bold, and they would know, being near at hand and painstaking folk. You rightly note the hostile demonstrations in the theatre. Even the legions, these that he recruited in Italy, are evidently very disaffected. But the man himself is his own worst enemy. You are right to be afraid of his plunging. He certainly will, if he gets desperate. That is a further reason for doing something in the Caelian spirit, though I hope with better fortune. But one step at a time. The first, whatever it is, you shall know immediately.

4 I shall give the young man what he needs, as you ask, and shoulder the entire Peloponnesus. He has good parts, if only * * * character. If that is altogether lacking now, still it can be acquired, or virtue is not teachable. And of that I cannot be persuaded.

205 (x. 13)

Scr. in Cumano Non. Mai. an. 49 (*§ 2*)

⟨CICERO ATTICO SAL.⟩

1 Epistula tua gratissima fuit meae Tulliae et mehercule mihi. semper s⟨p⟩ecu⟨la⟩m aliquam adferunt tuae litterae. scribes igitur, ac si quid ad spem poteris ne dimiseris. tu Antoni leones pertimescas cave. nihil est illo homine iucundius. attende πρᾶξιν πολιτικοῦ. evocavit litteris e municipiis denos et IIII viros. venerunt ad villam eius mane. primum dormiit ad H. III, deinde, cum esset nuntiatum venisse Neapolitanos et Cumanos (his enim est Caesar iratus), postridie redire iussit; lavari se velle et περὶ κοιλιολυσίαν γίνεσθαι. hoc here effecit. hodie autem in Aenariam transire constituit ⟨ut⟩ exsulibus reditum polliceretur. sed haec omittamus, de nobis aliquid agamus.

2 Ab Axio accepi litteras. de Tirone gratum. Vettienum diligo. Vestorio reddidi. Servius prid. Non. Mai. Minturnis mansisse dicitur, hodie in Liternino mansurus apud C. Marcellum. cras igitur nos mature videbit mihique dabit argumentum ad te epistulae. iam enim non reperio quod tibi scribam. illud admiror quod Antonius ad me ne nuntium quidem, cum praesertim me valde observarit. videlicet aut aliquid atrocius de me imperatum est ⟨aut⟩ coram negare mihi non vult quod ego nec rogaturus eram nec, si impetrassem, crediturus. nos tamen aliquid excogitabimus.

Ep. 205] *novam ep. constituit* ς: *cum superiore in codd. cohaeret* **1**, 2 speculam *Boot*: secum Ω*W*: secum spem *Moser* 3 ac si quid *Manutius*: aliq- Ω*W* 4 cave *ORW*: ne Δ (ve *M*(?)) 5 πρᾶξιν *Victorius*: ΠΡΧΙΝ *RMW*: ἀρχὴν *O*δ 6 viros ς: viri Ω*W* ad villam *Victorius*: duellam Ω*W* dormiit ς: -mit Ω*W* 9 velle et *OW*: vellet *Md*: velle *ERbms* 10 ut *add. Lambinus* 11 polliceretur *OMW*: -cetur *ER*δ **2**, 1 ab axio *O*: ad a- (a da-) *R*Δ*W*: a Q. A- *Buecheler* 5 quod Ω: quid δ 7 aut *ORMW*: *om. E*δ 8 aut *add. Schütz*

205 (x. 13)

Cumae, 7 May 49

CICERO TO ATTICUS

1 Your letter gave great pleasure to my Tullia and for that matter to me. Your letters always bring some glimmer of hope. So please go on writing, and if you can say anything tending to hope, don't let it slip. Mind you don't let Antony's lions frighten you. He is really the most agreeable fellow. What do you think of the following act of statesmanship? He summoned by letter the Boards of Ten and Four from the towns. They arrived at his country house early in the morning. First he slept till 9 o'clock. Then, being informed that the bodies from Naples and Cumae (with whom Caesar is annoyed) had arrived, he told them to come back next day, as he wanted to take a bath and *satisfaire à ses besoins.* This was yesterday's achievement. Today he has arranged to cross over to Aenaria to promise the exiles their recall. But enough of all this, and to our own concerns!

2 I have had a letter from Axius. Thanks about Tiro. I am Vettienus' good friend. I have given Vestorius your letter. Servius is said to have spent the night of 6 May at Minturnae and to be staying this evening with C. Marcellus near Liternum. So he will see me in good time tomorrow and will provide me with material for a letter to you—I have now quite run out of topics. I am surprised that Antony has not so much as sent me a message, particularly as he has been most attentive to me in the past. I suppose he has either received some drastic orders concerning me or else does not want to refuse to my face what I had no intention of asking and would not have trusted if I had obtained it. I shall think of something or other none the less.

3 Tu, quaeso, si quid in Hispaniis; iam enim poterit audiri et omnes ita exspectant ut, si recte fuerit, nihil negoti futurum putent. ego autem nec retentis iis confectam rem puto neque amissis desperatam. Silium et Ocellam et ceteros credo retardatos. te quoque a †curto† impediri video; etsi, ut opinor, habes †εκιταονον†.

206 (x. 14)

Scr. in Cumano viii Id. Mai. an. 49

⟨CICERO ATTICO SAL.⟩

1 O vitam miseram maiusque malum tam diu timere quam est illud ipsum quod timetur! Servius, ut antea scripsi, cum venisset Non. Mai., postridie ad me mane venit. ne diutius te teneam, nullius consili exitum invenimus. numquam vidi hominem perturbatiorem metu; neque hercule quicquam timebat quod non esset timendum: illum sibi iratum, hunc non amicum; horribilem utriusque victoriam cum propter alterius crudelitatem, alterius audaciam, tum propter utriusque difficultatem pecuniariam; quae erui nusquam nisi ex privatorum bonis posset. atque haec ita multis cum lacrimis loquebatur ut ego mirarer eas tam diuturna miseria non exaruisse. mihi quidem etiam lippitudo haec, propter quam non ipse ad te scribo, sine ulla lacrima est, sed saepius odiosa

---

3, 2 fuerit ς: -int Ω*W* 3 putent *ER*: -em *O*Δ*W* 5 curto Ω*W*: Curtio *Victorius* 6 ΕΚΙΤΑΟΝΟΝ *RMmZ*[1]: ἐκ τῶν ἀγώνων *c*: ἔκπλουν *Baiter*: ἐπιστόλιον *Rothstein* **Ep. 206**] *novam ep. facit E*: *cum superiore cohaeret in* Ω*W* 1, 10 *antecedenti vocabulo cohaeret in PMm*: *om.* Σ*bdsW* 3 postridie *W*: pridie Ω mane *W*: *om.* Ω*C* 6 sibi illum *W* 9 pecuniariam *Odms*: -niam *ERMW*:- niarum *b* quae erui *Gronovius* (qua e- *Bosius*): qu(a)e frui *E* (qua ef-) *OPW*: qua f- *R*Δ 12 quam *ERm*: quam quod *OMW*: quam quidem *bds*

3 Pray let me know if anything happens in Spain. The news may soon be out, and everyone is waiting for it under the impression that if things go well the job is as good as done. I myself do not think that all will be over if Spain is held or that everything is lost if Spain goes. I imagine that Silius and Ocella and the rest have been delayed. I see that you too are held up by * , though I believe you have a passport (?).

206 (x. 14)

Cumae, 8 May 49

CICERO TO ATTICUS

1 A wretched life we lead! To be so long prey to fear is surely worse than the actuality we are afraid of. Servius, having arrived on the Nones of May (see my earlier letter), came to my house early next morning. Not to keep you in suspense, we found no future in any plan. Never have I seen a man in such a quaver! Yet I must admit that none of his bogies was imaginary. 'Pompey was angry with him, Caesar no friend. The victory of either was a dreadful prospect, not only because one was cruel and the other unscrupulous, but because of the straits both were in for money, which could only be extracted from private property.' As he said all this he shed so many tears that I wondered such length of misery had not dried them up! As for me, even this ophthalmia which prevents me writing to you in my own hand doesn't bring tears, but it annoys me

2 est propter vigilias. quam ob rem quicquid habes ad consolandum collige et illa scribe, non ex doctrina neque ex libris (nam id quidem domi est, sed nescio quo modo imbecillior est medicina quam morbus)—haec potius conquire, de Hispaniis, de Massilia; quae quidem satis bella Servius adfert, qui etiam de duabus legionibus luculentos auctores esse dicebat. haec igitur si habebis et talia. et quidem paucis diebus aliquid audiri necesse est.

3 Sed redeo ad Servium. distulimus omnino sermonem in posterum, sed tardus ad exeundum; multo se in suo lectulo malle, quicquid foret. odiosus scrupulus de fili mili⟨ti⟩a Brundisina. unum illud firmissime adseverabat, si damnati restituerentur, in exsilium se iturum. nos autem ad haec et ⟨id⟩ ipsum certo fore et quae iam fiebant non esse leviora, multaque colligebamus. verum ea non animum eius augebant sed timorem, ut iam celandus magis de nostro consilio quam adhiben⟨dus⟩ videretur. qua re in hoc non multum est. nos a te admoniti de Caelio cogitabamus.

207 (X. 15)

Scr. in Cumano fort. vi Id. Mai. an. 49

⟨CICERO ATTICO SAL.⟩

1 Servius cum esset apud me, Cephalio cum tuis litteris VI Id. venit; quae nobis magnam spem attulerunt meliorum rerum de octo cohortibus. etenim haec quoque quae in his

---

2, 1 consolandum *C*: -sulandum *EO*: -sulendum *R*Δ: con (*reliqua desunt*) *W* 7 talia] alia *Otto* **3,** 2 est *post* tardus *add. Lambinus*, erat *Wesenberg* multo se . . . foret *Victorius*: multos . . . fore Ω*W* 3 militia *P*: milia Ω*W* 6 id *add. Lambinus* certe ς fiant *Ernesti*: fierent *Wesenberg* 8 celandus *Manutius*: -um *O*Δ*W*: et laudum *R* 9 adhibendus *Vrsinus*: ad idem Ω*W*: ad id adh- *Madvig* 10 -bamus *bds*WZ^{β}: -bimus Σ*Mm*

Ep. 207] *novam ep. faciunt Pms*: *uno tenore* Ω*W* **1,** 3 h(a)ec Ω*W*: h(a)e *d*: e(a)e *ms*

2 the oftener because I am so much awake. So please collect anything you have to offer in the way of comfort and send it, I don't mean from philosophy and books (that I have at home, but somehow the medicine is not strong enough for the malady) —no, but scrape up the news about Spain and Massilia, that sort of thing. As brought by Servius it sounds pretty satisfactory, and he says there is respectable authority for the report about the two legions. That's what I want then, and more of the same order. You are bound to hear something in the next few days.

3 To go back to Servius; we adjourned our talk till tomorrow, but he is reluctant about leaving; says he would much prefer to die in his own bed, whatever betide. His son's service at Brundisium is an awkward snag. One thing he declared very firmly, that if condemned persons were restored he would go into exile. To that I said that this would certainly happen and that what was already going on was no less deplorable, giving many examples. But instead of giving him courage this only made him more timorous, so that I now think he must be kept in the dark about my plan rather than called into partnership. So there's not much to hope for in that quarter. Following your admonition I am not forgetting Caelius.

207 (X. 15)

Cumae, 10 (?) May 49

CICERO TO ATTICUS

1 While Servius was at my house Cephalio arrived with your letter, on the 10th. This brought us great hope of better things, in connexion with the eight cohorts. And those in this area

locis sunt labare dicuntur. eodem die Funisulanus a te attulit litteras in quibus erat confirmatius idem illud. ei de suo negotio respondi cumulate cum omni tua gratia. adhuc non satis faciebat; debet autem mihi multos nummos nec habetur locuples. nunc ait se daturum; cui expensum tulerit morari; tabellariis, si apud te esset qua satis †fecisses†, dares. quantum sit Eros Philotimi tibi dicet.

2 Sed ad maiora redeamus. quod optas, Caelianum illud maturescit; itaque torqueor utrum ventum exspectem. vexillo opus est; convolabunt. quod suades ut †palam†, prorsus adsentior itaque me profecturum puto. tuas tamen interim litteras exspecto. Servi consilio nihil expeditur; omnes captiones in omni sententia occurrunt. unum C. Marcello cognovi timidiorem, quem consulem fuisse paenitet. ὢ πολλῆς ἀγεννείας! qui etiam Antonium confirmasse dicitur ut me
3 impediret, quo ipse, credo, honestius. Antonius autem VI Id. Capuam profectus est. ad me misit se pudore deterritum ad me non venisse quod me sibi suscensere putaret. ibitur igitur, et ita quidem ut censes, nisi cuius gravioris personae suscipiendae spes erit ante oblata; sed vix erit tam cito. Allienus autem praetor putabat aliquem, si ego non, ex collegis suis. quivis licet dum modo aliquis.

4 De sorore, laudo. de Quinto puero, datur opera; spero esse meliora. de Quinto fratre, scito eum non mediocriter laborare

---

5 in Σδ: *om. MW* idem illud Σ*W*: il- id- Δ 8 expensum *e.q.s. ita Manutius*: ex .P. (.p.) sustulerit moram tabellarius si a- te esse quas Ω*W* (*sed tantum* moram *e.q.s. habet W*) 9 fecisses Ω (*abscisum in W*): -set *Pius*: *fort.* facere posses **2,** 3 palam] *fort.* clam 4 profecturum δ: profut- Ω*W* 6 Marcellum *Schütz* 9 quo *Manutius*: quod Ω*W* **3,** 3 me ς: se Ω*W* suscensere *MW*λ (-ri *MW*): succ- Σδ (*sed* -ri *E*δ) 7 aliquis *O*(*?*): -uos *R*Δ*W*

too are said to be wavering. The same day Funisulanus brought me a letter from you in which the same report is repeated more positively. I made him a more than liberal answer about his own affair, giving you all credit. So far he has not been meeting his obligations—he owes me a tidy sum and is not considered well off. Now he says he will pay; that a debtor of his is behind time; that, if you have funds of his with which to meet the debt (?), you may hand the amount over to the couriers. Philotimus' man Eros will tell you the figure.

2 But to return to more important matters, you will be delighted to hear that the Caelian business is ripening. For that reason I am in a torment of indecision whether I ought to wait for a wind. A standard is all they need; they will flock to join it. I quite agree with you about secrecy (?), and that is how I think I shall set off. But in the meanwhile I await a letter from you. Servius' views take me no further. All manner of quibbles arise against every proposal. He is the only man I have met more timid than C. Marcellus, who is sorry he was ever Consul. *Quelle bassesse*! He (Marcellus) is actually said to have encouraged Antony to stop me leaving, I suppose to give his
3 own conduct a better complexion. Antony left for Capua on the 10th. He sent word to me that he had been deterred from calling on me by a feeling of embarrassment because he fancied I was annoyed with him. I shall be off then, and in the manner you recommend, unless some hope of assuming a more important role offers itself beforehand. But it scarcely will so soon. Praetor Allienus thinks that if I don't one of his colleagues will. Anyone may for aught I care so long as somebody does.

4 About your sister, I quite approve. About young Quintus, I am doing what I can and I hope there is some improvement.

de versura, sed adhuc nihil a L. Egnatio expressit. Axius de duodecim milibus pudens! saepe enim ad ⟨me⟩ scripsit ut Gallio quantum is vellet darem. quod si non scripsisset, possemne aliter? et quidem saepe sum pollicitus, sed tantum voluit cito. me vero adiuvarent his in angustiis. sed di istos! verum alias. te a quartana liberatum gaudeo itemque Piliam. ego, dum panes et cetera in navem parantur, excurro in Pompeianum. Vettieno velim gratias quod studiosus, et, si quemquam nactus eris qui perferat, litteras des ante quam discedimus.

208 (x. 16)

Scr. in Cumano prid. Id. Mai. an. 49

CICERO ATTICO SAL.

1 Commodum ad te dederam litteras de pluribus rebus cum ad me bene mane Dionysius †fuit†; cui quidem ego non modo placabilem me praebuissem sed totum remisissem, si venisset qua mente tu ad me scripseras. erat enim sic in tuis litteris quas Arpini acceperam, eum venturum facturumque quod ego vellem. ego volebam autem vel cupiebam potius esse eum nobiscum. quod quia plane, cum in Formianum venisset, praeciderat, asperius ad te de eo scribere solebam. at ille perpauca locutus hanc summam habuit orationis ut sibi ignoscerem; se rebus suis impeditum nobiscum ire non posse. pauca respondi, magnum accepi dolorem, intellexi fortunam

---

4, 3 versura *Vrsinus*: us- Ω*W* 4 ad me scripsit ς: ads- Ω*W* 7 in] *hic desinit W* sed di(i) istos Z^1: sed(d)ust- Ω 9 panes et *EδC*: paves et *M* pavescet *OR*: panis et *Boot*: navis et *Muretus* 10 et si *scripsi*: sit *OM*: sit si *Rms*: si *bd*: est; si *Victorius*

Ep. 208] *novam ep. faciunt EPms*: *uno tenore ORMbd* **1,** 2 fuit *del. Kayser*: venit *Mueller* 3 remisissem *E*Δ: perm- *OR*

About my brother, I can tell you that he is very much concerned to raise money to pay you, but he has not yet squeezed anything out of L. Egnatius. As for Axius and the 12,000, he has his nerve! He wrote to me repeatedly asking me to give Gallius as much as he wanted. Even if he had not written, could I have acted differently? I did make promises more than once, but he wanted that much and wanted it quickly. The money would have come in useful to me in these hard times. Confound them! However, another time. I am glad you are rid of your fever and Pilia too. While the bread, etc., is getting ready for the ship I am running over to my place at Pompeii. Please thank Vettienus for his zeal. If you find anyone to carry a letter, please send one before we leave.

208 (x. 16)

Cumae, 14 May 49

CICERO TO ATTICUS

1 I had just sent off a letter to you on various matters when Dionysius arrived at my place bright and early. I should not only have shown a placable spirit towards him, I should have forgiven the whole episode if he had come in the frame of mind you had led me to expect. You said in the letter which I received at Arpinum that he would come and do what I wanted. Now I wanted or rather earnestly desired him to stay with us; and because when he visited Formiae he categorically refused to do that I used to write to you about him rather harshly. However he had very little to say, and the gist of it was that I must excuse him; he was involved in business of his own and could not go with us. I did not say much in

ab eo nostram despectam esse. quid quaeris? fortasse miraberis: in maximis horum temporum doloribus hunc mihi scito esse. velim ut tibi amicus sit; hoc cum tibi opto, opto ut beatus sis; erit enim tam diu.

2 Consilium nostrum spero vacuum periculo fore; nam et dissimulavimus nec, ut opinor, acerrime adservabimur. navigatio modo sit qualem opto, cetera, quae quidem consilio provideri poterunt, cavebuntur. tu, dum adsumus, non modo quae scieris audierisve sed etiam quae futura providebis scribas velim.

3 Cato, qui Siciliam tenere nullo negotio potuit et, si tenuisset, omnes boni se ad eum contulissent, Syracusis profectus est ante diem viii Kal. Mai., ut ad me Curio scripsit. utinam, quod aiunt, Cotta Sardiniam teneat! est enim rumor. o, si id fuerit, turpem Catonem!

4 Ego, ut minuerem suspicionem profectionis aut cogitationis meae, profectus sum in Pompeianum a. d. iiii Id. ut ibi essem dum quae ad navigandum opus essent pararentur. cum ad villam venissem, ventum est ad me: centuriones trium cohortium, quae Pompeiis sunt, me velle postridie convenire. haec mecum Ninnius noster; velle eos mihi se et oppidum tradere. at ego tibi postridie a villa ante lucem, ut me omnino illi ne viderent. quid enim erat in tribus cohortibus? quid si plures? quo apparatu? cogitavi eadem illa Caeliana quae legi in epistula tua quam accepi simul et in Cumanum veni eodem die; et simul fieri poterat ut temptaremur. omnem igitur suspicionem sustuli.

2, 2 nec *scripsi*: et Ω, *quo servato* non *ante* acerrime *add. Madvig* (*addere noluerat Lambinus*) asservabimur *Lambinus*: -mus Ωλ 4 poterunt *E*δ: potue- *ORM* 5 scieris *ER*δ: scies *OM* **3,** 2 se ad eum Σ: se ad eum se *M*: ad eum se δ **4,** 1 ego *E*δ: ergo *ORM* 4 ventum est *M*: venerunt Σδ 5 Pompeis *Brunus* (M^4): -pei(i) Ω postridie δ: posse die Ω convenire *CZ*: *om.* Ω 7 a villa *Manutius*: ad villam Ω 9 cogitavi (*ex* -abi) *M*: -abit *OR*: rogitavi *bd* (*de ms tacet Sjögren*) 10 et Ω: ut ς: atque *Schmidt* 11 simul *secl. Baiter*

answer, but I was bitterly hurt. Clearly he scorned us in our present plight. Well, there it is. Perhaps you will be surprised when I tell you that among the distresses of this present time I count this as one of the greatest. I hope you may keep his friendship, and in expressing that wish I am wishing you prosperity; the one will last just so long as the other.

2 I hope my plan won't involve any risk. I have concealed my intention and I don't think I shall be very closely watched. If only sailing conditions are satisfactory, all other contingencies that can be rationally foreseen will be provided for. So long as I am here please write not only what you get to know or hear but what you see ahead.

3 Cato, who could have held Sicily without any difficulty (and if he had, all the honest men would have joined him), left Syracuse on 23 April, so Curio has written to me. Let us hope Cotta holds Sardinia, as they say he will—there is a rumour. A sorry figure Cato will cut if he does!

4 In order to draw off suspicion as to my departure or intentions I left for Pompeii on the 12th, meaning to stay there while the necessaries for the voyage were got ready. On my arrival at the house I had a visit to inform me that the Centurions of the three cohorts stationed at Pompeii desired to meet me next day. Our friend Ninnius discussed this with me, told me they wanted to put themselves and the town in my hands. As for me, I was off and away from the house next morning before daybreak, so that they should not get so much as a sight of me. For what was the use of three cohorts, or even more, supposing there had been more? What equipment had they? I thought of those same Caelian ideas which I read in the letter of yours that I received as soon as I got back to Cumae later in the day; and besides, it could have been a trap. So I removed all suspicion.

5 Sed, cum redeo, Hortensius venerat et ad Terentiam salutatum deverterat. sermone erat usus honorifico erga me. iam eum, ut puto, videbo; misit enim puerum se ad me venire. hoc quidem melius quam collega noster Antonius, cuius inter lictores lectica mima portatur.

6 Tu quoniam quartana cares et novum morbum removisti sed etiam gravedinem, te vegetum nobis in Graecia siste et litterarum aliquid interea.

209 (X. 17)

Scr. Cumano xvii Kal. Iun. an. 49 (§ *4*)

⟨CICERO ATTICO SAL.⟩

1 Prid. Id. Hortensius ad me venit scripta epistula. vellem cetera eius. quam in me incredibilem ἐκτένειαν! qua quidem cogito uti. deinde Serapion cum epistula tua; quam prius quam aperuissem, dixi ei te ad me de eo scripisse antea, ut feceras. deinde epistula lecta cumulatissime cetera. et hercule hominem probo; nam et doctum et probum existimo. quin etiam navi eius me et ipso convectore usurum puto.

2 Crebro refricat lippitudo, non illa quidem perodiosa sed tamen quae impediat scriptionem meam. valetudinem tuam iam confirmatam esse et a vetere morbo et a novis temptationibus gaudeo.

3 Ocellam vellem haberemus; videntur enim esse haec paulo faciliora. nunc quidem aequinoctium nos moratur quod valde perturbatum erat. id si traxerit, utinam idem maneat

---

5, 1 cum] dum *Lambinus* 2 iam *Wesenberg*: tam Ω: tum δ **6,** 1 novum *OMbdCZ*^{l}λ: nedum (ne dum) *RmsZ*^{b}: non modo *vel* non modo veterem *Lambinus* 2 te *R*δ: teque *OM*

Ep. 209] *novam ep. faciunt Pms*: *uno tenore* Ω **1,** 2 *fort.* eius modi 4 ei *Manutius*: et Ω 5 lecta *Manutius*: scripta Ω: aperta *Klotz*: stricta (*mallem* strictim lecta) *Tyrrell* 6 probo nam (pro b-) Ω: bonum *F*δ: *om. Ant.*
2, 1 refricatur *Corradus* **3,** 1 Ocellam *Victorius*: c- Ω 3 traxerit *scripsi*: cras erit Ω : transierit *Ziehen*

5 Back again, I found that Hortensius had arrived and turned out of his road in order to call on Terentia and pay his respects. He had spoken of me very politely. I expect I shall be seeing him presently as he has sent a boy to tell me he is coming. That's an improvement anyway on my colleague Antony—who has an actress carried in a litter among his lictors.

6 Now that you are free of your fever and have shaken off your recent complaint and your cold too, see that we find you hale and hearty in Greece and send a line or two in the meanwhile.

209 (x. 17)

Cumae, 16 May 49

CICERO TO ATTICUS

1 Hortensius called on the 14th after my letter was written. I could wish the rest of him were to match. Quite extraordinary *empressement* towards me! I mean to make use of it. Then came Serapion with your letter. Before I opened it I told him that you had already written to me about him, as was the fact. Then, after reading the letter, I said what else there was to say in terms as handsome as I could make them. I really do like him. He seems a cultured person and an honest one. In fact I think I shall avail myself of his ship and of his company on board her.

2 My ophthalmia often irritates me, not that it is so very bad, but it's bad enough to interfere with my writing. I am glad to hear that your health is now fully restored, both from the old complaint and the recent attacks.

3 I wish we had Ocella with us, now that things seem to be a little easier than I had expected. It is just the unusually rough equinox that is holding up us now. If that lasts, I only hope

Hortensius! si quidem, ⟨ut⟩ adhuc erat, liberalius esse nihil potest.

4 De diplomate admiraris quasi nescio cuius te flagiti insimularim; negas enim te reperire qui mihi id in mentem venerit. ego autem, quia scripseras te proficisci cogitare (etenim audieram nemini aliter licere), eo te habere censebam et quia pueris diploma sumpseras. habes causam opinionis meae. et tamen velim scire quid cogites in primisque si quid etiam nunc novi est. XVII Kal. Iun.

210 (X. 18)

Scr. in Cumano xiv Kal. Iun. an. 49 (§ *1*)

⟨CICERO ATTICO SAL.⟩

1 Tullia mea peperit XIIII Kal. Iun. puerum ἑπταμηνιαῖον. quod εὐτόκησεν gaudeam; quod quidem est natum perimbecillum est. me mirificae tranquillitates adhuc tenuerunt atque maiori impedimento fuerunt quam custodiae quibus adservor. nam illa Hortensi⟨a⟩na omnia †fuere infantia ita fiet† homo nequissimus a Salvio liberto depravatus est. itaque posthac non scribam ad te quid facturus sim sed quid fecerim; omnes enim Κωρυκαῖοι videntur subauscultare quae loquor.

2 tu tamen si quid de Hispaniis sive quid aliud perge, quaeso, scribere nec meas litteras exspectaris, nisi cum quo opto pervenerimus aut si quid ex cursu. sed hoc quoque timide scribo;

---

4 ut *add. Faërnus* **4,** 1 insimularim *Corradus*: -rem Ω 4 nemini *s*: -nit (-nit-) *Mm*: -nem *ORbd* 6 cogites *ms*: -et Ω

Ep. 210] *novam ep. facit E* (*inc. v.* 3, me): *uno tenore ORΔ* **1,** 2 gaudeo ς: -ebam *Manutius*: est quod gaudeam *Tyrrell* 4 maiori *Lamb.* (*marg.*): -re Ω 5 Hortensiana ς: -ina Ωλ fuerunt *Wesenberg* inania *Orelli*: fatua *Reid* id ita fit *Wesenberg* **2,** 3 cursu ς: -sus Ω

Hortensius stays of the same mind, for so far nothing could be more forthcoming.

4 You express surprise about the passport, as though I had accused you of some misdemeanour, and say you can't imagine how I got such an idea. Well, since you had written that you were planning to leave and since I had heard that no one was allowed to do so otherwise, that was why I thought you had one, and also because you had taken out a passport for your boys. So now you know why I thought what I did. Anyhow I should like to know your plans, and also more especially any news there may yet be. 16 May.

210 (X. 18)

Cumae, 19 May 49

CICERO TO ATTICUS

1 My Tullia has given birth to a seven months' child, a boy, on 19 May. For her safe delivery let me be thankful. As for the baby, it is very weakly. I have been held up until now by some extraordinary calms which have been a greater hindrance than the watch set over me—that stuff of Hortensius' was just words (?). You will find it so (?): the scoundrel has been perverted by the freedman Salvius. So henceforward I won't write to you what I am going to do, only what I have actually done. Every spy in the country seems to have an ear
2 cocked to catch what I say. However, on your side pray go on sending me news about Spain or anything else you have,

ita omnia tarda adhuc et spissa. ut male posuimus initia sic cetera sequuntur.

Formias nunc sequimur; eaedem nos fortasse furiae persequentur. ex Balbi autem sermone quem tecum habuit non probamus de Melita. dubitas igitur quin nos in hostium numero habeat? scripsi equidem Balbo te ad me ⟨et⟩ de benevolentia scripsisse et de suspicione. egi gratias; de altero
3 ei me purgavi. ecquem tu hominem infeliciorem? non loquor plura, ne te quoque excruciem. ipse conficior venisse tempus cum iam nec fortiter nec prudenter quicquam facere possim.

---

5 eedem *s*: c(a)edem *Ebd*: eadem *ORMm*: eodem Z^{1} furi(a)e *ΣbdsZ*^{1}: -ia *Mm* 8 et de *Orelli*: de *ERδ*: e *O(?)M*: de eius *Schmidt* 9 de altero; de altero *Boot* 10 purgavi Σδ: -ga *M* ecquem ς: eo q- Ω

but don't expect to hear from me until we arrive where I hope we shall—or perhaps I may send something on the voyage. But I hesitate to write even this much, everything has so far been so slow and sticky. We started badly and the sequel corresponds.

Now I am for Formiae. Perhaps the same avenging powers will follow me there. To judge from Balbus' talk with you, my idea about Malta does not find favour. Can you any longer doubt that Caesar regards me as an enemy? I have written to Balbus saying that I had heard from you both about his good will and about his suspicions, and offering him my thanks and, on the second point, my exculpations. Is there an unluckier
3 fellow in the world? I won't run on, for fear of distressing you too. For myself it is more than I can bear to find that a time has come when I can no longer act either boldly or wisely.

COMMENTARY

133 (VII. 10)

What happened after C.'s return *ad urbem*, despite his personal efforts to stem the tide, is general history; on the question of the responsibilities assigned to him by the Senate or by Pompey see Appendix II. Before leaving Rome early on 18 January in the panic evacuation which followed news of Caesar's advances in the north, he dispatched this note to Atticus, who remained. Pompey had left for Campania the previous evening.

1 **exirem** Though he had been *ad urbem*, not *in urbe*, C. uses the normal word for leaving town.

2 **laureatis** Lictors' *fasces laureati* were the outward sign of the title of *imperator* conferred upon a commander by his men (Mommsen, *St.* I, p. 374). C. soon found his lictors an encumbrance; cf. 135 (VII. 12). 4.

3 **quid agam sqq.** Cf. 2 (I. 6). 2 n.

4 **consili** The evacuation of Rome; cf. 134 (VII. 11). 3; 145 (VII. 21). 1, etc.

6 **nescio adhuc** Taken, as used to be customary, with *coartatus*, there was no sense to be got out of *adhuc*, since Pompey had only left Rome a few hours previously. The conjectures and interpretations in T.–P.'s note are not worth discussing, especially as the transfer of a comma is all that is wanted: cf. 169 (IX. 2*a*). 3 *nos adhuc quid Brundisi actum esset plane nesciebamus*; *Fam.* IX. 7. 2 *nihil adhuc scimus*; Ov. *Met.* IX. 554 *quid liceat nescimus adhuc*; Sen. *Contr.* II. 3. 4, X. 1. 4; Plin. *Paneg.* 79. 2. *adhuc* quite often follows its verb at the end of a sentence or clause, e.g. 165 (VIII. 15). 2 *offici me deliberatio cruciat cruciavitque adhuc*; Q. *Fr.* II. 12. 2 *certi nihil est adhuc, sed veremur. in oppidis. . .stupens* is an afterthought giving C.'s idea of Pompey's situation as it must be henceforward. There is nothing wrong with *coartatus*—a great man like Pompey could not spread himself in these petty places: cf. 158 (VIII. 8). 1 *in Apuliam se compegerat.* For *oppidis* cf. 96 (V. 3). 1 *in oppidis enim summum video timorem.*

7 **omnes** I.e. all republicans, C. included. Watt substitutes *omnino* (concessive), but I see no real difficulty in the vulgate: cf. 152 (VIII. 2). 3 *nos interea ne Capuae quidem sed Luceriae* (written from Formiae).

consistet The chances seem heavy against *consistat*, especially in view of *cedet* following; see however K.–S. II, p. 395.

10 **vel. . .venerit** Cf. 12 (I. 12). 4 n. *vel* implies *si rem nullam habebis.*

134 (VII. 11)

Leaving Rome before daybreak on the 18th, C. could easily arrive at Formiae on the evening of the 19th. §5 suggests that this letter was written shortly after his arrival there; its successor in the collection belongs to the 22nd (see introd. note). We have two letterless days between the 18th and the 22nd; therefore, since C. says in 139 (VII. 15). 1 that he had written every day since leaving the capital, two letters must be missing (cf. 138 (VII. 14). 2). One of them may be assumed to have been dispatched on the 20th to report his arrival at his villa. This letter is therefore best assigned to the 21st.

1, 2 **Cingulum** Held perhaps by Attius Varus (cf. 137 (VII. 13*a*). 3), but not for long: cf. Caes. *B.C.* I. 15. 2.

inquit Not 'people say'. The subject, when unexpressed, is always a particular person, real or imaginary, to whom the writer cannot or will not put a name (cf. *Thes.* VII. 1779 ff.). Some hold that Pompey is that person here, and that the items of intelligence were reported by him to the Senate either in his speech on the 17th (Schmidt, *Briefwechsel*, p. 115) or in a dispatch subsequently (E. Fraenkel, *Eranos* 54 (1956), p. 190, n. 1). The first hypothesis would point to the 18th or 19th as the date of writing, which in view of §5 is not probable. As for the second, where was the Senate? Pompey would not be sending dispatches to the laggards in the capital. And how was Atticus to understand? Besides it is improbable that Labienus' defection, treated in 135 (VII. 12). 4 f. as a rumour not yet definitely confirmed, had been officially notified by Pompey. We might suppose that the reports had been quoted in a letter of Atticus, if we did not know that C. had not yet received one (cf. 135 (VII. 12). 1 n.). The only way out seems to be to understand with E. Meyer (*Caesars Monarchie*[3], p. 89, n. 5) that C. is quoting from a source he does not trouble to name ('ein Bote oder ähnl.'). The use of *inquit* with citations from unnamed authors or proverbial sayings is essentially similar.

Anconem amisimus This news had reached Rome before the evacuation (*Fam.* XVI. 12. 2). On the form of the accusative, from *Ancon* (Ἄγκων), see Neue–Wagener, *Formenlehre*[3], I, p. 499. In 142 (VII. 18). 2 and elsewhere C. uses the Latin form *Ancona* (cf. *Thes.* II. 29).

3 **Labienus** Recently put in charge of Cisalpine Gaul by Caesar, who according to Hirtius (*B.G.* VIII. 52. 3) had been warned of his disloyalty but refused to believe the reports.

5 **τοῦ καλοῦ** Cf. 39 (II. 19). 1 n.

8 **nullo publico consilio** The state having had no hand in determining the matter: cf. *Lig.* 3 *si illud imperium esse potuit quod ad privatum clamore multitudinis imperitae, nullo publico consilio deferebatur*; *Pis.* 77 *se contra armatum tribunum pl. sine publico consilio decertare nolle* et sim.

9 **patriam** = πόλιν.

χρεῶν ἀποκοπάς, φυγάδων καθόδους On the first cf. Adam on Plat. *Rep.* 566A. In *Leg. Agr.* II. 10 *restitutio damnatorum* is included among proceedings wrongly accounted 'popular', *qui civitatum adflictarum perditis iam rebus extremi exitiorum solent esse exitus*; cf. 199 (x. 8). 2 *exsulum reditum et tabulas novas.*

10 **τὴν θεῶν κ.τ.λ.** Eur. *Phoen.* 506, where Pearson notes that 'the deification of abstractions is characteristic of Euripides'.

11 **unam sqq.** Cf. *Fam.* II. 12. 2 (to Caelius) *cum una mehercule ambulatiuncula atque uno sermone nostro omnis fructus provinciae non confero*, VII. 11. 2 (to Trebatius) *una mehercule collocutio nostra pluris erit quam omnes Samarobrivae*; 84 (IV. 10). 1. D. L. Drew (*Cl. Rev.* 52 (1938), p. 9) suggests that C. was thinking here of Alexander's meeting with Diogenes (cf. *Tusc.* V. 92), 'the classic, if not unique, instance of ethical collision between sun-bathing and tyranny'.

12 **lucrativo** Clearly a phrase of Atticus'. *lucrum* is something one has not paid for, 'thrown in': cf. Varro, *L.L.* V. 176 *lucrum ab luendo, si amplius quam ut exsolveret quanti esset ⟨re⟩ceptum*; Ter. *Phorm.* 246 *quicquid praeter spem evenit, omne id deputare esse in lucro* (cf. *Fam.* VII. 24. 1), also *de lucro (alicui) vivere* (*Fam.* IX. 17. 1; Liv. XL. 8. 2), *lucri facere* (with various nuances, but 'get for nothing' in Sen. *Contr.* X. 5. 20 *putent se alienas sententias lucri fecisse*). Atticus may be supposed to have called the sunshine at his home *lucrativus* because it did not have to be paid for, perhaps poking fun at his own economical housekeeping (cf. Nep. *Att.* 13. 6). Watt surprisingly prints *Lucretilino* (Faërnus), from Lucretilis, a mountain or possibly group of mountains in the Sabine country (see Philipp, *RE.* XIII. 1656). There is surely very little likelihood that Atticus' *suburbanum* (*Ficulense*: cf. 126 (VII. 3). 6 n.) lay so far out in the hills.

14 **illius** I can see no reason why C. should have to write *istius* twice.

2, 1 quid si sqq. The sequence of thought could have been made clearer. Atticus or someone is supposed to raise an objection: 'It is all very fine to call Caesar a pitiable lunatic, but if you wanted to be a tyrant (you say it's the last thing you do want), might you not be acting as he acts?' C.'s first answer is that the harm is not in the wish for despotic power (cf. Juv. X. 95 *quidni / haec cupias? et qui nolunt occidere quemquam / posse volunt*) but in the attempt to implement it. Then, feeling that this retort does not really represent his position (cf. *Off.* III. 37 *in ipsa enim dubitatione facinus inest*, 49 *hoc enim ipsum utile putare quod turpe sit calamitosum est*), he dismisses it (*sed*) and puts forward another: the wish itself is the worst thing that can happen to anyone (so there can be no question of himself or any rational person indulging it)—the worst thing, that is, but one, its fulfilment.

5 **σοι** A necessary correction: cf. 14 (I. 14). 4 n. (*auditori*). The scribe repeated CO. For σχολάζω, 'give lectures', see L.–S.–J.

3, 1 **per fortunas** Cf. 104 (V. 11). 1 n. The question amounts to an appeal for enlightenment.

2 **quid...reliquerit** *Catil.* II. 13 *quaesivi quid dubitaret proficisci*; *Div.* I. 59 *visum tibi esse...C. Marium...quaerere ex te quid tristis esses* et sim. The alternative is Watt's *quod...reliquit* (*Mnemos.* Ser. 4, 16 (1963), p. 391: 'the subjunctive *reliquerit* has attracted but few comments, and those few are fatuous').

3 **tum nihil absurdius** Sc. *videbatur. tum* = τότε, i.e. 'at the time' (cf. *rursus autem* below). Taken as 'moreover' the word is meaningless, for ἀπορῶ is not a direct criticism of Pompey. No doubt it may be taken as *implying* a criticism (that his action made no sense), but in that case *nihil absurdius* would not constitute a further, separate criticism. Watt substitutes *tamen*, perhaps rightly.

ergo...venirent Perhaps a question, as some editors make it. The argument is a *reductio ad absurdum*: if Pompey is willing to abandon Rome to Caesar, he would do the same in case of a foreign, Gallic invasion, and that in the eyes of all patriots would be an unthinkable disgrace. Not 'you would have done the same (i.e. no more) if the Gauls were coming upon us'.

4 **parietibus** C. may have had in mind Thuc. VII. 77. 7 ἄνδρες γὰρ πόλις, καὶ οὐ τείχη οὐδὲ νῆες ἀνδρῶν κεναί (cf. I. 143. 5; Herod. VIII. 61. 2). So Pompey to the Senate in Appian's speech (*B.C.* II. 37) οὐ γὰρ τὰ χωρία καὶ τὰ οἰκήματα τὴν δύναμιν ἢ τὴν ἐλευθερίαν εἶναι τοῖς ἄνδρασιν.

5 **aris et focis** Cf. 136 (VII. 13). 1 *illa templa et tecta.*

Themistocles...Pericles Cf. Plut. *Pomp.* 63 αἰτιᾶται καὶ Κικέρων ὅτι τὴν Θεμιστοκλέους ἐμιμήσατο στρατηγίαν μᾶλλον ἢ τὴν Περικλέους, τῶν πραγμάτων τούτοις ὁμοίων ὄντων οὐκ ἐκείνοις; 199 (X. 8). 4 *Pompeium...cuius omne consilium Themistocleum est.* K. von Fritz (*Trans. Am. Phil. Ass.* 73 (1942), p. 151; cf. p. 152) was not entitled to quote C. as saying 'that Pompey had quoted Themistocles as his model' in support of his contention that Pompey's decision to evacuate Italy in case of an open conflict with Caesar was taken half a year before its outbreak.

fluctum sqq. C.'s (if C. is to be identified with Pompey's critic) answer to Pompey's appeal to precedent. After his buoyant language in December (cf. 131 (VII. 8). 4) Pompey was in no position to make the obvious rejoinder that in terms of comparative force available Caesar was as irresistible as Xerxes.

7 **anno...quinquagesimo** Cf. K.–S. I, p. 404.

9 **οὕτως κ.τ.λ.** *Il.* IX. 524 (οὕτω καὶ τῶν).

4, 1 **rursus** Cf. Liv. I. 59. 6 *ubi eo ventum est, quacumque incedit armata multitudo, pavorem ac tumultum facit; rursus, ubi anteire primores civitatis vident, quicquid sit, haud temere esse rentur.*

2 **exitum habiturum** In modern slang 'there may be a future in it'.

3 **nescio istic** Cf. 116 (VI. 2). 8 *tibi nescio*. Perhaps read *nescio* ⟨*an*⟩ *istic* (Ernesti) or *nescio istic*⟨*ine*⟩ (Wesenberg). Terence's *nescio alias* (*Heaut.* 396), *deos nescio* (*ibid.* 1038) are only partially parallel.

4 **denique** The image of Pompey the Great as a fugitive was even more affecting to the public mind than that of Rome deserted.

7 **qualia sint** Not so much 'what they mean' as 'what they come to'—assessment rather than interpretation.

5, 1 **negotio** See Appendix II.

2 **haec Campania** 'This part of Campania', i.e. the north: cf. 114 (V. 21). 8 *in hac mea Asia*; *Flacc.* 64 *haec cuncta Graecia quae fama...floruit* (as opposed to Hellenistic extensions). The expression would be less open to question if C. were writing from Campania itself (Formiae lay a few miles over the Latian side of the Liris), but strict geographical precision need not be demanded; nor do we know the exact limits of the *regio* assigned to C. by the Senate. Sternkopf's *haec et Campana maritima ora* is more specific; but surely C. would have written merely *haec maritima ora*.

4 **vagus** Cf. 150 (VII. 26). 3 *dum existimabam vagos nos fore*.

5 **ὁρμή** Usually taken in the philosophical sense, *appetitio qua ad agendum impellimur* (*Acad.* II. 24); hence 'aim', 'motive'. But Caesar's motive was plain to C.'s eyes already: τὴν θεῶν μεγίστην ὥστ' ἔχειν τυραννίδα. What he would want to know and what Atticus might be able to tell him was the direction in which Caesar was moving (should *quae* be *qua*? Cf. Ov. *Met.* V. 651 *qua veniat...rogatus*). ὁρμή = 'forward rush', *impetus* (cf. 153 (VIII. 3). 4 *impetu huius belli*). The traditional misinterpretation, not shared by certain early scholars, originated in a not altogether lucid note of Victorius, in which he strangely seems to quote in its favour Dio, XLI. 5. 2 πρέσβεις πρὸς τὸν Καίσαρα...ἀπέστειλεν, εἴ πως τὴν ὁρμὴν αὐτοῦ ἐκφυγὼν ἔπειτ' ἐπὶ μετρίοις τισὶ συμβαίη.

7 **acquiesco** Cf. 135 (VII. 12). 3 *acquiesco enim* (sc. *ad te scribens*); 177 (IX. 10). 10 *perlegi omnis tuas et in eo acquievi*; 321 (XIII. 13–14). 3 *crebro regusto tuas litteras; in iis acquiesco*; Fronto *ad Ant. Imp.* II. 3 *in litteris tuis, ut aequum est, acquiescit*.

135 (VII. 12)

Probably to be assigned with Bayet (p. 87, n. 4) to the 22nd rather than the 21st (Schmidt, *Briefwechsel*, p. 120; cf. §2). Two letters to Terentia and Tullia (jointly), dated 22 January from Formiae and 23 from Minturnae (*Fam.* XIV. 18 and 14), show correspondences with this and the next letter to Atticus respectively which make it probable that the letters related were written at the same time. See below on §6 (*Romae*) and 136 (VII. 13). 1. It is of course possible that both pairs were written on the nights before they were dispatched, i.e. the 21st and 22nd.

1, 1 unam Answered in this letter. Evidently it had not arrived when C. wrote 134 (VII. 11).

2 **aliam** It arrived later; cf. 140 (VII. 16). 1.

6 **rogas curem** Cf. K.–S. II, p. 229.

2, 2 Libonem L. Scribonius L. f. Libo came of an old praetorian family and may himself have already held that office (cf. Broughton, p. 248); as early as 56 he is found supporting Pompey in the Senate (*Fam.* I. 1. 3). His daughter had married Pompey's younger son Sextus, and he counted among Pompey's closest intimates. As his Legate he had just been driven from Etruria by Mark Antony (cf. Broughton, p. 269). Later he served as a naval commander in the Adriatic, but seems to have made his peace with Caesar after Pharsalia. The chances of politics after Caesar's death made him Octavian's brother-in-law and Antony's colleague in the Consulship of 34.

plena. . .omnia Cf. 136 (VII. 13). 2 *nihil esse timidius constat, nihil perturbatius* (sc. *Pompeio*).

3 **cohortes** Belonging to the 'Appian' legions; cf. 136 (VII. 13). 2 n.

4 **Teani** Sc. *Apulum*, earlier called Teate, about 25 miles north of Luceria.

6 **quo aut qua** Sc. *discessurus sit.* Spain seemed at this time the most likely destination (cf. 141 (VII. 17). 1). *qua* is not 'where' but 'by what route'; cf. 153 (VIII. 3). 5 *qua autem aut quo nihil scimus.*

8 **Φαλαρισμόν** I.e. *Schrecklichkeit*: cf. *Off.* II. 26 *Phalaris, cuius est praeter ceteros nobilitata crudelitas.* Atticus thought that Caesar would play not only the tyrant but the savage tyrant, Phalaris rather than Pisistratus (cf. 144 (VII. 20). 2).

9 **rerum prolatio** The *iustitium*, involved in the Senate's *decretum tumultus* (cf. Mommsen, *St.* III, p. 1248).

10 **aerarium** According to Caesar (*B.C.* I. 14. 1) the Consul Lentulus was instructed by the Senate to remove the public funds and actually opened the Inner Treasury, but fled incontinent (18 January): cf. 145 (VII. 21). 2.

3, 7 nullo consilio. . .meum consilium C. plays on two senses, 'judgement' and 'advice'. With respect to the latter cf. 153 (VIII. 3). 3 *nihil nisi contra consilium auctoritatemque meam.*

9 **tenent** Cf. 38 (II. 18). 1 n.

11 **puerorum** Cf. 195 (X. 4). 5; 200 (X. 9). 2.

4, 3 M'. . . .Lepidus M'. Aemilius M'. f. Lepidus, Cos. 66. A hesitant republican, he probably ended like his colleague Vulcatius as a member of

Caesar's Senate. In the sixties he had counted as a leading optimate (Ascon. 60. 21, 79. 20; *Phil.* II. 12), but nothing is heard of him afterwards except in these letters of early 49.

4 **L. Torquatus** Cf. 92 (IV. 18). 3 n. Praetor this year, as generally supposed (but cf. 161B (VIII. 11B). 1 n.), he was probably with C. at Formiae (138 (VII. 14). 2 n.).

5, 6 **cui prosit** I.e. the Republic, no longer existing in its institutional form.

7 **nos** 'We here' perhaps rather than 'I' (not anyhow 'myself I think it true').

6, 1 **domesticis. . .tenes** Cf. *Fin.* III. 1 *suis se finibus tenere iubeamus*; Liv. VII. 38. 2 *neque. . .fama Italiae se finibus tenuit*; 217 (XI. 6). 2 *me domo tenui* et sim. Atticus continued to stay out of public sight: cf. 161 (VIII. 11). 7 *scio equidem te in publicum non prodire.*

2 **formam** 117 (VI. 3). 4 n.

3 **de Terentia et Tullia** See the letters to them dated 22 and 23 January (*Fam.* XIV. 18 and 14).

4 **Romae sqq.** Cf. *Fam.* XIV. 18. 1 *considerandum vobis. . .puto quid faciatis, Romaene sitis an mecum an aliquo tuto loco.* But *Romaene* (Reid) need not be written here: cf. K.–S. II, p. 525.

136 (VII. 13)

C. wrote *Fam.* XIV. 14 to his wife and daughter from Minturnae on 23 January; this letter to Atticus was probably written at the same time in view of the coincidences between the two, and probably before daybreak; also before C.'s interview with L. Caesar, which took place *mane* (137 (VII. 13*a*). 2).

1, 1 **Vennonianis** Cf. 115 (VI. 1). 25 n. The nature of the business is unknown.

Labienum sqq. Cf. *Fam.* XIV. 14. 2 *Labienus rem meliorem fecit; adiuvat etiam Piso, quod ab urbe discedit et sceleris condemnat generum suum.* Contrast the depreciatory tone of 135 (VII. 12). 5. C. now has no doubts about the truth of the report.

2 **qui** In loose construction, as though the agent were implied in the act: cf. Caes. *B.C.* III. 83. 3 *unam fore tabellam qui liberandos omni periculo censerent, alteram qui capitis damnarent, tertiam qui pecunia multarent*; Sall. *Orat. Phil.* 12 *neque mihi satis consili est, metum an ignaviam an dementiam eam appellem, qui videmini tanta mala. . .prohibere ne conari quidem.*

ut aliud nihil C. writes *ut nihil aliud* in 225 (XI. 14). 1; 282 (XII. 42). 1; 390 (XV. 12). 2, but *si nihil aliud* in 35 (II. 15). 2 and *Verr.* II. 1. 152.

si is usual in later writers (Livy, Seneca the Younger, Curtius), though *ut aliud nihil* occurs in Sen. *Contr.* IX. praef. 3.

3 **ad summam profectum aliquid** Cf. Liv. XXXI. 34. 1 *Philippus aliquid et ad caritatem suorum et ut promptius pro eo periculum adirent ratus profecturum se si* sqq., also *id.* III. 61. 12 *parvaque certamina in summam totius profecerant spei*, XXXI. 37. 5 *in summam etiam belli profectum foret*; Quint. *Inst.* I. 1. 19 *hoc per singulos* (sc. *annos*) *prorogatum in summam proficit*; Tac. *Ann.* XIII. 38. 1 *nihil in summam pacis proficiebatur. summam* = *summam rem* (cf. Liv. XXXVI. 34. 7 *ad summam rem pertinere*) or *summam rerum* (Caes. *B.C.* III. 51. 4; Liv. VIII. 4. 1).

4 **Pisonem** L. Calpurnius L. f. Piso Caesoninus, C.'s old enemy as Consul in 58. A good deal is known about him, caricature allowed for, from the invective in 55; see R. G. M. Nisbet's sketch, introductory to his edition. His later career was 'moderate and statesmanlike', including the Censorship in 50, 'neutrality' in the Civil War, and opposition to Antony in 44 followed by attempted peacemaking. In 50 he was still unfriendly to C. (Caelius, *Fam.* VIII. 12. 2). His daughter Calpurnia had married Caesar in 59.

5 **grave** Cf. *Verr.* II. 2. 139 *inimici iudicium grave videretur*; *Catil.* I. 16 *cum sis gravissimo iudicio taciturnitatis oppressus* et sim.

quamquam C. qualifies his satisfaction: in this war public opinion after all would hardly count.

15 **animadvertis** I.e. 'in your letter'. The point about Picenum seems to have been made by Atticus.

Picena Cf. 158 (VIII. 8). 1 *Picenum amiserat culpa*. But just in what way Pompey had shown ignorance of affairs in Picenum, his home territory, we do not know. Caesar had seized Ancona in the extreme north of the district, but his main campaign there opened in February. In 145 (VII. 21). 1 Pompey is charged with ignorance of his own forces as well as the enemy's.

16 **sine consilio** Unwise and irrational. Not 'lacking in policy (as opposed to generalship)', though that would fit the context. *consilium* was held to be the especial virtue of the younger Africanus as a commander: cf. *Verr.* II. 5. 25.

17 **condicio** For the singular cf. 138 (VII. 14). 1 *probata condicio est* et sim.

2, 1 ac καίτοι.

4 **ad urbem** Cf. 114 (V. 21). 3 *cum Pompeius propter metum rerum novarum nusquam dimittatur.*

5 **duabus...legionibus** The two 'Appian' legions (cf. 139 (VII. 15). 3 n.) detached from Caesar's army some six months earlier. The Senate having decreed that Pompey and Caesar should each contribute a legion for service against the Parthians, Pompey made his contribution by asking

Caesar to return a legion which he had previously borrowed from himself. Two legions were accordingly released by Caesar, but retained in Italy (cf. 128 (VII. 5). 4 n.), the Parthian threat having subsided, *propter metum rerum novarum*. Their loyalty was naturally suspect (cf. 144 (VII. 20). 1); 162A (VIII. 12A). 3; 162C (VIII. 12C). 3; 162D (VIII. 12D). 1. *invidiose* is certainly preferable to *insidiose*; Sjögren quotes Caes. *B.C.* I. 4. 5 *infamia duarum legionum permotus quas ab itinere...converterat* (sc. *Pompeius*); cf. Vell. II. 45. 3 *neque...quisquam aut expulsus invidiosius aut receptus est laetius*.

6 **invitorum** Cf. 145 (VII. 21). 1 *nec nomina dant; deficit enim non voluntas sed spes*.

8 **commissum** *committere ut faciam* may amount to 'be unwise enough to do', 'make the mistake of doing': cf. 161D (VIII. 11D). 3 *nec...placuit committere ut temeritas nostra non solum nobis sed etiam rei publicae noceret*.

9 **ut...traderemus** Plut. *Caes.* 34 reads like an echo of this passage: οἰκτρότατον δὲ θέαμα τῆς πόλεως ἦν, ἐπιφερομένου τοσούτου χειμῶνος, ὥσπερ νεὼς ὑπὸ κυβερνητῶν ἀπαγορευόντων πρὸς τὸ συντυχὸν ἐκπεσεῖν κομιζομένης.

3, 2 **in Graeciam** C. did not at this time expect Greece to become a theatre of war. He thought that if Pompey left Italy he would go to Spain (141 (VII. 17). 1).

3 **barbarorum** Cf. 180 (IX. 13). 4 *auxiliis Gallorum*. Rhetoric apart (cf. Luc. I. 481 ff.), C. may have been thinking of the Gaulish cavalry (cf. 130 (VII. 7). 6) and the Alaudae: cf. Dio, XLI. 8. 6 μέτριον οὐδὲν οὐδὲ ἐς τὸν Καίσαρα ὑπώπτευον ἀλλὰ καὶ πολὺ πλείω καὶ δεινότερα, ἅτε καὶ βαρβαρικοῦ τὸ πλεῖστον τοῦ στρατοῦ αὐτοῦ ὄντος πείσεσθαι προσεδόκων. Cf. also 161 (VIII. 11). 4 *conculcari...Italiam videbis...aut* ⟨*alterius aut*⟩ *utriusque mancipiis ex omni genere collectis*.

5 **paulum respiro** Writing to Terentia and Tullia the previous day C. had expressed confidence in Dolabella's protection (*Fam.* XIV. 18. 1 *Romae vos esse tuto posse per Dolabellam*), but in *Fam.* XIV. 14. 1 from Minturnae he is less secure (*sin homo amens diripiendam urbem daturus est, vereor ut Dolabella ipse satis nobis prodesse possit*). Dolabella was with Caesar and high in his favour (cf. 185 (IX. 16). 3).

6 **aliter...consulendum** In his own case safety would not be first.

7 **ad opiniones** *ad* 'by the standard of', 'with reference to' is well within ordinary usage: cf. *Planc.* 39 *dubitatis...quin vos M. Laterensis...non ad sententiam legis sed ad suam spem aliquam de civitate delegerit?*; *Parad.* 47 *est enim* (sc. *mea pecunia*) *ad vulgi opinionem mediocris, ad tuam nulla, ad meam modica* (sim. *Off.* III. 84; *Div.* II. 70); *Off.* I. 85 *procuratio rei publicae ad utilitatem eorum qui commissi sunt, non ad eorum quibus commissa est, gerenda est*; Sall. *Orat. Macr.* 13 *nomina rerum ad ignaviam mutantes*; Nep. *Epam.* 2. 3

haec ad nostram consuetudinem sunt levia et potius contemnenda, Eum. 8. 3 *hiberna sumpserant non ad usum belli sed ad ipsorum luxuriam*; Sen. *Ep.* 16. 7. *si ad naturam vives, numquam eris pauper: si ad opiniones, numquam eris dives.*

ne reprehendamur Cf. *Fam.* XIV. 18. 1 *rursus illud me movet quod video omnis bonos abesse Roma et eos mulieres suas secum habere,* 14. 1 *reliquum est. . .vestri similes feminae sintne Romae; si enim non sunt, videndum est ut honeste vos esse possitis.*

9 **Peducaeo** Sex. Peducaeus Sex. f., under whose father C. served in Sicily as Quaestor (cf. 1 (I. 5). 4 n.). Münzer's view that the father is meant here and in several subsequent passages cannot be accepted: cf. Introd. p. 34, n.2. Appian (*B.C.* II. 48) mentions a Sex. Peducaeus as Caesarian governor of Sardinia in 48, who was probably a different man—if Appian confused the praenomina he might be either C. Peducaeus who died at Mutina (cf. *Fam.* X. 33. 4) or T. Peducaeus who was Consul Suffect in 35 (Broughton, p. 406). There is a similar doubt about a Tribune of 55 (? Cf. *ibid.* p. 220, n. 2) and a triumviral commander in Spain in 40 (*ibid.* p. 385). Nor does Caelius' reference (*Fam.* VIII. 14. 1) to a Sex. Peducaeus acquitted of an unnamed charge in 50 make matters any clearer (to say nothing of the *praefectus* (?) L. Peducaeus in *Flacc.* 68; cf. Broughton, p. 178). C. had a very high respect for this Sextus (177 (IX. 10). 10; 190 (X. 1). 1; 416 (XV. 13). 3; 420 (XVI. 11). 1), and I should find it hard to apply his language to a Caesarian careerist. Two old friends were invited to Atticus' deathbed, Balbus and Peducaeus (Nep. *Att.* 21. 4).

10 **splendor** Cf. 113 (V. 20). 4 n. (*Sex Lucilius*).

4, 3 **nam acta sqq.** Cf. 32 (II. 11). 1 n.

4 **μάντις δ' ἄριστος** ὅστις εἰκάζει καλῶς. From an unknown play of Euripides (Nauck, 973). C. translates in *Div.* II. 12 *bene qui coniciet, vatem hunc perhibebo optimum.*

5, 1 **aenigma sqq.** C. begins his next letter with the announcement that he has solved the riddle. The persons intended were the Oppii from Velia (probably the town on the coast of Lucania rather than the district on the Palatine, since from 155 (VIII. 7). 3 they appear to have been neighbours of Atticus on the Quirinal). They seem to have been bankers (cf. 155 (VIII. 7). 3; 195 (X. 4). 12; 198 (X. 7). 3), with whom Terentia had dealings (cf. 146 (VII. 22). 2; 160 (VII. 26). 3 n.). According to the MSS at 137 (VII. 13*a*). 1 Atticus had called them *de Velia saccones. sacco* from *saccus*, 'money-bag', may seem a good enough word to invent for a banker, but it would hardly have baffled C. ἐν αἰνιγμοῖς we expect a play on words, like Κροτωνιάτου in 118 (VI. 4). 3 and φιλοτιμίαν in 123 (VI. 9). 2. *succones* from *suc(c)us* = ὀπός fills the bill. Moreover *sucos(s)us* is a vulgarism for 'rich' in Petr. 38. 6. *Oppiorum* in the MSS is clearly a gloss which has replaced the enigmatic word of the original, but as Watt points out (*l.c.* p. 391) *ex Velia* is probably genuine 'since a glossator, with his eye on the second passage, would hardly have changed *de* to *ex*'.

2 **numero Platonis** Cf. *Rep.* 546.

137 (VII. 13*a*)

The letter is better assigned to the 24th (to avoid a day's gap; cf. 139 (VII. 15). 1) than to the 23rd. On the 24th C. left Minturnae for Cales on his way to Capua, pursuant to Pompey's wishes (138 (VII. 14). 2). These will have reached him by messenger or letter later in the day since he says nothing about leaving here.

1, 1 **aenigma** The substantive could be dispensed with but there is no sufficient reason to exclude it.

2 **dices** 'You will be meaning' or 'it will turn out that you mean': cf. K.–S. I, p. 142 f. *dicis* is usually read, but Bosius' 'exaratum reperi in Tornesiano et Crusellino *saccones dicis*' is probably only a mistake, the note being concerned with *saccones*.

2, 1 **L. Caesarem** Cf. 91 (IV. 17). 5 n. On his mission, see Appendix III.

Minturnis C. may well have written *Menturnis*, the older spelling (cf. *C.I.L.* X, p. 595). It is supported by the MSS in *Fam.* XIV. 14. 2, and in the letters to Atticus the Mediceus has it more often than not; but Σ generally favours the other.

2 **non hominem** Cf. Petr. 38. 15 *phantasia, non homo* et sim.

scopas solutas As useless as the twigs of a broom untied: cf. *Orat.* 235 *ut in proverbio est* (*etsi humilius dictum est, tamen simile est*), *scopas, ut ita dicam, mihi videntur dissolvere.*

3, 1 **Teanum** Sc. *Sidicinum.*

3 **scribam** This promise is not redeemed in any extant letter: cf. 140 (VII. 16). 1 n.

4 **a Teano** The preposition may be used or omitted in such cases: cf. K.–S. I, p. 478.

5 **mansit** C. can hardly have already received news from Venafrum, but he knew that this was Pompey's intention. Both *mansit* and *profectus est* are generally supposed to be epistolary tenses and untrue as to fact, since in writing to Pompey on 15 February (161B (VIII. 11B). 2) C. says that Pompey left Teanum on the day he himself arrived at Capua; and that day was certainly 25 January (139 (VII. 15). 2). But this can scarcely be correct; for in travelling from Minturnae to Cales on the 24th C. must have passed through Teanum, and if Pompey had still been there he would surely have mentioned it in 138 (VII. 14). 1, where he rather implies the contrary (*cum is esset cum*

consulibus Teani). Therefore his statement here is true, that in 161B (VIII. 11B). 2 a μνημονικὸν ἁμάρτημα.

9 **Thermus** Cf. 106 (V. 13). 2 n. On Curio's approach Thermus evacuated Iguvium and fled south. His troops deserted on the way (Caes. *B.C.* I. 12. 2).

P. Attius P. Attius Varus, a *praetorius*. C. may be mistaken about the place (cf. 134 (VII. 11). 1), since Caesar (*B.C.* I. 12. 3) speaks of Attius as holding Auximum further to the east. He too evacuated, and was pursued and worsted by a detachment of Caesarians. He is next found in Africa, his former province (*ibid.* 31. 2), where he irregularly seized control (cf. Appendix VI, p. 468) and where his defeat of Curio gave his party their one major success in the war. He probably fell at Munda.

138 (VII. 14)

From his *deversorium* at Cales (cf. 155 (VIII. 3). 7) C. proceeded to Capua on the 25th, Pompey having asked him to concert recruiting activity there with the Propraetor M. Considius (161B (VIII. 11B). 2).

1, 1 **cum...lippirem** If the text is sound *cum* is temporal (cf. K.–S. II, p. 344). C. will hardly have meant that he went from Cales to Capua or wrote his letter *in spite of* his eye trouble (if he had meant the latter he would have written *scripsi* rather than *dedi*). He probably mentioned the circumstance to account for the fact that the letter was not in his own hand (cf. 137 (VII. 13a). 3 fin.; 162 (VIII. 12). 1; 163 (VIII. 13). 1; Q. *Fr.* II. 2. 1 *parvula lippitudine adductus sum ut dictarem hanc epistulam*), though as his words stand he does not say so. Did a copyist substitute *dedi* for *dictavi*?

4 **condicio** Cf. *Fam.* XVI. 12. 3 (27 January, to Tiro) *feruntur omnino condiciones ab illo, ut Pompeius eat in Hispaniam, dilectus qui sunt habiti et praesidia nostra dimittantur; se ulteriorem Galliam Domitio, citeriorem Considio Noniano (his enim obtigerunt) traditurum; ad consulatus petitionem se venturum, neque se iam velle absente se rationem haberi suam; se praesentem trinum nundinum petiturum.*

8 **posse** Better than deletion of *esse*; *spero pacem nos habere* seems rather too confident.

2, 2 **coloni** Pompey's veterans and others who had received lands under Caesar's agrarian law in 59. Although C. went to Capua and cast an eye on the recruiting operations there he seems to have taken no active part (cf. 141 (VII. 17). 4; 161B (VIII. 11B). 2).

gladiatores Cf. Suet. *Iul.* 10. 2. C. received a letter from Caesar about these gladiators and replied to it early in February (cf. 152 (VIII. 2). 1).

3 **ante...scripseram** In a lost letter, probably dispatched on the 20th,

after C.'s arrival at Formiae (cf. 134 (VII. 11), introd. note). Schmidt would assign it to the 24th, which by his dating lacks a letter, i.e. the previous day; obviously a longer interval is likely from the wording. This passage throws considerable suspicion on Caesar's narrative in *B.C.* I. 14. 4 f. *Capuae primum sese confirmant et colligunt dilectumque colonorum qui lege Iulia Capuam deducti erant habere instituunt; gladiatoresque, quos ibi Caesar in ludo habebat, ad forum productos Lentulus libertatis ⟨spe⟩ confirmat atque his equos attribuit et se sequi iussit; quos postea monitus ab suis, quod ea res omnium iudicio reprehendebatur, circum familiaris conventus Campaniae custodiae causa distribuit.* We know from C. that the instructions disposing of the gladiators were Pompey's, not Lentulus', though Lentulus may have carried them out. Now since the Consuls did not leave Teanum for Capua before the 23rd (137 (VII. 13*a*). 3), then, if Caesar's account is to be believed, Pompey's orders must have been sent to Lentulus later and have arrived after the scene in the Capuan forum. Yet C. at Cales knew of them, though not seemingly of Lentulus' proceedings, on the morning of the 25th. All this can hardly be fitted together without straining probabilities. It looks much more likely that Lentulus took Pompey's instructions to Capua on the 23rd and carried them out on the 24th; and that Caesar's account is based on rumour, possibly arising from an earlier expression of intention by Lentulus. The false report which had reached C. from Torquatus several days previously may be connected.

Torquati L. Torquatus was at Formiae by 10 February (147 (VII. 23). 1; cf. 135 (VII. 12). 4), Aulus apparently not, though he was there later on (175 (IX. 8). 1). Aulus therefore is the more likely to have been the writer of the letter, but no praenomen is needed in the text since Atticus already knew who was meant.

5 **scutorum** Often interpreted 'heavy-armed gladiators'. But it is hard to believe that a gladiator was ever called a 'shield', even though Livy can write (XL. 14. 11) *quattuor gladiis domus tua capi et expugnari potuit?*, even harder to suppose that Caesar's *ludus* contained 500 (let alone 1,000 or 5,000) gladiators so armed, though one type at least, the *Samnes*, did carry a *scutum*. There is nothing against taking the word in its ordinary sense; commentators cite *Mil.* 64 *domus in clivo Capitolino scutis referta. secutorum* (Victorius) seems to be anachronistic (cf. Friedländer, *Sittengeschichte Roms*[9], IV. pp. 262 f.).

7 **provisum** *profixum* in the Mediceus is at least as likely to have come from *provisum* as from *profectum* (Orelli). C. seems anxious to stress (cf. *sane*. . .*sane*) that, whatever his other shortcomings, in this matter at least Pompey had shown *consilium*. Perhaps his revived hope of peace had made him momentarily less censorious.

3, 1 videas. . .sit So to Terentia and Tullia (*Fam.* XIV. 14. 1) *videndum*

est ut honeste vos esse possitis (sc. *Romae*). Cf. Varro, *L.L.* X. 19 *illud videndum, ut satis sit verecundi etiam illam in eandem arenam vocare pugnatum*; Petr. 106. 3 *vide ut possit illis ignosci quos ad poenam ipse deus deduxit.*

3 **scripsi. . .antea** In *Fam. l.c.* and 136 (VII. 13). 3.

7 **quod** I.e. *quam rem*, Dolabella's role in the Civil War. For the neuter cf. K.–S. I, pp. 61 ff. and 296 (XIII. 1). 2 *quod si efficias. quem* (Watt) does not seem requisite.

8 **sed id fit** *sed* is resumptive.

10 **ad pacem** Apart from Cratander's margin, a direct object after *hortari* would be very suspicious: cf. *Thes.* VI. 3011. 27 and 145 (VII. 21). 3 *ipse me Caesar ad pacem hortatur.*

139 (VII. 15)

2, 1 **pridie. . .dedi** *heri* might have been misunderstood 'the day before you read this letter'.

3 **stare condicionibus** So to Tiro (*Fam.* XVI. 12. 4 of 27 January), *sin autem ille suis condicionibus stare noluerit*; cf. *Off.* III. 96 *stare conventis* et sim.

5 **non auditus** *non* is the simplest supplement. The palaeographical advantage of *haud* (Bosius), slight in view of the ease with which *non* drops out of MSS, is more than offset by its rarity in C. with verbs other than *scio* (*an*); cf. K.–S. I, p. 816. There are other possibilities (see App. Crit.); but cf. *Fin.* V. 27 *est enim infixum in ipsa natura. . .sic ut contra si quis dicere velit non audiatur*; Liv. XXII. 60. 16 *P. Sempronium. . .non audistis arma capere . . .iubentem.*

in consilio I.e. at the meeting of Senators present: cf. Liv. XLII. 62. 11 *Romana constantia vicit in consilio.* Favonius may or may not have had a better hearing in private.

Cato Given command of Sicily, probably *pro praetore* (Broughton, p. 263).

10 **Postumius** The second Sallustian Letter to Caesar (9. 4) mentions a Senator L. Postumius as a hanger-on of the nobility in combination with Favonius: cf. *Philol.* 108 (1964), pp. 108 f., where I should have pointed out (on the question of authenticity) that this very combination is suspicious; the present passage might well have put it into a Pseudo-Sallust's head. Postumius is in all probability to be identified with the T. Postumius of *Brut.* 269, who perished in the Civil War, *non minus vehemens orator quam bellator.* His official rank is uncertain; but since he was evidently subordinate

to Cato he may have been his Quaestor (I withdraw the view expressed in *Cl. Quart.* N.S. 10 (1960), p. 256, following Münzer and Broughton, that he was a *praetorius*). The evidence of the Sallustian epistle can be disregarded.

11 **Furfanioque** T. Furfanius Postumus, a friend of C.'s (cf. *Fam.* VI. 8. 3 and VI. 9), had served on Milo's jury (*Mil.* 74 f.). He appears to have been Quaestor or *proquaestor pro praetore* in Sicily, though the fact that Caesar made him Proconsul of the same province in 45 does not prove conclusively that he was not governing there as a *praetorius* in 49 (cf. the case of Hither Spain governed by M. Lepidus as Proconsul in 48 and 44). The Senate probably distrusted him as a Caesarian sympathizer.

13 **quam** = *perquam*. As T.–P. say, there is no reason to deny C. this colloquialism, and *quam* is more likely to have been omitted than added by a scribe.

Fannium Cf. 44 (II. 24). 3 n. Whether he actually went to Sicily is doubtful (cf. 165 (VIII. 15). 3 n.).

3, 3 **interposita esse** *dicunt* is understood from *negant* as often.

4 **facturum ut...deducat** 'Aliquanto gravius hoc est, quam si scripsisset: *eum puto praesidia esse deducturum*' (Boot). The exact force of the periphrasis varies with the context. Sometimes one can render 'be sure to' (cf. 375 (XIV. 21). 2 *idque se facturos esse iurarent ut arma omnes haberent eaque duumviri omnibus mensibus inspicerent*), or 'contrive to' (*Q. Fr.* III. 5. 4 *facerem tamen ut possem*), or 'decide to' (236 (XI. 23). 2 *eo feci ut celeriter eunti darem*), or (with a negative) 'refrain from' (52 (III. 7). 2 *non faciam ut enumerem miserias omnis*). Here the suggestion is of reluctance on the part of the agent. Cf. *dare operam ut...*, *non committere ut....*

6 **quo ingressus est** For the ablative cf. *Thes.* VII. 1574. 1.

8 **quae in urbe est** This would have seemed more logical after *omnem*, unless *in urbe* is to be taken 'in the city generally'.

9 **in aerario** Cf. 135 (VII. 12). 2 n.

10 **Appianas** These are the two legions withdrawn from Caesar's army in 50 (cf. 136 (VII. 13). 2 n.). According to Plutarch (*Pomp.* 57) 'the army which Pompey had lent to Caesar' was brought back from Gaul by one Ἄππιος, whom Münzer (*RE.* III. 2854. 4) would identify with C. Claudius Pulcher's elder son, Appius *maior* (cf. 62 (III. 17). 1 n.). Here, however, and in 144 (VII. 20). 1 the name is corrupt in the MSS; hence Watt (cf. *l.c.* p. 392) prefers to read *Attianas* (*-arum*). But no known At(t)ius can be referred to here, and his statements that Appius is equally a shadow, if not a ghost, and that Appius as a gentile name is seldom attested at this time, ignore Münzer's theory.

140 (VII. 16)

1, 1 primas Cf. 135 (VII. 12). 1.

3 **de mandatis sqq.** There is nothing in 139 (VII. 15) about Labienus' arrival (at Teanum), only incidental reference to Caesar's message, nothing about the reply from Pompey and the Consuls. In 137 (VII. 13*a*). 3 C. promised a fuller account of what happened when Labienus got to Teanum, but if he wrote one it has not survived. Can he be thinking of another letter, now lost, dispatched from Capua on the 27th? If so, he will have written *a.d.V* by mistake, since *V* is not likely to be a corruption of *IIII*. If not, his memory has mixed up 137 (VII. 13*a*). 3 and 138 (VII. 14). 1 with 139 (VII. 15).

2, 5 si. . .venerit Temporal rather than conditional: cf. 30 (II. 12). 3 n. There was nothing at this time to stop Pompey going to Picenum.

6 **Labienum. . .non dubitantem** Cf. 198 (X. 7). 3 *Curio mecum vixit, iacere Caesarem putans. . .Siciliaeque diffidens.*

3, 2 referrent Sc. *rem*; likewise in 114 (V. 21). 12 *refero ad Scaptium*; *Fam.* III. 12. 2 *ad me ne referrent* et sim. Cf. *Caec.* 17 *ut in pauca conferam.*

141 (VII. 17)

1, 1 sunt Cf. 218 (XI. 7). 1 *gratae tuae mihi litterae sunt, quibus accurate perscripsisti omnia* sqq. There is no need to take the statement generally, as in *Fam.* XI. 15. 1 *etsi mihi tuae litterae iucundissimae sunt.*

de pueris Cf. 136 (VII. 13). 3.

4 **etiam nunc** This must not be taken as intended to convey that Atticus and Peducaeus had *more* reason to leave now than before. The fact was just the contrary. Indeed C. had earlier been inclined to think that they ought to leave (cf. 136 (VII. 13). 3; 138 (VII. 14). 3), but the opening of negotiations with Caesar had changed his mind, just as with regard to his wife and daughter (cf. 140 (VII. 16). 3). I am tempted to delete *etiam*, which can hardly be taken apart from *nunc.*

7 **detraxit** The threat of Caesarian confiscations and depredations would naturally bring values down after the evacuation of the city. Atticus owned much real estate in Rome (Nep. *Att.* 14. 3).

iocari A reliable sign with C. of relatively good spirits.

2, 5 quae. . .venturae essent Cf. 13 (I. 13). 2 n. (*committendae* sqq.).

7 **Σηστιωδέστερον** Cf. 62 (III. 17). 1 n.

8 **omniaque et** *et* need not be changed to *ei* (Koch): cf. Sjögren, *Comm. Tull.* p. 113, citing *ad Brut.* 25. 4 *omnia iam ultroque deferenda putat.*

9 **amentissimus** C. ignores the crux of the matter, that Caesar was being asked to give up his military advantage without any real guarantee that the terms would be observed by the other side.

17 **acerrimus** Cf. 142 (VII. 18). 2 *Caesarem quidem L. Caesare cum mandatis de pace misso tamen aiunt acerrime dilectum habere, loca occupare, vincire praesidiis.*

3, 1 **Trebatius** C. Trebatius Testa, some fifteen or twenty years C.'s junior and a friend of long standing (*Fam.* VII. 17. 2), already in 54 eminent as a jurisconsult (*ibid.* VII. 5. 3). C. recommended him in that year to Caesar, under whom he served in Gaul. C.'s side of a lively correspondence with him survives. A Caesarian in the Civil War, he remained in Caesar's entourage (cf. Suet. *Iul.* 78. 1), and lived to a ripe old age (cf. Sonnet, *RE.* VIA. 2259. 29). C. dedicated his *Topica* to Trebatius, and Horace makes him his interlocutor in *Sat.* II. 1. Plutarch's account (*Cic.* 37), according to which C. replied to his letter in anger, is notably careless if based upon this passage.

5 **omnes abessemus** C. is probably thinking of Consulars, particularly the older ones. The passage shows that Caesar and Sulpicius Rufus were personally on good terms.

4, 3 **me...suscepisse** Cf. Appendix II, p. 440.

8 **improbis...invidis** *improbis* of course refers to Caesar and his followers. *invidis* can only be understood as Caesar's enemies, not surely with reference to envy of C. himself despite *Fam.* V. 21. 2 *cui* (sc. *mihi*) *nisi invidisset is quem tu numquam amasti* (sc. *Pompeius*)...*et ipse beatus esset et omnes boni.* Commentators cite from C.'s letter to Caesar in March, 178A (IX. 11A), 2 *iudicavique eo bello te violari contra cuius honorem populi Romani beneficio concessum inimici atque invidi niterentur*; but this is as patently insincere as his praise of Caesar's *admirabilis ac singularis sapientia* (§1), of which he writes to Atticus (188 (VIII. 9). 1) *non sum veritus ne viderer adsentari cui tali in re libenter me ad pedes abiecissem* (cf. *Deiot.* 11 *nihil de conspiratione audiebat certorum hominum contra dignitatem tuam*). As an expression of his private mind this passage is unique. Elsewhere Caesar is condemned wholesale (132 (VII. 9). 3 f.; 134 (VII. 11). 1; 141 (VII. 18). 2; *Fam.* XVI. 11. 2, 12. 2, 4); the stock charge against Pompey, so far as war-guilt is concerned, is that he 'fostered' Caesar instead of checking him in time (126 (VII. 3). 4; 128 (VII. 5). 5; 129 (VII. 6). 2; 130 (VII. 7). 6; 142 (VII. 18). 2; 153 (VIII. 3). 3; 158 (VIII. 8). 1; *Fam.* XVI. 11. 3). I am therefore strongly tempted to read *im⟨pro⟩vidis* (with reference to Pompey's political blindness rather than to his supposed military incompetence as in 144 (VII. 20). 2 *improvidi et neglegentes duces*). But C.'s mind did vary at this period and the MSS may have the benefit of the doubt. Possibly Trebatius' letter had complained of the *invidia* of Caesar's enemies as Caesar himself does in *B.C.* I. 7. 1. For the combination cf. *Off.* I. 77 *ab improbis et invidis.*

11 **sin autem otium aut** For *autem etiam* editors with weaker digestions than Sjögren (and, in this instance, Watt) have written ⟨*pax*⟩ *aut etiam*

(Schütz), ⟨*aut pax*⟩ *aut etiam* (Wesenberg), ⟨*otium*⟩ *aut etiam* (Tyrrell). But *autem* so often follows *sin* that it may as well be kept.

5, 2 **mulieres** Pomponia may have been in the party (see below), but C.'s letter was doubtless to Terentia and Tullia, like *Fam.* XIV. 14 and 18.

142 (VII. 18)

1, 1 **mulieres nostrae** Probably including Pomponia (cf. 138 (VII. 14). 3), who would naturally join her husband and son, though *tuaque...pertulerunt* will refer to Tullia and Terentia.

6 **iussi sumus** The Consuls appear to have issued an edict summoning certain persons (Senators?) to Capua for a meeting on the 5th: cf. 161B (VIII. 11B). 2.

7 **contioni** Held by whom? Possibly by the Pompeian Tribune L. Metellus (cf. 172 (IX. 6). 3 n.). Pompey had been making speeches in the Italian towns (cf. 145 (VII. 21). 1 fin.), but *populo* implies Rome. Nor would C. have been so elated (cf. 143 (VII. 19). 1) otherwise.

9 **iacebit** Of reputation (cf. 91 (IV. 17). 2 n.).

vicerit The sense should be plain from 132 (VII. 9). 3 and 139 (VII. 15). 3 *vicerit enim si consul factus erit, et minore scelere vicerit quam quo ingressus est*, and was so to Corradus. But why should C. have left the apodosis *vicerit* to his correspondent's imagination? It is much more likely to have dropped out of the text after *acceperit*.

2, 1 **Cassium** Q. Cassius Longinus.

4 **vincire** *devincire* Müller, comparing *Leg. Agr.* II. 86 (add I. fr. 2 *cetera oppida praesidiis devincient*).

7 **cum Pompeio...eamus** That Pompey should go to Spain was one of Caesar's peace conditions: cf. 141 (VII. 17). 2. Wrongly Manutius and others 'si erit ut consistere in Italia non possimus'.

8 **optima** See App. Crit. *-ima* may have disappeared before *ī ma-* leaving *opt*, whence easily *opto*: cf. Sen. *Ep.* 101. 12 *quod est in malis optimum*. *opto in malis* might pass as a survival in a stock phrase of the preclassical sense of *optare*, 'choose', also found in Augustan poetry, but the simple correction is preferable. *optio* (Gruter) and *opto* ⟨*ut*⟩ *in malis* (Purser: 'I pray for this considering the evil state we are in') seem less likely.

9 **ne data quidem occasione** Evidently with reference to the law of the Ten Tribunes (cf. 124 (VII. 1). 4 n.); had Caesar been refused the right to stand in absence, he would not have stood at all. In his disgust C. seems to forget that Caesar might still have returned to stand in person, as he now offered to do.

reppulimus 'Averted', as of a calamity or danger (cf. e.g. *Phil.* II.

113 *servitus* (sc. *est*) *postremum malorum omnium, non modo bello sed morte etiam repellendum*).

3, 5 docto homine *doctus* is often almost untranslatable because of the difference between ancient and modern, or pagan and Christian, ideas with regard to accomplishments, culture, and learning. A good commentary here and elsewhere (as *Fam.* III. 10. 7, V. 19. 2, VI. 5. 4, 22. 2; Q. *Fr.* I. 1. 7, 28) is *Part. Orat.* 90 *hoc primum intellegamus, hominum esse duo genera, alterum indoctum et agreste, quod anteferat semper utilitatem honestati, alterum humanum et politum, quod rebus omnibus dignitatem anteponat.* The link between culture and conduct still held for Apuleius: cf. *Met.* X. 2 *habebat iuvenem filium probe litteratum atque ob id consequenter pietate, modestia praecipuum.*

7 **tamen** 'Though I know he ought to have come with me, yet...'.

si erit...invito Cf. 159 (VIII. 10) *me nihil ab ipso invito contendere.* Even if the war continued, C. did not want Dionysius worried so long as his own movements remained uncertain: cf. 150 (VII. 26). 3 *Dionysio, dum existimabam vagos nos fore, nolui molestus esse.* But when the time came he himself wrote a letter of summons (*arcessi*) and appeal, which Dionysius rejected (156 (VIII. 4). 1). How Atticus was to avoid 'troubling him against his will' *if* it became necessary to send for him, C. does not explain; but perhaps he was too deeply hurt and annoyed by the tutor's behaviour to write logically. Otherwise *si* has to be replaced by *nisi*. Scribes quite often mix up the two as e.g. in 29 (II. 9). 2; 160 (VIII. 9*a*). 2; 253 (XIII. 16). 1; 276 (XII. 37). 3.

4, 1 ab Egnatio Cf. 31 (IV. 12). 1 n. 'sumptam ab Egnatio debitore suo pecuniam tibi numeret' (Manutius). This would not have been a case of *delegatio* since Quintus evidently wanted to make Egnatius pay himself and then to settle with Atticus.

3 **Q. Titinius** Cf. 114 (V. 21). 5 n.

4 **idemque** Usually taken adversatively, 'he has no money for travel, and *yet* he is not calling in his loans'. But the second statement supports the first. Titinius was not asking his debtors to pay up nor raising the interest on loans overdue because he knew they could not be expected to find the money.

5 **L. Ligus** Probably the friend mentioned in 360 (XIV. 6). 1 (not the hostile Tribune of 58; cf. 97 (V. 4). 2 n.).

6 **domi** I.e. 'in ready money'.

10 **μηδὲ δίκην** δικάσῃς πρὶν ἀμφοῖν μῦθον ἀκούσῃς: cf. Hes. fr. 338, Merkelbach-West; Leutsch-Schneidewin, *Corp. Paroem. Gr.* II, p. 759.

12 **quicquid est** 'Whatever it amounts to' (not 'such as it is'): cf. Lucr. III. 135, V. 1252 *quicquid id est.* Similarly *quid est hoc?* 'what is one to make of this?', and so on.

143 (VII. 19)

On the face of it *non dederim* in the first sentence implies that 142 (VII. 18) was suppressed and this letter substituted. But how then did 142 (VII. 18) get into the collection? Schmidt (*Briefwechsel*, p. 126) says it was added to 143 (VII. 19); but why in that case does C. say that he had not dispatched it? What happened may be imagined thus: C. wrote 142 (VII. 18) before dawn; then at daybreak, as he was about to set out for Capua, a spate of bad news arrived, under the influence of which he decided on the spur of the moment not to send what he had written, and substituted this hasty note, which he dispatched forthwith. Later, perhaps on the evening of the 3rd at his stopping-place (probably Cales) *en route*, he reread 142 (VII. 18) and decided to send it after all—it contained several private items which would need to be transmitted anyhow. He therefore dispatched it, no doubt adding or meaning to add a covering note, which he may have forgotten to enclose or which may have disappeared subsequently.

2 **plena spei bonae** The 'public' part of 142 (VII. 18) could not be called exactly cheerful, but it does assume the likelihood of a peaceful settlement; and that, despite the doubt professed in §1 and the lugubrious resignation of §2, was C.'s real hope, now dashed.

3 **contionis** Cf. 142 (VII. 18). 1 n.

5 **Furni** Cf. 95 (V. 2). 1 n. He enclosed Curio's letter.

6 **legationem** The word must not be pressed: cf. 7 (I. 11). 1 n. L. Caesar was not *legatus* in an official sense (Appendix III).

144 (VII. 20)

1, 2 **cave...consulibus** Lit. 'don't suppose anything worth less than these Consuls': cf. Pollio, *Fam.* X. 31. 5 *hac enim legione noli acrius aut pugnacius quicquam putare esse*, also *Fam.* X. 12. 1 *cave enim putes ullas umquam litteras gratiores quam tuas in senatu esse recitatas*. For *minoris* (sc. *preti*) cf. Liv. XXVIII. 28. 9 *vos...minoris certe omnes pretii quam Albius et Atrius sunt*; Petr. 42. 4 *minoris quam muscae sumus* and 126 (VII. 3). 5 n. (*pluris*). Such expressions derive from the slave market (cf. Caelius Sabinus *ap.* Gell. IV. 2. 5 *quanto ob id vitium minoris erit*). The alternative rendering 'don't suppose that anything is of less importance to these Consuls (than waging war)' is certainly possible, but less natural. C.'s poor opinion of the pair, repeated in the next letter (§1 *nihil in consulibus*), antedated their entry into office (cf. 122 (VI. 8). 3 *at a quibus victus!*).

3 **quorum** 'De structura cf. Madvig ad Cic., De fin., I, 18, 60 *quarum potiendi spe*' (Moricca): but *quos sperans me auditurum aliquid* is not Latin.

'*quorum*. . .*aliquid* (i.e. *spe audiendi ex iis aliquid*) varie temptata; cfr. Madv. de fin. IV. 13,[32]' (Sjögren): genitives like *haec Epicuri* or *quid simile Milonis?* only prove that *quorum aliquid* might mean 'something in the Consuls'. Malaespina in the sixteenth century could do better than this: he explained 'quarum ego rerum spe audiendi aliquid'. But *quorum* as indefinite neuter (cf. 113 (V. 20). 1 *quae cognosce*; 178A (IX. 11A). 3 *quae si tantum* sqq., et sim.) is dubious in an oblique case (cf. however *meorum* in 410 (XVI. 5). 5), and after *consulibus* lends itself to misinterpretation. Probably something has dropped out—not *iussu* or *vocatu* which would anticipate *ut eram iussus*, but perhaps *ad congressum* (cf. *Phil.* XII. 26 *nempe in Antoni congressum colloquiumque veniendum est*).

6 **adhuc, id est Nonis** The only objection to these words from Cratander's margin is the following *nondum* where we should expect *non*; but this seems a natural pleonasm in familiary style. Possibly however *non* was expanded to *nondum* after *adhuc*. . . . *Nonis* had dropped out of the text.

7 **inanes, imparati** There has been some unwarrantable tampering with these epithets: for the first cf. 357 (XIV. 3). 1 *cum inanes redissent*; Plaut. *Most.* 571 *hic homo inanis est* et sim.

8 **Appianarum** Cf. 139 (VII. 15). 3 n.

9 **ruere** Cf. 145 (VII. 21). 3 *sed antiquiores litterae quam ruere coepit.* Caesar's advance down Picenum had just begun. It meant war.

2, 1 **καὶ συναποθανεῖν** Sc. θέλω? Possibly from an unknown play.

te id consulo Cf. *Thes.* IV. 584. 36 (add Petr. 88. 1 *consulere prudentiorem coepi aetates tabularum*, where editors suppose a lacuna in the text).

4 **coniungendi** For this reflexive use of the gerund cf. K.–S. I, pp. 108 ff.

5 **Phalarimne** Cf. 135 (VII. 12). 2 n.

Pisistratum The type of a benevolent despot: cf. *Ath. Pol.* 16. 2.

9 **ad suas Nonas** With a note of contempt. *ad* is literally 'by': cf. 140 (VII. 16). 2 *Capuam venire iussi sumus ad Non. Feb.*

145 (VII. 21)

The gap of two days, 6 and 7 February, probably contained at least one lost letter: cf. 146 (VII. 22). 2 n.

1, 1 **istinc** Not from Rome itself, but from the north.

5 **Calibus** Cf. 138 (VII. 14), introd. note.

6 **nihil in consulibus** Cf. 206 (X. 14). 3 *in hoc non multum est*; *Comm. Pet.* 27 *nemo erit*. . .*in quo modo aliquid sit, qui* sqq.

8 **φαινοπροσωπεῖν** Cf. 376 (XIV. 22). 2 φαινοπροσωπητέον *ergo.*

2, 3 **de sanctiore aerario** Cf. 135 (VII. 12). 2 n. This reserve treasury for emergencies was maintained from the *aurum vicesimarium* (5% tax on manumissions) and probably other sources, such as spoils of war: cf. Kubitschek, *RE.* I. 671 f. The keys seem to have been kept by the City Quaestors (cf. Mommsen, *St.* II, p. 132).

4 **quis sinat?** A nonsensical question, taken literally. But 'who would allow?' is a rhetorical way of saying 'would they be allowed?': cf. Sen. *Dial.* X. 3. 5 *quem tandem longioris vitae praedem accipis? quis ista sicut disponis ire patietur?* and *Propertiana*, p. 73. Little is known about the state of things in Rome between its evacuation by the republicans and the establishment of Caesar's authority, but the *improbi* may well have been strong enough to make unsupported entry by the Consuls a dangerous undertaking.

5 **ut prius ipse in Picenum** C.'s next words show that it is quite a mistake to regard Lentulus' answer as an insult. He meant it seriously, not knowing that Picenum had already been overrun. Pompey himself had recently held out hopes of a republican return to Rome following his own entry into Picenum (140 (VII. 16). 2).

3, 3 **quid me deceat** Sc. σκέμμα *magnum est*, in resumption of *quid agam. quod* is usually read, but *quid agam quod me deceat* is an odd phrase and the relative clause superfluous and awkward after a long parenthesis.

4 **ad pacem** I.e. *ut de pace agam.*

6 **tamen** Understand *si minus, tamen...*; or read *tantum*?

7 **ista** C.'s house and other interests in the capital.

146 (VII. 22)

1, 1 **qui...sit** I.e. every part of Italy which Caesar had not already occupied was his for the taking.

3 **celeritatem** Cf. 160 (VIII. 9*a*). 2 *sed hoc* τέρας *horribili vigilantia, celeritate, diligentia est.* Antony in 44 was said *Caesariana uti celeritate* (422 (XVI. 10). 1).

5 **non quo minus...dominationis** Cf. *Off.* II. 23 *malus enim est custos diuturnitatis metus.* Caesar was well aware of this: see his own letter, 174C (IX. 7C). 1.

7 **quorum** The needy adventurers who were a prominent part of Caesar's entourage, the νέκυια as Atticus called them (cf. 187 (IX. 18). 2).

8 **†sit** Perhaps read with T.–P. *recte sit.⟨sed⟩ censeo cedendum* (sc. *Roma*). For *recte sit* (i.e. 'let us hope that fears of a massacre turn out liars after all') cf. 197 (X. 6). 1 n. Watt (*l.c.* pp. 392 ff.) conjectures *recte autem* (or *sed recte*) *censes* (Schütz) *non cedendum* (sc. *Italia*), arguing that C. was averse to leaving Italy and that Atticus advised him against it: cf. 147 (VII. 23). 2 *de me autem*

ipso tibi adsentior, ne me dem incertae et periculosae fugae; 148 (VII. 24) *ego a consilio fugiendi, ut tu censes, absum*. But from what follows (*ego quid agam?* sqq.) it is plain that this advice, which was sent on 7 February (cf. 177 (IX. 10). 5), had not yet reached him. Nor would a declaration of his own view (*recte*) be compatible with his present state of ἀπορία.

2, 1 **Oppiis** Cf. 136 (VII. 13). 5.

2 **atque adeo** Corrective rather than augmentative. There would be no need to talk to Terentia's agent when Terentia herself was returning to Rome so soon. In his next letter (§2) C. says that he had told Atticus of his intention to send the women back to Rome; he will have done so in a lost letter from Capua on 6 or 7 February, unless it was from Cales on the 4th. A fragment of this letter, or of another from the same period, survives in 177 (IX. 10). 6, where see note.

7 **nullo modo quidem** Cf. *Tusc*. V. 35 '*aliter id scire non potes?*'—'*nullo modo*'; Colum. *R.R.* IX. 8. 6 *quoniam interdum...vel mediocre pecus, nam malum nullo quidem modo, parandum est*. The former vulgate, now discarded by Bayet and Watt, is insensitive: *equidem* (Bücheler) *a te petam consilium, ut soleo*. Why should C. have written *equidem* (he might no doubt have written *nullo modo equidem*: cf. 188 (VIII. 9). 2 '*num igitur peccamus?*' *minime vos quidem*), and why not *peto*? Also *etsi* or *quamquam* would have preceded *explicari*.

147 (VII. 23)

1, 1 **Domitium** At Corfinium (cf. Appendix IV, pp. 448 ff).

2 **Lentulo** P. Lentulus Spinther held Asculum with ten cohorts but fled at Caesar's approach (*B.C.* I. 15. 3).

3 **Thermo** Cf. 137 (VII. 13*a*). 3 n.

6 **M'. Lepidum** Cf. 135 (VII. 12). 4 n.

7 **C. Cassium** He seems to have come to Formiae from Capua (cf. 145 (VII. 21). 2.

10 **plane iam captos** Cf. 161D (VIII. 11D). 4 fin. For *plane* in correction of *paene* see below *capti plane sumus*, also 143 (VII. 19). 1 *plane oppressi videmur*; 161D (VIII. 11D). 2 *me ipsum plane exceptum putabam*; 172 (IX. 6). 2 *ut plane interclusi captique simus*.

12 **et non...opponimus?** For *et* introducing an indignant question cf. *Thes*. V (ii). 890. 68.

14 **oppressi, capti** Cf. 83 (IV. 6). 2 *oppressus et captus*; *Verr*. II. 5. 122 *qui...oppressus a praedonibus et captus est*; Liv. XXIV. 47. 6 *se...captos oppressosque a paucis esse*, XXV. 31. 5 *civitatem...ne...captam et oppressam tenerent*.

2, 2 ut scripseram Cf. 146 (VII. 22). 2 n.

4 **quasi hunc gradum** *hunc quasi gradum* Boot, comparing *Leg. Agr.* II. 38 *hunc quasi gradum quendam atque aditum ad cetera factum intellego.* This may well be right (cf. 180 (IX. 13). 1).

5 **de me** Atticus' advice, in a letter of 7 February, is cited verbatim in 177 (IX. 10). 5.

6 **ipso** *ipse*, printed by Sjögren, is no less objectionable here than in his text of *Fam.* V. 2. 3.

8 **possum** Cf. 152 (VIII. 2). 4 *ego pro Pompeio libenter emori possum.*

etsi vivere No need to supply ἀβίωτον vel sim. The aposiopesis is easily intelligible: cf. 83 (IV. 16). 2 n. (*ferrei*).

3, 1 Capua Does this stand for the Campanian area (cf. *Fam.* XVI. 11. 3 *nos Capuam sumpsimus*) or for the republican military headquarters, as one might have said 'Chantilly' in 1916?

2 **nisi. . .fuerit** Nothing is gained by reading *nisi qui deus iuverit* (or *fecerit*); C. would hardly make Pompey's action depend on divine intervention. Sjögren compares Q. Cicero, *Fam.* XVI. 27. 2 *nisi aliquid firmius fuerit.* Cf. 190 (X. 1). 3 *si quid eius modi evenerit ut arcessamur.*

5 **Caesaris litterarum** Cf. 145 (VII. 21). 3.

148 (VII. 24)

2 **Cassio** Sc. *redduntur. Cassi* seems quite unnatural, despite *tuam epistulam* in 33 (II. 13). 1.

3 **Lucretio** Cf. 89 (IV. 16). 5 n. He may or may not be the commander at Sulmo mentioned in 156 (VIII. 4). 3 and Caes. *B.C.* I. 18. 1. If he was, he may be supposed (as T.–P. suggest) to have come to Capua for consultation with the Consuls.

Nigidium Cf. 22 (II. 2). 3 n.

4 **Vibullium** L. Vibullius Rufus, Pompey's *praefectus fabrum* (cf. 174C (IX. 7C).2). Pompey had made him his envoy to C. in 56 (*Fam.* I. 9. 10) and to Caesar in 54 (*Q. Fr.* III. 1. 18). On his activity in Picenum and the number of troops under his command see Gundel, *RE.* VIIIA. 2011. In fact he joined Domitius at Corfinium and was captured there (and released) later in the month. Captured a second time in Spain in 48, he was sent by Caesar with peace proposals to Pompey (*B.C.* III. 10). He is last heard of as Pompey's messenger to Milo prior to the latter's descent on Italy late in that year (*ibid.* III. 22. 1; or possibly the message was delivered in the previous year as Vibullius was on his way from Italy to Spain). He was not a Senator (cf. Caes. *B.C.* I. 23. 2).

6 **VI milia** See App. Crit. As generally supposed, Domitius had twelve cohorts (162A (VIII. 12A). 3), which at full strength would give him 7,200 men. Appian (*B.C.* II. 32) however says that he left Rome with 4,000 men. See Appendix IV, p. 448, n. 8.

7 **consules discessisse** If this was true, Lentulus at any rate seems to have returned later: cf. 161D (VIII. 11D). 3.

149 (VII. 25)

On the date cf. 150 (VII. 26). 1 n. (*hoc biduo*).

1 **veras** Strictly this applies to the reports in the letter rather than to the letter itself: cf. *firmas* below.

2 **Cephalio** This *tabellarius* crops up several times in letters of 49–47. He seems to have belonged to C., not Atticus (cf. especially 227 (XI. 16). 4).

3 **vobis** Including perhaps Philotimus, Peducaeus, and others. If Cephalio had belonged to Atticus C. would probably have written *a te*.

etiam a te Atticus had written optimistically for once.

firmas Not 'decided' or 'confident' but 'solid', i.e. reliably based,—really (like *veras* above) describing not so much the letter as the reports it contained: cf. 235 (XI. 25). 2 *rumor est non firmus ortus*; *Fam.* XII. 4. 2 *eo firmiora videntur esse quae nuntiantur* (somewhat similarly Plaut. *Most.* 1104 *firmiora consilia*, 'more reliable counsels').

5 **firmum** Surely a necessary addition: cf. 135 (VII. 12). 2 *vereor ne exercitum firmum habere non possit*; 140 (VII. 16). 2 *scribit paucis diebus se firmum exercitum habiturum*; 145 (VII. 23). 1 *litteras accepi Domitium exercitum firmum habere*; 153 (VIII. 3). 3 *cum firmo exercitu*; 162C (VIII. 12C). 3 *exercitum firmum habere oportet*. Though C. thought that Pompey was *in fuga* he knew that he had *some* forces; cf. 147 (VII. 23). 3 *ut Pompeius istas Domiti copias cum suis coniungat*. It is hardly possible to accept Ernesti's suggestion 'nisi vero propterea dixit Cicero non habere exercitum quia firmus non esset'.

6 **malas...concidit** Cf. Plut. *Cat. Min.* 53 πολὺν ἔφη (sc. ὁ Κάτων) περὶ τὰ θεῖα πλάνον εἶναι καὶ ἀσάφειαν, εἰ Πομπήϊον ἐν οἷς ὑγιὲς οὐδὲν οὐδὲ δίκαιον ἔπραττεν ἀήττητον γενόμενον νῦν, ὅτε τὴν πατρίδα βούλεται σῴζειν καὶ τῆς ἐλευθερίας ὑπερμάχεται, προλέλοιπε τὸ εὐτυχεῖν.

8 **ars...regere** Cf. Liv. II. 43. 10 *adeo excellentibus ingeniis citius defuerit ars qua civem regant quam qua hostem superent*. C. says *erat* because he is thinking of Pompey's past errors: cf. Ov. *Fast.* II. 125 *quid volui demens elegis imponere tantum / ponderis? heroi res erat ista pedis.*

150 (VII. 26)

Dated by Schmidt (*Briefwechsel*, pp. 133 f.) 15 February on the strength of 151 (VIII. 1). 1 *cum ad te litteras dedissem, redditae mihi litterae sunt a Pompeio*, since Pompey's letter arrived that day (161B (VIII. 11B). 1). But this letter answers one from Atticus of 11 February (cf. §2 n.) and is therefore unlikely to have been written so late. Atticus' letter might be expected to reach Formiae on the 12th and the reply to be dispatched on the 13th; but as the 13th seems to be included in *hoc biduo* (§1) it may be that for some reason it was not written until the evening of that day. The letter of the 15th referred to in 151 (VIII. 1). 1 must have perished. The reference there to a letter from Philotimus suggests that this had been specifically mentioned, but there is no such mention in 150 (VII. 26).

1, 4 hoc biduo 12 February (after dispatch of the gloomy 149 (VII. 25)) and 13. Alternatively 149 (VII. 25) may have been dispatched on the 11th fairly soon after 148 (VII. 24) and better news have arrived later that day.

5 **fuga** Cf. 147 (VII. 23). 3 *in fuga omnes sunt.*

interdicta 'Et invidiose et false dictum, quasi Caesar iam putaret sibi tamquam praetori arrogandum esse ius in cives' Manutius.

6 **si...offendero** Ennius' translation (Ribbeck³, I, p. 53) of Creon's words to Medea (Eur. *Med.* 352) εἴ σ' ἡ 'πιοῦσα λαμπὰς ὄψεται θεοῦ... θανῇ, quoted in *Rab. Post.* 29 as typical tyrant's talk; cf. Ter. *Eun.* 1064 *si te in platea offendero hac post umquam...periisti.* What threats of Caesar are referred to we do not know.

7 **de Afranio** Supposed to be on his way from Spain to Italy: cf. 152 (VIII. 2). 3; 153 (VIII. 3). 7.

2, 1 me integrum Reid (*Hermath.* XII (1903), p. 261) proposed *mihi*, comparing *Fam.* I. 9. 10 *ut integrum mihi...reservarem*, VIII. 6. 5 (Caelius) *de Dolabella integrum tibi reserves suadeo* (T.–P. add *Fam.* V. 2. 8 *respondit sibi non esse integrum*). But it is not true that the accusative can be paralleled only in Tac. *Hist.* IV. 52; cf. *Flacc.* 51 *ego me ad id quod adtulerit integrum conservabo.* As to the sense, Atticus had advised C. not to leave Italy if Pompey did so in a letter of 11 February, to which this is evidently a reply: C. and others in a similar position should remain severally 'on their watch towers' (cf. 177 (IX. 10). 6 n.). He may well have suggested that by avoiding complete commitment against Caesar C. would be preserving himself as an available intermediary.

3 **certe videri possum** Some take *videri* with emphasis: 'I may *seem* so.' But how was Atticus to know? I formerly (*Towards a Text*, p. 36) proposed *certen videri possum?* (for *certen* cf. also *Leg.* I. 3), holding with Madvig 'nullo modo Cicero se ad turpem causam propensiorem videri posse

concedit, quaeque sequuntur, ad omnem huiusmodi reprehensionem removendam pertinent'. Watt prints *certe videri ⟨non⟩ possum* from Ed. Romana, remarking (I cannot agree) that 'the alternative suggestions which have been made are poor by comparison' (*l.c.* p. 394, n. 2). Certainly the words cannot be taken ironically, as Manutius wished, but it now seems to me that C. may simply be agreeing that his conduct might be badly construed: cf. 161D (VIII. 11D). 7 to Pompey *ego me in hac omni causa facile intellegebam pugnandi cupidis hominibus non satis facere*. What follows is not exactly directed 'ad omnem huiusmodi reprehensionem removendam', but rather to explaining *why* he had laid himself open to such criticisms. *ridere* (Madvig) is an unhappy suggestion.

me ducem...negavi esse Cf. 114 (V. 21). 11 *negavi me audire*; Plaut. *Curc.* 597 *nego me dicere*; Ascon. 54. 12 *cum ei praemium lege daretur, negavit se eo uti*; Tac. *Ann.* I. 29. 1 *negat se terrore et minis vinci*. This probably alludes to C.'s command (cf. Appendix II).

5 **quod multo rectius fuit** Not surely the execution of the Catilinarians (Corradus, etc.) but the rejection of Caesar's overtures in 59.

7 **verbis** No doubt from Pompey's letter to Caesar composed by Sestius (141 (VII. 17). 2; cf. 188 (VIII. 9). 2).

8 **ego scio sqq.** This cryptic utterance (in form reminiscent of Plaut. *Men.* 246 *ego illum scio quam cordi sit carus meo*, *Mil.* 1325 *scio ego quid doleat mihi*) may have had to do with some *arcanum*. But probably the fear C. has in mind is that which he hints less ambiguously in 161D (VIII. 11D). 7 and 199 (X. 8). 5: namely, that should Pompey and Caesar make up their differences he himself, if he took a strong anti-Caesarian line, might be thrown to the wolves. In that case *quem metuam* refers to Pompey's possible treachery rather than to Caesar's hostility, which would hardly have called for such obliquity of phrase.

3, 1 **HS XX** Probably the matter of the Oppii: cf. 136 (VII. 13). 5 n.

2 **vagos** Cf. 134 (VII. 11). 5.

3 **de eius officio** Had Atticus written that Dionysius was *in officio*, ready to do what he should?

diem ex die *diem* is syntactically governed by *exspectabam*.

5 **certe** Not 'my boys will certainly winter in Formiae' (Winstedt, ignoring *videntur*).

hiematuri 15 February, current calendar = 16 December, Julian calendar.

et ego? nescio Orelli's punctuation. But perhaps *num* or *an* has fallen out.

7 **quod habebo certi** It is not quite clear whether this refers to C.'s own plans or to news generally.

8 **Parthicus casus** I.e. an unexpected deliverance like the Parthian withdrawal in the preceding summer (cf. 121 (VI. 6). 3 n.). There is no reference to a possible retreat by Caesar, still less to a Parthian invasion, as Manutius supposed.

151 (VIII. 1)

C. probably wrote during the night of 15–16 February: see below on §2.

1, 1 **litteras** Not 150 (VII. 26), where see introd. note.

redditae On the 15th: cf. C.'s reply, 161B (VIII. 11B). 1. This letter of Pompey's is lost, the received opinion identifying a part of it with 161A (VIII. 11A) being certainly wrong: see *ad loc.*

2 **quas. . .scripsisset** The subjunctive shows that this was stated by Pompey. If the paradosis *quae* were right the clause *quae. . .scripsisset* should either have preceded *de rebus in Piceno gestis* or have followed *de dilectu Domiti* since both items are included in *cetera.* Vibullius' report probably concerned the first only.

3 **nec tam laeta** Editors read *nec tamen* ⟨*tam*⟩ *laeta* (Bosius). There is little or nothing to choose. Even though Pompey's account was less cheerful than Philotimus' it was fairly encouraging, at least as regards affairs in Picenum: cf. 152 (VIII. 2). 4; 161B (VIII. 11B). 1.

4 **quam. . .scripserat** Orelli's addition of *quae* is unnecessary, since *ea* can be understood, somewhat as in 62 (III. 17). 2 *cetera. . .intellego esse languidiora quam alii ostendunt*: cf. 411 (XVI. 4). 4 *paratiorem enim offendi Brutum quam audiebam*; *Fam.* VI. 12. 3 *minus enim te firmum sermo Eppuleiae. . . lacrimaeque. . .declarabant quam significant tuae litterae.*

5 **ipsam. . .epistulam** I.e. a copy. If C. had been going to send the original, which he was not likely to do, he could have sent it at once.

6 **cras. . .mittam** This was done: cf. 152 (VIII. 2). 4.

7 **ipsius manu** The rest of the letter was dictated.

9 **pro relicto** I.e. *pro relicta re*: cf. 227 (XI. 16). 5 *id enim mihi erit pro desperato. derelicto* seems to be a conjecture: cf. *Brut.* 263 *hunc facilem et cottidianum novisse sermonem num pro relicto est habendum?*, where *relicto* has been variously emended (to *derelicto* by Lambinus).

11 **non parcere** Pompey was sacrificing these areas by not defending them. It is very doubtful whether *parcere* means 'take thought for' in Virg. *Aen.* X. 880 *nec divom parcimus ulli*, and such a meaning certainly ought not to be assumed in C.

2, 1 hominemque certum M. Tullius: cf. 161B (VIII. 11B). 4.

2 **me non quaerere sqq.** What follows is hardly so much as a travesty of the reply actually sent (161B (VIII. 11B)). It is ridiculous to suppose that C. was deliberately deceiving Atticus, to whom he sent a copy of the reply eleven days later. The discrepancy can be simply explained if the tenses (*rescripsi*, etc.) are understood as epistolary; C. had not yet written to Pompey, and when he did come to write his feelings had had time to subside, so that the answer turned out very differently from his first intention. This letter to Atticus appears to have been written in the night of 15–16 February (cf. the complaint of sleeplessness at the end); C. probably wrote to Pompey the following day. But it is also possible that he had already written, though not dispatched, an answer to Pompey on the lines indicated to Atticus, and changed it after further reflection.

ubi tutissimo essem Quoted twice by Charisius (*G.L.K.* I. 192. 23, 217. 12), with *essent* in both places.

9 **stabilis** Madvig's objection to *stabilis* (*Adv.* III, p. 178 'locum *stabilem* Latine dici, in quo aliquis consistat nec ultra fugiat, prorsus nego') is scarcely warranted; his own *ut locus standi sit* seems much more dubious Latin. Livy can describe a town as *fide praefectorum principumque...stabile atque inexpugnabile* (XXVIII. 6. 11).

3, 1 quo minus...fugae T.–P. were right to suggest a stop after *fugae*. These words cannot be attached to what follows (*eundum...dissentire*) with any respect for logic. Usage too supports a backward reference, regular in such phrases. The verb is usually indicative: cf. 226 (XI. 15). 2 *quo minus debes mirari* sqq.; Lucr. VI. 1012 *quo minus est mirum....si* sqq.; Sall. *Cat.* 37. 8 *quo minus mirandum est* sqq.; Ov. *Her.* 17. 19 *quo magis admiror quae sit fiducia coepti* (cf. *ex Pont.* II. 3. 21); Plin. *N.H.* II. 117 *quo magis miror* sqq. (also IX. 144, XV. 44; Quint. *Inst.* IV. 2. 111, XI. 3. 148; Plin. *Ep.* VII. 17. 2), XII. 2 *quo magis ac magis admirari subit* sqq., 18 *quo magis mirum est* sqq.; Quint. *Inst.* XII. 10. 74 *quo minus mirum est quod* sqq.; Plin. *Ep.* IV. 21. 5 *quo minus te mirari oportebit quod* sqq.; Tac. *Ann.* II. 37. 1 *quo magis mirum fuit quod* sqq.; IV. 31. 2 *quo magis mirum habebatur* sqq. The subjunctive is found occasionally, as in Plin. *N.H.* VIII. 54 *quo minus mirum sit* sqq., IX. 3 *quo minus miremur* sqq.; Quint. *Inst.* IX. 4. 139 *quo minus id mirere in pedibus orationis.*

4 **eundum** T.–P. compare 207 (X. 15). 3 *ibitur igitur*; 354 (XIII. 42). 3 *eatur.* But *sed* may have dropped out before or *tamen* after (cf. §4 *ibimus tamen Luceriam*).

9 **M'. Lepidi sqq.** Vulcatius (cf. 160 (VIII. 9*a*). 1) and Sulpicius (cf. 141 (VII. 17). 3) may have already returned to Rome, if indeed the former ever left. Lepidus probably returned on 7 March (167 (IX. 1). 3).

4, 1 unus The *boni* having been dismissed.

152 (VIII. 2)

1, 1 vero The opening words answer some apologetic phrase in Atticus' letter.

2 **diligentia mea** Not 'my energy in the discharge of my duties'. When writing to Atticus C. was not apt to make much of his responsibilities as ἐπίσκοπος, whatever they really amounted to (cf. 141 (VII. 17). 4), and the reports which had worried Atticus evidently concerned not these but his contacts with Caesar. *diligentia* will therefore mean 'punctiliousness' towards Atticus himself, who if the reports had been true might well have felt hurt at C.'s 'casualness' (*neglegentia*) in failing to keep him informed.

4 **Capua** On the second visit, 4–7 February.

5 **gladiatoribus** Cf. 138 (VII. 14). 2.

8 **si quo** *quo* lit. = 'to any quarter'.

2, 3 μέμψιν An admirable correction: cf. 321 (XIII. 13–14). 2 *neque...potero* μέμψιν *effugere.*

4 **qui magis effugiam?** If people are going to attribute to C. things he never wrote (*fingere*), then how will avoidance of writing help him to escape criticism? For *qui magis* cf. *Acad.* II. 90 *qui magis haec crederet si essent quam credebat quia videbantur?*, 96 *hoc negas te posse nec approbare nec improbare: qui igitur magis illud?*; *Rep.* III. 43 *urbs illa praeclara...arx visenda...templa, muri, nihilo magis efficiebant, Dionysio tenente, ut esset illa res publica*; Nep. *Paus.* 3. 5 *hinc tamen se expedivit, neque eo magis carebat suspicione*. If *effugias* is kept, the second person must be taken generically with Manutius ('id est, nihilo magis effugiam'); but it is much easier to suppose that a copyist confused the persons, as copyists often did. Put into Atticus' mouth *qui...effugias* stultifies *verum tamen* and turns the sense upside down. Moreover *qui magis* = *quo modo melius* would be peculiar Latin.

9 **existimem** The subjunctive might be explained as courteous, the apodosis of an implied condition, 'if I were to be asked'; more probably it is due to *mihi videris* = *puto*: cf. *de Orat.* II. 26 *iam mihi videor navasse operam quod huc venerim.*

3, 3 hoc miserius Best taken with what follows.

4 **vagamur egentes** 'This is a peevish, petulant, and somewhat hysterical paragraph' (T.–P., pointing to the next letter, §7 *scripsique sedatiore animo quam proxime scripseram*).

5 **quotannis** An exaggeration surely, though Pompey may have had other dangerous illnesses before the celebrated one in 50.

8 **ita multi sqq.** The interrogative punctuations, essential to sense, are due to Reid.

9 **suburbanis...hortis** Cf. 130 (VII. 7). 6 n. (*horti et Tusculanum*).

10 **nos** The expatriated Pompeians generally (cf. 213 (XI. 3). 3 n. (*sumus*)). Capua, not being Rome, would have been bad enough as a headquarters, the remoter Luceria was worse.

12 **Afranium** Cf. 150 (VII. 26). 1 n.

Petreium M. Petreius, now governing part of Further Spain as Pompey's Legate. Praetor before 63, he commanded the government forces in the final battle with Catiline as Legate of the Consul Antonius. After the Pompeian collapse in Spain he fought for the Republic in Greece and Africa, where he and Afranius met their deaths.

13 **parum est dignitatis** Cf. Liv. XXX. 30. 28 *quia parum dignitatis in legatione erat.* Here ironical, in keeping with the angry tone of the passage. C. cannot be serious. For one thing it was not the personal eminence of Afranius and Petreius which made them worth waiting for but the armies they would bring with them. For another, Labienus, after his career in Gaul, would hardly be described except in irony as inferior in *dignitas* to the *praetorius* Petreius, even if he had not himself held the Praetorship; but a much discussed passage of Hirtius (*B.G.* VIII. 52. 2) almost certainly means that in 50 he was thinking of becoming a candidate for the Consulship. So far as birth went, as the son of a Roman Knight he was Afranius' superior and perhaps Petreius' also. Nor do C.'s references to him in 135 (VII. 12). 5, etc. suggest that he was regarded in Pompeian circles as 'transfuga vilis, ut scribit Lucanus' (Boot).

illud There are various guesses as to what has dropped out here and after *hic quidem quae est.* The double gap suggests Greek, and the context suggests something like φρόνημα ἀριστοκρατικόν in the first and ἀριστοκρατία in the second. Watt (*l.c.* p. 394 f.) suggests Καλλιόπειον and σπουδή (or προθυμία); but it seems likely that the lost expressions were related to one another. C.'s point probably is that there is no use in asking him to seek *famam laudesque bonorum* in the present circumstances.

15 **istic** *tum* is the vulgate, and C. has usually been held (as by Watt, *l.c.*) to refer to the great days of 63, which sacrifices the contrast between *ostendit* ('promised') and *adest.* He surely has in mind the period immediately before the outbreak of the war (so Corradus). The corruption of *quis istic* to *quis tu* is no palaeographical problem.

4, 3 **διπλῆ** A sign (>) used by grammarians to draw attention to a passage, e.g. to mark the appearance of a new speaker in the text of a play.

6 **ita** *ut tu,* which Wesenberg proposed to add or substitute, does not seem indispensable: cf. 60 (III. 15). 3 *non ita laudat Curionem.*

7 **ut. . .putes** We should expect *te putare. significas ut putes* is not good Latin for 'signify that you think' (contrast Caes. *B.C.* I. 86. 2 *significare coeperunt ut statim dimitterentur*). C. seems to have written *ut putes* carelessly

(as though *alia significas ac solebas* had preceded), in definition of *aliquanto secus quam solebas* (I have not attempted to reproduce this in translation). Apparently he misinterpreted Atticus' letter (cf. 177 (IX. 10). 6).

10 †**sed cur** Having settled that neither expediency nor duty require him to leave Italy, C. turns to face the next argument. *sed cur*, 'but why (do you ask)?', is not in logic demonstrably wrong, but like many others I find it hard to believe that it is right. *sed tu* conceivably may be, though an imaginary objection does not seem to be so introduced elsewhere; so may *videtur* (with the preceding sentence). *sequitur* (*se q tur?*) would have led more easily to the corruption: cf. 389 (XV. 11). 3 *sequebatur ut mecum ipse*; *Rab. Post.* 29 '*moreretur*', *inquies; nam id sequitur*. Watt deletes 'ut ex additamento *sed tur⟨pe⟩* ortum'.

poterisne...tyrannum Cf. *Off.* I. 112 *Catoni...moriendum potius quam tyranni vultus aspiciendus fuit.*

11 **quasi intersit sqq.** As Boot remarks, C. takes a different view in *Fam.* VI. 4. 3 *in malis omnibus acerbius est videre quam audire* and elsewhere.

12 **XXX** 'Nedum unus' (Manutius).

13 **pedem porta non extulit** Cf. 122 (VI. 8). 5.

14 **praecipua** Perhaps, as surmised by Mongault, this alludes to Terentia (or Philotimus?), perhaps to C.'s financial position generally (cf. 211 (XI. 2). 2). Bayet suggests 'le ménage Tullia-Dolabella'.

16 **ego...quid ero?** A postscript: see Appendix IV, pp. 454 f.

17 **inflammaram** Evidently at Atticus' request: cf. *Fam.* V. 20. 9 *hanc epistulam cur conscindi velim causa nulla est* (in reply no doubt to a promise or offer by the recipient).

ad Pompeium Perhaps *profectus sum* vel sim. has dropped out, perhaps more: Appendix IV, *ibid.*

18 **quid ero?** Cf. 60 (III. 15). 2 n. A camp was not the place for C. (cf. 367 (XIV. 13). 2).

153 (VIII. 3)

On C.'s movements after he left Formiae see Appendix IV, pp. 455 ff.

1, 4 **quod...suspicor** It is noteworthy that C. writes of the evacuation of Italy as something still only on the cards. Pompey's message to the Consuls, as described by himself in 162A (VIII. 12A). 3, was definite, and C. tells Pompey in 161D (VIII. 11D). 1 that he was informed of its content before he left Formiae (cf. Appendix IV. pp. 454f.). Of course there was the chance that Pompey might change his mind; and perhaps C. so disliked the idea that he could not bring himself to write as though it was settled. But it looks as though von Fritz is right in suggesting that the message was less categorical than Pompey later represented it (see also Appendix IV, p. 450, n. 1).

2, 5 **optimorum et clarissimorum** Elsewhere described in very different terms (cf. e.g. 151 (VIII. 1). 3 fin.). There is no actual inconsistency, since the epithets refer to political attitude and standing, not to mind or morals; but there is certainly a discrepancy in tone. Here C. is, so to speak, on his high horse, and to have expressed his real opinion of Scipio, Domitius, Appius and the rest would not have suited the posture.

8 **a me...provisum** Cf. Introd. pp. 24 f.

14 **qui fuerit** Cf. 55 (III. 10). 2 n.

15 **†fore** For *fore* commentators compare *de Orat.* II. 334 *subest ille timor...ne dignitatem quidem posse retineri*, which would make a better parallel if the paradosis were *se* (or *me*) *fore*. *forte* makes better sense since in a Pompeian victory C.'s position as a non-combatant would certainly be dangerous, whereas the disgrace might be a matter of opinion. But *forte* = *fortasse* or *si forte* is not Ciceronian.

16 **Pompeius** An unconscious switch from the general to the particular.

rem publicam recuperarit Not 'again grasps the helm' (How): cf. *Har. Resp.* 54 *habuit regalem potestatem* (sc. *Sulla*), *quamquam rem publicam recuperarat* et sim. Pompey might become a despot like Sulla, but his régime would bear more semblance of constitutional propriety than Caesar's. The phrase is in the same key as *optimorum et clarissimorum civium*.

3, 3 **addo...meam** Cf. 135 (VII. 12). 3.

4 **omitto illa vetera** A fine specimen of Ciceronian paraleipsis.

5 **legibus...ferendis** In 59.

7 **adiunctor** Suetonius (*Iul.* 22. 1) and Dio (XXXVIII. 8. 5) say that Transalpine Gaul was added to Caesar's command by the Senate. Plutarch (*Caes.* 14) ignores this: Πομπήϊος...συνεπεκύρου τῷ δήμῳ τοὺς νόμους, Καίσαρι δὲ τὴν ἐντὸς Ἄλπεων καὶ τὴν ἐκτὸς ἅπασαν Κελτικὴν προσθεὶς τὸ Ἰλλυρικὸν μετὰ ταγμάτων τεσσάρων εἰς πενταετίαν.

8 **augur** Cf. 30 (II. 12). 1.

ille...studiosior So (though not of Pompey) to Lentulus Spinther (*Fam.* I. 9. 14) *usus es quibusdam nobilissimis hominibus fortioribus in me restituendo quam fuerant idem in tenendo.*

9 **propagator** By the lex Pompeia Licinia in 55. Commentators compare Liv. XXIII. 25. 11 *consuli propagari in annum imperium*; Suet. *Aug.* 23. 1 *praesidibus provinciarum propagavit imperium.*

11 **contendit sqq.** Cf. 124 (VII. 1). 4 n. (*Ravennae*).

12 **lege quadam sua** *quadam* seems to suggest a doubt as to the validity of Pompey's confirmation of the privilege: cf. *ibid.* n. (*ratio absentis*).

13 **Marcello** Cf. Caelius, *Fam.* VIII. 8. 4, 9, VIII. 9. 5. On the view advocated by Cuff the Kalends of March were those of 50 (cf. 130 (VII. 7). 6 n. (*transierit*)).

14 **restitit** See also App. *B.C.* II. 26.

15 **in qua sumus** Palaeographically almost identical with -*m que sum* of the Mediceus, which is otherwise hard to account for ('mero errore' Watt): cf. 191 (X. 1*a*) *haec...*ἄλη *in qua nunc sumus*; 195 (X. 4). 6 *in hac vita et fuga*; 202 (X. 11). 2 *in hac mea fuga*, 3 *his ipsis malis in quis sumus*; *Fam.* IV. 13. 4 *in istis molestiis in quibus es hoc tempore.*

4, 3 **pecunia** Cf. 139 (VII. 15). 3; 145 (VII. 21). 2.

4 **causa** A cause, as it were, functioning, i.e. a movement sufficiently organized for men to be able to enlist in its support; cf. 55 (III. 10). 1 n.; 126 (VII. 3). 5 n.

6 **impetu** 'Forward rush'; cf. 134 (VII. 11). 5 ὁρμῇ *Caesaris* and *Man.* 34 *tanti belli impetus*; Luc. II. 448 *primo terrore ruentis...belli.*

7 **maritima opportunitas** How compares Liv. XLV. 30. 4 *maritimas quoque opportunitates ei* (sc. *terrae*) *praebent portus* sqq.; contrast 161B (VIII. 11B). 3 *hanc oram...quae et opportunitatem et dignitatem habet*, where *opportunitatem* refers to the import of corn.

8 **†invite cepit** See Appendix II, p. 439.

9 **sine *** causa** Many corrections have been proposed, mostly idle. Diplomatic probability apart, *diffidens causae* (Müller) is the best. The most popular is *in ea causa* (Lambinus), with a comma after *cupidi*; but *dixi... pecunia* does not follow happily (better to stop after *cupidi*, understanding the verb from what precedes (†*cepi*), but that too does not read convincingly). Probably words have fallen out after *sine*, e.g. *sine* ⟨*copiis dux esse nolui in ea*⟩ *causa*.

ordinum Senate or Knights. Cf. 130 (VII. 7). 5.

10 **dolor** Cf. 74 (IV. 2). 2 n.

11 **sensissem** The assimilation of mood is not uncommon: cf. K.–S. II, pp. 202 ff. Presumably C. refers to things he had witnessed during the fortnight he spent *ad urbem* in January.

multitudo et infimus quisque Cf. 126 (VII. 3). 5 *omnem illam urbanam ac perditam plebem*; Sen. *Ep.* 104. 31 *si animo complecti volueris illius imaginem temporis, videbis illinc plebem et omne erectum ad res novas vulgum, hinc optimates et equestrem ordinem, quicquid erat in civitate sancti et electi, duos in medio relictos, rem publicam et Catonem.*

12 **multi...cupidi** Cf. Luc. I. 181 *hinc usura vorax avidumque in tempora faenus / et concussa fides et multis utile bellum.*

5, 3 **quod...fugam** Cf. Appendix IV, pp. 450 f., where add this passage.

eam Del. Boot. But *fugam sequor* amounts to *fugientes* (or *fugientem*) *sequor* (cf. 155 (VIII. 7). 1 n.), not *fugam capesso*; and Müller's comparisons with 161D (VIII. 11D). 5 *quid tu sis secutus*, etc. are quite astray.

4 **quanam** 'No editor thinks *quanam* (Frederking, *Philol.* 58 (1899), p. 630; he also conjectured *quonam* ⟨*modo*⟩) worth recording. It is clearly right, since the answer concerns route, not destination' (*Towards a Text*, p. 37). 'The following sentence does *not* prove that this question "concerns route, not destination" ' (Watt, *Journ. Rom. Stud.* 50 (1960), p. 278). Further elucidation seems to be required. Pompey is in course of flight, and the supposition is that C. follows him. If he asks *quonam?*, 'whither?', his question is idle because the answer is obvious—'wherever Pompey goes'. True, Pompey's ultimate destination was uncertain, but that in itself did not make him difficult to follow—he was certainly going across the Adriatic to Greece (162A (VIII. 12A). 3). The immediate question was 'how?', that is 'by what route?', as the answer makes clear. C. cannot go *with* Pompey because Caesar bars the route to Luceria. He would therefore have to take ship from the west of Italy, a dangerous and unpleasant undertaking in mid-winter. The Tuscan Sea, *mare inferum*, had a bad reputation: in *de Orat.* III. 69 C. calls it *barbarum, scopulosum atque infestum* in contrast with the Ionian, *Graecum quoddam et portuosum.*

7 **cum fratre** C.'s difficulty about his brother appears in a letter of 6 March (167 (IX. 1). 4): *frater accedit, quem socium huius fortunae esse non erat aequum. cui magis etiam Caesar irascetur; sed impetrare non possum ut maneat.*

8 **in utraque. . .re** I.e. to go with Quintus or without him. That is still the main dilemma, though the mention of young Marcus had indicated further perplexities. The alternative punctuation *cum fratre an sine eo? cum filio, an quo modo?* imports confusion.

11 **populare** Cf. 161D (VIII. 11D). 7 *ut mea persona semper ad improborum civium impetus aliquid videretur habere populare.*

12 **fascis. . .laureatos** Cf. 133 (VII. 10).

13 **ut iam** Cf. *Fam.* I. 9. 13 *ut iam sit in iis culpa qui me non defenderunt* et sim.

6, 2 **L. Philippus** L. Marcius Philippus, Consul in 91 and father of the homonymous Consul of 56 who married Caesar's niece Atia. He held the Censorship under Cinna's régime in 86, but when Sulla returned to Italy joined him at once. On his behaviour and that of other Consulars during Sulla's absence cf. E. Badian, *Studies in Greek and Roman History*, pp. 215 f.

L. Flaccus L. Valerius Flaccus, Cos. 100, Cens. 97 (to be distinguished from his Marian namesake, Consul Suffectus in 86) became Princeps Senatus in 86. As Interrex in 82 he proposed the law conferring dictatorial powers on Sulla (*Leg. Agr.* III. 5).

6 **Thrasybulus** His formal banishment by the Thirty (Xen. *Hell.* II. 3. 42) will have followed his flight.

sed. . .sententia Watt (*l.c.* pp. 395 f.) correctly explains the general sense, which has been misunderstood (e.g. by How, 'the policy and resolution of Mucius is thoroughly well grounded'). Mucius' line might not be the best, but he had a definite *ratio* (course of conduct chosen on rational grounds: cf. e.g. 20 (I. 20). 2 init.) and *sententia* (as we might say 'point of view')—it was not cowardice or folly that made him stay in Rome. The same could be said for Philippus, though his *ratio* differed somewhat from that of Mucius, who stayed behind only because he could not bear to attack his *patria*. I do not follow Watt in retaining *certe*; cf. *Tusc.* II. 5 *certis quibusdam destinatisque sententiis. certa ratio* is common in C. (e.g. *Verr.* I. 48 *habeo autem certam viam atque rationem qua omnis illorum conatus investigare et consequi possim*).

7 **et. . .datum** This defines Philippus' *ratio, et servire* and *et non amittere* being correlated.

11 **accipere** This obvious supplement clears up the passage satisfactorily. *vereor* or *vide* need not be supplied before *ne*: cf. K.–S. II, pp. 254 f.

12 **rem** Not just the question of the Triumph, but the whole dilemma —to go or to stay.

13 **quid. . .potest?** *quid* = *quid aliud*. The choice must be made, there is no other way; cf. Watt, *l.c.* p. 396.

18 **in Caieta** I.e. in the harbour (*Caietae portus*); cf. 8 (I. 3). 2 n.

7, 5 etsi. . .scripserat In his letter sent by D. Laelius: cf. 162A (VIII. 12A). 3 and Appendix IV, pp. 449 f.

6 **Fausto** Cf. 84 (IV. 10). 1 n. He was now *proquaestor pro praetore* (cf. Broughton, p. 261). The ethic dative is defended by 162D (VIII. 12D). 1 (Pompey) *qui ex dilectibus conscripti sunt consulibus*, and is probably repeated from Pompey's letter. The actual enrolment would be done by subordinates.

7 **a consule** Cf. 162A (VIII. 12A). 3. C. in his excitement may possibly have written the plural by mistake, but *cos.* and *coss.* are often confused.

ad consules Cf. Appendix IV, p. 453, n. 1.

8 **spes. . .pugnasse** Quite a natural expression, since although the events (if true) would already have taken place reliable knowledge of them had still to come.

10 **Trebonio** Cf. 82 (IV. 8*a*). 2 n. In the autumn of 50 he was in sole command of four legions in the Belgic territory (Hirt. *B.G.* VIII. 54. 4), and had doubtless been ordered to march part of his army to the Pyrenees. Caesar placed him in command of the operation against Massilia (*B.C.* I. 36. 5).

11 **Fabium** Cf. 126 (VII. 3). 3 n. Orelli's conjecture *Fadium* identifies

him with M. 'Fadius' Gallus (cf. 162 (VIII. 12). 1 n.). But Gallus was a friend of C.'s as well as Atticus', was in Italy at this time, and his nomen was Fabius, not Fadius.

cum * cohortibus A number, e.g. *V*, appears to have dropped out.

summa Cf. 117 (VI. 3). 5 *summa haec est* et sim. *summa* is usually taken with *spes*, but Afranius' march seems more naturally presented as the main result to which the rumoured Pompeian successes contributed.

14 **ad Capuam. . .ad Luceriam** 'The preposition is inserted because the meaning is "to the neighbourhood of Capua or Luceria." As both places were held for Pompey, Caesar could not count on admission within their walls' (How). A clear case (*ad* here might be taken as = *adversus*) is 161D (VIII. 11D). 3 *te. . .ad Corfinium esse venturum*.

15 **Leptam** Cf. 110 (V. 17). 2 n.

ne quo inciderem This 'could mean "lest I should run into anything"' (Watt, *l.c.* p. 396). That is what it does mean, 'anything' being a euphemism for 'anything unpleasant', as in phrases like *ne quid accidat*: cf. *de Orat.* II. 301 *permulta. . .sunt circumspicienda ne quid offendas, ne quo irruas*. It could not mean 'for fear of falling in with him (Caesar) anywhere', which would require *ne quo* ⟨*loco*⟩ as read by Watt. C. is of course thinking of Caesar, but prefers to put his fears less directly.

154 (VIII. 6)

The sequence 154–7 (VIII. 6, 7, 4, 5), first advocated in 1956 (*Journ. Rom. Stud.* 46, pp. 62 ff.) has been adopted (without acknowledgement) by Bayet and Watt. See Appendix IV, pp. 457 ff.

1, 1 ista epistula Cf. 33 (II. 13). 1 n. The letter is lost. It was evidently sealed after writing, ready for early dispatch next day.

de nocte Cf. 75 (IV. 3). 4 n.

2 **C. Sosius** Nothing else is known of him apart from the reference in 167 (IX. 1). 2. He is to be distinguished from Antony's lieutenant, who became Consul in 32.

4 **cuius quaestor fuit** Perhaps during Lepidus' Consulate in 66.

ad consules See Appendix IV, p. 453, n. 1.

2, 1 XIII Kal. Cf. 161D (VIII. 11D). 3; 162D (VIII. 12D). 1.

3, 2 pridie See Appendix IV, pp. 457 ff.

4 **magnum nomen sqq.** Cf. *Man.* 13 *cuius adventu ipso atque nomine . . .impetus hostium repressos esse intellegunt ac retardatos*; *Bell. Afr.* 31. 6 *ipsius nomen auctoritasque magna ex parte eorum exercitus minuebat audaciam*; Liv. II. 9. 5 *adeo valida res tum Clusina erat magnumque Porsennae nomen* et sim. I do

not think C. intended a play on Pompey's cognomen, though it may have been in his mind.

5 **nihil sqq.** *timiditas* seems certain; *levitas* (Boot) would not balance *fortiter*. For the rest see App. Crit.

5, 1 **ab altera** Cf. 125 (VII. 2). 2. Not 'the second attack'.

155 (VIII. 7)

1, 3 **talem civem** C.'s opinion of Domitius personally was poor enough (cf. 151 (VIII. 1). 3). But this is supposed to be a *vox populi*, and *talem* need not primarily refer to Domitius' personal qualities. Cf. 160 (VIII. 9*a*). 1 *quod talibus viris non subvenit*.

quos una scit esse I.e. Lentulus Spinther and other Senators, Vibullius Rufus, and a number of young men of rank, also many Knights and municipal dignitaries (Caes. *B.C.* I. 23. 2). *scis esse* (Victorius) has found unreflecting acceptance through the centuries. Why should C. make the interlocutor tell him that he, C., knew who was at Corfinium? The point is that Pompey knew, and so would surely come to the rescue.

4 **XX** The two 'Appian' legions: cf. 162A (VIII. 12A). 2.

XXX Cf. Caes. *B.C.* I. 17. 2 *se cohortisque amplius XXX*. The figures quoted by Pompey in 161A (VIII. 11A) add up to 31 cohorts; cf. Appendix IV, p. 448, n. 8.

6 **cui** Sc. *fugae* rather than *Pompeio*: cf. 153 (VIII. 3). 5 n. (*eam*).

video...quid sentias From the burnt letter of *c.* 14 February: cf. 152 (VIII. 2). 4 fin.

2, 1 **ego...non habeo** A celebrated epigram: cf. Introd. pp. 61 f.

2 **meum** Cf. 124 (VII. 1). 4 *si enim castris res geretur, video cum altero vinci satius esse quam cum altero vincere*, also Atticus as cited in 177 (IX. 10). 7.

8 **ista...istum** 'Nec ea, quae nunc Romae geruntur, nec Caesarem adspicere possum' (Boot). This is probably right (cf. 171 (IX. 5). 1 fin.; 180 (IX. 13). 4 init.; 189 (IX. 19). 2), though the words can be and have been interpreted with reference to Pompey's flight and Pompey.

10 **memet ipso** Cf. 50 (III. 5) *inimici mei mea mihi, non me ipsum ademerunt* and 60 (III. 15). 2 n.

3, 1 **viatico** In case he should join Pompey: cf. 153 (VIII. 3). 6 *navis et in Caieta est parata nobis et Brundisi*.

a Moneta The temple of Juno Moneta on the Capitol, the Roman mint. How C. expected to raise funds there is uncertain. Possibly bullion could be exchanged for money, or possibly he had deposited a sum in the temple (cf. 393 (XV. 15). 1 n.).

2 **Oppiis** Cf. 136 (VII. 13). 5 n. *contubernalibus* suggests that they may

have been Atticus' close neighbours: cf. Q. *Fr.* II. 4. 2 *domus utriusque nostrum aedificatur strenue...spero nos ante hiemem contubernalis fore.*

156 (VIII. 4)

1, 2 **tuo...meo** Cf. 131 (VII. 8). 1.

3 **testimoni** The genitive after *vereor*, attested in Terence, etc. and Apuleius, is unique in the classical period: cf. K.–S. I, p. 469. Watt reads *ne tui* (sc. *iudici*) *testimonium*, perhaps rightly.

6 **motum...gubernabimus** As of a ship in rough seas: cf. Val. Max. IX. 12. praef. *medii temporis cursus, prout fortuna gubernaculum rexit, modo aspero modo tranquillo motu peragitur.* Rather differently *Nat. Deor.* II. 15 *statuat necesse est ab aliqua mente tantos naturae motus gubernari* (cf. *Fin.* V. 71 *omnes motus fortunae*). Curtius has *quoniam facilius est vobis adversam quam secundam regere fortunam* (X. 2. 22).

7 **contempti** To recommend such a person to others was a signal token of regard.

10 **efferrem** See Sjögren, also Peterson's apparatus to *Verr.* II. 2. 91 *hiemi fluctibusque sese committere maluit quam non istam communem Siculorum tempestatem calamitatemque vitaret.*

14 **Aristoxenum** Of Tarentum, especially noted for his writings on music. He was Dicaearchus' contemporary and fellow-pupil (of Aristotle); cf. *Tusc.* I. 41. Dicaearchus' literary letter to him is mentioned in 305 (XIII. 32). 2.

non unum hominem The archetype of Σ probably omitted *hominem*, that of Δ *non unum*: cf. Vatinius, *Fam.* V. 10*a*. 1 *hominem unum omnium crudelissimum.*

2, 1 **sed sit** The paradosis *sed est memoria bona* is generally printed in quotations marks as a retort from Atticus or some imaginary defender of Dionysius; but 'Einwürfe werden nicht mit *sed* gemacht' (Müller, *Rhein. Mus.* 53 (1898), p. 127, proposing *scilicet* or *si*). Memory was more valued in C.'s day than now, for obvious reasons: cf. Reid on *Fin.* I. 34.

4 **tam humili sqq.** 'Were he never so humble', etc.: cf. *ad Brut.* 23. 1 *quibus igitur litteris tam accurate scriptis adsequi possum subtilius ut explicem...?*; *de Orat.* I. 226 *quis hoc philosophus tam mollis...probare posset?* For the sense cf. *Comm. Pet.* 45 ff.

3, 1 **navem** Cf. 153 (VIII. 3). 6.

4, 1 **C. Atium Paelignum** Not a Senator; cf. Caes. *B.C.* I. 18. 1. Caesar says that he and Lucretius had seven cohorts in Sulmo and that both *de muro se deiecerunt.* At(t)ius was captured and released.

2 **Q. Lucretium** Cf. 89 (IV. 16). 5 n.

3 **scis** C. might reasonably assume that the news had reached Rome along the Via Tiburtina before it got to Formiae. But Bayet and Watt print as a question, perhaps rightly.

157 (VIII. 5)

1, 2 auctoritate tua I.e. by you as *auctor*: cf. 160 (VIII. 9*a*). 1 *tua... auctoritas*, 'your advice'.

5 **cerritior** This conjecture should need no vindication.

6 **postea...tum eum isse** *postea* cannot mean 'after writing my last letter' for *quod ad te non scripseram* clearly implies that C. could have told Atticus if he had chosen. I can only suppose that it relates to the incident to which he goes on to allude, which must have happened at some earlier time. It was apparently so well known to Atticus that *tum* ('on that occasion') was a sufficient reminder.

7 **πολλὰ κ.τ.λ.** The line is not found elsewhere, but an Alexandrine source (perhaps Callimachus: see Pfeiffer, fr. 732) is suggested by Catullus' apparent imitation (64. 111) *nequiquam vanis iactantem cornua ventis*.

8 **suo capiti** Cf. Otto, *Sprichwörter*, p. 75.

sed vide Cf. 41 (II. 21). 3 *ac vide mollitiam animi*.

11 **Pollicem** Mentioned in several later letters.

a pedibus meis Cf. *Deiot.* 2 *qui...servum...a legatorum pedibus abduxerit*; *Verr.* II. 1. 92 *servos artifices pupilli cum haberet domi, circum pedes autem homines formosos et litteratos, suos esse dicebat*; Plaut. *Most.* 857 *equidem haud usquam a pedibus abscedam tuis* (slave to master); Petr. 68. 4 *servus qui ad pedes Habinnae sedebat*; Sen. *Ep.* 27. 6 *habebat ad pedes hos a quibus subinde cum peteret versus quos referret saepe in medio versu excidebat*; Mart. XII. 87. 2 *dum neglegentem ducit ad pedes vernam* et sim. Similarly *ad manum* (cf. Wilkins, *de Orat.* III. 225). *meum* (Victorius) need not be considered.

2, 1 exspectatione Corfiniensi Sjögren (*Eranos*, 10 (1910), pp. 145 f.) cites Caelius, *Fam.* VIII. 8. 4 *exspectatione Galliarum* and *ad Brut.* 5. 2 *erat exspectatio reliquiarum Antoni*. The difficulty does not lie in the expression *exspectatio Corfiniensis*: see Reid's comment *ap.* T.–P. and cf. phrases like 364 (XIV. 10). 1 *Capitolino die*; *Fam.* III. 8. 9 *sententia bima*; Liv. XL. 12. 7 *nocturno argumento*; Quint. *Inst.* XII. 10. 4 *Peloponnesia tempora*. It lies in the statement 'that the safety of the state depended on the expectation and not on the thing expected' (T.–P. VI, p. 116). *ad Brut.* 2. 2 *nos exspectatio sollicitat, quae est omnis iam in extremum adducta discrimen* is not parallel even if the text is sound—suspense can reach a crisis; but Watt marks a lacuna after *sollicitat*. The simplest remedy here is to delete *in* (*i* was written twice). *qua* depends on *Corfinium*, understood from *Corfiniensi*: cf. Sall. *Iug.* 66. 2 *Vagenses quo Metellus...praesidium imposuerat*; Just. XXXVI. 2. 1 *Iudaeis origo Damascena*,

Syriae nobilissima civitas; Eur. *Andr.* 652 οὖσαν μὲν Ἠπειρῶτιν, οὗ κ.τ.λ.; *Hec.* 710 Θρῄκιος ἱππότας, ἵνα κ.τ.λ.; K.–S. I, pp. 30 f.

2 **decernetur** Even after the news of Pompey's 'desertion' and the loss of Sulmo, which temporarily plunged him into despair (155 (VIII. 4). 3 *confecta res est*), C. still seems to hope against hope that Domitius with his thirty cohorts may give a good account of himself. Perhaps *decernitur* (R) should be read.

5 **in sumptum** Cf. 154 (VIII. 6). 5.

158 (VIII. 8)

1, 1 sic enim sqq. Cf. 195 (X. 4). 4.

2 **aluerat** Cf. 153 (VIII. 3). 3.

5 **culpa** Cf. 220 (XI. 9). 1 *nihil mihi mali casus attulit, omnia culpa contracta sunt*; Nep. *Iphicr.* 1. 2 *nusquam culpa male rem gessit. sua* (Ernesti) is unnecessary.

2, 3 ad oculos Watt (cf. *l.c.* p. 397) reads *ob*, comparing *versari, ponere ob oculos* (*ante oculos* is commoner).

4 **πρὸς ταῦθ' ὅ τι χρὴ κ.τ.λ.** Lines of Euripides, adapted by Aristophanes, *Ach.* 659. Cf. 115 (VI. 1). 8 n. The original had πᾶν instead of πάντ(α).

7 **πολλὰ χαίρειν** Commentators point to the Latin counterpart *multam salutem (dicere)* in *Fam.* VII. 33. 2.

159 (VIII. 10)

On the date see Appendix IV, p. 459.

4 **in nummis** Cf. *Verr.* II. 1. 199 *habet idem in nummis, habet in urbanis praediis*; Hor. *Sat.* I. 2. 13 *dives agris, dives positis in faenore nummis.*

6 **servulis** Cf. 163 (VIII. 13). 2 *villulas...nummulos suos*; *Nat. Deor.* III. 86 *at enim minora di neglegunt, neque agellos singulorum nec viticulas persequuntur.*

7 **ut magistrum** Despite his incompetence alleged in 156 (VIII. 4). 1. But in anger C. sometimes wrote more than he meant. In any case Dionysius might be difficult to replace in existing circumstances. For the wording cf. e.g. *Cluent.* 14 *discedit a Melino Cluentia ut in tantis iniuriis non invita, ut a viro non libenter.*

9 **volui te scire** *id* may well have dropped out, but need not be added: cf. Sjögren, *Comm. Tull.* pp. 115 f.

160 (VIII. 9a)

1, 1 εὐγενῆ tua consilia Offered in a letter of the 22nd from which C. cites the key passage in 177 (IX. 10). 7: *si M'. Lepidus et L. Vulcatius* *remanent, ⟨manen⟩dum puto, ita ut, si salvus sit Pompeius et constiterit alicubi, hanc* νέκυιαν *relinquas et te in certamine vinci cum illo facilius patiare quam cum hoc. . .regnare.*

pro temporibus 'To suit the times', or perhaps 'considering the times' (with the implication that any course must be dangerous in such circumstances).

5 **sed me. . .pignora** Cf. 126 (VII. 3). 3 fin.

8 **reliqui. . .tuendi** By 'recovering the future' C. means that by eventually joining Pompey he will make amends for present inactivity; by 'maintaining the present', that the conduct towards Caesar recommended by Atticus (we do not know exactly what it was, but it is not hard to guess) will enable him to get through the interval without too much loss of dignity and self-respect.

10 **quaerere** Rarely in C. = *consequi*. But in *Tim.* 46 he translates ὅτι μὴ κακῶν αὐτὸ ἑαυτῷ γίγνοιτο αἴτιον by *quatenus non ipse bene factus sua culpa sibi aliquid miseriae quaereret.*

11 **conservatorem inimicorum** Caesar had freely released his prisoners at Corfinium (*B.C.* I. 23).

2, 1 **Balbus minor** L. Cornelius P. f. Balbus, nephew of Balbus *maior*. He received Roman citizenship in 72 along with his uncle (Plin. *N.H.* V. 36). This unsuccessful mission to Lentulus Crus, which he later made the subject of a play (Pollio, *Fam.* X. 32. 3), is the first known step in a career which culminated thirty years afterwards in a Triumph *ex Africa*. During the Civil War he was mostly in Caesar's entourage and received the Quaestorship in 44 (Broughton, p. 325). The aforementioned letter of Asinius Pollio, under whom he served the next year in Spain, throws a lurid light on his activities there.

occulta via Formiae lay on the main route from Rome to Brundisium. C. can hardly mean that Balbus travelled along byroads, but he may have travelled at night.

3 **Romam ut redeat** Possibly 'on condition he return to Rome': cf. 161 (VIII. 11). 5 *cum litteris Caesaris praemiorumque promissis si Romam revertisset.* But it may be doubted whether C. would have so used *ut* without a negative, though *Phil.* XII. 24 *qui Terminalibus nuper in suburbium, ut eodem die reverterer, ire non sum ausus* has some similarity.

4 **posse non arbitror, [ni]si erit conventus** Manutius found a reading *nisi non erit* in a MS belonging to a friend, and thence proposed *posse arbitror nisi non erit conventus.* Lambinus followed him. Three centuries later Nipperdey (*Philol.* 3, (1848), pp. 148 f.) observed that 'etwas zu leugnen ausser für den Fall, in welchem es allein möglich ist, ist nicht witzig, sondern abgeschmackt': hence *posse arbitror, si erit conventus.* But

non can stand. If Balbus did *not* meet Lentulus, there could hardly be any possibility of his persuasions succeeding; but even if he did, it was unlikely.

7 **ad unam illam** Cf. 197 (x. 6). 2 *si ab uno illo cavero*; *Amic.* 88 *una illa subeunda est offensio* et sim. *illam* may refer to something in Atticus' letter, a reference to Φαλαρισμός (cf. 135 (VII. 12). 2) or the like; cf. 44 (II. 24). 1 *illam celeritatem.* Or perhaps it is simply 'the cruelty we have in mind'; cf. Q. Cicero, *Fam.* XVI. 16. 1 *indignum illa fortuna* ('the fortune that was his', i.e. slavery). Anyway *illam* balances *haec*, and corrections (*Cinnanam, Sullanam*) are worse than needless.

9 **tu, puto, hoc credis** Heavily ironical: cf. 12 (I. 12). 3 *quod te moleste ferre certo scio*; Sen. *Contr.* VII. 1. 17 *quid de me iudicaturus es si fecero? puto, difficulter postea in me parricidium credes.*

12 **XI Kal.** The omission of *Kal.* in the paradosis could be defended from 113 (v. 20). 2 and 381 (xv. 4). 1, but is awkward here because the numeral might at first sight be taken with *legiones.*

13 **plane...nescio** Cf. *Fam.* XII. 22. 2 *quid futurum sit plane nescio.*

161 (VIII. 11)

1, 4 **illud quidem** *tamen* of the paradosis is untenable. T.–P. punctuate after *licet* and render 'that, in spite of what I have implied (about its uselessness), I do all day'. But C. has implied nothing about the uselessness of lamentation.

5 **etiam...nostris** Boot refers to 37 (II. 17). 1 *ne et opera et oleum philologiae nostrae perierit.*

7 **vis** 'Essence', 'true nature': cf. *Inv.* I. 91 *mala definitio est cum... communia describit, hoc modo: 'seditiosus est is qui malus atque inutilis civis est'. nam hoc non magis seditiosi quam...alicuius hominis improbi vim describit*; *de Orat.* I. 21 *vis oratoris.*

libris Best added, though *scripta* is sometimes omitted after possessive pronouns where the meaning is immediately obvious (cf. 80 (IV. 5). 1 n. (*mea*)).

8 **tenesne** Sc. *memoria*: cf. *Balb.* 56 *Tusculanum...ad Metellum pervenisse de Vennoni Vindicis* (so read for *Vindici*) *bonis non tenebat.*

9 **quo** Note the verbal ambiguity. At first sight one is tempted to understand as *ad quem* (as Watt, reading *volumus*, presumably does). Cf. *Q. Fr.* I. 1. 4 *ac mihi quidem videntur huc omnia referenda iis qui praesunt aliis ut ii qui erunt in eorum imperio sint quam beatissimi.*

10 **quinto...libro** *de Republica*, §8.

2, 4 **nec vero sqq.** Cf. Appendix IV, pp. 450 f.

8 **Sullani regni** Cf. 174 (IX. 7). 3 *mirandum enim in modum Gnaeus noster Sullani regni similitudinem concupivit*; *Har. Resp.* 54 *dissensit cum Mario ...L. Sulla; horum uterque ita cecidit victus ut victor idem regnaverit.*

3, 4 **iamque mari magno** From Ennius' *Alexander*. The passage is cited in *Div.* I. 67:

iamque mari magno classis cita
texitur; exitium examen rapit.
adveniet, fera velivolantibus
navibus complebit manus litora.

6 **'Ιλιάς** A proverbial expression (Leutsch–Schneidewin, *Corp. Paroem. Gr.* II, p. 34; cf. Dem. *Fals. Leg.* 148 κακῶν 'Ιλιάς; Plaut. *Mil.* 743 *odiorum Ilias* et sim.), here specially appropriate.

4, 1 **remansimus** *remansisti* might have been expected: cf. 74 (IV. 2). 3 *mihi restitui.*

2 **occurrimus** Simply 'met' rather than 'went to meet' (as in 287 (XII. 46). 2 *occurram etiam, si necesse erit*); cf. Sen. *Contr.* VII. 7. 15 *festinavi nec occurri*; Liv. XXXIX. 6. 1 *quibus* (sc. *comitiis*) *occurrere non potuit*; Plin. *Ep.* VI. 34. 3 *vellem Africanae* (sc. *ferae*), *quas coemeras plurimas, ad praefinitum diem occurrissent.*

4 **aut alterius sqq.** The first of the two supplements is plainly right and the second must be at any rate near to the original. *singulorum* is needed to balance *universae*. But Madvig is not to be followed in changing *in mancipiis* to *immanibus copiis* vel sim. *mancipia* is just the term C. would use for the 'barbarian' auxiliaries on both sides.

7 **universae** Sc. *Italiae* (which Wesenberg proposed to add): cf. *Fam.* XII. 4. 1; *post Red. ad Quir.* 1; *Phil.* IV. 13. For the corruption cf. 90 (IV. 15). 7 *epistulae / epistulam*. But other possibilities (*universorum, universus, universae rei p(ublicae)*) are by no means excluded.

5, 1 **quod quaeris sqq.** A letter written about this time by C. to Caesar thanking him for his clemency to Lentulus Spinther (cf. 178A (IX. 11A). 3 *cum antea tibi de Lentulo gratias egissem*) may have been a reply to Caesar's letter here mentioned. But how did Atticus know of the latter? There is nothing about it in the extant correspondence. Written after the capture of Corfinium it may have reached C. on the 24th, and he may have sent a copy to Rome after dispatching 159 (VIII. 10).

quod saepe Sc. *scripsit* (though C. will also be thinking of messages sent through others: cf. 145 (VII. 21). 3; 147 (VII. 23). 3). The ellipse is of a common type; cf. 14 (I. 14). 4 n. (*illo tempore*). Here, it is true, the complete expression would be *scripsit quod saepe scripserat*, but this is naturally understood.

6, 1 **neglegentiam** 'Carelessness', 'casualness'. Cf. 2 (I. 6). 1 n.

7, 2 **Parthicis rebus** Cf. 121 (VI. 6). 3 n.

6 **adferri** Cf. K.–S. I, p. 703.

Demetrio Magnete Cf. 86 (IV. 11). 2 n. After another request (162 (VIII. 12). 6) Atticus sent the book, which C. returned a fortnight later when he gave up the idea of making a public (?) appeal for peace (176 (IX. 9). 2).

7 **missum...mittas** Cf. 306 (XII. 6). 2 *librum...mitte. tuus est enim profecto, quoniam quidem est missus ad te*; *Nat. Deor.* I. 16 *liber Antiochi nostri, qui ab eo nuper ad hunc Balbum missus est* et sim.

161A (VIII. 11A)

This is plainly *not* the letter mentioned in 151 (VIII. 1). 1 and 152 (VIII. 2). 4, which C. answered with 161B (VIII. 11B). That was a letter of some length giving information about Vibullius' operations in Picenum and Domitius' troop levies. Equally unacceptable is Schmidt's theory (*Briefwechsel*, p. 134) that this is the postscript written in Pompey's own hand (cf. 151 (VIII. 1). 1 *sed in ea Pompei epistula erat in extremo ipsius manu 'tu censeo Luceriam venias; nusquam eris tutius'*). For (*a*) though the sense of the last sentence is the same as in the quotation sent to Atticus, the wording is considerably different and there is no apparent reason why C. should have changed it. Moreover his language in 151 (VIII. 1). 1 suggests that he quoted the entire postscript. (*b*) C. had already sent a copy of Pompey's longer letter to Atticus (152 (VIII. 2). 4). Why then should he send the postscript now? And why accuse Pompey of *neglegentia* if this was only a postscript to a longer letter? (*c*) This note, though short, contained (or seemed to contain) important information. If C. had received it, why does he say nothing about Fabius' report either to Atticus in his letter of the 15th or in his reply to Pompey—particularly as it ran counter to the optimistic information sent by Philotimus (147 (VII. 23). 1), which the earlier part (according to this theory) of Pompey's letter evidently corroborated, though in a 'less cheerful' form (cf. 151 (VIII. 1).1; 152 (VIII. 2). 4; 161B (VIII. 11B). 1 (n.b. *nunc quoniam...in spe firmiore sumus*)).

It is therefore clear that 161A (VIII. 11A) is a complete letter written soon after the longer one which C. had received on 15 February. It may have arrived on the 17th or 18th after he had left Formiae. Why then does he send it to Atticus on the 27th as the letter to which he replied in 161B (VIII. 11B)? The answer is simple: he made a mistake. The enclosure of this correspondence with Pompey may have been a sudden thought which occurred to him as he wrote, and there is no reason to think that he reread the letters carefully beforehand. The similar invitations to go to Luceria in both letters made it easy to confuse them.

1 **Q. Fabius** Perhaps Q. Fabius Vergilianus, who had been Ap. Pulcher's Legate in Cilicia (*Fam.* III. 3. 1 f.; 4. 1). He seems to have brought a letter from Vibullius (cf. 162B (VIII. 12 B). 1).

2 **XII** Cf. 162A (VIII. 12A). 1.

3 **habuisse in animo** On the reason why Domitius changed his mind cf. 162B (VIII. 12B). 1; 162C (VIII. 12C). 1; Appendix IV, p. 449, n. 5.

4 **C. Hirrum** Cf. 89 (IV. 16). 5 n. Probably now a Legate under Pompey, he fled from Camerinum to Corfinium with six cohorts, according to Caes. *B.C.* I. 15. 5. He is usually supposed to have been captured there and released with the rest, but he is not among the five captured Senators mentioned by Caesar (*ibid.* I. 23. 2). He will therefore have left the town before it fell and joined Pompey.

161B (VIII. 11B)

On the time of writing cf. 151 (VIII. 1). 2 n.

CN. MAGNO The use of Pompey's cognomen is contrary to C.'s ordinary practice (cf. 16 (I. 16). 11 n.); but Pompey had so styled himself, and C. had to follow suit.

1, 6 **navem** Cf. 153 (VIII. 3). 6 fin.

10 **praesidia** According to Caes. *B.C.* I. 24. 3 the Praetor Rutilius Lupus was in Tarracina with three cohorts until the fall of Corfinium. He then abandoned the town (cf. 162A (VIII. 12A). 4), but was deserted by his troops and, according to one report, returned to Rome (cf. 167 (IX. 1). 2).

11 **nemo** C. Cassius may have left some time after 11 February (cf. 149 (VII. 25)). But M'. Lepidus appears to have remained at Formiae until 7 March (cf. 167 (IX. 1). 2); perhaps C. thought him too old and inactive to count. A. Torquatus too seems to have left about the same time (cf. 175 (IX. 8). 1), but may have arrived after the 15th: cf. 138 (VII. 14). 2 n.

12 **M. Eppium** M. Eppius M. f. (cf. *Fam.* VIII. 8. 5) later served as Legate under Metellus Scipio in Africa, where he was captured after Thapsus and pardoned by Caesar (*Bell. Afr.* 89. 5). *hominem* reflects his social inferiority to the aristocrat Torquatus.

13 **L. Torquatum** It seems hardly credible that C. should not have added *praetorem* here, if in fact Torquatus held the office. The assumption that he did rests on Caesar's statement (*B.C.* I. 24. 3) that after the capture of Corfinium the Praetor L. Manlius (Mallius in the oldest MSS) fled from Alba (doubtless Alba Fucens: cf. *ibid.* I. 15. 7) with six cohorts. Torquatus had been at Formiae up to 10 February (cf. 147 (VII. 23). 1), and it is possible

that Caesar's L. Manlius (or Mallius) is a different man. Other possibilities are that Caesar made a mistake about his office or that *praetor* after his name is a copyist's anticipation of *Rutilius Lupus praetor* almost immediately following. Torquatus' forthcoming Praetorship is mentioned in *Fin.* II. 74, but the year in which the dialogue is set is otherwise uncertain.

2, 1 omnino C. seems to have intended a continuation such as 'but I did not stay there, since all was going forward satisfactorily'.

eo ipso die In fact Pompey seems to have left Teanum on 24 January whereas C. arrived in Capua the following day: cf. 137 (VII. 13*a*). 3 n. (*mansit*).

2 **volueras** Cf. 138 (VII. 14). 2.

3 **M. Considio** M. Considius Nonianus, Praetor perhaps in 52 (cf. Münzer, *RE.* IV. 914. 39), had been named by the Senate as Caesar's successor in Cisalpine Gaul (*Fam.* XVI. 12. 3).

4 **T. Ampium** T. Ampius T. f. Balbus, Tr. pl. 63, Pr. 59, and governor of Asia the following year. A henchman of Pompey (cf. Vell. II. 40. 4), who backed him in an unsuccessful candidature for the Consulship (Schol. Bob. (Stangl), p. 156) and defended him alongside C. in the courts (*Leg.* II. 6; cf. Quint. *Inst.* III. 8. 50), his party zeal earned him the name of *tuba belli civilis* (*Fam.* VI. 12. 3). C., a close friend (*Fam.* XIII. 70), probably obtained Caesar's permission for his return to Italy in 46; see the letter addressed to him in exile, *Fam.* VI. 12.

5 **L. Libonem** Cf. 135 (VII. 12). 2 n. The absence of praenomen might possibly be due to Libo's familiarity with Pompey, but in the official style of this letter we expect one.

6 **quoad consules** Until 28 January (140 (VII. 16). 2).

8 **fuissem** Sc. *ibi*, understood from *Capuam*: cf. *Rosc. Am.* 74 *qui Romam multis annis non venit neque umquam plus triduo fuit.*

triduum Cf. 109 (V. 6). 2 n. In fact C. spent only two clear days in Capua on his second visit, as on his first: 5 and 6 February (144 (VII. 20). 1; 145 (VII. 21). 1). But he did not get back to Formiae till the 8th, and his reluctance to tell Pompey plainly how very brief these expeditions of duty really were is understandable (note *quoad consules* above in lieu of a date).

3, 2 opportunitatem Cf. 151 (VIII. 1). 2 *hortatusque sum ut oram maritimam retineret, si rem frumentariam sibi ex provinciis suppeditari vellet.*

4 **opus est esse qui praesit** I.e. 'I must stay at my post': cf. Appendix II, p. 454.

6 **quo die** 17 January, though C. in fact left early on the 18th. *discessimus* may refer to the republican leaders generally (cf. 133 (VII. 10) n. (*omnes*)).

4, 1 M. Tullium Cf. 97 (V. 4). 1 n.; 151 (VIII. 1). 2 init.

161C (VIII. 11C)

Date and place established in 161D (VIII. 11D). 4.

1 **s.v.b.** *si vales benest.* A common prefatory formula (usually *e(go) q(uoque) v(aleo)* vel sim. follows) in official letters, found also in others not formal, as Cicero's to Terentia. *e.* (*est*) is sometimes added here, but cf. 174B (IX. 7B).

tuas litteras 161B (VIII. 11B).

161D (VIII. 11D)

1, 1 **misissem** The pluperfect can be explained as used 'neglegentia quadam', C. having in mind that the dispatch of the letter preceded Pompey's receipt of it: cf. (with Sjögren) Madvig on *Fin.* II. 54.

2 **suspicionem nullam habebam** Cf. §5 *nam suspicione adsequi non potui* sqq. The statement is untrue (cf. 151 (VIII. 1). 2), though later C. did think for a short time that Pompey would stay and fight after all (153 (VIII. 3). 7; 154 (VIII. 6). 3; 158 (VIII. 8). 2).

6 **mandatis** Laelius brought an oral message (cf. 162A (VIII. 12A). 3 *mandaram*) as well as a letter (cf. 153 (VIII. 3). 7 *scripserat*).

7 **D. Laelio** D. Laelius D. f., whose father had been one of Pompey's Legates against Sertorius, was not directly descended from the consular Laelii of the second century: cf. *Flacc.* 18 *honesto loco natus* (C. would certainly have called him *nobilis* in that context if he had been able). His unsuccessful prosecution of Flaccus in 59 was his first notable act. As Pompey's *paternus amicus et pernecessarius* (*Flacc.* 14) he is found as Tribune in 54 helping Gabinius (Val. Max. VIII. 1. Abs. 3), and was an active Pompeian admiral in 48. But after Pharsalia he was one of the first to make his peace (cf. 218 (XI. 7). 2). D. Laelius Balbus, who resisted Sextius' invasion of Africa Vetus in 42 and finally committed suicide, was probably his son, ancestor of the imperial Laelii Balbi (Münzer, *RE.* XII. 412 f.). Caelius' supposed reference in *Fam.* VIII. 4. 2 to *Laelios et Antonios et id genus valentis* is almost certainly corrupt (cf. *Philol.* 105 (1961), p. 85).

2, 1 **C. Messius** Cf. 73 (IV. 1). 7 n.

4 **quod...putabam** Quoted by Nonius (p. 455, Lindsay), as is also §3 *admoniti sumus...Caesare*, with the reference *ad Pompeium lib. IIII*: cf. Büchner, *RE.* VII A. 1199 f.

3, 1 **litterarum** Text in 154 (VIII. 6). 2.

20 **rei publicae noceret** If they fell into Caesar's hands.

21 **si etiam** Cf. 92 (IV. 18). 5 *si etiam sapis*; *Thes.* VII. 934. 75.

4, 1 tuas litteras 161C (VIII. 11C).

3 **cum accepissemus** Probably without any causal sense; cf. *cum misissem* in §1.

8 **regionibus exclusi** The text needs explanation, not emendation. *regionibus* means 'by whole districts', i.e. large tracts of country: cf. Curt. IV. 2. 16 *exhauriendas esse regiones ut illud spatium exaggeraretur*; Ov. *Her.* XV. 125 *quamvis regionibus absis* (Palmer wrong, Purser right), *Met.* XII. 41 *quamvis regionibus absit.* Wesenberg's *regionibus* ⟨*suis*⟩ is quite misguided, though ⟨*a suis*⟩, 'from their own side', would make for clarity: cf. 162B (VIII. 12B). 1 *prius quam Caesar...me abs te excludere posset.*

praesidia atque...arma Cf. 170 (IX. 3). 1 *cum ea* (sc. *Italia*) *tota armis praesidiisque teneatur.* The distinction is between stationary troops (and the posts they occupy: cf. *Bell. Alex.* 23. 1 *a regis amicis qui in Caesaris essent praesidiis*) and troops on the move.

5, 3 reiciebam See Appendix II, p. 439.

8 **omnia prius...quam sqq.** This kind of expression is regular in poetic ἀδύνατα (cf. *Propertiana*, pp. 44 f., 277). Of course this statement is as insincere as the following expression of trust in Pompey's wisdom. Its covert sting is sharpened by the pretence that withdrawal from Italy had been inconceivable to patriots like C. himself; but there would be no point in it at all if Pompey's intention had been previously declared or generally expected by his supporters. See Appendix IV, pp. 450 f.

11 **quid tu secutus sis** Cf. 74 (IV. 2). 4 n. (*quid...secuti*).

6, 7 civili perniciosissimo bello Watt brackets *civili*, presumably as a gloss, a suspicion which had also occurred to T.–P. Purser suggests *civili bello perniciosissimo.* But the paradosis is defended not only by 189 (IX. 19). 1 *in civili nefario bello*, but by several other passages in which a colouring epithet is sandwiched between specifying adjective and substantive: *Div.* I. 20 (*de Consulatu suo*) *civilem...ingentem cladem*; *Brut.* 76 *illud Punicum acerrimum bellum*; *Off.* II. 57 *aedilicio maximo munere*; *Fam.* V. 2. 6 *fraternam plenam humanitatis ac pietatis voluntatem*; Nep. *Att.* 14. 3 *nullam suburbanam aut maritimam sumptuosam villam*; Liv. XXIII. 37. 2 *ligneam ingentem admotam urbi turrem.* Cf. Liv. XXVIII. 41. 3 *prioris Punici perpetrati belli titulus.* In *Phil.* V. 40 we have *periculosissimum civile bellum maximumque* (cf. *Marc.* 24 *in tanto civili bello*), followed shortly by *bellum acerbissimum civile.*

7, 5 ad eas *ea* is defended by Sjögren (*Comm. Tull.* p. 167) as a neuter of general reference, citing passages such as *Nat. Deor.* II. 15 *ut...cum videat omnium rerum rationem, modum, disciplinam, non possit ea sine causa fieri iudicare*: cf. K.–S. I, p. 61 f. But the pronoun here is so closely connected with the single substantive *condiciones* that the neuter seems extremely unlikely.

6 **honorifice** In a way (i.e in terms) complimentary to Caesar (not 'conciliatory' or 'honourable'): cf. 150 (VII. 26). 2; 188 (VIII. 9). 2.

duxi meam rationem Cf. 132 (VII. 9). 4 *habe meam rationem*; *Verr.* II. I. 126 *debere eum aiebant suam quoque rationem ducere.*

10 **si. . .deferebatur** Cf. 162 (VIII. 12). 2 *cavi ne animum eius offenderem cui Pompeius iam armatus armato consulatum triumphumque deferret.*

12 **amplissimus** It is hard to see how the Triumph offered to Caesar was particularly glorious except in so far as his own achievements made it so. *amplissime* ('in the most handsome terms') would fit better here than in 125 (VII. 2). 6.

proeliis Cf. 16 (I. 16). 1 *vis scire quo modo ego minus quam soleam proeliatus sim*; *Fam.* IX. 11. 2 *quod scribis proelia te mea causa sustinere. procellis,* Corradus' conjecture revived by Madvig, does not seem obligatory.

13 **ut. . .videretur** This is a tortuous sentence in an uneasy letter, but while recognizing the difficulty of *ut* I do not think it necessary to substitute *quod* or *et* or *cum*. C. is very apt to use *videri* in a consecutive clause when he wants to make a comment for which he prefers not to take full responsibility: cf. 19 (I. 19). 3 *hoc idem post me Pompeio accidit, ut nos duo quasi pignora rei publicae retineri videremur* and other passages cited in *Towards a Text*, p. 39. This is exactly similar, except that he imagines himself as making the comment *ut. . .habere videretur* (i.e. *quasi haberet*) in circumstances which might have arisen, but in fact have not. If they had, he could have said *isdem proeliis subicior, ut. . .videatur.*

14 **populare** As one might speak of a popular target or victim. Cf. 153 (VIII. 3). 5 *quod putabit fortasse in nobis violandis aliquid se habere populare.*

atque *neque* (Müller) is read by nearly all modern editors, even the most conservative, but the paradosis is perfectly acceptable. C. means that there was no need for him to work all this out for himself since threats had been made early and openly. It is in no way unlikely that such threats were uttered against him in public by Caesarian politicians before the outbreak of war.

8, 1 **quam ob rem** There are two ways of interpreting *quam brevem*, both inadmissible. (*a*) Understand *rationem*. But in such a case one says 'you have in brief an account. . .' (cf. *ad Brut.* 23. 11 *habes rationem mearum sententiarum* sqq.), not 'you have in brief *this* account. . .'. (*b*) *quam* = *perquam* (which Reid conjectured): cf. 139 (VII. 15). 2 n. In a familiar, colloquial passage this use of *quam*, frequent in comedy, may pass well enough; but nothing could be less familiar than this letter. Besides C.'s exposition is not as brief as all that. *quam* could be deleted with Madvig (so Watt), but the change here adopted (or *quam* ⟨*ob rem*⟩ *brevem*, suggested verbally by

Professor D. L. Page as an alternative) seems preferable. *Part. Orat.* 113 *quam ob rem haec sint dicta de causa* is closely analogous.

rationem nostram Or perhaps 'my policy'.

2 **reliqui facultatem** Apparently 'means of disposing of the rest as I would have chosen'. But the expression seems very harsh and perhaps some verb like *recuperandi* (cf. 160 (VIII. 9*a*). 1 *reliqui temporis recuperandi rationem*) has dropped out after *reliqui*. The sense anyway is that up to the breakdown of peace negotiations in late February C. had been deterred by the considerations aforesaid from taking too active a part, while afterwards, when he wished to join Pompey in Apulia, it was no longer possible.

3 **neque. . .umquam fui** Had C. forgotten or did he expect others to forget his professions of friendship for Caesar in the late fifties? He can hardly be accusing himself of hypocrisy. He may of course be thinking of certain Pompeians who, unlike Cato and Domitius, actually had been friends of Caesar, e.g. Labienus and Lentulus Spinther. And no doubt there is a covert reminder of Pompey's own past, even though he is distinguished from the critics by *quod idem te intellexeram velle*.

162 (VIII. 12)

1, 1 **lippitudo** Cf. 138 (VII. 14). 1 n. Possibly however, as Orelli suggested, C. used the Greek equivalent λήμη.

2 **Gallo Fabio** M. Fabius Gallus (cf. 112 (V. 19). 1 n. (*Apellae*)), on whose *nomen gentile*, which editors since Orelli had disguised as Fadius, see *Cl. Rev.* N.S. 12 (1962), pp. 195 f. A friend of long standing (*Fam.* XV. 14. 1; cf. IX. 25. 2, XIII. 59; 349 (XIII. 49)) and, like Atticus and Papirius Paetus, an Epicurean (*Fam.* VII. 26. 1), he was the recipient of four extant letters (*Fam.* VII. 23–6), all probably belonging to 46–45.

5 **vaticinationem** Cf. 161 (VIII. 11). 3.

8 **†quo tibi sqq.** This seems irretrievably corrupt. The botch provided in some texts (including the most recent), *quo quia tibi perexiguo opus est*, may be ignored; and Madvig's *quo tibi quidem perexiguo opus est; explicari* ⟨*enim*⟩ *mihi* is far from convincing. Something like *ad scribendum quid mihi faciendum putes* is wanted after *sumeres aliquid temporis*. And would C. tell Atticus that the thing would take very little time (cf. §4), even in compliment to his facility as a writer? I do not forget 395 (XV. 18). 2 *tribues nobis paulum operae; nec enim multum opus est.*

2, 3 **tum. . .nolui** See Appendix II, p. 438. The v. l. *imparatam* has no authority, though *qua* conjecture there is something to be said for it as making clearer the point of *ignaviae dedecus*. But then *iam* has to go.

4 **ignaviae dedecus** 'numquam mihi persuadebitur dici posse

ignavia delectus pro neglegentia in delectu habendo' Orelli. Defending *delectus* in Χάριτες *Fr. Leo dargebracht*, pp. 291 ff. Sjögren was washing a stone. But even Sjögren did not put it in his text, as Watt surprisingly does (*dil-*). *dedecus* is virtually certain. C. means that having no resources at his back he knew that he could do nothing effective as commandant in Capua and, if he had to surrender the place, might come to be suspected of actual treachery.

6 **Fabatum** L. Roscius Fabatus, Praetor this year. In 54 he had been Caesar's Legate (*B.G.* v. 24. 2, etc.: surely not Quaestor only five years before his Praetorship; cf. Drumann–Groebe, III, pp. 697 f.). On his part in the negotiations cf. Appendix III, pp. 446 f. He died in 43, fighting for the Republic in the first battle of Mutina (*Fam.* x. 33. 4). The praenomen *L.* can be dispensed with (L. Caesar had, of course, to be distinguished from his famous kinsman).

3, 3 **erat deliberationis** The subject is *id*: cf. 133 (VII. 10) *consili res est*; *de Orat.* II. 370 *id est consili*; Caes. *B.G.* VII. 38. 6 *quasi vero consili sit res*; Liv. XXII. 53. 6 *negat consilii rem esse*; 126 (VII. 3). 3 *habet enim res deliberationem*; also 398 (XV. 21). 2 n.

obire The verb suggests the fulfilment of a task: cf. *obire negotium, facinus, munus. obire diem, vadimonium* et sim. are less relevant since *id* = *mare transire* rather than *tempus maris transeundi*.

4 **cum praesertim, sqq.** See Appendix IV, pp. 455 ff.

5, 2 **illorum temporum** 58–57. So 169 (IX. 2*a*). 1 *illorum temporum culpam*; *Fin.* II. 72 *temporibus illis quae nota sunt omnibus*.

3 **memini sqq.** See Introd. pp. 17 f.

5 **calculos** 'Counters', i.e. 'principles of action'. Not 'let us go over the old calculation afresh'.

7 **paulo salubrioribus** *salubribus* has been defended by Ter. *Heaut.* 205 *paulo qui est homo tolerabilis*. But it is hard to believe in one such Ciceronian example of the positive beside scores of the comparative.

6, 9 **librum** Cf. 161 (VIII. 11). 7 n.

162A (VIII. 12A)

On the date see Appendix IV, p. 453.

1, 3 **cum omni copia** The singular seems to have no special significance; the *Thesaurus* (IV. 905. 18) provides plenty of examples. The notion that it may denote 'a hastily raised and irregular levy' is sufficiently refuted in §4.

5 **iter habebant** Before they joined Domitius at Corfinium. Vibullius,

who was Pompey's own emissary to Picenum (Caes. *B.C.* I. 15. 4), and Hirrus with him will have been on their way to join the main army when, perhaps of their own volition or perhaps by Domitius' orders, they halted to strengthen the garrison at Corfinium. Pompey's language to Domitius in 162B (VIII. 12B). 2 fin. shows that he felt he had a moral right to these troops, though they were under Domitius' command. The indicative *habebant* states the fact; it cannot be epistolary since the following sentence shows that Pompey did not suppose that these troops actually had escaped the net.

6 **ut neque. . .neque** Madvig's *et* may look more elegant, but the sequence of *ut* clauses, the second depending on the first, is unobjectionable (cf. e.g. 326 (XIII. 19). 5 *ut non sim consecutus ut superior mea causa videatur*). But perhaps *ut* should be omitted, as in Σ (apart from O) and many editions. In that case, however, the first *neque* must be allowed a dual function, in correlation with *implicaretur* on the one hand and with the following *neque* on the other, a construction not found in C. but not uncommon in historical writing (cf. Leumann–Hofmann, *Lat. Gramm.* p. 663). It occurs in Caesar's letter 172A (IX. 6A) *cum Furnium nostrum tantum vidissem neque loqui neque audire meo commodo potuissem.*

7 **ad castra facienda** Sc. *contra Caesarem.* Cf. Lepidus, *Fam.* X. 34. 1 *castra ad flumen Argenteum contra Antonios feci*, also 162 C (VIII. 12C). 2.

2, 5 **quod. . .misi** Cf. 153 (VIII. 3). 7 *etsi Brundisium Scipionem cum cohortibus duabus praemiserat*, on the strength of which editors add *duas* after *quod.* Pompey was not bound to repeat the number here and it would be rather odd to mention the strength of the force sent to Brundisium while giving no figure for Canusium (in fact presumably four cohorts). *quas* of $Z^{(b)}$ λ would be a point in favour of *quod duas* if we could be confident that it came from Z; but this is very doubtful, since the citation *quas Brundisium praesidium misi* was made for the sake of *praesidium* and *quas* (ed. Iens.) was the vulgate. The collators may easily have failed to notice that Z in fact had *quod.*

3, 1 **mandaram** Cf. 161D (VIII. 11D). 1.

5 **legit** Lit. 'picked', here = *conscripsit* (cf. 153 (VIII. 3). 7).

9 **possim** Something has fallen out, perhaps in the nature of Wesenberg's *ipse autem fortasse possit*, though this contradicts §1. Pompey would hardly say here that Domitius could *not* extricate himself (*neque ipse possit* Tyrrell, *auctore Lambino*) since that would be no reason for not going to his assistance. Also *per montis* would become superfluous. But the gap may be wider.

10 **dubio animo** Cf. 136 (VII. 13). 2 n.

4, 1 **†altia** *talia* is palaeographically the easiest change, but *atque ita* is much more likely to have been what Pompey wrote. Many other variants have been suggested, some innocuous (e.g. *nec aliter*), others involving a good deal of rewriting.

2 **M. Marcello** Perhaps *a* should be added, though the dative would not certainly be inadmissible even in C.: cf. K.–S. I, pp. 324 ff. Some editors read *C. Marcello* against the authority of Z and probabilities both palaeographical and historical. For C. Marcellus (Cos. 50) did not cross to Greece with Pompey (cf. 203 (X. 12). 3), Marcus almost certainly did: cf. *Cl. Quart.* N.S. 10 (1960), p. 253, n. 7, adding Val. Max. IX. 11. 4 *Pompeianae militiae comes.*

5 **eodem Brundisium** Müller, while deleting the name of the town with Manutius and others, compares 353 (XIII. 52). 2 *eodem ad me cum revertere*, where *eadem* (Moricca, and so Reid here) is only a possibility. Cf. Liv. XXIII. 34. 2 *eodem ad Iunonis Laciniae*, XLI. 17. 8 *eodem Pisas*; Nep. *Epam.* 5. 2. *indidem Thebis.* There is the less cause for suspicion here in that Pompey would naturally want to make his instructions absolutely clear.

7 **quae arma...ea** Cf. K.–S. II, p. 290 (add Liv. XXXVIII. 44. 5 *signa aliaque ornamenta, quae quererentur ex aedibus suis sacris sublata esse, de iis...placere ad collegium pontificum referri*).

9 **P. Lupum** Cf. 161B (VIII. 11B). 1 n. (*praesidia*). P. Rutilius Lupus, probably son of his namesake, Consul in 90, appears as Tribune in 57–56 to have combined hostility to Caesar (Q. *Fr.* II. 1. 1) with support for Pompey (*Fam.* I. 1. 3, 2. 2). The report in 167 (IX. 1). 2 of his return to Rome was probably untrue since in 48 he was serving under Pompey in Greece (Caes. *B.C.* III. 56. 3).

C. Coponium Later a Pompeian naval commander in the Adriatic (*ibid.* III. 5. 3, etc.). His wife saved him in the proscriptions of 43 (App. *B.C.* IV. 40), and he figures as a witty and respected Senator in 32 (Vell. II. 83. 3).

162B (VIII. 12B)

On the date cf. Appendix IV, p. 449.

1, 2 **de re publica** I.e. on the military situation. The political situation (so Winstedt translates) was not engaging either Domitius' or Pompey's attention at the time.

5 **ut Vibullius mihi scripserat** This letter had probably been brought by Q. Fabius (cf. 161A (VIII. 11A). *scribit* below evidently refers to a later letter, reporting Domitius' change of plan. See Appendix IV, *ibid.*

7 **illa causa** More plainly stated at the beginning of the next letter.

12 **aut...aut** Caesar might either be close enough on Domitius' heels to interfere with his march or (as he actually did) might get to the

south of him and so prevent him marching at all.

2, 1 etiam Cf. 87 (IV. 13). 2 n.

3 **ad me venires** *me* is a necessary addition: 'man kann ja auch jemand nur bitten, irgendwohin zu kommen, nicht an einem Orte anzukommen' (Otto, *Rhein. Mus.* 41 (1886), p. 371: he compares 161A (VIII. 11A) *censeo ad nos Luceriam venias*; 162C (VIII. 12C). 1 *in Samnium ad me venturum*, 3 *ut...ad me venias*). The tense is determined by *destiti* in the parenthetic clause instead of by the main verb—not a rare phenomenon in C.: cf. K.-S. II, p. 195.

5 **villas** This may point to local people rather than to Roman magnates, who would not be so likely to have country houses in this area: cf. 163 (VIII. 13). 2.

aequum est Cf. 162A (VIII. 12A). 1 n.

7 **missum facias** Sjögren refers to P. Thielmann, *Arch. Wölffl.* 2 (1885), p. 547. *missos* would of course be normal.

162C (VIII. 12C)

On the background and purpose of this letter see Appendix IV, pp. 451 ff.

1, 1 M. Calenius Unknown. The name occurs in three inscriptions, one of them at Cales (*Thes.* Suppl. 79. 70).

6 **animo magno** I.e. regardless of personal risk: cf. 35 (II. 15). 2 n.

rem agere Not = *rem gerere*; there is no specifically military implication, though *bellum agere* (cf. *pacem agere*) occurs in Sallust, Nepos, etc. (*Thes.* II. 1834. 41). Cf. *Dom.* 139 *qui...ageret illam rem ita raptim et turbulente uti* sqq.; Q. *Fr.* I. 1. 31 *in omnibus rebus quas statues, quas decernes, quas ages* et sim.

13 **Bussenius** Another unknown.

14 **Curionem** He had taken Iguvium for Caesar about 19 January (*B.C.* I. 12. 1 f.). About 17 February he was put in charge of the second Caesarian camp at Corfinium (*ibid.* 18. 5). Of his movements in the interval we have no definite information, so that this passage gives no sure ground for aspersions on Pompey's intelligence arrangements.

16 **quae si copiae sqq.** An awkwardly constructed sentence, but not so awkward as to excuse current misinterpretations. Neither the first nor the second *ut* means 'although'. They are explanatory, = *ita ut*. Pompey is *explaining* what he thinks Caesar will do. The sending of forces to Alba (Fucens), in order to cut off Domitius from the west, and the refraining from battle are hinges, not snags, in Caesar's trap. For this use of *ut* cf. e.g. 14 (I. 14). 3 *ornatissimeque de meo consulatu locutus est, ut ita diceret, se...referre.*

2, 2 hoc Cf. 162D (VIII. 12D). 2; *Thes.* VI. 3072 f. It cannot be a coincidence that the MSS of C.'s correspondence show this form almost exclusively in the letters of others, Pompey, Plancus, D. Brutus, Lentulus.

3 **M. Tuscilio** There is epigraphic evidence of Tuscilii in Pompey's country of Picenum (cf. Münzer, *RE.* VIIIA. 1462).

4 **duae legiones** *hae* (cf. 162A (VIII. 12A). 2 *his duabus legionibus*) should perhaps be added.

3, 1 deducturi sunt *ad me* (Wesenberg) vel sim. is to be understood rather than added to the text. Pompey's vagueness is probably deliberate: cf. Appendix IV, pp. 452 f. For the verb cf. Sall. *Orat. Phil.* 17 *praesidia deducta atque imposita.*

6 **amplum...magnum** There must surely be *some* distinction between these adjectives. Perhaps *magnum* refers only to numbers while *amplum* is more general, suggesting the balance of various arms together with equipment, officers, etc.

8 **summae** I can hardly believe that Pompey wrote the paradosis *summam*, whereas a copyist unfamiliar with the expression *summa res publica* might easily make *summae* agree with *rationem.*

4, 1 †sic adpoete† The vulgate *Sicca abs te* is much less than certain, at least so far as the name is concerned. Its only known possessor is C.'s friend (cf. 48 (III. 2). n.) and there is nothing to connect him with either Domitius or Pompey.

162D (VIII. 12D)

1, 4 te implicet Nothing can well be done with *per* (*praeter*) in the MSS except to delete it. Tmesis seems out of the question since *perimplicare* is a hardly conceivable verb, and my conjecture *penitus implicet* lacks a satisfactory parallel.

7 **voluntate...confido** For the ablative cf. K.–S. I, p. 399.

10 **etiam** = *adhuc.*

11 **consulibus** Cf. 153 (VIII. 3). 7 n. (*Fausto*).

2, 2 hoc Cf. below and 162C (VIII. 12C). 2 n.

3 **adversarium** Genitive; cf. Neue–Wagener, *Formenlehre*[3], I, p. 179. Sjögren compares *Div.* II. 52 *quod ni fecisset, uno in loco omnes adversariorum copiae convenissent.* The proposed changes (⟨*ad*⟩ *adversarium, adversari in unum*) are clearly unnecessary.

5 **quantum** Cf. 54 (III. 9). 2 n., also Plancus, *Fam.* X. 24. 3 *quantum autem in acie tironi sit committendum nimium saepe expertum habemus.*

noti Cf. Liv. XXXV. 3. 4 *in aciem exire non audebat novo milite et ex multis generibus hominum collecto necdum noto satis inter se, ut fidere alii aliis possent.*

163 (VIII. 13)

The dates of this and the following letters are fixed by 166 (VIII. 16). 2 *IIII Non.*

1, 1 lippitudinis sqq. Cf. 138 (VII. 14). 1 n.

3 **nactus...esset...tramisisset** Epistolary tenses.

2, 2 municipales How points out that there is no sharp distinction between these and the *rusticani*, citing *Verr.* II. 1. 127 *homines rusticanos ex municipiis* and *Rosc. Am.* 43 *homines illius ordinis ex municipiis rusticanis* ('In fact most country proprietors, such as Sex. Roscius, would be *municipes* of country towns (*ibid.* 15)').

3 **villulas...nummulos** Cf. 160 (VIII. 10) *de servulis suis.*

7 **impendere** Cf. 161 (VIII. 11). 3 *tanta malorum impendet* Ἰλιάς.

164 (VIII. 14)

1, 7 crede mihi Cf. 103 (V. 10). 1 n.

11 **mutum...a litteris** Ovid has the simple ablative, *Tr.* V. 7. 62 *et fiat potius vox mea muta sono.* For such alternations cf. K.–S. I, p. 374. *ab*, 'in respect of', follows a variety of adjectives (cf. *ibid.* p. 496), but especially those expressive of lack or absence, as *vacuus* (*Inv.* II. 24, etc.), *nudus* (*post Red. ad Quir.* 16; *Dom.* 58), *inops* (*ibid.*): cf. Plaut. *Poen.* 1186 *a culpa castas* (and Gell. III. 5. 1 *a stupro integer*); Cato, *R.R.* 33. 3 *vinea a vite calva*; Colum. *R.R.* XII. 18. 7 *die quieto a ventis* (and Gell. II. 30. 3 *undae...a vento...tranquillae*), VII. 12. 2 *desidemque ab opere suo*; Quint. *Decl.* 272 *securis ab omni cogitatione bellorum.*

13 **bidui aut tridui** Cf. 52 (III. 7). 1 *quadridui* et sim. *biduum abest* means 'is absent for two days'. *bidui via* (T.–P., comparing Caes. *B.G.* VI. 7. 2, etc.) accounts neatly for the corruption; but this could easily be due to a copyist's failure to understand the genitives, and *via* lacks Ciceronian parallel.

14 **proximi** For *primus* and *proximus* confused see Housman on Man. V. 218 (I suspect that *Verr.* II. 2. 100 *primis illis temporibus* is yet another example). It would be quite unnatural for a contemporary to look upon the operations at Brundisium as the 'first stage in the war', even if *primi temporis* were a natural way to express that.

17 **Feralibus** 21 February.

18 **diariis** Like T.–P. I see no serious reason to alter this.

2, 5 auctores M'. Lepidus and Vulcatius Tullus: cf. 177 (IX. 10). 7.

6 **quod...desiderat?** Cf. 160 (VIII. 9*a*). 1.

9 **haec** 'Quae in Italia a Caesare fiunt' (Corradus).

13 **tecum tamquam mecum loquor** Cf. Sen. *Ep.* 3. 2 *tam audaciter*

cum illo (sc. *amico*) *loquere quam tecum*, 27. 1 *sic itaque me audi tamquam mecum loquar*; Plin. *Ep*. V. 1. 12 *non aliter tecum quam mecum loqui soleo*.

3, 4 **modo sqq.** As Wesenberg saw, a phrase such as *modo ad Pompeium festinare, quod falsum est* (Purser) must have disappeared before *modo*. The words *lepidi quo cum lepidus* remain mysterious. Without them the text so supplemented would make satisfactory sense, with them there seems nothing to be done. Some conjectures run up against the point that M'. Lepidus was clearly still at Formiae (cf. also 167 (IX. 1). 2). Others introduce a play on the name, unsuitable to the tone of the passage.

6 **itineribus occultis** Cf. *Verr*. II. 3. 219 *avaritiae, quae antehac occultis itineribus atque angustis uti solebat* and 160 (VIII. 9*a*). 2 *occulta via*. Lambinus also suggested *deviis*; cf. 364 (XIV. 10). 1 *itineribus deviis*.

7 **adipiscendi** C. cannot seriously be supposed to have used the old form *apisci* in this one place out of scores (I do not count *Leg*. I. 52, where editors have imported it).

ne id quidem scit Watt rightly discards Madvig's needless conjecture *is*. ⟨*nam*⟩ *ne id quidem* would be better though still unnecessary: cf. 224 (XI. 13). 1 *ne id quidem verum est*; Ter. *Eun*. 321 *PA. quid? virgo quoiast? CH. nescio hercle.* . . .*PA. ubi habitat? CH. ne id quidem.*

8 **sane molestum** Surely ironical. To expect Caesar to return the money (HS 6,000,000 according to *B.C.* I. 23. 4) was going rather far. None the less Caesar did restore it (*ibid*. Cf. App. *B.C.* II. 38, 41), though, as he says, the money was public funds supplied by Pompey to pay the troops.

165 (VIII. 15)

1, 1 **Aegypta** A freedman, apparently of C.'s, in 45 (276 (XII. 37). 1).

2 **Pinario** Cf. 115 (VI. 1). 23 n.

3 **praemissus** 'Sent ahead' by Caesar to Pompey. Caesar (*B.C.* I. 34. 1) says that he let Vibullius go free at Corfinium, but nothing about a mission to Pompey. No doubt the story was untrue, as C. implies, so far as Vibullius was concerned. But Caesar did send another *praefectus fabrum* of Pompey's (cf. 174C (IX. 7C). 2) to Pompey with a message (*B.C.* I. 24. 4 f.), so the report may simply have confused the names. Vibullius did go on a peace mission from Caesar to Pompey later in the war (*ibid*. III. 10). Certainly Atticus was not referring to his mission from Pompey to Spain (*ibid*. I. 34. 1); that would make C.'s answer *qui omnino non est visus a Caesare* pointless.

7 **†aut hemonis** αὐθήμερον, adjective rather than adverb, is perhaps the best of many guesses. Atticus, who may have had reasons for wanting to stay in Rome as long as possible, might well write that he meant to be off the day Caesar arrived.

fugam intendis Cf. Introd. p. 37. Watt's complaint (*l.c.* p. 398) that *intendere* in the sense of 'purpose' or 'intend' with the accusative of a noun is very doubtful Ciceronian Latin seems captious, since C. does so use *animo intendere* (once, in *Phil.* x. 9) and the same construction without *animo* is found in Sallust and Livy (*Thes.* VII. 2116. 84). If there were any need to suspect the vulgate, which is practically the paradosis, it would be easier to suppose that *animo* has fallen out than that '*fugam intendis*' (*sic*) 'is a scribe's latinization of the corresponding Greek words φυγὴν διανοῇ'.

8 **cum fascibusne sit** As Caesar's appointed successor in Transalpine Gaul.

2, 3 **Iovi ipsi iniquum** A proverb, here of course with reference to Pompey, for violent anger or truculence: cf. *Fam.* x. 12. 4 *venit paratus Servilius Iovi iniquus*; Otto, *Sprichwörter*, p. 179 (where add Sil. x. 53 *nunc Hannibal ipsi / (tam laetus bello est) ausit certare Tonanti*, 67 *quippe furit Poenus, qui nunc contraria bella / ipsi ferre Iovi valeat*).

6 **pluma aut folio** Cf. Plaut. *Men.* 487 *homo / levior quam pluma, Poen.* 812 *levior pluma est gratia*; Ov. *Am.* II. 16. 45 *verba puellarum foliis leviora caducis, Her.* v. 109 *tu levior foliis, Fast.* III. 481 *Bacche levis leviorque tuis, quae tempora cingunt, / frondibus, ex Pont.* IV. 3. 33 *quolibet est folio, quavis incertior aura.*

7 **cruciat cruciavitque adhuc** Watt reads *cruciavit cruciatque* on his own conjecture, comparing passages like 58 (III. 14). 1 *minus moleste feremus nos vixisse et adhuc vivere* (*l.c.* p. 398). But the reason why the normal order is here inverted seems sufficiently obvious. Having stated in the present tense the considerations which do *not* influence him (*nec me movet...nec me consules movent*) C. naturally uses the same tense in stating his real motive, and then as an afterthought adds that this has been his motive all along (cf. 176 (IX. 9). 4 *nam me adhuc tuae litterae sustentarunt*).

3, 1 **recentissima** A passage from it is quoted in 177 (IX. 10). 8.

3 **nec...Pompeium sqq.** Similarly Balbus, 165A (VIII. 15A). 1. He and C. were doubtless right (cf. Caes. *B.C.* I. 26. 5). In his present humiliating position peace with any semblance of honour was no longer possible for Pompey.

6 **memento** Senators (and C. evidently has only Senators in view) other than the Consuls or those charged with an office or mission outside Italy had to obtain special permission to go overseas (cf. Mommsen, *St.* III, pp. 912 f.).

7 **Appium** Still Censor, unless he had resigned.

fere In 167 (XI. 1). 4 C. Cassius is mentioned as another exception. It is difficult to believe that there were not more.

ius...transeundi I.e. without the special license normally required.

Before leaving Rome Pompey had secured a senatorial decree to indemnify magistrates absenting themselves from the capital (Dio, XLI. 6. 2), and this may have covered absence from Italy *rei publicae causa* for private members also.

8 **cum imperio** C. himself of course was *cum imperio*, but he is thinking of provincial office actually current; cf. 167 (IX. 1). 4.

9 **Scipio** Appointed governor (Proconsul) of Syria in succession to Bibulus (Caes. *B.C.* I. 6. 5).

Sufenas Cf. 90 (IV. 15). 4 n. His province is unknown (cf. 115 (VI. 1). 13 n.).

Fannius Cf. 44 (II. 24). 3 n. He was to have been sent ahead of Cato to Sicily, probably as Propraetor, in late January (139 (VII. 15). 2), but either never went or returned after Cato's arrival there.

Voconius He and his province are unknown. He may have been a son of Q. Voconius Naso, one of the jury at the trial of Cluentius in 66 (*Cluent.* 147). Cf. 255 (XII. 17) *Nasone*.

Sestius C.'s appointed successor in Cilicia (Plut. *Brut.* 4).

10 **quibus...provincias** Cf. Mommsen, *St.* I, p. 53; H. Last, *Journ. Rom. Stud.* 37 (1947), p. 160.

11 **sed nihil differo** Cf. 244 (XII. 7). 1 *sed quid differo?* Despite the point just made C.'s mind is really made up (for the moment) in favour of what he believes to be Atticus' opinion, and further argument is unnecessary. The vulgate *decerno* (for the paradosis *desero*; cf. 162 (VIII. 12). 5 *sed nihil praescribo*) is at odds with the next words.

165A (VIII. 15A)

1, 2 **virtutis** The genitive after *dignus* seems to have been something of a vulgarism at this time: cf. K.–S. I, pp. 398 f.

4 **potestate** Cf. 6 (I. 10). 2 *confido illum fore in officio et in nostra potestate.*

5 **si...reicis** The present belongs to ordinary usage, of which C. has many examples: cf. K.–S. I, p. 146. It is especially frequent when the protasis expresses a wish or command with reference to the near future and the apodosis offers an assurance.

7 **magis opto quam spero** So Caesar in a letter to Balbus, *ap. Q. Fr.* II. 11. 4 *id erat eius modi ut magis optandum quam sperandum putarem.* Cf. 233 (XI. 19). 1 *cogis me sperare quod optandum vix est*; *Fam.* IV. 1. 2 *mihi venire in mentem nihil potest non modo quod sperem sed vix iam quod audeam optare.*

9 **et** = *etiam* ('when *X* happens, then *Y* too will happen'). Cf. in §2 *si voluerit...incipiam sperare etiam* sqq.

2, 1 meum Added as though *consulem* were part of the name; cf. the headings of C.'s letters to Dolabella, 371A (XIV. 17A) = *Fam.* IX. 14 and 402 (XV. 14). 2. Weiske's deletion of *consulem*, approved by Watt, is unwise. Balbus probably owed his Roman citizenship to Lentulus Crus, whence his nomen Cornelius.

voluisti Apparently with reference to advice given by C. to Lentulus before the evacuation of Rome.

3 **qui...diligam** Similarly Antony (199A (X. 8A). 1 *mihi neminem esse cariorem te excepto Caesare meo*. For *qui* cf. Lucr. V. 3 *quisve valet verbis tantum qui fingere laudes / pro meritis eius possit* et sim. (K.–S. II, pp. 298 f.). *tanti facio* amounts to *tantum diligo*. I do not think it justifiable to substitute *ut*, though in 174B (IX. 7B). 3 Balbus writes *te...tanti facio ut paucos aeque ac te caros habeam.*

3, 2 quo modo in eius modi re Cf. 174 (IX. 7). 3 *sana mente scriptas litteras quo modo in tanta insania*; *Fam.* IX. 16. 1 *quo modo in tali re atque tempore.* Similarly 395 (XV. 18). 2 *ut in his*; *Fam.* IV. 9. 3 *ut in tali re.*

4 **Balbi** Cf. 160 (VIII. 9*a*). 2.

tuique Cf. *Fam.* IV. 4. 5 *Servius tuus vel potius noster*, Trebonius, *ibid.* XII. 16. 1 *adulescente tuo atque adeo nostro (nihil enim tibi a me* (so read: cf. *Philol.* 105 (1961), p. 268) *potest esse seiunctum).*

5 **quaeque** Perhaps = *et quaecumque* as often (after preceding *quicumque*, etc.) in the poets: cf. Housman on Man. III. 68 (note and addenda), *Propertiana*, p. 286.

166 (VIII. 16)

1, 2 hoc...mari I.e. *mari infero*, the Tyrrhenian.

3 **illuc** Not necessarily Brundisium. If C. had been thinking seriously of joining Pompey at this time he would rather have made his way to Greece, where for all he knew Pompey already was (cf. §2 fin. and 163 (VIII. 13). 1).

11 **etiam** *Caesari* must be understood in both exclamations and the second is in aggravation of the first, not a new departure such as would have been marked by the paradosis *autem.*

se venditant Cf. 16 (I. 16). 16 *valde te venditavi* et sim. Not 'are selling themselves'.

deum Sc. *faciunt*: cf. Ter. *Ad.* 535 *facio te apud illum deum.* The reading is not certain (see however below on *propitium...iratum*). *ad eum* of Σ may not impossibly represent *ad caelum* (sc. *ferunt*)—the ellipse would not be startling in so common a phrase. *ad eum* (sc. *obviam eunt*, ἀπαντῶσι) by itself is intolerably flat, awkward too as anticipating *quas fieri censes* ἀπαντήσεις *ex oppidis* below. Watt's *ad⟨ulantur⟩ eum* would similarly anticipate *quos honores*.

2, 2 Pisistratus Cf. 144 (VII. 20). 2.

fecit The choice lies between *fecit...est* and *fecerit...erit* and the former is clearly more apt to the context.

3 **propitium...iratum** These terms give some little support to *deum* above, since C. almost always applies the former to deities (*Nat. Deor.* II. 145 is an exception); for the combination cf. *Cael.* 42 *huic homini ego fortasse et pauci deos propitios, plerique autem iratos putabunt*; *Pis.* 59 *neque propitii cuiquam esse solent* (sc. *di*) *neque irati*; Plaut. *Curc.* 557 *quoi homini di sunt propitii, ei non esse iratos puto.*

4 **ἀπαντήσεις** Cf. 21 (II. 1). 5 n. (*non est itum obviam*). Official deputations seem to be in mind here, though of course private individuals would also go to meet Caesar, as Atticus and Peducaeus later did (cf. 188 (VIII. 9). 2).

5 **credo...magis** Cf. 171 (IX. 5). 3 fin.

7 **iudices de CCCLX** Personally chosen by Pompey in 52 for the trial of Milo and others: cf. Mommsen, *St.* III, p. 532, n. 5, *Str.* p. 199, n. 2.

9 **minas** '*minas* in Cratander is obviously a gloss' (How). So indeed it might seem. But is *nescio quas Lucerias* really possible, even though C. had written in a recent letter (161 (VIII. 11). 4) of threats of proscription current among the Pompeians at Luceria? *Fam.* VII. 11. 2 *una mehercule collocutio nostra pluris erit quam omnes Samarobrivae* is sometimes cited in support. But it is not the plural *Lucerias* that makes the difficulty but what it has to signify. Everyone must judge for himself. I find it hard, though not quite impossible, to believe that C. wrote the vulgate. If on the other hand *minas* was the original the corruption can be explained. *minas* in minuscule might look very like *lueras* or *luerias*; for confusion between *n* and *ri* cf. 136 (VII. 13). 1 *picena / puteria* (N); 190 (X. 1). 3 *iri si / nisi* (M), also 231 (XI. 25). 3 *miserrima / miserum ea* (confusion between *n* and *r* is commoner, e.g. 25 (II. 5). 3 *certius / recentius*; 39 (II. 19). 2 *per(a)eque / de re qu(a)e / denique*; 239 (XII. 3). 1 *auctione / auctore*). A copyist who had recently transcribed 161 (VII. 11). 4 might easily do the rest. That seems more likely than Baiter's *Lucerinas minas*, not to speak of Boot's *delicias*.

11 **αἰδέομαι Τρῶας** Cf. 25 (II. 5). 1 n.

17 **cogitabam** Sc. *ire*, as in 176 (IX. 9). 2 *Arpinum...cogito*. Cf. 120 (VI. 7). 2 *Rhodum volo.*

167 (IX. 1)

1, 2 VIIII Cf. 164 (VIII. 14). 1 *Feralibus*.

4 **moverat** Sc. *castra*. So *Bell. Afr.* 7. 1, *Bell. Hisp.* 20. 1 (?), and often in Livy.

7 **κενόσπουδα** Not 'matters of mere curiosity' (L.–S.–J.). What was happening at Brundisium was far from being that. But C.'s anxieties were κενόσπουδα because σπουδή about them was κενή; it is no use to worry without data: cf. 164 (VIII. 14). 2 *dices 'quid igitur proficis qui anticipes eius rei molestiam quam triduo sciturus sis?'* ἀκενόσπουδος in *Fam.* XV. 17. 4 ('shunning vain pursuits' L.–S.–J.) is similar; Cassius is told that he will be wise not to concern himself to no purpose, i.e. not to worry about politics under Caesar. Contrast 327 (XIII. 21*a*). 1 περὶ μικρὰ σπουδάζειν.

quae tamen...necesse est *tamen* implies, not 'whether these events are important or not', but 'whether I worry or not'.

2, 6 **Sosium** Cf. 154 (VIII. 6). 1 n.

Lupum Cf. 162A (VIII. 12A). 4 n.

7 **ius dicere** Cf. 179 (IX. 12). 3 *praetores ius dicunt.* As regards Lupus the report was probably false (cf. 162A (VIII. 12A). 4 n.).

8 **diem conterere** Cf. 160 (VIII. 9*a*). 1 *Lepido...nam fere* συνδιημερεύομεν.

3, 3 **ἀναπάντητον** Properly perhaps, as T.–P. point out, 'free of ἀπάντησις', parties of welcome from the towns on the way, rather than merely 'where one would meet nobody'.

6 **mihi** The ethic dative is tantamount to an exclamation mark: cf. *Catil.* II. 10 *qui mihi accubantes in conviviis...eructant sermonibus suis caedem bonorum.*

7 **tempestivis** Cf. 180 (IX. 13). 6 *quas enim eos cenas et facere et obire scripsit ad me Sextus, quam lautas, quam tempestivas!*; *Fam.* IX. 16. 8; *Mur.* 13.

4, 1 **nam** 'Occupatory', as much as to say 'it is no use telling me that I shall be following the example of others'.

2 **genero** Pompey had married Scipio's daughter Cornelia three years previously.

3 **iratum** For Scipio's anti-Caesarian role before the outbreak of war cf. Caes. *B.C.* I. 1–6; Plut. *Caes.* 30.

4 **eodem timore** Understand *est* (cf. 107 (V. 14). 4 *magno timore sum*), or, perhaps better, *proficiscitur* (causal ablative).

inimicitiarum As with Curio, Caelius Rufus, and Dolabella. The genitive depends on *timore.*

5 **et tamen** The sense seems to be 'I speak of fear of Caesar, but as a matter of fact everyone except Appius and C. Cassius has an official reason for leaving Italy'.

reliqui Sc. *nostri ordinis*: cf. 165 (VIII. 15). 3 n. (*memento*).

6 **pro quaestore** I.e. *proquaestor pro praetore* (cf. Broughton, p. 261). A proposal to send Faustus to Mauretania in January had been vetoed by a Caesarian Tribune (Caes. *B.C.* I. 6. 4).

liceret 'Would be open (if I liked to consider the other alternative)': cf. 177 (IX. 10). 7 n. (*dubitares*).

7 **huius fortunae** Cf. 186 (IX. 17). 2 *in hac...fortuna.*

10 **non sermo bonorum** Contrast 166 (VIII. 16). 1 *non me igitur is ducit sed sermo hominum qui ad me ⟨a⟩ Philotimo scribitur.* C. knew that his obligation to Pompey was not in reality a very powerful argument, at least not in Atticus' eyes, and therefore puts it forward most emphatically when he is most averse to the course indicated (cf. Introd. p. 42).

12 **ne id quidem roganti** I.e. *id ne roganti quidem.*

nec suam...publicam If Pompey was not fighting for himself, all the less reason to join him on personal grounds.

168 (IX. 2)

1 **die tuo** 'The day of your attack.' Atticus' fever being a quartan, this establishes a sequence of attacks on 4, 7, 10, 13 March—a point of relevance to the dating of the letters.

3 **IIII Non.** Cf. 177 (IX. 10). 8.

διάλειψιν *remissionem*, more probable than λῆψιν (*accessionem*) both diplomatically—(ν)δια would be more easily dropped in 177 (IX. 10). 8 than intruded here—and because Atticus would naturally write after the abatement rather than after the attack. Both would occur on one day: cf. Cels. III. 15. 4 *post febrem oportebit ungui et vehementer perfricari, cibum et validum et fortiter adsumere, vino uti quantum libebit; postero die...tertio die* sqq.

169 (IX. 2a)

The 'longer letter' (168 (IX. 2) init.) which C. was expecting was sent on 5 March (177 (IX. 10). 9), and will have arrived on the 7th after the dispatch of 168 (IX. 2).

1, 1 **quam nihil praetermittis** Cf. *Fin.* I. 57 *videtisne quam nihil praetermittatur quod vitam adiuvet...?*

3 **gaudes: ac proponis** The two statements contrast with one another and should be punctuated accordingly.

4 **detrahatur** Cf. 172 (IX. 6). 6 *molior...ut mihi Caesar concedat ut absim cum aliquid in senatu contra Gnaeum agatur.*

5 **'di' inquis 'averruncent!'** Hardly a quotation from Atticus' letter, since *contra igitur?* is an objection raised by C. *inquis* is normally used with

imaginary sayings (cf. 174 (IX. 7). 5 n.; 177 (IX. 10). 7 n.), and so probably here; though *et de triumpho erit integrum* below could well be an actual quotation.

8 **otioso** In effect 'neutral': cf. *Marc.* 18 *quidam* (sc. *Pompeiani*) *enim non modo armatis sed interdum etiam otiosis minabantur.*

9 **triumpho** Cf. 153 (VIII. 3). 6.

11 **olim** In 59: cf. 39 (II. 19). 4.

15 **honos** C.'s MSS nearly always attest this form: cf. *Thes.* VI. 2916. 30.

2, 1 **offensa** This un-Ciceronian alternative to *offensio* is probably quoted from Atticus. Caelius has it in 200A (X. 9A = *Fam.* VIII. 16). 2.

4 **queretur** Cf. 199 (X. 8). 5 *non simul cum Pompeio mare transiimus. omnino* ⟨*non*⟩ *potuimus; exstat ratio dierum. sed tamen* (*fateamur enim quod est*) *ne contendimus quidem ut possemus.*

7 **putat** *scit* again might seem more natural, but perhaps *putat* lends a touch of modesty. These warnings of C.'s will have been given before the war broke out.

8 **pecunia** In the Treasury: cf. 135 (VII. 12). 2 n. (*aerarium*).

11 **τίς δ' ἐστὶ κ.τ.λ.** From Euripides, play unknown (Nauck, 958).

13 **ut scribis** In the passage quoted in 177 (IX. 10). 9: *postea, si opus fuerit, non erit difficile, et illi, quoquo tempore fuerit, erit* ἀσμενιστόν.

nam quod ais *nam* is 'occupatory'. For Atticus' own words see again 177 (IX. 10).

14 **temperatius** *temperantius*, a non-Ciceronian form, cannot be defended like *offensa* above since we happen to know from 177 (IX. 10). 9 that Atticus wrote *temperate.*

17 **constantia** Even if Caesar's force (*vires*) proved superior, persistent resistance or refusal to co-operate on the part of the *boni* would drive him to harsh measures. Perhaps, however, C. is here thinking only of the fighting republicans, as in 172 (IX. 6). 4 *cum bonis esse*, who might maintain the struggle even after defeat (as they actually did).

3, 2 **Postumus Curtius** Curtius Postumus, a former client of C.'s (cf. 172 (IX. 6). 2 n.), is generally identified with the M. Curtius whom he recommended to Caesar for a Military Tribunate in 54 (*Q. Fr.* II. 14. 3, III. 1. 10; cf. *Philol.* 105 (1961), pp. 81 f.). He often appears in the Correspondence as a zealous adherent of Caesar, who apparently raised him to the Praetorship (cf. 292 (XII. 49). 2). Dessau, however, identified him with Caesar's protégé C. Rabirius Postumus (son of C. Curtius, adopted by his uncle Rabirius), defended by C. in 54/53: cf. *Hermes*, 46 (1911), pp. 613 ff., 47 (1912), p. 320. If that is correct the man recommended by C. in 54 must be a different person, for Rabirius would have needed no recommendation to his old friend Caesar (cf. *Rab. Post.* 43 *veterem amicum suum*). We have no other evidence as to Postumus' praenomen, the reading *Curtius* in 363 (XIV. 9). 2 being quite hypothetical.

3 **eripiebat sqq.** Postumus did these things 'with his mouth', as representing Caesar: cf. Liv. XXXV. 49. 5 *rex contra peditum equitumque nubes iactat et consternit maria classibus suis* (i.e. *se constraturum ostendit*); Sen. *Lud.* 3. 2 *patere mathematicos aliquando verum dicere, qui illum ex quo princeps factus est. . .omnibus mensibus efferunt.* This figure is naturally commoner in poetry (cf. *Cl. Quart.* 43 (1949), p. 28, adding Sil. x. 335).

tenebat Asiam sqq. Not without grounds. L. Antonius, in charge of Asia as *proquaestor pro praetore* (Broughton, p. 260) was a Caesarian sympathizer. So probably was T. Furfanius Postumus in Sicily (cf. 139 (VII. 15). 2 n.), though Cato may already have taken over there. Africa was temporarily under the Legate Q. Ligarius (see Appendix VI, p. 467); ultimately he joined Pompey, but was probably expected to support Caesar, as his brothers appear to have done (*Lig.* 5, 34 ff.). M. Aurelius Cotta, who held Sardinia in late March (Caes. *B.C.* I. 30. 2), was a firm republican (cf. 208 (X. 16). 3), but sentiment in the province was for Caesar (*B.C.* I. 30. 3).

170 (IX. 3)

1, 1 **Domiti filius** Cn. Domitius L. f. Ahenobarbus, destined to become a partisan of Antony and Consul in 32. His mother was Cato's sister, Porcia.

3 **Dionysius** Probably C.'s reader (*anagnostes*) and librarian, who stole his books and ran away in 46 to avoid the consequences (*Fam.* XIII. 77. 3, v. 9. 2, etc.).

8 **armis praesidiisque** Cf. 161D (VIII. 11D). 4 n. But 'armed detachments' may be all that is meant here.

10 **nihil potest. . .tramitti** Nothing is gained by taking *potest* impersonally and *nihil* as = *nullo modo* (cf. 128 (VII. 5). 3 *ego in Tusculanum nihil sane hoc tempore*).

2, 4 **transisse** Sc. *Gnaeum*, though *eum* in the next sentence refers to Caesar: cf. 21 (II. 1). 5 n.

171 (IX. 5)

1, 1 **die tuo** In view of Nepos' statements (*Att.* 21. 1, 22. 3) that Atticus died on 31 March three months after his 77th birthday *natali* must be an erroneous gloss. His letter, a reply to 167 (IX. 1) of the 6th, will have been written on the 7th, ὑπὸ τὴν διάλειψιν no doubt (cf. 168 (IX. 2). 1 n.), given to Philotimus on the 8th, and delivered at Formiae late on the 9th.

6 **gratulationi** A simple dative of purpose would be difficult to justify. Rather take with *obtulisse*, *gratulationi* (*Caesaris*) loosely amounting to *Caesari gratulationis causa.*

7 **iam, inquam** *iam, iam inquam*, may well be right, since *inquam* is normally used in reiteration (cf. *Thes.* VII. 1784); but does it not here point back to earlier gloomy forecasts, as 169 (IX. 2*a*). 2 fin.?

10 **Q. Fufius** Cf. 14 (I. 14). 1 n.

11 **levitatem** He probably contrasted the vote on 1 December, in favour of Curio's motion for the resignation of both Caesar and Pompey from their commands, with later proceedings.

12 **†cur tum** Despite 172 (IX. 6). 2 *quovis potius certe quam ut Curtium videat* I do not think *Curtium* satisfactory here; the sentence runs much better without it. And why Curtius rather than Fufius? Perhaps *curtū* was only a dittography of *curia.*

2, 2 **'dic, M. Tulli'** Cf. 126 (VII. 3). 5.

6 **me. . .movent** Without *me* this must be taken as a general statement, which is just, but only just, possible in view of the following example of the Allia battle.

10 **diem. . .Alliensis pugnae** 18 July.

11 **religiosus** Otherwise *nefastus* or *ater.*

3, 3 **sermonesque** Presumably before the outbreak of hostilities.

6 **αὐτίκα κ.τ.λ.** *Il.* XVIII. 96.

11 **officia** The duties (i.e. their performance) owing to Pompey under the four aspects mentioned; not, as commonly supposed, 'sc. *a Pompeio in me collata*'. Pompey's past 'offices' could not now be bought. Lehmann compares *Verr.* II. 5. 23 *haec vero, quae vel vita redimi* ('bought off') *recte possunt, aestimare pecunia non queo.*

14 **illa. . .decreta** During Pompey's late illness or after his recovery. *optimatibus* above = *bonis*, including *municipales.*

15 **'timent' inquies** Cf. 166 (VIII. 16). 2 *'metuunt' inquies.*

172 (IX. 6)

1, 3 **conventum** Cf. 160 (VIII. 9*a*). 2.

4 **Albae** Cf. Caes. *B.C.* I. 24. 3 and 161B (VIII. 11B). 1 n. (*L. Torquatum*). Caesar's lieutenant Vibius Curius may possibly be the Proconsul to whom in 45 or thereabouts C. wrote a letter of recommendation (*Fam.* XIII. 49).

6 **ad urbem** Holding *imperium* Caesar could not legally pass the city boundary, though he seems in fact to have done so: cf. 194 (X. 3*a*) n. (*Regia*); 195 (X. 4). 8 n. (*Metellum*).

2, 1 **ut aiunt** Cf. 208 (X. 16). 3 *utinam, quod aiunt, Cotta Sardiniam teneat.*

2 **non improbo** *non probo* would prompt the question, why should C.

disapprove of Domitius going to Spain? There is no obvious answer. He would hardly blame Domitius for preferring *not* to join Pompey after the 'desertion' at Corfinium, though he would admire his magnanimity if he did; and he goes on to say that *anything* would be better than remaining in Italy. The MSS often drop *in-*, *im-* (*ī*).

4 **patronus** This could hardly refer to the Military Tribunate, even if it is the same man (cf. 169 (ix. 2*a*). 3 n.). C. does not use *patronus*, where individuals are concerned, in the general sense of 'patron' (cf. 16 (i. 16). 10 n.). He must have defended Curtius in the courts, even if Curtius and Rabirius Postumus were not one and the same.

7 **interclusi captique** Cf. 226 (xi. 15). 2 *alii capti, alii interclusi.*

3, 1 **litterae** The letter cannot be Clodia's. She would not have written *dicitur* and *dicunt*, and she would have known that only part of the Pompeian force crossed on the 4th. Pompey himself followed with the remainder on the 17th. Presumably C.'s unnamed correspondent in Capua had been given a garbled version of Clodia's letter. The last sentence, *de hac re. . .transiit*, used to be taken for a comment of C.'s own and printed at the beginning of the next paragraph.

4 **milia triginta** According to C.'s later information the true figure was 15,000 (cf. 176 (ix. 9). 2 n.). Plutarch (*Pomp.* 62) says that the Consuls took 30 cohorts, which squares with Caesar's statements that 20 cohorts, out of a total of five legions (*B.C.* iii. 4. 1), remained in Brundisium (*ibid.* i. 25. 2). Clodia had presumably referred to the entire Pompeian force, but even so her figure was an exaggeration, based no doubt on a theoretical allowance of 6,000 men to a legion. But Pompey's legions were in fact much below strength (*ibid.* iii. 4. 2).

5 **et tribuni pl.** It seems more than possible that *et pr.* fell out before *et tr.*, as also perhaps in 360 (xiv. 6). 2 *consules et tribunos pl.* Cf. 411 (xvi. 4). 1 *tantum addi placuit, quod erat 'coss.' solum, ut esset 'pr., tr. pl., senatui'*; Q. *Fr.* iii. 4. 6 *et Appium consulem secum habebit et praetores et tribunos pl.*; *Fam.* xvii. 11. 2 *senatus consulibus, praetoribus, tribunis pl. et nobis qui pro consulibus sumus, negotium dederat* (sim. Caes. *B.C.* i. 5. 3); Varro, *L.L.* vi. 91 *consules praetores tribunosque plebis collegasque tuos.* Of the Praetors of 49 C. Coponius, M. Favonius, and P. Rutilius Lupus (not to include L .Torquatus) were active Pompeians, and the first two at any rate were probably with Pompey at Brundisium. Manutius' *consules et duo tribuni pl.* is not a necessary change, since *qui fuerunt cum eo omnes* applies to the Tribunes as well as the Senators. The translation 'all with wives and children' leaves bachelors unaccounted for.

7 **praecidisse** 'Cut off the forepart' ('rostra defregisse' Ernesti): cf. *Div.* i. 32 *cotem novacula posse praecidi.* T.–P. suggest *percidisse*, 'smashed', but

we should rather expect *concidisse* (cf. Liv. XXXVIII. 39. 2 *naves. . .concideret cremaretque*). The report was false (176 (IX. 9). 2).

8 **L. Metello** Son of L. Caecilius Metellus, Verres' successor in Sicily and Consul in 68. Concerning his defiance of Caesar in the matter of the Treasury cf. 195 (X. 4). 8 n. We do not know which of Ap. Pulcher's three sisters was his mother-in-law.

4, 1 **ante** Previously C. had been worried about the difficulty of his position (cf. 169 (IX. 2*a*). 1 init.); *now* he is overwhelmed by the thought of its dishonour.

5 **οὐδέ μοι κ.τ.λ.** *Il.* X. 93.

11 **filia** Cf. 199 (X. 8). 9 of 2 May *tamen nos recte facere et bene audire vult.* Yet Tullia at that time was begging for delay (§1). C. later blamed his family for his final decision to leave: 220 (XI. 9). 2 *cessi meis vel potius parui.* His son seems to have been consistently in favour of that course: cf. 200 (X. 9). 2 fin.; 202 (X. 11). 3 fin.

5, 2 **ne me proiciam** Cf. 177 (IX. 10). 8 *si una proieceris te.*

6 **mi Tite** Cf. 36 (II. 16). 3 *o noster Tite*—the only other place in the correspondence where Atticus is addressed by his praenomen.

6, 4 **Furnius** Cf. 95 (V. 2). 1 n.

ut quidem scias quos sequamur Commentators from Manutius onward have misunderstood this in various ways. Q. Titinius, a wealthy Senator of long standing and a friend of Atticus and C. (cf. 114 (V. 21). 5 n.), is one of the optimates of 171 (IX. 5). 3—rich, respectable quasi-neutrals, who professed republican sympathies while in reality playing Caesar's game; such, among the Consulars, were Vulcatius, M'. Lepidus, and, for the time being, Sulpicius (who also sent his son to serve with Caesar: cf. 187 (IX. 18). 2 *quid quod Servi filius, quod Titini in iis castris fuerunt quibus Pompeius circumsederetur?*). These were the people whom Atticus had held up as models (cf. 126 (VII. 3). 3, 177 (IX. 10). 7). Now Titinius had shown where he and his kind really stood (see also on 176 (IX. 9). 1).

filium Called Pontius Titinianus in 189 (IX. 19). 2, adopted therefore by a Pontius. He may possibly be the Pontius mentioned in *Phil.* XIII. 3 as a boon-companion of Antony's.

5 **sed** Resumptive. The mention of Titinius was incidental.

maiores. . .quam vellem To C. in his present mood Caesar's gratitude for his passivity is part and parcel τοῦ αἰσχροῦ: cf. 147 (VII. 23). 3.

8 **fuissemus. . .defuisset** The two verbs *can* be taken together as protasis and apodosis: cf. *Har. Resp.* 7 *diem dixisset ut iecerat, fecissem ut ei statim tertius a praetore dies diceretur.*

9 **σύν τε δύ' ἐρχομένω** καί τε πρὸ ὃ τοῦ ἐνόησεν | ὅππως κέρδος ἔῃ (*Il.* X. 224).

7, 1 **acta ne agamus** He continues to do just that: cf. 389 (XV. 11). 2.

3 **populari via** 20 (I. 20). 3 *me hanc viam optimatem. . .tenere* and *Catil.* IV. 9 *hanc. . .in re publica viam quae popularis habetur* are compared. For the sense cf. 150 (VII. 26). 2; 161D (VIII. 11D). 7; 199 (X. 8). 5.

7 **videtur. . .his** Schütz might well take these words for a gloss. As they stand in the MSS *his* must be the Pompeians, and we have a feeble repetition of the preceding sentiment. But *his*, as generally, means the Caesarians (cf. e.g. 178 (IX. 11). 4 *sed certe et haec perdita sunt et illa non salutaria*), and *sed* or *sed nunc* must be supplied.

172A (IX. 6A)

If Furnius arrived at Formiae on 11 March (cf. 172 (IX. 6). 6) he will have left Caesar about the 5th, half way between Arpi (cf. 170 (IX. 3). 2) and Brundisium (cf. 181A (IX. 13A). 1).

CAESAR IMP. Caesar's style of address is less formal than Pompey's, and he does not use the title of Proconsul, which C. might have been reluctant to reciprocate.

1 **neque loqui** Cf. 162A (VIII. 12A). 1 n.

8 **consilio** Cf. 178A (IX. 11A). 1.

9 **ad propositum revertar** Cf. 355 (XIV. 1). 2 *sed ad propositum*. C. in his letters usually has *ad prima redeo* (*ad primum revertor* 226 (XI. 15). 3). Caesar means that his main object in writing is to apologize for not writing at greater length, as he does by implication in the opening words of his note.

173 (IX. 4)

Since this letter was to have been sent the day before Atticus' quartan attack (§3) and was in fact sent before the 17th (176 (IX. 9). 1 θέσεις *meas commentari non desino*), it can be assigned to the 12th (cf. 168 (IX. 2). 1 n.), the only day without a letter between the 6th and 14th (inclusive). It can further be identified with the letter mentioned in 174 (IX. 7). 1, which was to have been dispatched on the 12th but did not go that day because the intended bearer did not leave. The 15th is unlikely, since *is qui hanc epistulam tulit* in §3 can hardly refer to Philotimus, who left on that day with 175 (IX. 8): cf. 176 (IX. 9). 3.

1, 4 **excluduntur** *excludentur* ('you will find that. . .') could be related to *tibi idem accidere certo scio*, but the present is far more natural. *-entur* may be an echo from *solent*.

7 **θέσεις** Cf. Quint. *Inst.* II. 4. 24 *sunt et illae* (sc. *theses*) *paene totae ad deliberativum pertinentes genus, ducendane uxor, petendine sint magistratus.*

2, 3 **εἰ. . .αἵρηται** τὸν καταλύοντα means, in effect, Pompey. The optimates should be alive to the risk that in pulling Caesar down they might be setting Pompey up (cf. 161 (VIII. 11). 2 *uterque regnare vult*; 174 (IX. 7). 3 *mirandum enim in modum Gnaeus noster Sullani regni similitudinem concupivit*; 198 (X. 7). 1 *regnandi contentio est*). This is so remote from the previous proposition as to justify the replacement of ἦ with εἰ, whereas ἦ διὰ παντὸς κ.τ.λ. and ἦ ἐφετέον κ.τ.λ. below are merely alternatives, not separate problems. There seems little to choose between αἵρηται and ἀρθῇ.

3, 4 **recte ambulavit** A man setting out from Formiae on the morning of the 12th and making good progress would reach Rome by the evening of the 13th.

174 (IX. 7)

1, 1 **epistulam** 173 (IX. 4).

3 **celeripes** Probably an ironic nickname: cf. *tardipes, segnipes, planipes, loripes, gracilipes. Callippides* (cf. 320 (XIII. 12). 3) is a needless piece of ingenuity. 'Fleet-foot' brought two letters (§2), a short one of 9 March (cf. 177 (IX. 10). 10) and a longer one, probably of the 10th.

Salvius Like Statius, an old praenomen in use as a slave name and then as a *nomen gentile*. Two persons so called are mentioned by C., a literary slave of Atticus' (336 (XIII. 44). 3; 412 (XVI. 2). 6) and an influential freedman of Caesar's (cf. 210 (X. 18). 1 n.). The former is doubtless meant here (correct Münzer, *R.E.* IA. 2022. 41).

4 **restillarunt** ἅπ. λεγ. in Classical Latin, but supported as against *instillarunt* or *stillarunt* by Z.

5 **τὸ συνέχον** 'The main point' (see L.–S.–J. s.v.) was to ease C.'s fears for his reputation. Nothing else counted, since there was nothing left now to hope for.

8 **uno** *hoc uno* would mean 'in the life-time of Caesar singly'. But that would imply that there *was* hope, since Pompey might win and Caesar be eliminated. On C.'s fears of a Pompeian despotism cf. 173 (IX. 4). 2 n.

2, 4 **Sexto** The younger Peducaeus: cf. 136 (VII. 13). 3 n.

5 **a quo** Peducaeus of course is meant, despite the intervening *tu*. Lehmann's supplement *fecisti* ⟨*quod me de eius iudicio certiorem fecisti*⟩ is neither elegant nor necessary.

3, 2 **idem** I.e. *ne arma capiam contra.*

5 **quo modo** = *ut.*

6 **πολίτευμα** *actionem* (cf. 174A (IX. 7A). 2 n.) the active pursuit of a political aim.

7 **periculum** Advocacy of peace from an independent standpoint might irritate the Caesarians.

9 **μή μοι κ.τ.λ.** *Od.* XI. 634. A compromise peace would thwart Pompey's ambitions.

11 **Sullani regni** Cf. 161 (VIII. 11). 2 n.

12 **nihil. . .tulit** Dissimulation being Pompey's habit.

14 **ut in Milone, ut in—** Milo, like Pompey, had helped to bring about C.'s restoration in 57. Whom else did C. have in mind? Not, I think, Sestius (the proposal to add *Sestio* (*Sextio*) before *sed* in the text goes back to Schütz); C. certainly defended him out of gratitude and despite some personal ill-feeling (cf. Q. *Fr.* II. 3. 5, 4. 1), but would scarcely have thought his a bad case. Possibly Lentulus Spinther, in the matter of Ptolemy Auletes' restoration.

sed hactenus Cf. 106 (V. 13). 1 n.

4, 1 **optima** Similarly in 46 *quid quaeris? nihil boni praeter causam* (*Fam.* VII. 3. 2).

3 **vastare, urere** Cf. *Phil.* XII. 9 *exhauritur, vastatur, uritur* (sc. *Gallia*); Liv. XXVI. 21. 15 *sociorum populi Romani agros urebant.*

4 **sed. . .perpeti** C.'s meaning would have been more obvious if he had written *omnino eadem metuo ab hac parte, sed si* sqq.

6 **ἀχαριστίας** Here Greek comes to aid in a genuine case of *patrii sermonis egestas.*

5, 2 **dum agamus** 'de triumpho' (Corradus): cf. 337 (XV. 1). 2 *ei legi et egi*. F. R. D. Goodyear (*Gnomon*, 34 (1962), pp. 779 f.) may, however, be right in suggesting that something has fallen out (it could be *rem* or *id*). There is nothing to be said for *dum vagamur* (Bosius).

ὁ πλόος ὡραῖος I.e. spring weather, it being now late January by the season. The phrase doubtless comes from Leonidas of Tarentum's poem (*Anth. Pal.* X. 1), which it begins (cf. 187 (IX. 18). 3 n.), though *he* may have taken it from Hes. *Op.* ὡραῖον μίμνειν πλόον.

3 **si modo. . .firmus** This looks like a quotation from Atticus' letter, though the wording *may* be C.'s own: cf. 169 (IX. 2*a*). 1. n. *firmus* = 'strong' (cf. 162A (VIII. 12A). 1 (Pompey) *satis firmus. . .ad castra facienda*; Plancus, *Fam.* X. 15. 2 *Antonius ab equitatu firmus esse dicebatur*); not 'resolute'.

5 **si valebit** Cf. 117 (VI. 3). 4 *valeat modo*; 152 (VIII. 2). 3.

tegulam Lit. 'roof-tile'.

7 **contra. . .auctoritatem** Better taken with *tene socio* than, as usually punctuated, with *cupio discedere*: cf. 177 (IX. 10). 3 *male Tarquinius. . .impie Coriolanus. . .recte Themistocles qui mori maluit* sqq.

6, 1 scirique sqq. The paradosis can be defended so far as the omission of *nos* is concerned; but why should C. be pleased to know that the *boni* had heard of his failure to join Pompey, which anyway could be no secret? What he wanted to hear from Atticus was that they did not condemn him for it. The exact wording is naturally uncertain; e.g. ⟨*nos ratione*⟩ *non profectos* (cf. 285 (XII. 44). 3 *ratione fecisti*) would do as well.

4 **homini...optimati** Ironical. C. believed Philotimus a swindler and ridiculed his pretensions to high aristocratic principles: cf. 200 (X. 9). 1 and 285 (XII. 44). 3. He might say in public *sunt etiam libertini optimates* (*Sest.* 97), but the actuality was too much for him.

7, 1 ut...desit *ut* is not 'supposing that', but explanatory as in *Fam.* IV. 13. 7 *extremum illud est ut te orem et obsecrem* (sim. XV. 4. 16). So with *reliquum est, proximum est, tertium est* (K.–S. II, p. 241). The force of 'finally' extends to the whole passage down to *quantum potest*. Then comes an afterthought.

5 **quantum potest** Cf. 87 (IV. 13). 1 *velim res istas...scribas ad me quantum pote*; Sjögren, *Comm. Tull.* pp. 165 f.

7 **in Epirum** Atticus had not taken the hint in 167 (IX. 1). 4 fin. He now responded well (cf. 179 (IX. 12). 1).

8 **ambulandum, ungendum** Atticus had probably ended his letter thus. Cf. *Cels.* III. 14. 1 *si vero tertiana...aut quartana est, mediis diebus et ambulationibus uti oportet aliisque exercitationibus et unctionibus.*

174A (IX. 7A)

This and the following are likely to have been dispatched on the same day. Both probably arrived on the 12th since they are not mentioned in 173 (IX. 4), and will therefore have left Rome on the 11th or possibly the 10th.

1, 1 nedum...sed etiam Cf. *Fam.* VII. 28. 1 *erat enim multo domicilium huius urbis...aptius humanitati et suavitati tuae quam tota Peloponnesus, nedum Patrae*; K.–S. II, p. 68. The inversion is unique in the classical period, but J. Campernass (*Glotta*, 6 (1914), pp. 164 f.) quotes several examples of *nedum ...sed etiam* et sim. from the *Acta Sanctorum.*

ut nos sumus C. might have written *quales*, but cf. *Fam.* XIII. 64. 2 *magnum theatrum habet ista provincia, non ut haec nostra.*

10 **non desineremus** Cf. 165A (VIII. 15A). 1.

2, 2 sit...opinari *sit* = ἐξῇ, an un-Ciceronian use tolerable in Balbus–Oppius: cf. K.–S. I, p. 669.

8 **in hac re** *in* (or *de*) is needed, not because *hac re* = 'things being as they are' lacks a parallel (174B (IX. 7B). 2 *hac re mihi placet* is not one; but cf. 372 (XIV. 19). 5 *tali re talique tempore*), but for sense.

si erit. . .rescriptum *si* = *simul atque*: cf. 30 (II. 12). 3 n.

11 **actioni** *rationi* is tempting, but cf. 183 (IX. 15). 2 *prima eius actionis horreo. actio* here appears to have a wider sense ('general political action, programme') than that of a particular political activity, such as we find in 176 (IX. 9). 2 *actio de pace*; *Dom.* 23 *improbitatem et legis et actionis tuae*, 40 *tua. . . omnis actio posterioribus mensibus fuit*; Liv. IV. 55. 5 *ea. . .res vires tribuniciae actioni adiecit.*

174B (IX. 7B)

1, 1 **s.v.b.** *si vales benest*: cf. 161C (VIII. 11C). n.

3 **ex quibus** A slip. Balbus mixes up *epistulam* with *litteras*; perhaps he had written *litteras* originally and then altered it to avoid an inelegant repetition—unless, of course, a copyist is to blame.

suam et Pompei So in the previous letter, *de reconciliatione gratiae suae et Pompei* (§1).

6 **pietate** Of obligation to a benefactor; so below.

2, 1 **hoc idem probaturum** An awkward conflation of *hoc probaturum* and *hoc idem sensurum.*

2 **humanitate** So in the previous letter (§2) *pro sua humanitate. . .pro sua indulgentia in suos.*

3 **cum. . .suscipias** I.e. *dummodo suscipias, suscipientem*: cf. *Fam.* XV. 17. 4 *cum sciam* (= *sciens*); *Mil.* 49 *sic Miloni, cum insidiator esset,. . .subsidendum atque exspectandum fuit*; *de Orat.* I. 167 *quod cum impetrasset causa caderet*; Tib. II. 3. 5 *o ego, cum aspicerem dominam, quam fortiter illic / versarem valido pingue bidente solum!*

7 **Lentulum** Cf. 165A (VIII. 15A). 2.

14 **qua optare** Cf. K.-S. II, p. 288.

15 **hac re** = *hanc ob rem.* Caelius, *Fam.* VIII. 11. 2 *quibus hac re ad intercessionem evocandam interpellantibus* and Val. Max. III. 6. 1 *nec hac re segniores Punicis exercitibus manus intulit* can be added to *Thes.* VI. 2746. 36 ff. Cf. *ea re* (as in 158 (VIII. 8). 1 *o rem turpem et ea re miseram!*), *qua re. hac re* also = *hoc modo* (cf. Ter. *Eun.* 172, 723; Val. Max. II. 7. 8, III. 1. 2, III. 3. Ext. 1). C. does not use the expression.

16 **praesidium petere** If C. took up a mediating role he might need to appear in public and to move about in Italy and in Caesar's camp. That Balbus' suggestion of a body-guard may have been made with ulterior motives is obvious enough. During Milo's trial, according to Asconius (40. 7), M. Marcellus and Milo himself asked the president of the court for protection against the mob and Pompey came into court with a body-guard in consequence. But from Balbus' words it would seem that he gave C. a special guard: cf. *Fam.* III. 10. 10 *me. . .armis denique texit suis.*

17 **praestabo** Cf. 102 (V. 9). 1 n.

3, 1 quam prudenter Cf. 174A (IX. 7A). 1.

3 **ita...moriar** Cf. Sen. *Dial.* v. 30. 5 *haec res sua in reges arma convertit fidissimosque eo compulit ut de morte eorum cogitarent pro quibus et ante quos mori votum habuerant.* Popma cites Sen. *Contr.* lib. 4 *ita mihi superstite filio mori liceat*, but I have not found the passage.

174C (IX. 7C)

This letter may be supposed to have reached Rome on the 11th and left Caesar about six days previously, somewhere on his march south.

1, 5 si possimus The subjunctive seems obligatory: cf. Caes. *B.C.* I. 83. 4 *illi vadum fluminis Sicoris temptare* (sc. *parant*) *si transire possent*; Liv. I. 57. 3, II. 35. 4, XXIII. 18. 1; Hor. *Ep.* II. 1. 164; K.–S. II, p. 425. To salve the indicative by taking *si possumus* separately, as in *Orat.* 19 *investigemus hunc igitur, Brute, si possumus*, mars the sense. Caesar could not doubt his ability to try out the policy, only its success.

7 **reliqui** Notably the Marian leaders and Sulla. In *Phil.* VIII. 7 C. reckons the war between Caesar and Pompey as the fourth civil war, but Caesar may also be thinking of certain foreign examples such as the Thirty in Athens.

2, 1 N. Magium Cf. 181 (IX. 13*a*) n. He was captured by Caesar after the fall of Corfinium and sent to Pompey with a request for a conference (*B.C.* I. 24. 4 f.).

2 **missum feci** A military expression, as T.–P. point out.

duo praefecti fabrum Cf. Caes. *B.C.* I. 24. 4 *N. Magius Cremona, praefectus fabrum Cn. Pompei.* The other was Vibullius Rufus, called simply *praefectus* in *B.C.* III. 10. 1 (like Magius above), who had been taken at Corfinium. The v.l. *partium* is certainly wrong. Caesar would not so have described Pompey's subordinate officers.

175 (IX. 8)

The last sentence fixes the date: cf. 168 (IX. 2). 1 n.

1, 1 III Id. See Appendix v.

3 **alter...paucos** Castiglioni's supplement *alter multos, ⟨alter paucos ante dies⟩* left nothing to be desired except a homoeoteleuton.

4 **corona** Cf. Caelius Sabinus *ap.* Gell. VI. 4. 3 *antiquitus mancipia iure belli capta coronis induta veniebant et idcirco dicebantur sub corona venire.* There could surely be no question of selling Pompey's captured soldiers *sub corona*, nor would that have been particularly suggestive of the proscriptions. But captured slaves might have been so sold; or possibly the phrase could cover

the sale of other booty. In any case the (unique) use here of the noun in the sense of 'auction' seems to support Gellius' alternative explanation that *corona* was the guard surrounding the captives.

5 **agro Sabino** Stronghold of antique virtues.

6 **nos quoque** Perhaps a genuine plural, including Quintus, etc.

2, 1 **coniectura** A guess guided by data: cf. 170 (IX. 3). 2 *coniectura tempestatum et dierum.*

4 **Μέντορ, κ.τ.λ.** *Od.* III. 22.

176 (IX. 9)

1, 2 **respondebo** Atticus' first letter, dispatched on 12 March, was in reply to 171 (IX. 5) of the 10th.

3 **adsentior** Cf. 126 (VII. 3). 3 n.

4 **de supero mari** Atticus' advice was to wait for the spring weather (cf. 174 (IX. 7). 5), from which we may infer that he also advised sailing from the western side of Italy. That is what C. finally did.

temptaboque Much the best correction of *plaboque*. *tē* having fallen out, there would be little difference—*l* is commonly confused with *t*.

ut. . .scripsi Cf. 169 (IX. 2*a*). 1; 172 (IX. 6). 6.

6 **oblivisci me scripsi** Cf. 171 (IX. 5). 3 init.

10 **colligamusque nos** Cf. *Tusc.* IV. 78 *quid est autem se ipsum colligere nisi dissipatos animi partis rursus in suum locum cogere?*

11 **σοφιστεύω enim** Arguing like a sophist on both sides. The function of *enim* is not very clear. Possibly something like *quod facio etiam nunc* has dropped out after *nos*.

rus C.'s villa at Formiae was no doubt thronged with visitors as ten years previously (cf. 34 (II. 14). 2). These excursions into the countryside will have given opportunities for quiet reflexion.

12 **θέσεις** Cf. 173 (IX. 4). 1.

13 **de optimatibus** Cf. 171 (IX. 5). 3 *optimatibus vero tuis nihil confido.* Clearly Atticus had made excuses for these people, especially that they were afraid (*ibid. 'timent' inquies.*), and maintained that their hearts were in the right place. C. waives argument, but reminds him of the proverb 'Dionysius at Corinth', for which cf. *Tusc.* III. 27 *Dionysius quidem tyrannus Syracusis expulsus Corinthi pueros docebat*; *usque eo imperio carere non poterat* and *Fam.* IX. 18. 1 *quod, ut Dionysius tyrannus, cum Syracusis pulsus esset, Corinthi dicitur ludum aperuisse, sic ego sublatis iudiciis, amisso regno forensi ludum quasi habere coeperim* (cf. Quint. *Inst.* VIII. 6. 52; in Sen. *Dial.* VI. 17. 5 *erit Dionysius ille tyrannus, libertatis iustitiae legum exitium, dominationis cupidus etiam post Platonem, vitae etiam post exilium*; *alios uret, alios verberabit* sqq. *vitae* ought

surely to be deleted as entirely beside the point). Its application here I take to be as follows: As the tyrant preferred the travesty of power to no power at all, so the optimates prefer the travesty of prominence to obscurity—they would rather be Caesarian figureheads than disappear. The following reference to Titinius and his son, which editors have been so far from understanding as to make it begin a new paragraph, rams the point home. Titinius' behaviour (cf. 172 (IX. 6). 6) shows the lengths such persons will go to curry favour with the victor.

17 **fac. . .destiteris** *fac ne destiteris* is an indefensible combination, though *fac ne desistas* would not be.

2, 1 **alteram** On 13 March, in reply to 172 (IX. 6) of the 11th.

2 **dimidio plus** Her 30,000 should have been 15,000 (not, as sometimes supposed, 20,000: cf. *Verr.* II. 3. 117); cf. 172 (IX. 6). 3 n.

3 **consules** I.e. *cos⟨s⟩*. Cf. *ibid. consules duo*; Caes. *B.C.* I. 25. 2, etc.

4 **discessu** I do not now feel able to retain *dispersu*. (*a*) Two can hardly be said to be 'scattered'. (*b*) C. would not have known that the Consuls intended to separate in Greece, if in fact they did. (*c*) It was the departure of the Consuls from Italy, not their subsequent movements, that ruled out negotiations. If *illorum* be taken as the Pompeians generally, these objections disappear; but that is clearly difficult. The substantive *dispersus* would be ἅπ. λεγ.

6 **Demetri librum** Cf. 161 (VIII. 11). 7.

7 **Philotimo** He left Formiae on the 15th (§3).

13 **sermonibus** Cf. Appendix IV, p. 450, n. 2.

Colchis From *Colchi*: C. does not use *Colchis, -idis*. Like some of the other names in this catalogue this would have required a preposition if it had stood alone (cf. 227 (XI. 16). 1 n. (*in ipsa Alexandria*)). Colchis furnished timber and other materials for shipbuilding (Strabo, XI. 2. 17), and Caesar (*B.C.* III. 3. 1) mentions Pontus among the places which supplied ships for Pompey's fleet.

16 **frumentarias provincias** Sicily, Sardinia, Africa.

17 **veniet** Sc. *Pompeius. venire* is often combined with an adjective, the verb having more or less significance according to the context: cf. *Propertiana*, p. 31.

22 **septemtrione** Cf. 172 (IX. 6). 3 *ex ea die fuere septemtriones venti.* The Pompeians would be carried up coast in the direction of Atticus' property.

24 **ipsa** I.e. as well as in other ways (cause, prestige, etc.).

25 **cum illum videro** *illum* because Caesar has just been referred to (*hunc*): cf. 182 (IX. 14). 2 *hic. . .illo*; 220 (XI. 9). 2 *se enim scire summo illum* (sc. *Quintum*) *in odio fuisse Caesari*; *illum* (sc. *Caesarem*) *tamen non modo favisse sed*

etiam tantam illi (sc. *Quinto*) *pecuniam dedisse honoris mei causa.* Not 'as more remote in idea and belonging to the other party'.

27 **Arpinum. . .cogito** Cf. 166 (VIII. 16). 2 *ego Arpinum cogitabam.*

29 **deterrima** *taeterrima* may well be right: cf. Caelius, *Fam.* VIII. 15. 1 *taeterrima hieme.* The weather may have been bad when C. wrote (though not bad enough to stop him going into the country (§1)); it cleared up on the 18th (180 (IX. 13). 2).

venisse From his province of Syria.

3, 1 **ais epistula** The simple ablative in such cases is quite common with relative pronouns as in 202 (X. 11). 1 *litteras. . .quibus. . .scribis,* not so common otherwise; but cf. *Fam.* III. 7. 2 *eadem. . .epistula petebas*; *Tusc.* IV. 4 *carmen quod. . .laudat epistula quadam*; Tac. *Agr.* 39. 1 *rerum cursum. . .nulla verborum iactantia Agricolae epistulis auctum*; Gell. II. 10. 3 *eadem epistula negat*; Plin. *N.H.* XXIX. 143 *sequenti dicemus volumine* et sim.

2 **eo serius** Cf. Appendix V.

5 **iste. . .sordidissimus** Who this is there is no saying; not necessarily one of the Praetors of 49 and in any case scarcely M. Lepidus, as supposed by Corradus and generally since. Lepidus was a *nobilis* of *nobiles, sordidissimus* would better suit a Fufius Calenus or a Vatinius. The only aristocrat to whom C. ever applies this adjective is L. Piso Caesoninus (*Pis.* 66, 99), and Piso's birth was not beyond reproach.

6 **idem qui semper** Cf. Ter. *Hec.* 544 *sed ut olim te ostendisti, eadem esse nil cessavisti usque adhuc.* Some read *ille idem* in view of M (*idem ille* would not be Ciceronian; cf. *Thes.* VII. 202).

8 **in ea epistula** 172A (IX. 6A); contrast C.'s answer to Caesar (178A (IX. 11A). 1), written after his talk with Matius (178 (IX. 11). 2).

10 **id quidem. . .hoc** Cf. 74 (IV. 2). 5 n. *id* for *hoc* in Σ is pretty certainly a copyist's error due to *id* preceding. Distinguish passages like *Tusc.* III. 71 *id quod alii rectum opinantes. . .id hi turpe putantes* (cf. Madvig on *Fin.* V. 22), where the repetition is rhetorical.

11 **sententia consulari** Carrying authority and delivered before other categories.

13 **ex tuis litteris** Perhaps the *uberrimae litterae* of 174 (IX. 7). 1.

15 **nos** Sc. *augures.* Gellius (XIII. 15. 4) cites from Messalla *de Auspiciis*: *praetor, etsi collega consulis est, neque praetorem neque consulem iure rogare potest, ut quidem nos a superioribus accepimus aut ante haec tempora servatum est et ut in commentario tertio decimo C. Tuditani patet, quia imperium minus praetor, maius habet consul, et a minore imperio maius aut maiori* (*maiore* codd.) *collega rogari iure non potest* (cf. Mommsen, *St.* II, p. 126). The argument is that Praetors were both like and less than Consuls; and a magistrate who was like a Consul could not be 'proposed' by one who was less than a Consul.

17 **numquam** *nusquam* has been defended by expressions such as *nusquam excessi* in *Fam.* X. 32. 5 (Pollio), but here it would suggest a wrong sense ('in any state').

21 **Galba...Antonio** Obviously all Augurs, though only Antony (elected in 50) is definitely attested as such by other evidence. The absence of the Caesarians P. Servilius Isauricus the Younger and L. Marcius Philippus (Tr. Pl. 49, Cos. Suff. 38) suggests that these should not be included in Broughton's list (p. 255) of the College in 50. Galba is doubtless Ser. Sulpicius Galba, formerly Legate of C. Pomptinus and then of Caesar in Gaul (*B.G.* III. 1, ff., VIII. 50. 3) and Praetor in 54 (cf. 92 (IV. 18). 4 n. (*latum de imperio*)). One of Caesar's assassins, he commanded a legion at the battle of Forum Gallorum and sent C. an extant account of it (*Fam.* X. 30). After his condemnation under the lex Pedia of 43 (Suet. *Galba*, 3. 2) no more is heard of him.

22 **Scaevola** Cf. 91 (IV. 17). 4 n.

Cassio The Caesarian Tribune Q. Cassius (cf. 113 (V. 20). 8 n.).

τότε κ.τ.λ. *Il.* IV. 182.

4, 1 **sed...vides** In my previous edition I ought to have followed my own admonition and begun a new paragraph here. The 'storm' is the threatened demand for support in the Augural College, which C. would have to refuse.

5 **vectigalibus** Caesar would not be able to keep up the ordinary corn distributions from public funds without *vectigalia*, revenues from the provinces, especially Asia (see on 180 (IX. 13). 4) and the east generally: cf. *Fam.* XV. 1. 5 *ut...summum periculum sit ne amittendae sint omnes hae provinciae, quibus vectigalia populi Romani continentur.* No taxes were now levied in Italy except the manumission tax (cf. 36 (II. 16). 1 fin.). The rendering 'without special imposts' would require *novis.*

illum Caesar, not Pompey as usually supposed. Here are two further reasons for fearing a food shortage in Rome: Caesar's adherents would drain what financial resources he had, and the Pompeian blockade (*bellum nefarium*) would interfere with supplies.

6 **Trebatium** Cf. 141 (VII. 17). 3 n.

10 **Phameam** Uncle or grandfather of Caesar's and Augustus' favourite Tigellius; for C.'s relations with both cf. 347 (XIII. 49) and *Fam.* VII. 24. The excellence of his dinners was long remembered (*ibid.* IX. 16. 8). His other names are unknown, but there is nothing to prove that he was a freedman, as sometimes stated.

11 **res publica** Here implying an ordered society.

12 **qui maxime meus** *es* should perhaps be added. Sjögren refers to

306 (XII. 6). 2 *sed longe oratio est et tu occupatus in meo quidem negotio*, where however λ has *occupatus es*, also to Leo, *Plautinische Forschungen*², p. 285.

sciebam sqq. Atticus bought land not for pleasure but as an investment: cf. Nep. *Att.* 14. 3 *nullos habuit hortos, nullam suburbanam aut maritimam sumptuosam villam, neque in Italia, praeter Arretinum et Nomentanum, rusticum praedium, omnisque eius pecuniae reditus constabat in Epiroticis et urbanis possessionibus*; Varro, *R.R.* I. 2. 8 *duo in primis spectasse videntur Italici homines colendo, possentne fructus pro impensa ac labore redire et utrum saluber locus esset an non.*

13 **quoto anno** The usual explanation 'in how many years you would recoup yourself for the purchase money' is sound as to general sense but quite mistaken as verbal analysis. Commentators cite Hor. *Ep.* II. I. 35 *chartis pretium quotus adroget annus*, which is no more illuminating than Frontin. *de Aquis*, praef. 3 *quoto post urbem conditam anno*. Turn rather to Sen. *Ben.* IV. 12. 3 *nemo Tusculanum aut Tiburtinum paraturus salubritatis causa et aestivi secessus quoto anno empturus sit disputat*: nobody argues in the case of such a property about how many years' purchase, what multiple of the annual yield, he is going to pay. *anno*, ablative of price not time, is seen to be business brachylogy for *fructu annuo*, the figure expressing the yearly income from the property. All that need be mentally added to C.'s wording is the verb *emas*. Thus Seneca interprets C. and C. in return guarantees Seneca's text against the tampering of Fickert and others.

quantum in solo Commentators compare Sen. *Quaest. Nat.* II. I. 2 *tertia illa pars de aquis terris arbustis satis quaerit et, ut iurisconsultorum verbo utar, de omnibus quae solo continentur*; *Dig.* VIII. I. 7 praef. *aut rei soli aut rei mobilis usus fructus legatur* et sim.

14 **digamma** διάγραμμα might perhaps mean 'register of taxable property' (see L.–S.–J. s.v.), but it remains possible that *digamma* had some relevant sense; though the suggestion that it stands for *F* = *faenus* or *fundi* on the back of a ledger is highly speculative.

16 **Marcellino consule** In 56.

17 **propter domum Anti quam tum habebam** C.'s Tusculan villa having been destroyed by Clodius, he had to decide after his restoration whether to rebuild it or to get a suburban estate somewhere else or to go without one altogether (cf. 74 (IV. 2). 7). The property at Lanuvium would have had the advantage of lying near the road between Rome and Antium, where C. at that time owned a house—the last extant letters from it belong to the first half of 56. Moreover the figure of HS 500,000 proposed by C. to Phamea was less than the sum required to rebuild the Tusculanum, being in fact the amount awarded to him in compensation for the latter *valde illiberaliter* (*ibid.* 5). Actually however as he remembered later on (180 (IX.

13). 6), the property for which he negotiated in 56 was not the Lanuvium but another. Modern editors write *domum antiquam ⟨quam⟩ tum habebam* after Lehmann (*Berl. Phil. Woch.* 9 (1889), p. 1036), whose 'excellent explanation' is rubbish. He did not even know that *hortulos* means not a garden but an estate near the capital (cf. 130 (VII. 7). 6 n.)

19 **egi...venale** As emended by Marshall and Lehmann and punctuated by Müller the sentence makes excellent sense, except with regard to the go-between, represented in the MSS by *predum. praedem in* many editions (including mine of 1961) will not do. C. would not require a surety before the property was for sale, nor would he be likely to mention his agent thus anonymously. Moreover *praes* (in contradistinction to *sponsor*) is used in connexion with debts to the state: see the definitions (Varro, *L.L.* v. 40, etc.) quoted by Lewis and Short. I know of no clear example in the classical period of *praes* relating to a purely private transaction. *predum* no doubt conceals a name, and the only name palaeographically very similar is *Precium*. On C.'s friend Precius, from whom he inherited in 50, see 123 (VI. 9). 2 n.

22 **eiusdem Antias** Better attested than *eius dementias*, which anyhow makes no tolerable sense.

cave contemnas Cf. Cato, *R.R.* I. 4 *caveto alienam disciplinam temere contemnas*; Petr. 38. 6 *reliquos autem collibertos eius cave contemnas.*

23 **addicta vastitati** Cf. 174 (IX. 7). 5 *promitto tibi...tegulam illum in Italia nullam relicturum*; 177 (IX. 10). 3 n. (*vastitatem*).

26 **d.** *dedi* or *data*. The Liberalia were on 17 March.

177 (IX. 10)

1, 3 **aegritudo** Cf. *Tusc.* III. 23 *ut aegrotatio in corpore sic aegritudo in animo.*

2, 4 **XIIII Kal Febr.** The day Pompey left Rome.

6 **aliud in alio** Different errors in different matters: cf. Cels. praef. 43 *ut eius interior aliqua pars aperiatur, et in alio alia*, III. 10. 2 *quorum quidlibet ex aceto impositum dolorem minuit, sed magis aliud in alio.* But *ex* rather than *in*, 'one error after another', might have been expected: cf. *Fam.* IX. 19. 2 *me cottidie aliud ex alio impedit* et sim.

8 **alienat quod** I prefer this to Madvig's *alienamur ⟨si quid⟩* because I think C. would have preferred the less personal way of putting this particular matter, that is if the verb is his and not part of a quotation. A quotation here has been plausibly suspected, but it need not have extended beyond the three adverbs.

9 **neglegentiaeque** Cf. 161 (VIII. 11). 6 n.

13 **dies et noctes** This or *dies noctesque* is what C. ordinarily writes, though he has *diem noctem* in *Div.* II. 59 and other variants elsewhere (*dies noctes* I have never found).

avis illa In Plato, *Epist.* VII. 348 a τὸ δὲ μετὰ ταῦτα ἐζῶμεν ἐγὼ καὶ Διονύσιος, ἐγὼ μὲν βλέπων ἔξω, καθάπερ ὄρνις ποθῶν ποθεν ἀναπτέσθαι, ὁ δὲ κ.τ.λ. C. quotes from the same letter in 180 (IX. 13). 4.

18 **quae...remansissent** Cf. 217 (XI. 6). 6 *omnes enim qui in Italia manserant hostium numero habebantur.* T.–P. cite Plut. *Pomp.* 61; App. *B.C.* II. 37; Dio, XLI. 6. 2.

3, 3 **mori maluit** The legend of Themistocles' suicide, found in Aristophanes (*Eq.* 83), survived Thucydides' disapproval (I. 138. 4). The earlier interpretation of it, which made him die ἀδύνατον νομίσαντα εἶναι ἐπιτελέσαι βασιλεῖ ἃ ὑπέσχετο, was supplemented by the more sentimental one adopted here (cf. Diod. XI. 58; Plut. *Them.* 31). C. himself vacillates; cf. *Amic.* 42, where Coriolanus and Themistocles are placed on a par, and *Brut.* 43, where Atticus is made to discredit both suicides as rhetorical fictions.

4 **qui...cecidit** So Justin, II. 9. 21. J. Miller (*RE.* VIII. 1704. 55) gives Ephorus as the source of this statement, belied by the silence of Herodotus and Thucydides.

6 **iure** This must mean that they could plead some constitutional justification, Sulla and Cinna as having been wrongfully deprived of a command and a Consulship respectively, Marius as Cinna's associate and as wrongfully exiled.

10 **Getarum...Colchorum** C. has been taken to task for exaggeration 'as these tribes do not appear in the list given by Caesar (*B.C.* III. 4)'. History however is one thing, prophecy another—and this prophecy never came to pass at all.

11 **vastitatem** *vastitas Italiae* 'would appear to be a kind of fixed and recognized expression in Latin' (T.–P. VI, p. 247, following J. H. Schmalz); add to the cited examples Tac. *Hist.* I. 50.

12 **mortalem esse...exstingui** Caesar might die in the course of nature or he might be eliminated in some other way, for example by assassination.

15 **oblectabat** Better in sense and palaeography than *sustentabat. lec* is more easily confused with *ten* or *tē* than *sus* with *ob*.

18 **sol...videtur** Cf. *Amic.* 47 *solem enim e mundo tollere videntur ei qui amicitiam e vita tollunt.* Otto (*Sprichwörter*, p. 327) interprets: 'ich hätte alles für möglich gehalten, ich hätte eher den Einsturz des Himmels erwartet'; but Atticus had surely meant that with the eclipse of Pompey's reputation the light had gone out of the Roman world. Cosmic metaphors suited Pompey (cf. 41 (II. 21). 4).

25 **scripsi** *scripsisti* can hardly be retained. C. had already given several reasons for staying—his alienation from Pompey, his horror of the war (backed by historical precedents), his hopes of peace, his inclination towards rest and domesticity. How could he proceed to lay the whole onus on Atticus? Nor is the distinction between *ea quae scripsisti* ('die Nachrichten... die du mir geschrieben hast' according to Schmidt, *Rhein. Mus.* 52 (1897), p. 153) and *auctoritas* made sufficiently clear; contrast *ad Brut.* 17. 1 *me quidem cum rationes quas collegeras tum auctoritas tua a nimio maerore deterruit.*

4, 3 **erat igitur** *igitur* as in 360 (XIV. 6). 1 and 415 (XVI. 7). 4, citing a document already referred to; cf. 368 (XIV. 14). 1 *itaque* and *Thes.* VII. 269. 50.

4 **illius** Verbally it is easier to take this of Caesar, because of *Gnaeus* before and *iste* after. The latter would be highly superfluous if *illius* = *Pompei.*

5 **omnino** μέν.

8 **tantum modo...ne** Cf. *Fam.* XVI. 12. 4 *tantum modo ut eum intercludamus.*

15 **ὑποκορίζῃ** Like King Charles II, who did not want to go on his travels again.

5, 5 **huius...civibus** An indignant statement rather than a question.

6, 2 **fugamne...nefandam** These words must have been taken from a lost letter of C.'s written on 6 or 7 February; cf. 146 (VII. 22). 2 n. Most modern texts have Otto's *fugamne defendam an moram utiliorem putem*, one of the worst of many guesses. Misled by him (*Rhein. Mus.* 41 (1886), p. 371) they imagine that the epithets *foedam* and *nefandam* beg the question which Atticus was asked to decide. Not at all. Neither alternative was good (*honestum*), but C. wanted to know, not without irony, which of the two was the more expedient (*utile*). A pejorative epithet for both is what his perplexity required: cf. 142 (VII. 18). 1 *utrum turpi pace nobis an misero bello esset utendum.* Delay was *nefanda* because it meant deserting Pompey and what C. always felt at bottom to be the cause of the Republic.

4 **tum ipsi Gnaeo** Does this refer to flight on Pompey's part or on C.'s? Surely the latter—if C. stayed he might help Pompey as a mediator. Either way *periculosam* applies only to *tibi.*

6 **vos** Including M'. Lepidus, etc. Surely not = C. and Pompey; the latter would have left Italy *ex hypothesi* and anyway could hardly remain *in specula.*

8 **sullaturit...proscripturit** Cf. Quint. *Inst.* VIII. 3. 32 *nec a verbis modo sed a nominibus quoque derivata sunt quaedam, ut a Cicerone 'sullaturit', ab Asinio 'fimbriatum' et 'figulatum'*, 6. 32 *vix illa quae* πεποιημένα *vocant,*

quae ex vocibus in usum receptis quocumque modo declinantur, nobis permittimus, qualia sunt 'sullaturit' et 'proscripturit'.

9 **cum tu. . .cederem** Cf. 152 (VIII. 2). 4.

10 **quaedam significari** *quaedam* could certainly well be spared, but cf. 293 (XII. 51). 1 *sed expecto te, a Peducaeo utique; tu autem significas aliquid etiam ante.*

12 **ego vero** Perhaps the first words of the letter: cf. 198 (X. 7). 1; Plin. *Ep.* IX. 20. 1, IX. 38.

15 **relinquitur** Sc. *Gnaeo.*

7, 4 **νέκυιαν** Atticus' name for Caesar's *entourage*, borrowed by C. in 178 (IX. 11). 2 and 187 (IX. 18). 2. Clearly it means more than 'rabble'. Atticus doubtless thought of the procession of ghosts in *Od.* XI, but why liken Caesar's followers to ghosts? Not, I think, because they were 'mere shadows of real men', or because they came up hungry for plunder as the ghosts for blood, but because many of them were outcasts from respectable society. They now emerged from the shades of bankruptcy or ἀτιμία, conjured up by the new Odysseus-magician (νέκυια = necromancy in Hellenistic Greek), Caesar.

8 **inquis** From Atticus' letter, in which *quidsi. . .discedunt* was an imaginary interjection by C.: cf. 169 (IX. 2*a*). 1 n.

9 **quod egeris. . .putabo** Cf. 332 (XIII. 24). 1 *quod egeris id probabo*; *Fam.* II. 18. 3 *tu quod egeris id velim di adprobent.* Hence the elliptical *quod egerit* (cf. 121 (VI. 6). 4 n.).

10 **dubitares** ' "Si alors tu eusses hésité (au cas où ces deux hommes se fussent retiré, *si isti discessissent*)." Car dans *si discedunt*, ἀπορῶ, est impliqué *si discesserint*, ἀπορήσω' (M. Bonnet, *Rev. de Phil.* 24 (1900), p. 54): cf. 90 (IV. 15). 4 *ne animum Publi offenderet* (sc. *si ego in ea causa verba fecissem*); 167 (IX. 1). 4 *ego unus cui utrumvis liceret.*

8, 3 **τὸ μέλλον ibi καραδοκήσεις** Cf. App. *B.C.* V. 127 καραδοκῶν τὸ μέλλον.

6 **ὑπὸ τὴν διάλειψιν** Cf. 168 (IX. 2) n.

9 **quamquam magna sollicitudine** A participle ('*ente*') may be understood: cf. Tac. *Hist.* I. 83 *quamquam turbidis rebus et diversis militum animis*, IV. 18 *quamquam rebus trepidis*, *Ann.* III. 30. 4 *quamquam prompto ad capessendos honores aditu*; Caes. *B.C.* I. 67. 5 *etsi aliquo accepto detrimento*; Madvig on *Fin.* V. 68; K.–S. I, pp. 779 f.

9, 1 **angerer** C. is perhaps rather thinking of his state of mind a few days later: cf. 172 (IX. 6). 4 f. For the mood cf. K.–S. II, p. 344.

5 **ita dico, si** Cf. 169 (IX. 2*a*). 2 fin. *ita* as in *Fam.* V. 19. 2 *libenter amplector talem animum, sed ita (non enim dimittam pudorem in rogando meum), si feceris id quod ostendis magnam habebo gratiam, si non feceris ignoscam.* Distin-

guish the common *ita si* = 'with the proviso that' (*ita* looking backwards, not forwards).

10, 7 ad ea tute hortare Lit. 'urge me to them', i.e. the remaining steps, *reliqua*.

9 **tamen** Cf. 136 (VII. 13). 1 *ut aliud nihil, hoc tamen profecit: dedit illi dolorem.*

178 (IX. 11)

1, 4 visum est Cf. *Verr.* II. 4. 91 *quod mihi numquam veri simile visum est*; Liv. XXVII. 7. 6 *quod mihi minus simile veri visum est*; also on 385 (XV. 8). 2. A verb is necessary (cf. Madvig on *Fin.* V. 68), and C. would not have written *vix verisimile est* (Reid) of something he now knew to be true, and *visum ē* is more likely than *videbatur* to have fallen out after *verisimile.*

5 **hortis** A villa in the suburbs of Puteoli (cf. 130 (VII. 7). 6 n.).

6 **gratias agens** For his release.

7 **C. Caecio** Cf. 180 (IX. 13). 7. The name Caecius occurs in inscriptions.

2, 1 Matius C. Matius, an old friend of C.'s (*Fam.* XI. 27. 2), closely attached to Caesar—he had been a link between them during their *rapprochement* in the mid-fifties (*ibid.*). Though with Caesar in Gaul, where he made friends with Trebatius Testa (*Fam.* VII. 15. 2), he avoided official rank; Münzer (*RE.* XIV. 2207. 17) compares his relations with Caesar to those of Maecenas with Augustus. His letter to C. after Caesar's assassination (*Fam.* XI. 28) is one of the most celebrated in the collection (recently discussed by B. Kytzler (*Historia* 9 (1960), pp. 96 ff. and A. Heuss (*ibid.* 5 (1956) pp. 53 ff., 11 (1962), pp. 118 ff.). The friend of Augustus mentioned by Pliny (*N.H.* XII. 13) and Tacitus (*Ann.* XII. 60. 6) may have been his son.—T.–P.'s remark that Trebatius seems to have been present at this interview is not proved by *Fam.* XI. 27. 3 (August 44) *quibus rebus interesse memini Trebatium*; but Trebatius does seem to have been with Matius at this time (cf. on 183 (IX. 15). 4) and 184 (IX. 15*a*) *pueri quos cum Matio et Trebatio miseram* shows that they visited Formiae together. It might therefore look as though *cum Trebatio* has fallen out after *Matius,* as I earlier suggested. But the matter can be explained without interference with the text. On the 20th Matius and Trebatius were at Minturnae, only nine miles south of Formiae (179 (IX. 12). 1). Prior to leaving for Capua (184 (IX. 15*a*)) they may have paid C. a joint visit on the 21st, of which he could have informed Atticus in a letter of the 22nd, now lost.

Quinquatribus The greater of the two festivals of that name in honour of Minerva. Its first and originally its only day was 19 March, five days from the Ides by inclusive reckoning.

4 **νέκυιαν** Cf. 177 (IX. 10). 7 n.

5 **epistulam...Caesaris** 172A (IX. 6A).

6 **antea** On 11 March.

3, 1 **Crassipes** Despite the coolness after his divorce from Tullia, indicated by his omission from C.'s mailing list the previous year (cf. 124 (VII. 1). 8), he and C. were now evidently on outwardly amicable terms.

4 **†qui...potius** The vulgate *qui* ⟨*pro sua*⟩ *prudentia potuit attendere* would imply that it needed a particularly clever or expert person to heed this talk, which is absurd. And I doubt whether C. wanted to pay a compliment to his former son-in-law. On the contrary I suspect that he wrote *quod* (or *quoad*) *sua prudentia potuit attendere*, 'so far as his sagacity enabled him to take it in', implying that too much in the way of accurate *rapportage* was not to be expected from this young man.

5 **inimicos...hostis** Cf. 39 (II. 19). 3 n.

4, 4 **illic** Overseas. C. thinks of the proposed blockade, etc.

5 **convenire** 'In urbe, ut eorum bona vendant' (Manutius).

7 **μακροψυχίαν** Rightly restored by Sjögren in place of μικροψυχίαν. If Pompey thought of retiring so far, it was not for refuge but to gather forces *pour mieux sauter*, as C. well recognized (cf. 177 (IX. 10). 3). μακροψυχίαν can now be supported by μακροψυχέω, μακρόψυχος = '(be) patient, dilatory' in papyri, and may fairly be rendered 'length of view' (not, of course, = μεγαλοψυχίαν, as commentators used to think). Pompey was planning a long war from distant bases, if the rumours were to be believed.

8 **cogitare** 'Think of'. There is no ellipse of *ire* here as in 176 (IX. 9). 2 *Arpinum cogito*.

12 **tantum** Read perhaps by a copyist as *iā n̄rūm*. Or *nostrum* may have arisen from *nostram* (so Müller).

178A (IX. 11A)

This replies to Caesar's letter 172A (IX. 6A), received more than a week previously. Lentulus Spinther's letter mentioned in §3 may have arrived on the 19th, and this one bears the impress of Matius' conversation the same day.

1, 2 **ad urbem** Cf. 172 (IX. 6). 1 n.

5 **admirabili...sapientia** This phrase and *aliquid impertias temporis* in §3 (which was misunderstood) came in for especially unfavourable comment when this letter was made semi-public property: cf. 188 (VIII. 9). 1.

2, 4 **cum primum potui** This implies that C. attended the Senate in January despite Pompey's advice (cf. 127 (VII. 4). 2).

5 **nec. . .attigi** Cf. Appendix II, p. 440.

7 **honorem** The privilege of standing for the Consulship *in absentia*. Or does C. mean the Consulship itself, politely assuming what was in fact the case, that if Caesar had been able to stand his election would have been a foregone conclusion?

8 **invidi** Cf. 141 (VII. 17). 4 n.

3, 5 **sperarem me a te** The pronouns are probably emphatic.

10 **antea** No doubt in reply to Caesar's letter mentioned in 161 (VIII. 11). 5.

12 **misit** See App. Crit. The mere addition of *putavi* after *accepisse* is hardly rotund enough. The missing words may have been something like ⟨*teneri non potui quin iterum tibi gratias agerem atque hoc ita significarem*⟩, *eandem* sqq.

179 (IX. 12).

The letter was not written immediately after receipt of Lepta's mentioned in §1, but only after receipt of another from Matius and Trebatius; so it may not have been written, and was anyhow doubtless not dispatched, till the following morning.

1, 7 **Mucianum exitum** Cf. 153 (VIII. 3). 6 n.

8 **expedita** Atticus had 'ironed out the difficulties'.

11 **Epirum** Cf. 174 (IX. 7). 7.

2, 1 **sum admiratus** 'Quum Cicero iam antea illum hominem cognovisset ingratissimum, cf. VIII. 4 [154], non poterat mirari ab eo se nunc relinqui. admirabatur potius Dionysium Attici litteris defendi vel excusari' (Boot). This may be right, but I am rather inclined to take *sum admiratus* with reference to the original revelation (now confirmed) of Dionysius' true character.

2 **Panaetius** Of Rhodes, the famous second-century Stoic who settled in Rome and lived on familiar terms with Scipio Aemilianus and his circle: cf. *Mur.* 66, etc.

3 **despecta est** So in 208 (X. 16). 1 *intellexi fortunam ab eo nostram despectam esse*. Cf. Caes. *B.C.* III. 103. 4 *neve eius fortunam despicerent*, 104. 1 *despecta eius fortuna*.

3, 5 **perscribunt** Cf. 91 (IV. 17). 2 n. (*perscriptionibus*).

4, 2 **ad finem** 'Tending towards an end': cf. 52 (III. 7). 2 *reliqua tempora sunt non tam ad medicinam quam ad finem doloris*. It would be a mistake to write *qui* (or *quae*) *finis*. Confusion of final *m* and *s* in the MSS is not uncommon: cf. e.g. 41 (II. 21). 4 *Protogenes/-em*; 73 (IV. 1). 4 *diem/dies*; 130 (VII. 7). 6 *dies/diem*; 135 (VII. 12). 5 *magistratus/-um*; 184 (IX. 15*a*) *Hispanias/-am*. By *huius* *vitae* C. surely means the life he is now leading: cf. 195 (X. 4). 6 *in hac vita et fuga*. He would not ask Atticus' advice on how to commit suicide (cf. Apul. *Met.* VI. 14. 1 *illic in⟨ventura⟩ vitae pessimae finem*).

3 **cum quidem** *quidem* is appropriate. It is just now, when his conduct seems to have been justified by the event, that C. regrets it most bitterly: cf. *Pis.* 21 *itaque discessu tum meo omnes illi nefarii gladii de manibus crudelissimis exciderunt, cum quidem tu...arbitria non mei solum sed patriae funeris abstulisti* et sim. In 1961 I made the mistake of printing the vulgate *cuidam*, which ought to mean 'to you know who' rather than 'to anybody'.

5 **illius** I.e. *Pompei*? Perhaps rather with *victoriae* as in 217 (XI. 6). 2 *praedam...illius victoriae*.

180 (IX. 13).

C. was sending a letter every day at this time (182 (IX. 14). 2 fin.; 185 (IX. 16). 1), so a letter dispatched on the 22nd will have been lost.

1, 1 οὐκ ἔστ' ἔτυμος λόγος From Stesichorus' palinode, which continues οὐδ' ἔβας ἐν νηυσὶν εὐσέλμοις (fr. 11, Diehl).

ratibus Cf. 179 (IX. 12). 1.

3 **εὐημερίαν quasi Caesaris** Perhaps the order should be changed (see App. Crit.), but in view of 131 (VII. 8). 3 *quantum quasi sit in trientis triente* I do not feel certain that it is wrong: cf. Lucr. III. 256 *in summo quasi corpore*, 440 *quod vas quasi constitit eius* et sim.

2, 1 XI Kal. Atticus' letter will have been written on the 19th or 20th, after receipt of 177 (IX. 10); cf. §3.

3, 1 συναγωγή In 177 (IX. 10).

12 **ab eisdem** The optimates, though Cato at least is acquitted in 60 (III. 15). 2. That Pompey was lured to disaster by the Catonian faction is certainly a tenable view, but it is not usually C.'s. He seems to have been seduced into it here by a rhetorician's desire to develop his similitude.

14 **potuit** 'Had the power (to help).' The parallel, C. realizes after having stated it, is not quite perfect. Pompey *did* not help before the catastrophe (in 58); C. (in 50–49) *could* not, or not enough.

15 **nec ego nunc** *nec* = *nec tamen* as often. C. now demolishes his own case.

4, 7 peditum A numeral has fallen out, perhaps also *eos*, though this can be understood from *Gallorum*.

8 **annos decem—** The sentence could be regarded as grammatically complete if *ita* above were understood as referring backwards (= *ita ut nulla sit spes reditus*). But it seems more likely that C. originally meant to add a clause like *ut...non videam* below.

9 **Asiae** Sjögren reads *Italiae*. But the Italian revenue cannot now have amounted to much (cf. 36 (II. 16). 1), so that in 176 (IX. 9). 4 Caesar is said (or as good as said) to have no revenues with which to maintain the corn distributions. The wealth of Asia (sometimes probably in the wider sense of Asia Minor) and the importance of its taxes for the Roman finances is much emphasized in the *pro Lege Manilia*, e.g. 14 *ceterarum provinciarum vectigalia . . .tanta sunt ut eis ad ipsas provincias tuendas vix contenti esse possimus, Asia vero tam opima est ac fertilis ut. . .facile omnibus terris antecellat*: see also on 176 (IX. 9). 4 (*vectigalibus*). The singular *vectigal* strictly means one year's revenue (cf. Caes. *B.C.* III. 32. 6 *insequentis anni vectigal*).

12 **oderunt. . .ludum** 'Hate the game' or 'hate school' (cf. Petr. 85. 4 *quia dies sollemnis ludum artaverat*), i.e. 'are tired of the business'. The saying is not found elsewhere, but that proves nothing (cf. *ludus est suggerendus* in 285 (XII. 44). 2). It is however suspicious that the omission of *ludum* improves the sense, leaving *illum* as object of *oderunt*. What follows has been much disputed both as to reading and interpretation, but I think there can be no reasonable doubt that *iste*, 'that man of yours', is some *vir bonus* whose conversation Atticus had reported without mentioning his name, and that *quia plus ostenderat quam fecit* (cf. 176 (IX. 9). 1 *fac ut ostendis*; *Fam.* V. 19. 2 *si feceris id quod ostendis*) refers to Pompey, whose pre-war confidence had been bitterly reproached by Favonius and Vulcatius Tullus in full Senate (Plut. *Pomp.* 63 ἐξηπάτηκας ἡμᾶς, ὦ Πομπήϊε): Boot's proposal *ac vellem scripsisses quisnam hoc significasset* therefore makes good sense.

16 **adhuc diligunt** I.e. approve of his behaviour since the invasion. Caesar was no favourite of the *municipia before* the war.

19 **αἱ γὰρ κ.τ.λ.** Also from Plato's seventh Epistle (329 d: cf. 177 (IX. 10). 2), which C. had evidently been reading.

5, 1 **ἀλίμενα** Not places inland (such as Arpinum: cf. 176 (IX. 9). 2 fin.). C. is not thinking of residence (there was no question of his *residing* at Brundisium), but of points of embarcation for Greece. ὑπηρεσίαν means 'ship's crew', as usual.

3 **suppetant** Usually altered to *suppeterent* in texts which keep *vellet* in 234 (XI. 24). 2 *equidem tibi potissimum velim, si idem illa vellet*. How far such variations of tense, common in Comedy, should be admitted into classical prose is doubtful (cf. K.–S. II, p. 401), but to substitute a palaeographically none too plausible conjecture in a familiar letter seems needlessly despotic.

6, 4 **fortiores** Sc. *nobis*. Cf. Nep. *Thras.* 2. 4 *nam iam tum illis temporibus fortius boni pro libertate loquebantur quam pugnabant.*

5 **Lanuvino** Cf. 176 (IX. 9). 4.

Troianum Cf. Liv. I. 1. 4 *Aeneam. . .ab Sicilia classe ad Laurentum agrum tenuisse. Troia et huic loco nomen est.*

somniabam C. was thinking of the Troianum, but dreamily, *somniantis more*, so that he mixed it up with the Lanuvinum. *somniaveram* of Ω has been taken to mean 'it was his Troianum I dreamt (of acquiring)'. But *somniare* would be a very odd verb for C. to use if that was what he meant. There was nothing fantastic about the villa or his offer to Phamea (cf. Plaut. *Curc.* 546 *quos Summanos somnias?* et sim.). The delusion was in his memory.

6 **Q** = 500,000; see H. Chantraine, *RE.* XXIV. 622. 38.

cuperem emeres From 176 (IX. 9). 4 it does not appear that C. thought of buying the place himself.

7, 1 **libello** Apparently some Caesarian pamphlet or notice that had come C.'s way.

3 **Caecius** Cf. 178 (IX. 11). 1 n.

διατροπήν Commonly taken as 'fiasco, debacle'; but such a sense is uncorroborated. Normally διατροπή means 'confusion, consternation, *animi perturbatio*' (L.–S.–J.), which fits well enough here. But *reformidat* should be understood 'is appalled by (shies away from) the memory of': cf. Ov. *Tr.* III. 6. 29 *mensque reformidat, veluti sua vulnera, tempus / illud, et admonitu fit novus ipse pudor*. It is less satisfactory to interpret 'fears the effect of the consternation created by Corfinium' (what effect was there to *fear*?). If Lentulus really intended to give up the Pompeian cause, he later changed his mind.

5 **prospecta re** *perspecta* may be right ('now that he sees the truth'—about Caesar's superiority in force and generalship); but for *res* = *eventus* cf. *Verr.* II. 5. 173 *si res aliter acciderit.*

181 (IX. 13*a*)

Clearly a new letter. Balbus' letter will have come in on the 23rd after 180 (IX. 13) had been dispatched: cf. 182 (IX. 14). 1.

1 **mene** Cf. 172 (IX. 6). 4 *mene non...cum Pompeio...esse...?. prospecta re. m-* was misread as *prospectaret n-*.

2 **N. Magium** Cf. 174C (IX. 7C). 2. Caesar (*B.C.* I. 26. 2 f.) tells a different story: greatly surprised that Magius was not sent back by Pompey, he made yet another attempt to arrange the desired personal interview, this time through his Legate Caninius Rebilus. The fact probably was that Magius did not return promptly (he was sent about 3 March), and when he did come back brought nothing of importance. Caesar's misstatement has been seized upon as evidence of unveracity, but a deliberate lie on such a detail would scarcely have been worth his while. What mattered was not whether Magius returned or not, but whether he had anything of interest to say. *A priori* it is

unlikely that he had, for Pompey was in no situation for peace talks (cf. 165 (VIII. 15). 3 n.).

6 **aedificaret** Cf. 238 (XII. 2). 2 *at Balbus aedificat.* The verb indicates that *horti* and *villa* amount to the same thing, except that the former must be near a town.

nostrum I.e., perhaps, *consularium*: cf. 141 (VII. 17). 3 n.

10 **sententia** To join Pompey in the spring.

181 A (IX. 13A)

1, 1 **litteras** Caesar seems to have written soon after his arrival before Brundisium, perhaps on the following day, 10 March. His letter will have arrived in Rome about the 22nd.

8 **aliquid me conficere** Lit. 'that I am accomplishing anything'—but *posse* may well have dropped out.

2, 3 **namque** If right, purely asseverative (cf. K.–S. II, p. 114), a use hardly found in classical prose.

4 **posse mihi viderer** *possem videri* ('I might perhaps manage to seem of use') *could* be regarded as an extension of an idiomatic use of *videri* mitigating an assertion which might otherwise sound presumptious: cf. e.g. *de Orat.* II. 129 *pauca enim sunt quae usu iam tractata et animo quasi notata habere videamur* (also 161D (VIII. 11D). 7 n.). But Madvig's correction is very easy and satisfactory.

182 (IX. 14)

1, 3 **Q. Pedio** Caesar's nephew, or possibly great-nephew, and his Legate in Gaul in 58–56 (?). He failed in his candidature for the Curule Aedileship in 54 (*Planc.* 54), but was Praetor in 48 and three years later celebrated a Triumph for successes in Spain (Broughton, p. 309). He died in office as Consul Suffect in 43, colleague of his kinsman Octavian.

8 **exitum** *exitu* may be right, but cf. *aditum prohibere* (*Cluent.* 200, etc.).

2, 3 **Cn. Carbonis, M. Bruti** The former, the principal Marian leader after Cinna's death, was captured and killed by Pompey in Sicily. The latter, Tribune in 83 and father of the 'liberator', joined Lepidus' revolt in 77 and met the same fate as Carbo when he surrendered to Pompey at Mutina.

5 **Curionem** Münzer (*RE.* IIA. 872. 38) surmises that Curio was sent to Rome as Caesar's representative after the fall of Corfinium.

6 **a se damnatos ambitus nomine** There is no need to consider ineptitudes like Purser's *se ambire reditionem.* Manutius saw that *ambitionem*

conceals *ambitu(s)*, reference to which is almost indispensable to balance *patriae proditores*. *nomine* is needed to account for the corruption (*se* having fallen out *a dam⟨natos am⟩bit' noie* becomes *ad ambitionem*): cf. Caes. *B.C.* III. 21. 4 *qui Clodio interfecto eo nomine erat damnatus*; Tac. *Ann.* XIII. 15. 4 *damnata veneficii nomine*. For the sense cf. 195 (X. 4). 8 *nihil esse certius quam ut omnes qui lege Pompeia condemnati essent restituerentur*.

quibus. . .fuisset Mommsen (*Str.* p. 874) conjectures that Pompey's bribery law of 52 punished offenders with exile for life. Its retrospective character brought a protest from Cato (Plut. *Cat. Min.* 48).

7 **ab illo** Sulla, not Pompey. The *patriae proditores* restored by him were most probably, I think, persons condemned by the Mamilian Commission of 109 in connexion with the Jugurthine scandals and/or under the lex Varia *de maiestate* of 90 for complicity in the Italian revolt. Sulla may well have brought back other survivors besides C. Aurelius Cotta (who as a relative of Caesar can hardly be specifically intended). Mommsen's suggestion (*Str.* p. 874, n. 7) of Catiline's uncle, L. Billienus (or Bellienus), is wrong; he was condemned (in 64) for murder, not treason (Ascon. 91. 1), and there is no reason to think that Pompey brought him home. *Fam.* VIII. 15. 2 refers to a different man (cf. *Proc. Cam. Phil. Soc.* N.S. 5 (1958–9), pp. 11 ff.).

8 **Milone** Caesar did not recall Milo and could hardly have thought his sentence unjust, but could still deplore Pompey's use of force to secure it.

9 **arma contra** Sc. *se tulisset*.

10 **Baebius** Several persons of this name and in this period are recorded.

non infans I.e. well able to express himself, not likely to spoil a good story in the telling: cf. Quint. *Inst.* XI. 1. 21 *si. . .disertus imperitum plane et infantem* (sc. *se*) *vocet*. See also on 92 (IV. 18). 1.

11 **†quis ulli** Seemingly a hopeless crux, unless Lambinus' *quis illa non dicat?* could be accepted in the sense 'who would *not* find a tongue for such a tale?', which I doubt.

13 **Anteros** Cf. 211 (XI. 1). 1. He will hardly be the man (probably a *tabellarius*) whom M. Cicero the Younger commended to Tiro in 44 (*Fam.* XVI. 21. 8), but may be distinguished from him by *Quinti*.

Quinti Cf. 207 (X. 15). 1 *Eros Philotimi* et sim. (K.–S. I, p. 414). *quin te* is usually omitted from the text; but how did it get there?

3, 2 **Id. Mart.** Actually Pompey sailed on the 17th (184 (IX. 15*a*)).

183 (IX. 15)

1, 1 **ut scires sqq.** Not quite accurate. The information was only added in postscript.

4 **veniam** Permission to be absent from any proceedings in the Senate directed against Pompey.

5 **impetrabo...ipso** Usually taken to imply 'I shall go and join Pompey'. But this C. intended to do anyway (§3), when opportunity served. Rather 'I shall do without his leave and stay away just the same'. Somewhat otherwise Caelius, *Fam.* VIII. 12. 1 *ab eo deprecarer iniuriam quem vitam mihi debere putaram impetrare a me non potui.*

Lepta Ziehen was clearly right. Caesar would not have given military information of this sort to C., and besides there is no mention of any letter from him to C. between 172A (IX. 6A) and 181A (IX. 13A). *Lepta* (cf. 179 (IX. 12). 1; 182 (IX. 14). 3) comes rather more naturally after *ut* than after *scripsit*, and would easily fall out in that position (*-leut⟨lepta⟩a-*).

2, 1 **prima eius actionis** *primas eius actiones* is an obvious normalization, but the paradosis is quite defensible. *actio* is Caesar's active political programme, as in 174A (IX. 7A). 2; for the genitive cf. *Fin.* III. 21 *prima naturae*; *Fam.* I. 9. 15 *summa pectoris*, X. 19. 2 *belli extrema*; K.–S. I, p. 433.

3 **augurum decretum** Cf. 176 (IX. 9). 3 fin.

4 **vexabimur** 'Fatigabor nuntiis' Boot, perhaps too specifically.

vel ut...vel Sjögren (*Comm. Tull.* p. 138) cites *Amic.* 64 *aut si in bonis rebus contemnunt aut in malis deserunt.*

6 **et magister equitum** Often omitted, since the Master of the Horse was nominated by the Dictator himself. Sjögren however compares Liv. VIII. 17. 3 *dictator ab consulibus...dictus P. Cornelius Rufinus, magister equitum M. Antonius*, IX. 7. 13 *Q. Fabium Ambustum dixerunt* (sc. *dictatorem*) *et P. Aelium Paetum magistrum equitum.* It must be admitted that the inaccuracy here is more gratuitous.—Sulla was elected Dictator in 82 by the Centuries under the presidency of the Interrex L. Valerius Flaccus, and made Flaccus himself his Master of the Horse.

7 **Q. Mucius** Cf. 153 (VIII. 3). 6 n.

8 **L. Scipio** Asiaticus (Asiagenus), Cos. 83. Pardoned once by Sulla, he was later proscribed and fled to Massilia.

3, 1 **τέτλαθι** *Od.* XX. 18 τέτλαθι δή, κραδίη: καὶ κύντερον ἄλλο ποτ' ἔτλης.

3 **hominum** *omnium* (Reid) was a quite needless suggestion: cf. 223 (XI. 12). 1 *sermones hominum sustinere*; Q. *Fr.* II. 11. 2 *magno hominum risu cavillatus* et sim.

9 **sed tu quid** Cf. 408 (XV. 29). 2 *sed tu quid ais* (and 330 (XIII. 33*a*). 1). Either this or *sed ⟨quid⟩ tu* (Purser, needlessly omitting *qui* after *omnia*: cf. *Phil.* VIII. 12 *sed quaeso, Calene, quid tu?*) seems preferable to *sed ⟨heus⟩ tu* (Schmidt) or *sed ⟨ubi⟩ tu* (Tyrrell) or to Sjögren's break after *acta essent.*

4, 2 **Trebatium** The vulgate (until 1961) *T. Rebilum* (cf. 126 (VII. 3). 3 n.) is untenable. Caninius Rebilus' praenomen was Gaius, not Titus (some indexes include both!), and C. never seems to have had any personal relations with him. Trebatius had apparently visited C. along with Matius on 21 March (cf. 178 (IX. 11). 2 n.). That he had intended to see C. again before the interview with Caesar (*ut constitueram*) appears from his and Matius' joint letter in 184 (IX. 15*a*) *Trebatius sedulo facit ut antecedat*. As early as the 17th C. had Trebatius in mind in this connexion (cf. 176 (IX. 9). 4). On the 27th he was in fact awaiting him (186 (IX. 17). 1). The interview with Caesar actually took place on the 28th, but C. was now expecting Caesar on the 27th (§1). He might well think that this would not leave Trebatius time to come ahead as he had promised.

4 **ἄλλα μὲν αὐτός** *Od.* III. 26 Τηλέμαχ', ἄλλα μὲν αὐτὸς ἐνὶ φρεσὶ σῇσι νοήσεις, | ἄλλα δὲ καὶ δαίμων ὑποθήσεται.

5 **mandata** Probably those conveyed by N. Magius. Caesar sent him to Brundisium about 3 March (174C (IX. 7C). 2), whereas the Consuls left on the 4th (172 (IX. 6). 3); so he may well have sent a message to them as well as to Pompey. Madvig's reconstruction of the corrupt words seems to be on the right lines. The reference can hardly be to the communication brought by L. Caesar on 23 January (137 (VII. 13*a*). 2). Atticus would scarcely have been interested in that by now, and *misi ad te ante* would be difficult to explain. The replies of Pompey and the Consuls on that occasion were not sent to Atticus by C., but were displayed in public (141 (VII. 17). 2).

8 **Philippus** L. Marcius L. f. Philippus, son of the famous trimmer (cf. 153 (VIII. 3). 6 n.). Politically he followed his father as a man of the centre. Married to Caesar's niece, but father-in-law of Cato and Hortensius, he seems to have fallen foul of no one as Consul in 56 and colleague of the strenuous Lentulus Marcellinus (cf. *Q. Fr.* II. 5. 2 *consul est egregius Lentulus non impediente collega*). In view of his family tie with Caesar he was not expected to take open part against him in 49 (cf. *B.C.* I. 6. 5), and Caesar for his part accepted his neutrality (195 (X. 4). 10). In 44 he gave counsels of caution to his stepson Octavian (Vell. II. 60. 1 f., etc.; cf. 390 (XV. 12). 2 n.), and in the struggle between Antony and the Senate played a moderating role (*Phil.* VIII. 28, etc.). The last fact recorded of him is Octavian's permission, also given to C., to absent himself from the Senate (*Epp. fr.* IV. 23B (Watt)). He and C. were on good enough terms, though his prosiness in talk might make him undesirable company (cf. 248 (XI. 9)).

Neapoli This Philippus is probably the man referred to as *duovir* in a marble tablet found at Herculaneum; cf. H. Bloch, *Gnomon*. 37 (1965), pp. 561 f.

5, 1 **de Dionysio** Cf. 179 (IX. 12). 2.

2 **antiquorum hominum** 'Id est simplicis ingenii et minime callidi' (Corradus, comparing ἀρχαῖος): Varro, *Menipp.* 167 *ego, unus scilicet antiquorum hominum, subductis superciliis dicam*: γαμήσει ὁ νοῦν ἔχων. For

the genitive cf. K.–S. I, p. 426. The omission of *unus* is exceptional; so in Greek one can say τὸν δὲ μὴ πανοῦργον τῶν ἀπαιδεύτων ἀεὶ ἐνομίζεν εἶναι (Xen. *Anab.* II. 6. 26) et sim.

5 **te ipsum. . .violavit** Atticus, it is implied, had some responsibility for Dionysius as his freedman and protégé.

7 **nec tamen. . .impono** *tamen* refers back to the previous sentences ('for all that I have said')—unless, as W. B. Sedgwick suggests, it has 'strayed in from the *nec tamen* of the next line but one'.

8 **oneris** Cf. 174 (IX. 7). 3 *vereor ne Pompeio quid oneris imponam.*

10 **nec. . .sibi** Cf. 179 (IX. 12). 2 *sed illum ulciscentur mores sui.*

Philargyro Perhaps a freedman of A. Torquatus mentioned in *Fam.* VI. 1. 6 of 46. The payment seems to have been overdue.

184 (IX. 15*a*)

That this is a new letter of the same day as the two preceding appears from §1 and from 185 (IX. 16). 1 *ne quem diem intermitterem.*

2 **cum Matio et Trebatio** Cf. 178 (IX. 11). 2 n.

11 **mandata** Probably connected with Caesar's advent.

185 (IX. 16)

1, 4 **opes** In the sense of political influence as in *Fam.* XIII. 4. 4 *pro meis pristinis opibus.*

6 **per litteras** This will be the letter referred to in 178A (IX. 11A). 3 *cum antea tibi de Lentulo gratias egissem.*

3, 3 **hanc adeo** *hanc* = *huius rei. adeo* emphasizes the pronoun (cf. *Thes.* I. 614. 72), or perhaps merely adds a certain liveliness (= δή).

neque. . .poterit Sc. *quin tibi suadeat ut ad urbem praesto sis*: cf. 195 (X. 4). 11. But if the text is sound Caesar expresses himself less clearly than usual. Madvig's *nec ideo* for *hanc adeo* is very attractive.

4 **sensus** I.e. *sensus communis*: cf. *Har. Resp.* 19 *nec denique hoc ipso huius gentis ac terrae domestico nativoque sensu Italos ipsos ac Latinos* (sc. *superamus*). A positively complimentary meaning is indicated by the context, though *sensus* could otherwise be merely 'disposition' (cf. Ter. *Ad.* 533 *ego illius sensum pulchre calleo. / cum fervit maxime tam placidum quam ovem reddo*; Plancus, *Fam.* X. 24. 5 *modestissimi atque humanissimi fuit sensus*).

186 (IX. 17)

1, 5 **ergo ei negandum est** Usually taken as a question. But C.'s mind was made up on this point.

6 **quid praeripio?** Cf. 190 (X. 1). 2 *nec praeripiam tamen.*

2, 5 **κινδυνώδη** Cf. 326 (XIII. 19). 1 *tu* ἀκίνδυνα *esse scribis.*
6 **haec** Sc. *cura.*

187 (IX. 18)

Probably written immediately after the interview with Caesar and dispatched early on the 29th. C. had repeatedly promised to write straight (*statim, continuo*) after the talk.

1, 3 **putaramus** As a matter of fact C. had *not* expected Caesar to be 'easy': cf. 183 (IX. 15). 3 *vix enim spero mihi hunc veniam daturum*: 186 (IX. 17). 1 *nec dubito quin a me contendat ad urbem veniam.* Atticus evidently had, and C. politely associates himself with the mistake (see on §3).

12 **aut non veniendum** Perhaps to be placed with δ after *adessem.* If the order of the paradosis is sound, 'notio dicendi post interiecta illa *aut non veniendum* quasi rursus emergit'. So Sjögren (*Symbolae Phil. O. A. Danielsson dicatae*, p. 372), comparing *inter alia Comm. Pet.* 3 (where however Watt prints Bücheler's conjecture) and Prop. III. 4. 12 ff.

2, 2 **ἥρως Celer** The best correction Lehmann ever made. Of the implausible guesses which jostle one another in Boot's or T.–P.'s notes the less said the better. Atticus would naturally be interested to hear of his brother (?)-in-law (cf. 29 (IV. 18). 5 n.) in Caesar's company. No less naturally ἥρως follows on νέκυια. Lehmann (*De Cic. ad Att.* pp. 210 ff.) did not explain just how he took his own restoration, which others have misunderstood. It is not that 'Pilius is a sort of hero in the midst of the "rabble rout"' or that he appeared 'der Verworfenste aus diesem ganzen "Orcus"'; he is called a hero, not without sarcasm, simply as participating in the νέκυια.

3 **Servi filius** Cf. 97 (V. 4). 1 n., also 189 (IX. 19). 2; 191 (X. 1*a*); 194 (X. 3*a*). 2.

Titini Cf. 172 (IX. 6). 6; 176 (IX. 9). 1; 189 (IX. 19). 2; 194 (X. 3*a*). 2. Lambinus' *Tulli* would be quite unwarranted even if Vulcatius Tullus had sent his son to Brundisium (but see on 194 (X. 3*a*). 2).

4 **sex legiones** Sc. *sunt* (rather than *habet*): cf. 130 (VII. 7). 6 *nunc legiones XI, equitatus tantus quantum volet* sqq.; 156 (VIII. 4). 3 *cum essent cohortes quinque*; *Fam.* VI. 18. 2 *exemplum Paciaeci litterarum, in quo erat illas XI esse legiones*; 353 (XII. 52). 1. *quippe hominum* CIↃ CIↃ.

6 **hoc fuerat extremum** Cf. §4 *extremum fuit de congressu nostro.* These words are certainly not to be expelled with Meutzner as a gloss on κατακλείς. *fuerat* is not a 'Tempusverschiebung' for the perfect (cf. K.–S. I, pp. 140 f.), but implies 'it had been settled (between us) that....': cf. Ter. *Hec.* 570 *hoc mi unum ex plurimis miseriis reliquum fuerat malum*; Liv. XXX. 30. 3

si hoc ita fato datum erat ut. . .ad pacem petendam venirem, laetor te mihi sorte potissimum datum a quo peterem. extremum = American 'deadline'.

3, 1 **καταχλείς** *clausula*: cf. 23 (II. 3). 4.

3 **vidisti. . .scripseras?** To be taken in one of two ways: (*a*) 'Have you seen Caesar as your letters pictured him (i.e. *facilem*)?' That makes doubtful, but not certainly impossible Latin (see on 125 (VII. 2). 3 *adulescentem ut nosti*). The question is then ironical, rubbing in Atticus' misjudgement of Caesar's attitude. (*b*) 'Have you "seen the great man", as you put it?' This gives *virum* its proper value and seems on the whole the better interpretation: cf. the forceful use of *videre* in *Catil.* I. 8 *nihil agis, nihil moliris, nihil cogitas quod ⟨non⟩ ego non modo audiam sed etiam videam planeque sentiam.* Atticus might well be curious to have a vivid account of Caesar and have written something like *omnia perscribas velim, ut virum non modo audiam sed etiam videam*. But his letters would have to be resurrected for certainty.—Editors have made havoc, treating *vidisti. . .ingemuisti?* as an imaginary interjection by Atticus with *certe* as C.'s answer. Against this (*a*) *vidisti. . .scripseras*, whether question or statement, is next to nonsense in Atticus' mouth. 'So you have seen him as you wrote that you would?' (the most natural way of taking it) might be in place if there were any implication of surprise as in 95 (V. 2). 2 '*non vidisti igitur hominem?*' *inquies*, but there can be none. C. had made up his mind (on Atticus' advice) to face Caesar as long back as the 11th (172 (IX. 6). 1), and in the intervening letters there is never any doubt on the point: cf. e.g. 183 (IX. 15). 1 *eum cum videro, Arpinum pergam*. On the other hand the common interpretation 'talem qualem scripseras, audacem et in victoria insolentem' (Boot) does not square with §1 *illa fefellerunt facilem quod putaramus*. Manutius' view that *virum* is opposed to *hominem* ('ut Atticus id verbum usurpet quo Cicero in epistola quadam usus erat, cum scriberet fortasse sic: *Ego cum virum videro*; ἐμφατικῶς de Caesare') is clearly useless as an explanation, though *virum* probably does convey something approximate to 'the great man'. (*b*) Why should C. use this device of question and answer to tell Atticus that he groaned? And when did he groan? Not during the interview, presumably. The idea of his groaning afterwards is odd to my mind, especially as he was very well satisfied with his own part in it (§1 fin.). *ingemiscere* occurs seven times elsewhere in the Letters, always of an immediate reaction to some thought or piece of news or event. Three times C. imagines his correspondent groaning at something in his own letter: 10 (I. 1). 1 *puto te in hoc aut risisse aut ingemuisse*; 147 (VII. 23). 1 *et non omnes nostra corpora opponimus? in quo tu quoque ingemiscis*; Q. *Fr.* II. 9. 2 *verebor ne quando ego tibi, cum sum una, molestus sim. video te ingemuisse.* Similarly here.

This I still think the best way to take the passage. But another possibility may be mentioned. We might write *vidisti igitur virum, ⟨aut⟩, ut scripseras, ingemuisti certe* (see App. Crit.). 'So you have seen the great man, or at any rate groaned, as you wrote you would.' But the implication as to what Atticus wrote in his letter seems less probable thus.

4 **certe** Even if C. had not succeeded in making Atticus *see* Caesar plain the account was *at any rate* evocative enough to distress him.

5 †**Pelanum** Not *Pedanum*, since Pedum seems to have lain 19 miles from Rome on the road to Praeneste—it had probably ceased to exist as a town, though the *regio Pedana* remained (cf. Hor. *Epist.* I. 4. 2 and Schol.). Caesar, moving Romewards along the Via Appia, would not be going there.

Arpinum Sc. *profectus sum* (epistolary perfect).

inde After a place-name obviously local, not temporal. If, as has sometimes been supposed, the letter had been written from Arpinum, C. would have said *hinc.*

6 **λαλαγεῦσαν** The spring swallow, from Leonidas of Tarentum's poem, *Anth. Pal.* x. 1. It starts ὁ πλόος ὡραῖος· καὶ γὰρ λαλαγεῦσα χελιδὼν | ἤδη μέμβλωκεν, χὠ χαριεὶς Ζέφυρος. (cf. 174 (IX. 7). 5 n.).

tu malim sqq. Mention of the swallow recalls Atticus' optimistic forecast of Caesar's attitude; C., let us suppose him to have written, having settled matters comfortably with Caesar, might then sit back and wait for the 'twitterer' (cf. 174 (IX. 7). 5). Otherwise the exhortation to 'let bygones be bygones' is meaningless (Atticus certainly must not be supposed to be telling C. that 'it was too late to join Pompey now': cf. 177 (IX. 10). 9; 189 (IX. 19). 2 *pergamus igitur quo placet* sqq.). *malum*, 'confound it!', must be rejected, though the form of prohibition *ne agas* is acceptable in a common saying (cf. K.–S. I, p. 188). Boot (*Mnemos.* 18 (1890), pp. 356 ff.) urged that C. always follows this exclamation with *iste* except in *Rosc Am.* 56 (where he emends). A more conclusive objection is that C., like others, only uses it in questions.

7 **illum** Pompey.

4, 1 **sed** Resumptive.

2 **extremum fuit** *de congressu nostro* is practically substantival, **τὸ τῆς συνόδου.**

188 (VIII. 9)

The letter replies to one from Atticus reporting unfavourable comment in Rome upon C.'s letter to Caesar, 178A (IX. 11A) of 19 or 20 March, which had been widely circulated. There can therefore be no question of following the MSS, in which it makes the first part of 160 (VIII. 9*a*) of 25 February; and *prid. Kal.* at the end has to be 31 March. C. must have written it not long before that date, since time has to be allowed (*a*) for 178A (IX. 11A) to reach

Caesar on his way from Brundisium to Rome, (*b*) for Caesar to send it on to Rome and for its dissemination there, and (*c*) for Atticus' comments to reach C. As there are no blank days in C.'s series to Atticus between 23 and 28 March inclusive, the date will be 29 or 30 March; more likely the latter, as 187 (IX. 18) was probably dispatched on the morning of the 29th. The place will be somewhere intermediate between Formiae and Arpinum.

1, 5 **non videbar...dicerem** Cf. *Fam.* XV. 21. 4 *in excitando autem et in acuendo plurimum valet si laudes eum quem cohortere.*

7 **cum...hortabar** Sjögren (Χάριτες *Fr. Leo dargebracht*, p. 290) defends *quo* as = *quo modo*. But praise of Caesar's wisdom was hardly a method of exhorting, though it might be called a method of persuading. And the choice between *quo* and *quō* is almost free.

10 **non est de pace sqq.** This is in fact the only possible interpretation of C.'s words in 178A (IX. 11A). 3, though a stupid or malevolent reader might easily misunderstand them.

2, 3 **scribens** The participle is loosely used as though *haec verba posuit* vel sim. were to follow. C. refers to Pompey's letter in reply to L. Caesar's message, actually composed by Sestius (141 (VII. 17). 2; cf. 150 (VII. 26). 2).

4 **amplioribusne** C. seems to be perversely understanding *amplissimi* as 'greater than all besides'; Sestius-Pompey of course meant 'very great'.

5 **ita tempus ferebat** Watt strangely punctuates as a question.

6 **vos duo tales** Atticus and Sex. Peducaeus. Understand *obviam itis* (or *ituri estis*)—as C. could not yet have heard reports of Caesar's arrival at the capital he must allude to an intention expressed in Atticus' letter. In the event the conduct of the pair did not lack *gravitas*, so at least C. declares in 191 (X. 1*a*).

quo...unde I.e. *in Hispanias* (not *ad urbem*) *a Brundisio* (i.e. *a Pompeio oppugnando*): cf. Sen. *Ep.* 29. 9 *qui intellegis unde quo evaseris.* Boot's conjecture enfeebles *quid acturo.*

189 (IX. 19)

Arrived at Arpinum on the 31st, C. will have celebrated his son's majority the next day and written this letter that evening or on the morning of 2 April: cf. §2 *senatus consulta facta quaedam iam puto*, with reference to the meeting called for 1 April (186 (IX. 17). 1).

1, 4 **ἀναθεώρησις** L.–S.–J. distinguish two senses, 'close examination' ('further reflection') and '*attention attracted* by an event', quoting this passage, 369 (XIV. 5). 1 and 370 (XIV. 16.) 2. The first is well attested both for the noun and for ἀναθεωρέω, the second has no support outside C. The two latter passages are in effect one, referring to Dolabella's lapse into grace in

April 44: *magnam* ἀναθεώρησιν *res habet* and again *o Dolabellae nostri magnam* ἀριστείαν! *quanta est* ἀναθεώρησις! There L.–S.–J.'s second sense fits better than here, but the evidence of contemporary usage to be found in three passages of Diodorus points to something rather different: XIII. 35. 4 μεγάλης δὲ οὔσης κατὰ τὴν νομοθεσίαν ἀναθεωρήσεως, *ibid.* ἔστι δὲ κατὰ τὴν λέξιν σύντομος καὶ πολλὴν τοῖς ἀναγινώσκουσιν ἀπολείπων ἀναθεώρησιν, (cf. Longin. 7. 3 ὅταν . . .μηδ' ἐγκαταλείπῃ τῇ διανοίᾳ πλεῖον τοῦ λεγομένου τὸ ἀναθεωρούμενον), XXIV (*excerpt. de Virt. et Vit.* p. 605) ἑκατέρα μὲν οὖν ἀπόφασις ἐδόκει τῷ συνεδρίῳ μεγάλην ἔχειν ἀναθεώρησιν (exactly parallel to C.'s *magnam* ἀναθεώρησιν *habet*). In these passages the ordinary sense of 'reflexion' is transferred from the thinker to the thing thought about, so that we get something like 'food for thought', 'thought-provoking quality'. So in C.

8 **civili nefario bello** Cf. 161D (VIII. 11D). 6 n.

10 **neque. . .putavi** The propriety of *neque. . .numquam* (cf. K.–S. I, pp. 827 f.) need not be canvassed, since neither *numquam* nor *umquam* has any business here. The following *numquam* accounts for the interpolation.

2, 1 **pergamus sqq.** A splenetic passage in the style of 167 (IX. 1). 3 f.

3 **una fugissemus** Sc. *Roma.* Cf. 213 (XI. 3). 3 n.

10 **Vulcati sententiam** No doubt this was in favour of opening negotiations with Pompey. Such a motion was in fact passed with Caesar's approval (*B.C.* I. 33. 1), and Atticus will have told C. that Vulcatius meant to put it (cf. 190 (X. 1). 2). What follows is bitter sarcasm in tune with the angry and contemptuous tone of the whole passage: 'After all, I need not worry which particular motion is passed. They are all in a tale (i.e. professing to desire peace, but really only concerned to protect themselves by truckling to Caesar). Though to be sure Servius will be very savage'—Sulpicius, as C. well knew, was the most innocuous of men. C. had no faith in these peace proposals (cf. 191 (X. 1*a*) *simulationem esse apertam*) and a poor opinion of Vulcatius' conduct, if, as seems very probable, he is the *emptus pacificator* and *nummarius* of the next letter.

12 **Cn. Pompeium** παθητικῶς: cf. 179 (IX. 12). 3.

13 **Pontio Titiniano** Cf. 176 (IX. 6). 6 n.

14 **hic** Titinius *père*. A relatively unimportant Senator might be afraid for his personal safety (though the concession is probably ironical: cf. 171 (IX. 5). 3), but for a patrician Consular like Sulpicius, on reasonably good terms with Caesar, that excuse would not wash.

ille vero— Aposiopesis, as Corradus said, rather than a question, as usually printed.

3, 3 **boni cives** Cf. 167 (IX. 1). 3 *cedamus igitur et ut boni cives simus bellum Italiae terra marique inferamus.*

infestum habebimus Cf. 409 (XVI. 1). 3 *Dymaeos. . .mare infestum habere nil mirum*; *Rep.* III. 24 *mare haberet infestum uno myoparone*. Similarly with *agros. . .vias* (*Tull.* 19), *oram* (Liv. XXXIV. 36. 3).

4, 1 **Cephalioni** Cf. 149 (VII. 25). n.

190 (X. 1)

1, 1 **Laterium** Cf. 77 (IV. 7). 3 n.

2 **ruinas** The collapse at Corfinium and to follow.

4 **Sexto etiam** *enim* in the MSS is accounted for by *enim* preceding, as in 164 (VIII. 14). 3 and 409 (XVI. 1). 5. It is just possible to understand with T.–P. '[I will not say I merely value], for I am delighted with the approval of Peducaeus', but C. would normally have written *nam* rather than *enim* in such a case.

5 **patris** Cf. 9 (I. 4). 1 n.

9 **μὴ μὰν κ.τ.λ.** Hector's words to himself (*Il.* XXII. 304). If the omission of ἀπολοίμην in the first line is genuine, it is probably due to the impropriety of the first person, though that did not prevent C. from writing it in *Fam.* XIII. 15. 2. T.–P. explain that it is left out because 'had C. on the 5th of December taken the less vigorous course, it would have been the course more likely to ensure his own safety'; but what can be understood with μέγα ῥέξας τι except ἀπόλοιο?

11 **vivit auctoritas** Cf. *Phil.* II. 12. *Q. Catulus, cuius semper in hac re publica vivet auctoritas.*

simillimus Cf. *Fin.* II. 58 *Sex. Peducaeus Sex. f., is qui hunc nostrum reliquit effigiem et humanitatis et probitatis suae filium.*

2, 2 **emptum pacificatorem** Whom? Curio (hardly the man for such a role), Balbus (not a Senator), L. Piso, and M. Lepidus have been proposed. But in all probability it is Vulcatius Tullus, as suggested by Corradus (though he preferred Sulpicius Rufus). He was expected to move for peace negotiations in the Senate (189 (IX. 19). 2). C.'s comments may be tinged with jealousy (cf. §3 and the next letter).

3 **consessu** Cf. *Fam.* IV. 1. 1 *in senatum sive potius in conventum senatorum.*

4 **meum** Sc. *consilium*, taking up *tuum consilium* above. There is some awkwardness in that *consilium* has to change sense from 'advice' to 'plan', so that *me* or *meum* ⟨*animum*⟩ or *me* ⟨*animo*⟩ may be right.

5 **qui enim. . .censes?** Wesenberg cites Q. *Fr.* I. 1. 17 *iam qui in eius modi rebus. . .cautus esse velim ac diligens, quo me animo in servis esse censes?*

Flavio If this is L. Flavius, Tr. Pl. 60, Pr. 58 (cf. 18 (I. 18). 6 n.), he must be supposed to have deserted his former patron, Pompey. In the event this appointment, with two legions, went to Curio (Caes. *B.C.* I. 30.

2). According to Appian (*B.C.* II. 40) and Plutarch (*Cat. Min.* 53) Cato was driven out of Sicily by Asinius Pollio (presumably sent in advance by Curio: cf. Broughton, p. 266); hence *Asinio* (Corradus).

8 **Solonis** Cf. Plut. *Sol.* 20, etc.

ut puto ⟨iam⟩ etiam mei The MS text can hardly be taken as an incidental profession of philhellenism, though C. does call Albucius *Graecum hominem* in *Prov. Cons.* 15 and was himself called Γραικὸς καὶ σχολαστικός in his earlier days (Plut. *Cic.* 5). He evidently meant that he too was now thinking of taking up residence in Athens. Hence Gronovius' *iam iam* for *etiam* (which is also sacrificed in Orelli's *et, ut puto, iam mei*). But *etiam* has its function, and I doubt if *iam iam* for *iam iamque* (as distinct from cases like *Phil.* II. 87 *iam iam minime miror* sqq.) is Ciceronian Latin.

11 **alterum** Ambiguous only in form, since Atticus could not fail to understand that C. was more determined to shun Caesar's party than Pompey's. This passage contains the first hint of a project more distinctly outlined in 198 (x. 7). 1 *nec tamen in acie ⟨me⟩ sed Melitae aut alio in loco simili ⟨vel⟩ oppidulo futurum puto.*

praeripiam Cf. 186 (IX. 17). 1 *sed quid praeripio?*

3, 2 **omnino** Concessive, answered by *sed tamen.*

4 **exspoliare...Pompeium** In Spain.

5 **nisi...quiescat** Ironical. C. feels sure that Caesar is *not* going to hold up his military plans.

nummarius The *emptus pacificator* of §2. *summarius*, a senseless mediaevalism, has had a remarkable vogue.

7 **sed tamen...σκεμμάτων** Many correctors have tried their hands here and many editors obelize; not so Sjögren, content to replace *sit* ων by *est* τῶν and with *probi est* to understand σκέψασθαι. The first step towards even an approximate reconstruction is to place a question mark after *probi est* (*hoc ipsum* signifies activity as a negotiator, *ire et redire*). The next is to understand σκεμμάτων as a partitive genitive of a kind not uncommon in Greek. C.'s *meaning* is then plain enough. 'It is a great question' (cf. 145 (VII. 21). 3 *ego quid agam* σκέμμα *magnum*) 'and one of the highest political relevance' (cf. 131 (VII. 8). 3 *est* πολιτικὸν σκέμμα *rectumne sit* sqq.; 132 (VII. 9). 2 *hoc* διευκρινήσεις πρόβλημα *sane* πολιτικόν) 'whether', etc. This might have been expressed in Latin *magna est quaestio et ex maxime civilibus*; with the Greek genitive it might have been *magnum est* σκέμμα *et* τῶν πολιτικωτάτων. As we have it, σκεμμάτων is attracted by a bold metathesis into the case of πολιτικωτάτων (σκέμμα (Orelli) for σκεμμάτων gets rid of this). As for *est* and *et*, I prefer the arrangement in the text to an earlier proposal *et magnum est et* τῶν or Orelli's *magnum est et* τῶν; but there is not much to choose.

11 **non puto** *non curo* (cf. *Sull.* 73 *non possunt omnes esse patricii; si verum quaeris, ne curant quidem*) is belied by *nihil enim. . .maioris consili esset* below.

12 **dixi** Cf. 187 (IX. 18). 1.

15 **boni viri et civis** High praise for a Caesarian, repeated in 203 (X. 11). 4.

16 **sola adhuc** I.e. since the war began. So probably above *nihil mihi adhuc accidit*.

191 (X. 1*a*)

Certainly a new letter. The first paragraph is plainly in answer to one just received.

1 **gravitatem** C. will have had Atticus' account of his and Peducaeus' meeting with Caesar: cf. 188 (VIII. 9). 2.

3 **†macum** Possibly the remains of a Greek word or words, though none that have been suggested have any plausibility. There is something to be said for Reid's *Mucianum* with reference to the Pontifex Maximus killed by the Marians because he urged peace with Sulla (*Rosc. Am.* 33; cf. 153 (VIII. 3). 6; 179 (IX. 12). 1; 183 (IX. 15). 2). Atticus may have warned C. against a similar fate. But the change is substantial, and an intrinsically neutral word does not quite fit the implications of *tam re. . .quam verbo*: cf. Sen. *Dial.* XII. 5. 6 *nunc in his quae mala vocantur nihil tam terribile ac durum invenio quam opinio vulgi minabatur. verbum quidem ipsum persuasione quadam et consensu iam asperius ad aures venit et audientes tamquam triste et execrabile ferit* sqq. It should be noted that *mortis instar* does not imply any previous reference to death. C. uses this expression freely for anything eminently disagreeable.

5 **ἄλη** For the metaphorical sense 'wandering of mind, distraction' L.–S.–J. cite only Eur. *Med.* 1285, on which D. L. Page has 'I observe no parallel. . .; and *literal* wandering is by no means out of place here'. If C.'s commentators were right this would be a parallel, but they are wrong: cf. 153 (VIII. 3). 3 *turpissima in qua sumus fuga* and the passages there cited.

10 **istum** Sulpicius Rufus. As he did not send his son to Brundisium to negotiate peace but to serve in Caesar's army (cf. 189 (IX. 19). 2; 194 (X. 3*a*). 2), the first *de pace* should be omitted as a copyist's anticipation (as irony it would be fatuous). Boot starts the parenthesis after *misit*, but I think *de pace* is better taken with *legatum iri*: cf. 193 (X. 3) *ecqui essent ad Pompeium. . .de pace legati*. For the positive *legatum iri arbitor* implied in the following negative cf. *Fin.* I. 2 *veritus ne movere hominum studia viderer, retinere non posse*; *Acad.* II. 126 *an Stoicis ipsis inter se disceptare, cum his non licebit?* In the outcome no envoys were sent because, according to Caesar (*B.C.* I. 33. 1), nobody was willing to take upon himself the risk of such a mission.

192 (x. 2)

Perhaps dispatched from Laterium immediately after receipt of Atticus' letter on the morning of 5 April (§1), in which case *sustinui* is epistolary perfect for future. Alternatively C. may have written the letter after arrival at Arcanum and dispatched it on the 6th. In that case it is, as usually supposed, the *epistulam longiorem* of 194 (x. 3*a*). 1. But in fact it is only very slightly longer than 194 (x. 3*a*), so possibly the longer letter is lost.

1, 2 **et inde** Sc. *profecturus*, southwards to Cumae. I see no advantage in *ut* (Wesenberg) for *et*.

3 **in Arcano** Cf. 94 (v. 1). 3 n.

5 **possent** Cf. K.–S. II, p. 202.

λαλαγεῦσα Cf. 187 (IX. 18). 3 n.

6 **stat** T.–P. compare 58 (III. 14). 2 *nos in Asiam convertemus, neque adhuc stabat quo potissimum. scio* is another possible substitute for *est*: cf. 38 (II. 18). 3 n.

2, 5 **Dionysium sqq.** In 208 (x. 16). 1 C. says that he was informed in a letter of Atticus' received at Arpinum that Dionysius would be coming to see him and would do what he wished. From his language here it is obvious that this letter had not yet reached him, so that *Arpini* in 208 (x. 16). 1 is probably a lapse of memory. Otherwise we must suppose that C. returned to Arpinum before he left for Cumae.

8 **nolo** Cf. 184 (IX. 15). 5 *nec tamen in hoc tibi quicquam oneris impono.*

193 (x. 3)

4 **ex senatus consulto** Cf. Caes. *B.C.* I. 33. 1.

5 **cum...scire cuperem** *cum* is the paradosis, so that the vulgate *ut ...scirem* is less 'scientific' than Lambinus' conjecture.

9 **a.d. VII Id.** Modern editors begin the next letter with this date.

194 (x. 3*a*)

1, 1 **epistulam...longiorem** Perhaps 192 (x. 2), or perhaps not: see there.

2 **Regia** Caesar's official residence as Pontifex Maximus on the east side of the Forum. Rosenberg (*RE.* s.v.) distinguishes between this and the *domus publica* mentioned in Suet. *Iul.* 46 as Caesar's residence after his election, considering the former as merely an *Amtshaus*. It appears from this passage that Caesar did enter the *pomerium* at this time. Cf. also 195 (x. 4). 8 n. (*Metellum*).

3 **istam reprehensionem** Generally, of compliance to Caesar (cf. 188 (VIII. 9)), rather than with reference to the interview at Formiae, at which C. had in fact shown himself far from compliant.

5 **etiam si nihil erit** Cf. 285 (XII. 44). 4 *etiam si nihil erit quod scribas... tamen id ipsum scribas velim te nihil habuisse quod scriberes, dum modo ne his verbis.*

2, 2 **facile patior.** A better punctuation than *facile patior quod scribit* sqq.: cf. 147 (VII. 23). 3 *cui* (sc. *Caesari*) *nos valde satisfacere multi ad me scripserunt, quod patior facile, dum* sqq. There was no obvious reason, none at least that C. would have cared to admit, why the remark about Servius and Titinius should have given him pleasure.

3 **Titinium** Cf. 187 (IX. 18). 2 and 189 (IX. 19). 2, where Servius and Titinius are similarly bracketed. Vulcatius Tullus on the other hand is distinguished from Servius in the latter passage, which would run very oddly if he too had sent his son to Brundisium. There is not much difference between *tullium* and *titinium* in minuscule.

195 (X. 4)

After 7 April the extant correspondence lapses for a week, during which C. left Arcanum and arrived in Cumae (§7).

1, 12 **quos propter omnia** For the 'ambiguous' metastrophe cf. 199 (X. 8). 8 *quos contra me senatus...armavit*; *Top.* 32 *quaerentibus eis quos ad id pertineret*; Housman on Man. I. 245. There is of course no real ambiguity.

2, 1 **nec remittit aliquid** 'Pronomen *aliquid* positum in sententia generaliter negante uno et altero exemplo defenditur (obscurato pronomine et cum verbo prope in unam notionem conflato), velut pro Mil. 88: *ne cum solebat quidem id facere, in privato eodem hoc aliquid profecerat*' (Madvig on *Fin.* II. 87). It is quasi-adverbial as in 322 (XIII. 14–15). 1 *etiam ad te aliquid pertinet* (cf. *Fin.* IV. 77 *urgent tamen et nihil remittunt*). Both *remittit* and *ingravescit* have medical associations (cf. *ardet*), though whether C. could have used these verbs unambiguously *sensu medico* with the invalid (not the disease) as subject I should not like to say. The younger Pliny (*Ep.* II. 20. 5) has *mox ingravescit* of a sick woman.

2 **expulit** Sc. *socium*. I do not feel that a supplement like *generum* is required.

3, 4 **ille quidem** *illud* need not be substituted: cf. *Thes.* VII. 354. 21–8.

4, 3 **florentissima** Cf. *Pis.* 38 *nunc meam spoliatam fortunam conferam cum florente fortuna imperatoris.* The epithet may seem inappropriate to *Pompey's* fortunes in April 49. But Pompey was still a great man, a commander of armies, and perhaps destined to lead them victoriously back to Rome.

conflictati Cf. Nep. *Timol.* I. 2 *non simplici fortuna conflictatus est.* For the zeugma cf. K.–S. II, p. 565 b (also 331 (XIII. 23). 3; 368 (XIV. 14). 2 fin.).

5 **in illis libris** *de Republica* (the passage is lost): cf. 258 (VIII. 8). I.

5, 4 **XIIII annis** Even in 63, C. implies, he saw that Caesar was the real danger to the state.

10 **excruciat** Cf. on 235 (XI. 25). 3 *huius miserrimae facilitate confectus conflictor.*

13 **et exspecto** Needless to delete *et* or change to *sed*. This is another reason why C. should not write more at the moment—he is waiting for more information.

6, 2 **multa et magna** Cf. 212 (XI. 2). I.

3 **compressi** Not 'kept to myself'. C. argues now that indulgence was *not* after all the root of the trouble (so too in 202 (x. 11). 3), and that he himself had *not* been over-indulgent.

5 **celaremus** Possibly the letter itself, more probably their reactions.

6 **videremur** I now prefer this to *videmur*, which would be more natural if *te celaremus* made the main point; but *quidem* shows that it only leads up to *sed...reddidisse.*

hoc...iter To Rome, evidently; we have no details.

7 **simulatioque pietatis** Quintus will have made his mother an excuse for the trip—perhaps he had accompanied her back to Rome from Formiae: cf. 116 (VI. 2). 2 *ac mihi videtur matrem valde, ut debet, amare*; 117 (VI. 3). 8 *miram in eo pietatem...perspexi.* The common view that he pretended to be going to Rome in order to put in a good word for his father with the Caesarians is manifestly foolish. C. seems to have learned the truth in part from Atticus (§5 fin.), but also from some other source (Hirtius?).

9 **suis** I.e. *Caesaris.* Cf. *de Orat.* III. 109 *placeatne a Karthaginiensibus captivos nostros redditis suis recuperari?*

rationibus Cf. *Vat.* 38 *graviterque etiam se ferre praetorem aliquem esse factum qui a suis rationibus dissensisset*; *pro Cornelio*, fr. B. VI. 7 *exemplum... meis alienissimum rationibus.* This is what Quintus was alleged to have said: cf. 125 (VII. 2). 7 n. (*in me ingratissimi*).

10 **et haec ipsa timide** Sc. *scribo* (cf. 39 (II. 19). 5 *haec scripsi properans et mehercule timide*; 210 (x. 18). 2 *sed hoc quoque timide scribo*), not *egisse* (cf. Caes. *B.G.* v. 33. 1 *tum demum Titurius...trepidare et concursare cohortesque disponere, haec tamen ipsa timide*). C. is clearly not making a point in Quintus' favour.

natura Natural disposition, ἦθος.

11 **Hortensi filium** Cf. 117 (VI. 3). 9 n.

13 **vita** Not to be taken literally. C. cannot have seriously believed that his life or his brother's was in danger. There are comparable exaggerations in *post Red. ad Quir.* 13 and *Dom.* 23, where his 'blood' stands for his exile. Cf. also *Quinct.* 39 *hominis propinqui sanguinem vitamque eripere conatur*, where the stake was really Quinctius' property and good name (cf. 98 f.). Or is *de sua vita* practically a periphrasis for *de se*? Cf. Ov. *ex Pont.* IV. 1. 26 *nunc quoque nil subitis clementia territa fatis / auxilium vitae fertque feretque meae* and C. Bailey on Lucr. III. 420.

14 **huic tu, huic tu** The occasion warrants the *pathos*: cf. 17 (I. 17). 6 n. (*vidi enim, vidi*).

16 **minora** Sc. *quam deferuntur*: cf. Quint. *Inst.* V. 13. 10 *id. . .minus esse quam adversarius dicat.*

quid futurum sit Sc. *de Quinto filio.*

18 **diligentiam** The oddity of *consilium non deest ad diligentiam* is palliated by the preceding *ad severitatem* ('with a view to strictness'); for the combination Schmidt compares Cato, *Fam.* XV. 5. 3 *severitatem diligentiamque sociis et rei publicae praesta. indulgentiam* is only superficially attractive; further indulgence to Quintus was scarcely in C.'s mind at this moment.

19 **nunc** The sentence might have been expected to continue with something like *omnia erunt difficiliora.* Apparently the force is, 'as things stand, all I can say is that. . .'. But *haec* may be correct.

7, 1 a Curione. . .venire Cf. *Acad.* I. 1 *nuntiatum est nobis a M. Varrone venisse eum.*

8, 1 praeteriit C. resumes writing after his interview with Curio, who passed his villa on the 14th (not the 13th, as T.–P.), leaving word as he did so that he would soon be back.

8 **interitum** Cf. 135 (VII. 12). 4 *eum finem statuit.*

finem illi fore Cf. Liv. XXV. 11. 10 *isque finis Hannibali fuit ea parte arcem oppugnandi*, XXIX. 32. 9 *is finis Bucari* (dat.) *sequendi fuit.* But *belli* may be right.

9 **propius factum esse nihil** Sc. *quam ut Pompeius* (*Brundisi*) *interiret*; cf. *Q. Fr.* I. 2. 15 *propius nihil est factum quam ut occideretur*; *Verr.* II. 5. 94 *neque quicquam propius est factum quam ut illud Vticense exemplum. . . transferretur ad Syracusas*; *Cluent.* 59 *nec quicquam propius est factum quam ut illum persequeretur et. . .reduceret.* The words make excellent sense after *tribunum pl.*, but will do well enough where they are.

10 **Metellum** Cf. 172 (IX. 6). 3 n. He attempted to stop Caesar removing the state treasure from the *aerarium*, planting himself in front of the door, which Caesar was about to break down, and only gave way when his life was threatened (Plut. *Caes.* 35, etc.). It seems that despite his *imperium*

Caesar entered the city in April (he was not named Dictator until later in the year (*B.C.* II. 21. 5)): cf. 194 (x. 3*a*). 1 n.

9, 1 quem exitum Cf. *Sest.* 93 *o di immortales! quemnam ostenditis exitum nobis? quam spem rei publicae datis?*

3 **†esset** Evidently the remains of a pluperfect, whether *exisset* (cf. 198 (x. 7). 3 *Siciliaeque diffidens si Pompeius navigare coepisset*) or *accessisset* (cf. 199 (x. 8). 4 *navigabit...maximis classibus et ad Italiam accedet*).

4 **sex tui fasces** As Propraetor by Caesar's appointment (*B.C.* I. 30. 2), i.e. *legatus pro praetore*, Curio was entitled to put laurels on his lictors' fasces in virtue of his Imperator's victories in Gaul. Only as such he ought not to have had six fasces, the number appropriate to Praetors and Propraetors of the Senate's appointment, but some smaller number, probably five (cf. Mommsen, *St.* I, p. 385, n. 3). If however he had been appointed by senatorial decree he would have had a right to the six fasces but not to the laurels.

5 **surrupto** L. Metellus had been obstructing Caesar in the Senate by his veto (*B.C.* I. 33. 3: cf. Caelius, *Fam.* VIII. 16. 1 *his intercessionibus plane incitatus est*), which must have been particularly galling to the professed champion of tribunician rights. *surrupto* conveys some way of circumventing the veto, perhaps by taking a vote unexpectedly when Metellus was not present.

7 **a me...proficiscentur** These words are of course part of what Curio said to C., quoting Caesar, who is the implied subject of *inquit*—as Sjögren (*Symbolae phil. O. L. Danielsson dicatae*, p. 323) and others failed to understand.

8 **quia duodecim nolui** I.e. 'I could have had just as many as I pleased'. Under the Republic persons with consular *imperium* had twelve fasces, but no *legatus* could be *pro consule* and Curio's reply is flippant. Such niceties, he implies, were out of date.

10, 2 Philippum Cf. 183 (IX. 15). 4 n.

11, 3 an quo modo dixerit *quo modo* makes better sense as relative, with *facturus* understood, than as interrogative. C. wants to know how Consuls were to be appointed for 48: would Caesar wait for the end of the year, after which an Interrex could hold elections? Or would he have them created in some other way, as by elections held under a Praetor (cf. 176 (IX. 9). 3; 183 (IX. 15). 2)? Instead of putting the second alternative directly C. alludes to a remark of Caesar's (probably made during their interview at Formiae) that the Consulship for 48 was being offered to him, though he did not want it; this he thinks may be in Caesar's mind, i.e. to accept the offer on his own behalf or that of others.

5 **ad summam** *En fin de compte.*

6 **faceret** Modern editors down to 1961 discredit *faceret*, nearly all in favour of *facere solet*. But *quod nullo negotio* (= *facile*) *faceret* may stand as legitimate, if idiomatic, Latin for 'as he might easily do' (cf. 'as well he might'). An oath cost Curio nothing, but whether he spoke the truth was another matter. For *facile* with a potential subjunctive cf. e.g. 42 (II. 22). 6 *quod facile sentias*; *Fam.* I. 7. 3 *quod facile intellexerim*; Curt. VIII. 2. 35 *quod facile appareret*. If C. had been referring to the future he might have written *iurabit, quod nullo negotio faciat*.

7 **quid enim?...dic, quid?** Cf. *Verr.* II. 1. 143 *corriguntur leges censoriae. quid enim? video in multis veteribus legibus...vult aliquid eius modi C. Verres. dic, quid addidit?* But there *quid enim?* means 'what of that?' or 'why not?', here apparently amounts to *quid ais?* or *quid ita?* (τί δή;), *enim* simply emphasizing *quid* as in Ov. *Met.* III. 262 *profeci quid enim totiens per iurgia?* or Juv. VII. 158 *quid enim scio?*

8 **quod me cuperet sqq.** Cf. 185 (IX. 16). 3.

12 **quam ipse...suspicandum** The sense I take to be 'how much it goes against the grain to suspect him', but no plausible restoration exists and I have none to offer. I do not think that *invito* is from *invitare*.

14 **quam minimo** Sc. *nobis constet*. But *minimum* is very likely right.

12, 1 †optimus *Oppios* (cf. 136 (VII. 13). 5 n.) is usually printed: 'tu Oppios Terentiae conciliabis, a quibus nummos petat' (Boot: cf. 198 (X. 7). 3). But the sense assigned to *dabis* is unexampled, so the correction seems unsafe. Perhaps ⟨*ab*⟩ *Oppiis*, 'drawing upon the Oppii'.

nullum More natural than *vanum* (Boot) or *minimum* (Purser) and palaeographically about as good.

4 **ego ad te habebo** *statim*, like *verum* in §10, seems to have been interpolated from the adjacent line.

196 (X. 5)

1, 1 antea In a lost letter. Several may have disappeared from 8–13 April.

2, 4 quodam Cf. 152 (VII. 9). 3 *quidam* = *Pompeius*, and Sjögren, *Symbolae phil. O. S. Danielsson dicatae*, p. 336. Note that Quintus is not mentioned by name in the previous letter.

'Αρκαδίαν The first word of the Delphic Oracle's answer to the Spartans (Herod. I. 66): 'Αρκαδίην μ' αἰτεῖς · μέγα μ' αἰτεῖς · οὔ τοι δώσω. T.–P. do well to point out that if we did not happen to know the rest of the line the single word quoted by C. would not have been illuminating.

5 **molestior** Cf. 197 (X. 6). 2 *si sine illo possem, regerem; quod tu potes.*

sed ignosco; magnum, inquam, opus est. modestior appears in Sjögren's (and Moricca's) text, in what supposed sense I cannot imagine.

3, 1 commodius Cf. 124 (VII. 1). 8 *locutus enim erat cum iis commode*; 308 (XIII. 3). 2 *misi ad te epistulam, quia commode scripta erat.*

Vettienus A man of business mentioned from time to time in the letters of 49–44. The variant spellings of his name in the MSS seem to point to *Vetienus*, a form which also appears in the Codex Bernensis of Valerius Maximus (VI. 3. 3). But cf. *C.I.L.* VI. 18668 *Bettiena*. Canuleius cannot be identified. Caesar had a Legate of that name in 48 (*B.C.* III. 42. 3).

2 **neglegentiam** Casualness rather than carelessness: cf. 202 (x. 11). 5 *quod* ἀποτόμως *ad me scripserat de nummis curandis*. Vettienus apparently went straight ahead with the purchase without further reference to C., and when he did write his style was unduly curt. For this use of the word see on 161 (VIII. 11). 6.

7 **cui vellem addici** As representing the purchaser. He would probably be a slave: cf. 338 (XIII. 46). 3.

diem pecuniae Sc. *solvendae*: cf. *de Orat.* I. 168 *vetus atque usitata exceptio...'cuius pecuniae dies fuisset'* et sim. (*Thes.* v (i). 1059. 32).

8 **stomachosius** Cf. 202 (x. 11). 5 θυμικώτερον *eram iocatus*.

11 **itinere** It seems that Atticus was still thinking of going to Epirus: cf. 198 (x. 7). 1; 205 (x. 13). 3; 209 (x. 17). 4.

197 (x. 6)

If 198 (x. 7) is assigned to 22 April this letter belongs to one of the five days preceding.

1, 2 recte sit Madvig thought that *recitet et* must represent something like *ire certum est*. In that case *tamen* (Schmidt) rather than *et tamen* would be appropriate. But cf. 203 (x. 12). 2 *sit modo recte in Hispaniis*; 204 (x. 12*a*). 3 *recte esse in Hispaniis*; 205 (x. 13). 3 *si recte fuerit* (sc. *in Hispaniis*).

4 **et quia festinabam** Cf. 228 (XI. 17). 1 *eo brevior est, et quod eram missurus nostros.*

2, 1 fit...sedulo A common expression in Comedy: cf. *Fam.* II. 11. 2 *sed tamen sedulo fit et in primis a Patisco*. Since Quintus junior had not yet returned from Rome (cf. 198 (IX. 7). 3), perhaps *fiet* should be read, and *regemus* in 198 (x. 7). 3. Cf. however *relaxat* below and 195 (x. 4). 6 *sed ipsius videremur vitam insuavem reddidisse*. C.'s efforts to discipline Quintus presumably started from the discovery of the latter's letter to Caesar, before his journey to Rome.

nosti reliqua In *Fam.* VII. 28. 2 *nosti cetera* follows an unfinished quotation. Here the meaning is simply 'I need not go on': cf. *Fam.* XIV. 3. 5 *sin autem—sed nihil opus est reliqua scribere.*

2 **†dem** The vulgate *dein* is far from certain. Perhaps something more significant, e.g. *de meo* (sc. *filio*) or *de nave*, lies behind the variants.

et amice...me mones Cf. 20 (I. 20). 2 *quod ad me de re publica scribis, disputas tu quidem et amanter et prudenter*; 426 (XVI. 15). 4 *tu quidem et prudenter et amice suades ut* sqq.; *Fam.* XI. 21. 4 *quod mihi praecipis ut caveam...et sapienter et amicissime praecipis.*

4 **mirabilia** Here in praise. C. had a high opinion of his nephew's abilities: cf. 116 (VI. 2). 2 n. (*magnum*).

198 (x. 7)

§2 gives the closest indication of date. On 28 April C. received a letter from Ser. Sulpicius written after the arrival of his own messenger Philotimus in Rome (*Fam.* IV. 2. 1). Philotimus therefore can hardly have left Cumae later than the 22nd.

1, 1 Apuliam et Sipontum Apparently Atticus now proposed to go to Sipontum in Apulia, there perhaps to wait for a passport to Epirus (cf. 205 (x. 13). 3). From *tergiversationem* it would seem that he had been careful to get approval from the Caesarian authorities for the journey.

2 **nec tuam sqq.** This savours of special pleading for Atticus' benefit. C. did not really believe that the war was *simply* a struggle between dynasts.

10 **loco simili vel oppidulo** I.e. in some other small island or in some little town on the mainland. This seems a simpler way of dealing with the passage than those previously proposed. C. has the diminutive also in Q. *Fr.* II. 11. 2.

12 **immo...voluisset** See Appendix VI, p. 463.

13 **meliore tempore** 'Licet mihi tempestatem idoneam exspectare, quoniam dubitandum mihi non est ut aut mari Hadriatico Dolabella aut freto Siciliensi Curio meam umquam navigationem impediant' (Manutius).

14 **Fretensi** *Fretense* (*mare*) is ἅπ. λεγ., but *Fretum* for *fretum Siculum* is common.

2, 1 velle Understand *cognovi* from *spes iniecta est.* To take *velle* as dependent directly on *spes* makes *quaedam* otiose and gives less appropriate sense. C. had been told in writing (by Trebatius: cf. *Fam.* IV. 1. 1) of Sulpicius' desire for an interview. On account of the latter's ill health they had not met since C.'s return from the East (*ibid.*).

2 **Philotimum libertum** *Not* Terentia's freedman (mentioned in §3), but one of C.'s own: cf. 309 (XIII. 33). 1 *professus est Philotimus libertus; nosti, credo, librarium.*

3 **litteris** *Fam.* IV. 1.

sin autem—Cf. *Fam.* xiv. 3. 5 *sin autem—sed nihil opus est reliqua scribere.*

4 **erimus nos qui solemus** Cf. 223 (xi. 12). 3 *ego tamen is ero qui semper fui.*

3, 1 **mecum vixit** Not 'stayed with me'. The expression need not so imply (cf. *de Orat.* i. 191 *C. Aculeonem, qui mecum vivit semperque vixit*; *Lig.* 11 *ne nobiscum vivat, ne sit in patria* et sim.), and Curio had his own *Cumanum* (195 (x. 4). 7).

2 **putans. . .diffidens** Cf. 140 (vii. 16). 2 *Labienum secum habet non dubitantem de imbecillitate Caesaris copiarum.*

6 **quod timueramus** Cf. 195 (x. 4). 6.

8 **regimus** Cf. 197 (x. 6). 2 n. (*fit. . .sedulo*).

199 (x. 8)

1, 2 **quas intercipi** I.e. *de quibus epistulas intercipi*: cf. 13 (i. 13). 2 n.

2, 3 **fieri** *nec honestum nec tutum* (Lehmann) or something of the sort (rather than *nequit* or *posse nego*) has fallen out.

11 **et dubitantem** *nec* for *et* is unnecessary once C.'s meaning is understood, as it was in essentials by A. Frederking (*Philol.* 59 (1900), pp. 155 f.). C. disagrees with the view that he should lie low in Italy if Caesar wins in Spain because Caesar victorious will be worse than Caesar defeated; and, that much granted, it follows that it will be better to leave *now*, while Caesar is doubtful of success, than later, when he is confident of it. For, as the next sentence explains, once Caesar wins, massacre and confiscation will be the order of the day. The words *et. . .suis rebus* are relevant, not indeed to the hypothetical problem of what to do if Caesar wins in Spain, but to the actual problem which is the main theme of the letter, namely, whether to await the outcome there before taking action.

3, 1 **indignitas** 'Sense of indignity.' This might imply indignation (so Caelius, *Fam.* viii. 17. 2; Hirtius, *B.G.* viii. 44. 2, and often in Livy) or shame, as in *Pis.* 99 *fruar tamen tua et indignitate et timiditate*—here apparently the former.

3 **praesto** I.e. in Rome.

Cloelium Sex. Cloelius, formerly known as Clodius (cf. 30 (ii. 12). 2 n. (*Athenione*)). We do not know why he is called Atticus' client.

†Cateli See App. Crit. On C. Ateius cf. 91 (iv. 17). 4 n.

Plaguleium One of P. Clodius' lieutenants (*Dom.* 89), presumably exiled along with Cloelius in 52.

4 **necessarios** It is hard to say whom C. had in mind. Possibly Milo,

though Caesar did not recall him. P. Sulla, C. Antonius, and A. Gabinius had been clients, but were hardly *necessarii*. Messalla Rufus (Cos. 53) was a friend, but never so far as we know a client.

5 **dolore...dedecore** Because their rehabilitation would be illegal.

9 **cum periculo** Because Pompey might take vengeance.

4, 3 **Themistocleum** Cf. 134 (VII. 11). 3.

9 **adversabimur** *classibus* seems best deleted as a marginal gloss, prompted by *maximis classibus* above. Schmidt's interpretation 'shall I go on board ship and fight against Pompey?' would hardly have occurred to Atticus.

11 **solus** The reference can hardly be to C.'s Consulship, when he had the backing of all *boni*. I think with Shuckburgh that it is to the interview with Caesar at Formiae on 28 March, or perhaps to Caesar's pressure in general at that time and C.'s refusal to yield. The stand C. had taken would make cowardice in the future all the more discreditable, especially as there would be less excuse for it.

5, 6 **omnino** Concessive.

10 **idem** 'Eadem mente, in eadem opinione constantes' (Corradus). The common interpretation, 'how little there was to choose between them' is less to C.'s purpose.

12 **adsequar** The vulgate *adsequor* is not a necessary change; cf. K.–S. I, p. 145.

6, 2 **ab Atto** Naevio: cf. *Div.* II. 80; Liv. I. 36. 3. C. recurs to this motif in a letter to A. Caecina several years later (*Fam.* VI. 6. 3 ff.). For the preposition cf. *Thes.* I. 22. 69.

3 **de tyrannis** In *Rep.* VIII and IX; cf. C.'s *Rep.* I. 65 ff.

7 **tam cito** *tamen*, the paradosis, might be defended: the clemency and affluence were never more than a pretence, but even that had not lasted long. But there is little question of MS authority in such a case.

8 **utatur** *utetur* may be right, but cf. 343 (XIII. 40). 1 *quid faciat...?* (also *Verr.* II. 2. 192), Catull. 106. 2 *quid credat?* The third person is commoner with reference to the past, as *Verr.* II. 2. 139 *quis censor...legem metueret...?* (cf. K.–S. I, p. 181); Ov. *Met.* V. 211 *sed quid agat?* (historic present) et sim.

7, 5 **Sardanapali vicem in suo lectulo** The text is gravely suspect. *vicem* = 'like' is paralleled only in a fragment of Sallust (Nonius (Lindsay), p. 799), and *suo* can be defended only by taking *in suo lectulo* ('in one's own bed') as a proverbial expression (it was no doubt well worn: cf. 206 (X. 14). 3 *multo se in suo lectulo malle, quicquid foret*; *Fin.* II. 97 *philosophi autem in suis lectulis plerumque moriuntur*; *Nat. Deor.* III. 84 *in suo lectulo mortuus*). But perhaps *suo* should be replaced by *meo* or simply deleted (cf. *Fam.* IX. 18. 2 *nisi forte mori melius fuit. in lectulo, fateor; sed non accidit*). In any case C. must be following Clitarchus' version of Sardanapalus' end (Athen. xii. 530 a), according to which he died in old age after losing his empire.

6 **ut ait Thucydides** i. 138. 3. The quotation, no doubt from memory, contains several minor inaccuracies.

11 **quo modo...quid** If Themistocles had seen into the future correctly he would have found a way to avoid *invidia* and would not have made promises to the Great King which he could not fulfil (cf. 177 (ix. 10). 3 n.).

13 **nox** The truth of the story that Scipio Aemilianus was murdered is also implied in *Amic.* 41 and *Rep.* vi. 12, nor (*pace* Münzer, *RE.* iv. 1458. 27) is the contrary implied in *Amic.* 12.

15 **dies Sullanus** In 88: cf. 174b (ix. 7b). 2 *temporibus Milonianis*; 364 (xiv. 10). 1 *illo...Capitolino die.*

callidissimo Cf. *Nat. Deor.* iii. 80 *omnium perfidiosissimus.* This aspect of Marius is ignored in C.'s speeches: cf. R. Syme, *Sallust*, pp. 163 f.

17 **quo diximus** Sc. *confirmari*: cf. K.–S. ii, p. 288.

8, 2 **qui quidem...acerrimus** Cf. 204 (x. 12*a*). 3 *nihil inimicius quam sibi ipse.*

4 **tempus est** T.–P. compare 254 (xii. 18). 1 *longumque illud tempus cum non ero magis me movet quam hoc exiguum.* As they say, C. is thinking of posthumous fame, not of personal immortality.

8 **quos contra** Evidently including Caesar, in whose complicity with Catiline C. believed, despite his denial at the time (cf. *Off.* ii. 84; Plut. *Crass.* 13; also Suet. *Iul.* 9. 2). On the metastrophe cf. 195 (x. 4). 1 n.

ne quid...acciperet The words of the *senatus consultum ultimum.*

9, 3 **πλουδοκῶν** ἅπ. λεγ.

9 **domesticas tricas** Among others her pregnancy (cf. 210 (x. 18). 1).

10, 7 **Melitae** Actually C. had told Curio that he intended to go to Greece (196 (x. 4). 10), but the principle was the same.

civili bello Cf. *Fam.* ii. 16. 1 *ut...quod initio semperque fugi, civili bello interessem.*

9 **ad Misenum** Contrast 374 (xiv. 20). 2 *Misenum venit Antonius*; 377 (xv. 1). 2 *venit enim Misenum.* Antony's house would be in the neighbourhood of the town. If *Misenum* was adjectival, meaning the villa itself as in *Phil.* 48 and 73 (cf. *mons, portus Misenus, promunturium Misenum*), the preposition would be *in* not *ad.*

199a (x. 8a)

If Antony wrote from near by he probably wrote on 1 May; but the letter could have been sent from anywhere. Caesar had left him in charge of Italy.

1, 4 **famam...magni esse** *falsam agnosce(re)* could have arisen from a rewriting of *falsa magni esse*. But though dispensable the words are not altogether beside the point. Were anybody else involved, Antony would not trouble about a rumour he believed to be false, but his care for C. is such that he cannot rest easy without definitely recognizing it as false, i.e. getting a denial from C. himself. *quoque* and *quamvis sit falsa* show his anxiety to make it clear that he does not credit the report.

5 **trans mare** Cf. Ter. *Ad.* 274 *tam ob parvulam / rem paene ex patria!* But T.–P. rightly urge that so harsh an ellipse would be out of keeping with the style of the letter, which is careful if not commendable.

12 **ζηλοτυπίᾳ** Usually explained as a reference to C.'s election as Augur in 53. But Antony did not stand that year, according to himself because he retired in C.'s favour, according to C. for less creditable reasons (*Phil.* II. 4). It is better to admit ignorance. In 44 C. attributes their partial estrangement to the enmity between himself and the connexions of Clodius (cf. his letter to Antony, 267B (XIV. 13B). 5), but that was after Antony's marriage to Clodius' widow some years later.

15 **maxime in suis** Perhaps to be taken together: cf. 176 (IX. 9). 4 *te, qui maxime meus.*

2, 5 **Calpurnium** Probably an unknown, and obviously *not* C.'s old enemy L. Piso Caesoninus (Cos. 58), who would hardly be at Antony's disposal for such a purpose and would need no such introduction to C. The L. Piso of *Phil.* X. 13 (also suggested) would have been called L. Piso rather than Calpurnius. Similarly with Calpurnius Bestia of *Phil.* XI. 11, etc.

199B (X. 8B)

Caesar evidently wrote about the same time as Caelius (200A (X. 9A)), so possibly from the country of the Intimilii in Liguria (*ibid.* introd. note). The repetitive style (*pro nostra benevolentia petendum...pro iure nostrae amicitiae a te peto*, *amicitia* three times, *abesse* three times) and the obliquities of the last sentence are signs of hasty composition.

2, 4 **periculi causa** They could not be sure that their neutrality would be respected. That might apply both to those who joined Pompey for fear of what Pompey might do to them later on if they did not (a fear no longer in C.'s case since, in Caesar's view, Pompey had as good as lost the war) and to those who feared (needlessly of course) Caesar himself, like Ap. Pulcher and the Marcelli (cf. 167 (IX. 1). 4). That Caesar is thinking rather of the latter group appears from the following words, which aim to show that C. has adequate evidence of Caesar's good intentions towards himself.

5 **vitae...iudicio** Caesar's *vita*, which of late particularly had shown

him as a man of mercy, is one ground for reassurance. The other is *amicitiae iudicium*, a difficult phrase which in the context seems best interpreted as 'the (favourable) judgment (on your part) implied in our friendship (i.e. in your friendship for me)'. *iudicium* is commonly so used: see T.–P. on *Fam.* X. I. 4 (Vol. VI, p. 7) and to the passages there collected add *Fam.* VI. 17. 2 *necessitudine nostra iudiciisque patris tui de me*, X. 3. 2 *familiaritatem cum studio meo tum iudicio tuo constitutam*, 26. 2 *non magis te quam de te iudicium reprehendo meum*; Sen. *Ben.* I. 15. 5 *Crispus Passienus solebat dicere quorundam se iudicium malle quam beneficium...et subiciebat exempla: 'malo' aiebat 'divi Augusti iudicium, malo Claudii beneficium'* (also *Cluent.* 196; *Prov. Cons.* 41; *Phil.* XIV. 13; *Leg.* III. 1; Mart. X. 73. 10). So *iudicare: Amic.* 85 *cum iudicaris, diligere oportet; non, cum dilexeris, iudicare*; Sen. *Ep.* 3. 2 *post amicitiam credendum est, ante amicitiam iudicandum.* In choosing Caesar as his friend C. had committed himself to a favourable view of Caesar's character—the commitment was mutual of course, but Caesar's side is not really to the point.

200 (X. 9)

Philotimus arrived at Cumae with Caesar's letter the same day, presumably 2 May, that C. received Antony's letter 199A (X. 8A): cf. 199 (X. 8). 10; 199A (X. 8A). 2 fin.

1, 2 saepe...mentientis Cf. 174 (IX. 7). 6. Philotimus was not likely to colour his news in favour of Caesar.

4 **repressisset** Because of the resistance of Massilia; cf. 201 (X. 10). 4. *tuo* in M may indeed represent *immo*, though it is unlikely to have been 'das misverstandene Siegel für *immo* = m̊'.

7 **in Germaniam** Cf. 197 (X. 6). 3. There is no need for *Galliam.* Pompey was supposed to be marching to Germany *en route* for Gaul.

8 **dum quid in Hispania** 'Dum sciamus quod [quid?] in Hispania actum sit' (Manutius).

2, 2 meo...capite I.e. *mei capitis periculo*: cf. Liv. II. 12. 10 *ut in singulas horas capite dimices tuo. de capite* would be more usual.

6 **unicum filium** Caelius wrote *si filius unicus* (200A (X. 9A). 2), so that this is an obvious correction of the paradosis *unicam filiam*. But I do not feel quite certain that C. himself did not make the substitution unconsciously (cf. 331 (XIII. 23). 3 n.). Tullia certainly meant more to him than Marcus, and he may have had Antony's letter in mind (199A (X. 8A). 1 *cum tanti facias Dolabellam ⟨et⟩ Tulliam tuam, feminam lectissimam*).

3, 2 ab Afranio Indirectly no doubt: cf. 88 (IV. 14). 2 n. (*a C. Caesare*).

4 **in credendo** Cf. 205 (X. 13). 2 *quod ego nec rogaturus eram nec, si impetrassem, crediturus.*

nam The thought is: 'I shall not trust him fully, but I cannot keep him altogether in the dark, for. . .'.

6 **†adicit a** *adigit ita* is usually read, perhaps rightly: cf. 201 (x. 10). 4 *rogor enim ab eius uxore et filio*. But *adigere* seems a rather strong word, and it is dubious usage in this sense (cf. *Thes.* I. 678. 35: the only classical example, from *Dom.* 78, is an improbable conjecture). Perhaps *agit ita*: cf. 45 (II. 25). 2 *ita enim egi tecum superioribus litteris*; *Fam.* IV. 2. 1 *sed tamen, postquam tuas litteras legi, Postumia tua me convenit et Servius noster. his placuit ut tu in Cumanum venires, quod etiam mecum ut ad te scriberem egerunt.* Servius did come to Cumae on the Nones (206 (x. 14). 1).

200A (X. 9A)

Caelius clearly wrote about the same time as Caesar. Early in March he had been sent to Liguria to deal with a rising of the Intimilii and from there had written to C. (*Fam.* VIII. 15. 2). Caesar probably found him there on his way to Massilia. C.'s reply also survives (*Fam.* II. 16).

1, 5 Cicero So in §5 (on *Fam.* VIII. 13. 2 see *Philol.* 105 (1961), p. 88). The simple vocative (without *mi*) is appropriate to a solemn warning.

8 **praedixisse** I.e. in this letter. *postquam Caesarem convenerim* surely does not refer to Caelius' meeting with Caesar at Ariminum in January (cf. *Fam.* VIII. 17. 1). Caesar would scarcely have been discussing what he would do after victory then, and Caelius' letter in March (*Fam.* VIII. 15) is quite out of tune with such warnings (cf. §1 *ecquem autem Caesare nostro. . .in victoria temperatiorem aut legisti aut audisti?*). The meeting therefore was that which had just taken place (§4), and the warning that which follows in the next sentence.

13 **intercessionibus** Cf. 195 (x. 4). 9 n. (*surrupto*).

2, 3 ut. . .habeamus *noli committere* (Lehmann) before *ut* restores grammatical sequence, but *si tibi. . .carae sunt* still remains without any appropriate apodosis. If anything has fallen out it is probably something like *haec omnia etiam atque etiam cogitabis* after *habeamus*; but it is possible that in this emotional appeal Caelius did not pause to clear up the complications of his syntax.

4, 7 percurrissem Cf. Neue–Wagener, *Formenlehre*[3], III, pp. 353 ff.

5, 5 oppidum An Italian town, that is.

201 (X. 10)

Written on 3 May (§3) (but dispatched on the 4th: see on next letter) after receipt of letters from Antony (§2) and Atticus (§4).

1, 1 epistulam 199A (x. 8A), not the letter cited in §2. *misi* = 'send herewith' is normally used of *separate* enclosures; besides, it is natural for C. to mention Antony's former letter before describing his own reply.

2 **†saepissime** Antony says nothing in 199A (x. 8A) about earlier letters from C. on the same theme, and C. cannot be supposed to have written back to him more than once, let alone 'over and over again'. Hence *aequissime*, etc., have been mooted; but it seems to me more likely that *sepissime* developed from a dittography of *scripsissem* or from *statim re-(scripsissem)*.

4 **amicitiae** Perhaps with Caesar (so Manutius) or with Caesar and Antony rather than with Antony alone, though Antony seems to have understood in the latter way if *nostrae* in §2 is sound.

7 **παραινετικῶς** This adverb excellently suits the beginning and end of Antony's letter. παροινικῶς (also Lambinus) would be glaringly inappropriate, τυραννικῶς of Cratander's text, which looks like a conjecture, at any rate less appropriate (cf. however 202 (x. 11). 3 *quoniam scripsit quid fieri vellet*). There is something amusing in C.'s indignation at the chilly reception accorded to his insincerities.

2, 1 †quia As Madvig saw, the former vulgate *quam verum est* will not do. Whether *quam* be taken as exclamatory or as the equivalent of *perquam* (an unlikely colloquialism here), this can only be understood as an emphatic endorsement of C.'s plan. In explanation (*nam*) follows a sound and obvious reason for *not* approving it: departure from Italy would be an unneutral act. Commentators are reduced to asserting that *quam verum* is ironic, or that *consilium* means, not the plan to go abroad, but the slight degree of hesitation conveyed by *nec id ipsum certum etiam nunc habere*. The latter view refutes itself. As for the former, it ought to be unimaginable that Antony should begin a letter to C. at this time with a piece of insulting, heavy-handed sarcasm. *quia* of Ω does not seem to help. If *verum consilium* is rightly interpreted here as 'a sound plan', something may have fallen out, e.g. *tuum consilium quam verum sit ⟨nescio⟩* or *⟨vide⟩ quam verum sit*. Otherwise *tuorum* might replace *tuum*, supposing C. to have mentioned that his Caesarian friends, Dolabella, etc., had counselled him to stay in Italy. That would give *verum consilium* its normal sense, 'sound' (or 'honest') advice: so in the passages cited in *Thes.* (iv. 455. 29) and in others there omitted (174A (ix. 7A). 1; *Q. Fr.* iii. 1. 20; *Amic.* 44; [Sall.] *Ep. ad Caes.* ii. 10. 3, 12. 2). On 80 (iv. 5). 1 *recta, vera, honesta consilia* see ad loc.

5 **me probare** I.e. *si probarem*—not implying that Antony *does* approve.

8 **amicitiae nostrae** Most naturally 'the friendship between you and me', though Caesar may just possibly be included. It would be odd for C. to

give (or be expected by Antony to give) Caesar his friendship with Antony as a reason for trust when his friendship with Caesar himself would constitute so much more cogent and courteous an argument. Or is *cum...pollicearis* merely a way of saying 'since you promise to do nothing rash'? *vestrae* cuts the knot, such as it is.

3, 1 **omnino** Concessive.

excipiam A hunting term which signifies lying in wait for a quarry or attacking it when it comes or both (cf. *Thes.* v (ii). 1254. 79, 1255. 32). So used absolutely in 25 (II. 5). 1 *excipiamus et exspectemus.*

3 **audiam** Cf. *Fam.* III. 5. 1 *et tuas litteras legi libenter et audivi Lucilium diligenter. ut ei persuadeam me* (Schütz) or *persuadere me* (Schmidt) would be much less graphic.

5 **certe** Even if κάρτει (Sjögren) = βίᾳ were Ciceronian Greek, the sense would be wrong. C. meant to escape by stealth, not force, though he does contemplate force as a possibility in 204 (X. 12*a*). 2.

6 **Curionem** See Appendix VI, pp. 462 ff.

σύνες ὅ τοι λέγω Pindar, fr. 105 (Snell), cited by Plato and Strabo.

dolor accessit The numerous proposed alterations are entirely needless. C. means that his earlier motives for leaving are now reinforced by his disappointment and irritation at the substance and tone of Antony's letter. So in 16 (I. 16). 9 *dolor accessit bonis viris, virtus non est imminuta*; Quint. *Decl.* 335 (Ritter, p. 318. 25) *accessit dolor.*

4, 1 **de Massiliensibus** Their refusal to admit Caesar (*B.C.* I. 34. 4).

2 **Ocellam** Perhaps the L. Livius Ocella whose existence and that of his homonymous son were ingeniously reconstructed by Cichorius (*Röm. Studien*, pp. 253 ff.) from scattered and corrupt testimonies. He is thus identified with the L. Cella (*pater*) of *Bell. Afr.* 89. 5 whom Caesar pardoned after Thapsus, the ex-Praetor Λεύκιος Πέλλα of Plut. *Brut.* 35 disgraced by Brutus at Sardis in 42, and the L. Julius Mocilla, likewise *praetorius*, of Nep. *Att.* 11. 2, befriended by Atticus after Philippi. There was also a Ser. Ocella of whom Caelius (*Fam.* VIII. 7. 2) writes scandalously in 50.

si possem palam Cf. 209 (X. 17). 3. Ocella was probably no more than a friendly acquaintance, not to be taken on the secret flight which C. now had in mind.

3 **quod...effeceram** Cf. 195 (X. 4). 10 fin.

hic ego...opus esse Not a complete change of subject. C. at this time thought of associating Sulpicius in his plans (cf. 206 (X. 14). 3).

5, 1 **hic tamen** No supplement is needed, the reference to Antony being perfectly plain ('this fellow' as opposed to Curio). *tamen* seems to have little more than transitional force—Antony's outrageous behaviour would be an additional reason for concerting plans for flight rather than otherwise—, dismissive of the topic of Servius (= δ'οὖν): cf. 333 (XIII. 25). 2 init.

2 **Cytherida** Antony's mistress, a *mima* and a freedwoman of Volumnius Eutrapelus (208 (X. 16). 8; *Phil.* II. 58; Plut. *Ant.* 9. Cf. *Fam.* IX. 26. 2). Later sources, as Servius on *Ecl.* X. 1, make her the Lycoris to whom Cornelius Gallus wrote his elegies.

alteram uxorem So distinguished from the inferior *amicae. altera* would efface this touch, and is discountenanced by the parallel description in *Phil.* II. 58, where Antony's wife (his cousin Antonia: cf. *Phil.* II. 99; Plut. *Ant.* 9) is not mentioned.

3 **et sunt amicorum** *mignons* as well as *mignonnes*. This seems preferable to Bosius' *amicarum sunt⟨an⟩ amicorum?* In *Phil.* II. 58 a *raeda cum leonibus* is recorded, but no other litters (except by implication that of Antony's mother, who followed in the rear); these *amici* may however be included among the *comites nequissimi* of that passage.

7 **parricidio** I.e. *patriae caede.*

6, 2 **ἀνηθοποίητον** ἅπ. λεγ. in the sense 'morally unformed'.

3 **nescio quid cogitans** Cf. *Leg. Agr.* II. 28 *ut aut lusisse in tantis rebus aut profecto nescio quid spectasse videatur.*

202 (X. 11)

heri vesperi in §4 puts this letter on 4 May (cf. 201 (X. 10). 3 *erat autem V Non. venturus vesperi*). *interim venit Philotimus* in §1 would suggest that 201 (X. 10) was written before Philotimus arrived at Cumae from Rome. But he arrived on 2 May (199A (X. 8A). 2), at any rate no later, and 201 (X. 10) was written on 3 May (as proved not only by the date in §3 but by the fact that C. did not dispatch it along with 200 (X. 9), also of 3 May, but with 202 (X. 11)). Unless Philotimus is the man mentioned in 198 (X. 7). 2 (but C. would surely have added *libertus* if he had been), the only valid explanation seems to be Schmidt's (*Briefwechsel*, p. 156): Philotimus was sent by C. on 3 May to meet Antony (or on some other errand), and while on the road was given Atticus' letter by its original messenger.

1, 4 **quae. . .scribis** Quintus senior had probably permitted himself some 'irresolute' remarks in writing to Atticus of his son's conduct.

10 **itinere** This obvious restoration ('offenbar oberflächliche Zustutzung' Müller, *Rhein. Mus.* 53 (1898), p. 130) is the best by far. I see nothing particularly 'merkwürdig' (Schmidt, *ibid.* 52 (1897), p. 167) in its combination with *sorore*. The journey is probably Atticus' (cf. 196 (X. 5). 3 fin.), who may have expressed regret that as he was soon leaving he could do

little to set things right between Quintus and Pomponia—once more at loggerheads, evidently (cf. 207 (x. 15). 4 *de sorore laudo*).

2, 3 $\overline{\text{XII}}$ A larger figure might have been expected in view of *nescio quis HS $\overline{XX}$* below, but see on 207 (x. 15). 4.

4 **filio** See again 207 (x. 15). 4 n. (*de duodecim milibus*).

si Lepta Sc. *utitur excusatione temporis.*

3, 2 de eius filio *eius* may be a gloss, as apparently in 221 (xi. 10). 1 *Patris eius*: cf. 217 (xi. 6). 7 *Quintum fratrem audio profectum in Asiam ut deprecaretur. de filio nihil audivi.*

13 **certiorem** Cf. 200 (x. 9). 2 fin. *certus* = *firmus*, *obstinatus* is unusual in classical prose, perhaps unique (cf. *Thes.* iii. 911. 72).

4, 1 sed Dismissive (= δ'οὖν). So in 91 (iv. 17). 4 *sed senatus hodie erat futurus* and elsewhere.

2 **ne id quidem** In fact Antony did not call (205 (x. 13). 2; 207 (x. 15). 3).

5 **cum illis illo** *illis* is an easy and almost necessary supplement. C. would hardly use the singular *illo* (= *meo*) after *pueris* and the reader would be tempted to take it with ἀφράκτῳ. As to the latter cf. 104 (v. 11). 4; 122 (vi. 8). 4.

7 **actuariola** *actuariae* were small, swift vessels (*naviculae celeres, dictae quod cito agi possint*, Non. (Lindsay), p. 857), though the size varied considerably. The diminutive is also found in 413 (xvi. 3). 6 and 414 (xvi. 6). 1.

9 **vir...bonus** Cf. 190 (x. 1). 3.

5, 1 Vettienum Cf. 196 (x. 5). 3.

4 **monetali** Cf. 417 (xv. 13*a*). 1 *Vettienum accusat* (*tricatur scilicet ut monetalis*). When the two passages are set together it is clear that Vettienus *was a monetalis* in a specific sense, which cannot be that of *triumvir monetalis*; for the joke here requires that the word should have two senses, that of *triumvir monetalis* and something else, and the later passage shows that this something else (which Vettienus actually was) could be associated with sharp practice (*tricae*). Perhaps 'money-changer'.

203 (x. 12)

The dates of this and the next two letters are determined by that of 205 (x. 13). Cf. T.–P.: 'The interview with Antony, who arrived on the evening of May 4 (398 [they mean 396 of their edition, i.e. x. 11]. 4), probably occurred on the 5th, and Cicero, as was his wont, wrote about it at once.' Antony in fact arrived on 3 May and had no interview with C. I do not think that *Trebatio narravit* necessarily implies that he had an interview with Trebatius after the dispatch of 202 (x. 11: cf. §4)—it might refer to an earlier conversation of which Trebatius had just told C.—, but if he did it was on the 4th, not the 5th. For Trebatius left Cumae for Rome on the 5th, bearing this letter (*ibid. ei ipsi cras ad te litteras dabo*).

1, 7 **Hortensium** Appointed by Caesar to a naval command on the Tyrrhene Sea (cf. Broughton, p. 267).

Reginus Probably C. Antistius Reginus, a Legate of Caesar's in 53 and onwards (*B.G.* vi. 1. 1, etc.). He appears to have been associated with Hortensius.

totus noster Cf. *Fam.* xv. 7 *sum totus vester.*

2, 1 **satis lacrimis** Sc. perhaps *egi* (cf. *agere armis, auctoritate, fraude, precibus*, etc.) rather than *datum est*. For παραποπλευτέον, which I ought to have mentioned in 1961 and now think sufficiently probable to print in the text, Emil Thomas compared παραποδύομαι, παραφίημι, etc. (*Stud. zur Lat. u. Gr. Sprachgeschichte*, pp. 122 ff.).

2 **onerariam** C. seems for the nonce to have in mind a different type of boat from the *actuariola* of the previous letter: cf. Lübeck, *RE.* I. 331. 20.

4 **maiora quaedam** Not, as usually held, identical with the 'Caelian' project: see Appendix vi.

5 **quamquam** The sense is: I speak of Spain, but Sicily itself is said to be in arms against Caesar.

3, 1 **C. Marcellum** Cf. 75 (iv. 3). 5 n.

fere Or *vere*: but *aut vere* might rather have been expected.

5 **adhibebo** Here apparently = *habebo* (*Thes.* vi. 2440. 15), *tractabo*. The nearest parallel is *Verr.* ii. 5. 70 *imperat Centuripinis ut is victu ceterisque rebus quam liberalissime commodissimeque adhiberetur* (*haberetur* dett.). In *Q. Fr.* i. 1. 16 *adhiberi liberaliter* may refer to dinner invitations, etc.

possem *possim* (Pius) has generally been read, but the imperfect is better. C. wishes he was able to take young Quintus properly in hand, but actually he is not able (cf. 202 (x. 11). 3 *quas tamen evellerem profecto si liceret; sed ea tempora sunt ut omnia mihi sint patienda*). This also fits *tamen* in the next sentence ('Quintus is a hopeless case, but all the same I don't want my harsh language about him to leak out'). The imperfect is naturally quite often used in wishes, as in *Fam.* xv. 21. 3 *cui quidem ego amori utinam ceteris rebus possem, amore certe respondebo.*

7 **concerpito** This injunction and Atticus' disregard of it are noteworthy.

204 (x. 12*a*)

1, 3 **ἀλλὰ τὰ μὲν κ.τ.λ.** *Il.* xviii. 112.

4 **ruamus** Here implying miscalculation rather than, as more usually, recklessness.

2, 4 **suspectus** Sc. *mihi.*

vi aut clam Cf. *Caec.* 92 *aut vi aut clam aut precario possedisse.*

5 †**forte sqq.** A *locus desperandus. forte ne cum tempestate* seems to contain an objection to the first alternative, that of exit by force, to balance the objection to the second, stealth, which follows with *in quo si quod* σφάλμα sqq. Further than this I find it impossible to go with any confidence, and previous attempts have yielded nothing worth consideration. Possibly C. wrote something to the effect that force would involve extra risk of sailing in bad weather, since the attempt once made any further delay would be out of the question.

6 **vides quam turpe sit** *est* can hardly be defended by 163 (VIII. 13). 2 *vide quam conversa res est* et sim. (cf. K.–S. II, pp. 490 f.) since the σφάλμα is hypothetical.

3, 1 **Caelio** See Appendix VI.

5 **diligentes** At pains to be well-informed.

6 **in theatro** The preposition is best added. In 39 (II. 19). 3 *populi sensus maxime theatro et spectaculis perspectus est* its absence may be due to the combination with *spectaculis* (so K.–S. I, p. 355).

4, 1 **suppeditabimus** For the absence of an object cf. 374 (XIV. 20). 3 *quod Ciceroni suppeditas, gratum*; 365 (XIV. 11). 2 *ut ei suppeditetur ad usum et cultum copiose.*

Peloponnesum And not only Arcadia (cf. 196 (X. 5). 2)—Arcadia standing simply for the task in hand, irrespective of the rest of the quotation.

2 †**hoc sit** *huic sit* or *in hoc sit* is useless patchwork, for the demonstrative is redundant if referred to *iuveni* (even *ei* would not be required). Perhaps *huic* ⟨*ad*⟩*sit*, 'if only this (*indoles*) might be supported by...'. For the Greek there are many guesses; mine is ἦθος ἄκακον καὶ ἄδολον. 'Parablepsy' from KA to KA would produce AKAIAΔOΛON, which is very close to Z^b. Cf. 197 (X. 6). 2 *nihil simplex, nihil sincerum.*

4 **ἀρετὴ non est διδακτόν** Platonic terminology (*Meno*, 71 a, etc.).

205 (X. 13)

1, 2 **speculam** An excellent conjecture. Plautus and C. have the diminutive several times (as *Fam.* II. 16. 5). *secum* is not required: cf. 222 (XI. 11). 1 *semper aliquid adferunt* (sc. *tuae litterae*) *quod velim*; 223 (XI. 12). 4 *semper enim adferunt aliquid mihi tuae litterae.*

3 **ad spem** Cf. 126 (VII. 4). 2 n.

4 **leones** Is this an obscure joke or did Antony really keep lions and perhaps take them around with him? The question is not answered by the

story in Pliny (*N.H.* VIII. 55) and Plutarch (*Ant.* 9) that he used lions to draw his carriage in 48–47.

5 **denos** Cf. Liv. XXIX. 15. 5 *ut consules, magistratus, denosque principes Nepete, Sutrio...Romam excirent* et sim. They were the *decem primi*, the ten leading Senators in Italian or provincial municipalities, who represented the whole senate on special missions (cf. Mommsen, *St.* III, p. 852 n.). *IIII (quaternos) viros* are the principal town magistrates, usually four in number (cf. 26 (II. 6). 1 n.).

9 **κοιλιολυσίαν** *alvi solutionem*, as in Soranus I. 46 μέθην, ἔμετον, κοιλιολυσίαν, and Bekker's *Anecdota*, p. 323 ὑπότριμμα...ᾧ πρὸς κοιλιολυσίαν ἐχρῶντο; cf. *Fam.* XVI. 18. 1 εὐλυσίαν κοιλίας. L.–S.–J., from whom I take the first two references, misunderstood C.

10 **Aenariam** Modern Ischia.

2, 1 **ab Axio** Cf. 202 (x. 11). 2. Bücheler's *a Q. Axio*, assuming corruption of *Q.* to *D.*, may be right; but except in 202 (x. 11). 2, where it may be thought to lend a certain *pathos*, C. does not put in Axius' praenomen, and had the less reason to do so here in that he had been so recently mentioned: cf. 207 (x. 15). 4.

2 **diligo** Cf. 202 (x. 11). 5 *quoniam...nos diligit, ipse quoque a nobis diligatur.*

reddidi Sc. *litteras a te missas*: cf. 196 (x. 5). 2 *epistulam ad Vestorium statim detuli*, and for the ellipse 383 (xv. 5). 1 *a Bruto tabellarius rediit. attulit et ab eo et Cassio. reddere* is often used of letters transmitted indirectly or by a friend instead of by the correspondents' *tabellarii* (e.g. 224 (XI. 13). 1; 228 (XI. 17). 1; 234 (XI. 22). 1).

3 **Liternino** Liternum (Torre di Patria) was just north of Cumae.

6 **ne nuntium quidem** A message did arrive later (207 (x. 15). 3).

3, 4 **Silium** Cf. 115 (VI. 1). 13 n.

Ocellam Cf. 201 (x. 10). 4 n.

5 **†curto** Editors generally read *Curtio*, i.e. M. Curtius Postumus (cf. 169 (IX. 2*a*). 3 n.), but there is no evidence to connect him with this context.

6 **†εκιταονον** The sense is indicated by 209 (x. 17). 4 *de diplomate admiraris quasi nescio cuius te flagiti insimularim.* ἔκπλουν is palaeographically easier (ΙΤΑ = ΠΛ) than ἐπιστόλιον. There is no exact parallel for either.

206 (x. 14)

1, 4 **nullius consili exitum** I.e. *nullum consilium exitum habere.*

8 **alterius...alterius** I.e. *Pompei...Caesaris.*

9 **quae** Sc. *pecunia.* For the construction *ad sensum* cf. K.–S. I, pp. 29 ff.

13 **sed saepius...vigilias** Usually understood 'but it is often dis-

agreeable by keeping me awake'. Dissatisfied with this Madvig conjectured *et per se odiosa est ⟨et⟩ propter vigilias.* But C. means that his ophthalmia annoyed him more often than it normally would have done *because* he was so much awake at night—his worries made him a bad sleeper (cf. 151 (VIII. 1). 4; 174 (IX. 7). 7; 177 (IX. 10). 1; 178 (IX. 11). 4); it prevented him from reading and writing easily during the watches: cf. 209 (x. 17). 2.

2, 3 **domi est** Cf. *Thes.* v (i). 1957. 16.

6 **de duabus legionibus** Presumably about their disaffection: cf. 204 (x. 12*a*). 3; 207 (x. 15). 1.

7 **et talia** The passages cited by Otto in *Rhein. Mus.* 21 (1886), pp. 372 f. would be more to the point if he had conjectured *et si quid aliud* rather than *et alia.*

3, 1 **omnino** Concessive.

2 **tardus ad exeundum** Sc. *ex Italia.*

in suo lectulo Cf. 199 (x. 8). 7 n. *mori* has to be understood, as in *Fam.* IX. 18. 4 *satius est hic cruditate quam istic fame.*

6 **fiebant** Cf. K.–S. II, pp. 542 ff.

8 **consilio** Flight from Italy.

9 **in hoc** I.e. *in Servio.*

207 (x. 15)

C. probably wrote this letter on the evening of the 10th after his talk with Servius and dispatched it on the 11th. The usual view that he wrote immediately before he left for Pompeii on the 12th (208 (x. 16). 4) is not proved by *excurro in Pompeianum* (§4), which need mean no more than *excurrere cogito.*

1, 3 **de octo cohortibus** Another rumour of disaffection among the troops in Italy. That there was some substance to these reports appears from the incident narrated in the next letter (§4).

4 **Funisulanus** Cf. 97 (v. 4). 1 n.

6 **gratia** Atticus must have put in a word on Funisulanus' behalf.

9 **†fecisses** *fecisset* would mean 'with which the debtor had paid Funisulanus'. But this would hardly be understood, unless *is* were supplied after *qua.* More probable perhaps that *fecisses* represents *facere posses,* with reference to the same debt (Funisulanus' own) as *satis faciebat.*

10 **Eros Philotimi** A slave of Philotimus', perhaps the man often mentioned in connexion with C.'s financial affairs in the letters of 46–44. Plutarch (*Apophth. Cic.* 21) has an anecdote about a slave of that name whom C. manumitted.

2, 1 **Caelianum illud** See Appendix VI.

3 **†palam** In view of *ibitur igitur, et ita quidem ut censes* below, this has

to be referred to C.'s departure from Italy, in which case *palam* can hardly stand. C.'s intention ever since 3 May had been to leave secretly; nothing had happened to change it: cf. 201 (x. 10). 3 *clam agam, cum paucissimis alicubi occultabor*; 203 (x. 12). 2 *occulte in aliquam onerariam corrependum*; 206 (x. 14). 3 *celandus magis de nostro consilio quam adhibendus*; 208 (x. 16). 2 *consilium nostrum spero vacuum periculo fore*; *nam et dissimulavimus nec, ut opinor, acerrime observabimur*—the alternative of violence mentioned in 204 (x. 12*a*). 2 would arise only if secrecy failed. Gronovius' ingenious idea that *palam* is from *pala*, with allusion to Gyges' ring, can hardly be taken seriously—even if Atticus had mentioned the ring in his letter, this way of putting things would be outrageously deceptive. The best way out is the boldest: *palam* should be *clam* (not that there is really anything particularly bold about such conjectures by proper critical standards, but they are apt to appear so to the unreflecting).

6 **captiones** Servius raised quibbling objections against every course proposed: cf. *Part. Or.* 133 *eamque sententiam quam significari posse dicet nihil habere aut captionis aut viti*; *Acad.* II. 45 *praestigiis quibusdam et captionibus*; 384 (xv. 7) *Servius. . .videtur. . .omnis captiunculas pertimescere*. '*captiones* proprie dixit cum loqueretur de iuris consulto' (Manutius).

Marcello *Marcellum* is unnecessary. For *unum* cf. 239 (XII. 3). 1 *unum te puto minus blandum esse quam me*.

9 **honestius** Sc. *maneret*.

3, 5 **Allienus** A. Allienus had been Q. Cicero's Legate in Asia: cf. *Q. Fr.* I. 1. 10 *Allienus autem noster est cum animo et benevolentia tum vero etiam imitatione vivendi*. As Caesarian Proconsul in Sicily from 48–46 (Broughton, p. 296) he received two recommendatory letters from C. (*Fam.* XIII. 78, 79), and in 43 was still *familiaris et necessarius* (*Phil.* XI. 32). He took a republican line after Caesar's death. Legate successively to Trebonius and Dolabella, he handed four legions, which he was bringing up from Egypt to join the latter, over to C. Cassius in Syria (Cassius, *Fam.* XII. 11. 1, etc.). On the significance of this passage see Appendix VI, pp. 463 f.

7 **dum modo aliquis** Cf. 314 (XIII. 7) *rescribes igitur quicquid voles, dum modo aliquid*.

4, 1 **sorore** Cf. 202 (x. 11). 1.

3 **L. Egnatio** Cf. 81 (IV. 12). n.

de duodecim milibus Clearly the sum mentioned in 202 (x. 11). 2. The idea that Axius was asking C. for a second loan is plainly wrong. For one thing he would hardly have had time to write or C. to promise 'often' since 4 May, the date of 202 (x. 11). Gallius must be Axius' son mentioned in that letter, his name changed by adoption. He cannot be M. Gallius Q. f. of 232 (XI. 20). 2, because he will have taken the praenomen of his adoptive father; but he could be this man's brother Q. Gallius, Pr. 43, son of C.'s former client Q. Gallius, Pr. 65 (cf. Vonder Mühll, *RE.* VII. 672), who was deposed from office by Octavian (App. *B.C.* III. 95; Suet. *Aug.* 27. 4). On 'M. Axianus' of 408 (XV. 29). 1 see *ad loc.*

4 **pudens** Axius was evading his obligations, like Dolabella in 373 (XIV. 18). 1 *o hominem impudentem! Kal. Ian. debuit, adhuc non solvit.*

6 **sum pollicitus** I.e. C. had tried to fob him off with promises, but he insisted on cash.

7 **adiuvarent** Usually understood 'they should have helped me rather' —but C. would have written *potius* not *vero*. Better make *duodecim milia* the subject.

di istos Sc. *perduint.*

9 **panes** 'Loaves.' The singular might have been expected, but there is nothing conclusive against the plural. It does seem rather odd however that C. should mention this item specially. Against *navis* is the following *cetera in navem* (*cetera ad navigandum* (cf. 208 (X. 16). 4) would then be logical).

208 (X. 16)

The date is shown by 209 (X. 17). 1 *prid. Id. Hortensius ad me venit scripta epistula.*

1, 1 **litteras** Presumably 207 (X. 15). Dionysius probably arrived on the 11th, the day before C. left for Pompeii.

2 **ad me. . .†fuit** *apud me esse* is usual, but cf. 195 (X. 4). 8 *fuit ad me sane diu* et sim. The difficulty here is that after *commodum. . .dederam. . .cum* the natural verb would be *venit*: cf. 169 (IX. 2*a*). 3 *vixdum epistulam tuam legeram cum ad me. . .Curtius venit* et sim. For the corruption Sjögren compares 161D (VIII. 11D). 4 *fuissent / venissent*, etc. Or *fuit* may be deleted: cf. 375 (XIV. 21). 2 *ad me autem, cum Cassi tabellarium dimisissem, statim Balbus.* There is no clear example of *esse* as a verb of motion in classical Latin.

3 **placabilem me praebuissem** Probably an echo of Atticus' letter.

totum Virtually adverbial.

4 **tuis litteris** Cf. 192 (X. 2). 2 n.

6 **volebam. . .cupiebam** Cf. Ov. *ex Pont.* III. 1. 35 *velle parum est: cupias, ut re potiaris, oportet.*

7 **cum in Formianum venisset** On 22 February (157 (VIII. 5). 1).

8 **praeciderat** Cf. 156 (VIII. 4). 2 *plane nulla exceptione praecidit.*

12 **despectam** Cf. 179 (IX. 12). 2 n.

15 **tam diu** Cf. *Fin.* II. 78 *manebit ergo amicitia tam diu quam diu sequetur utilitas.*

2, 2 **nec** A negative is plainly essential; for *et. . .nec* cf. 161D (VIII. 11D).

6 *quae et nunc adflicta est nec excitari...potest* et sim. (*Thes.* v (ii). 889. 48). Lambinus, who first suggested adding *non* before *acerrime*, was put off by the inconsistency with 210 (x. 18). 1 *custodiae quibus adservor* (cf. 204 (x. 12*a*). 2 *mirificae sunt custodiae*), but that is easily explained. When C. wrote 208 (x. 16) he had been temporarily reassured by Terentia's report of Hortensius' visit (§5).

3, 1 **Cato** Later authorities, as Plutarch (*Cat. Min.* 53) tend to justify Cato's action; Caesar (*B.C.* I. 30. 5) is non-committal.

4 **Cotta** M. Aurelius Cotta was in fact expelled from Sardinia by the inhabitants before the arrival of Caesar's Legate Valerius, and fled to Africa (Caes. *B.C.* I. 30. 2 f.; Dio, XLI. 18. 1). He can hardly be the son of M. Cotta, Cos. 74 (cf. 261 (XII. 22). 2 n.), who had successfully prosecuted his father's former prosecutor C. Carbo about ten years previously (cf. Münzer, *RE.* XVIII. 1021 f.); for *he* undertook the prosecution the day he donned his *toga virilis* (Val. Max. v. 4. 4), which makes him too young to be governing Sardinia in 49.

4, 1 **profectionis aut cogitationis** See Appendix VI, p. 467.

5 **haec mecum** Sc. *collocutus est* vel sim. Boot was right to punctuate so as to make it clear that *velle...tradere* represents Ninnius' gloss on the Centurions' message. 364 (XIV. 10). 3 is somewhat similar: *ibi eum Balbus mane postridie, eodemque die mecum in Cumano: illum hereditatem aditurum.*

6 **Ninnius** Cf. 68 (III. 23). 4 n.

7 **tibi** Cf. K.–S. I, *ibid.*

9 **eadem illa Caeliana** Cf. Appendix VI, *ibid.*

5, 1 **cum redeo** *dum* is not necessary. For *cum* with the historic present and a past tense in the main clause see T.–P.'s note (add Liv. III. 46. 10 *profectus Verginius prima vigilia erat, cum postero die...litterae redduntur*).

ad Terentiam salutatum Cf. 28 (II. 8). 1 n. (contrast Ter. *Phorm.* 311 *ego deos penatis hinc salutatum domum / devertar*). Terentia (and Tullia) had rejoined C. at Cumae and was head of the household in his absence (cf. 3 (I. 7). 1 n. *apud matrem*).

4 **hoc quidem melius** Sc. *fecit*: cf. *Off.* III. 49 *melius hic quam nos, qui piratas immunis, socios vectigalis habemus*; Hor. *Sat.* I. 2. 90 *hoc illi recte* et sim. Antony, C.'s fellow-Augur, had not had the courtesy to call.

cuius...portatur Cf. 201 (x. 10). 5. 'Si haec verba ipsius Ciceronis sunt, non interpolatoris, ut mihi videntur, dicendum erit Antonii mentionem scribenti bilem movisse' (Boot).

6, 1 **novum morbum** The δυσουρία of 201 (x. 10). 3: cf. 209 (x. 17). 2 *valetudinem tuam iam confirmatam esse et a vetere morbo et a novis temptationibus gaudeo. non modo* (or *non modo veterem*) for *novum* is not required (cf. 60 (III.

15). 5 n. (*sed etiam*)), neither is Fr. Schmidt's dubiously appropriate *seda* for *sed.*

2 **siste** Originally a legal term, 'produce' in court. Commentators quote Gell. XVIII. 10. 7 *fac. . .sistas hunc nobis sanum atque validum* (cf. Prop. III. 17. 41 *tu modo servitio vacuum me siste superbo* and Plautine usages like *aliquid salvum sistere*). So without accompanying adjective in 70 (III. 25) *ut te ante Kal. Ian. ubicumque erimus sistas.*

209 (X. 17)

1, 1 vellem cetera eius 'Admodum dure supplent: essent his similia quae dixit' Boot. There is little plausibility in the same editor's *vellem spectasses* or in Madvig's *bella* (Lipsius), *ut cetera eius*, or in Schmidt's *vellem cernere potuisses* or in Müller's *vellem* ⟨*tam laudare possem*⟩ *cetera eius.* If change were needed it would be easy to write *vellem cetera eius* ⟨*modi*⟩ (cf. 306 (XII. 6). 2 *etsi tua quidem sunt eius modi omnia*) or to add *sic* before *vellem.* But the sense seems sufficiently obvious, in view of Hortensius' notorious shortcomings. For *cetera* cf. Tac. *Hist.* I. 5 *nec enim ad hanc formam cetera* (sc. *Galbae*) *erant* (otherwise *Q. Fr.* III. 14 *cetera eius suscipio* and 379 (XII. 38*a*) *cetera Antisthenis*). The genitive here is of a common type, such as may follow *omnia, multa,* etc.

2 **ἐκτένειαν** Not pejorative as L.–S.–J. represent: cf. 317 (XIII. 9). 1 *nihil possum dicere* ἐκτενέστερον, *nihil* φιλοστοργότερον.

3 **Serapion** Surely not the geographer mentioned in 24 (II. 4). 1.

4 **aperuissem** Cf. K.–S. II, p. 370. The subjunctive need not be understood as implying a purpose behind C.'s procedure: cf. *Rab. Perd.* 25 *quae causa ante mortua est quam tu natus esses* (needlessly 'emended').

5 **lecta** *aperta* and *stricta* are superfluous attempts to get closer to the *ductus litterarum*—superfluous because *scripta epistula* and *scripsisse* foregoing sufficiently account for *scripta* in the MSS.

7 **navi** Serapio seems to have been leaving Italy in a ship owned by himself, unless 'his ship' means 'the ship in which he is sailing'. C.'s plans were evidently not yet so firmly fixed in detail that they could not be adjusted to new opportunities.

ipso According to one suggestion as tutor to the young Ciceros. But probably C. plays on two senses of *uti*, 'use' and 'cultivate' (cf. Hor. *Ep.* I. 12. 22 *utere Pompeio Grospho* et sim.).

2, 1 refricat Sc. *me*. But *refricatur* may well be right.

3 **vetere. . .novis** Cf. 208 (X. 16). 6 n.

3, 1 Ocellam Cf. 201 (X. 10). 4; 205 (X. 13). 3.

haec 'Things here', i.e. the business of his departure, which now looked 'a little easier' because of Hortensius' attitude. If secrecy were not required Ocella could have been a fellow-passenger.

3 **si traxerit** For the intransitive dictionaries quote Cels. II. 8. 24 *si quis etiam in eo morbo diutius traxit* and Flor. IV. 2. 12 *decem annos traxit ista dominatio*; cf. 412 (XVI. 2). 4 *quin etiam idcirco trahebam ut quam diutissime integrum esset.* I formerly preferred Ziehen's *si transierit* ('once it blows over'), but the apodosis would then more naturally be an action than a state. No doubt *utinam maneat* can be taken as amounting to *profectionem ne impediat*, but still the sequence seems rather awkward. Palaeographically there is not much to choose, since *s* and *x* are often confused. *si* ἀκραὲς *erit* (Bosius) is only worth mentioning because it appears in certain texts (accompanied in T.–P.'s by *inde* (Reid) for *id* because equinoxes do not blow).

4, 1 diplomate Cf. 205 (x. 13). 3. Later C. uses the word in writing to a Pompeian exile of his passport back to Italy (*Fam.* VI. 12. 3).

7 **etiam nunc** Even at this late stage.

210 (x. 18)

1, 1 ἑπταμηνιαῖον For this form, besides the classical ἑπτάμηνος, see L.–S.–J.

2 **gaudeam** Cf. K.–S. I, p. 180. The mood implies 'I ought to be glad that Tullia is safe, though the baby is a poor thing'. It did not live long.

3 **tranquillitates** After the storm: cf. 207 (x. 17). 2.

5 **Hortensiana** On *Hortensina* cf. 16 (I. 16). 10 n.

omnia Cf. 124 (VII. 1). 5 *omnia illa prima . . .* ἐπίτηκτα *fuerunt. fuere* for *fuerunt* in what follows is to be rejected (cf. Nisbet on *Pis.* 96). *fuerunt inania* (cf. *Fam.* VII. 11. 2 *sin autem ista sunt inaniora*; 229 (XI. 17*a*). 3 *quod inane esset etiam si verum esset*) is the most obvious expression for C. to have used, though *fuerunt fatua* comes closer to the paradosis. *ita fiet* is generally supposed to be equivalent to *sic erit* (C. says *illud profecto est* for this in *Phil.* II. 2), but there seems to be no parallel (*factum est ita* in 131 (VII. 8). 4 is hardly good enough).

6 **Salvio** Probably Caesar's freedman mentioned in *Q. Fr.* III. 2. 21, 2. 1 and *Fam.* IX. 10. 1, where (to Dolabella) C. calls him *Salvio nostro.*

8 **Κωρυκαῖοι** The coast near Mt. Corycus in Ionia was a haunt of pirates, who had the peculiar habit of spying on their prey in the harbours so as to attack them later. Hence the proverb τοῦ δ' ἄρ' ὁ Κωρυκαῖος ἠκροάζετο (cf. Leutsch–Schneidewin, *Corp. Paroem. Gr.* I, pp. 104 f.).

2, 5 eaedem Preferable to *eadem* ('on the same road') or *eodem*. C. would naturally say 'the same avenging demons (that have dogged me so far)'. He seems to feel that his ill-luck is a judgement on his failure in loyalty to Pompey.

9 **benevolentia. . .suspicione** Schmidt (*Rhein. Mus.* 52 (1897). p. 16) complains that it is not immediately clear what good will and what suspicion are meant; but no doubt it would be if we had Atticus' account before us. Presumably Balbus had been talking to him about the prevalent rumours that C. intended to leave Italy.

APPENDIX I

EPHEMERIS: 18 JANUARY – 19 MAY 49

Bearings are easily lost in the abundant correspondence of these months. The following abstract of Cicero's personal activities ignores some minor questions. For evidence as to dates and places, see notes. Four periods may be conveniently distinguished:

1. 18 January (Cicero's flight from Rome) to 3 February (Cicero abandons hope of current peace negotiations).
2. 4–23 February (news of the fall of Corfinium).
3. 24 February–28 March (interview with Caesar).
4. 29 March–19 May (last letter to Atticus before leaving Italy).

In the first period, after a few days of confusion, Cicero's hopes are focused upon the interchanges conducted through L. Caesar. Their breakdown is succeeded by a short spell of dejection and personal perplexity, but from 9–23 February he hangs upon military developments, which had suddenly appeared to be taking a more favourable turn. The third period, after the republican debacle at Corfinium, is one of gloom, hesitation, and expectancy; certain now of Pompey's intention to evacuate Italy, Cicero's mind fluctuates as he waits for the upshot at Brundisium, then for his own interview with Caesar victorious. The letters of April and May reflect a more settled state of nerves and purpose. Cicero's resolution to leave Italy is pretty well fixed, and he waits for the 'spring swallow' and for suitable ways and means.

During the first three periods his base was Formiae. The fourth, after an excursion to Arpinum, seems to have been entirely spent at Cumae, apart from a curtailed visit to Pompeii on 12 May. At the end of May Cicero left for Formiae (210. (x. 18). 2), whence he took ship on 7 June (*Fam.* XIV. 7). When possible the place where he spent the preceding night is given after each date.

I

18 January[1]	Rome. After penning a hasty note to Atticus (133 (VII. 10)) Cicero sets out before daybreak for Formiae, probably in company with his brother and their sons. Their wives and Tullia remain in Rome.

[1] 1 December, Julian calendar.

19 January	Tarracina, or some other place on the Via Appia, from which Cicero probably dispatched a lost letter to Atticus. He would arrive at Formiae in the evening.
20 January	Formiae. Another lost letter to Atticus.
21 January	Formiae. 134 (VII. 11) dispatched. Cicero sees the Consul Lentulus and Scribonius Libo (135 (VII. 12). 2), and discusses the future with M'. Lepidus and L. Torquatus (*ibid.* 4).
22 January	Formiae. Cicero dispatches 135 (VII. 12) to Atticus (also *Fam.* XIV. 18 to Terentia and Tullia), undecided and distressed (§3). Later he goes to Minturnae.
23 January	Minturnae. After dispatching 136 (VII. 13) and *Fam.* XIV. 14 to Terentia and Tullia, but still in the morning, Cicero sees L. Caesar, who is on his way to Pompey at Teanum Sidicinum (137 (VII. 13*a*). 2).
24 January	Minturnae. After dispatching 137 (VII. 13*a*), dictated because of ophthalmia, Cicero receives word from Pompey asking him to go to Capua and help with recruiting. He sets out accordingly and spends the night at his *deversorium* in Cales.
25 January	Cales. Cicero dispatches 138 (VII. 14), then leaves for Capua. There he confers with the Consuls, Cato, and other Senators (Pompey had left Teanum for Apulia on the 23rd), and attends to recruiting business with Ampius Balbus and Libo (139 (VII. 15). 2; 161B (VIII. 11B). 2).
26 January	Capua. 139 (VII. 15) dispatched.
27 January	Capua. *Fam.* XVI. 12 dispatched to Tiro and perhaps a lost letter to Atticus. About this time Cicero writes to his wife and daughter telling them to consult Atticus about whether to stay in Rome or leave (140 (VII. 16). 3).
28 January	Capua. Returning to Formiae, Cicero spends the night at Cales. There, in the afternoon, he receives a letter from Atticus and replies with 140 (VII. 16). Probably by the same messenger he writes to his wife and daughter telling them to remain in Rome (141 (VII. 17). 5).
29 January	Cales. Cicero returns to Formiae.
1 February	Formiae. About this time Cicero receives and answers a letter from Trebatius conveying Caesar's wish that he should go back to Rome (141 (VII. 17). 3 f.).
2 February	Formiae. 141 (VII. 17) dispatched, largely about peace

	prospects. Terentia and Tullia (perhaps also Pomponia) arrive at Formiae (142 (vii. 18). 1).
3 February	Formiae. Cicero leaves for Capua with his brother, the Consuls having required their presence on the 5th. Before setting out he writes 142 (vii. 18), but on receiving letters from Atticus and others which dissipate hopes of peace, dispatches 142 (vii. 19) instead. Later he sends 142 (vii. 18) after all. Presumably lodges for the night at Cales.

II

4 February	Cales. Cicero gets to Capua in a rain-storm (144 (vii. 20). 1), but finds the Consuls not yet arrived.
5 February	Capua. 144 (vii. 20) dispatched. Lentulus Crus arrives late in the day, but Cicero finds nothing toward in him or in the town (145 (vii. 21). 1). During his stay (4th–7th) he answers a letter from Caesar asking him to use his influence for peace (*ibid.* 3) with a brief but friendly counter-exhortation to the same (152 (viii. 2). 1), and probably writes at least one lost letter to Atticus, asking for advice and signifying his intention to send the women back to Rome (cf. 146 (vii. 22). 2 n.).
6 February	Capua.
7 February	Capua. C. Cassius arrives from Pompey with instructions for the Consuls, which Lentulus rejects (145 (vii. 21). 2). Cicero leaves Capua for Formiae, breaking the journey as usual at Cales.
8 February	Cales. 145 (vii. 21) dispatched before dawn. Cicero returns to Formiae.
9 February	Formiae. 146 (vii. 22) dispatched—an appeal for advice. In the evening a letter from Philotimus brings good news of the military situation to the north-east, heartening the republicans in Formiae, though Cicero himself is sceptical (147 (vii. 23). 1). However he gives up for the time his intention to send the women back to Rome (*ibid.* 2).
10 February	Formiae. 147 (vii. 23) dispatched. A letter to Cassius from a friend in Capua temporarily dispels the previous day's optimism.
11 February	Formiae. 148 (vii. 24) dispatched. A cheerful letter comes in from Atticus.

12 February	Formiae. Cicero replies in 149 (VII. 25).
13 February	Formiae. Cicero writes 150 (VII. 26) in brighter mood (*omnia erant facta hoc biduo laetiora*).
14 February	Formiae.
15 February	Formiae. Cicero dispatches a lost letter to Atticus, then receives one from Pompey recommending him to come to Luceria.
16 February	Formiae. Before dawn, unable to sleep, Cicero writes 151 (VIII. 1) to Atticus informing him of Pompey's letter, to which he later dispatches a reply, 161B (VIII. 11B), by the hand of his former *scriba*, M. Tullius.
17 February	Formiae. Cicero writes 152 (VIII. 2) before daybreak, accompanying it with a copy of Pompey's letter and of his own reply to a letter of Caesar's (cf. 161 (VIII. 11). 5) dispatched the same day. He adds a postscript announcing his immediate departure for Luceria, following receipt of Pompey's decision to evacuate Italy, as brought to the Consuls by D. Laelius. Having set out with Quintus and the boys (161D (VIII. 11D). 1), he hears in Teanum Sidicinum that Caesar is on the march towards Capua and decides to await developments in Cales, probably arriving there the same evening. About this time he receives a further (very brief) letter from Pompey, 161A (VIII. 11A).
18 February	Cales. At night Cicero writes a long, deliberative letter to Atticus, 153 (VIII. 3). While so engaged he receives word or copy of Pompey's letter to the Consuls announcing Caesar's investment of Corfinium and decides to return to Formiae. He sends Lepta with a letter to Pompey.
19 February	Cales. Cicero dispatches 153 (VIII. 3) and returns to Formiae with his party. In the evening he writes a lost letter to Atticus, enclosing the text of Domitius' last dispatch to Pompey (154 (VIII. 6). 3). After this letter is sealed, C. Sosius arrives with the text of that letter of Pompey to the Consuls (*ibid.* 2) which Cicero had already seen or heard about at Cales.
20 February	Formiae. Cicero dispatches 154 (VIII. 6), including the text of Pompey's letter.
21 February	Formiae. Cicero dispatches 155 (VIII. 7). In the course of the day comes news of the fall of Sulmo and Pompey's retreat on Brundisium (156 (VIII. 4). 3).
22 February	Formiae. Before dawn Cicero dispatches 156 (VIII. 4)

	about the tutor Dionysius, to whom he addresses a 'strong' letter in the same package. In the evening Dionysius himself arrives. Cicero sends 157 (VIII. 5) by special messenger to inform Atticus and retrieve the 'strong' letter.
23 February	Formiae. Cicero dispatches 158 (VIII. 8) after hearing of the surrender at Corfinium. Dionysius declines to stay with him and is dismissed.

III

24 February	Formiae. Cicero dispatches 159 (VIII. 10) about Dionysius. In the evening Balbus *minor* arrives (160 (VIII. 9*a*). 2), charged by Caesar with a message for Lentulus Crus and one for Cicero himself (161 (VIII. 11). 5).
25 February	Formiae. Cicero dispatches 160 (VIII. 9*a*). He is spending most of his time with M'. Lepidus (§1).
26 February	Formiae.
27 February	Formiae. Cicero receives a letter, 161C (VIII. 11C), from Pompey urging him to come to Brundisium. He replies with 161D (VIII. 11D), and sends copies of the correspondence to Atticus along with a despairing letter of his own, 161 (VIII. 11).
28 February	Formiae. Cicero dispatches 162 (VIII. 12) by Fabius Gallus, enclosing copies of letters written by Pompey to the Consuls and to Domitius between 11 and 16 February, 162A–D (VIII. 12A–D). He asks for Demetrius of Magnesia's treatise 'On Concord'. His eye trouble is worse. About this time he writes to Caesar (probably in answer to a letter received) thanking him for the release of Lentulus Spinther at Corfinium (178A (IX. 11A). 3), and to Balbus on his nephew's visit (165A (VIII. 15A). 3).
1 March	Formiae. Awaiting news from Brundisium Cicero dispatches 163 (VIII. 13)—mention of talks with local townsmen and landowners.
2 March	Formiae. Still waiting for news, Cicero dispatches 164 (VIII. 14).
3 March	Formiae. 165 (VIII. 15) dispatched to Atticus together with a copy of a letter from Balbus, 165A (VIII. 15A), just received.
4 March	Formiae. Cicero dispatches 166 (VIII. 16), still waiting for news of Pompey's escape and Caesar's return (§2 fin.).

5 March — Formiae.

6 March — Formiae. Cicero dispatches 167 (IX. 1), still waiting.

7 March — Formiae. Cicero dispatches 168 (IX. 2), still waiting. M'. Lepidus leaves for Rome (167 (IX. 1). 2).

8 March — Formiae. Curtius Postumus calls. 169 (IX. 2*a*) dispatched. Domitius junior passes through the town and sends a message to Cicero (170 (IX. 3). 1).

9 March — Formiae. Cicero dispatches 170 (IX. 3). Still no news from Brundisium. Q. Fufius calls.

10 March — Formiae. Cicero dispatches 171 (IX. 5), still waiting.

11 March — Formiae. Having received a letter from Balbus reporting Lentulus Crus' departure for Greece, but still no direct news from Brundisium, Cicero writes 172 (IX. 6). Then comes a letter from Capua (added in postscript) reporting (erroneously) that Pompey embarked on the 4th and plunging Cicero into a paroxysm of distress. Furnius arrives with a courteous note from Caesar, 172A (IX. 6A).

12 March — Formiae. Cicero writes, but lacks opportunity to dispatch, 173 (IX. 4), mainly a collection of topical θέσεις.

13 March — Formiae. In reply to a consoling letter from Atticus received the previous day Cicero writes 174 (IX. 7), enclosing a letter (174A (IX. 7A)) from Balbus and Oppius, another (174B (IX. 7B)) from Balbus, and Caesar's letter (174C (IX. 7C)) to the pair. Cicero has decided to await Caesar at Formiae (§2) and later on to leave Italy himself (§5), though still waiting for the outcome at Brundisium. While he is at dinner, Statius brings a letter from Atticus.

14 March — Formiae. Cicero replies with 175 (IX. 8). He is expecting Caesar at Formiae on the 22nd.

15 March — Formiae. Having temporarily given up hope of peace Cicero sends back Demetrius' book (176 (IX. 9). 2).

16 March — Formiae. Three letters come in from Atticus.

17 March — Formiae. Cicero replies in 176 (IX. 9).

18 March — Formiae. Cicero sends 177 (IX. 10), συναγωγὴν *consiliorum tuorum* (180 (IX. 13). 3). Furius Crassipes calls, with reports of ferocious talk in Pompey's circle (178 (IX. 11). 3).

19 March — Formiae. Cicero hears from Lentulus Spinther, now at Puteoli and full of temporary gratitude for his release by

	Caesar. C. Matius calls, holding out hopes of a mediatory role for Cicero. Under this influence Cicero writes 178A (IX. 11A) to Caesar.
20 March	Formiae. Cicero sends 178 (IX. 11), enclosing a copy of his letter to Caesar. While reading one from Atticus, he gets letters from Lepta and Matius–Trebatius reporting Pompey under siege at Brundisium.
21 March	Formiae. 179 (IX. 12), written in agitation perhaps on the previous day, dispatched. Later perhaps a visit from Matius and Trebatius.
22 March	Formiae. Cicero hears from Dolabella, whose letter (dated Brundisium, 13 March) belies alarmist reports of Pompey's situation (180 (IX. 13). 1).
23 March	Formiae. Cicero dispatches 180 (IX. 13). He is thinking himself of escape by sea (§5), but still awaits news. He hears from Balbus (181 (IX. 13A)), who encloses a letter of Caesar's.
24 March	Formiae. Cicero sends 181 (IX. 13*a*), with a copy of Balbus' letter. He has no hope of peace. Then comes a letter from Q. Pedius containing an extract from a letter of Caesar's on siege operations at Brundisium (182 (IX. 14). 1). 'A certain Baebius' retails from Curio Caesar's fierce talk against Pompey.
25 March	Formiae. After writing 182 (IX. 14) Cicero adds before daybreak a postscript announcing news just received of Pompey's embarkation on the 15th (two days out) and Caesar's expected arrival at Capua on the 26th. A subsequent letter from Capua gives warning of Caesar's arrival at Formiae on the 27th; Cicero passes on the news in a second letter (183 (IX. 15) dispatched the same day. On receipt of a letter from Matius and Trebatius correcting the date of Pompey's embarkation, he sends a copy to Atticus, with a postscript on Caesar's movements (184 (IX. 15*a*)).
26 March	Formiae. Cicero dispatches 185 (IX. 16), enclosing a copy of a letter from Caesar received that day.
27 March	Formiae. Cicero dispatches 186 (IX. 17); he is expecting Trebatius.
28 March	Formiae. The interview with Caesar takes place, described in 187 (IX. 18).

IV

29 March	Formiae. After dispatching 187 (IX. 18) Cicero sets out for Arpinum. Terentia and Tullia may now have returned to Rome (cf. 191 (X. 1*a*)).
30 March	From a place *en route* Cicero dispatches 188 (VIII. 9), answering criticisms of his letter 178A (IX. 11A) to Caesar.
31 March	Cicero arrives in Arpinum (188 (VIII. 9). 3).
1 April	Arpinum. Cicero gives his son the *toga virilis.*
2 April	Arpinum. 189 (IX. 19) dispatched.
3 April	Arpinum. On the first stage of his journey back to the coast Cicero moves to his brother's house at Laterium, from which he writes 190 (X. 1).
4 April	Laterium. 191 (X. 1*a*) dispatched.
5 April	Laterium. Cicero sets out to reach Minturnae on the 6th, but pauses at Quintus' Arcanum to wait for news of peace moves in Rome while preparations for his departure from Italy go forward.
6 April	Arcanum. Cicero dispatches 192 (X. 2).
7 April	Arcanum. 193 (X. 3) dispatched. Cicero receives a letter from Caesar of which he sends a copy along with 194 (X. 3*a*).
8–13 April	Within this period Cicero makes his way from Arcanum to Cumae.
14 April	Cumae. Cicero writes 195 (X. 4), in anxiety about young Quintus' meetings with Hirtius and Caesar. He hears that Curio, who had arrived in the district the previous evening, is coming to call and later resumes his letter with an account of their interview.
15 April	Cumae. Curio calls again (196 (X. 5). 2).
16 April	Cumae. 196 (X. 5) dispatched.
17–21 April	Cumae. On one of these days Cicero dispatches 197 (X. 6); he is now only waiting for the weather. Curio is a frequent visitor (198 (X. 7). 3). The younger Quintus returns (*ibid.*).
22 April	Cumae. Cicero sends *Fam.* IV. 1 to Ser. Sulpicius in Rome and 198 (X. 7) to Atticus. He now thinks of staying out of the war, perhaps in Malta.
22–27 April	Cumae (?). Nothing is known of Cicero's activities during these days.
28 April	Cumae. Cicero receives a letter from Sulpicius, then

	meets Postumia and young Servius. Writes *Fam.* IV. 2 inviting Sulpicius to Cumae, also probably *Fam.* V. 19 to Mescinius Rufus.
29 April–1 May	Cumae. Another blank.
2 May	Cumae. Cicero writes 199 (X. 8), enclosing 199A (X. 8A) from Antony, who is expected at Misenum. Philotimus arrives with discouraging news of the war in Spain (200 (X. 9). 1) and a letter from Caesar, 199B (X. 8B), appealing to Cicero not to leave Italy. Probably along with this Cicero receives 200A (X. 9A) from Caelius Rufus, which reduces his son and nephew to tears. He replies with *Fam.* II. 16.
3 May	Cumae. Cicero writes 200 (X. 9), enclosing Caelius' letter. He is still thinking of Malta. Another letter from Antony (σκυτάλη Λακωνική) arrives, the text of which Cicero includes in 201 (X. 10). Antony himself arrives at Misenum (202 (X. 11). 4).
4 May	Cumae. 202 (X. 11) dispatched. Trebatius is with Cicero (§4).
5 May	Cumae. Trebatius tells Cicero (after a visit to Misenum?) that Antony has received instructions not to let him go abroad. C. Marcellus is at Liternum (205 (X. 13). 2), in contact with Cicero (203 (X. 12). 3). Sicily is rumoured to be rallying to Cato (*ibid.* 2). 203 (X. 12) dispatched.
6 May	Cumae. 204 (X. 12*a*) dispatched—first mention of the 'Caelian' project. Ser. Sulpicius arrives at Minturnae (205 (X. 13). 2).
7 May	Cumae. 205 (X. 13) dispatched. Tullia is now with Cicero (§1), also, no doubt, Terentia (208 (X. 16). 5). Sulpicius stays the night with Marcellus at Liternum (§2).
8 May	Cumae. Unsatisfactory interview with Sulpicius described in 206 (X. 14). Cicero still thinking about 'Caelius' (§3).
9 May	Cumae. Probably another interview with Sulpicius (206 (X. 14). 3).
10 May	Cumae. Cicero sees Sulpicius again, but to no purpose (207 (X. 15). 2). Antony leaves for Capua, sending an apologetic message for his failure to call (*ibid.* 3). The 'Caelian' project is ripening (*ibid.* 2).
11 May	Cumae. 401 (X. 15) dispatched. Cicero plans a visit to his Pompeianum (§4), to divert suspicion during preparations for his voyage (208 (X. 16). 4).

12 May	Cumae. Cicero leaves for Pompeii. On his arrival he receives a message from the Centurions of three cohorts stationed there requesting an interview. Ninnius tells him that they want to hand over their men and the town (208 (x. 16). 4). Cicero also has a talk with M. Marius (*Fam.* VII. 3. 1).
13 May	Pompeii. To avoid the Centurions Cicero scurries off back to Cumae before daybreak. Hortensius had called in his absence to pay his respects to Terentia (208 (x. 16). 5). News received of Cato's evacuation of Sicily (*ibid.* 3).
14 May	Cumae. 208 (x. 16) dispatched. Hortensius calls and is very forthcoming (209 (x. 17). 1).
15 May	Cumae. Cicero finds writing difficult because of his ophthalmia (209 (x. 17). 2).
16 May	Cumae. 209 (x. 17) dispatched.
17–19 May	Cumae. On the 19th Tullia gives birth to a child, announced in 210 (x. 18).

APPENDIX II

CICERO'S COMMAND IN 49

Italiae regiones discriptae sunt, quam quisque partem tueretur. nos Capuam sumpsimus. So Cicero to Tiro in a letter dated 12 January 49 (*Fam.* XVI. 11. 3). This seemingly simple statement of fact is the fountainhead of a perplexed stream of controversy on Cicero's official role in the first six weeks of the Civil War.[1] Whatever else is doubtful, it has generally been taken as outside dispute that Cicero did officially accept charge of Capua and its *regio* of Campania. According to one view he remained nominally responsible until automatically relieved by the collapse of the republican cause in Italy, according to another he resigned within a few days to take a less onerous post.[2] Neither is tenable.

Three later letters of Cicero's make reference to 'Capua' in this sense, and I think there should be no doubt, despite some textual uncertainties, that in all of these he writes of himself as having *refused* the command. I take the last in time, 162 (VIII. 12). 2 of 28 February:

omnia sunt integra nobis; nihil praetermissum est quod non habeat sapientem excusationem, non modo probabilem. nam certe neque tum peccavi cum imperatam iam Capuam, non solum ignaviae dedecus sed etiam perfidiae suspicionem fugiens, accipere nolui neque *et sqq.*

accipere nolui can mean only one thing in a passage like this: 'I declined to accept.' If Cicero meant that he had withdrawn an acceptance already given, that at any rate is not what he says. Nor is it linguistically possible to interpret 'I was reluctant to accept'; that requires *nolebam*. Besides, if Cicero had actually taken and kept the Capuan command, he would not have needed to justify any initial reluctance, but rather his failure to discharge its responsibilities, even to the extent of residing in the town. It is to be noted that, if the text is sound,[3] he speaks of having been 'actually ordered' to take, not merely offered, the post. Who ordered him? Probably Pompey, rather than the Senate, for it was Pompey who assigned him the function which he actually accepted (cf. 134 (VII. 11). 5 and below). In decreeing the distribution of Italy into *regiones* the Senate may well have entrusted Pompey with

[1] See especially Schmidt, *Briefwechsel*, pp. 116 ff.; Sternkopf, *Wochenschr. f. klass. Phil.* 16 (1899), pp. 485 ff.; Sjögren, Χάριτες *F. Leo dargebracht* (1911), pp. 291 ff.; J. D. Duff, *Journ. Phil.* 33 (1914), pp. 154 ff.; T.–P. IV, pp. 559 ff.; Rice Holmes, *Roman Republic*, III, pp. 365 ff.

[2] On T.–P.'s variant see below, p. 454.

[3] On the v.l. *imparatam* see note *ad loc.*

the appointment of their commandants; and Pompey's nomination could morally though not technically be regarded as an order.

Second, 161D (VIII. 11D). 5 of 27 February (to Pompey):

quod cum ita sit, maxime vellem primum semper tecum fuissem; quod quidem tibi ostenderam cum a me Capuam reiciebam. quod feci non vitandi oneris causa sed quod videbam teneri illam urbem sine exercitu non posse, accidere autem mihi nolebam quod doleo viris fortissimis accidisse.

This passage, almost contemporaneous with that just discussed, follows the same lines. Even if 162 (VIII. 12). 2 were not there to guide, it would be perverse to understand *cum. . .reiciebam* with Duff as 'when I wished to refuse charge of Capua'.[1] Cicero would not have made so much of mere unwillingness, soon overborne; and *feci* surely implies a definite act of rejection. If however he were alluding to the resignation of a post initially accepted, he might have been expected to write *deponebam* rather than *reiciebam*.

Finally 153 (VIII. 3). 4 of 18 February:

†invite cepit† Capuam, non quo munus illud defugerem sed. . .dixi ipsi (*sc.* Pompeio) me nihil suscepturum sine praesidio et sine pecunia.

The vulgate *invite cepi* (see App. Crit.) is bad Latin. Cicero would have written *invitus*. Commentators quote *de Orat.* II. 364 *quem ego paulo ante sciebam vel pudentius vel invitius (nolo enim dicere de tam suavi homine fastidiosius) ad hoc genus sermonis accedere*. But because Cicero once allowed himself to use the adverb (its only occurrence in classical Latin apparently) where it was stylistically impossible for him to use the adjective, we are not therefore justified in accepting it where he was subject to no such temptation. And what he says about the language he used to Pompey implies refusal, not reluctant acceptance—'Capua' could not have been accepted as a sinecure. *non recepi* (Lehmann) or *hinc reieci* (Sternkopf) will represent the sense.

Instead of 'Capua' Cicero accepted a commission described to Atticus in a letter of 20 January or thereabouts as follows (134 (VII. 11). 5): *ego negotio praesum non turbulento. vult enim me Pompeius esse quem tota haec Campan⟨i⟩a et maritima ora habeat* ἐπίσκοπον, *ad quem dilectus et negoti summa referatur. itaque vagus esse cogitabam. haec*, if the reading is sound, shows that only the neighbouring part of Campania (Cicero wrote from Formiae) is included, and elsewhere he writes of his responsibility as though it was virtually confined to the coast: cf. 138 (VII. 14). 3 *in ora maritima. . .cui ego praesum*;

[1] Similarly Billerbeck: 'als ich die Auftrag nach Capua zu gehen ernstlich von mir abzulehnen suchte'.

161B (VIII. 11B). 1 (to Pompey) *in ea ora ubi praepositi sumus* (cf. *ibid.* 3 *si tenendam hanc oram putas. . .opus est esse qui praesit*); *Fam.* XVI. 12. 5 (to Tiro, 27 January) *ego adhuc orae maritimae praesum a Formiis. nullum maius negotium suscipere volui quo plus apud illum* [sc. *Caesarem*] *meae litterae cohortationesque ad pacem valerent.* It was probably understood between Cicero and Pompey that his supervisory role would not amount to anything very active (cf. 153 (VIII. 3). 4 above). So far as Campania as a whole was concerned, both the Consuls were on the spot to supervise or supplement the recruiting activities of zealots like Scribonius Libo, Faustus Sulla, and T. Ampius Balbus. Accordingly Cicero, who had at first expected to be much on the move, spent most of his time undisturbed at his Formian villa. On 24 January he had word from Pompey asking him to go to Capua and help with the levy (138 (VII. 14). 2)—evidently a special request, which so far from showing that Capua was Cicero's official sphere rather implies the contrary. Cicero complied, but when he got there found his presence superfluous and stayed only three nights (161B (VIII. 11B). 2).

Such a function, in practice merely titular, could be represented in different ways to different people, a flexibility which Cicero found convenient. To Atticus on 18 February he says that he had had nothing whatever to do (153 (VIII. 3). 5), and to his Caesarian friend Trebatius (141 (VII. 17). 4) and to Caesar himself (178A (IX. 11A). 2) he claims to have taken no part in the war; whereas in his letter to Pompey of 16 February (161B (VIII. 11B)), he represents his post as one of real responsibility. Granted that his language goes further in both directions than the truth quite warranted, it is fair also to allow that the truth in this instance could easily seem a matter of interpretation.

Cicero's statement to Tiro on 12 January has still to be accounted for. The simplest answer to that problem is a linguistic one: *sumpsimus* is an epistolary tense. On 11 January, let us say, Cicero received Pompey's 'order' to 'take Capua'. His first impulse was to accept. Writing to Tiro he puts his intention, after the manner of Roman correspondence, as though it were the accomplished fact which it presumably would be by the time the letter came to be read. But soon afterwards he changed his mind, and told Pompey that he would not undertake the charge without troops and money. So they reached a compromise, by which Cicero avoided the stigma of unemployment while at the same time escaping substantial commitment and thus preserving intact his potential usefulness as an intermediary. The last consideration may have appealed to Pompey, who anyhow was hardly in a position to force the pace.

APPENDIX III

THE CREDENTIALS OF L. CAESAR AND L. ROSCIUS[1]

In 49 B.C., on 24 January by the contemporary calendar, now running over six weeks ahead of schedule, nearly a fortnight after Caesar had crossed the Rubicon and nearly a week after the republican exodus from Rome, Cicero at Minturnae wrote to Atticus, who had remained behind, as follows (137 (VII. 13*a*). 2):

> L. Caesarem vidi Minturnis a.d. VIII Kal. Febr. mane cum absurdissimis mandatis, non hominem sed scopas solutas, ut id ipsum mihi ille [sc. Caesar] videatur irridendi causa fecisse, qui tantis de rebus huic mandata dederit; nisi forte non dedit et hic sermone aliquo adrepto pro mandatis abusus est.

In fact it turned out that L. Caesar's *mandata* were authentic and Cicero soon ceased to think them *absurdissima*. Caesar (I reserve 'Caesar', *tout court*, for the great man) was offering peace terms—that Pompey should go to Spain, that troops recruited in Italy for the Republic should be disbanded, that free elections should be held, and that Caesar for his part should resign his command on 1 July and come to Rome in person to stand for the Consulship—much the same terms as Curio had put before the Senate on 1 January. L. Caesar submitted them to Pompey and the Consuls at Teanum Sidicinum on 23 January and they were approved (final dispositions being left to the Senate), subject to Caesar's withdrawing his forces from the places he had occupied in Italy outside his province. With this condition Caesar would not comply, and the negotiations, of which Cicero had high hopes for a week or so, came to nothing.

Apart from Cicero, ancient information about these negotiations comes from two sources, Caesar and Dio Cassius. The former tells us (*B.C.* I. 8) how he harangued his troops and, satisfied with their reactions, marched to Ariminum (on 11 January). Then:

> Eo L. Caesar adulescens venit, cuius pater Caesaris erat legatus. is reliquo sermone confecto, cuius rei causa venerat, habere se a Pompeio ad eum privati offici mandata demonstrat: velle Pompeium se Caesari purgatum, ne ea quae rei publicae causa egerit in suam contumeliam vertat. semper se rei publicae commoda privatis necessitudinibus habuisse potiora. Caesarem quoque pro sua dignitate debere et studium et iracundiam suam rei publicae dimittere neque adeo graviter irasci inimicis ut cum illis nocere se speret rei publicae noceat.

[1] Read to the Society for the Promotion of Roman Studies in 1958 and published in its journal (50 (1960), pp. 88ff.). The paper is here reprinted by kind permission of the Society, with mechanical alterations.

pauca eiusdem generis addit cum excusatione Pompei coniuncta. eadem fere atque eisdem verbis praetor Roscius agit cum Caesare sibique Pompeium commemorasse demonstrat.

Caesar goes on to say that, having found two suitable persons to convey his wishes to Pompey, he requested each of them (*petit ab utroque*), since they had brought Pompey's message to him, not to object to taking his own demands to Pompey, in the hope that at the cost of a little trouble they might be able to end great quarrels and release all Italy from fear. Then follow the proposals mentioned above. With this message (*acceptis mandatis*) Roscius, with L. Caesar, arrived in Capua, where they found the Consuls and Pompey (a slight inaccuracy: they found them at Teanum).

All this is food for learned debate. The problem of L. Caesar's time-table has produced many pages of anxious chronology. The content of his message, which raises far-reaching questions concerning Caesar's good faith both as author and as politician, has been elaborately discussed by K. von Fritz.[1] I shall be sparing of dates and cautious of wide issues. I want to consider L. Caesar's status. Who commissioned him? How did this loose broom get his chance to change history?

To begin with, who was he? Historians usually record that he was a relative of Caesar, not always that Caesar was his second cousin twice removed; the patrician Julii being at this time split into two branches, the elder represented by this Lucius and his homonymous father, the younger by the future dictator and his cousin Sextus. This latter branch had a Marian connexion, whereas Lucius' grandfather, Consul in 90, and his great-uncle Gaius provided the Marians with two of their most distinguished victims. Lucius' father, who held the Consulship in 64, was a respectable person of generally conservative inclinations, which seem however to have been to some extent deflected by a personal connexion with the great Caesar, under whom he served as Legate. Mark Antony, who proscribed him, was his sister's son. In the Civil War he stayed in the background, probably in Italy. His son was at this time a young man (though Caesar's *adulescens* serves to distinguish him from his father and need not imply extreme youth) who had probably got no further along the *cursus honorum* than the Quaestorship, if so far. Unlike Lucius senior he turned out an active Pompeian until he was captured and put to death after Thapsus.

The second messenger (if such he was), the Praetor L. Roscius Fabatus, had served in Gaul as Caesar's Legate or Quaestor. Caesar had already mentioned (*B.C.* I. 3. 6) that in the senatorial debate on 6 January the Censor L. Piso (Caesar's father-in-law) and this Roscius volunteered (*pollicetur*) to go to his

[1] *Trans. Am. Phil. Ass.* 72 (1941), pp. 125–46.

camp in order to inform him of the proceedings and asked for six days in which to do so. But this was not conceded.[1] Little more is known of Roscius, except as a participant in these negotiations, down to his death in the first battle of Mutina, but a lex Roscia of 49 concerning the grant of citizenship to the Transpadane Gauls probably took its name from him. If so, he must have remained in Rome during his Praetorship as a member of the Caesarian Senate.

There are two points in Caesar's account which do not tally with what most modern writers have to say. (*a*) Nearly everyone has assumed that L. Caesar and Roscius came to Ariminum jointly. Caesar's language seems to me to imply the contrary—they said much the same things but said them separately. First Lucius is introduced and his message retailed, then Roscius. And Caesar's request that they should return to Pompey with his own proposals is made individually—so at least I understand *petit ab utroque*. (*b*) Caesar leaves us with an impression of informality: *nactus idoneos homines* suggests that L. Caesar and Roscius just happened to be around. And he requests them to carry his counter-message *as a favour*—they must not mind the trouble. If they were official envoys from the Senate, and that has been the majority view, Caesar's presentation must have been intended to mislead, at any rate as regards Lucius. Consider the sentence *is reliquo sermone confecto, cuius rei causa venerat, habere se a Pompeio ad eum privati offici mandata demonstrat*. If L. Caesar was sent officially by the Senate it would be deceptive if not downright false to tell us that he came to deliver a private message from Pompey.

It was accordingly suggested by Nissen,[2] and again by E. Meyer[3] and again by von Fritz,[4] that Caesar *is* out to mislead here, that he wanted to conceal from his readers the truth—that the Senate had sent official representatives to negotiate and persuade him to keep the peace. In the sentence I have just quoted Meyer and von Fritz take *reliquo sermone confecto* as Caesar's way of slurring over the official part of Lucius' communication. I grant that these words must not be translated as Peskett's Loeb version translates them, 'when their first greetings were over'. They do imply that Lucius had other things to talk about besides Pompey's message; and *cuius rei causa venerat* suggests that Pompey's message was not the *ostensible* reason for Lucius' presence in Ariminum. But was the ostensible reason an official mission? Might not Lucius have had private business with his father's

[1] Caesar's next sentence says that some senators also advocated the dispatch of *legati* to Caesar; the implication is clear that Roscius and Piso were proposing to go only in a private or semi-private capacity.

[2] *Historische Zeitung*, 46 (1881), p. 94, n. 1.

[3] *Caesars Monarchie*, p. 295.

[4] *l.c.* p. 131.

imperator, enough to form a pretext for the journey? The answer will become clearer later on.

To turn to Dio. Here is a translation of the relevant passage, beginning at XLI. 5. 1:

Accordingly Pompey, in view of what he was told about Caesar and because he had not yet any adequate force ready, seeing too that people in the capital, both ordinary folk and more especially the party men, feared war from their memories of Marius and Sulla and wanted to find a safe way out of it, changed his mind and sent as envoys to Caesar his kinsman L. Caesar and the Praetor L. Roscius (they had volunteered their services) to see whether he could escape Caesar's attack and come to a settlement on reasonable terms. Caesar replied by repeating the proposals in his letter to the Senate, including his wish for an interview with Pompey. Most people did not like the sound of this, fearing lest the two might reach an accord at their expense. But when the envoys spoke largely in praise of Caesar and ended by promising that no one would suffer any harm at his hands and that his troops would be disbanded forthwith, they were delighted, and sent the same envoys back to him, and went on clamorously demanding wherever and whenever they could that both together should lay down their arms. Pompey took alarm at this, for he was well aware that Caesar stood much higher than himself in the popular favour, and went off to Campania before the envoys returned....

The most remarkable point in Dio's account is that he makes the two envoys go twice to Caesar before the evacuation of Rome. This, despite L. Holzapfel's defence,[1] is generally agreed to be a blunder, as running counter to the evidence of Caesar and Cicero and involving difficulties of time-table. Dio's reference in his preceding chapter to Labienus' desertion as having already taken place is a similar error, universally acknowledged.

It is to be noted that in Dio Roscius and L. Caesar are joint envoys and that they are sent in the first instance not by the Senate but by Pompey.

Most of the modern authors whom I have consulted present both as the Senate's ambassadors, officially sent to inform Caesar of the *senatus consultum* which required him to resign his command and, as some add, to negotiate with him. So O. E. Schmidt,[2] Tyrrell-Purser,[3] Vonder Mühll,[4] Broughton,[5] and among historians Holzapfel,[6] Groebe,[7] Gelzer,[8] Meyer,[9] Adcock,[10] Rice Holmes,[11] Bloch-Carcopino,[12] von Fritz.[13] A substantial minority—

[1] *Klio*, 3 (1904), pp. 213ff. [2] *Briefwechsel*, p. 123. [3] IV, Appendix II.
[4] *RE*. IA. 1122. 42. [5] P. 265. [6] *l.c.* p. 131.
[7] Drumann–Groebe, III, p. 120, n. 9; *RE*. X. 224. 37.
[8] *Pompeius*, p. 213. [9] *op. cit.* pp. 295ff.
[10] *Cambridge Ancient History*, IX, p. 639.
[11] *Roman Republic*, III, p. 3—contradicted however in pp. 358ff.
[12] *République romaine*, pp. 522ff. [13] *l.c.* p. 131.

Lange,[1] Drumann,[2] Ferrero,[3] Heitland,[4] Marsh,[5] Miltner,[6]—follow Dio in making them Pompey's personal emissaries. Nissen[7] throws out a tentative theory that Roscius represented the Senate and L. Caesar only Pompey.

Even if Cicero's letters did not exist there would be remarkably little to be said for the majority opinion. Caesar and Dio, we have seen, discountenance it. Add that if Roscius and L. Caesar were really a senatorial embassy, its constitution would be extraordinary. When the Senate sent envoys to treat with Antony six years later it chose its three most eminent Consulars. A mere Praetor accompanied by an *adulescens* (even though distantly related) would surely have looked to Caesar more like an insult than a serious mission.

But Cicero's letters do exist, and I will ask the reader to go back to the one I quoted at the beginning of this paper. I am afraid I may be abusing his patience when I point out that if the Senate had appointed L. Caesar (according to Holzapfel they did so on Cicero's own motion) Cicero would have known of it; and that if Cicero *did* know of Lucius in such a capacity he could not so criticize Caesar's choice of him as the bearer of his own terms. Cicero's view of Lucius as an irresponsible good-for-nothing, whose message might have nothing more behind it than a scrap of casual conversation, cannot by any possibility be squared with his supposed status of Legatus.

The only historian in whom I have found any real appreciation of the importance of this paragraph is F. B. Marsh, who writes as follows:[8]

> It is also held that they were charged not only with a private message from Pompey, but also with an official message from the senate informing Caesar of the decree which required him to give up his provinces on a certain day or be declared a public enemy. Caesar, however, says nothing of a message from the senate.... Moreover, if the senate had sent them to make an official comunication to Caesar, it seems difficult to explain the surprise felt by Cicero at the choice of L. Caesar as envoy, since it would have been obvious that he was sent to deliver a reply to the senate because he had been the bearer of a message from the senate, and Cicero could hardly have written to Atticus.... If Cicero knew why the 'untied broom' had been selected such language is rather curious. It seems to be probable, therefore, that the two envoys were not the bearers of any official communication, but only of a private message from Pompey.

This is good as far as it goes, though 'impossible' would be a more appropriate term than 'difficult', and 'idiotic' than 'rather curious'. But the argument should have been pursued further. Cicero could not have written

[1] *Röm. Alterthümer*, III, pp. 401f. [2] Drumann–Groebe, III, pp. 120f.
[3] *Grandezza e Decadenza di Roma*, II, p. 315. His note is on the right lines.
[4] *Roman Republic*, III, pp. 281f. [5] *History of the Roman World*, III, Appendix 8.
[6] *RE.* XXI. 2182. 46. [7] *l.c.* p. 94. [8] *op. cit.* pp. 400f.

what he wrote if he had thought that Lucius went to Ariminum on behalf of the Senate; and by the same token he could not have written it if he had thought that Lucius went on behalf of Pompey. How could he suggest that the choice of Lucius was a deliberate insult on Caesar's part if he knew that Lucius was Pompey's messenger? And why should he then have doubted that Caesar was, indeed, answering Pompey's communication through the channel by which it had reached him? Clearly he did not know. Moreover none of his ten subsequent references to Lucius and his missions contains a hint of awareness that these were initiated by Pompey. Always he writes of Caesar's message (*mandata*) from Ariminum to Campania and of Pompey's reply (*responsa*).

Yet in face of Caesar's testimony and Dio's it can hardly be questioned that Lucius *was* sent by Pompey in the first instance, so that Cicero's ignorance of the fact after their talk at Minturnae was due either to accident or to deliberate concealment on Lucius' part. The first alternative being clearly improbable, the conclusion follows that Pompey's message was confidential and that Cicero and his like were ignorant of it because Pompey preferred to have them so. Nor are his motives hard to guess. Dio tells us that many people were nervous lest Pompey and Caesar should form another coalition; and when Tyrrell–Purser remark that 'Cicero never hints at any such possible treachery on the part of Pompey' they only reveal their failure to grasp the implications of 150 (VII. 26). 2; 161D (VIII. 11D). 7 and 199 (X. 8). 5; passages which show a lively consciousness of the danger that, as in 58, Cicero might himself be thrown to the wolves as a result of an accord between the two dynasts. But direct evidence is really unnecessary. Given Pompey's past, suspicions were inevitable, and it is obvious that he would have wished to avoid any action likely to stimulate them, even if he had in reality only the most loyal intentions towards his new allies. His message as Caesar reports it does, indeed, contain nothing to which Cato or Domitius could have objected, but I am not the first to suspect that Caesar's account may be incomplete. 'Auch ist es wahrscheinlich', writes Nissen,[1] 'dass der junge Lucius Cäsar noch anderes zu bestellen hatte als die Phrasen, die wir in den Denkwürdigkeiten lesen.' 'It is impossible not to suspect,' writes Adcock,[2] 'both that something more seductive was suggested and that the suggestion was intended to gain time by delaying Caesar's advance.' Whether that was Pompey's object or whether he was really exploring the possibilities of a settlement with his old associate can only be a matter of speculation.

To Cicero, L. Caesar was evidently the principal agent in these interchanges. His only reference to Roscius is in 162 (VIII. 12) of 28 February,

[1] *l.c.* p. 94, n. 1.

[2] *Cambridge Ancient History*, IX, p. 639.

condiciones pacis per L. Caesarem et Fabatum adlatas—another nail in the coffin of the senatorial embassy, since had Roscius and L. Caesar been officially associated the superior in rank would have taken the lead. The available evidence suggests that Roscius went unofficially to Ariminum in pursuance of his offer[1] to carry information to Caesar and perhaps in the hope of setting on foot negotiations. As a sympathizer with Caesar it would be a natural thing for him to do. How far Pompey was responsible for his going and what relation his message bore to L. Caesar's are questions which we have not sufficient evidence even to discuss.

[1] See above, pp. 442 f.

APPENDIX IV

EXSPECTATIO CORFINIENSIS[1]

The rapid thrusts with which Caesar opened his campaign in 49 and created the panic which on 17–18 January sent Senate and magistrates helter-skelter down the Appian Way were followed by a lull, while he waited for reinforcements from Gaul and explored, with whatever degree of sincerity, the possibilities of a peaceful accommodation. About 3 February he was on the move again. Joined by his Twelfth legion he overran Picenum and, on the 5th or later,[2] began an advance down the coast road from Firmum, south through Castrum Truentinum to Aternum. From there he turned south-west through the country of the Marrucini, to reach Corfinium on 14 or 15 February.

A large republican army had been concentrated in or near this town under a commander whose personality contained its fate.[3] L. Domitius Ahenobarbus, now in the eyes of his party legitimate governor of Transalpine Gaul, had been elected to the Consulship, as Cicero almost puts it,[4] in his cradle, fifth in an unbroken sequence of nine generations of consular Ahenobarbi, and enormously wealthy to boot. His career bespeaks courage, energy, and tenacity. Cicero, whose candidature in 64 relied largely on Domitius' support,[5] thought him a fool.[6] What his brother-in-law Cato thought after the electoral scandal of 54[7] is not on record. It hardly mattered. Neither scandal nor fiasco could cost Domitius his place in the front line. He had brought twelve cohorts from Rome, and not later than 8 February was joined by about nineteen more in retreat from Picenum.[8] Their

[1] The paper published in *Journ. Rom. Stud.* 46 (1956), pp. 57 ff. is here reprinted by permission with some modifications.

[2] Cf. Rice Holmes, *Roman Republic*, III, pp. 375 ff.

[3] The traditional condemnation of Domitius' conduct at Corfinium has been challenged by K. von Fritz in his paper 'Pompey's Policy before and after the Outbreak of the Civil War of 49 B.C.' (*Trans. Am. Phil. Ass.* 73 (1942), pp. 145ff.) and by A. Burns, 'Pompey's strategy and Domitius' stand at Corfinium' (*Historia* 15 (1966), pp. 74 ff.). They are right to urge that there was more than blind obstinacy in the case. But Domitius' experience in military matters, if he had any, did not entitle him to defy the warnings of a general with Pompey's record, even though he was technically not under Pompey's orders. To do so was to court disaster; and it is no excuse to argue that if Pompey had allowed his hand to be forced the result might have been different.

[4] 82 (IV. 8*a*). 2.

[5] 10 (I. 1). 4.

[6] 151 (VIII. 1). 3.

[7] Cf. 91 (IV. 17). 2.

[8] Cf. 161A (VIII. 11A); 162A (VIII. 12A). 1; Caes. *B.C.* I. 15. 3, 17. 2. The exact

commanders, Vibullius Rufus and Lucilius Hirrus, were henchmen of Pompey's (the latter a relative), but at Corfinium took their orders from Domitius. Not all of this force was in Corfinium itself, part being stationed at Alba Fucens and Sulmo.[1]

About 150 Roman miles away by road were Pompey's headquarters at Luceria. He had two legions, those detached from Caesar shortly before the war,[2] and some raw levies. But six of his veteran cohorts were garrisoning Canusium, further south on the road to Brundisium, and Brundisium itself.[3]

On the other side of Italy the Consuls were raising troops for the Republic. Their headquarters were at Capua.[4] Not far away, at his Formian villa, sat Cicero, charged with certain supervisory responsibilities which weighed among the lightest of his cares.

From 162B (VIII. 12B). 2 we learn that Pompey, foreseeing disaster if the army at Corfinium did not get out while it could, had been urging Domitius to join him at Luceria. On the 10th he had word that Domitius had indeed decided to start south on the 9th. The message was brought by one Q. Fabius, who left Corfinium on the 8th, and Pompey passed it on to Cicero (161A (VIII. 11A)). Vibullius had written likewise, but soon wrote again to report that Domitius was not marching after all,[5] news which provoked the first of Pompey's three extant letters to the latter, 162B (VIII. 12B). This second letter of Vibullius' will have been dispatched not later than the 9th and have arrived at Luceria on the 11th. Since every hour counted if Domitius was to be saved from Caesar and himself, Pompey's letter should be assigned to that day rather than the following. There is certainly no need to be so imprecise as Tyrrell–Purser (followed by Sjögren and Moricca), 'between February 10 and 16'.

While awaiting further news Pompey took an important step. Probably on the 13th or 14th, certainly no later than the early morning of the 15th,[6]

size and composition of Domitius' force is a matter of debate; cf. Rice Holmes, *op. cit.* III, pp. 368 ff.; Burns, *l.c.* pp. 81 ff.

[1] 162A (VIII. 12A). 1. [2] Cf. 136 (VII. 13). 2 n. [3] Cf. 162A (VIII. 12A). 2 n.

[4] The Consuls remained in this part of Italy until about 18 February, when they left to join Pompey, but after 5 February, when Lentulus was at Capua (145 (VII. 21). 1), their movements are otherwise unknown: cf. von Fritz. *l.c.* p. 157.

[5] Burns (*l.c.* pp. 82ff.) argues that Domitius altered his plan in consequence of the accession of Vibullius' force on 8 February. If so it is strange that Vibullius should have given not this reason but another and nugatory one to Pompey, who professes himself at a loss to understand the change (162B (VIII. 12B). 1).

[6] Schmidt, *Briefwechsel*, pp. 136 f.; von Fritz, *l.c.* p. 156.

he sent a message to the Consuls in Campania by the hand of his family friend, the *tribunicius* D. Laelius. He states its contents in his letter to the Consuls, 162A (VIII. 12A). 3

D. Laelio mandaram, quod maiores copias sperabam nos habituros, ut, si vobis videretur, alter uter vestrum ad me veniret, alter in Siciliam cum ea copia quam Capuae et cirum Capuam comparastis et cum iis militibus quos Faustus legit proficisceretur, Domitius cum XII suis cohortibus eodem adiungeretur, reliquae copiae omnes Brundisium cogerentur et inde navibus Dyrrachium transportarentur.

That was Pompey's first official notice of his intention to evacuate Italy,[1] how long previously formed no one can say for certain. In two rather highly wrought passages (161 (VIII. 11). 2; 177 (IX. 10). 6) Cicero accuses him to Atticus of having planned evacuation from the outset of the war and years earlier. Modern scholars tend to agree.[2] But Cicero's ordinary view was different. Pompey was ἀστρατήγητος (136 (VII. 13). 1), ἀστρατηγητότατος

[1] Von Fritz (pp. 159 ff.) argues that the message was not so definite as Pompey later represented it, a view which may seem to be borne out by Cicero's language in 153 (VIII. 3). 1 (see note *ad loc.*); on the other hand 161D (VIII. 11D). 1 *certior tui consili factus* tells against it. The message was not entirely oral as von Fritz supposes; cf. 153 (VIII. 3). 7 *scripserat ad consules.*

[2] A number are cited by Burns, *l.c.* p. 91, n. 89. Von Fritz (*l.c.* pp. 151 f.) points to two passages in the Letters as proving that Pompey had told Cicero personally of this intention early in the war, despite the latter's emphatic denial in a letter to Pompey himself (161D (VIII. 11D). 6). But (*a*) Pompey's words cited in 177 (IX. 10). 2 of 18 March *Sulla potuit, ego non potero?* do not 'certainly point to a plan of conquering Italy from the East', nor does Cicero say (as von Fritz says he says) that he used them on 17 January. All Cicero's references to Pompey's 'Sullaturient' designs (cf. 161 (VIII. 11). 2; 174 (IX. 7). 3; 177 (IX. 10). 6; 198 (X. 7). 1) come after the fall of Corfinium. They could be based on hearsay. (*b*) 'In a letter of March 17 [176 (IX. 9). 2] Cicero says that he himself was present when Pompey discussed in detail his plans for a blockade of Italy.... Since Cicero when he wrote this letter had not met Pompey since January 23 the discussion referred to must have taken place between January 16 and 23.' Cicero almost certainly did not see Pompey on 23 January or at any other time after they left Rome until his own arrival in Greece. He says nothing about *Pompey* discussing a blockade; *sermonibus interfui* may refer to talks with leading republicans such as those mentioned in 135 (VII. 12). 2. It is doubtless true that the idea of withdrawal from Italy was in the air in the days following the flight from Rome, even though Appian's statement (*B.C.* II. 37; cf. Dio, XLI. 7. 3) that Pompey intimated this as a possibility to the Senate on 17 January is hard to believe in face of Cicero's silence. Finally, as von Fritz recognizes (p. 152), nothing of this sort said by Pompey after the shock of Caesar's invasion would prove that his plan was settled in advance of it.

(166 (VIII. 16). 1). The way the capital was abandoned, especially the failure to remove the State treasure which Pompey afterwards tried vainly to retrieve (145 (VII. 21). 2), is not indicative of foresight. As for Pompey's confident talk before the war ('I have only to stamp my foot', etc.) and his sanguine letter to Cicero late in January (140 (VII. 16). 2), they *may* have been only meant to hearten waverers; but they have the ring of 1939. On 27 February Cicero writes to Pompey that an evacuation of Italy was the last possibility that would ever have entered his, Cicero's, head (161D (VIII. 11D). 5). This was a *façon de parler* (see my note *ad loc.*), for he had discussed the possibility with Caelius Rufus in December[1] and written of it to Atticus within a few days of leaving Rome.[2] But it is surely evidence that Pompey had given no distinct intention either publicly or to Cicero in private. Many or most of his supporters doubtless felt the same indignation and repugnance as did Cicero and Atticus.[3] All we know of Domitius suggests that no man would be less likely to see the necessities of the case as Pompey now saw them, and Pompey's first extant letter to him significantly contains no hint in that direction.

This needs to be remembered in reading Pompey's next letter, 162C (VIII. 12C). On 16 February he had received a reply to 162B (VIII. 12B) to the effect that Domitius proposed to wait and see what the enemy did. If Caesar moved down the coast, Domitius would march at once into Samnium to join Pompey;[4] otherwise he would stand fast at Corfinium and resist if attacked. In a final effort to avert the catastrophe he foresaw Pompey answered the same day with 162C (VIII. 12C), a remarkable document.[5] Consider his position. Here was the last chance, if indeed a chance remained, of saving the northern army. Doubtless Pompey would have liked to tell Domitius some home truths, but that would not get him out of Corfinium. Neither could he give an order, for Domitius was not his subordinate. He

[1] *Fam.* II. 16. 3; cf. Schmidt, *Briefwechsel*, p. 95.

[2] Cf. 135 (VII. 12). 2; but on 2 February he writes as though the idea had been given up: 141 (VII. 17). 1 *cum fuga ex Italia quaeri videbatur.*

[3] Cf. 177 (IX. 10). 4, 6.

[4] 162C (VIII. 12C). 1 *si secundum mare ad me ire coepisset, confestim in Samnium ad me venturum*, on which von Fritz (p. 154, n. 45) comments: 'this makes sense only if the plan had been to fight Caesar in Italy, and would have been perfectly insane, if Domitius had previously been informed that Italy was to be evacuated as early as possible'. It has to be remembered however that Domitius' route to Pompey lay through Samnium, Luceria being only a few miles within the Apulian border.

[5] Its deliberately ambiguous quality was appreciated by von Fritz, who rightly calls it a masterpiece of evasion and obscurity (p. 155), though I do not think he read between the lines quite correctly.

must persuade; and to persuade he must deceive, for to deal frankly, to communicate the plan of evacuation sent to the Consuls two days previously, could only confirm Domitius in his recalcitrance.[1] Word of Laelius' message, which did not reach Cicero at Formiae until the 17th, was not likely to reach Domitius before the arrival of 162C (VIII. 12C). If only he could be induced to retreat immediately, his eyes would not be opened until he was safely at Luceria. But what then? What would Domitius and his optimate friends have to say when the truth came out—that he had been lured from his stronghold on a pretence of united resistance only to take part in an ignominious flight overseas, deliberately kept in ignorance of the plan dispatched to the Consuls? Pompey must therefore choose his phrases with an eye to later recrimination.[2] Especially he must insert some reference to Laelius' message which, while not arousing Domitius' suspicions more than could be helped, might be adduced in evidence that Pompey had not designedly kept him in the dark—only expressed himself obscurely in the haste of an emergency.

Accordingly §§2 and 3 contain only vague hints of the coming evacuation. They could be read and were meant to be read by Domitius as implying that further retreat would be necessary only if the junction of forces at Luceria did not take place. With a strong army the risk of encirclement could be faced (*aut exercitum firmum habere oportet quo confidamus perrumpere nos posse. . .*). Given unity *possumus etiam nunc rem publicam erigere*—an echo of 162B (VIII. 12B). I *contractis nostris copiis spero nos et rei publicae et communi saluti prodesse posse*, on which the reader could put his own construction. Yet there is nothing at which Domitius could point an accusing finger later on and say 'this was a pledge'. There *is* a reference to Laelius' mission, so obscure and apparently casual that scholars have tried to clarify it by altering the text: §3 *consules praesidia omnia deducturi sunt aut in Siciliam ituri*. If Pompey had wanted to be explicit he might have added *Brundisium* after *omnia* as Schmidt does, or written Holzapfel's *et* for *aut* or Sternkopf's *aut huc aut*. Even so, the mention of Sicily would remain strangely at variance with the statement a few lines previously that the Consuls had decided to

[1] Cf. von Fritz, p. 170: 'The evidence concerning Domitius is perhaps less definite but his attitude at Corfinium together with the explanation he gave of his actions (*Att.* VIII. 12C. 1) leave hardly any doubt that he would have followed Pompey's orders if he had known of his inflexible decision concerning the grand stategy of the war.' If there was an inflexible decision and Domitius had been informed of it in advance, he might have acquiesced, though even this seems open to doubt. At any rate Pompey could not hope to convert him at this late stage, by letter.

[2] Von Fritz (p. 155) misses this point.

come at once to Luceria. But Pompey did not want to be clear or consistent here. *aut in Siciliam ituri* would be read by Domitius in the light of the next sentence (*nam aut exercitum firmum habere oportet...aut regiones eius modi obtinere e quibus repugnemus*) as an afterthought, part of a vaguely foreshadowed plan of retreat which would never come into operation if Pompey's inadequate forces were strengthened by the accession of his own. But the true purpose would only be served later on, when words began to pass in the *praetorium*.

Before the letter was dispatched Pompey heard again from Domitius (cf. §4, a postscript), and on the next day came Domitius' announcement of Caesar's arrival before the town. Pompey had every right to say 'I told you so', and in his reply, 162D (VIII. 12D), he said it. He also made it plain that he had no intention of committing his own small and unreliable forces, and urged Domitius even now to extricate himself if possible.

Besides this to Domitius, Pompey wrote to the Consuls[1] twice. First the brief note preserved in 154 (VIII. 6). 2, an urgent summons to join him (the Sicily plan being now out of date). Therewith went a copy of Domitius' final dispatch.

A much longer letter, 162A (VIII. 12A), explaining and justifying the policy of retreat was written, as editors except T.–P. perceive, later on the 17th or, more probably, on the 18th or even 19th. It is an elaborate document which must have taken some time to compose; the consultations mentioned in §4 with M. Marcellus and others probably took place in the interval between the two letters; and whereas the short letter reached its destination on the 18th, the contents of this were evidently unknown to Cicero when he wrote 157 (VIII. 5), not earlier than the evening of the 22nd,[2] an indication that it did not reach the Consuls before they left for Luceria, as they probably did on the 18th;[3] finally the difference in Pompey's instructions as given in his two letters to the Consuls suggests that the interval was more than half a day.[4]

[1] Cicero says *ad consules* in 154 (VIII. 6). 1 and 158 (VIII. 8). 2; but he refers to the same letter in 161D (VIII. 11D). 3 as *ad Lentulum consulem*, and Pompey himself uses the singular. Probably identical letters by separate messengers were sent to both Consuls because of the urgent operational nature of the contents in order to expedite reactions if they should not be together.

[2] Cf. §2 *novi si quid esset scripsissem*. He had evidently heard nothing beyond the bare fact of Pompey's retreat when he wrote the postscript to 156 (VIII. 4) on the morning of the 22nd.

[3] Pompey writes on the 20th of them having joined his army in Apulia (161C (VIII. 11C).

[4] So von Fritz, p. 159, n. 70. In this later letter Pompey uses plurals, *vos*, so probably only one copy was sent.

We may now turn to Cicero at Formiae. On the 15th he received a letter from Pompey, recommending him to proceed at once to Luceria.[1] Cicero's responsibilities in Campania, whatever they actually amounted to, gave him an excuse to temporize. His answer to Pompey, 161B (VIII. 11B), urges that if the coast was to be held, as seemed to him both possible and desirable, someone must be in command on the spot: *si tenendam hanc oram putas... opus est esse qui praesit.* So far from 'being in fact a resignation of his office'[2] this implies that Cicero will remain at his post until further directions. That is obvious from the words themselves and had already been stated in §1: *nunc quoniam auctoritate et consilio tuo in spe firmiore sumus,*[3] *si teneri posse putas Tarracinam ⟨et⟩ oram maritimam, in ea manebo.* If however Pompey decides upon concentrating all forces available, then Cicero will at once comply (*sin omnia unum in locum contrahenda sunt, non dubito quin ad te statim veniam*). So in writing to Atticus on the night of 15–16 February Cicero assumes that he will be going to Luceria (151 (VIII. 1). 4 *ibimus tamen Luceriam*), but clearly has no idea of setting out until he hears further from Pompey (cf. §2).[4] Nor is any such intention apparent in his next letter, 152 (VIII. 2), written before daybreak on the 17th, until we come to the last sentence, which runs in the MSS as follows:

> ego XIII Kal., cum eadem lucerna hanc epistulam scripsissem qua inflammaram tuam, Formiis ad Pompeium, si de pace ageretur, profectus;[5] si de bello, quid ero?

Clearly the text is defective. Perhaps the only change necessary is *profecturus* (ed. Rom., vulg.) for *profectus*; *profectus sum* can be understood after *ad Pompeium*. But the sentence still has somewhat of a makeshift look, and Atticus could not but be taken aback at so abrupt an announcement. Two possibilities need to be considered in the light of Cicero's letter to Pompey ten days later (161D (VIII. 11D). 1). There Cicero says that he made up his mind to leave after learning of Pompey's plan (to evacuate Italy) as com-

[1] The contents are known only from Cicero's description in 151 (VIII. 1). 1. 161A (VIII. 11A) came in later, perhaps on the 17th or 18th after he had left Formiae: see note *ad loc.*

[2] As T.–P. IV, p. 560.

[3] To Cicero as to Domitius Pompey had written nothing to suggest what was at any rate by now his real strategic purpose.

[4] This letter must have been written before 161B (VIII. 11B); cf. my note on 151 (VIII. 1). 2 *me non quaerere*. The account in the earlier version of this paper (p. 60) is thereby invalidated.

[5] With variants *praefectus* and *praefectis*.

municated through Laelius: *interim nondum meis litteris ad te perlatis ex iis mandatis quae D. Laelio ad consules dederas certior tui consili factus non exspectavi dum mihi a te litterae redderentur confestimque cum Quinto fratre et cum liberis nostris iter ad te in Apuliam facere coepi.* Obviously this happened after he had written the main part of 152 (VIII. 2), which has nothing about of evacuation or Brundisium (cf. §3 *nos interea ne Capuae quidem sed Luceriae*). The final sentence must be a postscript, added after news of Pompey's message had come in. But why in that case does Cicero say nothing of the message itself? One possible answer is that the postscript was dashed off in a tearing hurry. The domestic confusion when Cicero announced that he, Quintus, and the boys must leave immediately can be imagined. Alternatively some lines of text may have dropped out after *tuam*. In his next letter to Atticus, 153 (VIII. 3), written on the night of the 18th, Cicero makes only incidental mention of Laelius' message (§7), in a manner which seems to imply that Atticus would already have heard about it (the possibility that he was told in a lost letter dispatched the following day cannot however be excluded).

His next movements are recorded in §2 of 161D (VIII. 11D):

cum Teanum Sidicinum venissem, C. Messius, familiaris tuus, mihi dixit aliique complures Caesarem iter habere Capuam et eo ipso die mansurum esse Aeserniae. sane sum commotus quod, si ita esset, non modo iter meum interclusum sed me ipsum plane exceptum putabam. itaque tum Cales processi *et sqq.*

At Cales Cicero spent the next two nights (unless indeed he went there from Teanum on the 18th), and on that of the 18th he wrote 153 (VIII. 3) on the great question—should he follow Pompey overseas or no? As he was writing, stirring news came in: §7 *sed ecce nuntii scribente me haec ipsa noctu in Caleno, ecce litterae Caesarem ad Corfinium, Domitium Corfini cum firmo exercitu et pugnare cupiente.* According to Cicero's own statement to Pompey in 161D (VIII. 11D). 3 the *litterae* consisted of (or included) Pompey's dispatch of the 17th *ad Lentulum consulem* (reproduced in 154 (VIII. 6). 2) with Domitius' last dispatch from Corfinium appended. *his ego litteris lectis,* he continues, *in eadem opinione fui qua reliqui omnes, te cum omnibus copiis ad Corfinium esse venturum.* Pompey's dispatch, it appears, was misinterpreted. When he told the Consuls that all forces must be concentrated *unum in locum* he was taken to mean, not Brundisium (cf. 162A (VIII. 12A). 4), but Luceria. Or perhaps he really did for the moment mean this, or thought it necessary to appear to mean it, for his instruction to leave an adequate garrison in Capua (dropped in his later letter, 162A (VIII. 12A)) seems senseless otherwise. At any rate his readers in western Italy thought that in the new situation he meant to march to Domitius' rescue. As Cicero put it some days later (158

(VIII. 8). 2 *fulsisse mihi videbatur* τὸ καλὸν *ad oculos eius et exclamasse ille vir qui esse debuit* πρὸς ταῦθ' ὅ τι χρὴ καὶ παλαμάσθων | καὶ πάντ' ἐπ' ἐμοὶ τεκταινέσθων· | τὸ γὰρ εὖ μετ' ἐμοῦ.

But according to J. D. Duff,[1] Cicero was lying:

'At Cales (*cum Calibus essem*), Cicero says to Pompey, he received a copy of a despatch sent by Domitius to Pompey, with a postscript from Pompey which convinced Cicero and all his companions that Pompey had no intention of leaving Italy at all but was on the point of marching north to Corfinium. In that case, Cicero had no longer any reason to proceed to Luceria. Now a letter to Atticus (VIII. 6), written on Feb. 23rd from Formiae, shows that this statement is simply untrue: that Cicero had given up all idea of proceeding to Luceria and had returned to Formiae before he ever saw this important despatch, which he represents as having had so much influence upon his movements. I cannot avoid the inference that he purposely misled Pompey on this point. He wished to conceal the fact that he had returned from Cales at once to Formiae; he wished to convey the impression that he had gone as far as was safe for him and had remained there until he discovered that it was quite useless for him to proceed to Luceria. As a matter of fact, he had done nothing of the kind.'

If Duff had really wished to avoid an inference damaging to Cicero's character he would scarcely have overlooked the sentence just cited from 153 (VIII. 3). 7, which stands as incontrovertible proof that Cicero *did* learn at any rate the substance of Pompey's dispatch at Cales on the night of the 18th. And the next sentences show that he did indeed draw the conclusions he says he drew in 161D (VIII. 11D):

non puto etiam hoc Gnaeum nostrum commissurum ut Domitium relinquat; etsi Brundisium Scipionem cum cohortibus duabus praemiserat, legionem Fausto conscriptam in Siciliam sibi placere a consule duci scripserat ad consules. sed turpe Domitium deserere erit implorantem eius auxilium.

There can be no question of deliberate falsehood here. What Duff intended by his statement that Cicero returned from Cales at once to Formiae and wished to conceal the fact I am not sure; at first sight it looks 'simply untrue'. If it is meant that Cicero tried to mislead Pompey into supposing that he had gone beyond Cales in the direction of Luceria, it must be answered that Cicero's letter neither says nor implies anything of the kind.

The passage which led Duff to his hasty and unjust conclusion must now be considered. In 154 (VIII. 6) Cicero sends Atticus the text of Pompey's (short) letter of the 17th to the Consuls, brought by the Praetor Sosius the previous evening. To be sure 154 (VIII. 6) was not written on the 23rd

[1] *Journ. Phil.* 33 (1914), pp. 157 ff. Purser (Tyrrell died in 1914) followed (T.–P. IV, pp. xxviii, n. 2, and 100), and Duff's presentation does not seem to have been challenged until 1956. Cf. von Fritz, p. 152, n. 34.

but, as Schmidt had proved twenty years before Duff wrote, before the 22nd—as I hope to prove presently on the 20th. But it certainly appears that Cicero did not possess the full text of Pompey's letter until the evening of the 19th. Possibly he only received an account of the contents at Cales, not the text itself; in that case his statement to Pompey that he read the letter at Cales is a lapse of memory. One would think however that every detail of this dramatic incident would be fresh in his mind on the 27th, even though the difference between reading the letter itself and reading a paraphrase is in no way material. Then there is another point: in this same letter, 154 (VIII. 6). 3, he says that he had already sent Atticus *pridie* the text of Domitius' dispatch (appended to Pompey's); and *pridie* means, as will presently be shown, the 19th. I do not think we can be quite certain what happened, but suggest that the messenger who brought Pompey's letter to Cales had been told by Lentulus to visit other notables besides Cicero. So although Cicero read the letter, he could not keep it and did not delay the messenger by taking a copy. But after dispatching 153 (VIII. 3) he somehow acquired a copy of Domitius' letter (but not of Pompey's) and sent that off to Atticus from Formiae on the evening of the 19th, just before Sosius arrived.

On the morning of the 19th Cicero returned to Formiae. Then come four letters, VIII. 4–7 in the traditional arrangement, which as everyone now agrees, cannot have been written in that order. Modern editors[1] date as follows:

154 (VIII. 6) is assigned to 21 February. It begins with a reference to a letter not now extant, written the previous evening and dispatched before dawn (*de nocte*). After it had been sealed, says Cicero, the Praetor C. Sosius arrived with a copy of Pompey's (short) letter to the Consuls. The text of this follows. Appended was a copy of Domitius' letter *quod ego ad te pridie miseram*. Cicero is all anxiety for the outcome but not unhopeful.

Next 156 (VIII. 4). Its date, before dawn of the 22nd, is guaranteed by 157 (VIII. 5). 1. All but the final paragraph concerns the ungrateful behaviour of the Greek tutor Dionysius, a favourite topic at this period. But at the end comes a momentous postscript: *Sulmone C. Atium Paelignum aperuisse portas, cum essent cohortes quinque, Q. Lucretium inde fugisse scis,*[2] *Gnaeum ire Brundisium, ⟨Domitium⟩ desertum. confecta res est.*

Next 157 (VIII. 5), again mainly about Dionysius, who arrived at Formiae from Rome the same evening. Some editions assign it to the 22nd, others to the 23rd.

Lastly 155 (VIII. 7), generally assigned to the 23rd.

[1] I.e. up to 1956. On Bayet and Watt see introd. note to 154 (VIII. 6).

[2] *scito* Schmidt; see note *ad loc.*

Schmidt, in 1893, was the first to draw attention to the manifest impossibility of the fairly sanguine Letter 6 having been written after the despairing postscript to Letter 4. What of Letter 7, which begins thus?—

Vnum etiam restat amico nostro ad omne dedecus ut Domitio non subveniat. 'at nemo dubitat quin subsidio venturus sit'. ego non puto. 'deseret igitur talem civem et eos ⟨quos⟩ una sci⟨t e⟩sse,[1] cum habeat praesertim XX ipse cohortis, XXX Domitius?' nisi me omnia fallunt, deser⟨et⟩.

Is it likely, is it even credible, that these words were written by a man who wrote *confecta res est* the day before? How should he thus speculate about what Pompey is going to do when he had already heard? How could he say *nemo dubitat quin subsidio venturus sit*, when the news of retreat on Brundisium was already out? 'Noch fehlte die Bestätigung, dass das Gerücht wahr sei', says Schmidt.[2] But Cicero does not give the news as a rumour but as a fact; and though he might not yet be quite certain of its truth, he could not wholly ignore it. The order must be, not 6, 4, 5, 7, but 6, 7, 4, 5. For corroboration, when Cicero wrote Letter 7 he thought that Atticus favoured his leaving Italy if Pompey left: §1 *nihil spectat nisi fugam, cui tu (video enim quid sentias) me comitem putas debere esse*. Now we know from 177 (IX. 10). 6 that in a letter of 19 February Atticus had vigorously repudiated the suggestion that he advocated such a course. Cicero quotes his words: *ego vero nulla epistula significavi, si Gnaeus Italia cederet, ut tu una cederes, aut si significavi, non dico fui inconstans sed demens*. And again: *nihil relinquitur nisi fuga, cui te socium neutiquam puto esse oportere nec umquam putavi.*[3] Obviously Cicero had not read this letter when he wrote 155 (VIII. 7). But a letter from Rome normally took not more than two days, sometimes less, to reach Formiae. How came it that this letter of the 19th had not arrived by the 23rd?[4]

I conclude then that 155 (VIII. 7) was written before the 22nd; and it was certainly written after 154 (VIII. 6). Had they been written the same day Cicero would probably have said so. Accordingly 154 (VIII. 6) belongs to the 20th, the lost letter therein mentioned to the 19th (dispatched before dawn of the 20th) and 155 (VIII. 7) to the 21st. This arrangement has the further convenience of removing doubt as to the meaning of *pridie* in §3—

[1] *scis esse* vulg. See note *ad loc.*

[2] *Briefwechsel*, p. 145.

[3] Atticus was answering 152 (VIII. 2) of the 17th: §4 *significas enim aliquanto secus quam solebas ut etiam Italia, si ille cedat, putes cedendum.*

[4] It is curious that he does not acknowledge its receipt in his extant letters. There seems no room for a lost letter on the 21st or 22nd, so his omission to do so has to be set down to his preoccupation with Dionysius.

it can only mean the 19th. The marked change of mood between 154 (VIII. 6) and 155 (VIII. 7) is nothing out of the way for Cicero. Some rumour or conversation which he does not mention may have been responsible.

As stated above, 156 (VIII. 4) is fixed to the early morning of the 22nd by 157 (VIII. 5). 1, where Cicero refers to a 'strong' letter addressed to Dionysius in the same bag. When Dionysius arrived in person he was naturally anxious to recover this letter before it should be forwarded to its intended recipient. 157 (VIII. 5) will therefore have been written and perhaps dispatched (by special messenger (cf. §1) that same evening.[1] The brief, dirge-like 158 (VIII. 8), written after a first report of the surrender at Corfinium, is most naturally assigned to the 23rd (hitherto to the 24th, as following 155 (VIII. 7)). To the 24th I assign 159 (VIII. 10), a brief account of Cicero's talk with and dismissal of Dionysius. It is usually dated the 26th, but the interview would surely take place on the morning after Dionysius' arrival, i.e. on the 23rd, and be reported to Atticus without delay. This leaves the 26th without an extant letter (in place of the 20th).

[1] Schmidt's theory (p. 144) that Dionysius returned to Rome on the night of the 22nd and that Cicero so informed Atticus in a lost letter dispatched the same night is wholly untenable. (*a*) The opening sentence of 157 (VIII. 5) is plainly the first announcement of the tutor's arrival. (*b*) Dionysius would surely have rested at least one night. (*c*) Cicero would not have been so concerned to recover his 'strong' letter if he had known what Dionysius came to say. (*d*) The report of their interview would have been given in the lost letter, not in 159 (VIII. 10).

APPENDIX V

LETTER 175 (IX. 8)[1]

This is a brief letter from Formiae answering a brief letter from Rome. It begins:

Cenantibus II Id. nobis ac noctu quidem Statius a te epistulam brevem attulit.

II is the reading of Σ supported by the Tornesianus (*teste Lambino*). The first hand of M read *.H.* (or *.II.*) *d.* The inferior members of Δ are divided between *II* and *H .II.*

II = *pridie* is permissible: see Sjögren on 122 (VI. 8). 1. But one consideration makes it probable, and another makes it virtually certain, that Atticus' letter did not arrive on 14 March 49 but on the previous evening, i.e. that *II* should be *III*.

(1) A messenger normally took a day and a half to two days over the journey between Rome and Formiae. On 16 March Cicero received a batch of three letters from Atticus handed to the courier (*datae*) on 12, 13, and 14 March respectively (176 (IX. 9). 1). The letter mentioned in 175 (IX. 8) was presumably 'posted' before the first of these; at the latest therefore early on 12 March. In the ordinary course of things it should have reached Formiae not later than the night of the 13th.

(2) In his next letter, 176 (IX. 9) of the 17th, Cicero mentions (§3) that Terentia's steward Philotimus, who had arrived in Formiae on the 9th (171 (IX. 5). 1; cf. Schmidt, *Briefwechsel*, p. 148) and whose return Atticus was expecting on the 14th, actually left on the 15th. He adds: *eo serius ad tuam illam epistulam, cui ego statim rescripseram, redditae sunt meae litterae.* From the wording alone it is plain that the letters here referred to are the most recent of the correspondence, i.e. 175 (IX. 8) and the letter which 175 (IX. 8) answers. Moreover 174 (IX. 7) of the 13th, even if we could suppose that it was not dispatched until the 15th, answers *two* letters from Atticus (§2). But if *tua illa epistula* is a letter received on the night of the 14th, Cicero's anticipatory excuse (*redditae sunt* is of course an epistolary perfect) for the late arrival of his answer is inexplicable. How could he have been expected to dispatch an answer to a letter received after dark before the following morning?

So Atticus' letter arrived during dinner on the 13th. Cicero wrote his reply early on the 14th (the date is fixed by a concluding reference to Atticus' quartan fever, see Schmidt, *l.c.*), probably expecting Philotimus to leave that day. But for some reason Philotimus' departure was delayed until the 15th, so that 175 (IX. 8) would arrive one day late.

[1] Reprinted, with mechanical changes, from *Mnem.* S. 4. 14 (1961), p. 323 by permission of the Editor.

APPENDIX VI

CAELIANVM ILLVD

Between the 6 and 14 May 49, writing to Atticus from his villa at Cumae where he 'sat waiting for a sail'[1] to take him overseas, Cicero makes several references to a project then in his mind which he calls 'Caelian'. He never explains its nature (Atticus, of course, knew) and modern discussions, which have been sparse,[2] in my opinion leave the riddle unsolved. Before coming to those passages in which the name Caelius occurs it will be convenient to take certain others, which are generally, though I think not altogether correctly, supposed to foreshadow them.

Since Cicero's unsatisfactory interview with Caesar at Formiae on 28 March (= 6 February, Julian) his mind had been pretty well made up to leave Italy as soon as spring set in to mitigate the danger and discomfort of the voyage. But his destination remained undecided. At the beginning of April he was thinking of staying out of the way of the war, perhaps in Athens.[3] On the 14th he told Curio, then preparing to take over Sicily for Caesar, that he was looking for a 'solitary retreat'[4] in Greece. He hoped that Caesar, who was reported to have sanctioned a similar plan in the case of his niece's husband, L. Philippus, would not object. Curio was all encouragement; Caesar, he was sure, would approve and he himself would be delighted to facilitate Cicero's journey through Sicily. About 22 April Cicero's thoughts had turned to Malta.[5] But on 3 May a letter from Mark Antony, left by Caesar in charge of Italy outside the capital, informed him plainly that his departure abroad could not be authorized except by Caesar himself, who was now at Massilia on his way to Spain. To obtain Caesar's consent, even if it were forthcoming, would mean a long delay. Cicero decided to do without it and to leave by stealth, if necessary even by force.[6]

[1] 199 (x. 8). 9 *sedeo enim* πλουδοκῶν.

[2] Cf. J. Ziehen, *Ephemerides Tullianae* (Budapest, 1887), pp. 24 ff.; Schmidt, *Briefwechsel*, p. 178; T.–P. IV, pp. xliii ff., 246; Tenney Frank, *Cl. Phil.* 14 (1919), pp. 287 ff.; M. Rothstein, *Bericht über die Sitzungen des Philologischen Vereins im Jahre 1927*, pp. 6 f. (a reference which I have at length succeeded in tracking down thanks to Professor F. M. Heichelheim).

[3] Cf. 190 (x. 1). 2.

[4] 195 (x. 4). 10 *me recessum et solitudinem quaerere.*

[5] 198 (x. 7). 1: cf. 199 (x. 8). 10; 200 (x. 9). 1, 3; 210 (x. 18). 2.

[6] 201 (x. 10). 3; 204 (x. 12*a*). 2.

And in his disappointment and annoyance he resolved on a course of action to which he alludes as follows:

201 (x. 10). 3 (3 May)
certe hinc istis invitissimis evolabo, atque utinam ad Curionem! σύνες ὅ τοι λέγω. magnus dolor accessit. efficietur aliquid dignum nobis.
203 (x. 12). 2 (5 May)
Sicilia petenda; quam si erimus nacti, maiora quaedam consequemur.
204 (x. 12*a*). 2 (6 May)
quod si nobis is cursus quem speraram pateret, effecissem aliquid profecto, ut tu optas et hortaris, dignum nostra mora.

What were these 'greater things', 'worthy of himself', 'worthy of his delay' (i.e. making up for his earlier inactivity)? T.–P.'s answer is perhaps the first that will come to mind: 'What if Cicero should now make Sicily another centre of Pompeian resistance?' He had a long-standing connexion with the province (though five years later he writes that nearly all his friends there were dead[1]), and he believed that the island could be held for the Republic.[2] But would Atticus, the last man one would say to counsel rash, let alone desperate courses, have 'prayed for' such a venture, urging Cicero with no support except such as an almost unarmed province could offer to try conclusions with Curio's three (or two or four) legions?[3] He was not such a fool, and neither, as Rice Holmes says,[4] was Cicero. There are other difficulties. Cicero's words on 6 May (204 (x. 12*a*). 2 *sed mirificae sunt custodiae et quidem ille ipse Curio suspectus* (sc. *mihi* rather than *istis*) seem to show that he was still hoping for Curio's help. And what would have been his position *vis-à-vis* Cato, the governor appointed by the Senate—the news of Cato's flight did not arrive until about 14 May? Finally the verbal sequence in 203 (x. 12). 2 is enough in itself to put this theory out of court. Having written 'I must make for Sicily; that once gained, I shall achieve greater things. If only all goes well in Spain!' Cicero could not continue *quamquam de ipsa Sicilia utinam sit verum!* and retail reports about the province rallying to Cato's side and of Cato's troop levies if these 'greater things' had meant no more nor less than doing Cato's job for him.

[1] 420 (XVI. 11). 7.

[2] 203 (x. 12). 2; 208 (x. 16). 3.

[3] Cf. Drumann–Groebe, III, p. 401, n. 10. Exactly when Curio landed we do not know, but to find the province *vacuam* (Caes. *B.C.* I. 31. 1) it must have been after Cato's evacuation of Syracuse on 23 April (208 (x. 16). 3). But his subordinate Asinius Pollio had gone ahead (cf. Broughton, p. 266).

[4] *Roman Republic*, III, p. 48, n. 4.

Two other passages strongly suggest that what Cicero had in mind concerned not war but peace. We must not forget that both before and after the opening of hostilities he had wanted peace, even on Caesar's terms, and had seen himself and been seen by others as uniquely qualified for the role of intermediary between Caesar and Pompey. Even when he reached Pompey's camp in Greece he sang the same song.[1] Atticus for his part had in March envisaged him as becoming a public advocate of peace.[2] Replying to that suggestion Cicero wrote that he was not afraid of the risk in such action (which might have been resented by Caesar) but of embarrassing Pompey.[3] But in early May the situation looked less unfavourable for such an attempt. The tide of Caesar's success was apparently on the ebb. Adverse reports were coming in from Massilia, Spain, and Sicily; in Rome he had lost popularity, and there were persistent rumours, not without foundation in fact, of disaffection among the Caesarian troops in Italy.[4] The picture had changed appreciably since the March days when Pompey lay beleaguered in Brundisium and could only be expected to regard the victor's terms, whatever they were, as an intolerable humiliation.

On 22 April Cicero writes[5] that he will leave Italy out of gratitude to Pompey, but probably take no part in the fighting. Atticus is supposed to object: '*nihil*' *inquies* '*iuvas eum in quem ingratus esse non vis?*' 'On the contrary' replies Cicero 'he would perhaps have wanted me to help him less' (*immo minus fortasse voluisset*). A dark saying, variously explained. I do not think Cicero means that Pompey might have wished him to be less active in his efforts for peace *before* the war. *iuvas* points to the future; nor could those efforts well be described as helping Pompey. T.–P. suggest that this 'is perhaps the first mention of the "Caelian business", some resort to force, possibly in Sicily, which Cicero was meditating at this time'. But would that have displeased Pompey? It rather looks as though a peace move was again in mind. Pompey might not like it, yet, after the war had gone so badly for him, it might fairly be regarded as 'help'.

The other piece which may fit this part of the puzzle comes from a letter of 12 May (207 (x. 15). 3): *ibitur igitur, et ita quidem ut censes, nisi cuius gravioris personae suscipiendae spes erit ante oblata; sed vix erit tam cito. Allienus autem praetor putabat aliquem, si ego non, ex collegis suis. quivis licet dum modo aliquis.*

[1] Cf. *Fam.* VII. 3. 2 (to M. Marius in 46) *desperans victoriam primum coepi suadere pacem, cuius fueram semper auctor; deinde, cum ab ea sententia Pompeius valde abhorreret, suadere institui ut bellum duceret.* Cf. *ibid.* IV. 14. 2.

[2] 174 (IX. 7). 3 *sin mihi Caesar hoc non concedat* (sc. *ut absim a senatu*) *video tibi placere illud, me* πολίτευμα *de pace suscipere.*

[3] *ne Pompeio quid oneris imponam* (*ibid.*).

[4] 204 (X. 12*a*). 3. [5] 198 (X. 7). 1.

Again T.–P. would link this to the 'Caelian' project 'of some appeal to arms in Sicily', but that makes Cicero contradict himself: he says he will leave Italy *unless* he sees hope of assuming a more important role. Therefore he envisages this role as played in Italy. Nor was it an appeal to arms: that is evident from the reference to Allienus, brief and cryptic as it is. The Praetor A. Allienus was an old and congenial friend of Cicero's and remained so to the end.[1] T.–P. incline to think that on this occasion he was speaking as an *agent provocateur*, laying a trap for 'the good Cicero, who was but a novice in intrigue' (Catiline might have disagreed). But even though Cicero saw or pretended to see another incident at this time as a possible Caesarian trap (see below), such suspicions are plainly implausible. The last thing that Antony or Caesar himself could have wished was to have to deal with Cicero as a detected insurrectionary. It is hardly less unlikely that Allienus was mooting a military uprising in good faith. Why should a Praetor, not one Praetor in particular but one or other of them (*aliquem*), be expected to lead such a movement? We happen to know the names of the eight Praetors in 49. Three, Coponius, Favonius, and L. Torquatus,[2] were almost certainly with Pompey and so do not come into the picture. That leaves (apart from Allienus himself) M. Lepidus, left by Caesar in charge of Rome, L. Roscius Fabatus, a moderate who had figured as a peace negotiator in January and a former Legate of Caesar's, and the pair mentioned in 167 (IX. 1). 2, C. Sosius and P. Rutilius Lupus, who, despite Pompeian sympathies, were reported at the beginning of March to have returned to Rome and to be going quietly about their duties.[3] This quartet is not easily imagined as seething with schemes of revolt, and their office (Lepidus being obviously out of account) would not seem to offer a particularly favourable springboard. If however it was a peace initiative that was contemplated, a member of the praetorian College, the highest regularly appointed magistrates left in Italy, with powers of convoking the Senate and submitting proposals,[4] would be in a good position to take the lead—failing Cicero himself. And so indeed commentators have generally interpreted the passage.

Granted that the 'greater things' which Cicero hoped to accomplish when safely out of Italy also had to do with peace, how did he intend to

[1] See my note on the passage.

[2] That is if he *was* Praetor this year, as generally supposed: see on 161B (VIII. 11B). 1. If not, there is one unknown.

[3] The report may not have been true in Rutilius' case, since he was later active in the war on Pompey's side: cf. 162A (VIII. 12A). 4 n.

[4] Cf. Mommsen, *St.* III, pp. 910 f. In practice the praetorian right of convocation was usually exercised by the Praetor Urbanus. We do not know who was Praetor Urbanus in 49.

proceed? The answer can only be speculative. He may have hoped for co-operation from Curio, who though certainly loyal to Caesar,[1] might have been prepared to allow Cicero some scope in this direction. At any rate it is likely that Cicero contemplated a public appeal, whether issued from Sicily or some other place such as Malta, addressed to both combatant leaders. So far he had made no open statement of his views on the war. A private plea for peace and offer of mediation addressed to Caesar in March had been given some publicity both by the writer and the recipient,[2] but this was necessarily in terms flattering to the latter. A public manifesto from a man of Cicero's rank, reputation, and literary skill, composed without fear, immediate anyhow, of unpleasant personal consequences, would have made a sensation, even if it had not changed the course of history. Atticus might well pray for and encourage such a step.

Coming now to the 'Caelian' project itself, we must be careful to distinguish it from these 'greater things' which I have been trying to clarify. Contrary to the views of T.–P. and Tenney Frank the two were not identical, neither did the latter spring out of the former as a mere crystallization of what had previously been vague. The first reference to 'Caelius' is found in the letter of 6 May (204 (x. 12*a*)) from which I have already quoted. After the remark (§2) about what he would have achieved, *dignum nostra mora*, if only he had been given free passage out of Italy, Cicero says that he must make his escape either by stealth or by force. He feels himself swept along by circumstances (*trahimur, nec fugiendum si quid violentius*). He continues: *de Caelio saepe mecum agito nec, si quid habuero tale, dimittam.* Obviously this *tale quid* is not the 'something worthy of my delay' of which he has already spoken in this and earlier letters. The sequence of sentences shows that quite plainly. Moreover when Cicero refers to the 'greater things' his language always implies full confidence in their practicability (*efficietur... consequemur. . .effecissem*); once he gets where he wants the rest will follow. But when he comes to 'Caelius' he says: 'if I get such an opportunity I shall not let it slip'. The chance might come his way, or it might not.

Cicero continues with a recital of Caesar's difficulties in Spain, Massilia, and Italy, evidently as factors both relevant and favourable to the sort of enterprise he had in view. He ends this part of his letter thus: *illud recte times ne ruat* (sc. *Caesar*). *si desperarit, certe ruet; quo magis efficiendum aliquid est*

[1] Tenney Frank's idea that Cicero 'contemplated an attempt to induce Curio to revolt to Pompey' hardly needs refuting. He actually takes 199 (x. 8). 2 *si pelletur* (sc. *Caesar ex Hispania*), *quam gratus aut quam honestus tum erit ad Pompeium noster adventus, cum ipsum Curionem ad eum transiturum putem?* as implying doubts of Curio's loyalty!

[2] 188 (VIII. 9). I.

fortuna velim meliore, animo Caeliano. sed primum quidque; quod, qualecumque erit, continuo scies.

Before discussing these words it will be well to cite the other three passages which refer directly to the 'Caelian' project:

206 (x. 14). 3. (8 May)
nos a te admoniti de Caelio cogitabimus.

207 (x. 15). 2. (10 May)
quod optas, Caelianum illud maturescit; itaque torqueor utrum ventum exspectem. vexillo opus est; convolabunt.

208 (x. 16). 4. (14 May)
cogitavi eadem illa Caeliana quae legi in epistula tua.

The second of these is the most illuminating of the series. It proves first that a definite enterprise was on hand—it was ripening. Second, the scene of the enterprise was outside Italy—Cicero wonders whether he ought not to leave at once, wind or no wind. Third, his talk of a standard and of people flocking to join it can hardly mean any but one thing: from some part of the Roman empire he had received an invitation to come and take over.

The rest of the direct evidence, such as it is, fits without difficulty into this framework. The name Caelius, used by Cicero as a sort of codeword, does not help. From 204 (x. 12*a*). 3 *fortuna velim meliore, animo Caeliano* it is clear that there really had been a Caelius who had made an attempt of the sort Cicero had in view, bravely, but unsuccessfully. That excludes Cicero's Caesarian friend M. Caelius Rufus; nothing in his career so far will fit. Nor has the identification, going back to Corradus, with 'one Caelius who raised a force in Italy against Sulla, as we read in Plut. *Pomp*. 7' (T.–P.) much to commend it. The name in Plutarch is uncertain; the Sangermanensis has κλοίλιος, the Laurentianus κοίλλιος. And Plutarch says nothing about 'raising forces against Sulla'; he merely states that when Pompey took up arms for Sulla in Picenum in 83 he was opposed by three Marian armies commanded by Carrinas, 'Caelius', and Brutus, and that after he had defeated the last named these three fell out among themselves and retreated ὡς ἕκαστος ἔτυχε. That is as much as we know of Plutarch's Caelius,[1] and it throws no light on Cicero's. If the two were one, then Cicero must refer to some episode in his career which has dropped out of history; and that gets us no forwarder.

The last passage, from the letter of 14 May, needs some elucidation. On 12 May Cicero left Cumae for his villa at Pompeii, intending to wait there

[1] Unless he was the C. Caelius who crushed a revolt of the Salluvii in 90 (Liv. *Epit*. 73). Münzer (*RE*. Suppl. III. 224) suggests that this man was the C. (Coelius) Antipater whom P. Albinovanus murdered along with other Marian officers in 82 (App. *B.C.* I. 91).

while preparations for his voyage were going ahead. His object, he explains, was to 'diminish suspicion of his departure or plan'.[1] This wording is curious. Ziehen[2] took *cogitationis* to mean a peace move in Italy; but if Cicero means anything more than 'my departure, or rather my plan to depart', he probably means the *Caelianum*. When he got to his villa he received a message from the Centurions of three cohorts stationed at Pompeii, asking for an interview next day. His friend L. Ninnius explained that they were going to offer to put the town and its garrison in Cicero's hands. His reaction was swift and sensible: he set off back to Cumae before dawn. What, he asks Atticus, was the use of three cohorts without supporting equipment, or of more for that matter? Then he adds by way of further exculpation that he had borne in mind those same *Caeliana* (Caelian considerations) which he read in the letter from Atticus he found waiting for him on his return to Cumae—and then the thing might have been a trap. T.–P. follow Boot in tampering with the text, substituting *equidem* for *eadem*. Presumably they had not realized when they wrote their note (as they had come to do by the time they wrote their introduction) that the Caelian enterprise was to be located outside Italy. If Cicero had started a revolt on the spot, it would have meant giving up his project—a consideration all the more powerful if, as I shall presently suggest, the Caelian project too had peace as its ultimate objective.

Where then did Cicero look to find people waiting to rally round his flag? Not Sicily, for reasons already given. The East, already in Pompey's hands, can be ruled out. So can Sardinia and Gaul, because Cicero's way thither did not lie through Sicily and for other reasons. There was nothing for Cicero to do in Spain. That leaves Africa.

We happen to know something of the situation there from Cicero's speech on behalf of Q. Ligarius three years later. About the end of the year 50, the governor, C. Considius Longus, had returned to Rome to canvass for the Consulship. As his successor the Senate had appointed L. Aelius Tubero, a friend and connexion by marriage of Cicero's. But Tubero was not present at the casting of the lots, and wished to be excused on the ground of ill-health; and though he did leave eventually, he did not arrive before the province had already fallen into other hands (*Lig.* 21f.). Considius had left it in charge of his Legate Q. Ligarius, another friend of Cicero's. What followed Cicero himself may tell (*ibid.* 3):

bellum subito exarsit, quod qui erant in Africa ante audierunt geri quam parari. quo audito partim cupiditate inconsiderata, partim caeco quodam timore, primo salutis, post etiam studi sui quaerebant aliquem ducem, cum Ligarius

[1] 208 (x. 16). 4 *ut minuerem suspicionem profectionis aut cogitationis meae.*
[2] *l.c.* p. 21.

domum spectans, ad suos redire cupiens, nullo se implicari negotio passus est. interim P. Attius Varus, qui praetor Africam obtinuerat, Vticam venit. ad eum statim concursum est. atque ille non mediocri cupiditate adripuit imperium, si illud imperium esse potuit quod ad privatum clamore multitudinis imperitae, nullo publico consilio deferebatur.

There was then a period during which Africa was, as Caesar says (*B.C.* I. 31. 2) *vacua*, and its inhabitants 'looking for a leader'. May they not have looked towards Cicero?

Unfortunately these events cannot be exactly dated. At the outbreak of the war Attius Varus commanded some troops in Picenum, first apparently at Cingulum (cf. 137 (VII. 13*a*). 3), then at Auximum. At Caesar's approach he fled the town and made for Africa (*B.C.* I. 31. 2 *protinus ex fuga in Africam pervenerat*). Caesar's account suggests that Auximum was captured at the beginning of the war, before the evacuation of Rome; so Münzer (*RE.* XIII. 519. 68) makes Varus arrive at Utica about the beginning of February. But it is generally accepted that Auximum fell in the early stages of Caesar's main advance south, which began at the end of January.[1] Even if Varus did not waste a day he can hardly have reached Africa before March. But Caesar's *protinus* need not be rigorously pressed. Cicero's account implies a considerable interval between the receipt of the news of the Civil War in the province and Varus' arrival. He might be expected to wait at any rate until the result of the Italian campaign was settled by Pompey's departure overseas on 17 March. The advices from Africa which on the theory here advanced were coming in to Cicero in the first half of May will have been sent in April. There is nothing to show that Varus had arrived by then.[2]

The objections which rule out Sicily do not apply to Africa. There was no Caesarian army in that province, and no Cato. Tubero had been nominated as governor by the Senate, it is true; but he was reluctant,[3] and as a friend and kinsman of Cicero's may well have been party to the scheme. Incidentally Cicero's narrative in the *pro Ligario* gains a certain piquancy from the hypothesis that he himself, unbeknown to Caesar whom he was addressing, might easily have played a principal role.

It is not necessary to assume that Cicero's object was merely to secure Africa for his party. Africa under his control would make a better platform than Malta from which to launch the bid for peace which, as has appeared,

[1] Cf. Rice Holmes, III, pp. 376 ff. He dates Caesar's arrival at Auximum to 29 January.

[2] G. Walser (*Historia*, 8 (1959), p. 91, n. 8) points out that Tubero's departure for Africa can hardly have taken place long after Cato's evacuation of Syracuse on 23 April.

[3] *Lig.* 21 *scio igitur Tuberonem domi manere voluisse.*

both he and Atticus had in mind. The latter would hardly have 'prayed for' the 'Caelian' enterprise and repeatedly urged his friend to 'think about' it if he had not envisaged it as presenting such a possibility. Further I think the passage above quoted (p. 465) from 204 (x. 12*a*) precludes the view that it was intended simply as a blow against Caesar. Atticus was afraid of Caesar 'plunging', i.e. taking to plunder and massacre of opponents in Italy. Cicero agrees: if Caesar gets desperate that is just what he will do. All the more reason, he says, for achieving 'something Caelian'. On the face of it, the seizure of Africa by Cicero, coming on top of other supposed reverses, would only bring Caesar nearer desperation; and it would not prevent him doing what he liked in Italy. The logic of the passage requires that the 'something Caelian' should be of a nature to persuade Caesar to hold his hand, a step towards peace rather than war.

It all came to nothing. In the two subsequent extant letters which Cicero wrote to Atticus before he left Italy, of 16 and 19 May, he says no more about the Caelian plan. The last words of the second, *ipse conficior venisse tempus cum iam nec fortiter nec prudenter quicquam facere possim*, suggest that it had been abandoned, though they may only relate to difficulties in the matter of his departure.[1] On 7 June, on the point of leaving, he writes to Terentia *et tamen eius modi spero negotia esse ut et vos istic commodissime sperem esse et me aliquando cum similibus nostri rem publicam defensuros* (*Fam.* XIV. 7. 2). This looks as though he meant by then to join Pompey, as he actually did. The loss of Sicily and Sardinia to the Caesarians and perhaps fresh news from Africa of Varus' seizure of power there, will have quenched his more ambitious schemes.

[1] Cf. the rest of the letter, which makes nonsense of T.–P.'s thesis that 'now that Sicily was in the hands of Curio, Cicero was powerless, and he might for all Antony or Caesar cared, go off to Pompey as soon as he pleased' (IV, p. xlv).

CONCORDANCE

This Edition	*Vulg.*	*Vulg.*	*This Edition*
133	VII. 10	VII. 10	133
134	VII. 11	VII. 11	134
135	VII. 12	VII. 12	135
136	VII. 13	VII. 13	136
137	VII. 13*a*	VII. 13*a*	137
138	VII. 14	VII. 14	138
139	VII. 15	VII. 15	139
140	VII. 16	VII. 16	140
141	VII. 17	VII. 17	141
142	VII. 18	VII. 18	142
143	VII. 19	VII. 19	143
144	VII. 20	VII. 20	144
145	VII. 21	VII. 21	145
146	VII. 22	VII. 22	146
147	VII. 23	VII. 23	147
148	VII. 24	VII. 24	148
149	VII. 25	VII. 25	149
150	VII. 26	VII. 26	150
151	VIII. 1	VIII. 1	151
152	VIII. 2	VIII. 2	152
153	VIII. 3	VIII. 3	153
154	VIII. 6	VIII. 4	156
155	VIII. 7	VIII. 5	157
156	VIII. 4	VIII. 6	154
157	VIII. 5	VIII. 7	155
158	VIII. 8	VIII. 8	158
159	VIII. 10	VIII. 9	188
160	VIII. 9*a*	VIII. 9*a*	160
161	VIII. 11	VIII. 10	159
161A	VIII. 11A	VIII. 11	161
161B	VIII. 11B	VIII. 11A	161A
161C	VIII. 11C	VIII. 11B	161B
161D	VIII. 11D	VIII. 11C	161C
162	VIII. 12	VIII. 11D	161D
162A	VIII. 12A	VIII. 12	162
162B	VIII. 12B	VIII. 12A	162A
162C	VIII. 12C	VIII. 12B	162B
162D	VIII. 12D	VIII. 12C	162C

CONCORDANCE

This Edition	*Vulg.*	*Vulg.*	*This Edition*
163	VIII. 13	VIII. 12D	162D
164	VIII. 14	VIII. 13	163
165	VIII. 15	VIII. 14	164
165A	VIII. 15A	VIII. 15	165
166	VIII. 16	VIII. 15A	165A
167	IX. 1	VIII. 16	166
168	IX. 2	IX. 1	167
169	IX. 2*a*	IX. 2	168
170	IX. 3	IX. 2*a*	169
171	IX. 5	IX. 3	170
172	IX. 6	IX. 4	173
172A	IX. 6A	IX. 5	171
173	IX. 4	IX. 6	172
174	IX. 7	IX. 6A	172A
174A	IX. 7A	IX. 7	174
174B	IX. 7B	IX. 7A	174A
174C	IX. 7C	IX. 7B	174B
175	IX. 8	IX. 7C	174C
176	IX. 9	IX. 8	175
177	IX. 10	IX. 9	176
178	IX. 11	IX. 10	177
178A	IX. 11A	IX. 11	178
179	IX. 12	IX. 11A	178A
180	IX. 13	IX. 12	179
181	IX. 13*a*	IX. 13	180
181A	IX. 13A	IX. 13*a*	181
182	IX. 14	IX. 13A	181A
183	IX. 15	IX. 14	182
184	IX. 15*a*	IX. 15	183
185	IX. 16	IX. 15*a*	184
186	IX. 17	IX. 16	185
187	IX. 18	IX. 17	186
188	VIII. 9	IX. 18	187
189	IX. 19	IX. 19	189
190	X. 1	X. 1	190
191	X. 1*a*	X. 1*a*	191
192	X. 2	X. 2	192
193	X. 3	X. 3	193
194	X. 3*a*	X. 3*a*	194
195	X. 4	X. 4	195

CONCORDANCE

This Edition	*Vulg.*	*Vulg.*	*This Edition*
196	x. 5	x. 5	196
197	x. 6	x. 6	197
198	x. 7	x. 7	198
199	x. 8	x. 8	199
199A	x. 8A	x. 8A	199A
199B	x. 8B	x. 8B	199B
200	x. 9	x. 9	200
200A	x. 9A	x. 9A	200A
201	x. 10	x. 10	201
202	x. 11	x. 11	202
203	x. 12	x. 12	203
204	x. 12*a*	x. 12*a*	204
205	x. 13	x. 13	205
206	x. 14	x. 14	206
207	x. 15	x. 15	207
208	x. 16	x. 16	208
209	x. 17	x. 17	209
210	x. 18	x. 18	210

INDICES

To Commentary and Appendices only. References to Commentary are by letter (serial number of this edition), paragraph and line of lemma.

Further indices are planned to appear in a separate volume at the end of the series.

I. INDEX NOMINVM

II. INDEX VERBORVM

A. Latinorum

III. INDEX RERVM